lonely planet

Bali & Lombok

Ryan Ver Berkmoes

Iain Stewart

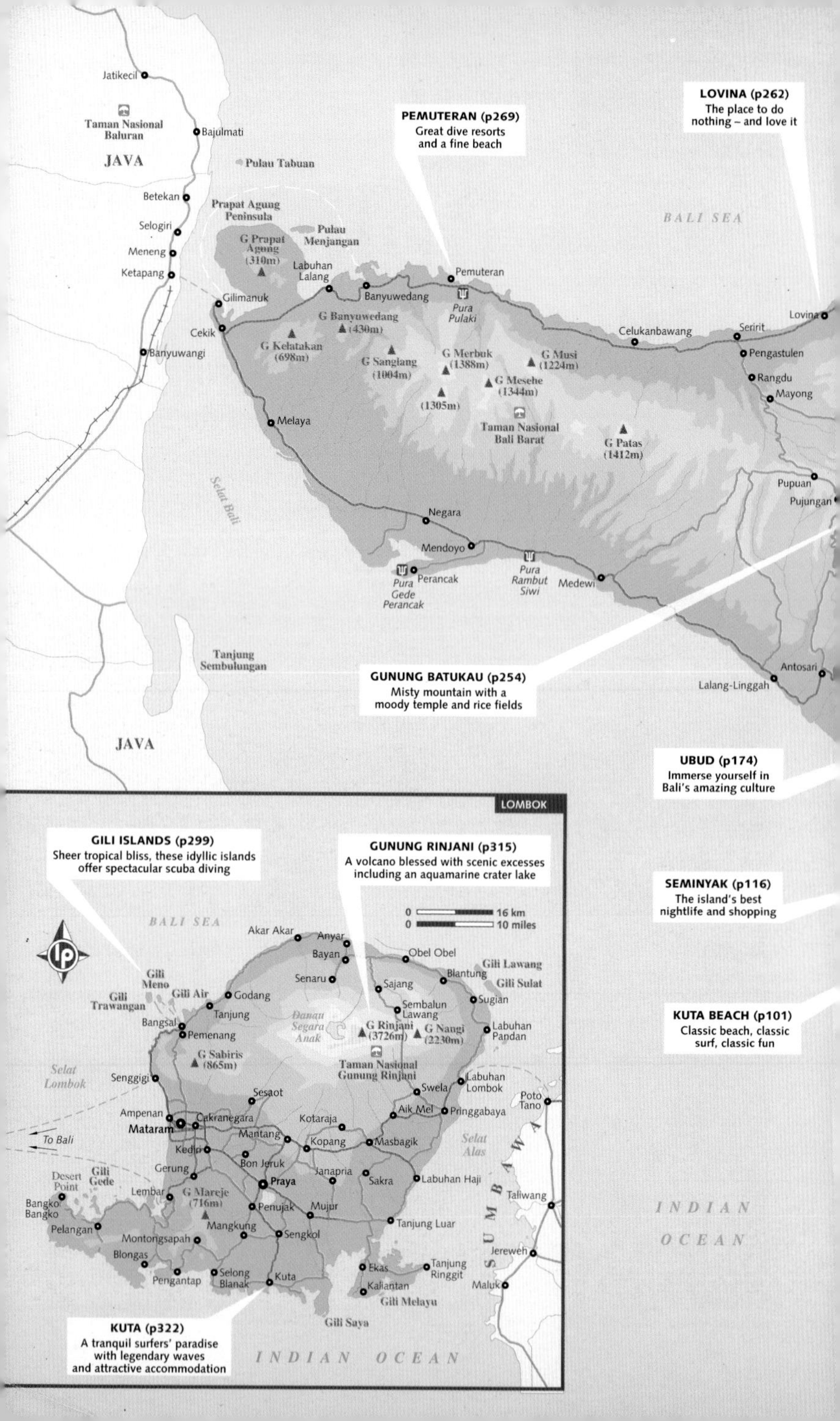

LOVINA (p262)
The place to do nothing – and love it
PEMUTERAN (p269)
Great dive resorts and a fine beach
GUNUNG BATUKAU (p254)
Misty mountain with a moody temple and rice fields
UBUD (p174)
Immerse yourself in Bali's amazing culture
SEMINYAK (p116)
The island's best nightlife and shopping
KUTA BEACH (p101)
Classic beach, classic surf, classic fun
LOMBOK
GILI ISLANDS (p299)
Sheer tropical bliss, these idyllic islands offer spectacular scuba diving
GUNUNG RINJANI (p315)
A volcano blessed with scenic excesses including an aquamarine crater lake
KUTA (p322)
A tranquil surfers' paradise with legendary waves and attractive accommodation
0 16 km
0 10 miles
Jatikecil
Taman Nasional Baluran
Bajulmati
JAVA
Pulau Tabuan
Betekan
Prapat Agung Peninsula
Selogiri
Meneng
Ketapang
G Prapat Agung (310m)
Pulau Menjangan
Labuhan Lalang
Pemuteran
Gilimanuk
Banyuwedang
Pura Pulaki
BALI SEA
Cekik
G Banyuwedang (430m)
G Kelatakan (698m)
G Sangiang (1004m)
G Merbuk (1388m)
G Musi (1224m)
G Mesehe (1344m)
(1305m)
Banyuwangi
Celukanbawang
Seririt
Lovina
Pengastulen
Rangdu
Mayong
Melaya
Taman Nasional Bali Barat
G Patas (1412m)
Selat Bali
Pupuan
Pujungan
Negara
Mendoyo
Pura Gede Perancak
Perancak
Pura Rambut Siwi
Medewi
Tanjung Sembulungan
Antosari
Lalang-Linggah
JAVA
BALI SEA
Akar Akar
Anyar
Bayan
Obel Obel
Gili Lawang
Blantung
Gili Sulat
Senaru
Sajang
Sugian
Gili Meno
Gili Air
Godang
Gili Trawangan
Tanjung
Sembalun Lawang
Bangsal
Pemenang
Danau Segara Anak
G Rinjani (3726m)
G Nangi (2230m)
Labuhan Pandan
G Sabiris (865m)
Taman Nasional Gunung Rinjani
Selat Lombok
Senggigi
Labuhan Lombok
Sesaot
Swela
Poto Tano
Ampenan
Cakranegara
Aik Mel
Pringgabaya
Mataram
Kotaraja
To Bali
Mantang
Kopang
Masbagik
Selat Alas
Kediri
Bon Jeruk
SUMBAWA
Gerung
Desert Point
Gili Gede
Janapria
Sakra
Labuhan Haji
Praya
Lembar
G Mareje (716m)
Taliwang
Bangko Bangko
Penujak
Mujur
Pelangan
Mangkung
Tanjung Luar
Montongsapah
Sengkol
INDIAN OCEAN
Jereweh
Blongas
Ekas
Tanjung Ringgit
Selong Blanak
Pengantap
Kuta
Kaliantan
Maluk
Gili Melayu
Gili Saya
INDIAN OCEAN

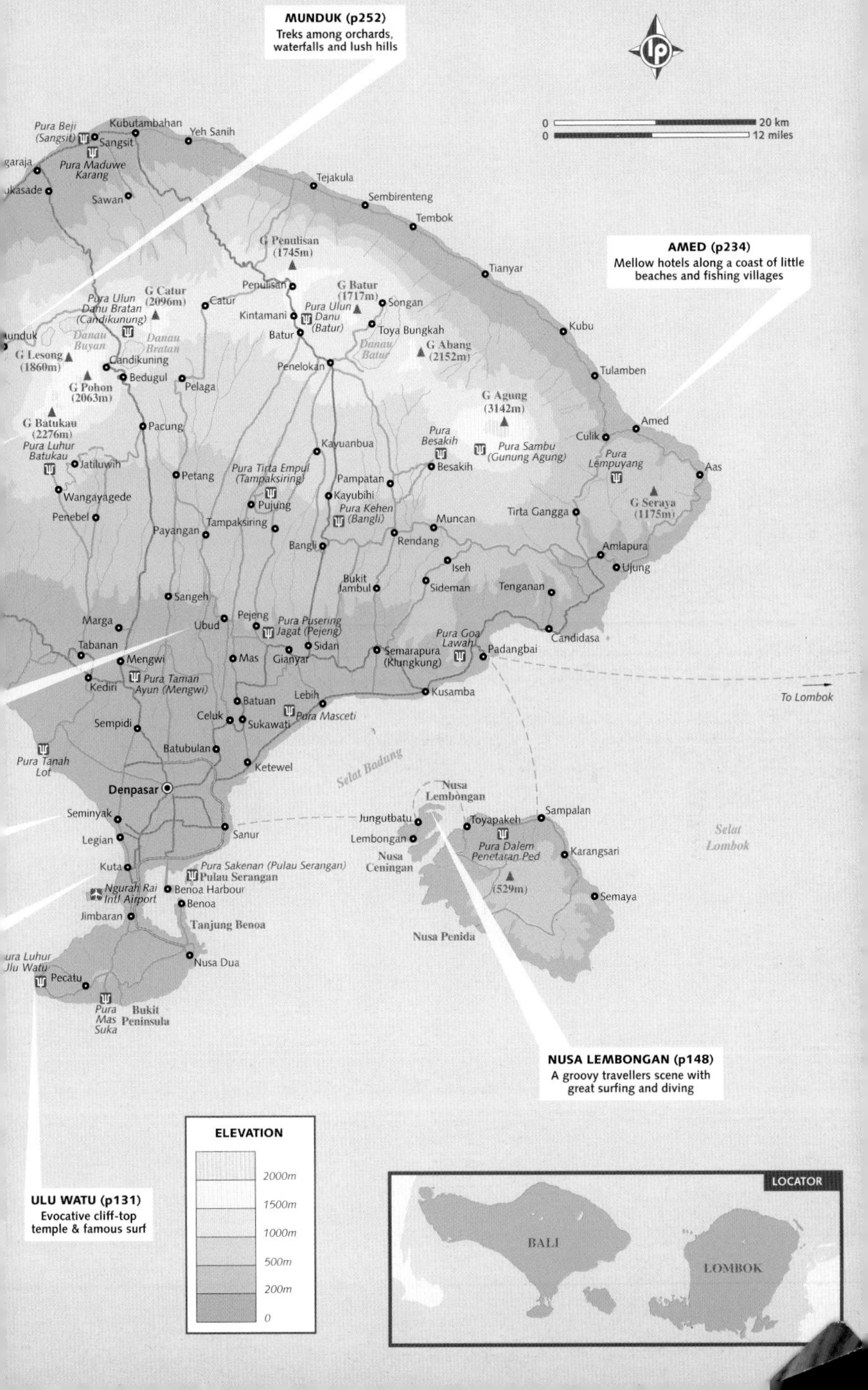

MUNDUK (p252)
Treks among orchards, waterfalls and lush hills
AMED (p234)
Mellow hotels along a coast of little beaches and fishing villages
NUSA LEMBONGAN (p148)
A groovy travellers scene with great surfing and diving
ULU WATU (p131)
Evocative cliff-top temple & famous surf
0
20 km
0
12 miles
Pura Beji (Sangsit)
Kubutambahan
Sangsit
Yeh Sanih
Pura Maduwe Karang
Sawan
Tejakula
Sembirenteng
Tembok
G Penulisan (1745m)
Tianyar
Penulisan
G Batur (1717m)
Songan
G Catur (2096m)
Catur
Pura Ulun Danu Bratan (Candikunung)
Kintamani
Pura Ulun Danu (Batur)
Toya Bungkah
Batur
Danau Buyan
Danau Bratan
Danau Batur
G Abang (2152m)
Kubu
G Lesong (1860m)
Candikuning
Bedugul
Pelaga
Penelokan
Tulamben
G Pohon (2063m)
G Agung (3142m)
G Batukau (2276m)
Pacung
Amed
Culik
Pura Luhur Batukau
Jatiluwih
Kayuanbua
Pura Besakih
Pura Sambu (Gunung Agung)
Pura Lempuyang
Aas
Petang
Pura Tirta Empul (Tampaksiring)
Pampatan
Besakih
Wangayagede
Pujung
Kayubihi
G Seraya (1175m)
Penebel
Pura Kehen (Bangli)
Tirta Gangga
Tampaksiring
Muncan
Payangan
Rendang
Bangli
Amlapura
Iseh
Ujung
Bukit Jambul
Sideman
Tenganan
Sangeh
Marga
Ubud
Pejeng
Pura Pusering Jagat (Pejeng)
Pura Goa Lawah
Candidasa
Tabanan
Sidan
Padangbai
Mengwi
Mas
Gianyar
Semarapura (Klungkung)
Pura Taman Ayun (Mengwi)
Kediri
Kusamba
To Lombok
Lebih
Batuan
Pura Masceti
Celuk
Sukawati
Sempidi
Pura Tanah Lot
Batubulan
Ketewel
Selat Badung
Denpasar
Nusa Lembongan
Seminyak
Jungutbatu
Toyapakeh
Sampalan
Sanur
Legian
Lembongan
Nusa Ceningan
Pura Dalem Penetaran Ped
Karangsari
Selat Lombok
Kuta
Pura Sakenan (Pulau Serangan)
Pulau Serangan
Ngurah Rai Intl Airport
Benoa Harbour
(529m)
Benoa
Semaya
Jimbaran
Tanjung Benoa
Nusa Penida
Nusa Dua
Pecatu
Pura Mas Suka
Bukit Peninsula
ELEVATION
2000m
1500m
1000m
500m
200m
0
LOCATOR
BALI
LOMBOK

Destination Bali & Lombok

Bali got a wave of publicity in 2006 when the world record for the most surfers to ride a single wave was set at Kuta Beach. Fifty-three people from around the world shared the moment.

If that news highlighted Bali as an incredible surf destination, it was but one of many superlative stories that could have been written. Jaded travellers the world over arrive in Bali and have their world-weary ways stripped away by the place that invented the word 'unique'.

Many try to pigeon-hole Bali as a cliché: but look a little deeper and you'll find a pervasive culture and beauty. Tiny offerings, with their brilliant bits of fresh flowers found in even the tiniest of niches. Dance performances, magical with their grace and charm. Lyrical local music playing live in even the most obscure corners. Balinese culture is no after-thought overlay, shucked on by only a few – it is a fundamental part of everyday life and it intrigues and entrances everyone who visits.

The beauty is a part of this cliché. But what can you do? Wild beaches stretching off to the horizon; rice terraces incredibly green and sinuous in their beauty; lush tropical forests where your biggest worry is a ripe fruit hitting your head. And these are just some of the images you'll savour.

And then there are the people. A cliché: you're unlikely to find a more joyous and delightful people anywhere! Travel here is just so easy. Whether in the resorts of the tourist areas or the remote corners of Bali and Lombok, you'll find it a breeze to catch your own personal wave here, no matter what form it may take.

OPPOSITE: TONY ARRUZA

GREGORY ADAMS

Beaches & Islands

PAUL BEINSSEN

Suit up, grab your board and get out into the surf in Legian (p102)

BERNARD NAPTHINE

Climb aboard a passenger boat for a trip to Gili Air (p300), Lombok

TIM ROCK

Exotic species abound in the waters off Bali and Lombok (p306)

STEPHANE VICTOR

Take some time out for an afternoon playing on the beach

Sample the waves at one of Bali's greatest surf sites, Bingin (p132) on the Bukit Peninsula

PAUL BEINSSEN

Culture

STEPHANE VICTOR

Enjoy the colourful costumes in a Gambuh dance performance (p206) in Ubud

Join in the fun and head to a festival at Pura Besakih (p216)

SARA-JANE CL

RICHARD I'ANSON

For traditional weaving, make your way to the village of Sukarara (p322)

GREGORY ADAMS

Marvel at the elaborate costumes of Legong dancers (p47)

Take in a Kecak dance performance (p197) at a temple in Ubud

STEPHANE VICTOR

Eating, Drinking & Merriment

JERRY ALEXANDER

Watch the sun sink into the ocean as you wait for your dinner in Jimbaran (p129)

Order from a long list of fresh tropical drinks, perfect to cool you down after a day in the sun

JERRY ALEXANDER

Treat yourself to an Asian fusion feast at the Jazz Café (p197) in Ubud

STEPHANE VICTOR

Treat Yourself

JERRY ALEXANDER

Settle back and relax in a traditional bath of essential oils and flower petals (p84)

STEPHANE VICTOR

Learn to create your own Balinese feast at one of Bali's famed cooking courses (p90)

Rejuvenate yourself with a soak in the hot springs at Air Panas Banjar (p268)

JERRY ALEXANDER

Getting Away From It All

JOHN BORTHWICK

Escape into the verdant surrounds of the Munduk waterfalls (p252)

CHRISTINE OSBORNE

For a little adventure, clamber into a raft for a white-water experience

Take a trip back into time, up into the rice terraces of Tegallalang (p205)

JERRY ALE

Contents

Regional Map Contents

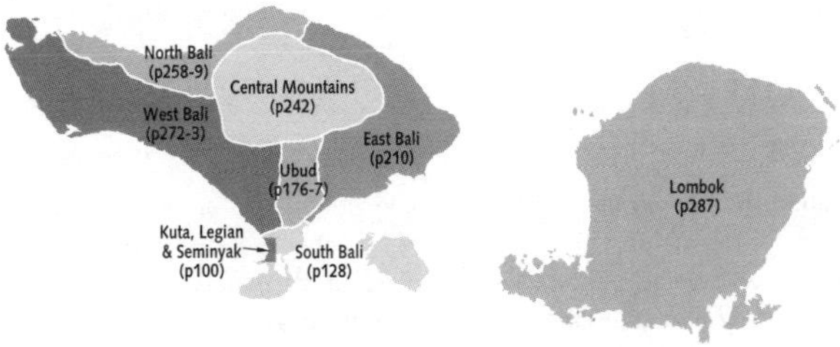

The Authors

RYAN VER BERKMOES

Ryan Ver Berkmoes first visited Bali in 1993. On his visits since he's explored almost every corner of the island – along with side trips to Nusa Lembongan, Nusa Penida and Lombok. Just when he thinks Bali holds no more surprises, he, for example, rounds a corner and is struck by the fabulous vistas from Jatiluwih. Better yet, he simply never tires of the place. Four times in two years shows that; sometimes his Bali social calendar is busier than anywhere. Off-island, Ryan lives in Portland, Oregon and vows to sample every last micro-brew in town – a lifetime avocation.

My Bali & Lombok

The beaches and nightlife of Seminyak are where I start. Once the jetlag is out of my system (oops, need another day by the pool for that), it's up on to Ubud to remind myself how Balinese culture is unlike anything in the world. From there (with a cheap room overlooking a river valley), I explore east – towards the Sidemen Rd and the beaches on the new coast road, and west – Jatiluwih and the mystical temple of Pura Luhur Batukau. After that, it's an undeveloped bit of the west coast. And along the way? Bintangs (or G&Ts) with friends new or old.

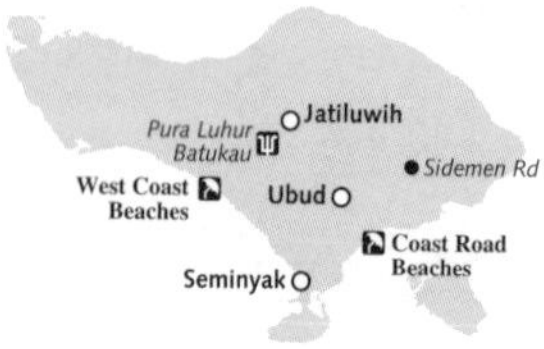

IAIN STEWART

Iain has explored many parts of the Indonesian archipelago, first visiting the country in 1992 when he journeyed between Sumatra and West Timor. He's returned several times since to dive the reefs of Sulawesi, haggle over ikat (patterned cloth) in Sumba and explore the remarkable islands of Bali and Lombok. A guidebook writer since 1997, Iain has written and co-written more than 20 titles, including contributing the Nusa Tenggara chapter of Lonely Planet's *Indonesia*. Iain lives by the sea in Brighton, UK, and revels in periodically exchanging the local pebble beach for a palm-fringed tropical version – especially if it's in Lombok's Gili Islands.

LONELY PLANET AUTHORS

Why is our travel information the best in the world? It's simple: our authors are independent, dedicated travellers. They don't research using just the internet or phone, and they don't take freebies in exchange for positive coverage. They travel widely, to all the popular spots and off the beaten track. They personally visit thousands of hotels, restaurants, cafés, bars, galleries, palaces, museums and more – and they take pride in getting all the details right, and telling it how it is. For more, see the authors section on www.lonelyplanet.com.

CONTRIBUTING AUTHORS

Dr Trish Batchelor wrote the Health chapter. Trish is a general practitioner and travel medicine specialist who works at the Ciwec Clinic in Kathmandu, Nepal, as well as a medical advisor to the Travel Doctor New Zealand clinics. Trish teaches medicine through the University of Otago, and is interested in underwater and high-altitude medicine and in the impact of tourism on host countries. She has travelled extensively through Southeast Asia, and loves high-altitude trekking in the Himalayas.

Philip Goad wrote the Contemporary Hotel Design boxed text. Philip is Professor of Architecture at the University of Melbourne. An architectural historian and contemporary design critic, he is the author of *Architecture Bali: Birth of the Tropical Boutique Resort* and, with Anoma Pieris, is co-author of *New Directions in Tropical Asian Architecture* (2004).

Janet de Neefe wrote the Food & Drink chapter. Originally from Melbourne, Janet is involved in the Ubud Writers Festival and is the owner of Casa Luna and Indus restaurants in Ubud. Passionate about Balinese food since her first visit in 1974, she has set up the Casa Luna Cooking School, now attended by visitors from all over the world. Janet lives with her husband, Ketut, and four children at the Honeymoon Guesthouse. Her memoir-cookbook, *Fragrant Rice,* details her life in Bali and how she has adapted to living there.

Getting Started

To get started for Bali, all you really need is a ticket. (Well maybe also a visa, passport, some money, but you get the idea.) The entire island is just so well set up for visitors, the Balinese are so welcoming and the climate and weather are so agreeable that you really can just hop on a plane and go.

Although Lombok is not quite as easy, you can still find your way around with little advance preparation. Simply getting to either place is the biggest hurdle (and it's low).

And if Bali and Lombok reward the spontaneous traveller, they also reward the traveller who plans. In Bali especially, you can stay at exquisite places, experience unique aspects of the culture and tailor your trip to a remarkable degree with advance work. If you want to make time for real discoveries or just discover some good bargains, you can reap the rewards of forethought.

See climate charts (p332) for more information.

Whatever your travel style, you'll find the real obstacles to independent travel in this part of the world are few. The islands are used to travellers of all stripes, English is widely spoken and the people truly live up to the shopworn cliché of 'friendly'.

WHEN TO GO

The best time to visit Bali, in terms of the weather, is during the dry season (April to September). The rest of the year is more humid, cloudier and has more rainstorms, but you can still enjoy a holiday.

There are also distinct tourist seasons that affect the picture. The European, American and Japanese summer holidays bring the biggest crowds – July, August and early September are busy. Accommodation can be very tight in these months and prices are higher. Many Australians arrive between Christmas and early January, when airfares to and from Australia are higher and flights can be booked solid. The school holidays in early April, late June to early July and late September also see more Australians, most of them on package tours to resort areas in southern Bali. Many Indonesians visit Bali around the end of December and during some Indonesian holidays. Outside

DON'T LEAVE HOME WITHOUT...

- Double-checking the fast-changing visa situation (p346).
- Sunscreen, sunglasses and a hat to deflect the fierce equatorial sun.
- Ascertaining your country's travel advice for Indonesia (p333).
- A travel insurance policy covering you for any sticky situations.
- Earplugs for the endless repetitions of 'Jammin'' at beach bars.
- Your favourite brand of wax for your surfboard.
- Comfortable but rugged walking shoes or sandals.
- Flip-flops in *your* size for hanging out by the pool.
- That clichéd extra bag for all the great stuff you'll buy.
- Sketch pad or camera for capturing the most beautiful place you'll ever see.
- That book you've been waiting to read.
- An iPod full of tunes to give your adventures a beat.

CLIMATE CHANGE & TRAVEL

Climate change is a serious threat to the ecosystems that humans rely upon, and air travel is the fastest-growing contributor to the problem. Lonely Planet regards travel, overall, as a global bene fit, but believes we all have a responsibility to limit our personal impact on global warming.

FLYING & CLIMATE CHANGE

Pretty much every form of motorized travel generates CO^2 (the main cause of human-induced climate change) but planes are far and away the worst offenders, not just because of the sheer distances they allow us to travel, but because they release greenhouse gases high into the atmosphere. The statistics are frightening: two people taking a return flight between Europe and the US will contribute as much to climate change as an average household's gas and electricity consumption over a whole year.

CARBON OFFSET SCHEMES

Climatecare.org and other websites use 'carbon calculators' that allow travellers to offset the level of greenhouse gases they are responsible for with financial contributions to sustainable travel schemes that reduce global warming – including projects in India, Honduras, Kazakhstan and Uganda.

Lonely Planet, together with Rough Guides and other concerned partners in the travel industry, support the carbon offset scheme run by climatecare.org. Lonely Planet offsets all of its staff and author travel.

these times Bali has surprisingly few tourists and there are empty rooms and restaurants everywhere.

Balinese festivals, holidays and special celebrations occur all the time, and most of them are not scheduled according to Western calendars, so don't worry too much about timing your visit to coincide with local events (see p336).

Just 8 degrees south of the equator, Bali has a tropical climate – the average temperature hovers around 30°C (around 85°F) all year. Direct sun feels incredibly hot, especially in the middle of the day. In the wet season, from October through March, the humidity can be very high and oppressive. The almost daily tropical downpours come as a relief, then pass quickly, leaving flooded streets and renewed humidity.

The dry season (April to September) is nicer, although this shouldn't be an overriding factor in your decision. The days are slightly cooler and obviously, for outdoor activities – such as getting a tan in Kuta or shopping in Seminyak – it's more fun if you're not getting drenched (but it still rains some). At any time of the year, you can escape the heat by heading to places like Ubud, where cool mountain air makes evenings a pleasure.

On Lombok, the west (where the main town and tourist areas are based) has a climate similar to South Bali but drier. The wet season, from late October to early May, is less extreme with December, January and February the wettest months. In the dry season, from June to September, temperatures will range from hot to scorching. At higher elevations it can get quite cold at night, so bring some extra layers of clothing. Clouds and mist usually envelop the slopes of Gunung Rinjani from early morning onwards, but the south coast is less humid and you'll enjoy clear skies almost every day. Travel on the island is slightly less convenient during Ramadan, the Muslim fasting month (the ninth month in the Muslim calendar), especially in the traditional rural areas. In the tourist areas though, there should be little difference in services.

HOW MUCH?

Cost to send an email taunting friends with all the fun you're having: under 500Rp

Simple beachside room with a great view: under US$20

Traditional gamelan music performance: 50,000Rp

Ticket for the speedboat ride of your life to Nusa Lembongan: US$25

Two dives at amazing Pulau Menjangan: US$60

TOP FIVES

Beaches

- Kuta Beach p95) – cynics aside, this long, curved, wide stretch of sand boasts great surf that swimmers and surfers alike can enjoy. It's a place enjoyed both by locals and visitors – especially at sunset when you hear a collective 'ahhhh'.
- Dream Beach (p131) – gorgeous white-sand beach on the Bukit Peninsula, backed by an impromptu resort. It's ramshackle in an endearing way and perfect for a snooze on the beach (but watch out for the encroaching golf course!).
- Pasir Putih (p230) – a little-known gem east of Candidasa, this crescent of palm-fringed white sand could be a postcard. You'll be delighted with the tremendous views of Nusa Penida and company across the water.
- Nusa Lembongan (p148) – there's a whole series of light-sand beaches at this relaxed and funky island off East Bali. Surf, dive, drink beer, hang out.
- Gili Island beaches (p299) – the beaches on these three islands are uniformly gorgeous, with circles of white sand, great snorkelling and a timeless traveller vibe.

Festivals

As well as the amazing selection of religious events that Bali offers, there is an impressive line-up of festivals to fascinate and transfix you. These events occur throughout the year and are scheduled using a Balinese calendar, very different from Western calendars. See p336 for details. The events below follow an annual schedule and are all worthy reasons to hop on a plane.

- Nyale Fishing Festival, held February or March, Kuta (p324). Thousands of Sasak fishermen build bonfires on the beach at Lombok's Kuta while myriad rituals take place.
- Bali Art Festival of Buleleng, held May or June, Singaraja (p259). Dancers and musicians from some of the region's most renowned village troupes perform over one week.
- Bali Arts Festival, held mid-June to mid-July, Denpasar (p170). Denpasar hosts a month of cultural performances by the best groups on the island, who compete for prizes.
- Kuta Karnival, held late September and early October, Kuta, Bali (p104). The always-near-the-surface zany side of Kuta is let loose though parades, arts competitions, cultural shows, beach sports tournaments, kite-flying contests and more.
- Ubud Writers & Readers Festival, held October, Ubud (p186). Top authors from around the world gather in a celebration of writing – especially that which touches on Bali.

Special Places

Travel is filled with moments where you stop, look around and with a sigh of contentment say, 'I'm so glad I'm here.' There's no shortage of places to do this on Bali and Lombok, but here are our favourite five. Now go find some of your own.

- The beach at Canggu (p125) – the surf is wild and woolly, the beach wind-blown and it's all a little rough-edged. A perfect spot for getting away from the beach hordes elsewhere.
- Pura Masceti (p209) – one of Bali's most important temples, it's newly accessible and on a great beach.
- Pura Luhur Batukau (p253) – a sacred temple well up the misty side of Bali's second-highest mountain is easily reached yet exudes serenity.
- Sidemen (p215) – immerse yourself in the verdant beauty of Bali's rice terraces and tropical river valleys.
- Gunung Rinjani (p314) – high on this volcano you can trek to Sembalun, nestled in a fertile valley. It's Shangri-la.

COSTS & MONEY

In Bali, you can spend as much as you want – there are fabulous resorts where a room costs US$500 or more a night, where dinner costs more than US$75 per person and you can be reborn in a spa for US$100 an hour. At the other extreme, you can find decent budget rooms easily for 50,000Rp and enjoy a fresh meal from a warung (food stall) for under 8000Rp. In short, Bali is a bargain for budget travellers and offers excellent value for those seeking every luxury.

In general, travellers who don't want air-con and hot water will discover they can get good rooms almost anywhere in Bali for under US$10. You can have an excellent three-course meal for US$6 (including a large bottle of beer) at many tourist restaurants, while US$15 can get you a gourmet delight at some of the finest restaurants around. See Accommodation (p328) for a full discussion of what kind of bed your money will buy you in Bali and Lombok.

Transport is affordable – remember that Bali is a small island. Public minibuses, buses and bemo (small minibuses) are the local form of public transport and they're very cheap – 30,000Rp will get you across the island. A rental motorcycle costs around US$4 per day and a small jeep runs about US$10 per day. You can charter a car *and* a driver for around US$25 to US$50 per day.

"you can spend as much as you want"

Nearly every museum, major temple or tourist site has an entry charge of about 4000/2000Rp per adult/child – it's a trifling amount. Galleries, bars and clubs are almost always free and the only place you'll really have to pay a premium is at a few attractions aimed at visitors such as animal parks, and adventure activities like river-rafting or water sports.

Overall, it's possible to live a simple life for under US$10 a day. This gets you a cheap room in Kuta, three solid meals at warung, one or more cold beers and all the free surfing you want on the beach. Spend more, say, US$50 a day and you'll pretty much be able eat, drink or do anything you want while enjoying a great midpriced room. Bali and Lombok really are that cheap.

TRAVEL LITERATURE

Books about Bali are common. Visit one of the bookshops on the island and you will have many choices, with new works appearing monthly. Titles dealing with Lombok, however, are a rarity.

Eat, Pray, Love is the publishing sensation that has women of a certain age flocking to Bali to find the answer to life's dreams. As the subtitle says, it is 'One woman's search for everything across Italy, India and Indonesia.' Author Elizabeth Gilbert ends up in Bali where she makes witty observations about local life and finds her own answer to everything: a rich Brazilian.

Diana Darling's *The Painted Alphabet* is based on a Balinese epic poem with all the usual ingredients: good, evil, a quest, baby swapping and various mystical events. It's a gentle and beguiling way to get your head into Balinese folklore.

A Patch of Paradise is Gaia Grant's search for 'real life in Bali'. Like many Westerners she was slowly drawn into the local culture and was ultimately transformed.

Bali Moon by Odyle Knight rounds out the subgenre of books about Western women who find more than an affordable holiday in Bali. The book will appeal to anyone who finds magic in crystals, as it recounts Knight's journey of spiritual discovery.

A House in Bali by Colin McPhee is the timeless classic about a Canadian who experienced Bali cultural and village life to the core in the 1930s.

Our Hotel in Bali by Louise Koke is another classic about Westerners on Bali in the 1930s. She and her husband Bob created the first-ever Kuta Beach hotel and had numerous delightful encounters along the way. It's a quick and fun read with lots of photos.

Many restaurants serve rice crackers, typically made with rice flour and soy beans, with your drinks.

Gecko's Complaint is a morality tale presented as an old Balinese children's fable. The recent Periplus edition is richly illustrated.

A Club of Small Men is a cute kids book based on Colin McPhee's 1930s children's orchestra.

INTERNET RESOURCES

Bali Advertiser (www.baliadvertiser.biz) This online edition of Bali's expat journal is filled with insider tips.

Bali Discovery (www.balidiscovery.com) Although run by a tour company, this site is easily the best source for Bali news and features, week in and week out. Excellent.

Lombok Network (www.lombok-network.com) Very comprehensive, this site brings together huge amounts of current information on the island.

LonelyPlanet.com (www.lonelyplanet.com) Share knowledge and experiences with other travellers about islands which have been Lonely Planet favourites from the start.

Stranger in Paradise (www.strangerinparadise.com) The online journal of the irrepressible Made Wijaya (p61) is filled with insightful and at times hilariously profane takes on local life.

Itineraries

CLASSIC ROUTES

TOTAL BALI & LOMBOK

Two Weeks

Start your trip in **Seminyak** (p116), with the best places to go out for a meal, a drink or more, and allow at least three days to experience the wild charms of **Kuta Beach** (p95). Once you're sated, head west, driving back roads around **Tabanan** (p275) and **Jatiluwih** (p254), where enormous bamboo trees hang over the roads and the rice terraces are some of the oldest on the island.

Continue west through **Taman Nasional Bali Barat** (West Bali National Park; p280). Stop here, or press on and settle in at **Pemuteran** (p269). From here, you can snorkel or scuba the untouched reefs at **Pulau Menjangan** (p282). Driving east, stop at **Lovina** (p262) and enjoy its laid-back beach-town vibe and then head up and over the string of volcanoes that are the heart – and soul – of the island.

Carry on through **Kintamani** (p246), where you'll be rewarded with vistas of Bali's big three: **Gunung Batur** (p242), **Gunung Abang** (p243) and the holiest of holies, **Gunung Agung** (p243). Coming back down on the wet side of the island, head straight to **Ubud** (p174), the spiritual centre of Bali. Nights of dance and culture are offset by days of walking through the serene countryside. Head down to Padangbai and catch the Perama boat to the beach resorts of **Senggigi** (p293) and then on to the great travellers' scene on the **Gili Islands** (p299).

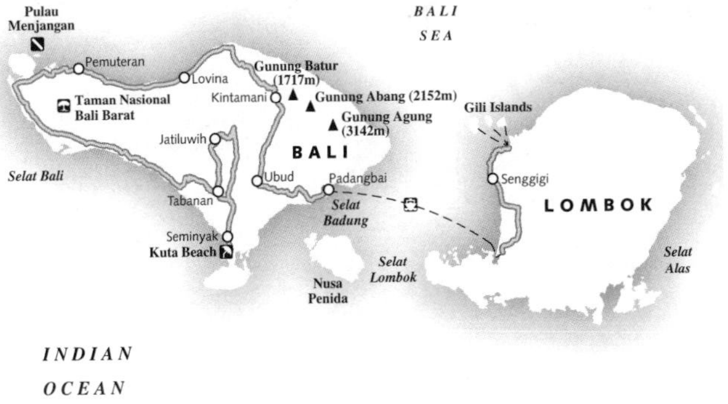

The best of everything in Bali and Lombok comes together on this two-week trip of tropical and cultural delights. Bask on the best beaches, drown in a sea of green rice paddies, let the aura of amazing temples flow over you like a warm bath and immerse yourself in Bali's incredible culture; it will be an island trip like no other.

TROPICAL PLEASURES

Two Weeks

Don't stray far from the airport, as **Kuta** (p95) in all its party glory is only 10 minutes away. Hit the bars and clubs after midnight and come back to earth on the beach by day. Be sure to get to the trendy restaurants and clubs of **Seminyak** (p116) before you leave this part of South Bali behind. Maybe you can learn how to surf, or brush up on your skills. Eventually, head south to sober up and mellow out. **Dream Beach** (p149) on the Bukit Peninsula always inspires snoozes – get some on the white sand here. When you're ready and rested, get a boat from **Sanur** (p139) to **Nusa Lembongan** (p148). This little island still has the classic, simple charm of a rural beach town, with a string of hotels – from basic to comfy – lining the sands. It's a timeless travellers' scene with a backdrop of excellent surfing and splendid snorkelling and diving.

Return to Bali and press on from Sanur to the beaches along the southeast coast. Try some of wild beaches around **Lebih** (p209), where the surf pounds the grey sand. Stop and test the waters with a little surfing, or grab a meal at one of the warung (food stalls) lining the roads to the beach. When you get to **Padangbai** (p221), stop. This fun little port town is an ideal place to hang around in for a couple of days before you hop a boat to Lombok, docking in **Senggigi** (p293), the heart of Lombok's beach scene. The coastline is lovely and as you're gazing back towards Bali you'll already feel you've made a journey – less people visit Lombok than Bali.

Now it's time to push on to the ultimate reward for your island adventure: the **Gili Islands** (p299). Depart from Senggigi and compare the scenes on Gili Trawangan, Gili Meno and Gili Air – then pick your favourite.

Surf and swim by day and party by night. Sleep? That will happen some time. Start in timeless Kuta, then sample hidden beaches and great travellers' scenes south of Bali and off its coast. Then it's over to Lombok for more day and night action.

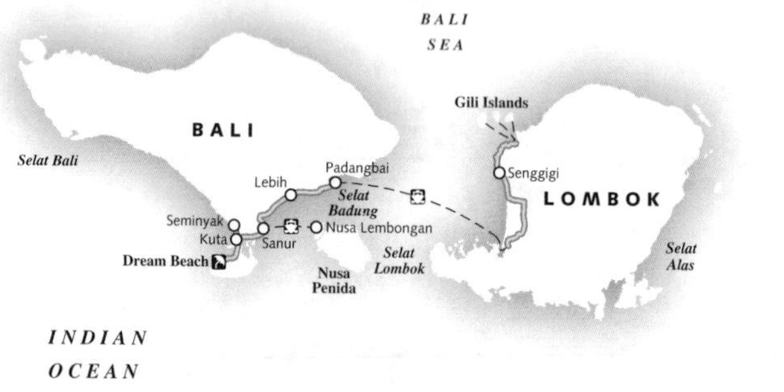

BEST OF BALI **One Week**

Start with a large room by the pool, or on the beach at one of the resorts in **Legian** (p95) or **Seminyak** (p116). Sample the **Kuta Beach** (p95) surf and head to Seminyak for world-class **shopping** (p123). Maybe a seafood dinner on **Jimbaran Bay** (p129), or a trendy restaurant in **Seminyak** (p120). Then hit the clubs in Kuta and Seminyak or a relaxed bar in **Legian** (p112).

Consider some day trips. Head down to surfing beaches like **Dreamlands** (p131) for sun and fun, then on to the spiritual centre (and monkey home) of **Pura Luhur Ulu Watu** (p132). Bali's ancient rice terraces will exhaust your abilities to describe green. Sample these in a drive up to the misty **Pura Luhur Batukau** (p253) followed by the terraces of **Jatiluwih** (p254).

In the east, the new coast road means that you can see wild and unvisited beaches like **Masceti** (p209) followed by the well-mannered royal town of **Semarapura** (p212) with its ruins. Head north up the breathtaking **Sideman Road** (p215), which combines ribbons of rice terraces with lush river valleys and cloud-shrouded mountains. Pass through **Muncan** (p208) and then go east to **Ubud** (p174), the crowning stop on any itinerary.

Bali's rich culture is most-celebrated and most-accessible in Ubud, as you can easily be enraptured by nightly dance performances. Hike through the surrounding rice fields to temples like **Yeh Pulu** (p201) and river valleys like the **Sungai Ayung** (p184). Take a break in **museums** (p175) bursting with paintings in the many styles reflecting Bali.

For pleasure, stay in one of the many **hotels** (p186) near the centre with views across rice fields and rivers. Sample a **spa** (p181) or two before you sample one of the myriad of great **restaurants** (p193) to choose from.

First time visitors to Bali as well as old hands love the island for its beaches, shopping, nightlife, culture and simply beautiful scenery. This itinerary gives you the best of all this and more. Start in the hedonistic south and end up in the cultured climes of Ubud. You may need more than a week!

ROADS LESS TRAVELLED

LEAVING THE CROWDS BEHIND **Two Weeks**

Escape the day-trippers' trails and explore the central mountains. Tackle **Gunung Agung** (p219), the spiritual centre of the island. Start early to reach the top and take in the views before the daily onslaught of clouds and mist.

Having climbed Bali's most legendary peak, head west to the village of **Munduk** (p252), which looks down to the north coast and the sea beyond. Go for a walk in the area and enjoy waterfalls, truly tiny villages, wild fruit trees and the sinuous bands of rice paddies lining the hills like ribbons. Then head south to the wonderful temple of **Pura Luhur Batukau** (p253), and consider a trek up Bali's second-highest mountain, **Gunung Batukau** (p254).

Now bounce across the waves to **Nusa Penida** (p153), the island visible from much of the south and east – it's lush, arid and almost unpopulated. Take in amazing vistas off its cliffs and the marine life, diving under the waves.

Head to Lombok and ignore the resorts in the east. Instead head south. Well off the beaten path, the south coast near Lombok's **Kuta** (p322) has stunning beaches and surfing to reward the intrepid. The little-driven back roads of the interior will thrill the adventurous and curious, with tiny villages where you can learn about the amazing local handicrafts. Many of these roads lead up the flanks of **Gunung Rinjani** (p314), the volcanic peak which shelters the lush and remote **Sembalun Valley** (p313). Trekking from one village to the next on the rim can take days, but is one of the great walks.

First have fun in Bali's south, then get the heck out! This trip takes you up Bali's stunning and spiritual peaks before sending you hiking lush hillside hideaways and on to mostly undiscovered Nusa Penida. Then it's off to the quietest parts of Lombok.

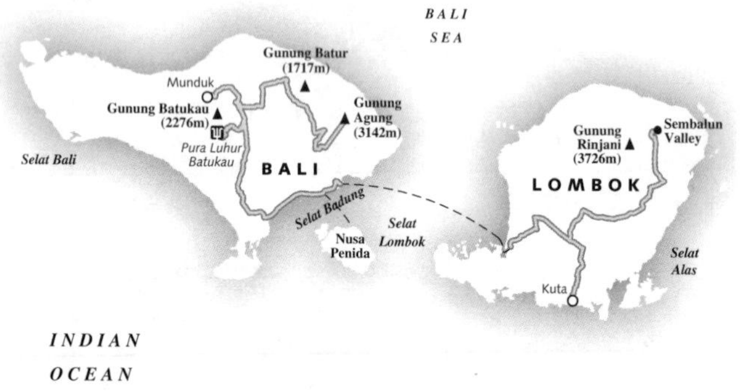

TAILORED TRIPS

SURFING SAFARI

You can have an endless summer in under a 100km radius in Bali. No matter what the season, there will be a break for you. Why not start where surfing in Asia was born – **Kuta Beach** (p95). After sampling the action there, head to the coast around **Canggu** (p125), where the water is wild and the beaches are all but empty. For a classic scene cruise north and then west to **Medewi** (p277), where people surf, sleep and then surf some more. When you're ready for a change of scenery, head back down south towards the Bukit Peninsula and the incredible challenges of the many amazing breaks around **Bingin** (p132) and **Ulu Watu** (p131). Here you can find legendary surfing in unadorned places where it feels as though little has changed in decades. Just working your way through the more than half-a-dozen breaks will take you days.

Once you move east to **Nusa Dua** (p133), you'll see that the towering luxury hotels aren't the only things rising above the horizon – there's often great surf as well. Move north along the coast to **Sanur** (p139) to wax your board... but why bother? Get one of the little boats and head out to **Nusa Lembongan** (p148) where you can get a room with a view of three legendary breaks for little more than the cost of good wax.

INCREDIBLE DIVES

Everyone can see the surfer on top of Bali's waves, but little do they realise that underwater there's even more action. Follow the coast around Bali and you'll be rewarded with one legendary dive spot after another, all with great dive shops and a place to kick back and relax in nearby towns. Head west to **Pulau Menjangan** (p282), in the Taman Nasional Bali Barat. It's renowned for its coral and the best local diving. The nearby **Pemuteran** (p269) hotels define relaxation, and you don't want to miss this diving. Staying at these wonderfully isolated resorts is yet another reason why this is a good place to hang up your flippers. **Lovina** (p262) is a good diving base. As well as being a relaxed beach town, you can reach many of Bali's best sites by day and still have time for one of the amazing local night dives.

Down the east coast is **Tulamben** (p238), where scores of people explore the shattered hulk of a WWII freighter. A smaller wreck lurks off the shores of **Aas** (p234) near Amed. **Padangbai** (p221) is another good diving base; there are lots of local sites to explore and the marine life encompasses everything from sharks to sunfish.

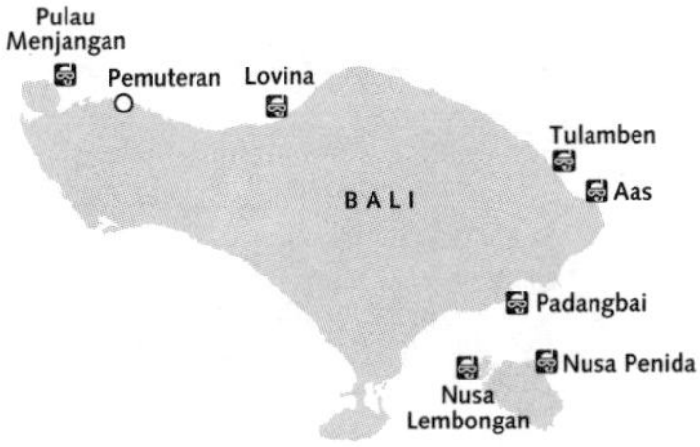

But wait, the brass ring for your dives might be in the distance offshore. The islands of **Nusa Penida** (p153) and **Nusa Lembongan** (p148) both have scores of demanding dives to challenge experienced divers. The rewards are deep grottoes, drop-offs, and everything from mantas to turtles.

SPOIL ME

Kilometre for kilometre, Bali has about the greatest density of fabulous resorts and spas you'll find anywhere. From incredible food to hedonistic pampering, you can give yourself every sensation you want and deserve. Massage, spa treatments or just lounging by a glittering pool, you'll find the peace and pampering you want. Two great hotels – the flashy **Legian** (p120), and the understated **Oberoi** (p119) – are just north of Kuta in Seminyak. They set the standards for the clean, tropical look that has come to be known as 'Bali Style'.

Great places circle the Bukit Peninsula like a pearl necklace. The **Four Seasons Jimbaran Bay** (p127) in Jimbaran, with its white sand and blue sea, pushes exclusivity while the **Ritz Carlton** (p129) pushes posh. Across the peninsula, the **Westin Resort** (p134) and the **Conrad** (p138) are fresh additions to Nusa Dua and Tajung Benoa. At the Conrad you can plunge off your own patio into the vast pool which encircles the hotel.

Some of the most famous places in Bali can be found in the lush lands around Ubud. Along the Ayung Valley, another **Four Seasons Resort** (p193) blends effortlessly with its verdant surrounds. The **Amandari** (p193) and the **Alila Ubud** (p193) both head the A-list going north along the valley.

Along the east coast with its remote beaches and its views of Nusa Penida, you can be pampered at two excellent places with sweeping views of Nusa Penida: the **Alila** (p225) near Manggis and, nearby, the stunning **Amankila** (p224).

BALI'S SPIRITUAL CENTRE

Start at **Pura Luhur Ulu Watu** (p132) right at the southern tip of Bali. On the Bukit Peninsula, it's one of only nine directional temples on the island, as well as being a sea temple honouring the many gods in the waters right around the island. Head east around the peninsula to **Pura Mas Suka** (p133), with its remote outlook over the Indian Ocean. From here go north, following the sea temples along the west coast of South Bali – **Pura Petitenget** (p117) in Seminyak is a classic example. Time your visit to **Pura Tanah Lot** (p272), one of the most important and photographed sea temples, for the morning when crowds are few. One glimpse of its perfect location and you'll understand why the hordes descend for sunset.

In **Ubud** (p174), settle in for a few days at one of the amazing hotels and experience Balinese art and culture. It won't take long to see how beauty of the mind and spirit merge so easily here. You will find the best of Balinese culture both here and in the surrounding villages.

Heading east, **Semarapura** (p212), commonly known as Klungkung, was once the centre of Bali's most important kingdom. While here, learn about how the Balinese held out against the Dutch among its fascinating palace ruins. Or, head into the verdant hills and valleys of East Bali to find your own spiritual centre. End your journey in **Amed** (p234), with its dramatic and contemplative ocean overlooks.

Snapshot

You see signs by the side of the road as you drive around Bali that read 'Bakso Babi'. An innocent-sounding little phrase but one that shows a sea change of attitudes on the island. No, it's not a nascent Balinese political party or a powerful independence slogan or even a cheer for a beloved local leader, rather it's a sign advertising pork meatballs. But in Bali such seemingly simple things are fraught with meaning – those little meatballs sold from carts trolling through neighbourhoods or waiting for peckish drivers are usually made from chicken or beef, meats that go down well with people of any religious faith, especially Muslims from the rest of Indonesia.

Certainly the Balinese (90% practise their own fascinating version of Hinduism) have always loved pork. Just look at the *babi guling* joints all over the island where you can get the succulent and richly seasoned roasted young pork. But a vendor putting 'Bakso Babi' on his cart has found a subtle but clear-cut way of saying 'I'm Balinese, I'm not from Java'. And the Balinese are there munching away in support.

Called 'Bali Krama', loosely 'Bali for the Balinese', the recent uptick in declarations of a more aggressive Balinese identity are notable. The Balinese normally prize a form of modesty and restraint that some mistake for politeness verging on meekness. So when they say to the rest of Indonesia 'you can't eat our meatballs' there's a lot more to it than what gets sold by the side of the road. Although it remains a remarkably tolerant society – there is no reported religious strife on the island – the Balinese can't help but feel threatened by forces in the rest of Indonesia.

As the island saw in October 2005 (p36), the bombings of 2002 were not unique and religious fanatics from elsewhere will come to Bali to make a statement. That so much of the economy now relies on tourism – it is the main producer of cash – means that carnage aside, being a stage for other's fanaticism has enormous costs. When tourists go elsewhere, as they have done, the entire island suffers. Families who sold their rice fields so that a child could go to tourism school and get a cash-paying job are left in a huge bind.

The ongoing downturn in tourism has had a big impact on the economy and is the number one topic of conversation. Even the tiniest village in the remote hills of East Bali has a couple of sons and daughters trying to send home money from tourist jobs in the south.

And matters in the rest of Indonesia have not helped. The string of horrible natural disasters, including those in nearby Java, have scared people away as has worries about bird flu (which also hasn't reached the island). Then there's the politicians in Jakarta, who are yelling about pornography and trying to pass legislation that would put Balinese customs, however modest, in their sights. Given the challenges that the nation faces you'd think the politicians might have better things to do. The strictly G-rated dances that entrance visitors in Ubud could very well be deemed pornographic under the proposed laws.

Meanwhile on Lombok, tourism has never really recovered after religious riots in 2000, and in some rural parts of the island, young people are adopting more militant and fundamentalist Islamic beliefs.

Battered on all sides by natural and manmade forces out of their control, is it any wonder that the Balinese want to stand up for themselves – even if for now it's just with meatballs?

FAST FACTS

Population: Bali 3.2 million; Lombok 3 million

Percentage of land in Bali used for rice production: 20%

Average monthly wage of a tourism worker: US$50-150

Average monthly wage of a farmer: under US$50

Percentage Balinese Hindu: Bali 92%; Lombok 93%

Serving of bakso babi: 4000Rp

Wet season: October to March

Dry season: April to September

Area: Bali 5620 sq km; Lombok 5435 sq km

History

There are few traces of Stone Age people on Bali, although it's certain that the island was populated very early in prehistoric times – fossilised humanoid remains from neighbouring Java have been dated to as early as 250,000 years ago. The earliest human artefacts found on Bali are stone tools and earthenware vessels dug up near Cekik in western Bali, estimated to be 3000 years old. Discoveries continue, and you can see exhibits of bones that may be 4000 years old at the Museum Situs Purbakala Gilimanuk (p283). Artefacts indicate that the Bronze Age began on Bali before 300 BC.

A serene little temple, Pura Gede Perancak (p279), marks the spot in West Bali where Nirartha landed in 1546.

Little is known of Bali during the period when Indian traders brought Hinduism to the Indonesian archipelago, although it is thought it was embraced on the island by the 7th century. The earliest written records are inscriptions on a stone pillar near Sanur, dating from around the 9th century AD; by that time Bali had already developed many similarities to the island you find today. Rice, for example, was grown with the help of a complex irrigation system, probably very like that employed now, and the Balinese had also begun to develop their rich cultural and artistic traditions.

If little is known about the earliest inhabitants of Bali, then even less is known about Lombok until about the 17th century. Early inhabitants are thought to have been Sasaks from a region encompassing today's India and Myanmar.

A Short History of Bali – Indonesia's Hindu Realm, by Robert Pringle, is a thoughtful analysis of Bali's history from the Bronze Age to the present, with excellent sections on the 2002 bombings and ongoing environmental woes caused by tourism and development.

HINDU INFLUENCE

Java began to spread its influence into Bali during the reign of King Airlangga (1019–42), or perhaps even earlier. At the age of 16, when his uncle lost the throne, Airlangga fled into the forests of western Java. He gradually gained support, won back the kingdom once ruled by his uncle and went on to become one of Java's greatest kings. Airlangga's mother had moved to Bali and remarried shortly after his birth, so when he gained the throne there was an immediate link between Java and Bali. At this time the courtly Javanese language known as Kawi came into use among the royalty of Bali, and the rock-cut memorials seen at Gunung Kawi, near Tampaksiring, are a clear architectural link between Bali and 11th-century Java.

After Airlangga's death, Bali remained semi-independent until Kertanagara became king of the Singasari dynasty in Java two centuries later. Kertanagara conquered Bali in 1284, but the period of his greatest power lasted a mere eight years, until he was murdered and his kingdom collapsed. However, the great Majapahit dynasty was founded by his son, Vijaya (or Wijaya). With Java in turmoil, Bali regained its autonomy, and the Pejeng dynasty, centred near modern-day Ubud, rose to great power. In 1343 the legendary Majapahit prime minister, Gajah Mada, defeated the Pejeng king Dalem Bedaulu and brought Bali back under Javanese influence.

Although Gajah Mada brought much of the Indonesian archipelago under Majapahit control, this was the furthest extent of their power. The 'capital' was moved to Gelgel, in Bali near modern Semarapura, around the late 14th century, and for the next two centuries this was the base for the 'king of Bali', the Dewa Agung. The Gelgel dynasty in Bali, under Dalem Batur Enggong,

TIMELINE

7th Century

Bali fully embraces Hinduism

1292

Bail gains independence from Java with death of Kertanagara

extended its power eastwards to the neighbouring island of Lombok and even westwards across the strait to Java.

The collapse of Majapahit into weak, decadent petty kingdoms opened the door for the spread of Islam, from the trading states of the north coast in to heartland Java. As the Hindu states fell, many of the intelligentsia fled to Bali. Notable among these was the priest Nirartha, who is credited with introducing many of the complexities of Balinese religion to the island, as well as establishing the chain of 'sea temples', which includes Pura Luhur Ulu Watu (p132) and Pura Tanah Lot (p272). The court-supported artisans, artists, dancers, musicians and actors also fled to Bali at this time and the island experienced an explosion of cultural activity. The great exodus to Bali was complete by the 16th century.

DUTCH DEALINGS

The first Europeans to set foot in Bali itself were Dutch seamen in 1597. Setting a tradition that has prevailed to the present day, they fell in love with the island and when Cornelius De Houtman, the ship's captain, prepared to set sail from the island, two of his crew refused to come with him. At that time, Balinese prosperity and artistic activity, at least among the royalty, was at a peak, and the king who befriended de Houtman had 200 wives and a chariot pulled by two white buffaloes, not to mention a retinue of 50 dwarfs, whose bodies had been bent to resemble the handle of a kris (traditional dagger). By the early 1600s, the Dutch had established trade treaties with Javanese princes and controlled much of the spice trade, but they were interested in profit, not culture, and barely gave Bali a second glance.

Bali – A Paradise Created, by Adrian Vickers, traces Balinese history and development by concentrating on the island's image in the West.

In 1710 the 'capital' of the Gelgel kingdom was shifted to nearby Klungkung (now called Semarapura), but local discontent was growing; lesser rulers were breaking away, and the Dutch began to move in, using the old strategy of divide and conquer. In 1846 the Dutch used Balinese salvage claims over shipwrecks as a pretext to land military forces in northern Bali, bringing the kingdoms of Buleleng and Jembrana under their control. Their cause was also aided by the various Balinese princes who had gained ruling interests in Lombok and thus were distracted from matters at home and also unaware that the wily Dutch would use Lombok against Bali.

In 1894 the Dutch, the Balinese and the people of Lombok collided in battles that would set the course of history for the next several decades. See the boxed text, p32.

The Balinese rulers of Lombok recognised Dutch sovereignty in 1844, however most of the island's population had other ideas and strife continued for more than 50 years.

With the north of Bali long under Dutch control and the conquest of Lombok successful, the south was never going to last long. Once again, it was disputes over the ransacking of wrecked ships that gave the Dutch an excuse to move in. In 1904, after a Chinese ship was wrecked off Sanur, Dutch demands that the rajah (lord or prince) of Badung pay 3000 silver dollars in damages were rejected, and in 1906 Dutch warships appeared at Sanur.

The Dutch forces landed despite Balinese opposition, and four days later had marched 5km to the outskirts of Denpasar. On 20 September 1906 the Dutch mounted a naval bombardment on Denpasar and began their final assault. The three princes of Badung realised that they were completely outnumbered and outgunned, and that defeat was inevitable. Surrender and exile, however, would have been the worst imaginable outcome, so they decided to take the honourable path of a suicidal *puputan* (a warrior's

1546
The charismatic priest Nirartha brings his own form of Buddhism to Bali

1597
The Dutch first visit Bali

THE BATTLE FOR LOMBOK

In 1894 the Dutch sent an army to back the Sasak people of eastern Lombok in a rebellion against the Balinese rajah (lord or prince) who controlled Lombok with the support of the western Sasak. The rajah quickly capitulated, but the Balinese crown prince decided to fight on.

The Dutch camp at the Mayura Water Palace was attacked late at night by a combined force of Balinese and western Sasak, forcing the Dutch to take shelter in a temple compound. The Balinese also attacked another Dutch camp further east at Mataram, and soon the entire Dutch army on Lombok was forced back to Ampenan where, according to one eyewitness, the soldiers 'were so nervous that they fired madly if so much as a leaf fell off a tree'. These battles resulted in enormous losses of men and arms for the Dutch.

Although the Balinese had won the first battles, they had begun to lose the war. They faced a continuing threat from the eastern Sasak, while the Dutch were soon supported with reinforcements from Java.

The Dutch attacked Mataram a month later, fighting street-to-street against Balinese and western Sasak soldiers and civilians. The Balinese crown prince was killed, and the Balinese retreated to Cakranegara (Cakra), where they had well-armed defensive positions. Cakra was attacked by a large combined force of Dutch and eastern Sasak. Rather than surrender, Balinese men, women and children opted for the suicidal *puputan* (a warrior's fight to the death) and were cut down by rifle and artillery fire. Their stronghold, the Mayura Water Palace, was largely destroyed.

The Balinese rajah and a small group of commanders fled to Sasari near Lingsar, and though the rajah surrendered, most of the Balinese held out. In late November 1894, the Dutch attacked Sasari and, again, a large number of Balinese chose the *puputan*. With the downfall of the dynasty, the local population abandoned its struggle against the Dutch. The conquest of Lombok, considered for decades, had taken the Dutch barely three months. The old rajah died in exile in Batavia (now Jakarta) in 1895.

fight to the death). First the princes burned their palaces, and then, dressed in their finest jewellery and waving ceremonial golden kris, the rajah led the royalty and priests and courtiers out to face the modern weapons of the Dutch.

The Dutch implored the Balinese to surrender rather than make their hopeless stand, but their pleas went unheeded and wave after wave of the Balinese nobility marched forward to their death, or turned their kris on themselves. In all, nearly 4000 Balinese died. The Dutch then marched northwest towards Tabanan and took the rajah of Tabanan prisoner, but he also committed suicide rather than face the disgrace of exile.

The kingdoms of Karangasem and Gianyar had already capitulated to the Dutch and were allowed to retain some of their powers, but other kingdoms were defeated and their rulers exiled. Finally, in 1908 the rajah of Semarapura followed the lead of Badung, and once more the Dutch faced a *puputan*. As had happened at Cakranegara on Lombok, the beautiful palace at Semarapura, Taman Kertha Gosa (p213), was largely destroyed.

With this last obstacle disposed of, all of Bali was under Dutch control and became part of the Dutch East Indies. There was little development of an exploitative plantation economy on Bali, and the common people noticed little difference between Dutch rule and rule under the rajahs. On Lombok, conditions were harder as new Dutch taxes took a toll on the populace.

For much of the 19th century, the Dutch earned enormous amounts of money from the Balinese opium trade. Most of the colonial administrative budget went to promoting the opium industry, which was legal until the 1930s.

1908 Last Balinese kingdom falls to the Dutch

1936 Two Americans build first hotel at Kuta Beach

WWII

In 1942 the Japanese landed unopposed Bali at Sanur (most Indonesians saw the Japanese, at first, as anticolonial liberators). The Japanese established headquarters in Denpasar and Singaraja, and their occupation became increasingly harsh for the Balinese. When the Japanese left in August 1945 after their defeat in WWII, the island was suffering extreme poverty, but the occupation had fostered several paramilitary, nationalist and anticolonial organisations that were ready to fight the returning Dutch.

In Praise of Kuta, by Hugh Mabbett, recounts Kuta's early history and its frenetic modern development.

INDEPENDENCE

In August 1945, just days after the Japanese surrender, Soekarno, the most prominent member of the coterie of nationalist activists, proclaimed the nation's independence, but it took four years to convince the Dutch that they were not going to get their great colony back. In a virtual repeat of the *puputan* nearly 50 years earlier, a Balinese resistance group called Tentara Keamanan Rakyat (People's Security Force) was wiped out by the Dutch in the battle of Marga in western Bali (p274) on 20 November 1946. The

THE TOURIST CLASS

Beginning in the 1920s, the Dutch government realised that Bali's unique culture could be marketed internationally to the growing tourism industry. Relying heavily on images that emphasised the topless habits of Bali's women, Dutch marketing drew wealthy Western adventurers who landed in the north at today's Singaraja and were whisked about the island on rigid three-day itineraries that featured canned cultural shows at a government-run tourist hotel in Denpasar. Accounts from the time are ripe with imagery of supposedly culture-seeking Europeans who really just wanted to see a boob or two. Such desires were often thwarted by Balinese women who covered up when they heard the Dutch jalopies approaching.

But some intrepid travellers arrived independently, often at the behest of the small colony of Western artists such as Walter Spies in Ubud (see p52 and p181). Two of these visitors were Robert Koke and Louise Garret, an unmarried American couple who had worked in Hollywood before landing in Bali in 1936 as part of a global adventure. Horrified at the stuffy strictures imposed by the Dutch tourism authorities, the pair (who were later married) built a couple of bungalows out of palm leaves and other local materials on the otherwise deserted beach at Kuta. Having recently been to Hawaii on a film shoot, Bob and Louise knew the possibilities of a good beach, which at that point was home to only a few impoverished fishing families. Robert left another lasting impression by teaching local boys to surf.

Word soon spread, however, and the Kokes were booked solid. Guests came for days, stayed for weeks and told their friends. The Dutch at first dismissed the Koke's Kuta Beach Hotel as 'dirty native huts', but soon realised that increased numbers of tourists were good for everyone. Other Westerners built their own thatched hotels, complete with the bungalows that were to become a Balinese cliché in the decades ahead.

WWII wiped out tourism and the hotels (the Kokes barely escaped ahead of the Japanese), but once people began travelling again after the war, Bali's inherent appeal made its popularity a forgone conclusion. The introduction of jet travel, reasonably affordable tickets and dirt cheap accommodation on beautiful Kuta Beach gave Bali an endless summer, which began in the 1960s.

In 1987 Louise Koke's long-forgotten story of Kuta Beach Hotel was published as *Our Hotel in Bali*, illustrated with her incisive sketches and her husband's photographs.

1946
Battle at Marga leads to independence for Indonesia

1963
Gunung Agung erupts, devastating East Bali

Dutch finally recognised Indonesia's independence in 1949, but Indonesians celebrate 17 August 1945 as Independence Day.

At first, Bali, Lombok and the rest of Indonesia's eastern islands were grouped together in the unwieldy province of Nusa Tenggara. In 1958 the central government recognised this folly and created three new governmental regions from the one, with Bali getting its own and Lombok becoming part of Nusa Tenggara Barat.

Bali and the Tourist Industry by David Shavit is a highly entertaining look at how tourism developed in Bali between the wars with the help of a menagerie of local and Western characters.

1965 COUP & BACKLASH

Independence was not an easy path for Indonesia to follow. A European-style parliamentary assembly was mired in internecine squabbles, with Soekarno as the beloved figurehead president. When Soekarno assumed more direct control in 1959 after several violent rebellions, he proved to be as inept a peacetime administrator as he was inspirational as a revolutionary leader. In the early 1960s, as Soekarno faltered, the army, communists, and other groups struggled for supremacy. On 30 September 1965, an attempted coup – blamed on the Partai Komunis Indonesia (PKI, or Communist Party) – led to Soekarno's downfall. General Soeharto (he didn't get the Muhammad moniker until the late '80s) emerged as the leading figure in the armed forces, displaying great military and political skill in suppressing the coup. The PKI was outlawed and a wave of anticommunist reprisals followed, which escalated into a wholesale massacre of suspected communists throughout the Indonesian archipelago.

Bali's airport is named for I Ngurah Rai, the national hero who died leading the resistance against the Dutch at Marga in 1946.

In Bali, the events had an added local significance as the main national political organisations, the Partai Nasional Indonesia (PNI, Nationalist Party) and PKI, crystallised existing differences between traditionalists, who wanted to maintain the old caste system, and radicals, who saw the caste system as repressive and who were urging land reform. After the failed coup, religious traditionalists in Bali led the witch-hunt for the 'godless communists'. Eventually the military stepped in to control the anticommunist purge, but no-one on Bali was untouched by the killings, estimated at between 50,000 and 100,000 out of a population of about two million, a percentage many times higher than on Java. Many tens of thousands more died on Lombok.

SOEHARTO COMES & GOES

Following the failed coup in 1965 and its aftermath, Soeharto established himself as president and took control of the government, while Soekarno was shoved aside, spending his final days under house arrest in the hills above Jakarta. Under Soeharto's 'New Order' government, Indonesia looked to the West in foreign policy, and Western-educated economists set about balancing budgets, controlling inflation and attracting foreign investment.

Politically, Soeharto ensured that Golkar (officially not a political party), with strong support from the army, became the dominant political force. Other political parties were banned or crippled by the disqualification of candidates and the disenfranchisement of voters. Regular elections maintained the appearance of a national democracy, but until 1999, Golkar won every election hands down. This period was also marked by great economic development in Bali and later in Lombok as social stability and maintenance of a favourable investment climate took precedence over democracy.

1965
Political and religious violence in Bali and on Lombok kills tens of thousands

1998
Soeharto resigns as president although his family retains control of several Bali resorts

LONELY PLANET 1975

A verdant tropical island so picturesquely and immaculately presented it could easily be a painted backdrop.

Kuta Beach At latest count there were over a 100 (over one hundred!) places to stay. One item you won't find on the menus are the 'special' omelettes and pizzas. About 400Rp for a large one – the special ingredients are the mushrooms. There's quite a rush on them at mid afternoon to ensure a good high by sunset.

Legian With Kuta getting bigger and more resort-like daily, a lot of people are moving 2km down the road to Legian, the mushroom village... They even has electricity now.

Tony Wheeler in South-East Asia on a Shoestring, *first edition (1975)*

In early 1997 Southeast Asia began to suffer a severe economic crisis, and within the year the Indonesian currency (the rupiah) had all but collapsed and the economy was on the brink of bankruptcy. To help deal with the continuing economic crisis, Soeharto agreed to the International Monetary Fund's (IMF) demand to increase the government-subsidised price of electricity and petrol, resulting in immediate increases in the cost of public transport, rice and other food staples. Riots broke out across Indonesia and although Bali and Lombok were spared most of the violence, their tourism-dependent economies were battered.

Unable to cope with the escalating crisis, Soeharto resigned in 1998, after 32 years in power. His protégé, Dr Bacharuddin Jusuf Habibie, became president. Though initially dismissed as a Soeharto crony, he made the first notable steps in opening the door to real democracy, such as freeing the press from government supervision. However he failed to tackle most of the critical issues dogging Indonesia such as corruption, and his cavalier handling of East Timor's independence helped to precipitate the 1999 massacres.

TERRORISTS & RECOVERY

In 1999, Indonesia's parliament met to elect a new president. The frontrunner was Megawati Sukarnoputri, whose party received the largest number of votes at the election. Megawati was enormously popular in Bali, partly because of family connections (her paternal grandmother was Balinese) and partly because her party was essentially secular (the mostly Hindu Balinese are very concerned about any growth in Muslim fundamentalism). However, the newly empowered Islamist parties helped to shift the balance of power. By astutely playing both the Islam card and using his long-standing relationship with Golkar leaders, Abdurrahman Wahid, the moderate, intellectual head of Indonesia's largest Muslim organisation, emerged as president.

Bali Blues by Jeremy Allan tells of the struggle by locals to survive in Kuta during the year following the 2002 terrorist attacks.

Outraged supporters of Megawati took to the streets of Java and Bali. In Bali, the demonstrations were typically more disruptive than violent – trees were felled to block the main Nusa Dua road, and government buildings were damaged in Denpasar and Singaraja. The election of Megawati as vice-president quickly defused the situation.

On Lombok, however, religious and political tensions spilled over in early 2000 when a sudden wave of attacks starting in Mataram burned Chinese-Christian businesses and homes across the island. The impact on tourism was immediate and severe, and the island is still trying to put this shameful episode behind it.

2000
Religious riots on Lombok devastate tourism

2002
Bombs in Kuta on October 22 killed over 200

LOCAL RULE BALI STYLE

Within Bali's government, the most important body is also the most local. More 3500 neighbourhood organisations called *banjars* wield enormous power. Comprising the married men of a given area (somewhere between 50 and 500), a *banjar* controls most community activities, whether it's planning for a temple ceremony or making important land use decisions. Decisions are reached by consensus and woe to a member who shirks his duties. The penalty can be fines or worse: banishment from the *banjar*.

Although women and even children can belong to the *banjar,* only men attend the meetings where important decisions are taken. Women, who often own the businesses in tourist areas, have to communicate through their husband to exert their influence. One thing that outsiders in a neighbourhood quickly learn is that one does not cross the *banjar*. Entire streets of restaurants and bars have been closed by order of the *banjar* after it was determined that neighbourhood concerns over matters such as noise were not being addressed.

As with his predecessor Soekarno, Wahid's moral stature and vast intellect did not translate into administrative competence. His open contempt towards squabbling parliamentarians did little to garner him much-needed support. After 21 months of growing ethnic, religious and regional conflicts, parliament had enough ammunition to recall Wahid's mandate and hand the presidency to Megawati.

Indonesia's cultural wars continued and certainly played a role in the October 2002 bombings in Kuta. More than 200 tourists and Balinese were killed and hundreds more were injured. Besides the obvious enormous monetary loss (tourism immediately fell by more than half), the blasts fuelled the ever-present suspicions the Hindu Balinese hold regarding Muslims (that the Muslim Javanese are trying to muscle in on the profitable Bali scene, and the Muslims from Indonesia are, in general, looking to show prejudice against non-Muslim Balinese) and shattered the myth of isolation enjoyed by many locals. See the boxed text, p102 for more on this and subsequent bombings which have dramatically changed life on the island.

For a different take on Bali, read Geoffrey Robinson's enlightening revisionist history *Bali, The Dark Side of Paradise*.

Blessedly the elections of 2004 managed to dispel fears and were remarkably peaceful. Susilo Bambang Yudhoyono (popularly known as 'SBY') beat incumbent Megawati Sukarnoputri. A former general and government minister, SBY promised strong and enlightened leadership. He has been put to the test numerous times since, with the tsunami that devastated Aceh in 2004, the spread of bird flu and the volcano eruption and tsunami which hit Java in 2006. So far there has been little to show that he'll enjoy more success than Soeharto, Wahid et al.

Meanwhile Bali continued to be affected by global politics. Its relationship with Australia became fractious over several high-profile arrests of Australians on drug charges and a perception that Indonesia had been lenient with many of those accused of the 2002 bombings which killed 88 Australians.

Still, tourism numbers had almost recovered by October 2005 when three suicide bombers killed 20 people – including five tourists – in Kuta and Jimbaran. Evidence collected in the following months showed that the attacks had been masterminded by a British- and Australian-educated engineer on behalf of a fundamentalist Islamic group based in Indonesia. Again tourism numbers suffered and the entire island's economy took a hit.

2004

Peaceful elections see Susilo Bambang Yudhoyono elected president of Indonesia

2005

Suicide bombers kill 20 in South Bali

The Culture

REGIONAL IDENTITY

Bali is commonly described as a heaven for its cheery, offering-proffering residents but it is a romanticism worthy of a tourist brochure at best. Life is often hard and the average Balinese person has a hardscrabble existence that would be familiar to people worldwide. However, the Balinese do excel in one key area – they have an undeniable talent for making use of every resource on the island: bamboo, vines, flowers and shells for their imaginative offerings; European perfumes, international CDs, brand-name clothing for rip-off copying. Even the tourist is a resource to be painted, oiled, massaged, manipulated, tattooed or plaited.

Balinese life centres around the village, and increasingly, the suburban neighbourhoods of the south. Every activity – from producing crops to preparing food, and from bargaining with tourists to keeping the youth employed – involves everybody. It is impossible to be a faceless nonentity on the island. This involvement with other people in the village extends to tourists. To make you feel welcome, Balinese will go out of their way to chat to you. But they won't talk about the weather or even the football. They are interested in you, your home life and your personal relationships. Chatting in Bali can get rather personal (see p57) but is never with malicious intent.

"Balinese are known for their sense of fun, their joy of life"

Balinese are known for their sense of fun, their joy of life, and their ability to adapt a situation to suit changing needs. The legend that tells of how a group of Balinese farmers promised to sacrifice a pig if their harvest was good is an example of this. As the bountiful harvest time approached, no pig could be found. Then they had an idea. The sacrifice had been promised after the harvest. If there was always new rice growing, the harvest would always be about to take place and no sacrifice would be necessary. Since then, farmers have always planted one field of rice before harvesting another.

Everybody loves children – visit Bali with your kids and you'll have a constant stream of people making sure they enjoy every moment. In one memorable scene, an otherwise irascible driver-tout dived to pluck a tourist child walking into the path of a taxi. Older children take care of the younger ones in their family or village. They're always seen carrying a child on their hips, all of them remarkably well-behaved and happy.

Women enjoy a prominent position in Bali, from manual labour jobs (you'll see them carrying baskets of wet cement on their heads) to almost every job in the tourist industry. In fact, the traditional female role of caring for people and preparing food means that many successful tourists shops and cafés were established by women.

Traditional Balinese society is founded on the Balinese Hindu religion and it permeates every aspect of life. There are temples in every village, shrines in every field, offerings made at every corner, nook and cranny. The Balinese feel that their religion should be an enjoyable thing, for mortals as well as the gods. It's summed up well in their attitude to offerings – once the gods have eaten the 'essence' of the food, you've still got enough left over to be satisfied (see p45).

The Balinese are a very proud, confident race, with a culture that extends throughout the generations. It's a culture they embrace with passion. After all, it's only a hundred years ago that 4000 Balinese nobility, dressed in their finest, walked out into the gunfire of the Dutch army rather than become colonial subjects (p31).

LIFESTYLE

For the average rural Balinese, the working day is not long. Their expertise at coaxing bountiful harvests from the fertile volcanic soil leaves them lots of quality time to chat or to prepare elaborate cultural events. In the towns, the working day is longer, but although routine observances may be less elaborate, they are undertaken with no less devotion.

Island of Bali, by Miguel Covarrubias, written in the 1930s, is still a fantastic introduction to the romance and seduction of the island and its culture.

In villages life is concentrated under the tropical vegetation of palm, breadfruit, mango, papaya, and banana trees. The centre of a village has an open meeting space, temples, the town market, perhaps a former prince's home, the *kulkul* (hollow tree-trunk drum used to sound a warning or call meetings) tower and quite likely a big banyan tree. The *banjar* (local division of a village consisting of all the married adult males) continues the strong community spirit by organising village festivals, marriage ceremonies, cremations and the local gamelan (traditional Balinese orchestra). The headquarters is the open-sided *bale banjar* (communal meeting place of a *banjar*) where you might see a gamelan practice, a meeting, food being prepared for a feast, or men preening their roosters for the next round of cockfights.

In the more urbanized south however, life embodies many of the same hassles of modern life anywhere. There's traffic, noise that drowns out even the loudest barking dog and various social ills such as drugs. There is though still a concept of village life under it all in that people are part of a greater group beyond their immediate family. This is important as women are finding much to do outside of the home, whether it's work or even cultural activities. Child care becomes an adult responsibility, not just a family or maternal one. In the end, an air-conditioned mall fills in for the village banyan tree as a meeting place for many.

Bali has three university campuses: in Singaraja, Denpasar and on the Bukit Peninsula.

Historically, the culture on Lombok is almost as rich as Bali's, but today it is no longer as colourful or as accessible as in Bali. Ancient traditions of worship, including elements of Hindu and animist beliefs, have all but died out as the vast majority of people now practise orthodox Islam. Nevertheless, small numbers of Wektu Telu (p316), a religion unique to Lombok, still exist and both Lombok's Balinese and Buginese communities help add to the diversity.

DON'T HANG THOSE UNDIES! *Janet de Neefe*

You might have noticed that the Balinese often dry their clothes on the grass in the fields or on low clothes racks. In Bali, clothing is considered unclean and should never occupy high sacred spaces. Even in my cupboard, my temple clothes occupy the top shelves with underwear strictly reserved for the lowest area.

When my husband Ketut, who is Balinese, saw our Hills Hoists and clothes lines in the suburbs of Melbourne, he was deeply offended. He ended up drying all his clothes, in the middle of winter, on a low bench in the backyard. Recently, he invited a priest to scan our Balinese compound for any negative energies that compounds tend to accumulate. When all was ready, Ketut did a final check of the property before the redeemed priest was about to arrive. Suddenly, he ran to me in a panic saying, ' you must go and tell the tourist to take all his washing down!' I ran to the front of our compound and was greeted with a riot of wet laundry in all shapes and sizes, flapping happily in the breeze. Our guest had decided to wash everything he owned. His sand shoes and wet underwear, shirts and other articles were stuck on branches, hung from lamps and stretched between the pillars out the front of his room. I quickly had to ask him if he could remove the garments until the priest was finished, and politely added that to display one's washing so high is very offensive for the Balinese. Since then, I have added a note in our guest rooms advising that all washing should only be hung to dry on the clothes racks provided.

Ceremonies & Rituals

Every stage of life, from conception to cremation, is marked by a series of ceremonies and rituals, which are the basis of the rich, varied and active Balinese cultural life.

BIRTH & CHILDHOOD

The first ceremony of Balinese life takes place when women reach the third month of pregnancy, with offerings to ensure the wellbeing of the baby. Soon after the birth, the afterbirth is buried with appropriate offerings. Twelve days later women are 'purified' through another ceremony. After 42 days, offerings are made for the baby's future.

Balinese education begins with six years of primary school, which most children attend – you'll see them walking along the roads in their uniforms.

The much-repeated Balinese names – which are gender neutral – carry a symbolic meaning, indicating social status and birth order. Low caste Balinese name their first child Wayan, Putu or Gede; the second is Made, Kadek or Nengah; the third is Nyoman or Komang; and the fourth is Ketut. The fifth, sixth, seventh and eighth children re-use the same set. The large number of Balinese named Anak Agung, a name denoting the child of a royal concubine, attest to the fertility of the Balinese rajahs (princes).

A child goes through 13 celebrations, or *manusa yadnya*. At 105 days, the baby is welcomed to the family and its feet are allowed to touch the ground for the first time – ground is considered impure, so babies are held until then. At 210 days (first Balinese year) the baby is spiritually blessed in the ancestral temple and there's a huge feast for the family and community.

A rite of passage to adulthood is the tooth-filing ceremony, when a priest symbolically files a teenager's (around 16 to 18 years) upper front teeth to produce a pleasing line. Crooked fangs are, after all, one of the chief distinguishing marks of evil spirits – just have a look at a Rangda mask! No-one may marry unless their teeth have been filed.

The Balinese tooth-filing ceremony closes with the recipient being given a delicious *jamu* (herbal tonic), made from freshly pressed turmeric, betel-leaf juice, lime juice and honey.

MARRIAGE

Every Balinese is expected to marry at a relatively young age. In rural areas this can be the late teens, and in the urban south it's after formal schooling is completed or a solid job secured. In general, marriages are not arranged, although there are strict rules that apply between the castes.

The respectable way to marry, known as *mapadik*, is when the family of the man visits the family of the woman and politely proposes. The Balinese, however, like their fun and often prefer marriage by *ngorod* (elopement). Nobody is too surprised when the young man spirits away his bride-to-be. The couple go into hiding and somehow the girl's parents, no matter how assiduously they search, never manage to find her.

Eventually the couple re-emerge, the marriage is officially recognised and everybody has had a lot of fun and games. Elopement has another advantage: apart from being exciting and mildly heroic, it's cheaper.

DEATH & CREMATION

The last ceremony, *pitra yadna* (cremation), is often the biggest, most spectacular, noisy and exciting event. Because of the burdensome cost of even a modest cremation ceremony, the deceased are buried, sometimes for years, and disinterred for a mass cremation with the cost shared among families. Brahmanas (high priests), however, must be cremated immediately.

The body is carried in a tall, incredibly artistic multitiered tower made of bamboo, paper, tinsel, silk, cloth, mirrors, flowers and anything else colourful, on the shoulders of a group of men. The number of tiers of the tower depends on the importance of the deceased. The funeral of a rajah or high priest may require hundreds of men to tote the 11-tiered structure.

COCKFIGHTS

Cockfights are a regular feature of temple ceremonies – a combination of sacrifice, sport and gambling. Men keep fighting cocks as prized pets, carefully grooming and preparing them for their brief moment of glory or defeat. Look for their hoop-shaped baskets near houses.

At the festival, the cocks are matched, a lethally sharp metal spur is tied to one leg, there's a crescendo of shouting and betting, the birds are pushed against each other to stir them up, then they're released and the feathers fly. It's usually over in seconds – a slash of the spur and one rooster is down and dying. After the bout, the successful gamblers collect their pay-offs and the winning owner gets to take the dead rooster home for his cooking pot. When travelling in rural Bali, you'll know there's a cockfight nearby when you see scores of vehicles and scooters parked near a temple but nobody in sight. The men are usually back behind the compound.

Although cock-fighting was once a method of keeping the small amounts of available cash in circulation, as more people in Bali hold jobs, wagering has exploded. It now diverts family income from school fees and credit payments.

Along the way, the group confuses the deceased's spirit so it cannot find its way back home. They shake the tower, run it around in circles, throw water at it and generally make the trip anything but a stately funeral crawl. Meanwhile, the priest halfway up the tower hangs on grimly, doing his best to soak bystanders with holy water. A gamelan sprints behind, providing an exciting musical accompaniment.

At the cremation ground, the body is transferred to a funeral sarcophagus which corresponds to the deceased's caste (p43) – a black bull for a Brahmana, white bull for priests, winged lion for a Ksatriyasa, and elephant-fish for a Sudra. Finally, it all goes up in flames and the ashes are taken to the sea to be scattered on the waves. With the material body well and truly destroyed, the soul is free to descend to heaven and wait for the next incarnation.

Reality Check

There is a growing problem with drug use among Balinese youth and on Lombok, especially with crystal meth – yabba – brought over from Java and sold cheaply to teenagers with access to cash raised from the tourism economy.

Local attitudes to sexuality differ to the Western misconceptions that still persist. For example, in rural areas people still bathe naked by the side of the road. This is not a show of exhibitionism, but a tradition; while bathing, they consider themselves invisible.

Begging has no place in traditional Balinese society – what you see in the south and at times in Ubud are either the mountain Aga people or families from Java.

Though unmarried Balinese girls are ostensibly virgins, discreet premarital sex is common, but generally restricted to couples who intend to marry. Sex workers and willing companions looking for some cash or merchandise on the side, however, are common in tourist areas. These people – of both sexes – are usually from another island, with Java being the primary source. In some cases they are from villages in the north and are counting on not being seen in the company of a foreigner by any one they know.

Balinese culture keeps intimacy behind doors. Holding hands is not customary for couples in Bali, and is reserved for small children; however, linking arms for adults is the norm.

ECONOMY

Bali's economy has traditionally been agricultural. A majority of Balinese worked in the fields, and agriculture still contributes about 40% of Bali's total economic output, although a much smaller proportion of its export income. Coffee, copra, seaweed (p150) and cattle are major agricultural exports – most of the rice goes to feed Bali's own population.

But tourism really is the engine of Balinese economic life. There's the money that pours in with visitors, and that which is made when people abroad buy Balinese goods. The value of handicrafts exported each year (whether silly and profane wood-carvings in a backpack or exquisite ikat cloth destined for a designer abroad) is at least US$1.5 billion.

Within the often-battered Indonesian economy, Bali is a relatively affluent province, with tourism providing a substantial hard-currency income, along with the craft and garment industries. Economic problems and unemployment elsewhere in Indonesia have led to an increasing number of people coming to Bali from other islands, hoping for work or for some other way to make money, and this is a continuing source of tension.

The Tourism Industry

Tourism accounts for about 40% of Bali's formal economy. This is achieved through the provision of accommodation, meals, services and souvenirs to visitors. You won't go anywhere in Bali and not see the importance of visitors to the island's livelihood. In many ways it underpins the economy, providing the funds needed for Bali to develop its infrastructure, educational system and more. The bombings of 2002 and 2005, coupled with bad relations with Australia, caused a plunge in visitor numbers that have sent shock waves throughout the island's economy. Shops and other businesses have closed by the score and the effects have been felt in the most remote villages as young people are no longer able to send home their earnings from tourism.

Farmers must join the local *subak* (rice growers' association). The *subak* ensures that water reaches all the paddies, so whoever's field is at the bottom is usually elected to lead the organisation since his happiness will mean others are happy as well.

In 2006, the total number of visitors was expected to be somewhere near 1.2 million, down 20% from the peak year of 2001. With the numbers of visiting Australians – who historically shared top visitor status with the Japanese – down more than 50%, Bali has had to rely more on tourists from Asia, North America and Europe. The entire industry is also undergoing a shift as the high end of the market continues to grow, seen in the hundreds of villas displacing rice fields north and west of Seminyak.

Lombok's tourism industry, though much smaller, has suffered several lean years since rioting provoked by religious and cultural tensions affected Senggigi in 2000. Though visitor numbers remain depressed in many parts of Lombok, the Gili Islands, particularly Trawangan, have largely bucked this trend.

STOPPING CHILD-SEX TOURISM IN BALI

Unfortunately, Indonesia has become a destination for foreigners seeking to sexually exploit local children. A range of socioeconomic factors render many children and young people vulnerable to such abuse and some individuals prey upon this vulnerability. The sexual abuse and exploitation of children has serious, life-long and even life-threatening consequences for the victims. Strong laws exist in Indonesia to prosecute offenders and many countries also have extraterritorial legislation which allows nationals to be prosecuted in their own country for these intolerable crimes.

Travellers can help stop child-sex tourism by reporting suspicious behaviour. Call the **Women & Children Care Unit** (☎ 0361-226 783, ext 127) of the Bali police. If you know the nationality of the individual, you can contact their embassy directly.

For more information, contact the following organisations:

Child Wise (www.childwise.net) This is the Australian member of ECPAT.

ECPAT (End Child Prostitution & Trafficking; www.ecpat.org) A global network working on these issues, with over 70 affiliate organisations around the world.

PKPA (Center for Study & Child Protection; ☎ 061 663 7821 in Medan, Sumatra) An organisation committed to the protection of Indonesia's children and the prevention of child-sex tourism.

The average Balinese earns US$100 a month in income, and restaurant, hotel and shop workers often make only half as much. Something to remember when you think about leaving a tip.

Although exact numbers are hard to come by, it's generally agreed that Bali has Indonesia's highest literacy rate.

POPULATION & MULTICULTURALISM

Bali is densely populated, with over 3.1 million people, almost all of the Balinese Hindu religion. Other residents come from Java, Sumatra and Nusa Tenggara; the Balinese tourist industry is a magnet for people seeking jobs and business opportunities.

The Balinese people are predominantly of the Malay race, descendants of the groups that travelled southeast from China around 3000 BC. Before that, ethnic strands have been traced to the Australian Aborigine, India, Polynesia and Melanesia, and a diverse range of physical features from those groups can be seen in Bali's population.

In Lombok, the majority of people live in and around the principal centres of Mataram, Praya and Selong. Almost 90% of the people are Sasak, with minority populations of Balinese, Chinese, Buginese, Javanese and Arabs. The Sasak are assumed to have come from northwestern India or Myanmar (Burma), and the clothing the women wear today – long black sarongs called *lambung* and short-sleeved blouses with V-necks – is very similar to that worn in those areas. The sarong is held by a 4m scarf called a *sabuk*, trimmed with brightly coloured stripes. Women wear very little jewellery and never any gold ornaments. Most Sasak people are Muslims, and many traditional beliefs are interwoven with Muslim ideology.

The Balinese of Lombok have retained their Balinese Hindu customs and traditions. They contributed to the emergence of Lombok's Wektu Telu religion (p316), and Balinese temples, ceremonies and processions are a colourful part of western Lombok's cultural life.

Ethnic minorities in Bali include the Bali Aga of the central highlands, whose Hindu traditions predate the arrival of the Majapahit court in the 15th

AVOIDING OFFENCE

Be aware and respectful of local sensibilities, and dress and act appropriately, especially in the rural villages and religious sites. When in doubt let the words 'modest' and 'humble' guide you.

- An increasing number of younger Balinese now adopt the dress of visitors, which means you'll see shorts everywhere. Overly revealing clothing is still frowned upon though – few want to see your butt crack.
- Many women go topless on Bali's tourist beaches, but bring a top for less touristy beaches (definitely if you're going to Lombok).
- Thongs (flip-flops) are acceptable in temples if you're otherwise well dressed, but if you are going to a government office, say to get a local driving licence, you need to look smarter.
- Take off your shoes before entering a mosque or someone's house.
- Don't touch anyone on the head, as it is regarded as the abode of the soul and is therefore sacred.
- Pass things with your right hand. To show more respect, pass something using both hands.
- Beware of talking with your hands on your hips as it is a sign of contempt, anger or aggression (as displayed in traditional dance and opera).
- Shaking hands is customary for both men and women on introduction and greeting.
- Beckon to someone with the hand extended and a downward waving motion. The Western method of beckoning is considered very rude.

BALI'S CASTES

Caste in Bali determines roles in religious rituals and the language to be used in social situations. This caste system derives from Hindu traditions on Java around 1350, and the structure, which suited Dutch interests, was entrenched during the colonial period.

Most Balinese belong to the common Sudra caste. The rest belong to the *triwangsa* (three people) caste which is divided into: Brahmana, high priests with titles of Ida Bagus (male) and Ida Ayu (female); Ksatriyasa, merchants with titles of Cokoda (males) and Anak Ayung (females); and Wesia, the nobility with titles of Gusti Ngura or Dewa Gede (male), and Gusti Ayu or Dewa Ayu (female). Despite the titles, the importance of one's caste is diminishing, as status now comes more from education, economic success and community influence.

Caste differences in language is overcome by the use of 'polite' forms of Balinese, or the use of the national Indonesian language (Bahasa Indonesia), itself a sign of status (for information on languages, see p373). In a traditional village, however, caste is still a central part of life, and absolutely essential to all religious practices.

century. There are Chinese in the larger towns, Indian and Arab merchants in Denpasar and thousands of permanent Western expatriate residents (p122). The island is a model of religious tolerance, with two Christian villages, some Chinese temples, a Buddhist monastery and Muslim communities, particularly around the ports of Gilimanuk, Singaraja, Benoa and Padangbai. Though Bali Hinduism largely defines the culture, in most cases, permanent residents professing other religions still refer to themselves as Balinese.

Ethnic minorities in Lombok include Chinese, brought over to serve as coolies in the rice paddies beginning in the 18th century. Many went on to set up their own businesses, which were singled out in the riots of 2000. The Arabs in Lombok are by and large devout Muslims, well educated and relatively affluent. In the late 19th century, Buginese from south Sulawesi settled in coastal areas and their descendants still operate much of the fishing industry.

MEDIA

Following the end of Soeharto's authoritarian rule, the press enjoyed a degree of freedom. However, it was short-lived. The courts have allowed defamation suits to be filed by government officials and businesspeople against editors and reporters using the Criminal Code instead of the Press Law. A consequence of this has been an increase in self-censorship.

Meanwhile, the influential *Jakarta Post* promotes a more humane civil society while serving the needs of its readers, both expatriate and Indonesian. In Bali visitors are likely to see scores of tourist-oriented publications which avoid serious controversy. The best source of local news in English is the Bali Discovery website (www.balidiscovery.com), which has a news section that draws from many local sources.

You may also see copies of the Indonesian edition of *Playboy* on newsstands. It's published in Denpasar, and despite having centrefolds featuring models wearing considerably more than the average tourist on Kuta Beach, it was chased out of Jakarta by Islamic protesters.

See p346 for details on broadcasting and other publications in Bali and Lombok.

The Sweat of Pearls: Short Stories About Women of Bali, by Putu Oka Sukanta, is a small collection of engaging stories about village life. Try to find a copy in one of the many used-book stalls.

RELIGION

Hinduism

Hinduism was the predominant religion in Indonesia (there are remarkable Hindu monuments on Java) until the great Hindu kingdom, the Majapahit, evacuated to Bali, taking their religion and rituals, and also the

TEMPLE ETIQUETTE

Foreigners can enter most temple complexes if decently dressed. Ususally, clean, tidy clothing and a *selandong* (traditional scarf) or sash to tie around your waist – some temples have these for hire for around 2000Rp, or a donation – is an acceptable show of respect for the gods.

Priests should be shown respect, particularly at festivals. Don't put yourself higher than them (eg by climbing on a wall to take photos).

Usually there's a sign at temple entrances warning you to be respectful, and asking that women not enter if menstruating. At this time women are thought to be *sebel* (ritually unclean), as are pregnant women and those who have recently given birth, or been recently bereaved.

art, literature, music and culture. While the Bali Aga retreated to the hills to escape this new influence, the rest of the population simply adapted it for themselves. The Balinese overlaid the Majapahit interpretation of Hinduism on their animist beliefs creating the unusual Balinese form of the religion.

Balinese worship the trinity of Brahma, Shiva and Vishnu, three aspects of the one god, Sanghyang Widi. The basic threesome is always alluded to, but never seen – a vacant shrine or empty throne tells all. Balinese temples come to life at the regular and colourful temple festivals (p337). A temple ritual involves major communal offerings, plus each family's own large and colourful offering, brought in in a spectacular procession. The betel on top of every offering symbolises the Hindu Trinity, as do the three basic colours used – red for Brahma, black or green for Wisnu, and white for Siwa. Conical shapes are models of the cosmic mountain and rice cookies represent plants, animals, people or buildings.

Islam

Islam is a minority religion in Bali; most who practise it are descendants of seafaring people from Sulawesi. Mosques are most often seen at seaports and fishing villages.

Gujarati merchants brought Islam to Lombok via the Celebes (now Sulawesi) and Java in the 13th century. The traditions and rituals affect all aspects of daily life. Friday afternoon is the official time for worship, when all government offices and many businesses close. Many, but not all, Muslim women in Lombok wear headscarfs, very few choose to wear the veil, and large numbers work in the tourism industry. Middle-class Muslim girls are often able to choose their own partners. In east Lombok most people practise a stricter, more conservative variety of Islam, and there is evidence that more radical, anti-Western beliefs are taking root with some youths.

The ancient Hindu swastika seen all over Bali is a symbol of harmony with the universe. The German Nazis used a version where the arms are always bent in a clockwise direction.

Wektu Telu

This unique religion originated in Bayan, in north Lombok. *Wektu* means 'result' in Sasak, while *telu* means 'three' and signifies the three religions that comprise Wektu Telu: Balinese Hinduism, Islam and animism. The tenet is that all important aspects of life are underpinned by a trinity. The Wektu Telu (p316) believe they have three main duties: to believe in Allah; to avoid the temptations of the devil; and to cooperate with, help and love other people.

The Wektu Telu have three days of fasting and prayer for Ramadan. They pray when and where they feel the need, so all public buildings have a prayer corner that faces Mecca. And, they believe that everything that comes from Allah is good, therefore pork is good.

ARTS

The richness of Bali's arts and crafts has its origin in the fertility of the land. The purest forms are the depictions of Dewi Sri, the rice goddess, intricately made from dried and folded strips of palm leaf to ensure that the fertility of the rice fields continues.

Until the tourist invasion, the acts of painting or carving were purely to decorate temples and shrines and to enrich ceremonies. Today, with galleries and craft shops everywhere, paintings are stacked up on their floors and you trip over stone- or woodcarvings. Much of it is churned out quickly, but you will still find a great deal of beautiful work.

Balinese dance, music and *wayang kulit* (a leather puppet used in shadow puppet plays) performances are one of the reasons that Bali is much more than just a beach destination. The artistry on display here will stay with you long after you've moved on from the island.

On Lombok you can find excellent crafts, including pottery in villages such as Banyumulek (p292). There are many shops and galleries with good items in Mataram (p290) and Senggigi (p298).

Richly illustrated, *The Art & Culture of Bali* by Urs Ramseyer is a comprehensive work on the foundations of Bali's complex and colourful artistic and cultural heritage.

Dance

BALI

You can catch a quality dance performance in Bali anywhere there's a festival or celebration, and you'll find exceptional performances in and around Ubud. Enjoying this purely Balinese form of art is reason enough to visit and no visit is complete without this quintessential Bali experience.

To see good Balinese dance on a regular basis, you'll want to spend some time in Ubud. For an idea of what's on, see p197. Performances typically take place at night and although choreographed with the short attention spans of tourists in mind they can last two hours or more. Absorb the hypnotic music and the alluring moves of the performers and the hours will, er, dance past. Admission to dances is generally around 50,000Rp. Music, theatre and dance courses are available in Ubud, where private teachers advertise instruction in various of the Balinese instruments (see p185).

A great resource on Bali culture and life is www.murnis.com. Click through to Culture to find explanations on everything from kids' names to what one wears to a ceremony and the weaving of the garments.

OFFERINGS

Although tourists in Bali may think they are the honoured guests, the real honoured guests are the gods, ancestors, spirits and demons that live in Bali. They are presented with offerings throughout each day to show respect and gratitude, or perhaps to bribe a demon into being less mischievous.

A gift to a higher being must look attractive, so each offering is a work of art. The basic form is fresh food arranged on a palm leaf and crowned with a *saiban* (palm leaf decoration). Once presented to the gods it cannot be used again, so new offerings are made again and again each day, usually by women (as more women hold jobs, you'll see easy-to-assemble offerings for sale in markets – much as you'll find quick dinner items in Western supermarkets).

While offerings come in many forms, typically they are little bigger than a guidebook. Expect to see flowers, bits of food – especially rice – and a few more unusual items such as Ritz crackers. More important shrines and occasions will call for more elaborate offerings, which can include dozens of citrus fruits and even entire animals cooked and ready for eating.

One thing not to worry about is stepping on offerings. Given their ubiquity it's almost impossible not to (just don't try to). In fact, at Bemo Corner in Kuta (p95) offerings are left in front of the shrine in the middle of the road where they are quickly run over by taxis. And across the island, dogs hover around fresh offerings ready to devour a bite or two, especially the crackers. Given the belief that gods or demons absorb the essence of an offering instantly, the critters are really getting leftovers.

For a perspective on the state of dance in Bali today from one of its top dancers, see the boxed text, p143.

Many tourist shows in South Bali hotels offer a smorgasbord of dances – a little Kecak, a taste of Legong and some Barong to round it off. Some of these performances can be pretty abbreviated with just a few musicians and a couple of dancers.

Belgian artist, Adrien Jean Le Mayeur, married renowned *Legong* (classic Balinese dance) dancer Ni Polok when he was 55 and she was 15. His house of antique carvings became a museum (see p140).

Balinese love a blend of seriousness and slapstick, and this shows in their dances. Some have a decidedly comic element, with clowns who convey the story and also act as a counterpoint to the staid, noble characters. Most dancers are not professionals. Dance is learned by performing, and carefully following the movements of an expert. It tends to be precise, jerky, shifting and jumpy, remarkably like Balinese music, with its abrupt changes of tempo and dramatic contrasts between silence and crashing noise. There's little of the soaring leaps or the smooth flowing movements of Western dance.

Every movement of wrist, hand and fingers is charged with meaning; and facial expressions are carefully choreographed to convey the character of the dance. Watch the local children cheer the good characters and cringe back from the stage when the demons appear.

Kecak

Probably the best known of the dances, the Kecak has a 'choir' of men who provide the 'chak-a-chak-a-chak' accompaniment, imitating a troupe of monkeys. In the 1960s, the tourist version of Kecak developed. This is easily found in Ubud and also at the Pura Luhur Ulu Watu (p132).

Kecak dances tell a tale from the *Ramayana*, one of the great Hindu holy books, about Prince Rama and his Princess Sita. The evil Rawana, King of Lanka, lures Rama away with a golden deer (Lanka's equally evil prime minister, who has magically changed himself into a deer). Then, when the princess is alone, he pounces and carries her off to his hideaway.

Dancing Out of Bali, by John Coast, tells of a ground-breaking international tour by a Balinese dance troupe in the 1950s.

Hanuman, the white monkey-god, tells Princess Sita that Rama is trying to rescue her and gives her Rama's ring. When Rama arrives he is met by the evil king's evil son, Megananda, who shoots an arrow that magically turns into a snake and ties Rama up. Fortunately, he is able to call upon a Garuda (mythical man-bird creature) who helps him escape. Finally, Sugriwa, the king of the monkeys, comes with his monkey army and, after a great battle, good wins out over evil and Rama and Sita return home.

Throughout the dance the chanting is superbly synchronised with an eerily exciting coordination. Add in the actors posing as an army of monkeys and you have unbeatable spectacle.

Barong & Rangda

This rivals the Kecak as Bali's most popular dance for tourists. Again it's a battle between good (the Barong) and bad (the Rangda). The Barong is a strange but good, mischievous and fun-loving shaggy dog-lion. The widow-witch Rangda is bad through and through.

The story begins with Barong Keket, the most holy of the Barong, enjoying the acclaim of its supporters – a group of men with kris (traditional daggers). Then Rangda appears, her long tongue lolling, terrible fangs protruding from her mouth, human entrails draped around her neck, and pendulous parody breasts. (In fully authentic versions – which are rarely seen by visitors – the Rangda is covered with real entrails from freshly slaughtered animals.)

The Barong and Rangda duel, and the supporters draw their kris and rush in. The Rangda throws them into a trance that makes them stab themselves. But the Barong dramatically casts a spell that stops the kris from harming them. They rush back and forth, waving their kris, rolling on the ground, desperately trying to stab themselves. It's all a conspiracy to terrify tourists in the front row!

Finally, the terrible Rangda retires and good has triumphed again. The entranced Barong supporters, however, still need to be sprinkled with holy water. Playing around with all that powerful magic, good and bad, is not to be taken lightly. A *pesmangku* (priest for temple rituals) must end the dancers' trance and a chicken must be sacrificed after the dance to propitiate the evil spirits.

Legong

This most graceful of Balinese dances is performed by young girls. It is important in Balinese culture that in old age a classic dancer will be remembered as a 'great Legong'.

Peliatan's famous dance troupe, often seen in Ubud, is particularly noted for its Legong Keraton (Legong of the Palace). The very stylised and symbolic story involves two Legong dancing in mirror image. They are dressed in gold brocade, their faces elaborately made up, their eyebrows plucked and repainted, and their hair decorated with frangipani. The dance relates how a king takes a maiden, Rangkesari, captive. When her brother comes to release her, Rangkesari begs the king to free her rather than go to war. The king refuses and on his way to the battle meets a bird with tiny golden wings bringing ill omens. He ignores the bird and continues on, meets Rangkesari's brother and is killed.

Balinese Music, by Michael Tenzer, features photographs, a sonography and a guide to all types of gamelan, each with its own tradition, repertoire and social or religious context.

Sanghyang

These dances were developed to drive out evil spirits from a village – Sanghyang is a divine spirit who temporarily inhabits an entranced dancer. The Sanghyang Dedari is performed by two young girls who dance a dream-like version of the Legong in perfect symmetry while their eyes are firmly shut. Male and female choirs provide a background chant until the dancers slump to the ground. A *pesmangku* blesses them with holy water and brings them out of the trance. The modern Kecak dance developed from the Sanghyang.

In the Sanghyang Jaran, a boy in a trance dances around and through a fire of coconut husks, riding a coconut palm 'hobby horse'. Variations of this are called Kecak Fire Dance (or Fire and Trance Dance for tourists) and are performed in Ubud almost daily.

Other Dances

The warrior dance, the Baris, is a male equivalent of the Legong – grace and femininity give way to energetic and warlike spirit. The Baris dancer must convey the thoughts and emotions of a warrior first preparing for action, and then meeting the enemy, showing his changing moods through facial expression and movement – chivalry, pride, anger, prowess and, finally, regret. It is one of the most complex of dances requiring great energy and skill.

The Ramayana ballet tells the familiar tale of Rama and Sita but with a gamelan gong accompaniment. It provides plenty of opportunity for improvisation and comic additions.

The giant puppet dances known as Barong Landung take place annually on the island of Serangan and a few other places in southern Bali. The legend relates how the demon Jero Gede Macaling popped over from Nusa Penida, disguised as a standing Barong, to cause havoc in Bali. A huge Barong puppet was made to scare him away. The dance, often highly comical, features two gigantic puppet figures – a horrific male image of black Jero Gede and his female sidekick, white Jero Luh.

The Richard Meyer gallery in Seminyak (p123) maintains a large collection of historic photographs of Balinese life and culture. Some are often on display and others may be viewed by request.

In the Topeng, which means 'Pressed Against the Face', as with a mask, the dancers imitate the character represented by the mask. The Topeng Tua is a classic solo dance where the mask is that of an old man. In other dances there may be a small troupe who perform various characters. A full collection of Topeng masks may number 30 or 40. Mask dances require great expertise because the dancer cannot convey thoughts and meanings through facial expressions – the dance has to tell all.

Dance in Bali is not a static art form. The Oleg Tambulilingan was developed in the 1950s, originally as a solo female dance. Later, a male part was added and the dance now mimics the flirtations of two *tambulilingan* (bumblebees).

You may often see the Pendet being danced by women bringing offerings to a temple. One of the most popular comic dances is the Cupak, which tells of a greedy coward (Cupak) and his brave but hard-done-by younger brother, and their adventures while rescuing a beautiful princess.

Drama Gong is based on the same romantic themes as a Balinese soap opera – long and full of high drama.

LOMBOK

Lombok has dances found nowhere else in Indonesia, but they are not widely marketed. Performances are staged in some luxury hotels and in the village of Lenek, known for its dance traditions. If you're in Senggigi in July there are also dance and *gendang beleq* (big drum) performances (p326).

The Cupak Gerantang is based on one of the Panji stories, an extensive cycle of written and oral stories originating on Java in the 15th century. It's often performed at traditional celebrations.

Another version of a Panji story is the Kayak Sando, but here the dancers wear masks. It is only found in central and eastern Lombok. The Gandrung follows a theme of love and courtship. It is a social dance, usually performed outdoors, most commonly in Narmada, Lenek and Praya.

A war dance, the Oncer (also called *gendang beleq*), is performed by men and boys. It is a highly skilled and dramatic performance, with dancers playing a variety of unusual musical instruments for *adat* (tradition, customs and manners) festivals, in central and eastern Lombok. The Rudat is danced by pairs of men in black caps and jackets and black-and-white check sarongs, backed by singers, tambourines and *jidur* (large cylindrical drums). The music, lyrics and costumes reveal both a mixture of Muslim and Sasak cultures.

The Tandak Gerok combines dance with music played on bamboo flutes and the *rebab* (a bowed lute), as well as singers imitating the sound of gamelan instruments. It is usually performed after harvesting or other hard labour.

Artists on Bali, by Ruud Spruit, is a well-illustrated description of the work of Nieuwenkamp, Bonnet, Spies, Hofker, Le Mayeur and Smit who studied and documented the culture and natural beauty of the island.

Music

BALI

Balinese music is based around an ensemble known as a gamelan, also called a *gong*. A *gong gede* (large orchestra) is the traditional form, with 35 to 40 musicians. The *gong kebyar* is the modern, popular form, and has up to 25 instruments. Although it sounds strange at first with its noisy, jangly percussion, it's exciting, enjoyable, melodic and at times haunting.

The prevalent voice is from the xylophone-like *gangsa*, which the player hits with a hammer dampening the sound just after it is struck. The tempo and nature of the music is controlled by the two *kendang* drums – one male and one female. Other instruments are the deep *trompong* drums, the small *kempli* gong and the *cengceng* cymbals used in faster pieces. Although some of the instruments require great skill, others do not which makes it a good village activity.

The pieces are learned by heart and passed down from father to son – there is little musical notation, although CDs are widely available. Look in music shops and department stores in South Bali and Ubud. It's traditionally a male occupation, although women have been known to play, and there are more ancient forms, such as the gamelan *selunding,* still occasionally played in Bali Aga villages like Tenganan in eastern Bali.

You can see instruments being made (usually to order) in Blahbatuh in eastern Bali and Sawan in northern Bali. Giant bamboo gamelan, with deep resonating tones, are made in Jembrana in western Bali.

LOMBOK

The *genggong,* a performance seen in Lombok, uses a simple set of instruments, which includes a bamboo flute, a *rebab* and knockers. Seven musicians accompany their music with dance movements and stylised hand gestures.

Theatre

Music, dance and drama are closely related in Bali. Balinese dance has the three elements working together, as does the *wayang kulit* drama performances, with the sound effects and the puppets' movements an important part of the show. The *arja* is a dance-drama, comparable to Western opera.

WAYANG KULIT

Wayang kulit has been Bali's cinema for centuries, but it is primarily a sacred matter. It has the sacred seriousness of classical Greek drama. (Indeed the word drama comes from the Greek *dromenon,* a religious ritual.) The word *wayang* means shadow and can refer to the puppets or the show. It may be derived from *hyang,* meaning ancestor or gods. Alternatively it may be from *bayan,* meaning shadow. *Kulit* means leather or hide.

Shadow puppet plays are more than entertainment, for the puppets are believed to have great spiritual power and the *dalang* (the puppet master and storyteller) is an almost mystical figure. A person of considerable skill and even greater endurance, he manipulates the puppets and tells the story while conducting the *gender wayang* (small gamelan orchestra) and beating time with his chanting. Having run out of hands, he does this with a horn held with his toes!

Perceptions of Paradise: Images of Bali in the Arts by Garret Kam is not only a detailed guide to Ubud's Neka Art Museum (p178) but is also a beautiful primer on Balinese art in general.

The *dalang*'s mystical powers are needed because the *wayang kulit,* like so much of Balinese drama, is about the eternal struggle between good and evil. Endurance is also required because a *wayang kulit* can last six or more hours, and the performances always start so late that the drama is only finally resolved as the sun peeps over the horizon.

The intricate lacy puppets are made of buffalo hide carefully cut with a sharp, chisel-like stylus and then painted. The figures are completely traditional – there is no deviation from the standard list of characters and their standardised appearance, so there's definitely no mistaking who's who.

The *dalang* sits behind a screen on which the shadows of the puppets are cast, usually by an oil lamp which gives a romantic flickering light. Traditionally, women and children sit in front of the screen, while the men sit with the *dalang* and his assistants.

Goodies are arrayed to the right and baddies to the left. Characters include nobles, who speak in the high Javanese language Kawi, and common clowns, who speak in everyday Balinese. The *dalang* also has to be a linguist! When the four clowns (Delem and Sangut are the bad ones, Twalen and his son Merdah are the good ones) are on screen, there is rushing back and forth, clouts on the head and comic insults. The noble characters are altogether more refined – they include the terrible Durga and the noble Bima.

Wayang kulit stories are chiefly derived from the great Hindu epics, the *Ramayana* and to a lesser extent the *Mahabharata*.

Puppets are made in the village of Puaya near Sukawati, south of Ubud, and in Peliatan, just east of Ubud, but they're easy to find in craft, antique and souvenir shops. Although performances are normally held at night (for performances in Ubud, see p198), there are sometimes daytime temple performances, where the figures are manipulated without a screen.

ARJA

An *arja* drama is not unlike *wayang kulit* in its melodramatic plots, its offstage sound effects and its cast of easily identifiable goodies, the refined *alus,* and baddies, the unrefined *kras*. It's performed outside, often with a curtain as a backdrop. Sometimes a small house is built on the stage, and set on fire at the climax of the story!

As the story is told by clown characters who describe and explain all the actions of the nobles, the dialogue uses both high and low Balinese. The plot is often just a small part of a longer story well known to the Balinese audience but very difficult for a foreigner to understand or appreciate.

Literature

The Balinese language has several forms, but only 'high Balinese', a form of Sanskrit used for religious purposes and to recount epics such as the *Ramayana* and the *Mahabharata,* is a written language. Illustrated versions of these epics inscribed on *lontar* (specially prepared palm leaves) are Bali's earliest books. The poems and stories of the early Balinese courts, from the 11th to the 19th centuries, were written in Old Javanese or Middle Javanese, and were meant to be sung or recited rather than read. Even the most elaborate drama and dance performances had no real written scripts or choreography, at least not until Westerners, like Colin McPhee, started to produce them in the 1930s.

Bali Behind the Seen: Recent Fiction from Bali, translated by Vern Cork and written by Balinese authors, conveys much of the tension between deeply rooted traditions and the irresistible pressure of modernisation.

In the colonial period, a few Indonesians began writing in Dutch, while Dutch scholars set about documenting traditional Balinese language and literature. Later, the use of Indo-Malay (called Bahasa Indonesia) became more widespread. One of the first Balinese writers to be published in that language was Anak Agung Pandji Tisna, from Singaraja in northern Bali. His second novel, *The Rape of Sukreni* (1936), adapted the features of Balinese drama: the conflict between good and evil, and the inevitability of karma. It was a popular and critical success. Most of the action in the novel takes place in a warung (food stall). An English translation is available at bookshops in Bali, and is highly recommended.

Most modern Balinese literature has been written in Bahasa Indonesia. Short stories are frequently published in newspapers and magazines, often for literary competitions. An important theme throughout these stories has been tradition versus change and modernisation, often elaborated as a tragic love story involving couples of different castes. Politics, money, tourism and relations with foreigners are also explored. Several anthologies translated into English are currently in print, some by Putu Oka Sukanta, one of Indonesia's most important authors of poetry, short fiction, and novels. Another novelist, Oka Rusmini, is both Balinese and female, which makes her book, *Tarian Bumi,* a story of generations of Balinese women, rather special. Other local writers of note include poet and novelist Pranita Dewi and the author Gusti Putu Bawa Samar Gantang.

It is striking how much has been published about Bali in the Western world, and (until recently) how little of it has been written by Balinese – it says a lot about the Western fascination with Bali. See p21 for recommendations of widely available works. The Lontar Foundation (www.lontar.org) is a nonprofit organisation run by Indonesian writers and is dedicated to getting at least 100 of the most important Indonesian books translated into English so that universities around the world can offer courses in Indonesian literature.

Cinema & TV

Fewer films have been filmed in Bali than one would expect. The main efforts have been location work for box-office hits like *Almayer's Folly* and *Toute la Beaute' du Monde*. However, the Bali Film Commission (www.balifilm.com) is doing its game best to lure filmmakers. It's even copyrighted the phrase 'Baliwood'.

The island is the site for numerous television documentaries, most focusing on some aspect of the culture or environment.

Long before the gorilla appears (!), you know *Road to Bali* is one of the lesser 'road' movies of Bob Hope and Bing Crosby. Few last long enough to see the pair vie for the affections of 'Balinese princess' Dorothy Lamour.

Painting

Balinese painting is probably the art form most influenced by Western ideas and demand. There are a relatively small number of creative original painters, and an enormous number of imitators. Originality is not considered as important in Bali as it is in the West. Even some renowned artists will simply draw the design, decide the colours and leave apprentices to apply the paint. Thus, shops are packed full of paintings in the popular styles – some of them are quite good and a few of them are really excellent. It's rare to see anything totally new.

Visit the Neka Art Museum and Museum Puri Lukisan in Ubud (p175) to see the best of Balinese art and some of the European influences that have shaped it. Visit commercial galleries like the Neka Gallery near Ubud and the Agung Rai Gallery to view high-quality work. If you buy a painting, consider buying a frame as well. These are often elaborately carved works of art in themselves.

See examples of some of the work by Bali's female artists that is on display, or available for sale, at www.seniwatigallery.com.

Traditional paintings faithfully depicting religious and mythological symbolism were customarily for temple and palace decoration. After the 1930s, Western artists introduced the novel concept that paintings could also be artistic creations which could be sold for money. The range of themes, techniques, styles and materials expanded enormously.

A loose classification of styles is: classical, or Kamasan, named for the village of Kamasan near Semarapura; Ubud style, developed in the 1930s under the influence of the Pita Maha; Batuan, which started at the same time in a nearby village; Young Artists, begun postwar in the 1960s, and influenced by Dutch artist Arie Smit; and finally, modern or academic, free in its creative topics, yet strongly and distinctively Balinese.

CLASSICAL PAINTING

There are three basic types of classical painting – *langse, iders-iders* and calendars. *Langse* are large decorative hangings for palaces or temples which display *wayang* figures, rich floral designs and flame-and-mountain motifs. *Iders-iders* are scroll paintings hung along the eaves of temples. Calendars are still used to set dates and predict the future. They include simple yellow calendars from Bedulu, near Ubud; more complex calendars from Semarapura and Kamasan; and large versions of the zodiacal and lunar calendar, especially the 210-day *wuku* calendar, which regulates the timing of Balinese festivals.

Langse paintings helped impart *adat* to the ordinary people in the same way that traditional dance and *wayang kulit* puppetry do. *Wayang* tradition can be seen in stylised human figures shown in profile, their symbolic

WESTERN VISITORS IN THE 1930S

When Gregor Krause's book *Bali: People and Art* was published in 1922, it became a bestseller. Krause had worked in Bangli as a doctor between 1912 and 1914 and his unique photography of an uninhibited lifestyle in a lush, tropical environment was one of the driving forces that promoted Bali as a tropical paradise for hordes of tourists in the 1930s. Western visitors included many talented individuals who helped rejuvenate dormant Balinese arts, and who played a great part in creating the image of Bali that exists today.

Walter Spies

German artist Walter Spies (1895–1942) first visited Bali in 1925 and moved there in 1927, establishing the image of Bali for Westerners that prevails today. Befriended by the important Sukawati family, he built a house at the confluence of two rivers at Campuan, west of Ubud. His home soon became a prime gathering point for Westerners who followed. He involved himself in every aspect of Balinese art and culture and was an important influence on its renaissance.

In 1932 he became curator of the museum in Denpasar, and with Rudolf Bonnet and Cokorda Gede Agung Sukawati, their Balinese patron, he founded the Pita Maha artists' cooperative in 1936. He co-authored *Dance & Drama in Bali*, published in 1938, and adapted a centuries old chant into the Kecak dance for the German film, *The Island of Demons*.

Rudolf Bonnet

Bonnet (1895–1978) was a Dutch artist whose work concentrated on the human form and everyday Balinese life. Many classical Balinese paintings with themes of markets and cockfights are indebted to Bonnet. He returned to Bali in the 1950s to plan the Museum Puri Lukisan in Ubud, and again in 1973 to help establish the museum's permanent collection.

Miguel Covarrubias

Island of Bali, written by this Mexican artist (1904–57), is still the classic introduction to the island and its culture. Covarrubias visited Bali twice in the early 1930s and was also involved in theatre design and printmaking.

Colin McPhee

Canadian musician Colin McPhee (1900–65) wrote *A House in Bali*, not published until 1944, but one of the best written accounts of Bali – his tales of music and house building are often highly amusing. After WWII, McPhee played an important role in introducing Balinese music to the West, and encouraging gamelan (traditional Balinese orchestra) to visit the US.

Robert & Louise Koke

This American couple opened the first hotel at Kuta Beach in 1936, which was an instant hit. Many of their decisions still resonate today. See above for more about the Kokes and the early days of tourism in Bali.

K'tut Tantri

A woman of many aliases, K'tut Tantri breezed in from Hollywood in 1932 inspired by the film *Bali, the Last Paradise*, an early example of soft-core ethnographic 'documentaries'. She dyed her red hair black (only demons have red hair) and was befriended by the prince of the Bangli kingdom. She opened a hotel first in collaboration with and then in competition with the Kokes.

After the war, however, only traces of the hotel's foundations remained. In the postwar struggle against the Dutch, K'tut worked for the Indonesian Republicans, and as Surabaya Sue, she broadcast from Surabaya in support of their cause. Her book, *Revolt in Paradise* (written as K'tut Tantri), was published in 1960.

Other Western Visitors

Others played their part in chronicling the period, such as writer Hickman Powell, whose book *The Last Paradise* was published in 1930, and German author Vicki Baum, whose book *A Tale from Bali*, a fictionalised account of the 1906 *puputan* (warrior's fight to the death), is still in print.

gestures, refined divine and heroic characters, and vulgar, crude evil ones. The paintings tell a story in a series of panels, rather like a comic strip, and often depict scenes from the *Ramayana* and *Mahabharata*. Other themes are the Kakawins poems, and indigenous Balinese folklore with its beliefs in demonic spirits – see the painted ceilings of the Kertha Gosa (Hall of Justice; p213) in Semarapura for an example.

The skill of the artist is apparent in the overall composition and sensitivity of the line work. The colouring is of secondary importance, often left to the artist's children. Natural colours were once made from soot, clay and pigs' bones, and artists were strictly limited to set shades. Today, modern oils and acrylics are used, but the range of colours is still limited. A final burnishing gives these pictures, known as *lukisan antic* (antique paintings), an aged look.

A good place to see classical painting in a modern context is at the Nyoman Gunarsa Museum near Semarapura (p215), which was established to preserve and promote classical techniques.

Scores of non-Balinese artists make their home on the island. One, Ashley Bickerton, who is formerly of New York, is renowned for his grotesque and funny paintings of human forms that often draw inspiration from tourist life on Bali. For more, see the boxed text, p122.

THE PITA MAHA

In the 1930s, with few commissions from temples, painting was virtually dying out. Rudolph Bonnet and Walter Spies (opposite), with their patron Cokorda Gede Agung Surapati, formed the Pita Maha (literally, Great Vitality) to encourage painting as an art form and to find a new market. The group had more than 100 members at its peak in the 1930s.

The changes Bonnet and Spies inspired were revolutionary. Balinese artists started painting single scenes instead of narrative tales and using everyday life rather than romantic legends as their themes: the harvest, the market, cockfights, offerings at a temple or a cremation. These paintings were known as the Ubud style.

Batuan, a noted painting centre, came under the influence of the Pita Maha, but its artists still retained many features of classical painting. They depicted daily life, but included many scenes – for example a market, dance and a rice harvest might all appear in a single work. The Batuan style is also noted for its inclusion of some very modern elements, such as sea scenes with the odd windsurfer.

Themes changed, and so did the actual way of painting. Modern paint and materials were used and stiff formal poses gave way to realistic 3D representations. More importantly, pictures were not just painted to cover a space in a palace or temple.

In one way, however, the style remained unchanged – Balinese paintings were packed with detail; a painted Balinese forest, for example, has branches, leaves and a whole zoo of creatures reaching out to fill every tiny space. You can see these glorious styles at the Museum Puri Lukisan in Ubud (p175) and in many galleries and art shops.

This new artistic enthusiasm was interrupted by WWII and Indonesia's internal turmoil. New work degenerated into copies of the original spirits, with one exception: the development of the Young Artists' style.

WOJ Nieuwenkamp: First European Artist in Bali, by Bruce Carpenter, is a fascinating depiction of Bali from 1904, when the Dutch artist Nieuwenkamp first arrived with a sketchpad and a bicycle.

THE YOUNG ARTISTS

Dutch painter Arie Smit was in Penestanan, just outside Ubud, in 1956, when he noticed an 11-year-old boy drawing in the dirt and wondered what he would produce if he had proper equipment. The story tells of how the lad's father would not allow him to take up painting until Smit offered to pay somebody else to watch the family's ducks.

Other 'young artists' soon joined that first pupil, I Nyoman Cakra, but Smit did not actively teach them. He simply provided the equipment and encouragement, and unleashed what was clearly a strong natural talent. An engaging new 'naive' style developed, as typically Balinese rural scenes were painted in brilliant technicolour.

The style is today one of the staples of Balinese tourist art. It is also known as work by 'peasant painters'. I Nyoman Cakra still lives in Penestanan, still paints, and cheerfully admits that he owes it all to Smit. Other 'young artists' include I Ketut Tagen, I Nyoman Tjarka and I Nyoman Mujung.

OTHER STYLES

There are some other variants to the main Ubud and Young Artists' painting styles. The depiction of forests, flowers, butterflies, birds and other naturalistic themes,for example, sometimes called Pengosekan style, became popular in the 1960s, but can probably be traced back to Henri Rousseau, who was a significant influence on Walter Spies. An interesting development in this particular style is the depiction of underwater scenes, with colourful fish, coral gardens and sea creatures. Somewhere between the Pengosekan and Ubud styles are the miniature landscape paintings that are popular commercially.

Murni (Gusti Kadek Murniasih) was one of Bali's most innovative contemporary artists before her death in 2006. She overcame a brutal childhood and went on to win praise for her taboo-breaking work. For more, see the boxed text, p180.

The new techniques also resulted in radically new versions of Rangda, Barong, Hanuman and other figures from Balinese and Hindu mythology. Scenes from folk tales and stories appeared, featuring dancers, nymphs and love stories, with an understated erotic appeal.

A growing number of Balinese artists receive formal art training. Others are influenced by artists who visit Bali. For details on Murni, an important female painter in Ubud who died in 2006, see p180. Or, to learn about how a prominent painter from outside Bali has been influenced by the island, see the boxed text, p122.

Crafts

Bali is a showroom for all of the crafts of Indonesia. A typical, better tourist shop will sell puppets and batiks from Java, ikat (cloth whose individual threads are dyed before weaving) garments from Sumba, Sumbawa and Flores, and textiles and woodcarvings from Bali, Lombok and Kalimantan. The kris, so important in a Balinese family, will often have been made in Java, which any Balinese will tell you is *the* place for a kris.

On Lombok, where there's never been much money, traditional handicrafts are practical items, skilfully made and beautifully finished. The finer examples of Lombok weaving, basketware and pottery are highly valued by collectors. Some traditional crafts have developed into small-scale industries and villages now specialise in them: textiles from Sukarara, batik paintings from Sade and Rembitan, and pottery from Penujak. Shops in Ampenan, Cakranegara and Senggigi have a good range of Lombok's finest arts and crafts, as do the local markets.

Pre-War Balinese Modernists 1928-1942: an additional page in art-history, by F Haks et al, is a beautiful book on the work of some brilliant but long-neglected Balinese artists.

OFFERINGS & EPHEMERA

Traditionally, many of Bali's most elaborate crafts have been ceremonial offerings not intended to last: *baten tegeh* (decorated pyramids of fruit, rice cakes and flowers); rice-flour cookies modelled into tiny sculptures and entire scenes with a deep symbolic significance; *lamak* (long woven palm-leaf strips used as decorations in festivals and celebrations); stylised female figures known as *cili,* which are representations of Dewi Sri (the rice goddess); or intricately carved coconut-shell wall hangings. Marvel at the care and energy that goes into constructing huge funeral towers and exotic sarcophagi, all of which will go up in flames.

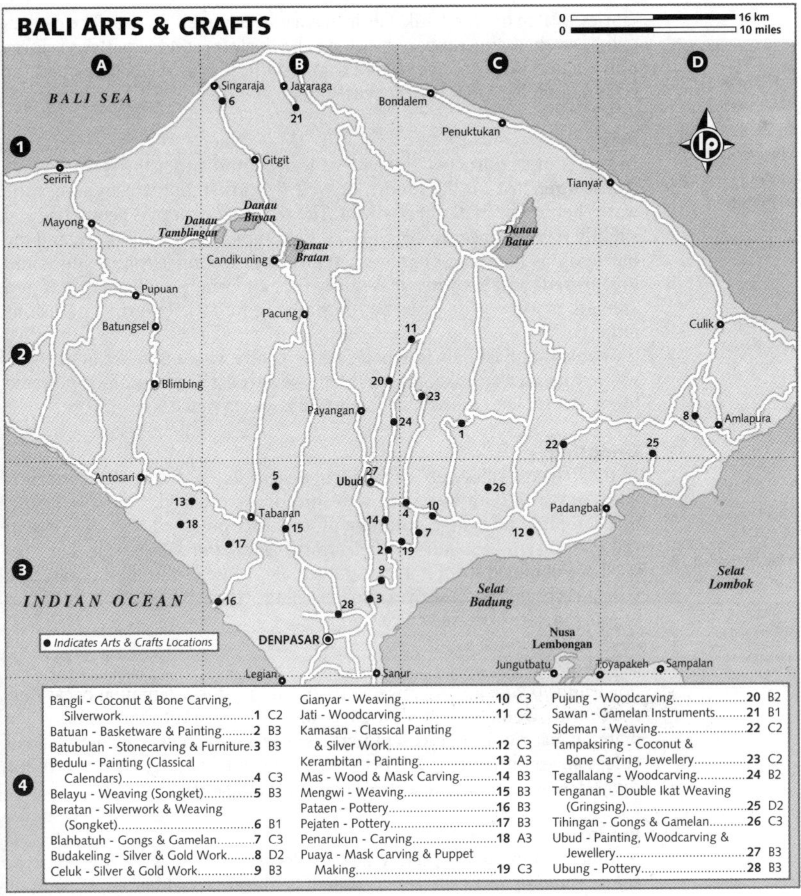

Bangli - Coconut & Bone Carving, Silverwork	1	C2
Batuan - Basketware & Painting	2	B3
Batubulan - Stonecarving & Furniture	3	B3
Bedulu - Painting (Classical Calendars)	4	C3
Belayu - Weaving (Songket)	5	B3
Beratan - Silverwork & Weaving (Songket)	6	B1
Blahbatuh - Gongs & Gamelan	7	C3
Budakeling - Silver & Gold Work	8	D2
Celuk - Silver & Gold Work	9	B3
Gianyar - Weaving	10	C3
Jati - Woodcarving	11	C2
Kamasan - Classical Painting & Silver Work	12	C3
Kerambitan - Painting	13	A3
Mas - Wood & Mask Carving	14	B3
Mengwi - Weaving	15	B3
Pataen - Pottery	16	B3
Pejaten - Pottery	17	B3
Penarukun - Carving	18	A3
Puaya - Mask Carving & Puppet Making	19	C3
Pujung - Woodcarving	20	B2
Sawan - Gamelan Instruments	21	B1
Sideman - Weaving	22	C2
Tampaksiring - Coconut & Bone Carving, Jewellery	23	C2
Tegallalang - Woodcarving	24	B2
Tenganan - Double Ikat Weaving (Gringsing)	25	D2
Tihingan - Gongs & Gamelan	26	C3
Ubud - Painting, Woodcarving & Jewellery	27	B3
Ubung - Pottery	28	B3

TEXTILES & WEAVING

The sarong is an attractive article of clothing, sheet or towel with a multitude of other uses. There are plain or printed cottons, more elegant batik designs, and expensive fabrics, suh as *endek* (elegant fabric, like *songket,* but the weft threads are predyed) and *songket* (silver- or gold-threaded cloth, hand-woven using a floating weft technique), that are necessary for special occasions – it is a religious obligation to look one's best at a temple ceremony. Dress for these occasions is a simple shirt or blouse, a sarong and a *kain,* a separate length of cloth wound tightly around the hips, over the sarong.

For more formal occasions, the blouse is replaced by a length of *songket* wrapped around the chest, called a *kamben*. Any market, especially those in Denpasar (p171) will have a good range of textiles.

Australian artist Donald Friend found the freedom to pursue his provocative art and lifestyle on Bali in the 1960s. Living in Sanur he created the Tanjung Sari Hotel, the island's first boutique hotel.

Batik

Traditional batik sarongs are handmade in central Java. The dyeing process has been adapted by the Balinese to produce brightly coloured and patterned fabrics. Watch out for 'batik' fabric that has been screen printed. The colours will be washed out compared with real batik cloth, and the pattern is often only on one side (the dye should colour both sides as the belief is that the body should feel what the eye sees).

Balinese Textiles by Hauser, Nabholz-Kartaschoff & Ramseyer is a large and lavishly illustrated guide detailing weaving styles and their significance.

Ikat

In this complex process, the pattern is dyed into either the warp threads (those stretched on the loom), or weft threads (those woven across the warp) before the material is woven. The resulting pattern is geometric and slightly wavy. Its beauty depends on the complexity of the pattern and the harmonious blending of colours, typically of a similar tone – blues and greens; reds and browns; or yellows, reds and oranges. Ikat sarongs and *kain* are not everyday wear, but they are not for strictly formal occasions either.

Gianyar, in East Bali, is a major textile centre with a number of factories where you can watch ikat sarongs being woven on a hand-and-foot-powered loom; a complete sarong takes about six hours to make.

Gringsing

In the Bali Aga village of Tenganan, in eastern Bali, a double ikat process is used, in which both warp and weft threads are predyed. Called *gringsing*, this complex and time-consuming process isn't practised anywhere else in Indonesia. Typical colours are red, brown, yellow and deep purple. The dyes used are obtained from natural sources, and some of the colours can take years to mix and age. The dyes also weaken the cotton fabric, so old examples of *gringsing* are extremely rare.

The Bali Arts Festival showcases the work of thousands of Balinese each June and July in Denpasar. See p336 for details.

Songket

For *kamben, kain* and sarongs worn exclusively for ceremonial occasions, the *songket* cloth, with gold or silver threads woven into the tapestry-like material, has motifs of birds, butterflies, leaves and flowers. Belayu, a small village in southwestern Bali between Mengwi and Marga, is a centre for *songket* weaving. *Songket* is also woven near Singaraja.

Prada

Another technique for producing very decorative fabrics for special occasions, *prada* involves the application of gold leaf, or gold or silver paint or thread to the surface of a finished material. Motifs are similar to those used in *songket*. The result is not washable, so *prada* is reserved for *kain* or for decorative wraps on offerings and for temple umbrellas. For *prada*, have a look at shops in Sukawati, south of Gianyar.

Weaving on Lombok

Lombok is renowned for its traditional weaving on backstrap looms, the techniques handed down from mother to daughter. Each cloth is woven in established patterns and colours, some interwoven with gold thread. Abstract flower and animal motifs sometimes decorate this exquisite cloth; look carefully to recognise forms such as buffaloes, dragons, crocodiles and snakes. Several villages specialise in weaving cloth, while others concentrate on fine baskets and mats woven from rattan or grass. You can visit factories around Cakranegara and Mataram that produce weft ikat on old hand-and-foot-operated looms.

Sukarara and Pringgasela are centres for traditional ikat and *songket* weaving. Sarongs, Sasak belts and clothing edged with brightly coloured embroidery are sold in small shops.

SMALL TALK

'Where do you stay?' 'Where do you come from?' You'll hear these questions over and over whether you're in a gallery, a café, walking down the street or just sitting in the shade. It's Balinese small talk and is traditional for locals who wish to change your status from complete stranger to a known quantity. It's all part of the culture.

Saying you're staying 'over there' and that you come from 'over there' can suffice as answers or you can go into detail. But expect follow-ups. 'Are you married?' It's easiest to say you are *sudah kawin,* 'already married'. 'Where's your partner?' A dead spouse is considered less of a tragedy than a divorced one. 'Do you want a boyfriend?' It's definitely easier to be 'married' than single.

'What's your religion?' If you have a strong conviction say so, otherwise just name whatever is common where you are from (you know, 'over there').

Don't get bent out of shape by this small talk, it's what makes Bali a sociable and enjoyable place.

WOODCARVING

A decorative craft, woodcarving was chiefly used for carved doors or columns; figures such as Garudas, or demons with a symbolic nature; minor functional objects, such as bottle tops; and the carved wooden masks used in Balinese dance. Yet, as with painting, it was the demand from outside that inspired new subjects and styles.

Ubud was a centre for the revolution in woodcarving. Some carvers started producing highly stylised figures. Others carved delightful animal figures, some realistic, some complete caricatures. More styles and trends developed: whole tree trunks carved into ghostly, intertwined 'totem poles', and curiously exaggerated and distorted figures which became baroque fantasies.

Almost all carving is of local woods, including *belalu,* a quick-growing light wood, and the stronger fruit timbers such as jackfruit wood. Ebony from Sulawesi is also used. Sandalwood, with its delightful fragrance, is expensive, soft and used for some small, very detailed pieces.

Tegallalang and Jati, on the road north from Ubud to Batur, are noted woodcarving centres. Many workshops line the road east of Peliatan (p205), near Ubud, to Goa Gajah (Elephant Cave). The route from Mas, through Peliatan, Petulu and up the scenic slope to Pujung is also a centre for family based workshops; listen for the tapping sound of the carvers' mallets.

Despite the emphasis on what sells, there's always something special, the technical skill is high and the Balinese sense of humour shines through – a frog clutching a leaf as an umbrella, or a weird demon on the side of a bell clasping his hands over his ears. It's difficult to separate traditional and foreign influences. The Balinese have always incorporated and adapted foreign themes into their work – religious figures based on Hindu mythology are very different to the equivalent carvings made in India.

In Lombok, carving usually decorates functional items, such as containers for tobacco and spices, and the handles of betel-nut crushers and knives. Materials include wood, horn and bone. A recent fashion is for primitive-style elongated masks, often decorated with inlaid shell pieces. Cakranegara, Sindu, Labuapi and Senanti are centres for carving.

Wooden articles lose moisture when moved to a drier environment. Avoid possible shrinkage by placing the carving in a plastic bag at home, and letting some air in for about one week every month for four months.

The website www.lombok-network.com gives details of Lombok customs, and the arts and crafts of various areas.

Mask Carving

A specialised form of woodcarving, only experts carve the masks used in theatre and dance performances such as the Topeng dance. The mask maker must know the movements that each performer uses so that the character can be shown by the mask.

Other masks, such as the Barong and Rangda, are brightly painted and decorated with real hair, enormous teeth and bulging eyes. Mas is recognised as the mask-carving centre of Bali, followed by the small village of Puaya, near Sukawati. The Museum Negeri Propinsi Bali in Denpasar (p168) has an extensive mask collection and is a great place to get an idea of different styles before buying anything.

STONE CARVING

Traditionally for the adornment of temples, stone sculptures haven't been affected by foreign influences, mainly because your average stone statue isn't a convenient souvenir. Stone carving is also Bali's most durable art form. Though it is soon covered in moss, mould or lichen, it doesn't deteriorate in the humid atmosphere.

Treasures of Bali by Richard Mann is a beautifully illustrated guide to Bali's museums big and small.

Stone carving appears in set places in temples. Door guardians are usually a protective personality such as Arjuna. Above the main entrance, Kala's monstrous face often peers out, his hands reaching out beside his head to catch any evil spirits. The side walls of a *pura dalem* (temple of the dead) might feature sculpted panels that show the horrors that await evildoers in the afterlife.

Even when decorating a modern building, stone carvers tend to stick to the tried and trusted – patterned friezes, floral decoration or bas-reliefs depicting scenes from the *Ramayana*. Nevertheless, modern trends can be seen and many sculptors are happy to work on nontraditional themes, such as Japanese-style stone lanterns or McDonalds' characters outside its Kuta store.

Much of the local work is made from a soft, grey volcanic stone called *paras*. It's a little like pumice, and so soft it can be scratched with a fingernail. When newly worked, it can be mistaken for cast cement, but with age, the outer surface becomes tougher and darker. Soft sandstone is also used, and sometimes has attractive colouring. Because the stone is light it's possible to bring a friendly stone demon back in your airline baggage. A typical temple door guardian weighs around 10 kg.

Batubulan (p172), on the main highway from South Bali to Ubud, is a major stone-carving centre. Stone figures from 25cm to 2m tall line both sides of the road, and stone carvers can be seen in action in the many workshops.

JEWELLERY

Bali is a major producer of jewellery and produces variations on currently fashionable designs. Very fine filigree work is a Balinese speciality, as is the use of tiny spots of silver to form a decorative texture – this is a very skilled technique, as the heat must be perfectly controlled to weld the delicate details onto the underlying silver without damaging it. Balinese work is nearly always handmade, rarely involving casting techniques. Most silver is imported, though some is mined near Singaraja in northern Bali.

A carefully selected list of books about art, culture and Balinese writers, dancers and musicians can be found at www.ganeshabooksbali.com/bookstore.html.

Celuk (p205) has always been associated with silversmithing. To see the 'real' Celuk, visit family workshops north and east of the main road. Other silverwork centres include Kamasan, near Semarapura in eastern Bali, and Beratan, south of Singaraja in northern Bali.

There's a wide range of earrings, bracelets and rings available, some using imported gemstones. Different design influences can be detected, from African patterning to the New Age preoccupation with dolphins and healing crystals.

You'll find many jewellery workshops in areas around Ubud. Tampaksiring, northeast of Ubud, has long been a centre for cheaper styles of fashion jewellery. Brightly painted, carved wooden earrings are popular and cheap.

KRIS

Often with an ornate, jewel-studded handle and sinister-looking wavy blade, the kris is the traditional and ceremonial dagger of Bali and other parts of Indonesia. A kris can be the most important of family heirlooms, a symbol of prestige and honour. It is supposed to have great spiritual power, sending out magical energy waves and thus requiring great care in its handling and use.

Trees have a spiritual and religious significance in Bali. The banyan is the holiest; creepers that drop from its branches take root, thus it is 'never-dying'.

OTHER CRAFTS

To see potters at work, visit Ubung and Kapal, north and west of Denpasar, respectively. Nearly all local pottery is made from low-fired terracotta. Most styles are very ornate, even functional items such as vases, flasks, ashtrays and lamp bases. Pejaten (p276), near Tabanan, also has a number of workshops producing small ceramic figures and glazed ornamental roof tiles. Some excellent, contemporary glazed ceramics are produced in Jimbaran, south of Kuta.

Earthenware pots have been produced on Lombok for centuries. They are shaped by hand, coated with a slurry of clay or ash to enhance the finish, and fired in a simple kiln filled with burning rice stalks. Pots are often finished with a covering of woven cane for decoration and extra strength. Newer designs feature bright colours and elaborate decorations. Penujak, Banyumulek and Masbagik are some of the main pottery villages, or head towards Mataram to visit the Lombok Pottery Centre (p290).

Lombok is noted for its spiral-woven rattan basketware; bags made of *lontar* or split bamboo; small boxes made of woven grass; plaited rattan mats; and decorative boxes of palm leaves shaped like rice barns and decorated with shells. Kotaraja and Loyok (p321) are noted for fine basketware, while Rungkang, near Loyok, combines pottery and basketware. Sayang is known for palm-leaf boxes.

Architecture

There is a spiritual and religious significance of Balinese architecture that is much more important than the physical materials, the construction or the decoration.

A village, a temple, a family compound, an individual structure – and even a single part of the structure – must all conform to the Balinese concept of cosmic order. It consists of three parts that represent the three worlds of the cosmos – *swah* (the world of gods), *bhwah* (the world of humans) and *bhur* (the world of demons). The concept also represents a three-part division of a person: *utama* (the head), *madia* (the body) and *nista* (the legs). The units of measurement used in traditional buildings are directly based on the anatomical dimensions of the head of the household, ensuring harmony between the dwelling and those that live in it. Traditionally, the designer of the building is a combination architect-priest called an *undagi*.

Architecture of Bali by Made Wijaya is a lavish book detailing the personal observations and conclusions of the Australian-born Bali landscape designer. The vintage photos and illustrations are worth the price alone.

The basic element of Balinese architecture is the *bale*, a rectangular, open-sided pavilion with a steeply pitched roof of thatch. Both a family compound and a temple will comprise of a number of separate *bale* for specific functions, all surrounded by a high wall. The size and proportions of the *bale*, the number of columns, and the position within the compound, are all determined according to tradition and the owner's caste status.

The focus of a community is a large pavilion, called the *bale banjar*, used for meetings, debates and gamelan (traditional Balinese orchestra) practice, among many other activities. You'll find that large, modern buildings such as restaurants and the lobby areas of resorts are often modelled on the larger *bale*, and they can be airy, spacious and very handsomely proportioned.

Bali Style by Rio Helmi and Barbara Walker is the coffee-table book that spawned enough imitations to pave Kuta Beach. First published in 1995, the book details the sort of clean and open-plan Bali design ethos that would become a cliché if it weren't simply so adaptable.

During the building process, if pavilions get beyond a certain size, traditional materials cannot be used. In these cases concrete is substituted for timber, and sometimes the roof is tiled rather than thatched. The fancier modern buildings – banks and hotels – might also feature decorative carvings derived from traditional temple design. As a result of this, some regard the use of traditional features in modern buildings as pure kitsch, while others see it as a natural and appropriate development of modern Balinese style. Buildings with these features are sometimes described as Baliesque, Bali baroque, or Bali rococo if the decoration has become too excessive.

Visitors may be disappointed by Balinese *puri* (palaces), which prove to be neither large nor imposing. The *puri* are the traditional residences of the Balinese aristocracy, although now they may be used as top-end hotels or as regular family compounds. They prove unimposing, as a Balinese palace can

LOMBOK ARCHITECTURE

Lombok's architecture is governed by traditional laws and practices. Construction must begin on a propitious day, always with an odd-numbered date, and the building's frame must be completed on that day. It would be bad luck to leave any of the important structural work to the following day.

In a traditional Sasak village there are three types of buildings – *beruga* (the communal meeting hall), *bale tani* (family houses) and *lumbung* (rice barns). The *beruga* and the *bale tani* are both rectangular, with low walls and a steeply pitched thatched roof, although, of course, the *beruga* is much larger. The arrangement of rooms in a *bale tani* is also very standardised. There is a *serambian* (open veranda) at the front and two rooms on two different levels inside – one for cooking and entertaining guests, the other for sleeping and storage.

THE VILLA BLIGHT

Like ducks in rice paddies after a rain, villas have appeared everywhere in Bali, especially in the south and along the coast stretching west to Pura Tanah Lot. But unlike ducks, the villas are far from beneficial to the landscape and although aimed at the affluent, they are really about as welcome as effluent.

True, many are creative works of architecture and some find innovative ways to celebrate Balinese design and art. But many more are generic boxes aimed at the *Wallpaper** magazine set: copy-cat fashion statements drawn from whim and catering to base instincts.

Made Wijaya, the renowned landscape architect, designer and author has watched the spread of villas with alarm. 'They are just trendoid and paranoid. The fortresslike gates are built bang on the road with intercom buzzers and flanking pots of horsehair grass – the lavender of metrosexuals.'

Wijaya, who is originally from Australia, has a deep understanding of Balinese culture. His look, which he describes as 'Bali baroque' – lots of traditional ornamentation and design cues – has been used to great effect on some of Bali's most sensitive and honoured projects such as the Oberoi in Seminyak and the Four Seasons in Jimbaran.

He decries the ethos behind the villas as 'aimed at people who'd go to Ibiza but come here for the cheap help.

'There's a small box for the maid and the driver doesn't even get a glass of water. Balinese design is about community and openness, but these things have a plunge pool surrounded by walls and a bland 'zen' design of black, white, brown and timber slats.

'They are treeless, birdless, loveless, godless environments with no shrines, no offerings… These things could be anywhere, whatever happened to local colour?'

never be built more than one storey high. This is because a Balinese noble could not possibly use a ground-floor room if the feet of people on an upper floor were walking above.

> The gate to a traditional Balinese house is where the family gives cues as to its wealth. They range from the humble – grass thatch atop a gate of simple stones or clay – to the relatively grand: bricks heavily ornamented with ornately carved stone and a tile roof.

THE FAMILY COMPOUND

The Balinese house looks inward – the outside is simply a high wall. Inside there is a garden and a separate small building or *bale* for each activity – one for cooking, one for washing and the toilet, and separate buildings for each 'bedroom'. In Bali's mild tropical climate people live outside, so the 'living room' and 'dining room' will be open veranda areas, looking out into the garden. The whole complex is oriented on the *kaja* (towards the mountains)–*kelod* (toward the sea) axis.

Many modern Balinese houses, particularly in Denpasar and the larger towns, are arranged much like houses in the West, but there are still a great number of traditional family compounds. For example, in Ubud, nearly every house will follow the same traditional walled design.

Analogous to the human body, there's a head (the family temple with its ancestral shrine), arms (the sleeping and living areas), legs and feet (the kitchen and rice storage building), and even an anus (the garbage pit). There may be an area outside the house compound where fruit trees are grown or a pig may be kept. Usually the house is entered through a gateway backed by a small wall known as the *aling aling*. It serves a practical and a spiritual purpose, both preventing passers-by from seeing in and stopping evil spirits from entering. Evil spirits cannot easily turn corners so the *aling aling* stops them from simply scooting straight in through the gate!

There are several variations on the typical family compound, illustrated on p62. For example, the entrance is commonly on the *kuah* (sunset side), rather than the *kelod* side as shown, but *never* on the *kangin* (sunrise) or *kaja* side.

THE FAMILY COMPOUND

1 Sanggah or Merajan Family temple
2 Umah Meten Sleeping pavilion for the family head
3 Tugu Shrine
4 Pengijeng Shrine
5 Bale Tiang Sanga Guest pavilion
6 Natah Courtyard with frangipani or hibiscus shade tree
7 Bale Sakenam Working and sleeping pavilion
8 Fruit trees & coconut palms
9 Vegetable garden
10 Bale Sakepat Sleeping pavilion for children
11 Paon Kitchen
12 Lumbung Rice barn
13 Rice-threshing area
14 Aling Aling Screen wall
15 Candi Kurung Gate with roof
16 Apit Lawang or Pelinggah Gate shrines

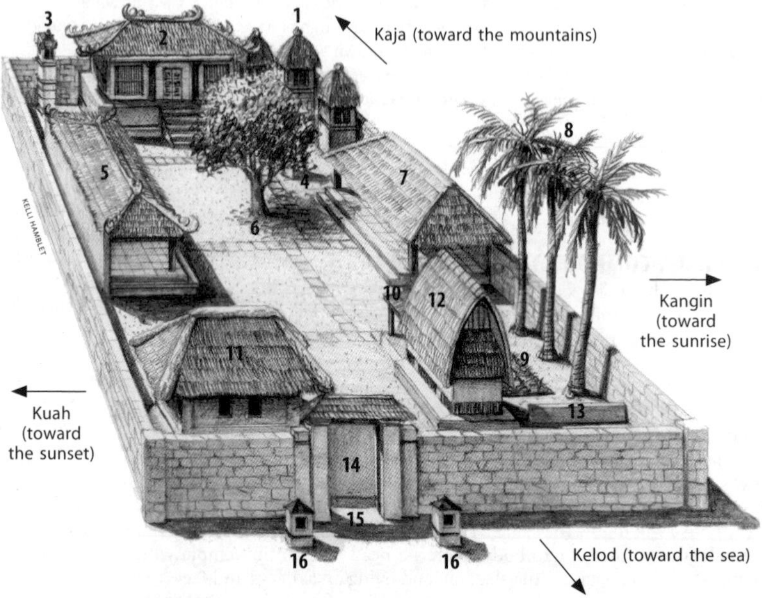

TEMPLES

Every village in Bali has several temples, and every home has at least a simple house-temple. The Balinese word for temple is *pura,* from a Sanskrit word literally meaning 'a space surrounded by a wall'. Similar to a traditional Balinese home, a temple is walled in – so the shrines you see in rice fields or at 'magical' spots such as old trees are not real temples. Simple shrines or thrones often overlook crossroads, to protect passers-by.

All temples are built on a mountains–sea orientation, not north–south. The direction towards the mountains, *kaja,* is the end of the temple, where

MAJOR TEMPLES

Bali has thousands of temples, but some of the most important are listed here, and shown on the colour highlights map, pp2–3.

Directional Temples

Some temples are so important they are deemed to belong to the whole island rather than particular communities. There are nine *kahyangan jagat,* or directional temples.

- Pura Besakih (p216) in Besakih, East Bali.
- Pura Goa Lawah (p221) near Padangbai, East Bali.
- Pura Lempuyang (p233) near Tirta Gangga, East Bali.
- Pura Luhur Batukau (p241) on Gunung Batukau, Central Mountains.
- Pura Luhur Ulu Watu (p132) at Ulu Watu, South Bali.
- Pura Masceti (p209) near Gianyar, East Bali.
- Pura Sambu (p210) remotely located on Gunung Agung, East Bali.
- Pura Ulun Danu Bratan (p250) in Candikuning (Danau Bratan), Central Mountains.
- Pura Ulun Danu (p242) in Batur, Central Mountains.

Most of these are well known and accessible, but some are rarely seen by visitors to Bali. Pura Masceti, on the coast east of Sanur, is easily reached on the new coast road but seldom visited, and it's a stiff walk to remote Pura Lempuyang.

Sea Temples

The 16th-century Majapahit priest Nirartha founded a chain of temples to honour the sea gods. Each was intended to be within sight of the next, and several have dramatic locations on the south coast. From the west, they include the following.

- Pura Gede Perancak (p279) – where Nirartha first landed
- Pura Rambut Siwi (p278) – on a wild stretch of the west coast
- Pura Tanah Lot (p272) – the very popular island temple
- Pura Luhur Ulu Watu (p132) – spectacular cliff-top view (one of the nine directional temples)
- Pura Mas Suka (p133) – at the very south of the Bukit Peninsula
- Pura Sakenan (p147) – on Pulau Serangan, southern Bali
- Pura Pulaki (p268) – near Pemuteran, in northern Bali

Other Important Temples

Some other temples have particular importance because of their location, spiritual function or architecture. They include the following.

- Pura Beji (p261) in Sangsit, northern Bali, is dedicated to the goddess Dewi Sri, who looks after irrigated rice fields.
- Pura Dalem Penetaran Ped (p153) on Nusa Penida is dedicated to the demon Jero Gede Macaling, and is a place of pilgrimage for those seeking protection from evil.
- Pura Kehen (p211) is a fine hillside temple in Bangli, eastern Bali.
- Pura Maduwe Karang (p261), an agricultural temple on the north coast, is famous for its spirited bas-relief, including one of a bicycle rider.
- Pura Pusering Jagat (p203), a temple at Pejeng, near Ubud, with an enormous bronze drum.
- Pura Taman Ayun (p274), the imposing state temple at Mengwi, is northwest of Denpasar.
- Pura Tirta Empul (p204), the beautiful temple at Tampaksiring, has springs and bathing pools at the source of Sungai Pakerisan (Pakerisan River), north of Ubud.

the holiest shrines are found. The temple's entrance is at the *kelod. Kangin* is more holy than the *kuah,* so many secondary shrines are on the *kangin* side. *Kaja* may be towards a particular mountain – Pura Besakih in eastern Bali is pointed directly towards Gunung Agung – or towards the mountains in general, which run east–west along the length of Bali.

Architectural Conservation In Bali by Edo Budiharjo examines the case for conservation of architectural heritage on the island of Bali, an important issue at a time when modern forms are appearing everywhere.

Temple Types

There are three basic temple types, found in most villages. The most important is the *pura puseh* (temple of origin), dedicated to the village founders and at the *kaja* end of the village. In the middle of the village is the *pura desa,* for the many spirits that protect the village community in daily life. At the *kelod* end of the village is the *pura dalem* (temple of the dead). The graveyard is also here, and the temple may include representations of Durga, the terrible side of Shiva's wife Parvati. Both Shiva and Parvati have a creative and destructive side; their destructive powers are honoured in the *pura dalem.*

Other temples include those that are dedicated to the spirits of irrigated agriculture. Rice-growing is so important in Bali, and the division of water for irrigation is handled with the utmost care, that these *pura subak* or *pura ulun suwi* (temple of the rice-growers' association) can be of considerable importance. Other temples may also honour dry-field agriculture, as well as the flooded rice paddies.

In addition to these 'local' temples, there are a lesser number of great temples. Each family worships its ancestors in the family temple, the clan worships in its clan temple and the village in the *pura puseh.* Above these are the state temples or temples of royalty, and often a kingdom would have three of these: a main state temple in the heartland of the state (such as Pura Taman Ayun in Mengwi, western Bali); a mountain temple (such as Pura Besakih, eastern Bali); and a sea temple (such as Pura Luhur Ulu Watu, southern Bali).

Scores of open-air carving sheds supplying statues and ornamentation to temples and shrines are a highlight of the road between Muncan and Selat in East Bali (see p220).

Every house in Bali has its house temple, which is at the *kaja-kangin* corner of the courtyard. There will be shrines to the Hindu 'trinity' of Brahma, Shiva and Vishnu; to *taksu,* the divine intermediary; and to *tugu,* the lord of the ground.

Temple Design

Temple design follows a traditional formula. A temple compound contains a number of *gedong* (shrines) of varying sizes, made from solid brick and stone and heavily decorated with carvings. See the boxed text, opposite, for an example.

Temple Decoration

Temples and their decoration are closely linked on Bali. A temple gateway is not just erected; every square centimetre of it is carved in sculptural relief and a diminishing series of demon faces is placed above it as protection. Even then, it's not complete without several stone statues to act as guardians.

The level of decoration varies. Sometimes a temple is built with minimal decoration in the hope that sculpture can be added when more funds are available. The sculpture can also deteriorate after a few years because much of the stone used is soft and the tropical climate ages it very rapidly (that centuries-old temple you're looking at may in fact be less than 10 years old!). Sculptures are restored or replaced as resources permit – it's not uncommon to see a temple with old carvings, which are barely discernible, next to newly finished work.

You'll find some of the most lavishly carved temples around Singaraja in northern Bali. The north-coast sandstone is very soft and easily carved,

TYPICAL TEMPLE DESIGN

1 Candi Bentar The intricately sculpted temple gateway, like a tower split down the middle and moved apart.
2 Kulkul Tower The warning-drum tower, from which a wooden split drum (*kulkul*) is sounded to announce events at the temple or warn of danger.
3 Bale A pavilion, usually open-sided, for temporary use or storage. May include a *bale* gong (3A), where the gamelan orchestra plays at festivals; a *paon* (3B) or temporary kitchen to prepare offerings; or a *wantilan* (3C), a stage for dances or cockfights.
4 Kori Agung or Paduraksa The gateway to the inner courtyard is an intricately sculpted stone tower. Entry is through a doorway reached by steps in the middle of the tower and left open during festivals.
5 Raksa or Dwarapala Statues of fierce guardian figures who protect the doorway and deter evil spirits. Above the door will be the equally fierce face of a Bhoma, with hands outstretched against unwanted spirits.
6 Aling Aling If an evil spirit does get in, this low wall behind the entrance will keep it at bay, as evil spirits find it difficult to make right-angle turns.
7 Side Gate (Betelan) Most of the time (except during ceremonies) entry to the inner courtyard is through this side gate, which is always open.
8 Small Shrines (Gedong) These usually include shrines to Ngrurah Alit and Ngrurah Gede, who organise things and ensure the correct offerings are made.
9 Padma Stone Throne for the sun god Surya, placed in the most auspicious *kaja-kangin* (mountain-sunset) corner. It rests on the *badawang* (world turtle), which is held by two *naga* (mythological serpents).
10 Meru A multiroofed shrine. Usually there is an 11-roofed *meru* (10A) to Sanghyang Widi, the supreme Balinese deity, and a three-roofed *meru* (10B) to the holy mountain Gunung Agung.
11 Small Shrines (Gedong) At the *kaja* (mountain) end of the courtyard, these may include a shrine to the sacred mountain Gunung Batur; a Maospahit shrine to honour Bali's original Hindu settlers (Majapahit); and a shrine to the *taksu*, who acts as an interpreter for the gods. (Trance dancers or mediums may be used to convey the gods' wishes.)
12 Bale Piasan Open pavilions used to display temple offerings.
13 Gedong Pesimpangan Stone building dedicated to the village founder or a local deity.
14 Paruman or Pepelik Open pavilion in the inner courtyard, where the gods are supposed to assemble to watch the ceremonies of a temple festival.

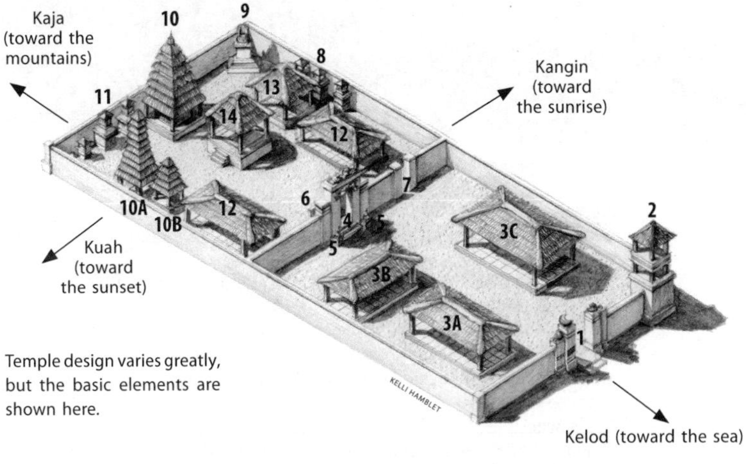

Temple design varies greatly, but the basic elements are shown here.

CONTEMPORARY HOTEL DESIGN

Intruding upon the serenity of Balinese cosmology and its seamless translation into the island's traditional architecture are tourists – interlopers, who, like Bali's many foreign visitors centuries ago, formed an intrinsic part of the island's myths and legends. Such legends describe tensions between the sacred and the profane, the high and the low, and it is these tensions that characterise boutique Bali hotels – the most accessible and significant examples of contemporary Balinese architecture. By their function, these hotels seem immediately alien to traditional Balinese culture. In all of them, however, despite obvious contradictions of commerce and privilege, there is the sincere attempt to define them as highly sophisticated architectures, albeit for hedonistic escape. These hotels are worth visiting because they heighten, even exaggerate, the sensation of being in Bali.

Hotels such as the pioneering Oberoi in Seminyak by Australian architect Peter Muller, his pièces de resistance, the Amandari, Ubud, and the Lombok Oberoi as well as those designed by another Australian, Kerry Hill; the Amanusa, Nusa Dua and the Alila (formerly Serai), near Candidasa employ the typical buildings and spaces of Bali: the walled house and garden compound and the village with its *bale* (an open-sided pavilion with a steeply pitched thatched roof), *bale agung* (village assembly hall), *bale banjar* (communal meeting place of a banjar; a house for meetings and gamelan practice) and *wantilan* (large bale pavilion used for meetings, performances and cockfights) structures. Yet such appropriation is not tokenistic. Much of the allure of these hotels is in the inclusion of traditional Balinese materials, crafts and construction techniques, as well as Balinese design principles that respect an archetypal approach to the world. Hence, a reflection on Balinese cosmology becomes an intrinsic part of each design. The inclusion of elaborate swimming pools and paradisaical garden designs by landscape architects like Made

TONY WHEELER

allowing local sculptors to give free rein to their imaginations; as a result, you'll find some delightfully whimsical scenes carved into a number of the temples.

Sculpture often appears in set places in Bali's temples. Door guardians – representations of legendary figures like Arjuna or other protective personalities – flank the steps to the gateway. Above the main entrance to a temple, Kala's monstrous face often peers out, sometimes a number of times – his hands reaching out beside his head to catch any evil spirits foolish enough to try to sneak in.

Elsewhere, other sculptures make regular appearances – the front of a *pura dalem* will often feature images of the witch Rangda and sculpted relief panels may show the horrors that await evil-doers in the afterlife.

TONY WHEELER

Wijaya and Ketut Marsa has added a further dimension to these free interpretations on tradition. Landscape has become one of the most powerful and seductive components of the Bali hotel experience, evidenced, for example, in the wonderful gardens of Bali's Four Seasons Resort at Jimbaran Bay.

Other designers have employed landscape but in a different way, drawing inspiration from the terracing of Bali's rural landscape or from water palaces like those at Tirta Gangga, Jungutan and Taman Ujung in East Bali. A feature of these sites are the *bale kambang* (water pavilions or 'floating palaces') that can also be found in the palaces of Klungkung and Karangasem, pavilions where kings would meditate and commune with the gods. For hotel designers, such an analogy is extremely attractive. Thus a hotel like Amankila near Manggis in East Bali adopts a garden strategy, with a carefully structured landscape of lotus ponds and floating pavilions that step down an impossibly steep site.

Another attraction of these buildings is the notion of instant age, the ability of materials in Bali to weather quickly and provide 'pleasing decay'. Two Ubud hotels that epitomise this phenomenon are Ibah Luxury Villas and Begawan Giri (now rebranded the COMO Shambhala). The latter is a private resort estate that comprises five uniquely styled residences designed by Malaysian-born architect Cheong Yew Kuan and where abstracted Balinese architectural principles are combined with exquisite craftsmanship. By contrast, at Sayan near Ubud, John Heah of Heah & Company (London), has created a completely new image for the Balinese hotel. The Four Seasons Resort at Sayan is a striking piece of aerial sculpture, a huge elliptical lotus pond sitting above a base structure that appears like an eroded and romantic ruin set within a spectacular gorge landscape.

Many of these hotels go close to that boundary where the reproduction is more seductive than the original. And it has to be said that the hotel was never a traditional building form in Bali! Each hotel has been designed not to mimic but rather to facilitate a consciously artificial reading of the place. These buildings need to be seen for what they are: thoroughly convincing architectures of welcome. They are skilful and highly resolved exercises in appealing to the most profound wants in Western society's eyes – the pleasures of the threshold; the pleasures of the perception of an exotic 'other'; and the pleasures of simply being in another highly sensitised state, and in what better place than Bali, Island of the Gods.

Philip Goad is professor of architecture at the University of Melbourne and author of Architecture Bali: Birth of the Tropical Boutique Resort.

Although overall temple architecture is similar in both northern and southern Bali, there are some important differences. The inner courtyards of southern temples usually house a number of *meru* (multiroofed shrines), together with other structures, whereas in the north, everything is grouped on a single pedestal. On the pedestal you'll find 'houses' for the deities to use on their earthly visits; they're also used to store religious relics.

While Balinese sculpture and painting were once exclusively used as architectural decoration for temples, you'll soon see that sculpture and painting have developed as separate art forms influencing the look of every aspect of the island. And the art of temple and shrine construction is as vibrant as ever: more than 500 new ones in all sizes are built every month.

When you stay in a hotel featuring *lumbung* design, you are really staying in a place derived from rice storage barns – the 2nd floor is meant to be airless and hot!

Environment

THE LAND

Bali is a small island, midway along the string of islands that makes up the Indonesian archipelago. It's adjacent to the most heavily populated island of Java, and immediately west of the chain of smaller islands comprising Nusa Tenggara, which includes Lombok.

The island is visually dramatic – a mountainous chain with a string of active volcanoes, it includes several peaks around 2000m. Gunung Agung, the 'Mother Mountain', is over 3000m high. The agricultural lands are south and north of the central mountains. The southern region is a wide, gently sloping area, where most of the country's abundant rice crop is grown. The northern coastal strip is narrower, rising rapidly into the foothills of the central range. It receives less rain, but coffee, copra, rice and cattle are farmed there.

Keeping birds has been a part of Indonesian culture for centuries. It's common to see caged songbirds and they are sold in most markets.

Bali also has some arid, less-populated regions. These include the western mountain region, and the eastern and northeastern slopes of Gunung Agung. The Nusa Penida islands are dry, and cannot support intensive rice agriculture. The Bukit Peninsula is similarly dry, but with the growth of tourism and other industries it's becoming more populous.

Bali is volcanically active and extremely fertile. The two go hand-in-hand because eruptions contribute to the land's exceptional fertility, and high mountains provide the dependable rainfall that irrigates Bali's complex and amazingly beautiful patchwork of rice terraces. Of course, the volcanoes are a hazard as well – Bali has endured disastrous eruptions in the past and no doubt will again in the future. Apart from the volcanic central range, there are the limestone plateaus that form the Bukit Peninsula, in the extreme south of Bali, and the island of Nusa Penida.

As with Bali, Lombok's traditional economy has driven intensive rice cultivation. The wooded slopes of Gunung Rinjani have provided timber as have the coconut palms which also provide fibre and food. The land use has been environmentally sustainable for many years, and the island retains a natural beauty largely unspoiled by industry, overcrowding or overdevelopment.

Birds of Bali by Victor Mason and Frank Jarvis is enhanced by lovely watercolour illustrations.

WILDLIFE

The island is geologically young, and while most of its living things have migrated from elsewhere, true native wild animals are rare. This is not hard to imagine in the heavily populated and extravagantly fertile south of Bali, where the orderly rice terraces are so intensively cultivated they look more like a work of sculpture than a natural landscape.

In fact rice fields cover only about 20% of the island's surface area, and there is a great variety of other environmental zones: the dry scrub of the northwest, the extreme northeast and the southern peninsula; patches of

GONE TO THE DOGS

For many people, the one off-note memory of their visit to Bali has been the hordes of mangy ill-tempered and ill-treated *anjing* (dogs). Why are there so many? Because for many Balinese they barely exist, inhabiting a lowly world of trash-eating and scavenging. Left to their own devices, the dogs keep reproducing and hanging around the fringes of society. Their reputation – and plight – is also not helped by the fact that many people consider them to be fraternisers with evil spirits (which is why they are always barking). Still Balinese fraternisation with dogs is on the upswing. Amid the mangy curs you'll find pampered pooches with healthy coats and cute collars.

THE WALLACE LINE

The 19th-century naturalist Sir Alfred Wallace (1822–1913) observed great differences in fauna between Bali and Lombok – as great as the differences between Africa and South America. In particular, there were no large mammals (elephants, rhinos, tigers etc) east of Bali, and very few carnivores. He postulated that during the ice ages, when sea levels were lower, animals could have moved by land from what is now mainland Asia all the way to Bali, but the deep Lombok Strait would always have been a barrier. Thus he drew a line between Bali and Lombok, which he believed marked the biological division between Asia and Australia.

Plant life does not display such a sharp division, but there is a gradual transition from predominantly Asian rainforest species to mostly Australian plants such as eucalypts and acacias, which are better suited to long dry periods. This is associated with the lower rainfall as one moves east of Java. Environmental differences – including those in the natural vegetation – are now thought to provide a better explanation of the distribution of animal species than Wallace's theory about limits to their original migrations.

Modern biologists do recognise a distinction between Asian and Australian fauna, but the boundary between the regions is regarded as much fuzzier than Wallace's line. Nevertheless, this transitional zone between Asia and Australia is still called 'Walacea'.

dense jungle in the river valleys; forests of bamboo; and harsh volcanic regions that are barren rock and volcanic tuff at higher altitudes. Lombok is similar in all these respects.

The Malay Archipelago by Alfred Wallace is a natural history classic by the great 19th-century biologist and geographer, who postulated that the Lombok Strait was the dividing line between Asia and Australia. The book remains in print.

Animals

Bali has lots and lots of lizards, and they come in all shapes and sizes. The small ones (onomatopoetically called *cecak*) that hang around light fittings in the evening, waiting for an unwary insect, are a familiar sight. Geckos are fairly large lizards, often heard but less often seen. The loud and regularly repeated two-part cry 'geck-oh' is a nightly background noise that visitors soon become accustomed to, and it is considered lucky if you hear the lizard call seven times.

Bats are quite common, and the little chipmunklike Balinese squirrels are occasionally seen in the wild, although more often in cages.

Bali has more than 300 species of birds, but the one that is truly native to the island, the Bali starling, is just about extinct (see the boxed text, p282). Much more common are colourful birds like the orange-banded thrush, numerous species of egrets, kingfishers, parrots, owls and many more.

Bali's only wilderness area, Taman Nasional Bali Barat (West Bali National Park, p280) has a number of wild species, including grey and black monkeys (which you will also see in the mountains and East Bali), *muncak* (mouse deer), squirrels and iguanas. Bali used to have tigers and, although there are periodic rumours of sightings in the remote northwest of the island, nobody has proof of seeing one for a long time.

There is a rich variety of coral, seaweed, fish and other marine life in the coastal waters. Much of it can be appreciated by snorkellers, but the larger marine animals are only likely to be seen while diving. The huge, placid sun fish found off Nusa Penida lure divers from around the world.

Dolphins can be found right around the island and have unfortunately been made into an attraction off Lovina.

ProFauna (www.profauna.or.id) is an Indonesia-based nonprofit that works to protect the environment. It's active in Bali and has worked on issues such as saving sea turtles.

INTRODUCED SPECIES

Bali is thick with domestic animals, including ones that wake you up in the morning and others that bark all through the night. Chickens and roosters are kept both for food purposes and as domestic pets. Cockfighting is a popular

SEA TURTLES

Both the green-sea and hawksbill turtles inhabit the waters around Bali and Lombok, and the species are supposedly protected by international laws that prohibit trade in anything made from sea turtles.

In Bali, however, green-sea turtle meat is a traditional and very popular delicacy, particularly for Balinese feasts. Bali is the site of the most intensive slaughter of green-sea turtles in the world – no reliable figures are available, although in 1999 it was estimated that more than 30,000 are killed annually. A survey conducted in the past few years suggests that 4000 or more turtles are smuggled off the island annually as part of illegal trade. It's easy to find the trade on the back streets of waterside towns such as Benoa. One irony is that tourism money helps more people afford turtle meat both for consumption and for religious rituals and offerings.

Many individuals and organisations are involved in protecting the species, including Heinz von Holzen, the owner of Bumbu Bali restaurant in Tanjung Benoa (p138), and the Reef Seen Turtle Project at Reef Seen Aquatics in Pemuteran (p269). Bali's Hindu Dharma, the body overseeing religious practice, has decreed that turtle meat is essential in only very vital ceremonies.

male activity and a man's fighting bird is his prized possession. Balinese pigs are related to wild boar, and look really gross, with their sway backs and sagging stomachs. They inhabit the family compound, cleaning up all the garbage and eventually end up spit-roasted at a feast – they taste a lot better than they look.

The environmental group, World Wide Fund for Nature (www.wwf.or.id), is active on both Bali and Lombok. It has programmes focused on reefs, sea turtles and more.

Balinese cattle, by contrast, are delicate and graceful animals that seem more akin to deer than cows. Although the Balinese are Hindus, they do not generally treat cattle as holy animals, yet cows are rarely eaten or milked. They are, however, used to plough rice paddies and fields, and there is a major export market for Balinese cattle to Hong Kong and other parts of Asia.

Ducks are another everyday Balinese domestic animal and a regular dish at feasts. Ducks are kept in the family compound, and are put out to a convenient pond or flooded rice field to feed during the day. They follow a stick with a small flag tied to the end, and the stick is left planted in the field. As sunset approaches the ducks gather around the stick and wait to be led home again. The morning and evening duck parades are one of Bali's small delights.

Plants

TREES

Almost all of the island is cultivated, and only in the Taman Nasional Bali Barat are there traces of Bali's earliest plant life. As with most things in Bali, trees have a spiritual and religious significance, and you'll often see them decorated with scarves and black-and-white check cloths. The *waringin* (banyan) is the holiest Balinese tree and no important temple is complete without a stately one growing within its precincts. The banyan is an extensive, shady tree with an exotic feature – creepers that drop from its branches take root to propagate a new tree. Thus the banyan is said to be 'never-dying', since new offshoots can always take root. *Jepun* (frangipani or plumeria trees), with their beautiful and sweet-smelling white flowers are also common in temples and family compounds.

Mangoes are one of the leading cultivated trees in Bali. You'll see these green heavy hangers growing almost everywhere; in gardens, fields and by the side of the road.

Bali has monsoonal rather than tropical rainforests, so it lacks the valuable rainforest hardwoods that require rain year-round. The forestry department is experimenting with new varieties in plantations around Taman Nasional Bali Barat, but at the moment nearly all the wood used for carving is imported from Sumatra and Kalimantan.

A number of plants have great practical and economic significance. *Tiing* (bamboo) is grown in several varieties and is used for everything from satay sticks and string to rafters and gamelan (traditional Balinese orchestral music) resonators. The various types of palm provide coconuts, sugar, fuel and fibre.

The brilliant red of a hibiscus flower is at the centre of many a Balinese temple offering and decoration. Although they last but a day, the flowers grow in such profusion that there is always a new supply.

FLOWERS & GARDENS

Balinese gardens are a delight. The soil and climate can support a huge range of plants, and the Balinese love of beauty and the abundance of cheap labour means that every space can be landscaped. The style is generally informal, with curved paths, a rich variety of plants and usually a water feature. Who can't be enchanted by a frangipani tree dropping a carpet of fragrant blossoms?

You can find almost every type of flower in Bali, but some are seasonal and others are restricted to the cooler mountain areas. Many of the flowers will be familiar to visitors – hibiscus, bougainvillea, poinsettia, oleander, jasmine, water lily and aster are commonly seen in the southern tourist areas, while roses, begonias and hydrangeas are found mainly in the mountains. Less-familiar flowers include: Javanese *ixora (soka, angsoka),* with round clusters of bright red-orange flowers; *champak (cempaka),* a very fragrant member of the magnolia family; flamboyant, the flower of the royal poinciana flame tree; *manori (maduri),* which has a number of traditional uses; and water convolvulus *(kangkung),* the leaves of which are commonly used as a green vegetable. There are literally thousands of species of orchid.

Besides providing the leaves for *lontar* books, *rontal* palms also supply the sap needed to make *tuac,* the brutal home-made palm beer that's been the basis for many a hangover.

RICE

Rice cultivation has shaped the social landscape – the intricate organisation necessary for growing rice is a large factor in the strength of Bali's community life. Rice cultivation has also changed the environmental landscape – terraced rice fields trip down hillsides like steps for a giant, in shades of gold, brown and green, green and more green.

The elaborate irrigation system used to grow rice makes careful use of all the surface water. The fields are a complete ecological system, home for much more than just rice. In the early morning you'll often see the duck herders leading their flocks out for a day's paddle around a flooded rice field; the ducks eat various pests and leave fertiliser in their wake.

There are three words for rice – *padi* is the growing rice plant (hence paddy fields); *beras* is the uncooked grain; and *nasi* is cooked rice, as in nasi goreng (fried rice) and *nasi putih* (plain rice). A rice field is called a *sawah.*

A harvested field with its left-over burnt rice stalks is soaked with water and repeatedly ploughed, often by two bullocks pulling a wooden plough. Once the field is muddy enough, a small corner is walled off and seedling rice is planted there. When it is a reasonable size it is replanted, shoot by shoot, in the larger field. While the rice matures there is time to practise the gamelan (traditional Balinese orchestral music), watch the dancers or do a little woodcarving. Finally, the whole village turns out for the harvest – a period of solid hard work. It's strictly men only planting the rice, but everybody takes part in harvesting it.

In 1969, new high-yield rice varieties were introduced. These can be harvested a month sooner than the traditional variety and are resistant to many diseases.

However the new varieties also have greater needs for fertilizer and irrigation water, which strain the imperilled water supplies. More pesticides are also needed; this has caused the depletion of the frog and eel populations, which depend on the insects for survival.

Although everyone agrees that the new rice doesn't taste as good as *padi* Bali, the new strains now account for more than 90% of rice. Small areas of *padi* Bali are still planted and harvested in traditional ways to placate the rice goddess, Dewi Sri. Temples and offerings to her dot every rice field.

Flowers can be seen everywhere – in gardens or just by the roadside. Flower fanciers should make a trip to the Danau Bratan area in the central mountains to see the Bali Botanical Gardens, or visit the plant nurseries along the road between Denpasar and Sanur.

Flowers of Bali and *Fruits of Bali* by Fred and Margaret Wiseman are nicely illustrated books that will tell you what you're admiring or eating.

NATIONAL PARKS

The only national park on Bali is Taman Nasional Bali Barat, p280. It covers 19,000 hectares at the western tip of Bali, plus a substantial area of coastal mangrove and the adjacent marine area, including some fine dive sites.

The Taman Nasional Gunung Rinjani (Gunung Rinjani National Park), on Lombok covers 41,330 hectares and is the water-collector for most of the island. At 3726m, Gunung Rinjani is the second-highest volcanic peak in Indonesia and is very popular for trekking, see p316.

The Indonesian Ecotourism Centre (www.indecon.or.id) is devoted to highlighting responsible tourism. It lists places in Bali and on Lombok that have made a commitment to the local environment and culture.

ENVIRONMENTAL ISSUES

A fast-growing population in Bali has put pressure on limited resources. The tourist industry has attracted new residents, and there is a rapid growth of urban areas, resorts and villas that encroach onto agricultural land.

Water use is a major concern. Typical top-end hotels use more than 500L of water a day per room and the growing number of golf courses – the new one on the arid Bukit Peninsula near Dream Beach is an outrage (see the boxed text, p131) – suck an already stressed resource. Water pollution is another problem both from deforestation brought on by firewood-

RESPONSIBLE TRAVEL

The best way to responsibly visit Bali and Lombok is to try to be as least-invasive as possible. This of course is easier than it sounds but consider the following tips:

Watch your use of water. Travel into rice-growing regions of Bali and you'll think the island is coursing with water, but demand is starting to outstrip supply. Take up your hotel on its offer to save itself big money, er, no, to save lots of water by not washing your sheets and towels every day. Cynicism aside, this will save valuable Balinese water. So too you can forgo your own private plunge pool at the high end or a pool altogether – although this is almost impossible at any price level.

Don't hit the bottle. Those bottles of Aqua (the top local brand of bottled water, owned by Danone) are convenient but they add up. The zillions of such bottles tossed away each year are a major blight. Still, you're wise not to refill from the tap so what do you do? Ask your hotel if you can refill from their huge containers of drinking water. In Ubud, stop by the **Pondok Pecak Library & Learning Centre** (Map p188; ☎ 976194; Monkey Forest Rd, Ubud) which will refill your water bottle and tell you which other businesses offer this service.

Support environmentally aware businesses. Several hotels have a strong conservation focus; they include the Udayana Eco Lodge near Jimbaran (p129), Hotel Santai in Sanur (p142), Hotel Uyah Amed (p236), Puri Lumbung in the cool highlands of Munduk (p253) and Taman Sari Bali Cottages in Pemuteran (p270).

Don't play golf. The resorts will hate this, but tough. Having two golf courses on the arid Bukit Peninsula is environmentally mental.

Conserve power. Sure you want to save your own energy on a sweltering afternoon, but using air-con strains an already overloaded system. Much of the electricity comes from Java and the rest is produced at the roaring and smoking plant near Benoa Harbour.

Don't drive yourself crazy. The traffic is already bad, why add another vehicle to it? Can you take a tourist bus instead of a chartered or rental car? Would a walk, trek or hike be more enjoyable than road journey to an over-visited tourist spot (Pura Tanah Lot comes to mind)?

For organisations that may be able to use your help in protecting the environment in Bali, see p346.

collecting in the mountains and lack of proper treatment for the waste produced by the population. The vast mangroves along the south coast near Benoa Harbour are losing their ability to filter the water that drains here from much of the island (the Mangrove Information Centre near Sanur has more on this, see p147).

Air pollution is another problem as anyone stuck behind a smoke-belching truck or bus on one of the main roads knows. And it's not just all those plastic bags and water bottles but just the sheer volume of waste produced by the ever-growing population that is another problem. What to do with it?

Just growing Bali's sacred grain rice has become fraught with environmental concerns. (See the boxed text, p147 for details.)

On the upside there is a nascent effort to grow rice and other foods organically, reducing the amount of pesticide and fertilizer run-off into water supplies. Things may finally be moving forward on starting a sewage treatment programme in the south (but it will take years and the money is not there) and proposals to expand the airport's runways have inspired efforts to protect the nearby mangroves.

The environmental group PPLH Bali in Sanur is active on a range of issues and is a great resource. See p127 for details.

Bali & Lombok Outdoors

It's so much more than a beach holiday with an overlay of amazing culture – Bali's an incredible place to get outside and play. Sure you may have to actually get up off the sand to do this, but the rewards are many. In waters around the island you'll find world-class diving that ranges from reefs to shipwrecks to huge, rare swimming critters.

When that water hits shore, it creates some of the world's best surfing. No matter what time of year you visit, you'll find legendary surf spots. Away from the waves, a passel of aquatic fun companies offer everything from parasailing to banana-boat racing.

On land, hikes abound through the luxuriant green of the rice fields and deep into the river valleys. In the cool mountains, trails lead past a profusion of waterfalls, lakes and lush forest. If you want to head high, you can climb any of the island's three main active volcanoes for views, vent holes and visions of a lunar landscape.

Lombok doesn't have the same level of organisation but it has fine diving, surfing – often in remote locations – and a famous volcano trek.

Bike tours down Bali's volcanoes are popular. The company takes you to the top and you ride a relatively quiet road partway down the hill through tropical forest, coffee plantations and terraced rice fields. See p363 for tour companies.

DIVING & SNORKELLING

With its warm water, extensive coral reefs and abundant marine life, Bali offers excellent diving and snorkelling possibilities. Reliable dive schools and operators all around Bali's coast can train complete beginners or arrange challenging trips that will satisfy the most experienced divers. The best sites can all be accessed in a day trip from the south of Bali, although the more distant ones will involve several hours travelling time. Lombok is close behind Bali for diving. It has good sites, especially around its northwest coast.

Snorkelling gear is available near all the most accessible spots, but if you're keen, it's definitely worthwhile to bring your own, and to check out some of the less visited parts of the coasts.

Sobek (☎ 0361-287059; www.balisobek.com) is Bali's largest activity and adventure operator. They have a huge range of tours, including rafting, trekking and biking. Their equipment is of a high standard.

Dive Costs

On a local trip, count on US$40 to US$75 per person for two dives, which includes all equipment. Many operators offer open-water diving certification for US$350 to US$400.

Dive Courses

If you're not a qualified diver, and you want to try some scuba diving in Bali, you have three options.

First, nearly all operators offer an 'introductory', 'orientation' or 'initial' dive for beginners, usually after classroom training and shallow-water practise. Courses are reasonably cheap (from around US$60 for one dive), but it is essential to stick to one of the recommended dive operators (see opposite).

Second, some of the larger hotels and diving agencies offer four- or five-day courses that certify you for basic dives in the location where you do the course. A resort course will give you a better standard of training than just an introductory dive, but it doesn't make you a qualified diver. These courses cost about US$300.

Finally, if you are serious about diving, the best option is to enrol in a full open-water diving course, which gives you an internationally recognised qualification. A four-day open-water course, to Professional Association of Diving Instructors (PADI) standards, with a qualified instructor, manual, dive table and certification, will cost about US$300 to US$400. Experienced divers can also upgrade their skills with advanced open-water courses in night, wreck and deep diving etc, from around US$200 for a three-day course.

Dive Operators

Major dive operators in tourist areas can arrange trips to the main dive sites all around the island. But distances can be long, so it's better to stay relatively close to your destination.

SINK OR SWIM: DIVING SAFELY

Diving is justifiably popular in Bali and on Lombok. But like all diving destinations, it is important to stay safe in and out of the water. Here are some tips to make your trip the best possible.

Choosing a Dive Operator

In general, diving in Bali and on Lombok is safe, with a good standard of staff training and equipment maintenance. However, as with anywhere in the world, some operations are more professional than others, and it is often difficult, especially for inexperienced or beginner divers, to select the best operation for their needs. Here are a few tips to help you select a well set-up and safety-conscious dive shop.

- Are its staff fully trained and qualified? Ask to see certificates or certification cards – no reputable shop will be offended by this request. Guides must reach 'full instructor' level (the minimum certification level) to be able to teach any diving course. To guide certified divers on a reef dive, guides must hold at least 'rescue diver' or preferably 'dive master' qualifications. Note that a dive master cannot teach – only fully qualified instructors can do that.
- Does it have safety equipment on the boat? At a minimum, a dive boat should carry oxygen and a first-aid kit. A radio or cell phone are also important.
- Is the boat's equipment OK and its air clean? This is often the hardest thing for the new diver to judge. A few guidelines are:
    1. Smell the air – open a tank valve a small way and breathe in. Smelling dry or slightly rubbery air is OK. If it smells of oil or car exhaust, that tells you the operator doesn't filter the air correctly.
    2. When the equipment is put together, are there any big air leaks? All dive centres get some small leaks at some time, however, if you get a *big* hiss of air coming out of any piece of equipment, ask to have it replaced.
- Is it conservation-oriented? Most good dive shops explain that you should not touch corals or take shells from the reef. It's also common for the better places to work with local fishermen to ensure that certain areas are protected. Some even clean beaches!

Safety Guidelines for Diving

Before embarking on a scuba diving or snorkelling trip, carefully consider the following points to ensure a safe and enjoyable experience:

- Possess a current diving certification card from a recognised scuba diving instructional agency (if scuba diving).
- Be sure you are healthy and feel comfortable diving.
- Obtain reliable information about physical and environmental conditions at the dive site (eg from a reputable local dive operation). Conditions vary greatly between dive sites around Bali and the islands. Seasonal changes can significantly alter any site and dive conditions.
- Be aware of local customs and etiquette about marine life and the environment.
- Dive only at sites within your realm of experience; if available, engage the services of a competent, professionally trained dive instructor or dive master.

RESPONSIBLE DIVING

Please bear in mind the following tips when diving and help preserve the ecology and beauty of reefs:

- Never use anchors on the reef, and take care not to run boats aground on coral.
- Avoid touching or standing on living marine organisms or dragging equipment across the reef.
- Be conscious of the effect from your fins. Even without contact, the surge from fin strokes near the reef can damage delicate organisms. Take care not to kick up clouds of sand, which can smother organisms.
- Practise and maintain proper buoyancy control. Major damage can be done by divers descending too fast and colliding with the reef.
- Do not collect or buy corals or shells or loot marine archaeological sites (mainly shipwrecks).
- Ensure that you take home all your rubbish and any other litter you may find as well. Plastics in particular are a serious threat to marine life.
- Do not feed the fish.
- Minimise your involvement with marine animals. Do not *ever* ride on the backs of turtles and learn as much as you can about the animals' natural habitat.

For tips on choosing a dive shop, see the boxed text, p75. Places with good dive shops in Bali include Sanur (p141), Padangbai (p156), Candidasa (p227), Amed (p234), Lovina (p263), Pemuteran (p269) and Nusa Lembongan (p150).

Diving & Snorkelling Sites

BALI

Bali's main diving and snorkelling sites including those places we've listed above with good dive centres. For details see those sections of the book. In addition, Nusa Penida (p153) and Pulau Menjangan (p282) in Taman Nasional Bali Barat (West Bali National Park) are renowned for their diving.

LOMBOK

There is some very good scuba diving and snorkelling off the Gili Islands (see the boxed text, p306), though some of the coral has been damaged by dynamite fishing. There are also some good reefs near Senggigi (p294). Quite a few dive operators are based on the Gilis and in Senggigi and many have good reputations.

Huge sunfish up to 2.5m in length and twice as high are a much treasured sight for divers. They can usually be found around Nusa Lembongan, Nusa Penida and at times off Tulamben. These gentle giants feed on jellyfish and plankton.

Equipment

All the equipment you need is available in Bali and on Lombok, but remember, you may not be able to get exactly what you want in the size you need. The quality is variable – some operators use equipment right to the end of its service life. Most dive operators in Bali include the cost of equipment in the cost of the dive, but if you have your own equipment (excluding mask, snorkel and fins), you'll receive a discounted rate. Tanks and weight belt – as well as lunch, drinking water, transport, guides and insurance – are generally included in dive trips.

The most essential basic equipment to bring is a mask, snorkel and fins – they're not too difficult to carry and that way you know they'll fit. At any area with coral and tourists you will be able to rent snorkelling gear for around

20,000Rp per day, but make sure that you check the condition of the equipment carefully before you take it away.

Also worth bringing, if you plan to do a lot of diving, is a thin, full-length wetsuit, which is important for protection against stinging animals and possible coral abrasions. A thicker one (3mm) would be preferable if you plan frequent diving, deep dives or a night dive – the water can be cold, especially deeper down.

Some small, easy-to-carry things to bring from home include protective gloves, spare straps, silicone lubricant and extra globes for your torch (flashlight). Most dive operators can rent good-quality regulators (about US$5 per day) and BCVs (aka BCDs or Buoyancy Control Devices; about US$5), but if you bring your own you'll save money, and it's a good idea especially if you're planning to dive in more remote and secluded locations than Bali, where the rental equipment may not be as good.

The Sanur-based environmental group PPLH Bali (see p127) has several programmes devoted to protecting Bali's reefs and educating people about their value.

HIKING & TREKKING

Bali does not offer remote 'wilderness treks'; as it's simply too densely populated. For the most part, you'll make day trips from the closest village, often leaving before dawn to avoid the clouds and mist that usually blanket the peaks by mid-morning – for most treks you'll go on you won't need camping gear.

Hiking is a good way to explore the wilds of Bali – you can trek from village to village on small tracks and between the rice paddies. Munduk (p252) is fast becoming one of the most popular places to hike, thanks to its lack of hassles and lush, waterfall-riven landscape.

You can easily go on short hikes, without guides, around Danau Buyan and Danau Tamblingan (p248), Tirta Gangga (p232), to splendid villages near Ubud (p180) and many more.

Several agencies offer organised walking and trekking trips. See the coverage for the destinations listed in the previous paragraphs.

On Lombok, the Gunung Rinjani area (p314) is superb for trekking.

Lombok's trekking favourite Gunung Rinjani is an active volcano and the third-largest in Indonesia. It rises to 3726m (12,224ft) and erupted as recently as 2004.

RAFTING

Rafting is very popular, usually as a day trip from either South Bali or Ubud. Operators pick you up from your hotel, take you to the put-in point, provide all the equipment and guides, and return you to your hotel at the end of the day. The best time is during the wet season (October to March), or just after; by the middle of the dry season (April to September), the best river rapids may be better called 'dribbles'.

SAFETY GUIDELINES FOR TREKKING

Before embarking on a trekking trip, consider the following points to ensure a safe and enjoyable experience:

- Pay any fees and possess any permits required by local authorities; often these will rolled into the guide's fee, meaning that it is all negotiable.
- Be sure you are healthy and feel comfortable walking for a sustained period.
- Obtain reliable information about physical and environmental conditions along your intended route, eg the weather can get quite wet and cold in the upper reaches of the volcanoes.
- Confirm with your guide that you will only go on walks/treks within your realm of experience.
- Carry the proper equipment. Depending on the trek and time of year this can mean rain gear or extra water. Carry a torch (flashlight); don't assume the guide will have one.

Most operators use the Sungai Ayung (Ayung River; see p184), near Ubud, where there are between 19 and 25 Class II to III rapids (ie potentially exciting but not perilous). As you float along, you can admire the stunning gorges and rice paddies from the boat. Sungai Telagawaja (Telagawaja River) near Muncan in East Bali (p208) is also popular. It is more rugged than the Ayung and the scenery is more wild.

Dress to get wet and bring something dry for afterwards. Companies will pick you up at your hotel in South Bali and Ubud.

Advertised prices run from around US$40 to US$70; discounts are common. Reputable operators include the big operators Sobek (see sidebar, left) and Bali Adventure Tours, plus the following:

Discovery Rafting (☎ 0361-764915; www.discoveryrafting.com) Sungai Ayung.

Telaga Waja Adventure (☎ 0361-727525; telagawajarafting@yahoo.com) Sungai Telagawaja.

SURFING

In recent years, the number of surfers in Bali has increased enormously, and good breaks can get very crowded. Many Balinese have taken to surfing, and the grace of traditional dancing is said to influence their style. The surfing competitions in Bali are a major local event. Facilities for surfers have improved, and surf shops in Kuta will sell just about everything you need.

www.surftravel.com.au is an Australian tour company with camps, yacht charters and a website with destination information, surfer reviews and more.

Equipment

A small board is usually adequate for the smaller breaks, but a few extra inches on your usual board length won't go astray. For the bigger waves – 8ft and upwards – you will need a gun. For a surfer of average height and build, a board around the 7ft mark is perfect.

If you try to bring more than two or three boards, you may have problem with customs officials.

There are surf shops in Kuta (p101) and elsewhere in South Bali (see p132). You can rent boards of varying quality and get supplies. If you need repairs, ask around, there are lots of places.

Other recommended equipment:

- Solid luggage for rugged airline travel
- Board-strap for carrying
- Tough shoes for walking down rocky cliffs
- Your favourite wax if you're picky
- Wetsuit or reef booties
- Wetsuit vest or other protective cover from the sun, cloudy days, reefs and rocks
- Surfing helmet for those rugged conditions (and riding a rented motor-cycle)

There are several surf schools that teach beginners in the waves off Kuta and Legian beaches. See p102 for details.

Surf Trips from Bali

Charter boats take groups of surfers for day trips around various local reefs, or for one-week 'surfaris' to great breaks on eastern Java (Grajagan, also known as G-Land has an incredible left), Nusa Lembongan, Lombok and Sumbawa, some of which cannot be reached by land. These are especially popular with those who find that the waves in Bali are too crowded. You'll see them advertised in numerous agents and surf shops in Kuta. Prices start at around 300,000Rp per person per week (seven days/six nights), including food. The most basic boats are converted Indonesian fishing boats with minimal comforts and safety equipment.

G-Land Bobby's Surf Camp (☎ 0361-755588; www.grajagan.com) is at Grajagan in East Java. It provides transport to/from Bali.

BALI SURF BREAKS

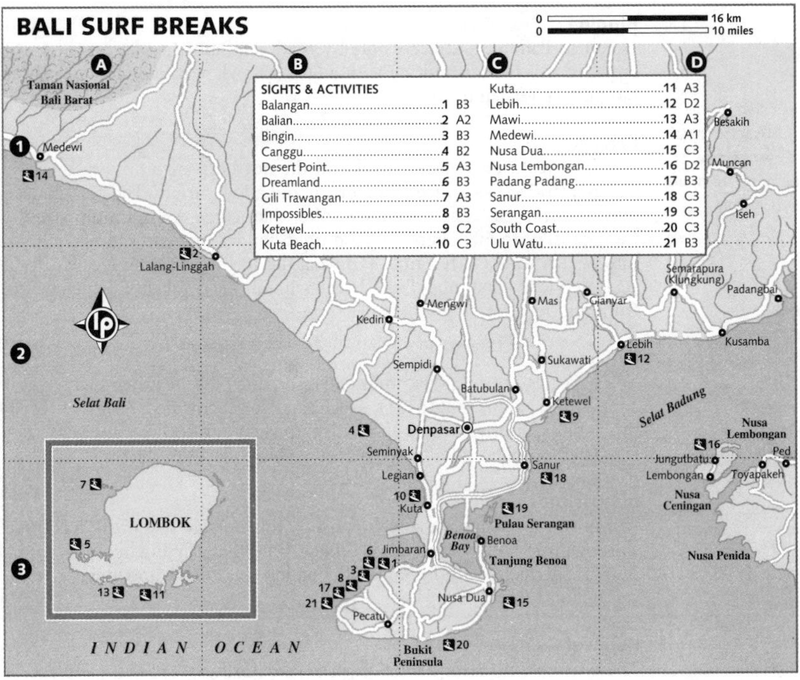

Where to Surf

BALI

Swells come from the Indian Ocean, so the surf is on the southern side of the island and, strangely, on the northwest coast of Nusa Lembongan, where the swell funnels into the strait between there and the Bali coast.

In the dry season (around April to September), the west coast has the best breaks, with the trade winds coming in from the southeast; this is also when Nusa Lembongan works best. In the wet season, surf the eastern side of the island, from Nusa Dua around to Padangbai. If there's a north wind – or no wind at all – there are also a couple of breaks on the south coast of Bukit Peninsula.

www.surftravelonline.com has information on remote Indonesian locations.

Balangan

Go through growing Pecatu Indah resort and follow the road around to the right past Dreamland to reach the Balangan warung (food stall). Balangan (p131) is a fast left over a shallow reef, unsurfable at low tide, good at midtide with anything over a 4ft swell; with an 8ft swell, this can be one of the classic waves.

Kuta's famous Tubes Surf Bar & Restaurant (p102) is a popular centre for anything to do with surfing – the Tubes tide chart is widely available.

Balian

There are a few peaks near the mouth of Sungai Balian (Balian River, p276 in western Bali – sea water here is often murky because the river can carry a lot of pollution. Look for the Taman Rekreasi Indah Soka, along the main road, just west of Lalang-Linggah. The best break here is an enjoyable and consistent left-hander that works well at mid- to high tide if there's no wind.

Bingin

North of Padang and accessible by road, this spot (p132) can now get crowded. It's best at midtide with a 6ft swell, when it manufactures short but perfect left-hand barrels.

www.indosurf.com.au has web links and surfing info and www.wannasurf.com has surf reports and a message board.

Canggu

North of Kuta-Legian-Seminyak, on the northern extremity of the bay, Canggu (p125) has a nice white beach and a few surfers. The peak breaks over a 'soft' rock ledge – well, it's softer than coral. An optimum size for Canggu is 5ft to 6ft. There's a good right-hander that you can really hook into, which works at full tide, and what the surf writer Peter Neely calls 'a sucky left ledge that tubes like Ulu but without the coral cuts', which works from midtide.

Dreamland

You have to go through Pecatu Indah resort and past the water-sucking golf course to reach this spot (p131), which can also get crowded. At low 5ft swell, this solid peak offers offers a short, sharp right and a longer more tubular left. There's quite a good scene here and cheap places to stay.

Impossibles

Just north of Padang Padang (opposite), this outside reef break has three shifting peaks with fast left-hand tube sections that can join up if the conditions are perfect (low tide, 5ft swell), but don't stay on for too long, or you'll run out of water.

Ketewel & Lebih

These two beaches (for Lebih, see p209) are northeast of Sanur, and access is easy from the new coast road. They're both right-hand beach breaks, which are dodgy at low tide and close out over 6ft. Most likely there are other breaks along this coast all the way to Padangbai, but they need a big swell to make them work.

Surfing Indonesia by Leonard and Lorca Lueras has about 80 pages on Bali. It has great photos, a comprehensive coverage of the waves, and some good surfing background.

Kuta Area

For your first plunge into the warm Indian Ocean, try the beach breaks at Kuta Beach (p95); on full tide go out near the life-saving club at the southern end of the beach road. At low tide, try the tubes around Halfway Kuta (p102), probably the best place in Bali for beginners to practise. Start at the beach breaks if you are a bit rusty. The sand here is fine and packed hard, so it can hurt when you hit it. Treat even these breaks with respect. They provide zippering left and right barrels over shallow banks and can be quite a lot of fun.

Further north, the breaks at Legian Beach (p95) can be pretty powerful, with lefts and rights on the sand bars off Jl Melasti and Jl Padma. At Kuta and Legian you will encounter most of the local Balinese surfers.

And again further north, there are more beach breaks off Seminyak (p101), such as the Oberoi, near the hotel of the same name. The sea here is fickle and can have dangerous rip tides – take a friend.

For more serious stuff, go to the reefs south of the beach breaks, about a kilometre out to sea. Kuta Reef, a vast stretch of coral, provides a variety of waves. You can paddle out in around 20 minutes, but the easiest way is by boat, for a fee. The main break is a classic left-hander, best at mid- to high tide with a 5ft to 6ft swell, when it peels across the reef and has a beautiful inside tube section; the first part is a good workable wave. Over 7ft it tends to double up and section.

The reef is well suited for backhand surfing. Unfortunately it's not surfable at dead-low tide, but you can get out there not long after the tide turns. The locals can advise you if necessary. It gets very crowded here, but if conditions are good there's another, shorter left, 50m further south along the reef, which usually has fewer surfers.

Medewi

Further along the south coast of western Bali is a softer left called Medewi (p277) – it's a point break that can give a long ride right into the river mouth. This wave has a big drop, which fills up then runs into a workable inside section. It's worth surfing if you feel like something different, but to catch it you need to get up early, because it gets blown out as the wind picks up. It works best at mid- to high tide with a 6ft swell. There's accomodation.

There are four 18-hole golf courses in Bali. One near Danau Bratan (p248), another near Pura Tanah Lot (p272) and two rather inappropriately on the arid Bukit Peninsula at Nusa Dua (p134) and a new one at Pecatu Indah (p134).

Nusa Dua

During the wet season you should surf on the east side of the island, where there are some very fine reef breaks. The reef off the Nusa Dua (p133) has very consistent swells. The main break is 1km off the beach to the south of Nusa Dua – go past the golf course and look for the whole row of warung and some boats to take you out. There are lefts and rights that work well on a small swell at low to midtide. On bigger days, take a longer board and go further out, where powerful peaks offer long-rides, fat tubes and lots of variety. Further north, in front of the Club Med, is a fast, barrelling right reef break called Sri Lanka, which works best at midtide and can handle swells from 6ft to 10ft.

Nusa Lembongan

In the Nusa Penida group, this island (p148) is separated from the southeast coast of Bali by the Selat Badung (Badung Strait).

The strait is very deep and generates huge swells that break over the reefs off the northwest coast of Lembongan. Shipwreck, clearly visible from the beach, is the most popular break, a longish right that gets a good barrel at midtide with a 5ft swell.

A bit to the south, Lacerations is a very fast, hollow right breaking over a very shallow reef – hence the name. Still further south is a smaller, more user-friendly left-hander called Playground. Remember that Lembongan is best with an easterly wind, as are Kuta and Ulu Watu, so it's dry-season surfing.

You can ride horses in Bali from stables in Kerobokan (p124), Yeh Gangga (p276), Ubud (p181) and Pemuteran (p269). Many people enjoy the chance to see nature at a relaxed pace and in some cases gallop through the surf.

Padang Padang

Just Padang for short, this super shallow, left-hand reef break (above) is just north of Ulu Watu towards Kuta. Again, check this place carefully before venturing out. It's a very demanding break that only works over about 6ft from mid- to high tide – it's a great place to watch from the clifftop.

If you can't surf tubes, backhand or forehand, don't go out: Padang is a tube. After a ledgey take-off, you power along the bottom before pulling up into the barrel. So far so good, now for the tricky part. The last section turns inside out like a washing machine on fast-forward. You have to drive high through this section, all the time while in the tube. Don't worry if you fail to negotiate this trap, plenty of other surfers have been caught too. After this, the wave fills up and you flick off. Not a wave for the faint-hearted and definitely not a wave to surf when there's a crowd.

Sanur

Sounds exciting! Sanur Reef (p132) has a hollow wave with excellent barrels. It's fickle, and doesn't even start till you get a 6ft swell, but anything over 8ft will be world-class, and anything over 10ft will be brown board shorts material. There are other reefs further offshore and most of them are surfable.

Hyatt Reef, over 2km from shore, has a shifty right peak that can give a great ride at full tide. Closer in, opposite the Sanur Beach Market, Tanjung Sari gives long left rides at low tide with a big swell, while Tanjung Right can be a very speedy wall on a big swell. The classic right is off the Grand Bali Beach Hotel.

Look for the free newspaper *Magic Wave,* which is distributed around Kuta and has full coverage of the Bali surfing scene.

Serangan

The abortive development at Pulau Serangan (Turtle Island) entailed huge earthworks at the southern and eastern sides of the island, and this has made the surf here much more consistent, though the landfill looks like a disaster. The causeway has made the island much more accessible, and several warung face the water, where waves break right and left in anything over a 3ft swell (see p147).

South Coast

The extreme south coast (p133), around the end of Bukit Peninsula, can be surfed any time of the year provided there is a northerly wind, or no wind at all – get there very early to avoid onshore winds. The peninsula is fringed with reefs and big swells are produced, but access is a problem. There are a few roads, but the shoreline is all cliff. If you want to explore it, charter a boat on a day with no wind and a small swell.

Nyang Nyang is a right-hand reef break, reached by a steep track down the cliff. Green Ball is another right, which works well on a small to medium swell, ie when it's almost flat everywhere else. Take the road to the Nikko Bali Resort & Spa, fork left just before you get there and take the steps down the cliff. The south coast has few facilities and tricky currents, and it would be a bad place to get into trouble.

www.surfaidinternational.org is a very well-regarded international surfer-run aid organisation that has done impressive work for the tsunami-ravaged islands off Sumatra.

Ulu Watu

When Kuta Reef is 5ft to 6ft, Ulu Watu (p127), the most famous surfing break on Bali, will be 6ft to 8ft with bigger sets. Kuta and Legian sit on a huge bay – Ulu Watu is way out on the southern extremity of the bay, and consequently picks up more swell than Kuta. It's about a half-hour journey from downtown Kuta by private transport.

Teluk Ulu Watu (Ulu Watu Bay) is a great setup for surfers – local boys will wax your board, get drinks for you and carry the board down into the cave, which is the usual access to the wave. There are warung and nearby there are cheap losmen (basic accommodation).

Ulu Watu has about seven different breaks. The Corner is straight in front of you to the right. It's a fast-breaking, hollow left that holds about 6ft. The reef shelf under this break is extremely shallow, so try to avoid falling headfirst. At high tide, the Peak starts to work. This is good from 5ft to 8ft, with bigger waves occasionally right on the Peak itself. You can take off from this inside part or further down the line. It's a great wave. At low tide, if the swell isn't huge, go further south to the Racetrack, which is a whole series of bowls.

At low tide when the swell is bigger, Outside Corner starts operating, fur ther out from the Racetrack. This is a tremendous break and on a good day you can surf one wave for hundreds of metres. The wall here on a 10ft wave jacks up with a big drop and bottom turn, then the bowl section. After this it becomes a big workable face. You can usually get tubed only in the first section. When surfing this break you need a board with length, otherwise you won't be getting down the face of any of the amazing waves.

Another left runs off the cliff that forms the southern flank of the bay. It breaks outside this in bigger swells, and once it's 7ft, a left-hander pitches right out in front of a temple on the southern extremity. Out behind the Peak, when it's big, is a bombora (submerged reef) appropriately called the Bommie. This is another big left-hander and it doesn't start operating until the swell is about 10ft. On a normal 5ft to 8ft day there are also breaks south of the Peak. One is a very fast left, and is also very hollow, usually only ridden by goofy-footers, due to its speed.

Observe where other surfers paddle out and follow them. If you are in doubt, ask someone. It is better having some knowledge than none at all. Climb down into the cave and paddle out from there. When the swell is bigger you will be swept to your right. Don't panic, it is an easy matter to paddle around the white water from down along the cliff. Coming back in you have to aim for the cave. When the swell is bigger, come from the southern side of the cave as the current runs to the north. If you miss the cave, paddle out again and repeat the procedure.

Bali-based Surf Travel Online (☎ 0361-750550; www.surftravelonline.com) has information on surf camps, boat charters and package deals for surf trips to remote Indonesian locations, as well as Nusa Lembongan.

LOMBOK

Lombok has some good surfing and the dearth of tourists means that breaks are uncrowded.

Desert Point

Located in an extremely remote part of Lombok, Desert Point (above) is legendary if elusive wave that was voted the 'best wave in the world' by *Tracks* magazine. Only suitable for very experienced surfers, on its day this left-handed tube can offer a 300m ride, growing in size from take-off to close-out (which is over razor-sharp coral). Desert Point only really performs when there's a serious ground swell and can be flat for days and days – May to September offer the best chance of the right conditions. The nearest accommodation is about 12km away in Pelangan, down a rough dirt track, so many surfers either camp next to the shoreline, or cruise in on surf safaris from Bali.

Indo Surf & Lingo (www.indosurf.com.au) by Peter Neely tells surfers where and when to find good waves around Bali and other Indonesian islands. The book also has a language guide with Indonesian translations of useful words. It's available at surf shops in the Kuta region.

Gili Trawangan

Much better known as a scuba diving mecca, Trawangan (p307) also boasts a little-known surf spot off its southwestern tip, offshore from the Vila Ombak hotel. It's a quick right-hander that breaks in two sections, one offering a steeper profile, and breaks over rounded coral. It can be surfed all year long but is best at high tide. There are no surf facilities in Trawangan, though both resident Westerners and locals may lend you a board.

Mawi

About 18km west of Kuta, Lombok the stunning bay of Mawi (above) has a fine barrelling left with a late take-off and a final tube. It's best in the dry season from May to October with easterly offshore winds and a southwest swell. As there are sharp rocks and coral underwater and the riptide here is very fierce, take great care. Unfortunately thefts have been reported from the beach, so leave nothing of any value and tip the locals to look after your vehicle.

WATER SPORTS

The east coast of South Bali is popular for water sports. The close-in reefs off Sanur and Tanjung Benoa (Benoa Headland) mean that the water is usually calm enough for a lot of aquatic fun. Parasailing, jet-skiing, water-skiing and banana-boat rides are just some of the choices. In Sanur (see p142) there are activity huts along the beach. In Tanjung Benoa (p137) several large water-sports centres are located on the beach. Most fetch and return patrons from

AHHH, A SPA

Whether it's a total fix for the mind, body and spirit, or simply the desire for some quick-fix serenity, lots of travellers in Bali are spending hours and days being massaged, scrubbed, perfumed, pampered, bathed and blissed-out. Sometimes this happens on the beach or in a garden, other times you'll find yourself in lavish surroundings.

Every upmarket hotel worth its stars has spa facilities (which are generally open to nonguests) offering health, beauty and relaxation treatments. Day spas are also common, particularly in Ubud (p181), Kuta (p103) and Seminyak (p104). The cost can be anything from a 20,000Rp beach rub to a multihour sybaritic soak for US$100 or more. However in general the costs are quite low compared with other parts of the world and the Balinese have just the right cultural background and disposition to enhance the serenity.

Massage and herbal body scrubs have an important place in Balinese family life. From birth, parents massage their children, and as soon as children are able it's normal for them to reciprocate. Anyone with an ailment receives a specially formulated scrub, and men provide and receive massage as much as women. The Balinese massage techniques of stretching, long strokes, skin rolling and palm and thumb pressure result in a lowering of tension, improved blood flow and circulation, and an all-over feeling of calm.

So what can you expect in a spa? It's usually a three-stage process – the massage, the scrub and the soak. Therapists are often female, although top-end spas may have male therapists. Many massage rooms are also set up with two massage beds, so you can have a massage alongside your partner or friend.

A basic therapeutic massage is a one-hour, top-to-toe, deep-tissue massage to relax the muscles, tone the skin and eliminate stress, while aromatherapy massages feature a choice of essential oils, such as ginger, nutmeg, coconut and sandalwood. Commonly offered massage options include Shiatsu, Thai and Swedish massage and reflexology (concentrating on pressure points of the feet). For something special, the 'four-hands' massage, where two therapists will treat you, is also an option at many spas.

Based on traditional herbal treatments, popular spa options include the *mandi rempah* (spice bath) and the *mandi susu* (milk bath). The *mandi rempah* begins with a massage, followed by a body scrub with a paste made from assorted spices, and ending with a herbal-and-spice hot bath. The *mandi susu* begins with a massage, followed by a herbal scrub and a milk-and-yogurt body mask. The treatment ends with a soak in a milk bath.

The most popular treatment though, is the Javanese *mandi lulur* body scrub. Based on the centuries-old Javanese palace ritual, the *mandi lulur* takes almost two hours but it feels longer as all sense of time is lost during the deep-tissue massage (ask for strong treatment if you dare). The massage is followed by a full body rub made from a vibrant yellow paste of turmeric, sandalwood and rice powder. This is allowed to dry and then gently rubbed off, exfoliating and polishing the skin. Next, a mixture of yogurt and honey is smoothed on, to moisturise and feed the skin and restore the perfect pH balance. After a quick rinsing shower, the highlight follows – a long and lovely bath in fragrant essential oils amid pale, floating frangipani petals. Refreshing hot ginger tea is normally served during the calming recovery time following the bath, when you'll feel so good you'll be dreamily planning another two hours of luxurious bliss.

all over the south. Costs for the various mechanized marvels can quickly add up to US$20 an hour or more. Just swimming off the beach is free.

For watery adventures after an island voyage, try one of the party boats making daily excursions to Nusa Lembongan (p148) and Nusa Penida (p153). There you have a full range of water sports based aboard a barge that often looks like something from the Kevin Costner dud *Waterworld*. It's all organised frolic and most basic activities like snorkelling the interesting reefs are included in the package cost (per person US$60 to US$80). Note that with pick-up and drop-off at your South Bali hotel, plus the boat ride to/from the barge it can be a very long day.

Food & Drink

Considered by many as one of the most dynamic islands in Indonesia, Bali has a fiery cuisine that matches the nature of its enigmatic folk, and one that is guaranteed to speed up the metabolism and have your blood flowing like the Sungai Ayung in the wet season! While the cuisine of Bali has remained a mystery to visitors for years (and it's still easy to eat Western cuisine for every meal, if that's your preference), times are changing. Balinese food is now more accessible than ever – be it on street corners or in restaurants frequented by tourists.

The finest Balinese food is found spilling out of even simple Balinese kitchens in your average village compound. It is here that the family cook takes the time to roast the coconut until the smoky sweetness kisses your nose, grinds the spices diligently to form the perfect paste and perhaps even makes fresh fragrant coconut oil in which to fry them. And when I say kitchen, don't for one minute imagine a stainless-steel work place with a fridge, oven and cupboards stacked with plates and cups. The favoured Balinese kitchen has a wood-fired oven that is fuelled by bamboo and sometimes even coffee wood that creates a smoky sweetness and wonderful flavour that modern cookers cannot reproduce.

The Food of Bali by Heinz von Holzen and Lother Arsana brings to life everything from *cram cam* (clear chicken soup with shallots) to *bubuh injin* (black-rice pudding). Von Holzen's books also include a forthcoming one on Balinese markets.

Compared with other Indonesian islands, Balinese food is more pungent and lively. The biting note of fresh gingers is matched by the heat of raw chillies, shrimp paste, palm sugar and tamarind. There is nothing shy about this cuisine and it is certainly not as sweet and subtle as the food of the neighbouring island of Java. But there is more to it than that – there is a multitude of layers that make the complete dish. A meal will contain the six flavours (sweet, sour, spicy, salty, bitter and astringent), which in turn promote health, vitality and stimulate the senses.

There are shades of South-Indian, Malaysian and Chinese flavours in Balinese food. It has evolved from years of cross-cultural cook-ups and trading with seafaring pioneers and perhaps even pirates, across the seas of Asia. The idea that you should only eat what is native to the soil doesn't apply in this part of the world, because even the humble chilli was introduced by the fearless Portuguese, along with a plethora of other colourful, edible exotica from the New World. In true Balinese-style, the village chefs selected the finest and perhaps most durable new ingredients and adapted them to the local tastes and cooking-styles of the people.

A bowl of cooked *kangkung* (water spinach) for dinner is guaranteed to give you a good nights' sleep as it is full of natural tryptophan.

Like Malaysian and Peranakan cooking, Balinese cuisine has a predominance of turmeric, ginger, chilli and coconut flavours, and shares many similar dishes with its South-east Asian neighbours. Other native ingredients such as the beloved candlenut, galangal and musk lime are fundamental to the cuisine of this region, as is the elegant, alluring lemongrass. Indian-style spices such as cinnamon, cardamom and cumin are seldom used in Bali. Emphasis is on the combination of fresh gingers, balanced by the complex sweetness of palm sugar, tamarind and shrimp paste along with the clean fresh flavours of lime-scented lemongrass, lime leaves and coriander seeds.

Bali has also become a place where global cuisines meet. Once famous only for its jaffles and black-rice pudding, Bali has become a culinary nirvana, offering the best of Indian, Moroccan, Italian, Chinese, Japanese, French, fusion and, of course, Indonesian food.

STAPLES & SPECIALITIES

Balinese cuisine is shaped around a lifestyle rich with ceremonies and cultural activity. Rice, the staple, has also played a leading role in determining the very nature of a meal and the way it's prepared. Many dishes are chopped

WE DARE YOU *Janet de Neefe*

One of my favourite drinks served at the Ubud market is *daluman*. Horrifying to most tourists, this wobbly green drink is full of natural chlorophyll and a bunch of health-giving nutrients. You could be forgiven thinking it's green slime or something scooped out of a Balinese river, but believe me, when served with palm-sugar syrup and a swirl of roasted coconut milk, it is sublime! It cools down a hot tummy and is said to help prevent stomach cancer.

Eels are an islandwide favourite and there is nothing tastier than deep-fried seasoned eel or even eel chopped and steamed in banana leaves, with freshly ground spices and a touch of delicate torch ginger.

For a refreshing treat, I dare you to try *es campur*. It is a mountainous mix of crushed ice, fresh fruits, fermented yam, seaweed jelly and lashings of sweetened condensed milk and iridescent pink syrup. I used to eat this soupy fruit salad when I was pregnant, much to the dismay of the Balinese, as pregnant women are not supposed to eat ice.

Bee larvae is a sweet, juicy delicacy in Bali. I always buy this golden honeycomb when it's available for the Casa Luna market tour and cook it up for the class. The baby bees are simmered with fragrant lemongrass, lime leaves and *salam* leaves and then mixed with roasted shredded coconut, lashings of chilli with shrimp paste and fried shallots. The subtle hint of honey and meaty texture of the bees, matched with gentle aromatics and spice is so delicious it makes you buzz!

finely to complement the cooked grains of rice and for ease of eating with the (right) hand. As you can imagine, the Balinese are very particular about rice – dry, fluffy grains are preferred.

Breakfast

In Bali, you can start the day with alluring flavours that will slap you out of that early morning slowness. The best breakfast food is usually found at the local market. Typical fare includes compressed rice cake mixed with steamed greens tossed with a freshly ground peanut sauce bursting with flavour; or soft, boiled rice topped with brilliant, chopped greens and sprouts mixed with a fiery *sambal* (chili paste) and roasted coconut, or you might like to eat plain, steamed rice with fried *tempe* (Indonesian soy-bean cake), crunchy anchovies, bitter greens and *sambal;* or a variety of satay from goat meat to pounded fish, roasted chicken, pork or even goat soup. If you have a sweet tooth, you can eat your way through endless rice porridges, temples cakes, squiggly rice cakes, boiled bananas and wash it all down with a green leafy drink or *cendol* (coconut milk and palm suagr). You can choose to sit in the lively ambience of the market or get your meal wrapped up in a banana leaf or brown paper and take it home. And that's just to start the day!

If you really enjoy spicy food, you can ask the staff in any restaurant to serve a fresh *sambal* of chopped chilli drowned in *kecap manis* (sweet soy sauce).

Lunch & Dinner

Lunch is eaten from 11am, and the regular fare is the famous *nasi campur. Nasi campur* simply means steamed rice and a mixture of side dishes. The combination of these is dependent on seasonal produce and economy. This is in fact the style of eating for just about every meal. Lunch constitutes the main meal of the day for it is at this time that the rice has finished a couple of hours of happy steaming and all the side dishes are ready and bubbling with vitality. The menu might consist of a stewy, meat dish such as *babi kecap* (pork in sweet soy sauce) or roast chicken, steamed greens with roasted or grilled coconut, fried tofu and *tempe* in a tomato-chilli sauce, fried fish and a spicy *sambal* or chilli seasoning. There are generally four or five side dishes that grace the plate and depending on family economics, dinner might just be a matter of leftovers. Dessert is a rarity; for special occasions, it will consist of fresh fruit or gelati-style coconut ice cream.

Mixing watermelon and palm sugar together is a major food no-no in Bali, and one that is bound to leave you with painful stomach cramps.

DRINKS

If you are a passionate wine drinker visiting Bali, you might do better to take up beer! Bintang, Bali Hai and now, the new organic, Storm beer will certainly quench your thirst on a hot day. Otherwise, Hatten wine makes an interesting local wine, and its glowing pink rosé has quite a following. Wine of the Gods, perhaps the finest local wine, actually imports freshly crushed grapes from Western Australia and bottles the wine in Denpasar.

Of course, if you want a more serious shot of alcohol, *arak* is probably the answer. *Arak* is the alcohol produced from fermented palm fruits and *tuak* is made from another type of palm. Drinking either of these is guaranteed to have you swaying like a palm tree with an immense hangover the next day. *Brem*, or rice wine, is a sweeter, milder brew that is not unlike sake. It is best served with lime juice and loads of ice. One of the most popular nonalcoholic local drinks on the island is *cendol*. This is an interesting, psychedelic mix of palm sugar, fresh coconut milk and crushed ice full of all sorts of known and unknown extra flavourings and floaties. My daughter's favourite is *es teler* which is a mix of soft avocado with young coconut and sago. Green coconut juice is the perfect tonic for upset tummies, hangovers and fevers. Mother Nature's perfect rehydration drink, it helps cool the body and replace all those electrolytes that tend to evaporate in tropical weather. Sometimes you will be greeted in the rice fields by farmers offering green coconut juice; they'll be eager to show their coconut-climbing skills to awe-struck tourists and make some pocket money on the side. Try it with ice and a squeeze of lime juice.

Green coconut juice is the perfect traditional remedy for heat stroke, Bali belly and fever.

Balinese ceremonies are determined by the phases of the sun, the moon and the stars, and you only have to glance at a Balinese calendar to see how many religious celebrations are held annually. For more information on the Balinese calendar, check out www.indo.com/culture/calendar.html.

CELEBRATIONS & CEREMONIES

Food is a major part of Balinese ceremonies, with the menu varying according to the size and importance of the occasion. A small home ceremony might include spit-roasted chicken, or smoked duck, whereas, with a grand affair, suckling pig is the desired fare. The preparations begin at dawn the day before with kilos of spices, exotic ingredients, meats and rice being cooked.

Men are ceremonial chefs for all festivities, becoming 'spice Gods' for the occasion and creating a celebratory extravaganza to honour the deities. The action begins in the early hours of the morning, when pigs, ducks or chicken are slaughtered and then prepared for a multitude of lively, spiced dishes that will be used as offerings to God and to feed all those who have

BABI GULING

Babi guling, or suckling pig, appears on the menu of most major household ceremonies, from a baby's three-month ground-touching ceremony to the fearful tooth-filing ceremony. I have seen these small, roasted *babes* delivered to our door so many times, wrapped in layers of plastic, ready to be sliced and served to friends, family and neighbours on a grand occasion. It is, by far, the most revered dish on the island.

In the early days, tourists were advised not to eat *babi guling* in order to avoid the renowned Bali belly, but nowadays you don't need to be sitting in a tight sarong at a ceremony to enjoy the succulent meat and spicy filling. The spice paste used includes chilli, turmeric, ginger, galangal, shallots, garlic, coriander seeds, aromatic leaves and is basted in turmeric and coconut oil. In the cuisine capital of the island, Ibu Oka's warung (food stall) in Ubud (p193) serves suckling pig every lunchtime and is jam-packed with lip-smacking tourists, brushing shoulders with Balinese, Indonesians and other Asians as they vie for a table at this popular, East–meets–West local eatery. Up to six freshly roasted pigs are brought in each day after 11am and if you are not there by 2pm, you will probably miss out. The meal includes slices of tender, roasted pork, homemade blood sausage, chopped greens, *sambal* (chilli sauce) and crisp pork crackling.

You can find this treat all over the island, from Gianyar to Tabanan.

helped prepare the food. It's community work at its best, sometimes with hundreds of men pounding meat and spices, chopping vegetables, boiling coconut milk, frying entrails and making Balinese satay. For my father-in-law's cremation, our garage became a production-line food hall, with more than 100 men preparing more than 800 satays and a whole range of other ceremonial, meaty dishes. *Lawar* is a celebratory favourite and consists of roasted shredded coconut, a fragrant coconut-milk broth, cooked greens, chopped fried liver, a drop of red, glossy, congealed blood, fried entrails, *sambal* and just about anything else that is sitting around. As you can imagine, this is not a dish for the faint-hearted.

White pepper is the preferred pepper in Asia, so don't be surprised if it is hard to find black pepper in restaurants.

WHERE TO EAT & DRINK

Balinese Food

It's everywhere, naturally. Balinese food can be enjoyed fresh from a street vendor, at world-class restaurants where it is elevated to culinary art, or at scores of places in between.

WARUNG

In between modern establishments are a million small cafés and local eateries known as warung or *kedais* (coffee houses). A warung is a small, no-frills local store–meets–restaurant with a couple of well-worn bench seats and long tables for hungry guests. A number of cooked dishes usually sit in a small glass cabinet at the entrance of the warung for all to see, and you can select from these or just order the house mixture or *nasi campur*. These roadside hang-outs are perfect for watching the world go by and are the gathering place for young and old alike. Seaside warung that hug the coastline serve a variety of fresh seafood; my favourite eating house, Merta Sari, near the bat caves in Kusamba (p221), serves up a meal that's hard to beat. Juicy, pounded fish satay, a slightly sour, fragrant fish broth, fish steamed in banana leaves, snake beans in a fragrant tomato-peanut sauce and a fire red *sambal* make up its renowned *nasi campur*. Other places around the coast also serve a wonderful selection of similar dishes but you'll have to hunt them down yourself.

Every town of any size in Bali and on Lombok will have a *pasar malam* (night market). You can sample a vast range of fresh offerings from warung (food stalls) and carts after dark.

A *warung lesehan* is a typical type of local eatery that you often find hugging the coastline or out in the villages, although there are also several of these open-style cafés in Denpasar. These simple above-ground wooden pavilions are furnished with low tables and bamboo mats where diners sit, sharing the space with other diners, the occasional tourist and the ubiquitous Balinese dog. Sometimes they are perched on the edge of the rice fields, offering a lovely view of ducks and endless green.

QUICK EATS

In every village in Bali you will find morning and afternoon food stalls or tables, usually perched under the enormous shade of the local banyan tree. These makeshift take-away affairs are a bit like meals-on-wheels, except that

BALI & LOMBOK'S TOP FIVE

- Bumbu Bali (p138) has superb and creative Balinese food in Tajung Benoa.
- Sate Bali (p121) delivers sumptuous traditional Balinese meals in Seminyak.
- Three Monkeys (p194) has a diverse menu in a magical Ubud setting.
- Café des Artistes (p196) is a cultured alternative with an enticing menu in a quiet part of Ubud.
- Qunci Restaurant (p298) is a hip hotel restaurant on the beach in Mangsit.

the wheels just happen to be the legs of the old granny selling the food. The table laden with all the cooked treats is carried by the seller to the selected destination and sold from there. When all is finished, the table, and empty pots and plates are carried back home. This is usually the best place to buy delicious rice puddings and sweet treats.

For an afternoon snack or light broth, you might want to sample the famous cuisine of the *bakso* or *kaki-lima* sellers. *Kaki-lima* translates as something five-legged and refers to the three legs of the cart and the two legs of the vendor. These mobile food merchants, usually from neighbouring Java, push their carts through the village streets in the late afternoon and sell light soups with *bakso* (Chinese-style meatballs). Of course, any meat product that sits in a glass cabinet in tropical heat requires a major dose of preservatives and probably lashings of MSG so, eat at your own discretion. Nowadays there is a movement in Bali to serve Balinese-style *bakso* in warungs. Signs displaying the words *Krama Bali* or *Bakso Babi* indicate they are serving freshly made *bakso*, usually with pork meatballs (p29).

Janet de Neefe's *Fragrant Rice* is part memoir, part cookbook and part cultural guide. It's a warm and informative telling of her deepening immersion into Balinese life, framed around traditional food and the rich rituals and customs that surround it.

International Food

You can eat well all over Bali and you are pretty much spoiled for choice. The classic modest traveller's café with a timeless mix of burgers, pizza, pasta and Indonesian dishes is found any place you find visitors.

But in places throughout South Bali, Ubud and parts of the east and beyond you can enjoy exceptional cuisine from all corners of the globe, often at prices that would make people at home weep. In particular, look to Seminyak and Ubud for dozens of innovative restaurants that beguile with choice and selection.

Most places serve breakfast through to dinner (8am until about 10pm – later at really trendy joints); in places where everything is fresh and the food service vendor is the produce market, you'll find kitchens are often very accommodating to special requests. If they have it they'll cook it how you want – although at times communicating this will be the biggest challenge.

Lonely Planet's *World Food Indonesia* by Patrick Witton has the low-down on Balinese high feasts as well as details of the cuisine for which the islands are known.

VEGETARIANS

Bali is a dream come true for vegetarians. Tofu and *tempe,* rich in protein, can be seen on many restaurant menus, and other wok-fried dishes, such as *cap cay* and *sayur hijau* can easily be ordered without meat. Salads abound in many modern restaurants, and that old rule of not eating raw foods in Bali no longer applies.

Vegetarian restaurants will of course be true to their name and there are many good Indian restaurants that also have vegetarian choices. Most vegetarian restaurants also cater for vegans, although you might need to double-check on shrimp paste.

'Aquatarians' (vegetarians who eat seafood) will find eating on the island full of wonderful choices. Freshly grilled seafood satay is often on sale around Bali in the afternoons, and seafood features on nearly all menus.

EATING WITH KIDS

Children are treated like deities in Bali and most places have child-doting staff that will grab yours and entertain them so you can enjoy a bit of quiet time together. In fact, children often seem as relieved as the parents to have someone else to play with! Most restaurants are happy to prepare different foods for frustrated children and, when in doubt, spaghetti, chips and ice cream will keep your young 'uns happy. Don't forget that kids aren't the intrepid travellers we would like them to be, so pay attention to their needs and don't expect them to like eating spicy foods and exotic dishes if they

LOMBOK'S SPICY FLAVOURS

The Sasak people of Lombok are predominantly Muslim, so the porky plethora found on Bali gives way to a diet of fish, chicken, vegetables and rice. In fact, rice here is of the finest quality, yet the drier climate means that sometimes only one crop can be produced a year. The fact that *lombok* means chilli in Indonesian makes sense, as Sasaks like their food spicy; *ayam taliwang* (whole split chicken roasted over coconut husks served with a peanut, tomato-chilli-lime dip) is one example. *Sares* is a dish made with chilli, coconut juice and banana-palm pith; sometimes it's mixed with chicken or meat. Three vegetarian dishes are *kelor* (hot soup with vegetables), *serebuk* (vegetables mixed with grated coconut) and *timun urap* (sliced cucumber with grated coconut, onion and garlic).

don't eat them at home. Even common favourites will taste different in Bali, especially when compounded with a hot, sticky climate, so patience and kindness are the keys for a bonding, stress-free family experience.

HABITS & CUSTOMS

It is not customary for the Balinese to talk while eating. I remember in the early days with my husband, eating meal after meal in silence, thinking how rude he was. In the meantime, he was thinking that when you give a Westerner a plate of food, they never stop talking. We eventually understood each other and now we sometimes eat in silence or talk softly while eating. If you wish to eat in front of a Balinese, it is customary to invite them to join you, even if you know they will say 'No', or you don't have anything to offer.

There are many interesting drinks you can try in Bali. One of my children's favourites is avocado milkshake with chocolate.

Remember, it is not a custom for Balinese to complain in restaurants and flexibility is the key to a happy holiday. If there is something you don't like about a meal, you can deliver a message much more effectively in Bali if it is done in a polite manner.

Balinese are formal about behaviour and clothing, so remember that it isn't polite to enter a restaurant without a shirt on, or eat a meal half-naked, no matter how many muscles or piercings you have. And while its OK to chomp on your food while eating, blowing your nose at the table is quite offensive.

You must not speak harshly of anything that lives in the rice fields, including ducks, eels, frogs and rats. Rice is the sacred grain and any creature that lives in these verdant fields must be treated with respect.

The right hand is the hand that gives and receives good things. It is the symbol of Brahma, the creator. The left hand is the hand that deals with unpleasant sinister elements. The tradition in local restaurants is to eat your meal with your right hand, thus explaining the bowl of water that is served with all Indonesian dishes (licking your fingers is not appreciated).

It is customary to wash your hands before eating, even if you choose to eat with a spoon and fork; local restaurants always have a sink outside the restrooms to lather up before the feast.

If you happen to be drinking coffee with a Balinese person, don't be surprised if they tip the top layer of their coffee on the ground. This is an age-old protection against evil spirits.

If you're invited to a Balinese home for a meal, it's OK to say you don't want second helpings or refuse food you don't like the look of. It's customary for Balinese to insist you eat more, but you may always politely refuse!

COOKING COURSES

It is said that the cuisine of a region always offers insight into the culture. When I first moved to Bali, I recorded Balinese recipes at ceremonies and felt like I was slowly excavating a precious ruin. The intrigue of this ancient cuisine certainly fired my own passion to learn more. Look for the famed cooking classes of Heinz von Holzen in Tanjung Benoa (p137), as well as good ones in Seminyak (p118) and Ubud (see p185).

EAT YOUR WORDS

Although you won't find the language much of a barrier, see the Language chapter (p373) for pronunciation guidelines.

For an exhaustive run-down of eating options on Bali, check out www.balieats.com. The listings are encyclopaedic, although criticism seems to exist only for places that have closed for competing media.

Useful Phrases

Here are some handy phrases that will help you enjoy a meal in Bali and on Lombok.

Where's a...?	*... di mana?*
food stall	*warung*
night market	*pasar malam*
restaurant	*rumah makan*
Can I see the menu, please?	*Minta daftar makanan?*
Do you have a menu in English?	*Apaka ada daftar makanan dalam baasa Inggeris?*
I'm hungry.	*Saya lapar.*
I'll try what they're having.	*Saya mau masakan seperti yang mereka pesan.*
Not too spicy, please.	*Kurang pedas.*
I like it hot and spicy.	*Saya suka masakan pedas.*
I don't eat...	*Saya tidak mau makan...*
chicken	*ayam*
fish	*ikan*
meat	*daging*
milk & cheese	*susu dan keju*
pork	*daging babi*
poultry	*ayam*
seafood	*makanan laut*
Thank you, that was delicious.	*Enak sekali, terima kasee.*
The bill, please.	*Minta bon.*
Do you accept credit cards?	*Bisa bayar dengan kartu kredit?*
Do you have a highchair for the baby?	*Ada kursi khusus untuk bayi?*
I'm a vegetarian/I eat only vegetables.	*Saya hanya makan sayuran.*
Do you have any vegetarian dishes?	*Apakah ada makanan nabati?*
Does this dish have meat?	*Apakah masakan ini ada dagingnya?*
Can I get this without the meat?	*Bisa minta masakan ini tanpa daging?*
What's that?	*Apa itu?*
Can you please bring me (some/more)...?	*Bisa minta... (lagi)?*
chilli sauce/relish	*sambal*
beer	*bir*
a napkin	*tisu*
pepper	*lada*
soy sauce	*kecap*
a spoon	*sendok*
coffee	*kopi*
tea (with sugar)	*teh manis*
tea (without sugar)	*teh pahit*
water	*air minum*

Food & Drink Glossary

Almost every restaurant in Bali – from humbled to fabled – will have a few of these classic dishes on the menu. Some can be found throughout Indonesia, others are unique to Bali and/or Lombok.

air botol, aqua – bottled water
air minum – drinking water
arak – spirits distilled from palm sap
ayam – chicken
ayam taliwang – whole split chicken roasted over coconut husks served with a tomato-chilli-lime dip (Lombok)
babi – pig
babi guling – spit-roast pig stuffed with a Balinese spice paste (Bali)
bakmi/mie goreng – rice-flour noodles fried with vegetables, and often meat and sauces
bakso ayam – light chicken soup with glass noodles and meatballs; a street-stall standard
bebek betutu – duck stuffed with Balinese spice paste, wrapped in coconut bark and banana leaves and cooked all day over smouldering rice husks and coconut husks (Bali)
brem – a type of rice wine, distilled from white and black rice (Bali)
bubuh injin – black-rice pudding made from black sticky rice and served with coconut milk (Bali)
cap cai – stir-fried vegetables (Chinese)
cendol – coconut milk drink mixed with palm sugar and crushed ice
daging sapi – beef
dingin – cold
es campur – a mixture of sliced fresh fruit, coconut fruits, seaweed jelly and fermented cassava served with shaved ice and sweet syrup
fu yung hai – a Chinese-style omelette with a sweet-and-sour sauce
gado-gado – steamed or salad vegetables tossed in a spicy peanut sauce
goreng – fried
isen – galangal, a gingerlike spice; also called *laos* and *lengkuas*
ikan – fish
jambu – guava
jeruk manis – orange
kacang – peanut
kari – curry
kelor – hot soup with vegetables (Lombok)
kentang – potatoes
kepiting – crab
kerupuk – rice crackers; also called *krupuk*
kodok – frog
kopi – coffee
krupuk udang– prawn crackers
lawar – a salad of chopped coconut, spices, meat (pork, chicken or liver) and sometimes blood
mangga – mango
mie kuah – noodle soup
nanas – pineapple
nangka – jackfruit
nasi campur – steamed rice served with a selection of meat and vegetable side dishes
nasi goreng – fried rice that includes Chinese greens and often meat; often served with satay and a fried egg
nasi putih – plain white steamed rice
pahit – 'bitter'; word meaning 'no sugar' in tea or coffee
panas – hot (temperature)
pepesan ikan – spiced fish wrapped in banana leaves and steamed or grilled
pisang goreng – fried banana fritters; a popular streetside snack
rambutan – red fruit covered in hairy spines, containing sweet white flesh
rendang – beef coconut curry

rijsttafel – literally, rice table; a Dutch adaptation of an Indonesian banquet encompassing a wide variety of dishes
sambal – chilli sauce or paste; contains chillies, garlic or shallots and salt
sares – chilli, coconut juice and banana-palm pith; sometimes mixed with chicken or meat (Lombok)
sate – grilled meat on skewers with peanut sauce; also spelled satay
sayur – vegetable
serebuk – vegetables mixed with grated coconut (Lombok)
serombotan – spicy salad of chilli, water spinach, bean sprouts, long beans, coconut milk and peanuts
soto ayam – light chicken soup
susu – milk
teh – tea
tempe – Indonesian soy-bean cake
timun urap – sliced cucumber with grated coconut, onion and garlic (Lombok)
tom – pounded duck, pork chicken or their livers, with spices and steamed in a banana leaves (Bali)
tuak – palm beer/wine
urab – greens with grated coconut, chilli, shallots and garlic

Kuta, Legian & Seminyak

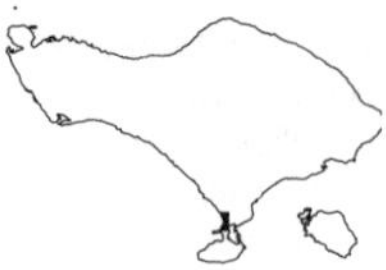

Few people can visit Bali and not spend time in Kuta, the original Balinese beach resort that defined the very idea of a beach holiday. Legian was a natural outgrowth to the north. Further north, however, Seminyak has become the centre for an altogether more stylish scene.

What links them all is a beautiful beach with pounding surf. Surfers, sun-seekers, strollers, loungers and more come here to play, party and relax in some combination depending on their moods. The entire region is devoted to catering to whims. Hotels, restaurants, bars, cafés, shops and a myriad more diversions by the thousand line the narrow and busy streets.

But within this vast area of development (many would say over-development), there are a multitude of neighbourhood personalities. Kuta is the original cheap and cheery party zone. The streets heave with traffic by day and crowds of boozing fun-seekers by night. Scores of cheap places offer deals that are amazingly cheap. Yes, a surfer can live here for US$10 a day.

Legian is further north and is where Kuta surfers go when they get married and have a steady job. The hotels are more commodious; many right on the beach. Commerce is aimed at a slower-moving, more affluent crowd. Tuban, between Kuta and the airport, is similar.

Seminyak is for the hedonist, the poser, the conspicuous consumer and the image conscious. It has top-end resorts, designer shops and a thriving nightlife.

North of here development tapers off, but villas and shops aimed at Westerners do dot the imperilled rice fields. Along the beach, the surf is wilder and the scene more remote.

HIGHLIGHTS

- Sunbathing and partying at **Kuta Beach** (opposite)
- Hitting the latest bars, restaurants and clubs of **Seminyak** (p121)
- Shopping yourself silly north to **Seminyak** (p123)
- Brunching on the beachside terrace of a café in **Legian** (p111)
- Exploring the wild and secluded beaches like **Echo Beach** (p125) north of Seminyak

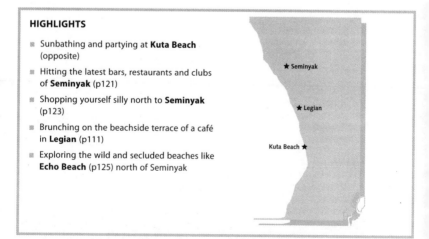

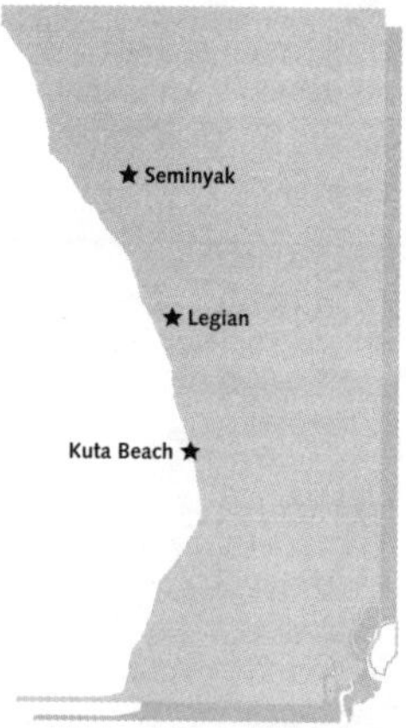

KUTA & LEGIAN

☎ 0361

Mention Bali and people often first think of Kuta. Hot, loud, frenetic and crowded are some of the adjectives you can use to describe the place. And just north in Legian, it's almost the same, only a little less so. South of Kuta, Tuban heaves with a huge mall but elsewhere is more subdued.

But if images of tourism gone mad are what you picture with Kuta and Legian, then you also need to understand that their amazing strength – and it is singular – is the beach. The stretch of Kuta Beach, which for most people also includes Legian Beach, is one fine crescent of surf and sand. And everything here derives from it. You can cut loose in hedonistic surf bars, eat at cheap and tasty restaurants aimed at the masses, stay in back-alley losmen (small, often family-run hotels) that are a steal at under US$10 a night, chill out at one of the many surfside hotels, shop for beachwear and much, much more.

Kuta and Legian may not be pretty but they're not dull. And amidst the rampant commercialism, you'll see the odd offering, a gentle smile and even the echo of a gamelan. And as frantic as the trio of neighbourhoods seems, a detour down a small *gang* (alley) can quickly transport you to a quiet and unhurried area.

HISTORY

Mads Lange, a Danish copra trader and 19th-century adventurer, set up a successful trading enterprise near modern-day Kuta in 1839. He mediated profitably between local rajahs and the Dutch, who were encroaching from the north. His business soured in the 1850s, and he died suddenly, just as he was about to return to Denmark. It's thought that his death may have been the result of poisoning by potential competitors. His **tomb** (Map p103; Jl Tuan Langa) is on his homesite just west of the night market.

Much to the annoyance of the Dutch Resident, Bob and Louise Koke's Kuta Beach Hotel thrived in the 1930s. The guests, mostly from Europe and the US, were housed in thatched bungalows built in an idealised Balinese style (the Resident called them 'filthy native huts'). After WWII, both Westerners and Balinese built their own hotels along the beach, although most visitors were still wealthy travellers who arrived from abroad on ocean liners.

Kuta really began to change in the late 1960s, when it became a stop on the hippy trail between Australia and Europe. At first, most visitors stayed in Denpasar and made day trips to Kuta. But as more accommodation opened, by the early 1970s Kuta had relaxed losmen in pretty gardens, friendly places to eat and a delightfully laid-back atmosphere. Surfers also arrived, enjoying the waves at Kuta and using it as a base to explore the rest of Bali's coastline. Enterprising Indonesians seized the opportunity to profit from the tourist trade, often in partnership with foreigners seeking a pretext to stay longer.

Legian, the village to the north, sprang up as an alternative to Kuta in the mid-1970s. At first, it was a totally separate development, but these days you can't tell where one ends and the other begins.

With an economy completely dependent on mass tourism, especially from Australia, the downturn in tourism after the 2002 and 2005 bombings has been felt here more than any other part of Bali.

ORIENTATION

The Kuta region is a disorienting place. It's flat, with few landmarks or signs, and streets and alleys that are crooked and often walled on one or both sides so it feels like a maze. Traffic is terrible and walking is often the quickest way to get around, although scooters speeding down narrow *gang* can cause peril.

Busy Jl Legian runs roughly parallel to the beach from Kuta north into Seminyak. At the southern end is Bemo Corner, a small roundabout at the junction with Jl Pantai Kuta (Kuta Beach Rd). This one-way street runs west from Bemo Corner and then north along the beach to Jl Melasti. Together, these are the main roads, although traffic and numerous one-way traffic restrictions will still have you tearing at your hair.

Between Jl Legian and the beach is a tangle of narrow streets, tracks and alleys, with a hodgepodge of tiny hotels, souvenir stalls, *warung* (food stalls), building construction sites and even a few coconut palms.

Most of the bigger shops, restaurants and low-rent nightspots are along Jl Legian and the main streets that head towards the beach. There are also tons of travel agents, souvenir

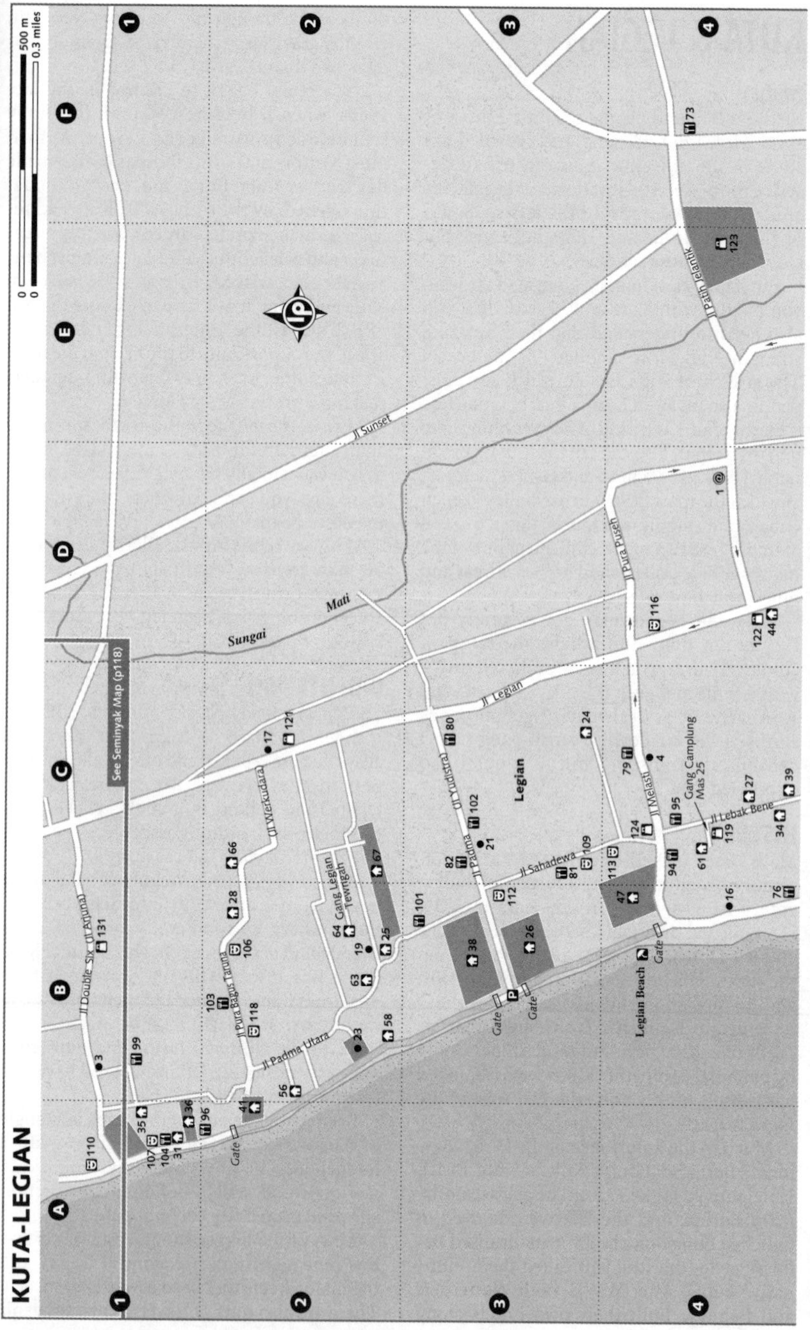
KUTA-LEGIAN
0 500 m
0 0.3 miles
See Seminyak Map (p118)
Jl Double Six (Jl Arjuna)
Jl Pura Bagus Taruna
Jl Padma Utara
(Jl Werkudara)
Gang Legian Tengah
Jl Padma (Jl Yudistra)
Jl Sahadewa
Jl Melasti
Jl Lebak Bene
Gang Camplung Mas 25
Jl Pura Puseh
Jl Legian
Jl Sunset
Sungai Mati
Jl Patih Jelantik
Legian
Legian Beach
Gate

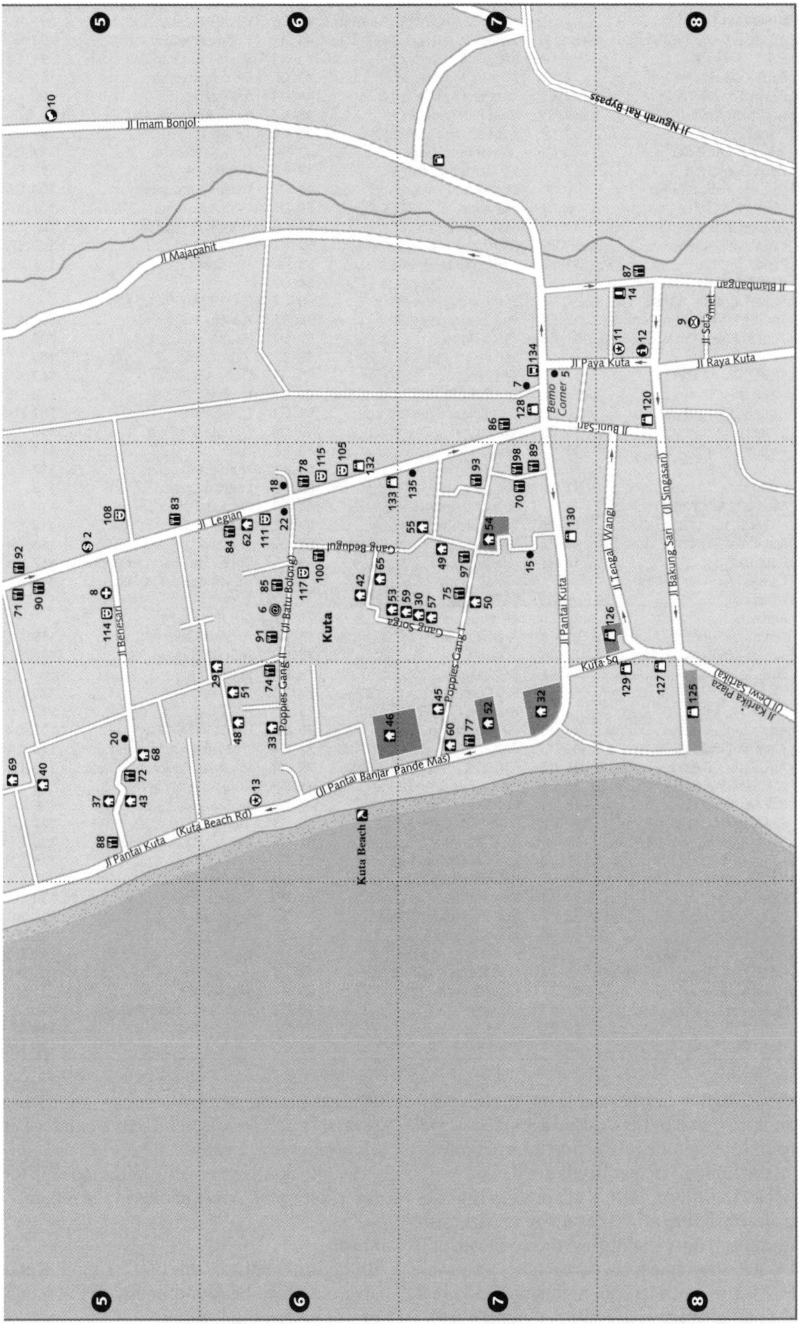
Jl Imam Bonjol
Jl Ngurah Rai Bypass
Jl Majapahit
Jl Blambangan
Jl Selamet
Jl Paya Kuta
Jl Raya Kuta
Bemo Corner
Jl Buni Sari
Jl Legian
Gang Bedugul
Jl Benesari
(Jl Batu Bolong)
Kuta
Gang Sorga
Poppies Gang II
Poppies Gang I
Jl Pantai Kuta
Jl Tengal Wangi
Jl Bakung Sari
(Jl Singasari)
Kuta Sq
Jl Kartika Plaza
(Jl Dewi Sartika)
(Jl Pantai Banjar Pande Mas)
Jl Pantai Kuta (Kuta Beach Rd)
Kuta Beach
5
6
7
8

INFORMATION
Austrian Consular Agent.......(see 123)
Bali@Cyber Café........................1 D4
Bank Commonwealth.................2 D5
Cevin Tour & Travel...................3 B1
Guardian Melasti........................4 C4
Hanafi..5 E7
Internet Outpost.........................6 D6
Kerta Bookshop...........................7 E7
Legian Medical Clinic..................8 D5
Main Post Office..........................9 E8
Netherlands Consulate.............10 F5
Periplus Bookshop.................(see 126)
Police Station.............................11 E8
Postal Agency......................(see 126)
Swiss Consular Agent...........(see 123)
Tourist Information Centre........12 E8
Tourist Police Post....................13 C6

SIGHTS & ACTIVITIES
AJ Hackett Bungy.................(see 110)
Aquatic Playground................(see 32)
Chinese Temple.........................14 E8
Dubious Gang............................15 D7
Jamu Spa...................................16 B4
Kudo's.......................................17 C2
Mandara Spa Hotel Padma Bali...................................(see 38)
Memorial Wall..........................18 D6
Putri Bali...................................19 B2
Quicksilver Boardriding School................................(see 31)
Redz..20 C5
School of Surf............................21 C3
Site of Sari Club........................22 D6
Spa..23 B2

SLEEPING
Ady's Inn...................................24 C3
Alam Kul Kul.........................(see 16)
All Seasons Resort.....................25 B2
Bali Mandira Hotel....................26 B3
Bali Matahari Hotel...................27 C4
Bali Niksoma Beach Resort......(see 23)
Bali Village Bagak Hotel............28 B2
Bendesa.....................................29 C6
Berlian Inn.................................30 D7
Blue Ocean................................31 A1
Hard Rock Hotel........................32 C7
Hotel Bounty.............................33 C6
Hotel Camplung Mas................34 C4
Hotel Kumala.............................35 A1
Hotel Kumala Pantai..................36 A1
Hotel Lusa..................................37 C5
Hotel Padma Bali.......................38 B3
Hotel Puri Tanah Lot..................39 C4
Hotel Sayang Maha Mertha......40 C5
Jayakarta Hotel.........................41 A2
Kedin's II...................................42 D6
Komala Indah I..........................43 C5
Kuta Lagoon Resort...................44 D4
Kuta Puri Bungalows.................45 C7
Kuta Seaview Cottages.............46 C6
Legian Beach Hotel...................47 B4
Lili Garden Cottages.................48 C6
Lima Satu Cottages...................49 D7
Masa Inn...................................50 D7
Mekar Jaya................................51 C6
Mercure Kuta............................52 C7
Mimpi Bungalows.....................53 D6
Poppies Cottages.......................54 D7
Puri Agung Homestay...............55 D7
Puri Tantra Beach Bungalows....56 B2
Rita's House..............................57 D7
Sari Beach Inn...........................58 B2
Sari Jaya...................................59 D7
Sari Yasa Samudra Bungalows..60 C7
Senen Beach Inn........................61 C4
Simpang Inn...............................62 D6
Sinar Indah...............................63 B2
Sri Beach Inn.............................64 B2
Suji Bungalow...........................65 D6
Su's Cottages II..........................66 C2
Three Brothers Inn....................67 C2
Un's Hotel..................................68 C5
Vilarisi Hotel..............................69 C5

EATING
Alleycats....................................70 D7
Aroma's Café.............................71 D5
Balcony.....................................72 C5
Bali Bakery................................73 F4
Bali Corner................................74 C6
Bamboo Corner.........................75 D7
Circle K North...........................76 B4
Circle K South...........................77 C7
ESC..78 D6
Gosha Bar & Restaurant...........79 C4
Hard Rock Café......................(see 32)
Indo-National............................80 C3
Indo-National............................81 C3
Joni Bar Restaurant...................82 C3
Ketupat......................................83 D5
Kopi Pot.....................................84 D6
Kori Restaurant & Bar...............85 D6
Kunti Japanese...........................86 E7
Kuta Night Market....................87 E8
La Cabana.................................88 C5
Made's Warung..........................89 D7
Mama's......................................90 D5
Ming Kitchen.............................91 D6
Nero Bar & Restaurant..............92 D5
Papa's Café............................(see 16)
Poppies Restaurant...................93 D7
Restaurant Puri Bali Indah.........94 C4
Sana Restaurant.........................95 C4
Seaside......................................96 A2
Swiss Restaurant..................(see 123)
TJ's..97 D7
Un's Restaurant.........................98 D7
Warung Asia..............................99 B1
Warung Indonesia...................100 D6
Warung Yogya.........................101 B3
Wayan & Friends.....................102 C3
Yut'z..103 B2
Zanzibar...................................104 A1

ENTERTAINMENT
Apache Reggae Bar..............(see 105)
Bounty.....................................105 D6
Capt Cook................................106 B2
De Ja Vu..................................107 A1
Dilenile....................................108 D5
Dolphin....................................109 C3
Double Six Club.......................110 A1
Fuel..111 D6
Hulu Café.................................112 B3
Legend.....................................113 C4
Oscar's Pub..............................114 D5
Paddy's....................................115 D6
Peanuts....................................116 D4
Tubes Surf Bar & Restaurant...117 D6
Ye Olde Foo-Kin Pub...............118 B2

SHOPPING
Apolina Gallery........................119 C4
Arin 93 Gallery........................120 E8
Bouchra.................................(see 131)
Djeremi Store...........................121 C2
IO & CO...................................122 D4
Istana Kuta Galleria..................123 E4
Jl Melasti Art Market...............124 C4
Jonathan Gallery....................(see 83)
Kuta Sq Art Market.................125 C8
Matahari..................................126 D8
Milo's.......................................127 C8
Ras Masta................................128 E7
RipCurl.....................................129 C8
Shafira..................................(see 131)
Spank!......................................130 D7
Sriwijaya..................................131 B1
Surfer Girl.................................132 D6
Uluwatu....................................133 D6

TRANSPORT
Bemos to Tegal, Jimbaran, Uluwatu & Nusa Dua...........................134 E7
Perama.....................................135 D7

shops, banks, moneychangers, motorcycle- and car-rental outlets, postal agencies, *wartel* (public telephone office) and internet cafés – all the holiday-maker needs are here.

North of Jl Melasti, Kuta merges into Legian, which has almost as many tourist businesses and only slightly less traffic. North of Jl Double Six/Arjuna, Legian becomes Seminyak (see p116), with its cool nightspots and great shopping. Somewhere south along Jl Kartika Plaza, Kuta merges with Tuban, which has several beach resorts, a huge mall and a fair amount of low-key life.

See 'Pick a Name, Any Name' (p116) for information on street names in the region.

Maps

Besides the maps in this book, simple Kuta-area maps can be found in any of the scores of free tourist publications.

INFORMATION

Bookshops

Little used bookshops and book exchanges can be found scattered along the *gang* and roads, especially the Poppies.

Kerta Bookshop (Map pp96-7; ☎ 758047; Jl Pantai Kuta 6B) A book exchange with a better than average selection of books. Many break the Sheldon-Brown-Steele pot-boiler mould.

Periplus Bookshop Discovery Shopping Mall (Map p103; ☎ 769757; Jl Kartika Plaza, Tuban); Bali Galleria shopping centre (Map p100; ☎ 752670; Ngurah Rai By Pass) Has the largest selection of new books in Bali.

Emergency

Police station (Map pp96-7; ☎ 751598; Jl Raya Kuta; 24hr) Next to the Badung Tourist Office.

Tourist police post (Map pp96-7; ☎ 7845988; Jl Pantai Kuta; 24hr) This is a branch of the main police station in Denpasar. Right across from the beach, the officers – who have a gig that is sort of like a Balinese Baywatch – are friendly.

Internet Access

There are scores of places to connect to the internet in Kuta, Legian and Tuban. Most have pokey connections and charge about 200Rp to 300Rp a minute. The following two places have fast broadband connections and offer numerous services, including wi-fi, CD burning, digital camera downloads and more. Connection rates average 500Rp per minute.

Bali@Cyber Café (Map pp96-7; ☎ 761326; Jl Patih Jelantik; meals 20,000-30,000Rp; 8am-11pm) Has a full range of computer options, parking and a good menu of snacks, meals and tasty smoothies.

Internet Outpost (Map pp96-7; ☎ 763392; Poppies Gang II; 8am-2am) Has desks, couches and cold drinks.

Laundry

Most hotels, even top-end ones, have a laundry service for a comparatively low price. Back-street laundries are only marginally cheaper – about 1500Rp for jeans, 1000Rp for a shirt or shorts, 500Rp for underwear – and you have less recourse if something goes awry.

Medical Services

See p364 for international medical clinics serving all of Bali.

Guardian Melasti (Map pp96-7; ☎ 765217; Jl Melasti; 8am-10pm) Modern chain pharmacy with prescription drugs.

Kimia Farma (Map p103; ☎ 757196; Jl Dewi Sartika 64; 24hr) Pharmacy popular with locals for cheap prices.

Legian Medical Clinic (Map pp96-7; ☎ 758503; Jl Benesari; on call 24hr) Has an ambulance and dental service. It's 300,000Rp for a consultation with an English-speaking Balinese doctor, or 700,000Rp for an emergency visit to your hotel room. It has a well-stocked pharmacy attached to the clinic.

Money

There are several banks along Jl Legian, at Kuta Sq and Jl Pantai Kuta. In addition, ATMs abound and can be found everywhere, including in the ubiquitous Circle K and Mini Mart convenience stores.

The numerous 'authorised' moneychangers are faster and efficient, open long hours and may offer better exchange rates. Be cautious, though, especially where the rates are markedly better than average. Extra fees may apply or, judging by the number of readers' letters we've received, they may be adeptly short-changing their customers.

Exchange counters run by international banks are a new phenomenon and should offer reliable service.

Bank Commonwealth Tuban (Map p103; ☎ 750049; Jl Dewi Sartika 8X; 11am-7pm); Legian (Map pp96-7; ☎ 758070; Jl Legian)

Post

Postal agencies that can send but not receive mail are common.

There are several cargo agencies in the Kuta area. If you've bought bulky items, the store will usually have arrangements with shippers to handle things for you. Or, for fast service, you can use one of the expensive international companies.

Main post office (Map pp96-7; Jl Selamet; 7am-2pm Mon-Thu, 7-11am Fri, 7am-1pm Sat) Is on a small road east of Jl Raya Kuta. It's small and efficient and has an easy, sort-it-yourself poste restante service. This post office is well practised in shipping large packages.

Postal agency (Map pp96-7; ☎ 761592; Kuta Sq; 10am-9pm) On the ground floor of the Matahari department store, they will mail packages.

Telephone

Wartel are concentrated in the main tourist areas, particularly along Jl Legian and along the main *gang* between Jl Legian and the beach. Hours are generally from 7am to 9pm, but some are open later. In most places, you can make international calls and send faxes (shop

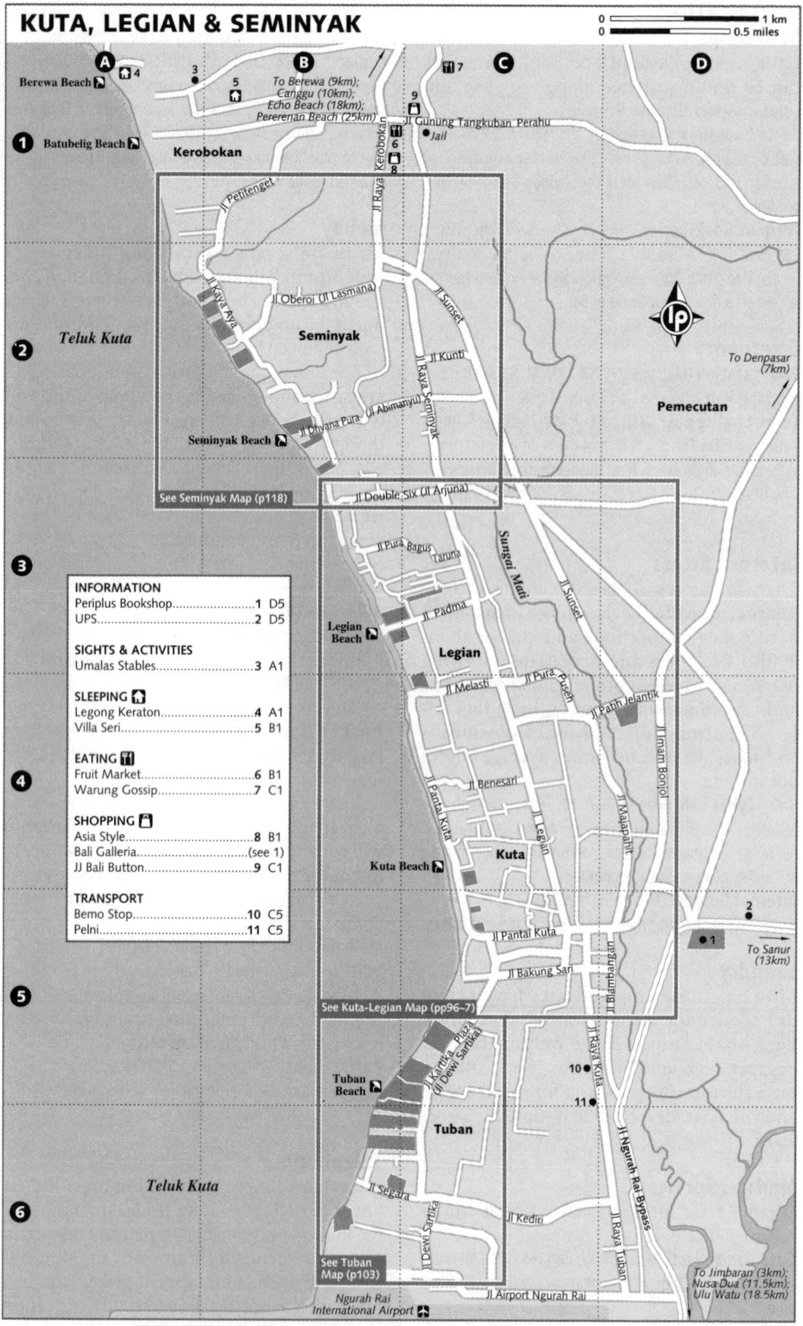
KUTA, LEGIAN & SEMINYAK
0 1 km
0 0.5 miles
A
B
C
D
1
2
3
4
5
6
Berewa Beach
Batubelig Beach
To Berewa (9km); Canggu (10km); Echo Beach (18km); Pererenan Beach (25km)
Jl Gunung Tangkuban Perahu
Jail
Kerobokan
Jl Petitenget
Jl Raya Kerobokan
Jl Kaya Aya
Jl Oberoi (Jl Lasmana)
Seminyak
Jl Sunset
Jl Kunti
Jl Raya Seminyak
Jl Dhyana Pura (Jl Abimanyu)
Seminyak Beach
Teluk Kuta
To Denpasar (7km)
Pemecutan
See Seminyak Map (p118)
Jl Double Six (Jl Arjuna)
Jl Pura Bagus Taruna
Sungai Mati
Jl Padma
Legian Beach
Legian
Jl Melasti
Jl Pura Puseh
Jl Patih Jelantik
Jl Imam Bonjol
Jl Benesari
Jl Pantai Kuta
Jl Majapahit
Jl Legian
Kuta Beach
Kuta
To Sanur (13km)
Jl Pantai Kuta
Jl Bakung Sari
Jl Blambangan
See Kuta-Legian Map (pp96–7)
Tuban Beach
Jl Kartika Plaza (Jl Dewi Sartika)
Jl Raya Kuta
Tuban
Jl Ngurah Rai Bypass
Teluk Kuta
Jl Segara
Jl Kediri
Jl Dewi Sartika
Jl Raya Tuban
See Tuban Map (p103)
Jl Airport Ngurah Rai
Ngurah Rai International Airport
To Jimbaran (3km); Nusa Dua (11.5km); Ulu Watu (18.5km)
INFORMATION
Periplus Bookshop....1 D5
UPS....2 D5
SIGHTS & ACTIVITIES
Umalas Stables....3 A1
SLEEPING
Legong Keraton....4 A1
Villa Seri....5 B1
EATING
Fruit Market....6 B1
Warung Gossip....7 C1
SHOPPING
Asia Style....8 B1
Bali Galleria....(see 1)
JJ Bali Button....9 C1
TRANSPORT
Bemo Stop....10 C5
Pelni....11 C5

around for international calls, as prices do vary), and arrange collect calls for a small fee.

Tourist Information

Other places that advertise themselves as 'tourist information centres' are usually commercial travel agents, and some can be helpful, especially for booking tours, activities and transport.

Tourist Information Centre (Map pp96-7; ☎ 766180; Jl Raya Kuta; 8am-3pm Mon-Thu, 8am-1pm Fri) Handles Kuta and the rest of Bali. Help is limited, however. It's best to have specific questions.

Hanafi (Map pp96-7; ☎ 756454; www.hanafi.net; Jl Pantai Kuta 1E) This gay-friendly tour operator and guide operates from a small veterinary clinic he shares with his sister. He's a valuable source of information on the gay scene, can also organise tours and has a small café here.

Travel Agencies

Many travel agents will arrange transport or car and motorcycle rental. They also sell tickets for tourist shuttle buses, Balinese dance performances, adventure activities and a variety of tours. Most will also change money and many can also book airline tickets.

Cevin Tour & Travel (Map pp96-7; ☎ 7437343; Jl Double Six 23) A reputable agent, popular with expats.

DANGERS & ANNOYANCES

Although the streets and *gang* are usually quite safe, beware of a dubious gang linking Poppies Gang I with Jl Pantai Kuta. Scooter-borne prostitutes (who may hassle single men late at night) consummate their business here. The continuing economic downturn has brought many illicit activities out into the open. Walking along you may hear: 'massage' followed by 'young girl' and the ubiquitous 'transport' followed by 'blow'.

Hawkers

Crackdowns mean that it's rare to find carts in the Kuta tourist area, but street selling is common, especially on hassle street, Jl Legian. The beach isn't unbearable, but the upper part has souvenir sellers and masseuses (who may grab hold of you and not let go). Closer to the water you can sunbake on the sand in peace – you'll see where the invisible line is.

Surf

The surf can be very dangerous, with a strong current on some tides, especially up north in Legian. Lifeguards patrol swimming areas of the beaches at Kuta and Legian, indicated by red-and-yellow flags. If they say the water is too rough or unsafe to swim in, they mean it. Red flags with a skull and cross-bones signal no swimming allowed.

Theft

This is not a big problem, but visitors do lose things from unlocked hotel rooms or from the beach. Going into the water and leaving valuables on the beach is simply asking for trouble (in any country). Snatch thefts are rare. Valuable items can be left at your hotel reception.

Water Pollution

The sea water around Kuta is commonly contaminated by run-off from both built-up areas and surrounding farmland, especially after heavy rain. Swim away from streams.

SIGHTS

The real sight here is of course the **beach**. After that, it's a lot of streets, alleys and hubbub – which can have their own fascination for wanderers, browsers and gawkers. You can find the odd non-touristy site like an old **Chinese Temple** (Map pp96-7; Jl Blambangan).

Reflecting the international character of the 2002 bombings (see p102), people from many nationalities pay their respects at the **memorial** (Map pp96-7). Listing the names of the 202 known victims, including 88 Australians and 35 Indonesians, it has an emotional effect on many who view it. Flower arrangements continue to arrive daily. Across the street, a vacant lot is all that is left of the Sari Club. Plans to turn it into a memorial park (www.balipeacepark.com) have so far proved difficult.

ACTIVITIES

From Kuta, you can easily go surfing, sailing, diving, fishing or rafting anywhere in the southern part of Bali, and be back for the start of happy hour at sunset.

Many of your activities in Kuta will centre around the superb beach. Hawkers will sell you sodas and beer, snacks and other treats, and you can rent lounge chairs and umbrellas (negotiable at 10,000Rp to 20,000Rp) or just crash on the sand. You'll see everyone from bronzed international youth strutting their stuff, to local families trying to figure out how to get wet *and* preserve their modesty. When the tide is out the beach seems to stretch forever and you may be tempted to walk for kilometres

THE BALI BOMBINGS

On Saturday, 12 October, 2002 two bombs exploded on Kuta's bustling Jl Legian. The first blew out the front of Paddy's Bar. A few seconds later, a far more powerful bomb obliterated the Sari Club. The blast and fireballs that followed destroyed or damaged neighbouring clubs, pubs, shops and houses.

Close to midnight on the busiest night of the week, the area was packed. More than 300 people from at least 23 countries were injured. The number dead, including those unaccounted for, reached over 200, although the exact number will probably never be known. Many injured Balinese made their way back to their villages, where, for lack of decent medical treatment, they died.

Indonesian authorities eventually laid the blame for the blasts on Jemaah Islamiyah, an Islamic terrorist group. Dozens were arrested and many were sentenced to jail, including three who received the death penalty. But most received relatively light terms, including Abu Bakar Bashir, a radical cleric who many thought was behind the explosions. He was convicted of conspiracy and sentenced to 30 months, a term that enraged many, especially in Bali and Australia.

Although it took three years, Bali had largely bounced back in terms of tourism by 1 October 2005. On this busy Saturday, three suicide bombers blew themselves up: one in a restaurant on Kuta Sq and two more at beachfront seafood cafés in Jimbaran. It was again the work of Jemaah Islamiyah, and although documents found later stated that the attacks were targeted at tourists, 15 of the 20 who died were Balinese and Javanese employees of the places bombed (the others were tourists: four Australians and one Japanese).

Those who suffered the most were those whose livelihoods depended on tourism. The local economy plunged as visitor numbers fell by half and stayed low for months afterwards. However, whereas the Balinese collectively went into a sort of shock after the first bombing ('How could somebody do this to our island?'), after the second the reaction was much more angry. Said one long-time local observer: 'They're pissed.'

north or south. Sunsets are a time of gathering for just about everyone in south Bali. When conditions are right you can enjoy a fuchsia-coloured show that photos just can't capture properly.

Surfing

The beach break called Halfway Kuta, offshore near the Hotel Istana Rama, is the best place to learn to surf. More challenging breaks can be found on the shifting sandbars off Legian, around the end of Jl Padma; and at Kuta Reef, 1km out to sea off Tuban Beach (see p78 for details on these surf breaks). Several shops on Jl Legian sell big-brand surf gear and surfboards. Smaller shops on the side streets hire out surfboards (for a negotiable 30,000Rp per day) and boogie boards, repair dings and sell new and used boards. Some can also arrange transport to nearby surfing spots. Used boards in good shape average US$200.

Quicksilver Boardriding School (Map pp96-7; ☎ 751214; qbs@quicksilver.co.id; Jl Double Six; half-day lesson US$40)

Redz (Map pp96-7; ☎ 763980; redzsurf@iol.it; Jl Benesari) They have a large selection of boards and gear.

Tubes Surf Bar & Restaurant(Map pp96-7; Poppies Gang II; 🕑 10-2am) The surfers' hang-out, it shows surfing videos and publishes a widely circulated tide chart. Also keep an eye out for free surfing magazines such as *Magic Wave*.

School of Surf (Map pp96-7; ☎ 750123; www.schoolofsurf.com; Jl Padma 51; classes from US$39) This surf school is associated with the Da Nui surf shop in Legian.

Waterbom Park

This popular theme park (Map p103; ☎ 755676; www.waterbom.com; Jl Kartika Plaza, Tuban; adult/child/family US$18.50/9.50/50; 🕑 9am-6pm), south of Kuta, is set on 3.5 hectares of landscaped tropical parks and has assorted water slides, swimming pools, play areas, a supervised park for children under five years old, and a 'lazy river' ride. Other indulgences include the 'Pleasure Pool', a food court and bar, and a Mandara Spa (opposite). There are lifeguards and it's well supervised.

Swimming Pools

Most hotels will allow nonguests to use their pool for a fee. The most impressive is the Hard Rock Hotel's **aquatic playground** (Map pp96-7; ☎ 761869; Jl Pantai Kuta; adult/child/family 100,000/

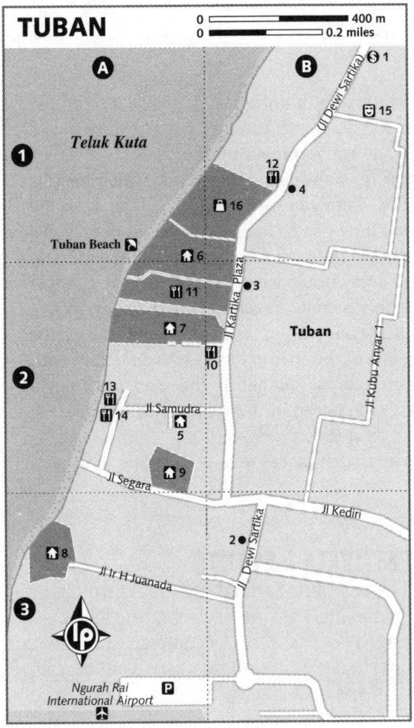

INFORMATION
Bank Commonwealth........................1 B1
Klmia Farma........................2 B3
Periplus........................(see 16)

SIGHTS & ACTIVITIES
Amazone........................(see 16)
Le Speed Karts........................3 B2
Mandara Spa Waterbom Park........................(see 4)
Waterbom Park........................4 B1

SLEEPING
Bakung's Beach Cottages........................5 A2
Discovery Kartika Plaza Hotel........................6 A1
Hotel Santika Beach........................7 A2
Patra Bali Resort & Villas........................8 A3
Rama Beach Resort........................9 A2
Sandi Phala........................(see 13)

EATING
Atmosphere Café........................(see 16)
Bread Talk........................(see 16)
C-Line Restaurant........................10 B2
Food Court........................(see 16)
Golden Lotus........................11 A2
Kafe Batan Waru........................12 B1
Ma Joly........................13 A2
Pantai Restaurant........................14 A2

ENTERTAINMENT
DeeJay Cafe........................15 B1

SHOPPING
Discovery Shopping Mall........................16 B1

50,000/250,000Rp; 8am-9pm). The vast, sinuous pool features two water slides and a sandy beach island. There are lifeguards, and if you need a snog, you can rent private cabanas for 100,000Rp.

Massages, Spas & Salons

The sybaritic pleasures of a massage or an interlude at a spa are an important part of many people's visit and choices are aplenty (see p84 for details). Scores of women offer massages on the beach. A reasonable price is about 20,000Rp for a half-hour massage and 40,000Rp for one hour, but you might have to bargain hard to get near this price if things are busy. Professional massages in your room or in a small massage establishment cost a negotiable 65,000Rp per hour. Most spas also offer facials, waxing and numerous indulgent services.

In the typically calm setting at **Jamu Spa** (Map pp96-7; ☎ 752520; www.jamutraditionalspa.com; Alam Kul Kul, Jl Pantai Kuta; traditional massage US$40; 9am-9pm) you can enjoy indoor massage rooms that open onto a pretty garden courtyard. If you've ever wanted to be part of a smoothie, here's your chance – treatments involve tropical nuts, coconuts, papayas and more, often in fragrant baths.

There are many **Mandara Spas** (www.mandaraspa-asia.com) in top-end hotels, including the Hotel Padma Bali **spa** (Map pp96-7; ☎ 752111; Jl Padma 1; massages from US$30; 10am-8pm). This divine spa is decorated with water features and impressive stone sculptural reliefs. Waterbom Park (opposite) also has a Mandara Spa where parents can find their own aquatic joy.

As stylish as its host hotel, **Spa** (Map pp96-7; ☎ 751946; Bali Niksoma Beach Resort, Jl Padma Utara; traditional massage 270,000Rp; 9am-9pm) offers private suites where you can indulge, from a pampering Bali coffee scrub to Shiatsu.

The delightfully relaxed spa at **Putri Bali** (Map pp96-7; ☎ 755987; Wisata Beach Inn, Jl Padma Utara; massage from 50,000Rp; 10am-9pm) offers a cream bath that has sent many spa-o-phile's heart a-twitter with delight. Located just off the main street, this lovely spa has very competitive prices.

Run by stylish hipsters, **Kudo's** (Map pp96-7; ☎ 756030; Jl Legian 456; 10am-8pm) is a high-concept salon that is *the* place to go for a cut and blow-dry. It's popular with brides before their Bali ceremony.

A WALK ON THE BEACH

That fabulous stretch of sand that starts in Kuta and runs north right past Seminyak can be the focus for a great day of exploring. Start where Jl Pantai Kuta meets the shore and head north. As your mood demands, frolic in and out of the surf while taking breaks on the sand.

As you pass Jl Melasti, the beach road is gated, making it a wide, quiet and pedestrian-friendly promenade. At various points, you'll find shady spots where you can relax and just soak up the sound of the waves while watching people stroll past. Time yourself so that by about noon you'll be at the patch of beach on the north edge of Legian where Jl Double Six meets the sand. Here you'll find a strip of outdoor cafés that are shady and enjoy ocean views. After lunch you can join locals and visitors in games like volleyball that give this popular beach relentless energy.

Continue north along the sand and ponder your massage options. Choose from one of the ladies on the beach or something more elaborate at one of the spas in the beachside hotels. With the afternoon starting to wind down, take a break on a rental lounger on the sand and enjoy a beverage from a vendor. Finally, as the sun sinks into the ocean in the west, finish up at Ku De Ta (p121), the popular beachside club that's a scene as well as a café.

Eventually, stop and have dinner at one of the many great places in Seminyak and then grab a cab home and collapse into bed.

Bungy Jumping

AJ Hackett Bungy (Map pp96-7; ☎ 731144; Jl Arjuna; US$59; noon-8pm daily, 2-4am Fri & Sat), beside the beach at the Double Six Club (p113) in Legian, has a great view of the coast (it means you can't see the hideous tower you're standing on – or bouncing from).

Activities for Children

Except for the traffic, the Kuta region is a pretty good place for kids. With supervision – and sunscreen! – they can cavort on the beach for hours. Almost all the hotels and resorts above the surfer-dude category have pools and the better ones offer kids' programmes.

Amazone (Map p103; Discovery Shopping Centre, Jl Kartika Plaza, Tuban; 10am-10pm) has hundreds of screeching arcade games on the top floor of the mall.

Just south of the very kid-friendly Waterbom Park (p102) is **Le Speed Karts** (Map p103; ☎ 757850; Jl Kartika Plaza, Tuban; five-min ride 60,000Rp; 10am-10pm) where you can zip around a tiny track.

TOURS

A vast range of tours all around Bali, from half-day to three-day tours, can be booked through travel agents or hotels in Kuta. These tours are a quick and easy way to see a few sights if your time is limited and you don't want to rent or charter a vehicle. See p328 for more information on the type of tours available.

FESTIVALS & EVENTS

The first **Kuta Karnival** (www.kutakarnival.com) was held in 2003 as way of celebrating life after the tragedy of 2002. It's become an annual event held in late September or early October, albeit with fits and starts. Events include parades, arts competitions, cultural shows, beach sports tournaments, kite-flying contests and more.

There are also surfing contests throughout the year.

SLEEPING

Kuta, Legian and Tuban have hundreds of places for you to stay. The top-end hotels are along the beachfront, midrange places are mostly on the bigger roads between Jl Legian and the beach, and the cheapest losmen are generally along the smaller lanes in between. Tuban and Legian have mostly midrange and top-end hotels – the best places to find budget accommodation are Kuta and southern Legian.

With hotel names, be sceptical about words such as 'beach', 'sea view', 'cottage' and 'bungalows'. Places with 'beach' in their name may not be anywhere near the beach and a featureless, three-storey hotel block may rejoice in the name 'cottages'. Note that hotels on Jl Pantai Kuta are separated from the beach by a busy main road south of Jl Melasti. North of Jl Melasti, though, the beach road is protected by gates that exclude almost all vehicle traffic. Hotels here have what is in effect a quiet, paved beachfront promenade.

Any place that is west of Jl Legian won't be more than a 10-minute walk to the beach.

Budget

The best budget accommodation is in a losmen with rooms facing a central garden. Look for a place that is far enough off the main roads to be quiet, but close enough so that getting to the beach, shops and restaurants isn't a problem. Luxuries like air-con and pools have become common even among the cheapies, although the cheapest are fan- and cold-water-only.

KUTA

Many of the cheap places are along the tiny alleys and lanes between Jl Legian and the beach in central Kuta. This is a good place to base yourself: it's quiet, but only a short walk from the beach, shops and nightlife. A few places on the eastern side of Jl Legian are close to the bars and restaurants, but can be noisy and a fair hike from the beach. Jl Benesari is a great place to stay, close to the beach and quieter than the Poppies Gangs. Gang Sorga is another top pick, with scores of options.

Puri Agung Homestay (Map pp96-7; ☎ 750054; off Poppies Lane I; s/d 30,000/50,000Rp) The budget winner in Kuta. Vampires (and partying surfers) will appreciate the dark, cold-water rooms at this attractive little place that features a tiny grotto-like garden.

Komala Indah I (Map pp96-7; ☎ 753185; Jl Benesari; r40,000-150,000Rp;) The rooms here are set around a pleasant garden. The cheapest of the 33 rooms have squat toilets, fans and twin beds only. Part of the Komala empire, there are adjoining ding repair and laundry places.

Rita's House (Map pp96-7; ☎ 751760; s/d 50,000/60,000Rp) Since 1971 this cheap, clean, cramped, cheerful 23-room losmen just north of Poppies Gang I has been renting rooms to weary surfers. The showers in the two-storey block are cold and the air is fan-driven.

Lili Garden Cottages (Map pp96-7; ☎ 750557; duarsa@dps.centrin.net.id; s/d 50,000/75,000Rp) There are 25 rooms (some with hot water) in substantial brick bungalows hidden away by dense foliage. Guests can share cooking facilities and there is a tiny café.

Mekar Jaya (Map pp96-7; ☎ 754487; off Poppies Lane II; r 60,000-70,000Rp) Twenty-five rooms in bungalows face huge, open and grassy grounds in the midst of Kuta. Tournament Frisbee players (or croquet buffs) will be thrilled. Rooms are simple with cold water.

Berlian Inn (Map pp96-7; ☎ 751501; off Poppies Gang I; s/d 60,000/80,000Rp, with hot water 90,000/120,000Rp) A stylish cut above other budget places, the 24 rooms in two-storey buildings here are quiet and have *ikat* (cloth with a pattern produced by dyeing the individual threads before weaving) bedspreads and an unusual open-air bathroom design.

Kedin's II (Map pp96-7; ☎ 763554; Gang Sorga; s/d 70,000/90,000Rp;) One of the best budget choices, the 16 cold-water rooms here have hints of style and are set in some fine gardens that feature a good-sized pool.

Bendesa (Map pp96-7; ☎ 751358; off Poppies Gang II; r 90,000-250,000Rp;) The 47 clean, simple rooms are quiet as the Bendesa is fairly isolated. There's an attractive new sinuous pool. The cheapest rooms – all clean – have cold water and fan.

GETTING AWAY FROM IT ALL

Dodging cars, motorcycles, touts, dogs and dodgy sidewalks can make walking through Kuta and Legian seem like anything but a vacation. It's intense and it can be stressful. You may soon be longing for uncrowded places where you hear little more the rustling of palm fronds and the call of a bird.

Think you need to book a trip out of town? Well, think again. You can escape to the country without leaving Kuta and Legian. All those teeming streets surround huge swaths of land and once you poke through the wall of commerce, you can be transported back to a Kuta and Legian of 30 years ago. The secret is to get off the streets and onto the *gang*. In Kuta this is hard as even these can be crowded, but take any alley or lane heading east of Jl Legian and you'll be in the quieter neighbourhood where the locals live.

Better still is Legian. Take any of the narrow *gang* into the area bounded by Jl Legian, Jl Padma, Jl Padma Utara and Jl Pura Bagus Taruna. Soon you'll be on narrow paths that go past local houses and the occasional simple *warung* (food stall) or shop. Wander at random and enjoy the silence accented by, yes, the sound of palm fronds and birds.

Mimpi Bungalows (Map pp96-7; ☎ 751848; kumimpi@yahoo.com.sg; off Gang Sorga; r 80,000R-150,000Rp;) The cheapest of the 10 bungalow-style rooms here are the best value. The private gardens boast orchids and shade, and the pool is good-sized.

Lima Satu Cottages (Map pp96-7; ☎ 754944; Gang Bedugul; s/d 120,000/170,000Rp;) On a *gang* of cheapies off Poppies Gang I, the 11 rooms here are in a three-storey block and are quite comfortable.

Masa Inn (Map pp96-7; ☎ 758507; www.masainn.com; Poppies Gang I; s/d 115,000/135,000Rp, with air-con 150,000/180,000Rp;) A friendly and central place, Masa Inn offers decent value. All rooms have hot water and the large pool is a popular hang-out.

Sari Jaya (Map pp96-7; ☎ 756909; off Gang Sorga; r with fan US$18, with air-con US$24;) A good-sized pool occupies the middle ground between two-storey blocks with 25 comfortable rooms. It's another of many good Gang Sorga choices.

Hotel Lusa (Map pp96-7; ☎ 753714; www.hotellusa.net; Jl Benesari; r US$11-37;) Older rooms here lack the flash of the rooms in a modern three-storey block but they are the better value. All guests of the 57 rooms can enjoy the pool, café and leafy grounds.

LEGIAN

The streets are wider and the pace is less frenetic than just south in Kuta. Budget places tend to be larger as well. Plunge into the interior for some quiet gems.

Sri Beach Inn (Map pp96-7; ☎ 755897; Gang Legian Tewngah; r 50,000Rp) Follow a series of paths into the heart of old Legian. When you hear the cock crowing, you're close to this old family-run place with eight simple, clean rooms. At night palms rustle overhead.

Senen Beach Inn (Map pp96-7; ☎ 755470; Gang Camplung Mas 25; s/d 50,000/60,000Rp) In a little *gang* near Jl Melasti, this low-key place is run by friendly young guys. Rooms have outdoor bathrooms and are set around a small garden. It's an atmospheric, quiet place to stay, with a small café.

Ady's Inn (Map pp96-7; ☎ 753445; off Jl Sahadewa; r 60,000-80,000Rp) Another hidden Legian find, there are eight simple bungalow-style units in a family compound down a long *gang*. Friendly dogs wander the expansive grounds.

Blue Ocean (Map pp96-7; ☎ 730289; r 120,000-130,000Rp, with air-con 150,000Rp;) Almost on the beach, the Blue Ocean is a clean and basic place with hot water and pleasant outdoor bathrooms. Many of the 24 rooms have kitchens and there's action nearby day and night.

Su's Cottages II (Map pp96-7; ☎ 752127; fax 750372; Jl Pura Bagus Taruna; r incl breakfast 150,000Rp-200,000Rp;) These 22 clean, bright rooms feature rattan beds. The two-storey blocks open onto an azure pool.

Sinar Indah (Map pp96-7; ☎ 755905; Jl Padma Utara; r 150,000-200,000Rp;) This standard, fairly basic losmen is handy at only five minutes to the beach. It offers 18 plain, clean rooms with hot water.

Hotel Puri Tanah Lot (Map pp96-7; ☎ 752281; tanalot@indo.net.id; Jl Lebak Bene; r with fan US$12-14, poolside with balcony & air-con US$18-20;) The 57 rooms are scattered about three- and four-storey blocks; all with satellite TV. It's very good value and the spacious garden is a bonus.

Midrange

The bulk of accommodation in the Kuta area falls into the midrange category, especially in Legian. Quality varies widely, with some places offering quite a bit in terms of location, amenities and service. Leave the latter for hapless groups.

TUBAN

There's midrange accommodation away from the surf and in the back streets east of Jl Kartika Plaza, but the places are out of the way and not very convenient for the beach or the nightlife areas.

Bakung's Beach Cottages (Map p103; ☎ 753941; www.bakungsbeach.com; Jl Samudra; r US$30-50;) This older, modest resort-style hotel has 107 clean and comfortable rooms with air-con and satellite TV. The two-storey blocks are set around a big pool.

Rama Beach Resort (Map p103; ☎ 751557; www.ramabeachhotel.com; Jl Jeggala; s/d US$60/70, bungalows US$80;) The beach in the name here is a three-minute walk away. This older 63-room resort has been tarted up with assorted fountain features, although some lucky guests may save their gushing for the bungalows with private pools.

KUTA

Most of these places are handy to the beach.

Suji Bungalow (Map pp96-7; ☎ 765804; www.sujibglw.com; off Poppies Gang I; r US$20-50;) This cheery place has a choice of 47 bungalows and rooms set in a spacious, quiet garden around a pool. It's not flash but it's better than many similarly priced options. There's a shady poolside café.

Sari Yasa Samudra Bungalows (Map pp96-7; ☎ 751562; fax 752948; Jl Pantai Kuta; s/d US$20/23, with air-con US$35/40; ✵ ☎) An excellent location directly opposite the beach makes this 50-room place fine value. It has pleasant bungalows set in richly planted gardens with a large pool.

Kuta Puri Bungalows (Map pp96-7; ☎ 751903; www .kutapuri.com; Poppies Gang I; r US$25-35, with air-con & hot water US$35-50; ✵ ☎) The 47 bungalow-style rooms here are well maintained and are nestled in verdant, tropical grounds. The pool has a shallow kids' area.

Un's Hotel (Map pp96-7; ☎ 757409; www.unshotel.com; Jl Benesari; s/d US$28/30, with air-con US$34/50; ✵ ☎) A hidden entrance sets the tone for the secluded feel of Un's. It's a two-storey place with bougainvillea spilling over the pool-facing balconies. The 30 spacious rooms have solar hot water, antiques and open-air bathrooms.

Simpang Inn (Map pp96-7; ☎ 761306; www.indo.com /hotels/simpanginn; Jl Legian 133; s US$25-48, d US$30-65; ✵ ☐ ☎) Perfectly clean and functional, the three-storey blocks here are set around a pool. If you want to be close to the Kuta clubs it's a good choice.

Hotel Bounty (Map pp96-7; ☎ 753030; www.bounty hotel.com; Poppies Gang II; r US$35-50; ✵ ☐ ☎) Two pools in leafy grounds are the draw here – one is quiet and low-key, the other is party central. The 166 rooms are comfortable and spread over several two-storey blocks.

Kuta Seaview Cottages (Map pp96-7; ☎ 751961; www .kutaseaviewhotel.com; Jl Pantai Kuta; r US$60-85; ✵ ☎) The 27 stylishly decorated cottages and 45 large rooms come complete with fresh flowers on the beds and a lovely garden setting. Right across the street from the beach, the pool area has surf views.

Poppies Cottages (Map pp96-7; ☎ 751059; www.pop piesbali.com; Poppies Gang I; r US$60-85; ✵ ☐ ☎) This Kuta institution has a lush, green garden setting for its 20 thatch-roofed cottages with outdoor sunken baths. The pool is surrounded by stone sculptures and water fountains in a garden that almost makes you forget you are in the heart of Kuta.

LEGIAN

Further north, many hotels have great locations on the beach. There's a crop of good-value places along Jl Lebak Bene.

Hotel Kumala (Map pp96-7; ☎ 732186; Jl Pura Bagus Taruna; r US$15-30; ✵ ☎) An amazing value, convenient to both Legian and Seminyak, the Kumala has large older-style rooms with teak furniture, modern bathrooms, and two pools in a garden filled with bamboo stands, frangipani and bougainvillea. Some cabbies call it the 'Kumala Grand'.

Hotel Sayang Maha Mertha (Map pp96-7; ☎ 751249; www.sayanghotel.com; off Jl Lebak Bene; r US$8-45; ✵ ☐ ☎) The 56 rooms here range from basic with cold water to quite comfortable with a range of amenities like satellite TV. It has a bar, billiards and a medium-sized pool, and is popular with surfers.

Bali Village Bagak Hotel (Map pp96-7; ☎ 753893; info@balivillagehotel.com; Jl Werkudara; r 200,000-250,000Rp; ✵ ☎) The only thing shoddy about this well-run place is the brochure, which notes that it is 'clowned' by graceful green waving palm trees. Actually the trees aren't funny at all. But you'll laugh at the good deal when you get into one of the 27 rooms. The best have good cross-breezes. Cheap long-term rates.

Three Brothers Inn (Map pp96-7; ☎ 751566; www .threebrothersbungalows.com; off Jl Padma Utara; r US$20-35, with air-con US$30-32; ✵ ☎) Twisting banyan trees shade scores of brick bungalows holding 90 rooms in the Brothers' sprawling and garden-like grounds. The fan rooms are the best option, but all rooms are spacious, some have lovely outdoor bathrooms, and most have solar hot water.

Bali Matahari Hotel (Map pp96-7; ☎ 763707; www .balimatahari.com; Jl Lebak Bene; r from US$25-35; ✵ ☎) Just off Jl Melasti, the Matahari has 38 small-ish rooms in a two-storey block. The contemporary architecture manages to make the tight space seem larger than it is (it does mean the pool is *close* to your door).

Vilarisi Hotel (Map pp96-7; ☎ 768010; www.vilarisi .com; Jl Lebak Bene 15x; r US$25-40; ✵ ☐ ☎) A five-storey hotel in the heart of Legian, the 34 rooms here are comfortable and feature shady balconies with good views from the upper floors and rooftop lounge. Outdoor tables at the café overlook the busy *gang* below.

Hotel Camplung Mas (Map pp96-7; ☎ 751461; www .camplungmashotel.com; Jl Lebak Bene; r US$26-40; ✵ ☎) Balinese stone architecture highlights the 69 bungalows set in walled compounds – if privacy is what you are after, this hotel is a good option. Even so, the rooms aren't overly exciting and you might just hit the beach five minutes away.

Hotel Kumala Pantai (Map pp96-7; ☎ 755500; www.kumalapantai.com; Jl Werkudara; r US$30-50;) One of the great deals in Legian. The 88 rooms are large with marble bathrooms that have separate shower and tub. The three-storey blocks are set in nicely landscaped grounds across from the beach. The breakfast buffet is bountiful.

Puri Tantra Beach Bungalows (Map pp96-7; ☎ 753195; puritantra@telkom.net; Jl Padma Utara 50X; s/d US$35/40) These six charming, traditional, fan-only cottages are a step back in time and make for a mellow retreat. All have outdoor bathrooms and are right on the beach, which is reached through a vivid red door.

Sari Beach Inn (Map pp96-7; ☎ 751635; sbi@indo.net.id; off Jl Padma Utara; r US$35-75;) Follow your ears down a long *gang* to the roar of the surf at this great-value beachside hotel. The 21 rooms have patios and the best have big soaking tubs. The cute grounds boast many little statues and water features.

All Seasons Resort (Map pp96-7; ☎ 767688; www.accorhotels.com/asia; Jl Padma Utara; r US$40-80;) This Bali branch of the stylish, yet cheap, chain has 113 compact but well-appointed rooms set around a pool and waterfall. All rooms have balconies and wi-fi access. Service is as bright as the décor.

Top End

A beachfront room is the goal of many. Note that those in Tuban and north in Seminyak (p118) are usually right on the beach – although Seminyak's beach is far superior. Beachfront hotels in Kuta front busy Jl Pantai Kuta while most of Legian's top hotels (and some more modest ones) front a fine swath of beach and a road closed to traffic, in effect a long promenade.

TUBAN

It's quieter here than Kuta but the action is a short walk north along the beach, which can get mighty small at high tide.

Discovery Kartika Plaza Hotel (Map p103; ☎ 751067; www.discoverykartikaplaza.com; Jl Kartika Plaza; r US$90-200;) The 312 spacious rooms at this large resort front expansive gardens and a gigantic swimming pool. For a real splurge, rent one of the private villas on the beach (units 2 to 7 are best). The Discovery Mall next door may be a plus or a minus, depending on your whim.

Hotel Santika Beach (Map p103; ☎ 751267; http://santika.net; Jl Kartika Plaza; r US$90-250;) A cute frangipani-lined entrance leads into these verdant grounds. Bungalows are secluded and have private gardens, and the 170 rooms have private balconies. The design is restrained compared to some of the big group-tour behemoths nearby.

Patra Bali Resort & Villas (Map p103; ☎ 751161; www.patra-jasa.com; Jl Ir H Juanada; r from US$90, villas from US$450;) Just beyond the south end of Tuban Beach, the Patra Bali has 228 rooms with colour and flair. The grounds and pools are immaculate, the rooms well equipped and the location quiet. Some villas feature private pools.

Sandi Phala (Map p103; ☎ 753 780; www.the-sandiphala.com; Jl Segara; ste from US$150;) Butlers buttle around the clock at this boutique hotel on a quiet bit of Tuban Beach. The 11 suites are done up in stark, dark shades that contrast with the windows overlooking the gardens. There's broadband internet in the rooms and artistic touches abound. The excellent Ma Joly restaurant (opposite) adjoins.

KUTA

Alam Kul Kul (Map pp96-7; ☎ 752520; www.alamresorts.com; Jl Pantai Kuta; r/villa US$75/250;) The Alam is an older hotel that has had a thoughtful redesign blending old and new design cues. It offers boutique charm amidst majestic, gnarled banyan trees. The 80 rooms and villas are nicely appointed. The Jamu Spa is on site (p103).

Mercure Kuta (Map pp96-7; ☎ 767411; www.accorhotels-asia.com; Jl Pantai Kuta; r US$90-180;) Across from the beach, the Mercure is a contemporary five-storey hotel with 129 rooms done up in Cubist style and featuring a lofty rooftop pool. The rooms facing the beach have some of Kuta's best views and feature balconies.

Hard Rock Hotel (Map pp96-7; ☎ 761869; www.hardrockhotels.com; Jl Pantai Kuta; r from US$120;) Nothing is understated about the swank 400 themed rooms, which all feel like a retail opportunity, what with the logo *everywhere*. The pool is ostentatious as well (which is a good thing; see p102). Staff are sharp and service is good – especially in the Megastore.

LEGIAN

Most of the top-end places in Legian are directly opposite the beach on stretches of road closed to traffic. These tend to be relaxed places favoured by families.

Legian Beach Hotel (Map pp96-7; ☎ 751711; www.legianbeachbali.com; Jl Melasti; r from US$100, bungalows from US$150;) Thatched bungalows are set among lovely gardens of tall coconut palms. The 206 rooms are comfortable, with extras like DVD players – you can see if that bootleg movie you paid a buck for actually works. The scenic pool area has fountains and a great view of the ocean from the swim-up bar.

Bali Niksoma Beach Resort (Map pp96-7; ☎ 751946; www.baliniksoma.com; Jl Padma Utara; r US$75-150, villa from US$400;) The mannered and minimalist style here comes right out of the pages of a design magazine. There are two multi-level pools, one of which seems to disappear into the ocean and horizon. The 58 rooms are exquisite and the villas sublime. There is a noteworthy spa (p103).

Jayakarta Hotel (Map pp96-7; ☎ 751433; www.jayakartahotelsresorts.com; Jl Pura Bagus Taruna; r US$110-200;) The Jayakarta fronts a long and shady stretch of beach. The palm-shaded grounds, 277 large rooms, several pools and various restaurants make it a favourite with mums, dads and kids. The beach is just out the back door.

Bali Mandira Hotel (Map pp96-7; ☎ 751381; www.balimandira.com; Jl Pantai Kuta; r US$120, cottage from US$150;) Gardens filled with bird of paradise flowers set the tone at the Bali Mandira. Cottages have modern interiors, and the bathrooms are partly open-air. A dramatic pool at the peak of a stone ziggurat housing a spa offers uninterrupted ocean views.

Hotel Padma Bali (Map pp96-7; ☎ 752111; www.hotelpadma.com; Jl Padma; r US$130-200;) Guests are protected from the wilds of Legian at this sprawling resort hotel. Grassy berms shelter the pool and offer lovely beach views for loungers. Many of the 405 artfully decorated rooms have DVD players, so you can stay in. It has a branch of the well-regarded Mandara Spa (p103).

EATING

There's a profusion of places to eat around Kuta and Legian. Travellers and surfers cafés with their cheap menus of Indonesian standards, sandwiches and pizza are ubiquitous. Other forms of Asian fare can be found as well and there are numerous places serving fresh seafood, steaks and pasta. Places with interesting kitchens can be found scattered throughout.

If you're looking for the laid-back scene of a classic travellers café, wander the *gang* and look for the crowds. Often what's busy one night will be quiet the next. For quick snacks and other victuals Circle K convenience stores are everywhere and open 24 hours. Many have cheap, good delis.

Tuban

The beachfront hotels all have restaurants. In most cases the best feature for non-guests is the beachside cafés, good for a tropical snack or a sunset drink.

The **Discovery Shopping Mall** (Map p103; Jl Kartika Plaza; above) is home to many places to eat. On the top floor there is a **food court** (meals 5000-10,000Rp) with scores of vendors selling cheap, fresh Asian food. You can eat outside on a balcony overlooking Kuta Beach. Near the entrance, **Bread Talk** (snacks 3000-7000Rp) is a wildly popular bakery where you grab tongs and choose your own goodies. There are also several trendy coffee places (and we're not talking about the international chain joint on level 1 that rhymes with 'pucks').

C-Line Restaurant (Map p103; ☎ 751285; Jl Kartika Plaza 33; dishes 20,000-50,000Rp) Local art lines the walls and bougainvillea shades the tables. Breakfasts, pasta, Indo standards, seafood and more are on the menu. The fruit juices are tops.

Kafe Batan Waru (Map p103; ☎ 766303; Jl Kartika Plaza; dishes 15,000-45,000Rp) The Tuban branch of one of Ubud's best cafés (p195) is a welcome addition to the local scene. It's a slickified version of a warung, albeit with excellent and creative Asian and local fare. There's good coffee, baked goods and newspapers on offer.

Pantai Restaurant (Map p103; ☎ 753196; Jl Segara; dishes 25,000-55,000Rp) Let your toes feel the sand at the beachside tables in this simple Jimbaran-style seafood restaurant. It's a little ramshackle, but the food's good.

Atmosphere Café (Map p103; ☎ 769501; Discovery Shopping Mall, Jl Kartika Plaza; dishes 20,000-60,000Rp; 11am-1am;) This posh, stylish café overlooks the surf. There's a large, umbrella-shaded patio and sleek lounge inside.

Golden Lotus (Map p103; ☎ 752403; Jl Kartika Plaza; dishes 40,000-100,000Rp;) This ever-popular Chinese restaurant is the best thing about the otherwise humdrum Bali Dynasty Hotel. The dining room and menu are posh Hong Kong.

Ma Joly (Map p103; ☎ 753708; Jl Segara; dishes 25,000-80,000Rp) A smart, open-air restaurant right on a private bit of beach, Ma Joly has a

French-accented menu and a good wine list. It adjoins the equally attractive Sandi Phala boutique hotel (p108).

Kuta

ON THE BEACH

Busy Jl Pantai Kuta keeps beachside businesses to a minimum in Kuta. Beach vendors are pretty much limited to drinks.

Circle K (Map pp96-7; Jl Pantai Kuta; sandwiches 15,000Rp; 24hr) This southern outlet of the cheerful chain has a deli counter where you can get freshly made salads and sandwiches. Picnic at one of the tables or skip across to the beach. There's another welcome location on a dreary stretch further north.

La Cabana (Map pp96-7; 766156; Jl Benesari at Jl Pantai Kuta; dishes 15,000-25,000Rp) A nice Kuta classic on an otherwise barren strip. Would you like a burger, pizza or maybe a rice dish? Sunsets here go well with beer.

CENTRAL KUTA

Kuta night market (Map pp96-7; Jl Blambangan; dishes 5000-10,000Rp; 6pm-midnight) This market bustles with locals and tourist workers chowing down on hot-off-the-wok treats, grilled goods and other fresh foods.

Bamboo Corner (Map pp96-7; Poppies Gang I; dishes 6000-9000Rp) This surfer classic has vegetarian plus local dishes. It's very popular and the fast turnover keeps things ultra fresh. The atmosphere can be best described as veteran.

Ming Kitchen (Map pp96-7; 765766; Poppies Gang II; dishes 12,000-25,000Rp; 24hr) Simple stir-fries are served here with a bit of style.

Alleycats Restaurant (Map pp96-7; 0813-3849 7592; off Poppies Gang I; dishes 15,000-30,000Rp) Two British expats serve up a range of evocative caff standards: beans with breakfast, butter on your sandwich at lunch.

Made's Warung (Map pp96-7; 755297; Jl Pantai Kuta; dishes 15,000-90,000Rp) Made's was the original tourist warung in Kuta. Time has only improved the offerings: a menu of Indonesian classics prepared and served with more attitude and authority than the usual warung.

TJ's (Map pp96-7; 751093; Poppies Gang I; dishes 25,000-60,000Rp) In the tradition of nearby Poppies and Un's, walls here open onto a lovely garden. Water courses through the dining room where Tex-Mex chow has been served up for years. The fun just keeps going.

Un's Restaurant (Map pp96-7; 752607; south of Poppies Gang I; dishes 25,000-80,000Rp) At night, little tea lights enliven the attractive, walled gardens here and make for a atmospheric setting. Look for fusion offerings with an international bent. The hotel (p107) is good value.

Poppies Restaurant (Map pp96-7; 751059; Poppies Gang II; dishes 30,000-90,000Rp) Poppies was one of the first restaurants in Kuta (Poppies Gang I is named after it), and is popular for its lush garden setting. There are little pebbles underfoot and it feels slightly mysterious in a romantic way. The delicious food is upscale western and Balinese. Poppies Cottages (p107) is one of Kuta's best.

ALONG JL LEGIAN

The possibilities of eating choices along Jl Legian seem endless, but avoid tables close to the busy street.

Aroma's Café (Map pp96-7; 751003; Jl Legian; dishes 20,000-45,000Rp) A gentle garden setting encircled by water fountains makes a fine place to face the start of the day over fine fresh juices, breakfasts and coffee. A long vegetarian menu is served throughout the day (the sandwiches are excellent), although the somnolent service could use a dash of protein.

Kopi Pot (Map pp96-7; 752614; Jl Legian; dishes 22,000-50,000Rp) Shaded by trees, Kopi Pot is an old tourist favourite popular for its coffees, milk shakes and myriad of desserts. The menu is typically varied. The multi-level, open-air dining area sits back from stinky Jl Legian.

Kunti Japanese (Map pp96-7; 761454; Jl Legian 14; dishes 25,000-30,000Rp) You know it's fresh because Kunti doesn't smell like fish. Poke into one of the tight tables for good sushi.

ESC (Map pp96-7; 756362; Jl Legian 61; dishes 25,000-80,000Rp; 24hr;) This high-concept place may be a bit much, both in style (motto: 'Urban Food Station') and price, but it does serve good fresh salads, sandwiches and baked goods in air-con comfort. There's also pricey internet access and wi-fi.

Nero Bar & Restaurant (Map pp96-7; 750756; Jl Legian; meals 20,000-80,000Rp; 10am-midnight) Nero has a slick, high-design interior and the international menu has a Mediterranean and seafood bent. It's all a bit chic with lots of dark colours and rattan.

Ketupat (Map pp96-7; 754209; Jl Legian; dishes 28,000-120,000Rp) Hidden behind the antique-filled Jonathan Gallery, Ketupat is a calm, serene oasis. The dining pavilions overlook an azure pool. Dishes originate from across Indonesia, including Javanese curries, such as *nasi* *hijau harum* (fried rice with greens, shrimps and herbs). An elaborate *nasi campur* is only 60,000Rp.

Mama's (Map pp96-7; ☎ 761151; Jl Legian; dishes 30,000-110,000Rp; 24hr) This German classic serves up schnitzel and other meaty dishes around the clock. The beer comes by the litre and the open-air bar is a merry place for enjoying satellite sports.

ON & NEAR POPPIES GANG II

Warung Indonesia (Map pp96-7; dishes 5000-16,000Rp) This is one of several similar, totally unpretentious cheapies on this lane serving up typical travellers fare. It has a genial mix of surfers and locals who enjoy the barbecued chicken.

Bali Corner (Map pp96-7; dishes 8000-20,000Rp) At the crossroads of a myriad of little lanes, this is one of the cheap travellers eateries with a classic menu. It serves up the usual range of Indonesian, Western and Chinese foods, and of course, the perennial crowd pleaser: pizza.

Balcony (Map pp96-7; ☎ 757409; Jl Benesari 16; dishes 20,000-80,000Rp) The Balcony has a breezy tropical design and sits above the hubbub below. It's a good place to celebrate a good day spent riding the waves; you can wash down grilled steaks and seafood with the various fruity drinks.

Kori Restaurant & Bar (Map pp96-7; ☎ 758605; Poppies Gang II; meals 15,000-90,000Rp) Kori's tables weave through a gorgeous assemblage of gardens and ponds. It has a good selection of pasta, upscale Indonesian, burgers and more. Good for a secluded rendezvous over a non-clichéd tropical drink in the flower-bedecked nooks out back. Some nights there's live jazz and blues.

EAST OF KUTA

Bali Bakery (Map pp96-7; ☎ 755149; Jl Imam Bonjol; meals 20,000-60,000Rp;) A classic Western bakery, there are fresh baguettes and much more daily. The chocolates are terrific. It also has a large and popular café with a good menu of salads, sandwiches and steaks. There's wi-fi and lots of international newspapers.

Swiss Restaurant (Map pp96-7; ☎ 761511; Istana Kuta Galeria, Jl Patih Jelantik; meals 30,000-80,000Rp) Relocated from Legian to this echoey mall, the Bali Swiss consul, Jon Zürcher, plays his violin many nights and hosts Balinese dancers on Thursday nights. This is the place for *raclette* and fondue.

Legian

Some of the beachside hotels have restaurants – often Italian – with nice views. Better still is the clutch of places at the end of Jl Double Six that afford views of sandy action by day, strolling fun-seekers by night and sunsets in between. Along the streets of Legian, the ho-hum mix with the superb, so take your time choosing.

Warung Yogya (Map pp96-7; ☎ 750835; Jl Padma Utara; dishes 10,000-15,000Rp) A real find in the heart of Legian, this barebones warung is spotless and serves up hearty portions of local food for prices that would almost tempt a local. The gado-gado comes with a huge bowl of peanut sauce.

Warung Asia (Map pp96-7; ☎ 742 0202; off Jl Double Six & Jl Pura Bagus Taruna; dishes 10,000-20,000Rp) Look down a couple of little *gang* for this gem of a spot. Traditional Thai dishes are served in a richly detailed open-air café. There's an authentic Italian espresso machine and lots of newspapers.

Wayan & Friends (Map pp96-7; ☎ 761024; Jl Padma; dishes 9000-40,000Rp) Don't want to burden Wayan and his pals by having them concoct a sandwich just for you? You can customise your own from the many choices. Wash it down with healthy fruit and vegetable juices. There's a kids' menu.

Restaurant Puri Bali Indah (Map pp96-7; ☎ 751644; Jl Melasti; dishes 12,000-60,000Rp) Listen to the woks roar in the open kitchen at this good Chinese choice. The menu is almost as long as the Great Wall, featuring dozens of seafood choices.

Joni Bar Restaurant (Map pp96-7; ☎ 751182; Jl Padma; dishes 17,000-46,000Rp) Take the plunge into the party atmosphere around the large swimming pool here and polish up your strokes. The Tex-Mex meals, live music and evening happy hour (6pm to 9pm) are popular.

Gosha Bar & Restaurant (Map pp96-7; ☎ 759880; Jl Melasti; dishes 20,000-85,000Rp) The scent of barbecued shrimp wafts through the airy bamboo interior here, where the focus is on charcoal-grilled seafood. Take a table on the tiled patio.

Indo-National (Map pp96-7; ☎ 759883; Jl Padma 17; dishes 20,000-90,000Rp) There's a big new location for Kerry and Milton Turner's always popular restaurant. Fortunately, the excellent fresh food and décor can still put you on cloud 9 (and out back there are some shady and romantic tables). People feel like regulars from the time they hit the genial bar. Order the heaping grilled seafood platter and Bali's best garlic bread – the prawn toast is tops.

Sana Restaurant (Map pp96-7; ☎ 767312; Jl Melasti; dishes 25,000-80,000Rp) Give the kid a hot dog at this bustling corner spot, which amends its long menu with a children's page. There's creative Indonesian and many grilled items served on the large patio or in the breezy room upstairs.

Yut'z (Map pp96-7; ☎ 765047; Jl Pura Bagus Taruna 52; dishes 30,000-90,000Rp) An upscale European restaurant, Yut'z overlooks the street and a small garden. The menu boasts many steaks, prices are good and there are daily specials. If you're a German breakfast fanatic, you can get your *Fruhstuck* fix here.

Papa's Café (Map pp96-7; ☎ 755055; Alam Kul Kul, Jl Pantai Kuta; dishes 30,000-100,000Rp) Enjoy ocean views at this breezy Italian café in the Alam Kul Kul hotel. The menu ranges from simple sandwiches to elaborate seafood dishes. There are more options like this place at neighbouring hotels.

DOUBLE SIX BEACH

These places are right on the beach, which is wildly popular with locals and visitors alike.

Zanzibar (Map pp96-7; ☎ 733529; Jl Double Six; dishes 20,000-45,000Rp) Sunset is prime time, but during the day you can enjoy the shade of the large trees overhead. Popular day and night, dishes are tasty variations on Bali menu classics like the *nasi* family and the burger bunch.

Seaside (Map pp96-7; ☎ 737140; Jl Double Six; dishes 25,000-70,000Rp) The curving sweep of seating at this sleek place provides beach views for one and all. The menu mixes faux Mexican with authentic fusion. The burgers and sandwiches are good. Just try to pass without plopping down on a bench for at least one drink.

ENTERTAINMENT

Around 6pm, sunset on the beach is the big attraction, perhaps while enjoying a drink at a café with a sea view. After a good dinner, many visitors are happy enough with another drink (or two) and a stroll in the cooler evening air. But a lot of people are on holiday and here to party, and in Kuta and Legian that means lots of drinking, dancing and late nights. The more sophisticated nightspots are mainly in Seminyak (p121), where the ambience is decidedly hipper, and where many clubs don't get going until after 11pm.

Watching DVD movies at a bar with a crowd is a Kuta tradition and you'll find scores of places in and around Poppies Gang II. Look for signs during the day or follow your ears at night. Expect anything with lots of guns and guys.

Bars & Clubs

Most bars are free to enter, and often have special drink promotions and 'happy hours' between about 5pm and 8pm. A cover charge is a rarity. Ambience ranges from the low-down vibe of the surfer dives to the high-concept nightclubs with their long drink menus and hordes of prowling servers.

At many of the more raucous clubs you'll see plenty of young women (usually from the north or a neighbouring island) looking to make a 'friend' – usually a Western guy who's a multiple of their age.

The swank clubs of Seminyak are most popular with gays and lesbians, but in general you can find a mixed crowd pretty much anywhere in Kuta and Legian.

TUBAN

DeeJay Cafe (Map p103; ☎ 758880; 2nd fl, Kuta Centre, off Jl Kartika Plaza 8x; 🕒 2-7am) In the post-midnight hours, this place rocks in the post-apocalyptic Kuta Centre, the run-down shell of a tourist mall. House DJs play tribal underground, progressive trance and more.

KUTA

Apache Reggae Bar (Map pp96-7; ☎ 761212; Jl Legian 146; 🕒 11pm-4am) One of the rowdier spots in Kuta, Apache jams in locals and visitors, many of whom are on the make. The music is loud, but that pounding you feel the next day is from the free-flowing *arak* (colourless, distilled palm wine) served in huge plastic jugs. A more sedate café is out front.

Bounty (Map pp96-7; ☎ 752529; Jl Legian; 🕒 10pm-6am) Set on a faux sailing boat amidst a mini-mall of food and drink, the Bounty is a vast open-air disco that humps, thumps and pumps all night. Climb the blue-lit staircase and get down on the poop deck to hip-hop, techno, house and anything else the DJs come up with. Frequent foam parties.

Dilenile (Map pp96-7; ☎ 0812 396 0982; off Jl Legian; dishes 7000-15,000Rp; 🕒 4-11pm) Run by an architect and antique collector, this little chill-out place down a *gang* has a French accent and lots of room for lounging. The tiny gleaming kitchen turns out some spectacular *mie goreng* (rice-flour noodles fried with vegetables, often meat and sauces).

Fuel (Map pp96-7; ☎ 765777; Jl Legian 62; 🕑 11am-5am) This high-concept café has a stark red and black design and popular features such as 'sexy dancers'. There are lots of shot specials and the motto is 'eat, drink, groove'.

Hard Rock Café (Map pp96-7; ☎ 755661; Jl Pantai Kuta; burgers 60,000Rp; 🕑 11-2am) A merchandising outlet disguised as a nightclub, the sprawling Hard Rock fronts the beach and is a magnet for local and Javanese yuppies. Slick bands play classic rock covers.

Oscar's Pub (Map pp96-7; ☎ 755674; Jl Benesari; 🕑 noon-midnight) A low-key pub with good drinks, snacks and a couple of tables outside.

Paddy's (Map pp96-7; Jl Legian 66; 🕑 4pm-4am) Reborn near Bounty after 2002, Paddy's is walled in front, but that doesn't mean that the pulse-pounding rock inside doesn't spill out onto the street. Lots of partiers drawn by the cheap beer specials.

Peanuts (Map pp96-7; ☎ 754226; cnr Jl Legian & Jl Melasti; 🕑 11pm-late) Testosterone-fuelled Peanuts attracts gigolos of all persuasions and their suitors. *Arak* and 'Jungle Juice' feature big time at this place, while the hawkish facade of the Screaming Eagle Bar could bring a sniffle to any marine.

Tubes Surf Bar & Restaurant (Map pp96-7; Poppies Gang II; 🕑 10-1am) A cavernous place that's deserted during the day, but attracts an enthusiastic crowd in the evening. The music is commercial and a long way from the bad cover bands found elsewhere. Kiosks open in the evening with info on surf lessons and trips. Beer specials pour forth.

LEGIAN

Most of Legian's bars are smaller and appeal to a more relaxed crowd of visitors than those in Kuta. The very notable exception is the area at the end of Jl Double Six.

Capt Cook (Map pp96-7; ☎ 761122; Jl Werkudara; 🕑 3-11pm; ⛶) You may not discover Hawaii at this corner place but you can explore the pool table or settle back for a lengthy voyage at the bar.

Dolphin (Map pp96-7; ☎ 755376; Jl Sahadewa; 🕑 3-11pm) A popular spot in the heart of Legian, the Dolphin draws crowds nightly bands playing everything from pop to country.

Hulu Café (Map pp96-7; ☎ 081-7470 8730; Jl Sahadewa; 🕑 4pm-1am) Everyone is singing 'Dancing Queen' at this small cabaret. Ten drag queens stage two shows nightly to orgasmic applause.

Legend (Map pp96-7; ☎ 755376; Jl Sahadewa; 🕑 3-11pm) A popular open-air spot, the Legend draws nightly crowds for 'Elvis Parsley' and live music shows, playing everything from pop to country.

Ye Olde Foo-kin Pub (Map pp96-7; ☎ 751802; Jl Werkudara 525; 🕑 3-11pm; ⛶) It's always nice to see a pub with a historical context. Burgers and more are served in a cool, woodsy bar that's probably more fun than the ones the Aussie patrons enjoy at home.

Jl Double Six

The eponymous club is the big destination here. There's usually another raucous post-midnight club running just next door (although the name changes by the season).

De Ja Vu (Map p96-7; ☎ 732777; Jl Double Six; 🕑 5pm-4am; ⛶) DJs are on duty from opening every night at this high-concept, glass-fronted club with beachfront tables outside.

Double Six Club (Map p96-7; ☎ 0812 462 7733; Jl Double Six; 🕑 11pm-6am) This renowned club got an upscale makeover to better compete with the clubs on Jl Dhyana Pura. The swimming pool is still there and so is the bungy jump (save the crowd and *don't* have that extra drink before leaping into the void; see p104). Top international DJs play a mix of dance tunes in a sleek open-air pavilion right out of *Wallpaper** magazine.

Balinese Dance & Music

The Ubud area (p197) is really the place to go for authentic dance, and you'll see offers in many hotels from tour operators. But note that you won't get back to Kuta until after 10pm with most of these.

SHOPPING

Many people spend – literally – a major part of their trip shopping. Kuta has a vast concentration of cheap places, as well as huge, flashy surf-gear emporiums on Kuta Sq and Jl Legian. As you head north along the latter into Legian, the quality of the shops improves and you start finding cute little boutiques, especially past Jl Melasti. Jl Double Six is lined with wholesale fabric, clothing and craft stores, giving it a bazaar feel. Continue into Seminyak (see p123) for absolutely fabulous shopping. Many better places purr with air-con.

In Tuban, the Discovery Shopping Mall is a huge hit, but nearby, Kuta Sq is not a fun date as the condo tout count is high and it's just not very appealing.

There are still scads of simple stalls (especially along the Poppies) where T-shirts, souvenirs and beachwear are the main lines, and where the price depends on your bargaining ability (p342). Many of these stalls are crowded together in art markets like the one near Kuta Sq (Map pp96-7) or the one on Jl Melasti (Map pp96-7). Here the 'art' refers to the creative application of Bintang logos to cotton.

Arts & Crafts

Shops in Kuta and Legian sell arts and crafts from almost every part of the island, from Mas woodcarvings to Kamasan paintings to Gianyar textiles. There are also many interesting pieces from other parts of Indonesia, some of questionable authenticity and value.

Apolina Gallery (Map pp96-7; ☎ 751334; Jl Lebak Bene; 🕑 10am-6pm) This offbeat place in Legian is run by half a dozen local artists. The paintings of artist Wahyoe Wijaya are on display, as well as all manner of items good, bad and profane.

Arin 93 Gallery (Map pp96-7; ☎ 776 5087; Jl Singasari) Heru Purnomo is a prolific painter of works, from the abstract to representational. Here you can see him work and take classes.

Ras Masta (Map pp96-7; ☎ 081-338686; Jl Pantai Kuta 8) Want to beat your bongo? This cool little shop sells custom-made drums and a plethora of other instruments.

Beachwear & Surf Shops

A huge range of surf shops sell big-name surf gear – including Mambo, RipCurl and Billabong – although goods may be only marginally cheaper than overseas. Local names include Surfer Girl and Quicksilver. Most have numerous locations in south Bali.

RipCurl (Map pp96-7; ☎ 765035; Kuta Sq) If everything in your luggage is looking a little tired and you want to make a bit of a splash, you can't go wrong in this big store with a huge range of beach clothes, water wear and surfboards.

Surfer Girl (Map pp96-7; ☎ 752693; Jl Legian 138) The winsome logo says it all about this vast store for girls of all ages. Clothes, undies, gear, bikinis, you name it.

Clothing

The local fashion industry has diversified from beach gear to sportswear to fashion clothing. From the intersection with Jl Padma, go north on Jl Legian to Seminyak for the most interesting women's (and men's) clothing shops.

Milo's (Map pp96-7; ☎ 754081; Kuta Sq Block E) Milo is a legendary local designer who arrived from Italy three decades ago and made his fortune designing and producing fine silk batik clothes. If cost is an issue, you might have to settle for just a scarf (2,000,000Rp). There's a small branch at Made's Warung II in Seminyak (p123).

Uluwatu (Map pp96-7; ☎ 751933; Jl Legian) The largest of numerous locations across southern Bali, this elegant shop showcases the collections of lace-accented linen and cotton clothing. The styles are simple and few tables wouldn't stand out with a set of Uluwatu table linens. The items are made in villages around Tabanan in West Bali.

IO & CO (Map pp96-7; ☎ 754093; Jl Legian 361) Gauzy, silky and fashionable women's wear in a sleek multi-level air-con shop. This Bali label also sells wholesale.

Spank! (Map pp96-7; ☎ 767 461; Jl Pantai Kuta) For thickos who don't get it, the monkey with a tanned arse logo says it all about this irreverent clothing shop. Fun and sassy clothes. There are some other interesting boutiques nearby.

Department Stores & Malls

Discovery Shopping Mall (Map p103; ☎ 755522; www.discoveryshoppingmall.com; Jl Kartika Plaza; 🕑 9am-9pm) Your eyes follow the beautiful sweep of sand south along the Kuta shore until you see…this! Huge and hulking, this enormous, enclosed Tuban mall is built on the water and is filled with stores of every kind, including a large Centro (☎ 769629) department store. It's proven a huge hit with locals and visitors alike who can look past the obvious aesthetic woes.

Matahari (Map pp96-7; ☎ 757588; Kuta Sq; 🕑 9.30am-10pm) This store has the basics – fairly staid clothing, a floor full of souvenirs, jewellery and a supermarket. You can find most things here, including some decent-quality luggage should you need extra bags to haul your loot home.

Bali Galleria (Map p100; ☎ 758875; Jl Ngurah Rai) A large open-air Western-style mall that is busy with locals and tourists alike. There are numerous large stores and plenty of well-known shops (Body Shop, Marks & Spencer etc). The duty-free emporium is big with the bus-tour set.

Istana Kuta Galleria (Map pp96-7; Jl Patih Jelantik) An enormous open-air mall that aspires to be something out of West Hollywood. For now it's a bit of dud but there are some interesting places amidst the empty storefronts. There is a hardware store in the rear if your needs run towards plungers or duct tape.

Fabric

Stroll Jl Double Six in Legian for a festival of open-air wholesalers selling fabrics, clothes and housewares. **Bouchra** (Map pp96-7; ☎ 733594; Jl Double Six 10) sells fabric with Gaugin-esque designs that's hand-painted in Denpasar. **Shafira** (Map pp96-7; ☎ 733593; Jl Double Six 9) has embroidered and sequin-covered fabrics good for cushions. **Sriwijaya** (Map pp96-7; ☎ 733581; Jl Double Six 35) makes batik and other fabrics to order in a myriad of colours.

Furniture

On Jl Patih Jelantik, between Jl Legian and Jl Pura Puseh there are scores of furniture shops manufacturing everything from instant 'antiques' to wooden Indians. However, a few make and sell teak outdoor furniture of very high quality at very low prices. A luxurious deck chair goes for about 200,000Rp to 250,000Rp. Most of the stores work with freight agencies and you can get eight of these chairs sent to Australia for about US$150.

Housewares

Djeremi (Map pp96-7; ☎ 744 6547; Jl Legian) Top-quality placemats, cushions, mosquito nets and more are stocked floor-to-ceiling. The workshop is nearby and you can get custom work.

Jonathan Gallery (Map pp96-7; ☎ 754209; Jl Legian 109) A horde of traditional art and antiques are beautifully displayed in this shop.

GETTING THERE & AWAY

Bemo

Dark blue public *bemo* (small pick-up truck) regularly travel between Kuta and the Tegal terminal in Denpasar – the fare should be 8000Rp. The route goes from a stop onto Jl Raya Kuta near Jl Pantai Kuta, looping past the beach and then on Jl Melasti and back past Bemo Corner (Map pp96-7) for the trip back to Denpasar.

Bus

PUBLIC BUS

Travel agents in Kuta sell bus tickets to Java and Lombok that depart from the Ubung terminal in Denpasar; keep in mind that you'll have to get yourself to Ubung. The tickets will be slightly more expensive than if you buy them at Ubung, but it's worth it to avoid a trip into Ubung and to be sure of a seat when you want to go. For public buses to anywhere else in Bali you will have to go to the appropriate terminal in Denpasar first, and pay your money there.

TOURIST SHUTTLE BUS

Shuttle bus tickets are sold at most travel agents – buy them a day ahead, or call the company and pay when you check in.

Perama (Map pp96-7; ☎ 751551; www.peramatour.com; Jl Legian 39; 7am-10pm) is the main shuttle bus operation in town, and will sometimes pick you up from your hotel for free (confirm this with them when making arrangements). Perama usually has at least one bus a day to all of its destinations. In busy seasons, there will be three or more to popular spots like Ubud.

Destination	Fare
Candidasa	40,000Rp
Lovina	70,000Rp
Padangbai	40,000Rp
Sanur	15,000Rp
Ubud	30,000Rp

GETTING AROUND

The hardest part about getting around the Kuta area is the traffic. It can be awful in the afternoon and evening, and anytime the vital streets like Jl Legian are closed for religious processions or for what seems to be constant construction.

See p353 for more details on getting around. Besides the frequent taxis, you can rent a scooter, often with a surfboard rack, or a bike – just ask where you are staying. One of the nicest ways to get around the Kuta and Legian area is by foot along the beach.

To/From the Airport

An official taxi from the airport costs 30,000Rp to Tuban, 45,000Rp to Kuta and 50,000Rp to Legian. To the airport, get a metered taxi for less than half.

Charter Transport

It's easy to find a vehicle to charter – just walk down a street and you will be assailed with offers of 'transport'. And, just in case you don't understand, the driver will effusively gesticulate the motions of driving a car.

A full-day, eight-hour charter should run between 300,000Rp and 400,000Rp, but more if it's non-stop driving over a long distance. You can estimate a price for shorter trips on a proportional basis, but you'll have to bargain. The 'first price' for transport can be truly outrageous.

Taxi

Plenty of taxis work the Kuta area. Most use their meters regularly and are relatively cheap. Taxis are indispensable for getting around town at night, and they can also be hired for longer trips anywhere in southern Bali, and even as far as Ubud. As always, the blue taxis of **Bali Taxi** (☎ 701111) are far and away the best bet.

SEMINYAK

Seminyak may be next immediately north of Kuta and Legian, but in many respects it feels like it's almost on another island. It's flash, brash, phoney and filled with bony models. It is the centre of life for hordes of the island's expats, many of whom own boutiques or design clothes, surf, or seem to do nothing at all.

It's also a very exciting place to be. It's home to dozens of restaurants and clubs. And it seems that when a hot new place opens, it's in Seminyak. Along Jl Legian and its successor in the north, Jl Raya Seminyak, and the odd side street, are a wealth of creative shops and galleries. World-class hotels line the beach. And what a beach it is, as deep and sandy as Kuta's but less crowded.

There's a lot of good and bad about Seminyak that seems to be taken from the pages of a glossy magazine, but there's also surprises. Not every beachfront hotel is world-class or charges world-class prices. All those restau-

PICK A NAME, ANY NAME

A small lane or alley is known as a *gang*, and most of them in Bali lack signs or even names. Some are referred to by the name of a connecting street, eg Jl Padma Utara is the *gang* going north of Jl Padma. Many are too small for cars, although this doesn't seem to stop some drivers from giving it a good go.

Meanwhile, some streets in Kuta, Legian and Seminyak have more than one name. Many streets are unofficially named after a well-known temple and/or business place, or according to the direction they head. In recent years there has been an attempt to impose official – and usually more Balinese – names on the streets. But the old, unofficial names are still common – the only place you're likely to encounter the new names is on some new, small street signs, and in some tourist brochures.

In this guide, all names are shown on the maps, but in the text, the street name that the business uses is the one given. For reference, here are the old (unofficial) and new (official) names, from north to south.

Old/unofficial	New/official
Jl Oberoi	Jl Laksmana
Jl Raya Seminyak	Northern stretch: Jl Raya Basangkasa
Jl Dhyana Pura/Jl Gado Gado	Jl Abimanyu
Jl Double Six	Jl Arjuna
Jl Pura Bagus Taruna/Rum Jungle Rd	Jl Werkudara
Jl Padma	Jl Yudistra
Poppies Gang II	Jl Batu Bolong
Jl Pantai Kuta	Jl Pantai Banjar Pande Mas
Jl Kartika Plaza	Jl Dewi Sartika
Jl Segara	Jl Jenggala
Jl Satria	Jl Kediri

rants and clubs combine to give the greatest choice of style and budget on Bali. And sure there are exclusive boutiques, but there are also workshops where everything is wholesale. And just when you've tired of trying to cross the street in front of zooming expats in SUVs, a religious procession comes through and shuts everything down.

In the end there's no way to characterise Seminyak. It has everything to offer and you'll only miss out if you don't give it a whirl.

ORIENTATION

The southern border of Seminyak runs north of Jl Double Six. Jl Raya Seminyak is the continuation of Jl Legian from Kuta and is lined with interesting shops and other businesses. Jl Dhyana Pura is lined with bars and restaurants and accesses many hotels. It is sometimes one-way.

Jl Oberoi heads west to the resort of the same name. From here things get real tricky as the road wanders north through a part of Seminyak that some people call Petitenget, is properly called Jl Pantai Kaya Aya, but is also known as both Jl Oberoi and Jl Laksmana! Either way, the road commonly called Jl Oberoi is home to a profusion of excellent restaurants, upscale boutiques and more. Meanwhile as Jl Seminyak continues north it changes to Jl Raya Kerobokan and is lined with many craft and furniture showrooms and workshops.

See 'Pick a Name, Any Name' (opposite) for more information on the confusing street names in the region.

INFORMATION

Seminyak shares many services with Kuta and Legian.

Bookshops

The Bali Deli (p118) and Bintang Supermarket (p121) have large book and periodicals sections.

Periplus (☎ 734843; Made's Warung II, Jl Raya Seminyak) Has the usual good selection of art books and periodicals.

Internet Access

Most of the top-end hotels have broadband connections for guests. A growing number of cafés and bars offer free wi-fi for patrons as noted in the listings.

Island Internet (Jl Raya Seminyak; per 30min 4500Rp; 🕑 8.30am-10pm) Located above a small market just north of Bintang Supermarket. Full-service shop with wi-fi.

Medical Services

Taiga Pharmacy (☎ 732621; Jl Raya Seminyak 19; 🕑 24hr) Has a full range of prescription medications.

Money

ATMs can be found along all the main roads.

Post

Postal agency (☎ 761592; Bintang Supermarket, Jl Raya Seminyak 17)

SIGHTS

North of the string of hotels on Jl Pantai Kaya Aya, **Pura Petitenget** is an important temple and the scene of many ceremonies. It is one of a string of sea temples that stretches from Pura Luhur Ulu Watu on the Bukit Peninsula, north to Tanah Lot in western Bali. The temple honours the visit of a 16th-century priest.

ACTIVITIES

Because of the limited road access, the beach in Seminyak tends to be less crowded than further south in Kuta. This also means that it is less patrolled and the water conditions are less monitored. The odds of encountering dangerous rip-tides and other hazards are ever present especially as you head north.

Spas

Spa (☎ 730622; Legian, Jl Pantai Kaya Aya; 🕑 10am-9pm) in the Legian is suitably lavish and clients can avail themselves of various private spa suites set among gardens.

At **Jari Menari** (☎ 736740; Jl Raya Seminyak 47; 🕑 10am-9pm), true to its name, which means 'dancing fingers', your body will be one happy dance floor. The all-male staff use massage techniques that emphasise rhythm. Fees start at 180,000Rp for 75 minutes.

Live the 1970s movie *Shampoo* at **Body Works** (☎ 733317; Jl Kayu Jati 2; 🕑 10am-9pm) where gossiping, beautifully coiffed hairdressers mingle with a gorgeous crowd. Massage starts at 139,000Rp.

The name says it all at **Chill** (☎ 734701; Jl Kunti; 🕑 10am-10pm). This zen place embraces reflexology with treatments starting at 80,000Rp.

Spa Bonita (☎ 731918; Jl Petitenget 2000x; 🕑 9am-9pm), part of the delightful Waroeng Bonita (p121), has a range of services in a simply elegant setting. Massages start at 85,000Rp for one hour.

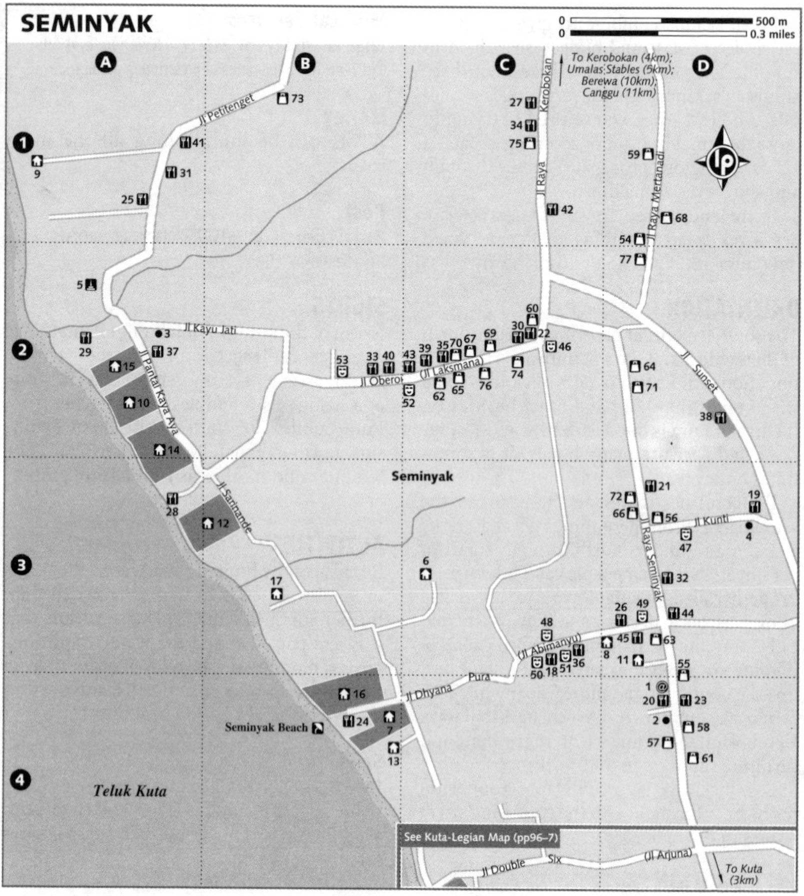

Cooking School

Sate Bali (☎ 736734; Jl Oberoi 22; course 325,000Rp) runs an excellent Balinese cooking course taught by noted chef Nyoman Sudiyasa. Students learn to prepare Balinese spices and *sambals*, which are then used to flavour duck, fish and pork. Not up to school? The restaurant is superb (p121).

SLEEPING

Seminyak isn't just about top-end hotels. There's a good bunch of cheaper places at the south and they're close to or even on the beach. If you're looking for the best places to stay in Bali, though, you will find several here, including the Legian and the Oberoi, both of which regularly feature on lists of the best hotels in the world. Seminyak is also home to villas available for holiday rental (p328).

Budget

Ned's Hide-Away (☎ 731270; nedshide@dps.centrim.net.id; Gang Bima 3; r from 80,000Rp) Named after Aussie icon Ned Kelly, this simple 15-room place is popular with those hoping to lie low between bouts of fun. Rooms have hot water and there's a character-filled bar. Look for the sign on Jl Raya Seminyak near Bintang Supermarket.

Galaxy Hotel (☎ 730328; galaxy_bali@yahoo.com; Jl Abimanyu 9A; r from 150,000Rp;) Right in the heart of the Dhyana Pura action, the Galaxy has 16 plain rooms, a busy bar and a brochure that is a balm for those tired of bikini-clad clichés. Weekly rates are really cheap.

INFORMATION
Island Internet....1 D4
Periplus....(see 32)
Postal Agency....(see 20)
Taiga Pharmacy....2 D4

SIGHTS & ACTIVITIES
Body Works....3 A2
Chill....4 D3
Jari Menari....(see 71)
Pura Petitenget....5 A2
Sate Bali....(see 37)
Spa Bonita....(see 41)
Spa....(see 10)

SLEEPING
Bali Agung Village....6 C3
Dhyana Pura Beach Resort....7 B4
Galaxy Hotel....8 D3
Hotel Intan Bali....9 A1
Legian....10 A2
Ned's Hide-Away....11 D3
Oberoi....12 B3
Raja Gardens....13 B4
Resor Seminyak....14 A2
Samaya....15 A2
Sofitel Seminyak Bali....16 B4
Villa Kresna....17 B3

EATING
Antique....18 C3
Bali Deli....19 D3
Bintang Supermarket....20 D4
Café Moka....21 D3
Corner Store....22 C2
Deli....23 D4
Gado Gado....24 B4
Hu'u....25 A1
Jef Burgers....26 D3
Kafe Warisan....27 C1
Ku De Ta....28 A3
La Lucciola....29 A2
Lazumba....30 C2
Living Room....31 A1
Made's Warung II....32 D3
Mykonos....33 B2
Padang Jaya....34 C1
Rumours....35 C2
Santa Fe Bar & Grill....36 C3
Sate Bali....37 A2
Seminyak Night Market....38 D2
Trattoria....39 C2
Tuesday Night Pizza Club....40 B2
Waroeng Bonita....41 A1
Warung Batavia....42 C1
Warung Murah....43 C2
Warung Ocha's....44 D3
Zula Vegetarian Paradise....45 D3

ENTERTAINMENT
Aina Bar....46 C2
Bottle Shop....47 D3
Bush Telegraph Pub....48 C3
Joulla's....49 D3
Kwin....50 C3
Q-Bar....51 C3
Street Life....52 C2
Zappaz....53 B2

SHOPPING
Alacazar....54 D1
Ashitaba....(see 56)
Biasa....55 D3
Biasa Art Space....(see 55)
Blue Glue....56 D3
Body & Soul....57 D4
Body & Soul Outlet....58 D4
Disini....59 D1
Divine Diva....60 C2
ET Club....61 D4
G&V Amazing Crafts....62 C2
Joe Joe....63 D3
Kemarin Hari Ini....64 D2
Lily Jean....65 C2
Luna Collection....66 D3
Morena....67 C2
Nôblis....68 D1
Paul Ropp....69 C2
Poon Studio....70 C2
Rama....71 D2
Rama Shinta Ki Jay....72 D3
Richard Meyer Culture....73 B1
Rio Helmi....(see 71)
St Isador....74 C2
Sunbek....(see 72)
Ticket to the Moon....75 C1
Toko Morocco....(see 60)
Tunas Maju Abadi....76 C2
You Like Lamp....77 D2

Midrange

OUR PICK Raja Gardens (☎ 730494; jdw@eksadata.com; Jl Abimanyu; r 200,000-300,000Rp;) Look for spacious, lush grounds in this quiet hideaway near the beach. The seven rooms are spotless and have touches of tropical style in their older and decidedly not trendy appointments. But the soft green pastels and open-air bathrooms, filled with plants, definitely have a tropical feel. The staff are unobtrusive but warm and experienced – they've seen it all before. It's a minute from the beach.

Bali Agung Village (☎ 730367; www.bali-agung.com; off Jl Abimanyu; r US$40-80;) Off a hidden back street of Seminyak, this attractive place has 41 rooms in bungalow-style units. The grounds are lush and there's a profusion of Balinese design touches. Look for the statue of a giraffe as you navigate in along the alleys.

Dhyana Pura Beach Resort (☎ 730442; www.dhyana pura-beach-resort.com; off Jl Abimanyu; r US$45-75;) A beach resort right out of the 1960s with an older clientele to match, this sprawling 120-room property has become a little shaggy around the edges but it's clean and the veteran staff welcoming. It's right on the beach.

Villa Kresna (☎ 730317; www.villa-kresna.com; Jl Sarinande 19; r US$40-85;) The beach is only 50m from this cute little property tucked away on a small *gang*. The 10 art-filled units are mostly suites, which have a nice flow-through design with both public and private patios. A small, sinuous pool wanders through the property.

Resor Seminyak (☎ 730814; www.resorseminyak.com; Jl Pantai Kaya Aya; r from US$70;) The grounds are spacious at this 60-room resort, which is good value at the low end of its prices. There are two pools and the poolside bar is lively. It fronts an attractive bit of beach.

Top End

Sofitel Seminyak Bali (☎ 730730; www.theroyal-seminyak.com; Jl Dhyana Pura; r from US$120, villas from US$500;) This hotel's beachside location is ideal and you can walk to the clubs and restaurants on Jl Dhyana Pura. The rooms are done in a smart contemporary style. What really sets the property apart are the private walled units, which feel like an old Balinese village.

Oberoi (☎ 730361; www.oberoihotels.com; Jl Oberoi; r from US$200, villas from US$400;) One of the world's top hotels, the beautifully understated Oberoi has been a refined beachside retreat since 1971. All accommodation has private lanais and as you move up through the food chain, additional features include private villas, ocean views and private, walled pools. From the café overlooking the almost private sweep of beach to the numerous luxuries, this is a place to spoil yourself.

Legian (☎ 730622; www.ghmhotels.com; Jl Pantai Kaya Aya; ste from US$300, villa from US$600;) The Legian is flashier than its main competitor, the Oberoi. All 67 rooms claim to be suites, even if some are just large rooms (called 'studios'). On a little bluff, the views are panoramic and of the many personal services offered you can enjoy gourmet dining at a table set up by the surf. The design mixes traditional materials with contemporary flair.

Samaya (☎ 731149; www.thesamayabali.com; Jl Pantai Kaya Aya; r from US$300;) There are 24 villas at this understated beachside luxury resort. Traditional grass roofs cover large, airy units with the now common stark and sombre colours contrasting with a light palette. All have private pools, from plunge to full-on depending on rate.

EATING

Seminyak is so spread out that you won't be walking among the many dining choices; rather you'll be choosing a neighbourhood first. Note that where indicated, some restaurants morph into clubs as the night wears on. Conversely, some of the places listed under Bars & Clubs also do decent food. Think of it as fusion fun.

Jl Dhyana Pura

Jef Burgers (☎ 081-7473 4311; Jl Dhyana Pura 24; dishes from 13,000Rp; 24hr) Like a downscale lunch counter, Jefs cooks up highly customisable burgers around the clock.

Zula Vegetarian Paradise (☎ 732723; Jl Dhyana Pura 5; dishes 15,000-40,000Rp; 8-4am) It's all vegetarian at this cute little place where you can get tofu cheese, a tofu spring roll, tofu cheesecake, not to mention a tofu-chickpea burger.

Santa Fe Bar & Grill (☎ 731147; Jl Dhyana Pura 11A; dishes 15,000-45,000Rp; 7-4am) Popular pizza and Southwest food draws people here at all hours, especially late when there's live music (mostly rock). Shots are popular.

Antique (☎ 739840; Jl Dhyana Pura; dishes 20,000-80,000Rp) Fresh food from around the archipelago features at this attractive restaurant. There's a good terrace shaded by a tree and decorative ironwork inspired by flowering vines. The Gold Black Rush is a surprising chocolate cake.

Gado Gado (☎ 736966; Jl Dhyana Pura; mains 70,000-150,000Rp) The location right on the beach is the primary draw here. To the sounds of surf, enjoy the good service and an interesting menu of Asian and Mediterranean fusion dishes. Brunch is popular.

Jl Raya Seminyak

Café Moka (☎ 731424; Jl Raya Seminyak; dishes 15,000-40,000Rp;) Enjoy French-style baked goods at this always-popular bakery. Fresh deli cuisine is served for lunch and dinner. The bulletin board is a window into the local expat community.

Warung Ocha's (☎ 736222; cnr Jl Raya Seminyak & Jl Dhyana Pura; dishes from 15,000Rp) Overlooking the busy intersection, this simple place serves spruced-up versions of traditional dishes (point and select from the display) at little tables with great views of the Seminyak scene.

Made's Warung II (☎ 732130; Jl Raya Seminyak; dishes 18,000-90,000Rp) This northern branch of the Kuta stand-by is set in a sheltered courtyard area. Well-prepared Indonesian food has always been the speciality here and there's a myriad of little touches that make it special. Shops line the periphery.

Jl Oberoi

Saddled by some with the unimaginative name 'Eat St', this restaurant row has scores of choices. Many use the newer name Jl Laksmana or Jl Pantai Kaya Aya further north.

Warung Murah (Jl Oberoi; dishes 5000-15,000Rp) Amidst the Jl Oberoi glitz, this simple, local place displays bowls and platters of fresh food at excellent prices. Enjoy a fried banana on the folding chairs out front.

Lazumba (☎ 731899; Jl Oberoi; dishes 15,000-40,000Rp;) This simple open-air café has superb Italian coffee, wi-fi and cool jazz wafting from the speakers.

Corner Store (☎ 730276; Jl Laksmana 10A; dishes 30,000-60,000Rp; 7am-5pm) Seminyak's fashionistas gather here most mornings (aka Tuck Shop) to dish the gossip and breakfast from dishes of upscale, healthy fare like organic muesli.

Mykonos (☎ 733253; Jl Oberoi 52; dishes 15,000-50,000Rp; 5pm-midnight) The island food of Greece comes to the island of Bali at this always busy vision in white. All the classics are here, from meze like tzatziki to various grilled souvlakis. Cheap wine fuels the fun.

Tuesday Night Pizza Club (☎ 730614; Jl Oberoi; pizza 25,000-130,000Rp; 🕑 6pm-midnight) Pizzas come in five sizes at this brightly lit joint and have a range of goofy names like Hawaii Five-O (ham and pineapple) and Blue Velvet (a tasty combo of blue cheese and crispy bacon). There's fast and efficient delivery.

Rumours (☎ 738720; Jl Oberoi 100; mains 20,000-60,000Rp; 🕑 6pm-midnight) This arch-rival of Trattoria is always packed thanks to good food at great prices. Such a concept! Terrace tables are always in demand. Steaks and pasta dominate the long menu.

Trattoria (☎ 737082; Jl Oberoi; mains 35,000-90,000Rp; 🕑 6pm-midnight) Enjoy authentic Italian cuisine at tables inside or out. The menu changes often but always features fresh pasta, grilled meats and seafood. Service is good and this place is justifiably popular.

La Lucciola (☎ 730838; Jl Pantai Kaya Aya; dishes 80,000-140,000Rp) A sleek beachside restaurant with good views from the 2nd-floor tables across a lovely lawn and sand to the surf. The bar is big with sunset watchers. The menu is a creative fusion of international fare.

Sate Bali (☎ 736734; Jl Oberoi 22; meals 195,000Rp; 🕑 11am-10pm) Some very fine traditional Balinese meals are served at this small but artful café run by chef Nyoman Sudiyasa. Prepare for an array of dozens of small plates of exquisite food. Service is sublime.

Ku De Ta (☎ 736969; Jl Oberoi; dishes 140,000-220,000Rp; 🕑 7am-1pm) Ku De Ta heaves with Bali's beautiful. Kids play in the stylish pool and enjoy free balloons while adults perfect their 'bored' look over drinks. Everyone ponders the gorgeous sunsets over the beach. The menu is a creative fusion mix; security is fairly tight.

Northern Seminyak

Seminyak Night Market (Jl Sunset; dishes from 2000Rp; 🕑 6pm-midnight) Enjoy delicious *bakso* (meat balls) and *soto ayam* (chicken soup) from scores of vendors. Few travellers make it to the market's new location along Jl Sunset.

Padang Jaya (☎ 486432; Jl Raya Kerobokan; dishes from 5000Rp) Join everyone else's driver at this classic Rumah Makan place where the food is fresh and displayed for your choosing pleasure.

Warung Batavia (☎ 731641; Jl Raya Kerobokan; dishes 6000-15,000Rp) This slightly upscale roadside place has a big choice of excellent, authentic Indonesian dishes. New creations stream forth from the kitchen.

Waroeng Bonita (☎ 731918; Jl Petitenget 2000x; dishes 20,000-60,000Rp) Balinese dishes such as *ikan rica-rica* (fresh fish in a spicy green chilli sauce) are the specialties at this cute little place with tables under the trees.

Hu'u (☎ 736443; Jl Pantai Kaya Aya; mains 50,000-100,000Rp; 🕑 11-2am) Like many of the fine open-air dining spots nearby, oodles of little tea lights provide a romantic glow at night. There's steak, seafood and a good selection of vegetarian dishes.

Living Room (☎ 735735; Jl Petitenget; mains 80,000-100,000Rp; 🕑 noon-midnight) At night hundreds of candles twinkle on and about the scores of outdoor tables at this open-to-the-stars restaurant (which has become more elegant after a cross-street move). The menu is Asian with good Thai, Vietnamese and Balinese dishes.

Kafe Warisan (☎ 731175; www.kafewarisan.com; Jl Raya Kerobokan; set dinner menus US$25-40; 🕑 noon-10pm) Chef Nicolas Tourneville gives fine French cooking a Mediterranean flair at one of Bali's finest restaurants. The tranquil setting looks out over rice paddies and the changing menu reflects what's in season locally – considering the quality, meals are fine value.

Self-Catering

Bali Deli (☎ 738686; Jl Kunti 117X; 💻) Almost at Jl Sunset, the lavish deli counter at this upscale market is loaded with imported cheeses, meats and baked goods. This is the place to get food from home. The cute café has wi-fi.

Bintang Supermarket (☎ 730552; Jl Raya Seminyak 17; 💻) Always busy, this large store has a supermarket with good prices and sells all manner of other goods. There's wi-fi at the café in front.

ENTERTAINMENT

Bars & Clubs

Jl Dhyana Pura boasts a line-up of trendy clubs that seem to change as often as, well, trends. Most cater to a mixed gay and straight crowd and a few favour the former. Note that where indicated, some of the places do good food in the evening, while some of the places listed under Eating also do music.

JL DHYANA PURA

One of the joys of Jl Dhyana Pura is bouncing from place to place all night/morning long. Many clubs snooze until after midnight.

Bush Telegraph Pub (☎ 732963; Jl Dhyana Pura 10XX; dishes 24,000-50,000Rp; 🕑 11-2am) The focus at this cavernous place is on sports TV. The only action you're likely to find is the latest from the world Formula One. You also can tuck into Australian pub fare.

Joulla's (☎ 732971; Jl Dhyana Pura 6XX; 🕑 10am-11pm) This relaxed open-air café-bar has a German accent and free wi-fi. Surf the web with a *weissbier* at the tables on the small terrace.

Kwin (☎ 762374; Jl Dhyana Pura 9; 🕑 8pm-3am) With a more mixed crowd than Q-Bar, the upper level is a good place to cool off and engage in running commentary on the clubbers passing by below.

Q-Bar (☎ 762361; Jl Dhyana Pura; 🕑 8pm-3am) This bright and always popular bar caters to gay clubbers. The music of choice is house. There are good views of the action – inside and out – from the upper floor.

JL PADMA

Bottle Shop (☎ 733963; Jl Kunti 6A; 🕑 11am-midnight; 💻) 'Shut up and drink' is the slogan at this simple place that opens up to the street. There's a small menu and free wi-fi. Settle in, have a cheap cold one and ponder your next move.

JL OBEROI

Hu'u (p121) and some of the other stylish open-air places north of Jl Oberoi along Jl Petitenget morph into clubs late in the evening.

Aina Bar (☎ 730182; Jl Oberoi; 🕑 6pm-2am) Mellow rock is the music of choice at this intimate little open-fronted bar. Pull up a stool and chat up the bartender.

SO YOU WANT TO LIVE IN BALI?

Numbers are fuzzy, but it's estimated that some 7000 people from other countries live more or less full-time on Bali. They come for the same reasons as many visitors (sun, surf, sex) or for more tangible reasons (culture, love, job) or just because it's really cheap ('A gardener, maid and driver for US$200 a month? Where's my ticket?!?').

You see them all over the south and Ubud and even scattered about the east, the north and the west; deeply tanned expats going – or not going – about their business every day. There's simply no way to generalise what they do, although the image of the Westerner idling away afternoons with US$1 Bintangs is common.

'You work?!?' That's the number 1 reaction Nicoline Dolman gets when she meets people and tells them she not only lives on Bali but also works there (as marketing manager for the Sofitel Seminyak Bali resort). 'People think I must be lounging by the pool all the time,' says Dolman, who came to Bali on a tourism internship, fell in love with the place and never left.

'I get paid in local wages, so you bet I work.'

Life in Bali has allowed her to grow in ways she wouldn't have at home. 'I've had to learn patience and I've come to prefer the Asian sense of respect for one another.'

Ashley Bickerton, the renowned American artist, has discovered rare qualities in Bali. 'There are places on this planet that have kinetic electricity and there are those that don't. Bali has it in spades. Like the great oceanic washes of opposing currents and upswellings that create nutrient-rich banks, Bali is ablaze with conflicting currents; edge is everywhere.'

And despite vowing that Bali wouldn't affect his work, Bickerton found that impossible.

'When I moved here from New York, I was adamant about not becoming one of those wispy fantasists that insist on portraying conventional island charm in dollops of pastel kitsch.

'Well, fast-forward 14 years and despite the protestations, I find the palette has dramatically shifted from primary colours and silvers to muted greeny, browny greys. It can only be the influence of the Batuan School. I never planned it!'

However, if Bali has shaped Bickerton and Dolman in ways they wouldn't have guessed, other expats want to shape Bali in more predictable ways.

'The rampant greed and short-sightedness running amok in Bali today threatens to strangle the very things that drew people here in the first place,' says Bickerton, while Dolman says she gets tired of idlers with attitudes out of tune with the local vibe. 'You meet someone and they say with a smirk, "I'm a fashion designer, you?"'

Still, neither would leave their life on Bali. 'Every time a long-term expat starts grumbling about moving on, they are invariably stumped by the same question, "Where?" says Bickerton, or as Dolman says, 'Other qualities aside, you've got a glass of beer, you're in the sun by that pool, why leave?'

Street Life (☎ 0183-3820 9567; Jl Oberoi 61; noon-midnight) A fun, lively open-air bar popular with expats on a budget.

Zappaz (☎ 7425534; Jl Oberoi; 11am-midnight) Brit Norman Findlay tickles the ivories nightly at this popular piano bar. The most enjoyable part of this performance is his enthusiastic patter with the crowd.

SHOPPING

Seminyak shops could occupy days of your holiday. Designer boutiques (Bali has a thriving little fashion industry), funky stores, slick galleries, wholesale emporiums and family-run workshops are just some of the choices.

The action picks up in the south from Kuta and Legian (p113) and heads north along Jl Legian and Jl Raya Seminyak (there's no exact demarcation between the two and some people call parts of the latter Jl Raya Basangkasa – yikes!). The retail strip branches off onto Jl Oberoi (lots of designer places) while continuing north on Jl Raya Kerobokan into Kerobokan itself (p125).

Jl Mertanadi is a quiet street of family-run places selling and making mostly housewares.

If you need help navigating this retail paradise, check out the Retail Therapy column in the *Bali Advertiser* (www.baliadvertiser.biz). It's written by the singularly named Marilyn (retailtherapym@yahoo.com.au) who brings a veteran retailer's keen eye to the local scene. For advanced studies, she's available for consultations.

Accessories

Rama (☎ 730115; Jl Raya Basangkasa 88) Amidst scores of so-so bead stores, this is one of the best. Antique and modern beads in a plethora of colours and styles.

Beachwear

Blue Glue (☎ 844 5956; Jl Raya Seminyak) Has a collection of Bali-made bathing suits from teensy to trendy.

Clothing

Biasa (☎ 730308; www.biasabali.com; Jl Raya Seminyak 36) This is Bali-based designer Susanna Perini's premier store. Her line of tropical ware for men and women combines cottons, silks and embroidery. Ex-husband Paul Ropp has a small shop across the street.

Body & Soul (☎ 733564; Jl Raya Seminyak) The flagship store in Bali for the Australian chain of beachy and cottony clothes. Many of the items here are Bali-made. Across the street, an outlet store (☎ 733011; Jl Raya Seminyak 16C) has hot deals on cool clothes.

Divine Diva (☎ 731903; Jl Oberoi 1A) It's like a Dove soap commercial for real women in this shop, filled with Bali-made breezy styles for larger figures.

ET Club (☎ 730902; Jl Raya Seminyak 14A) Out of this world prices on designer knock-offs and bohemian bags, belts, shoes and clothes.

Joe Joe (☎ 732678; Jl Raya Seminyak 43) Bling bling! Sequin-encrusted bags and purses glitter in the lights here. Styles range from vintage to far-out.

Lily Jean (☎ 734864; Jl Oberoi 102X) Saucy knickers underpin flouncy, sexy and gauzy women's ware; most is Bali-made.

Morena (☎ 745 3531; Jl Oberoi 69) Puerto Rican-born Wilma sells her line of sexy, floaty and colourful women's clothes here. Go ahead, prance on the beach.

Paul Ropp (☎ 734208; www.paulropp.com; Jl Oberoi) Elegant main store for one of Bali's premier high-end fashion designers. Most goods are made just a few kilometres away. And what goods they are – rich silks and cottons, vivid to the point of gaudy, with hints of the tie-dyed 60s.

Sunbek (☎ 732715; Jl Raya Seminyak 6) Rather than the usual tourist junk, this shop sells exquisite ikat clothes, bags and housewares.

Tunas Maju Abadi (☎ 730010; Jl Oberoi 117) A small workshop that makes custom leather and suede clothes. Make a splash with your own Nemo-brand custom-made wetsuit (a shorty goes for US$95).

Galleries

Biasa Art Space (☎ 744 2902; Jl Raya Seminyak 34) This stunning gallery is owned by Biasa designer Susanna Perini. Changing exhibits highlight bold works.

Kemarin Hari Ini (☎ 735262; Jl Raya Basangkasa) Glass objects created with laminated Japanese paper sparkle in the light at this airy gallery. It also has the bold acrylic works of painter Ngurah Atmaja.

Poon Studio (☎ 0817352754; Jl Oberoi 21) Above-average local talent display their works here. Think edgy and tangy.

Richard Meyer Culture (☎ 744 5179; Jl Petitenget 200X) This gallery sells works – mostly photos – by renowned contemporary Bali artists. Its openings are always events and it's been lauded for its conservation and historical collection.

Rio Helmi (☎ 735688; www.riohelmi.com; Jl Raya Basangkasa 88) This small gallery of the noted Ubud-based photographer shows his work and that of many others.

Housewares

Alacazar (☎ 0818-0553 1857; Jl Mertanadi) Whimsical painted furniture and carved wooden figures with elongated forms that look like Gumby on a bad day. Many items come from carving villages near Ubud.

Ashitaba (☎ 737054; Jl Raya Seminyak 6) Tenganan, the Aga village of East Bali (p225), produces the intricate and beautiful rattan items sold here. Containers, bowls, purses and more (from US$5).

Disini (☎ 746 4260; Jl Mertanadi 67A) Higher end interior items like modern-style ikat and cool statuary fill this attractive shop. Almost everything is made in Bali and profits are ploughed back into the villages.

G&V Amazing Crafts (☎ 743 3853; Jl Oberoi 99x) Antique Balinese décor and contemporary bits are combined in this large shop. Look for gems like an old Dutch basinet.

Nôblis (☎ 0815-5800 2815; Jl Mertanadi 54) Feel like royalty here with everything from knock-offs of items from the various French Louis's, to regal bits of décor from around the globe.

Rama Shinta Ki Jay (☎ 081-2360 6979; Jl Raya Seminyak 70) Dedicated to all things incense, this shop is an orgasm for your nose. Sniff out the sandalwood section.

St Isador (☎ 738836; Jl Oberoi 44) The workshops upstairs spew forth lovely bed linens, cushions and other items made from fabrics imported from across Asia. A beautiful scene.

Ticket to the Moon (☎ 735131; Jl Raya Kerobokan 14) Is it furniture if it fits in your backpack? Very cool hammocks (160,000Rp) are the thing here, with a range of models, including one for babies.

You Like Lamp (☎ 733755; Jl Mertanadi 32) Why yes, we do. All manner of endearing little paper lamps – many good for tea lights – are sold here cheap by the bagful. Don't see what you want? The staff working away on the floor will rustle it up immediately.

Jewellery

Luna Collection (☎ 0811-398909; Jl Raya Seminyak) Handmade sterling silver jewellery in a range of designs. The local craftsmen are quite creative and just browsing is a treat.

Toko Morocco (☎ 733238; Jl Oberoi 1B) How about a US$25 Buddha head, perfect for a pendant? This shop bulges with trinkets, beads, silver and other cheap and cheerful jewellery.

GETTING THERE & AROUND

Most transport information is the same as for Kuta (p115). Metered taxis are easily hailed. A trip from the airport in an official airport taxi costs 60,000Rp, to the airport less than half that. A taxi to the heart of Kuta will be about 12,000Rp. You can beat the traffic and have a good stroll by walking the beach south. Legian is about 20 minutes away.

NORTH OF SEMINYAK

☎ 0361

Growth is marching north and west along the coast, much of it anchored by the continuing beaches. Kerobokan is rivalling Seminyak for the affections of local expats. Villas and large shops dot the imperilled rice fields. Traffic can be an evil spirit: like elsewhere, road-building is a decade or two behind settlement.

Small roads lead off the main clogged artery to Pura Tanah Lot and to beaches at Berewa, Canggu, Batu Mejan (Echo Beach) and Perenan Beach. These are uncrowded and wild, with pounding surf, deadly swimming and sweeping views to the south.

Getting to most of the places listed is really only convenient with your own transport or by taxi. Think 20,000Rp or more from Kuta.

KEROBOKAN

Lots of interesting little places can be found here, a trend sure to continue. To get here from Kuta and points south, follow Jl Legian north, through its Jl Raya Seminyak phase until it becomes Jl Raya Kerobokan just north of Seminyak. One notable landmark is the **jail**, home to Schapelle Corby and other prisoners.

Activities

Umalas Stables (Map p100; ☎ 731402; www.balionhorse.com; Jl Lestari 9X), 5km north of Seminyak, has a stable of 30 horses and ponies, and offers one-hour rice field tours for US$30, and two-/three-hour beach rides for US$50/70. Lessons in beginner to advanced equestrian events such as dressage and showjumping can also be arranged.

Sleeping

For a romantic getaway, **Villa Seri** (Map p100; ☎ 730262; www.villaseri.com; Br Umalas Kauh; r from US$65, villas from US$135;) is a great little hideaway. A recent revamp has only improved a lovely property. Rooms are more refined, with stylish stone bathrooms, kitchens in the villas and more. The beach is a 10-minute walk.

Eating

About 1km north of the jail, off Jl Raya Kerobokan, **Warung Gossip** (Map p100; ☎ 0817 970 3209; Jl Pengubengan Kauh; meals 15,000-20,000Rp; noon-4pm) is always popular thanks to its top-notch versions of Balinese warung staples. Get a plate, tell the staff what you'd like and soon you'll be enjoying a fine lunch at one of the shady tables. There's also a café area for more formal dining.

At the corner of Jl Raya Kerobokan and Jl Gunung Tangkuban Perahu there's a scrumptious little **fruit market** (Map p100).

Shopping

Buy 'em by the kilo at **JJ Bali Button** (Map p100; ☎ 730001; Jl Gunung Tangkuban Perahu). Zillions of beads and buttons made from shells, plastic, metal and more are displayed in what first looks like a candy store. Elaborately carved wooden buttons are 700Rp.

Typical of some of the posher emporiums here, **Asia Style** (Map p100; ☎ 734599; Jl Raya Kerobokan 3) has Chinese antiques collected in Bali, vintage travel posters, crepe-silk sarongs (250,000Rp) and a whole lot more.

BEREWA

The greyish beach, secluded among stunning paddy fields, is 6km along the beach from Kuta (by car it's closer to 15km). The turn-off is along the road heading west from Kerobokan. There are some decent cafés and warung in the village, 200m from the beach.

Legong Keraton (Map p100; ☎ 730280; www.legongkeratonhotel.com; Berewa Beach; r US$55-85;) A very attractive 40-room hotel right on the beach, this place is very well run and makes a good get-away. The grounds are shaded by palms and the pool borders the beach. The best rooms are in bungalow units facing the surf.

CANGGU

A popular surf spot, Canggu draws a lot of locals at weekends. On the way you'll spot quite a few satellite dishes poking above the rice paddies denoting the locations of expat villas. Every road going towards the ocean ends at a beach where there's usually a warung or two. For details on surfing here, see p78.

Right at Canggu Beach, **Hotel Tugu Bali** (☎ 731701; www.tuguhotels.com; Jl Pantai Batu Bolong, Desa Canggu; r US$200-500;) is an exquisite hotel surrounded by rice fields and beach. It blurs the boundaries between a museum and gallery, especially the Walter Spies and Le Mayeur Pavilions, where memorabilia from the artists' lives decorates the rooms. The stunning collection of antiques and artwork begins in the lobby and extends throughout the hotel. There's a spa and numerous customised dining options. The artful rooms have wi-fi.

To get to Canggu, go west at Kerobokan and south at Kayutulang. Taxis from Kuta will run 40,000Rp or more.

ECHO BEACH

The next popular beach northwest of Canggu Beach is Echo Beach, or Batu Mejan. Besides the surfers' warung, there's the **Beach House** (☎ 738471; Jl Pura Batu Mejan; dishes 5000-40,000Rp), which faces the waves and draws stylish loungers. It has a variety of couches and tables where you can hang out, watch the waves and enjoy the menu of breakfasts, sandwiches and salads.

PERERENAN BEACH

Yet to be found by the right developer, this is the beach if you want your sand wind-swept and your waves unridden. It's southeast of Pura Tanah Lot; you get here from the south via Seseh.

Once you've found it, why leave? The friendly guys at **Pondok Wisata Nyoman** (☎ 081-2390 6900; Jl Raya Pantai Pererenan; r 100,000Rp) have four simple rooms (although the bathrooms are a tad arty) just behind the beach. There's a tiny café nearby and that's it.

South Bali

Much of South Bali was once home to little more than a few sand-pounding fishermen. But oh how times change! Once making merry on the sand became popular, it guaranteed that South Bali would be the focus for visitors to the island.

Kuta, Legian and Seminyak are the tourist hub. But from there spokes of interest radiate throughout this dry region, surrounded by blue ocean and most of Bali's best surf breaks.

The Dutch made Denpasar an administrative centre, and today it is the centre for Bali's commercial life and much of its population. It can both appeal and repel with its frenetic pace. That's not the case just east in Sanur, a pleasant enclave of mellow beach resorts and many foreign residents.

Dangling below Ngurah Rai airport, the gently domed Bukit Peninsula combines wild beaches and surf breaks near the culturally vital Ulu Watu temple with the more genteel climes of Jimbaran. The latter is home to discreet luxury resorts and beachside seafood joints for the masses.

On the east side, Nusa Dua is a gated enclave of huge resort hotels. To the north, Tanjung Benoa has more local flavour and is popular for the watersports possible just offshore.

Further offshore, and easily seen from anywhere facing east, the islands of Nusa Lembongan and Nusa Penida lure fun-seekers and the adventurous. Diving is world-class around the islands. Surfers and those looking for a mellow vibe flock to Lembongan, while Penida is for those who want to discover life that's been unchanged for decades.

HIGHLIGHTS

- Relishing freshly grilled seafood and the sunsets from **Jimbaran Beach** (opposite)
- Watching a full moon rise over Nusa Penida from **Sanur** (p139)
- Discovering the Bukit Peninsula's hidden beaches such as **Dreamland** (p131)
- Tossing a banana to a monkey at **Pura Luhur Ulu Watu** (p132)
- Absorbing Balinese culture at Denpasar's **Museum Negeri Propinsi Bali** (p168)

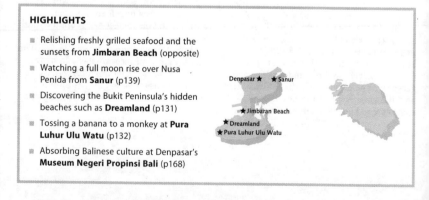

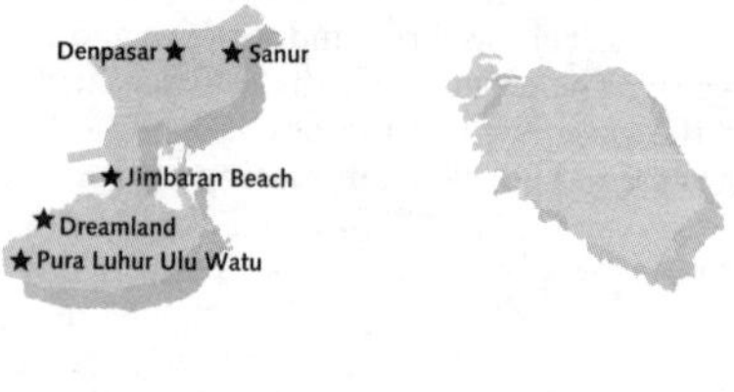

HISTORY

Following the bloody defeat of the three princes of the kingdom of Badung in 1906, the Dutch administration was relatively benign, and southern Bali was little affected until a fateful day in 1936 when Californians Bob and Louise Koke opened their idea of a little tropical resort on then deserted Kuta Beach.

Mass tourism took off – or landed – in 1969 when Ngurah Rai international airport opened. The first planned tourist resort was conceived in the early 1970s, by 'experts' working for the UN and the World Bank. As luxury hotels were built at Nusa Dua, unplanned development raced ahead from Kuta to Legian. People made the most of their opportunities, and small-scale, low-budget businesses were set up with limited local resources.

At first tourism development was confined only to designated areas such as Kuta, Sanur and Nusa Dua, but the boom of the 1990s saw it spreading north and south of Kuta, extending beyond Jimbaran Bay, and north of Nusa Dua to Tanjung Benoa. All the while, real estate speculators grabbed prime coastal spots around the Bukit Peninsula and north along the beach from Seminyak.

The annual cycle of more visitors bringing more money was disrupted after the millennium by the seemingly never-ending series of terrorist attacks, natural disasters elsewhere in Indonesia, various economic crises and other unsettling events that persuaded many visitors to stay home.

Pain was felt throughout tourist-dependent South Bali; slowly but surely though, visitors returned, development continued on parts of the Bukit Peninsula and Nusa Lembongan and somehow the traffic – which never got better – got worse.

BUKIT PENINSULA

☎ 0361

Hot and arid, the southern peninsula is known as Bukit (*bukit* means 'hill' in Indonesian), but was known to the Dutch as Taffelhoek (Table Point). Once a reserve for royal hunting parties – and a place of banishment for undesirables – the Bukit Peninsula was sparsely inhabited. Its only significant site was Pura Luhur Ulu Watu, the culturally significant 'sea temple' at the southwestern tip of the peninsula.

Today the peninsula is a busy part of Bali where the hubbub begins immediately south of the airport. Quiet Jimbaran has a picture-perfect beach and bay, while surfers revel at places such as Dreamland and Ulu Watu. The south coast is barren and dramatic. But in the east, Nusa Dua soldiers on, a vast gated resort with calm seas and scores of resorts and thousands of hotel rooms. Bukit has a multitude of personalities you'll want to get to know.

JIMBARAN

Just south of Kuta and the airport, Teluk Jimbaran (Jimbaran Bay) is a superb crescent of white sand and blue sea, fronted by a long string of seafood *warung* (food stalls), and ending at the southern end in a bushy headland, home to the Four Seasons Jimbaran Bay. It's mostly a somnolent kind of place except in the evenings as the sun goes down, when the tourists arrive and enjoy the spectacle while feasting on freshly caught grilled fish at any number of simple beachside joints. Once it's dark, you can see twinkling lights far out to sea: fishing boats bringing aboard the next night's meals.

Facilities are limited. Jl Raya Ulu Watu has some small markets and Jl Ulu Watu II has ATMs and mini-markets. For most things head to Kuta or Nusa Dua. Expect to pay 1000Rp for vehicles to the beach.

Sights & Activities

The temple **Pura Ulun Siwi** (Map p130) dates from the 18th century. In the mornings, the streets are the scene of the **morning market**, which sells some amazingly huge cabbages.

The **Ganeesha Gallery** (Map p130) at the Four Seasons Jimbaran Bay (see p129) has exhibitions by international artists and is worth a visit – walk south along the beach.

One of the best in Bali, the smelly, lively and frenetic **fish market** (Map p130) is well worth an early morning exploration. And out on the water, Jimbaran is a good place to access the surf breaks off the airport. See p82 for details.

Sleeping

The Jimbaran area is home to some of South Bali's most luxurious resorts, as well as more modest accommodation.

BUDGET

Villa Batu (Map p130; ☎ 703186; Jl Pantai Jimbaran; r 120,000-480,000Rp; ❄ 🏊) This rambling place

SOUTH BALI

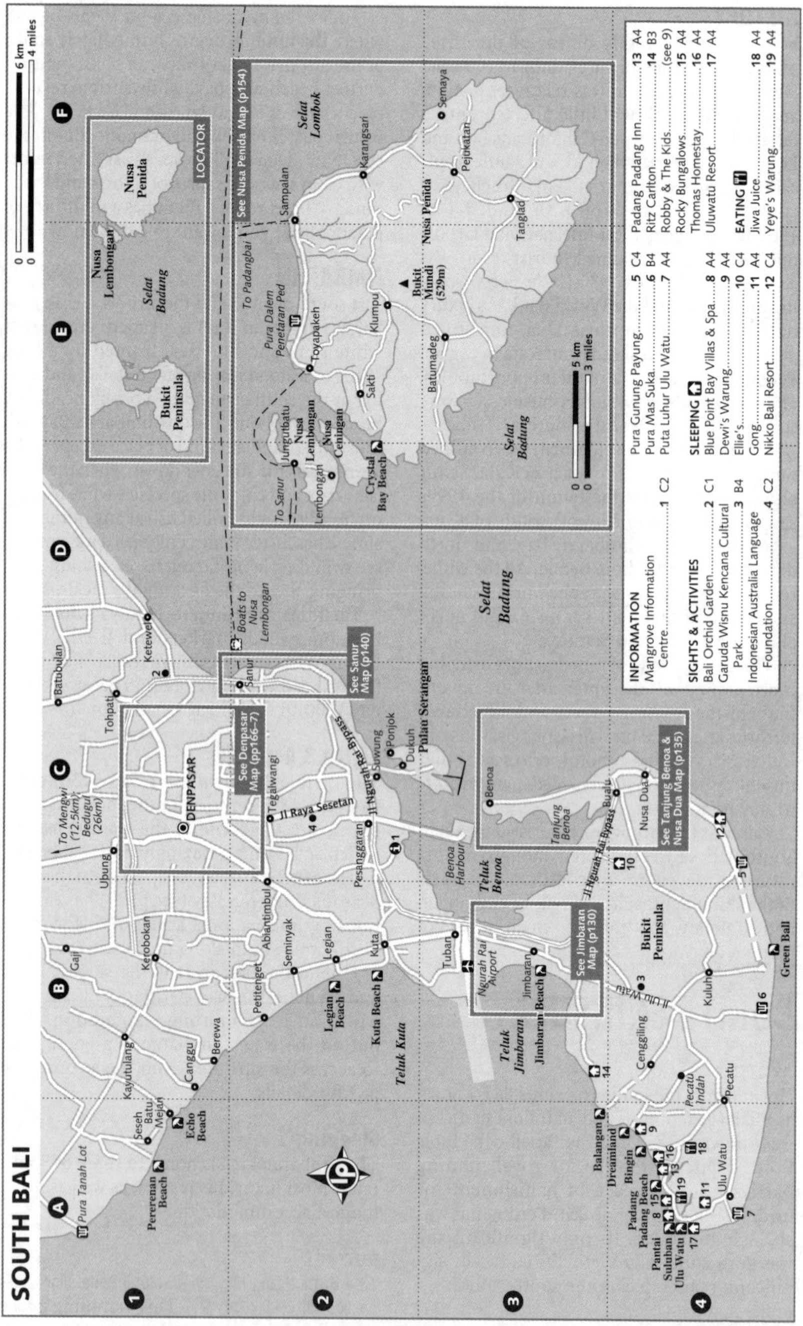
SOUTH BALI
0 6 km
0 4 miles
A B C D E F
1 2 3 4
LOCATOR
Bukit Peninsula
Selat Badung
Nusa Lembongan
Nusa Penida
See Nusa Penida Map (p154)
Selat Lombok
Sampalan
Karangsari
Semaya
Pejukatan
Tanglad
Nusa Penida
Bukit Mundi (529m)
Klumpu
Batumadeg
Sakti
Toyapakeh
Pura Dalem Penetaran Ped
To Padangbai
Jungutbatu
Nusa Lembongan
Nusa Ceningan
Lembongan
To Sanur
Crystal Bay Beach
0 5 km
0 3 miles
Selat Badung
Boats to Nusa Lembongan
Batubulan
Tohpati
Ketewel
See Sanur Map (p140)
Sanur
See Denpasar Map (pp166-7)
DENPASAR
To Mengwi (12.5km); Bedugul (26km)
Ubung
Tegalwangi
Jl Raya Sesetan
Jl Ngurah Rai Bypass
Suwung
Ponjok
Dukuh
Pulau Serangan
Pesanggaran
Benoa Harbour
Teluk Benoa
Benoa
Tanjung Benoa
Bualu
Nusa Dua
See Tanjung Benoa & Nusa Dua Map (p135)
Jl Ngurah Rai Bypass
Bukit Peninsula
Green Ball
Abiantimbul
Seminyak
Legian
Kuta
Tuban
Ngurah Rai Airport
See Jimbaran Map (p130)
Jimbaran
Jimbaran Beach
Jl Ulu Watu
Kuluh
Gaji
Kerobokan
Petitenget
Legian Beach
Kuta Beach
Teluk Kuta
Teluk Jimbaran
Berewa
Canggu
Kayutulang
Seseh
Batu Mejan
Echo Beach
Pererenan Beach
Pura Tanah Lot
Cenggiling
Pecatu Indah
Pecatu
Ulu Watu
Balangan
Dreamland
Bingin
Padang Padang Beach
Pantai Suluban
Ulu Watu
INFORMATION
Mangrove Information Centre....1 C2
SIGHTS & ACTIVITIES
Bali Orchid Garden....2 C1
Garuda Wisnu Kencana Cultural Park....3 B4
Indonesian Australia Language Foundation....4 C2
Pura Gunung Payung....5 C4
Pura Mas Suka....6 B4
Puta Luhur Ulu Watu....7 A4
SLEEPING
Blue Point Bay Villas & Spa....8 A4
Dewi's Warung....9 A4
Ellie's....10 C4
Gong....11 A4
Nikko Bali Resort....12 C4
Padang Padang Inn....13 A4
Ritz Carlton....14 B3
Robby & The Kids....(see 9)
Rocky Bungalows....15 A4
Thomas Homestay....16 A4
Uluwatu Resort....17 A4
EATING
Jiwa Juice....18 A4
Yeye's Warung....19 A4

has smallish rooms with open-air cold-water bathrooms. Some have air-con, others share a modest pool. There's a modest café in front.

Jimbaran Ocean Cottages (Map p130; ☎ 702253; info@kirakira-stay.com; Jl Pantai Jimbaran 3; r 150,000Rp, with air-con 200,000-250,000Rp;) Things are pretty tight here but you cannot beat the location across from the beach. All 15 rooms have hot water and there is a nice café on the 2nd floor with good views.

MIDRANGE

Hotel Puri Bambu (Map p130; ☎ 701377; www.puribambu.com; r US$40-70;) A mere 200m from the beach, it's an attractive, low-key and good-value option. It has 48 standard rooms in three-storey blocks around a pool.

Udayana Eco Lodge (Map p130; ☎ 747 4204; www.ecolodgesindonesia.com; s/d 550,000/600,000Rp;) Inland near Udayana University, this lodge has grand views over South Bali from its perch on a knoll in 70 hectares of bushland. The 15 rooms are comfortable and there is an inviting common area with a fine library. You can join in the fun of Sunday cricket matches.

TOP END

At this price level, scout around for deals during slack periods.

Puri Kosala (Map p130; ☎ 701673; www.purikosala.com; Jl Yoga Perkanti 2; villas US$135-180;) With only six comfortable cottages, this secluded resort makes for a good getaway. It's close to the beach and has a large pool and interesting gardens.

Pansea Puri Bali (Map p130; ☎ 701605; www.pansea.com; Jl Yoga Perkanti; cottages US$150-250;) Set in nice grounds complete with a figure-eight pool that looks onto open ocean, the 41 cottages have private gardens, deeply shaded patios and stylish room design. Huge-screen TVs should lure couch potatoes.

Hotel Intercontinental Bali (Map p130; ☎ 701888; www.bali.intercontinental.com; Jl Ulu Watu; r from US$155;) With 425 rooms, the Intercontinental is really a megalopolis, but it's a beautiful behemoth, decorated with Balinese arts and handicrafts. The plethora of pools feed each other and meander through the grounds. There is a good kids' club and the crescent of beach is fine.

Ritz Carlton (Map p128; ☎ 702222; www.ritzcarlton.com; r US$200-400, villas US$300-750;) The luxury here is hidden in vast private grounds and a compound overlooking the sea located three kilometres southwest of Jimbaran. Rooms are spacious and set in large blocks. With 290 rooms and 48 villas, this is the place for people who want a grand and lavish resort setting. The Ritz jealously guards its own gorgeous beach.

Four Seasons Jimbaran Bay (Map p130; ☎ 701010; www.fourseasons.com; villas with/without ocean frontage US$695/585;) The 147 villas are designed in a traditional Balinese manner complete with a carved entranceway, which opens onto an open-air dining pavilion overlooking a water-sucking plunge pool. The spa is guests-only, which keeps the riff-raff out – maybe they can keep eating cake. The Ganeesha Gallery with its regular exhibitions of fine Balinese art draws many visitors.

SOUTH BALI

Eating

The warung are the destination of tourists across the south. Jimbaran's three groups of **seafood warung** do fresh barbecued seafood every evening (and noon at many). The open-sided affairs are right by the beach and perfect for enjoying sea breezes and sunsets. Tables and chairs are set up on the sand – almost to the water's edge.

The usual deal is to select your seafood fresh from iced displays or tanks and pay according to weight. Expect to pay around 35,000Rp per 100g for live lobster, 15,000Rp to 20,000Rp for prawns, and 7500Rp for fish, squid and clams. Prices are open to negotiation and the accuracy of the scales is a joke among locals.

At the best places the fish is soaked in a garlic and lime marinade, then doused with chilli and oil while grilling over coconut husks. At night you can't see the thick clouds of smoke from the coals. But you can hear the roaming bands, who perform tunes from the 'I've got to be me' playlist. Many people actually join in.

The longest row of restaurants is at the **northern seafood warung**, south of the fish market. This is the area where you will be taken by a taxi if you don't specify otherwise. Most of these places are restaurant-like with tables inside and out on the immaculate raked sand. Call for free transport to/from much of the south. Recommendations include:

Pudak Cafe (Map p130; ☎ 0813-3855 3800; Jl Pantai Kedonganan) Many fish displays.

Sharky's (Map p130; Jl Pantai Kedonganan) Takes credit cards.

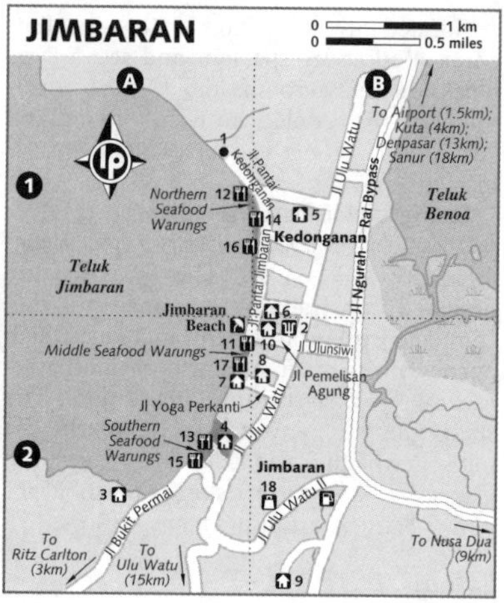

SIGHTS & ACTIVITIES

Fish Market	1 A1
Ganeesha Gallery	(see 3)
Pura Ulun Siwi	2 B2

SLEEPING

Four Seasons Jimbaran Bay	3 A2
Hotel Intercontinental Bali	4 A2
Hotel Puri Bambu	5 B1
Jimbaran Ocean Cottages	6 B1
Pansea Puri Bali	7 A2
Puri Kosala	8 B2
Udayana Eco Lodge	9 B2
Villa Batu	10 B2

EATING

Cafe Nyoman	11 A2
Pudak Cafe	12 A1
Roma	13 A2
Sharky's	14 B1
Teba Cafe	15 A2
Uluwatu Cafe	16 A1
Warung Bamboo	17 A2

SHOPPING

Jenggala Keramik Bali	18 B2

Uluwatu Café (Map p130; Jl Pantai Kedonganan) Comfy rattan furniture.

The **middle seafood warung** are in a compact group just south of Jl Pantai Jimbaran and Jl Pemelisan Agung. These seafood warung are the simplest affairs, with old-fashioned thatched roofs and wide-open sides. The beach is a little more natural, with the fishing boats resting up on the sand. Don't plan on getting any public transport out here though. Recommendations for warung along this part of the beach include the following:

Cafe Nyoman (Map p130; ☎ 703170; Jl Pantai Jimbaran)
Warung Bamboo (Map p130; ☎ 702188; off Jl Pantai Jimbaran)

The **southern seafood warung** are just north of the Four Seasons Jimbaran Bay. In many ways the warung are like the three bears: this group is not as formal as the northern group, not as rickety as the middle group – they are just right. There's a parking area off Jl Bukit Permai and the places are right in a row. The beach here is well-groomed with nice trees. Call for transport. Recommendations:

Roma (Map p130; ☎ 702387; off Jl Bukit Permai) Redolent with garlic.
Teba Cafe (Map p130; ☎ 0817-346 068; off Jl Bukit Permai) Lots of special platters.

The luxury hotels have nice cafés and restaurants right on the beach and can be a fine place to visit for brunch or lunch with a view.

Shopping

Jenggala Keramik Bali (Map p130; ☎ 703310; Jl Ulu Watu II; 9am-6pm) A modern warehouse with air-con showcases beautiful ceramic homewares. There's a viewing area where you can watch production, and a café. Ceramic courses are available for adults and children (US$10/50 for one/six sessions). The outlet store for Jenggala is Gudang Keramik in Sanur (p146).

Getting There & Away

Public bemo from Tegal terminal in Denpasar go via Kuta to Jimbaran (10,000Rp), and continue to Nusa Dua. They don't run after about 4pm, but plenty of taxis wait around the beachfront warung in the evening to take replete diners back to Kuta (about 30,000Rp) or wherever. If you're dining at the seafood warung, call to try to arrange free transport.

CENTRAL BUKIT

Jl Ulu Watu goes south of Jimbaran, climbing 200m up the peninsula's namesake hill, affording views over southern Bali.

For years the only tourist facilities on the west coast of the Bukit were a few warung at the surf breaks, but in the late 1990s speculation ran rampant. Most of it came to little beyond a few scars on the land, with one notable exception.

Garuda Wisnu Kencana Cultural Park (GWK; Map p128; ☎ 703603; admission 15,000Rp, parking 5000Rp; 8am-6pm) is the yet to be completed huge cultural park that is meant to be home to a

A GIANT SPONGE

Begun in the boom-boom 1990s and stalled by the economic crisis later in the decade, Pecatu Indah is a 400-hectare resort complex rising between central Bukit Peninsula and the coast. The land is arid but that hasn't stopped the developers from planning a huge hotel, condos, houses and, worst of all, an 18-hole golf course. Follow the grand boulevards and you can see that the course doesn't benefit from any water-conserving measures such as shade. You do see a lot of water trucks driving around.

Meanwhile, with greens almost overlooking Dreamland, the future of the many vendors and families working there is in doubt. There is talk that the entire beach area might be seized for something upscale – something that uses a lot of water no doubt.

66m-high statue of Garuda. This Brobdinagian dream is supposed to be erected on top of a shopping and gallery complex, for a total height of 146m. Touted as the biggest and highest statue in the world, it is to be surrounded by performance spaces, art galleries, a food court and an adventure playground.

Well that's the plan. So far the only completed part of a statue is the large bronze head. The buildings that do exist are mostly empty. At least the parking lot has good views over South Bali. Despite annual pronouncements of imminent resumption of construction, you're more likely to see a guard chipping golf balls or a cow chewing a cud than a huge erection of a sacred statue.

As it stands – or doesn't – the deserted site is not worth going out of your way for except for the views.

Sleeping

With great views north across much of southern Bali, **Ellie's** (Map p128; ☎ 770517; www.ellies-Bali.com; Jl Tanan Lawangan, Mumbul; r US$25-45;) is one of the Bukit's best deals. The best rooms at this family-run place have sweeping views and shady balconies. There's a nice pool, a café, library, DVD player and more. The access road is off Jl Ngurah Rai By Pass in the village of Mumbul three kilometres west of Nusa Dua.

DREAMLAND

Once a remote surf break, **Dreamland**, as it's commonly known, is now a trendy scene. Reached by passing through the vast development of Pecatu Indah (above), this perfect cove of a beach is surrounded by cliffs. On most days, those in the know line the sands watching surfers and taking comfort at the growing number of simple bamboo-topped warung. It's all a little wild: planning is non-existent as is pavement (after the grand boulevard ends) and it's not uncommon to see a cow wandering past lithe Versace-clad beauties.

Another noted surf break, **Balangan**, is north of Dreamland. Follow the paved road around and look for the path. For details about surfing at these two, see p79. Both are treacherous for swimming.

Dewi's Warung (Map p128; ☎ 081 5555 1722; r 150,000-250,000Rp) is right on the beach. The seven simple rooms have fans and stunning views. Nearby, **Robby & The Kids** (Map p128; ☎ 081-2367 9212; robbyandrosita@hotmail.com; r 50,000Rp) has four very basic rooms and tables on the sand. No extra credit for guessing who owns the place.

Dreamland (Lemongkak to the locals) is four kilometres off the Ulu Watu road. Pass through the grand gates of Pecatu Indah and follow the grand boulevard – and golf course – until the road ends. There you pay an entrance fee of 5000Rp to drive another few hundred metres and park on the deeply rutted terrain. The best route is to go as far to the right as possible as this puts you close to the beach and saves a long walk down the cliff.

Taxis from the Kuta area cost from 30,000Rp to 40,000Rp per hour for the round trip and waiting time.

ULU WATU & AROUND

The important temple, **Pura Luhur Ulu Watu** (Map p128), adds a cultural dimension to the west coast of the Bukit Peninsula, which among surfers is one of the world's most fabled spots.

The surf breaks here are always popular and the area boasts numerous small inns and warung that sell and rent surfboards, and provide food, drink, ding repairs or a massage – whatever you need most. **Pantai Suluban** is the only good place to swim in the area. From its bluff, you get a good view of all the area surf breaks.

Coming from the east to Suluban you will first encounter a gated parking area (car/motorcycle 2000/1000Rp), which is about a 400m walk from the water. Continuing over a bridge, there is an older parking area (car/motorcycle 1000/500Rp) that is a hilly 200m from the water. Watch out for 'gate-keepers' looking for bonuses.

Sights & Activities

SURFING

A paved road goes northwest from Pecatu village (turn right at the small temple), passing a rugged small side road branching off to **Bingin,** a popular beach with savage surf and a renowned left break. **Impossibles** is nearby, **Padang Padang** is about one kilometre on and there is parking just north of a bridge.

Ulu Watu (Ulu's) is a legendary surf spot – the stuff of dreams and nightmares. It's about one kilometre south of Padang Padang and its legend is matched closely by nearby **Pantai Suluban.** Since the early 1970s these breaks have drawn surfers from around the world. The left breaks seem to go on forever.

See p79 for more on surfing in this area.

PURA LUHUR ULU WATU

This **temple** (Map p128; admission 3000Rp, incl sarong & sash rental; parking 1000Rp; ☉ 8am-7pm) is one of several important temples to the spirits of the sea along the south coast of Bali. In the 11th century, the Javanese priest Empu Kuturan first established a temple here. The temple was added to by Nirartha, another Javanese priest who is known for the seafront temples at Tanah Lot (see p272), Rambut Siwi (see p278) and Pura Sakenan (see p147). Nirartha retreated to Ulu Watu for his final days when he attained *moksa* (freedom from earthly desires).

The temple is perched precipitously on the southwestern tip of the peninsula, atop sheer cliffs that drop straight into the pounding surf. You enter through an unusual arched gateway flanked by statues of Ganesha. Inside the walls of coral bricks are covered with intricate carvings of Bali's mythological menagerie. Only Hindu worshippers can enter the small inner temple.

The real attraction is the location – for a good angle, especially at sunset, walk around the cliff top to the left (south) of the temple.

Watch out for monkeys, which – when not reproducing – like to snatch sunglasses, handbags, hats and anything else within reach.

An enchanting **Kecak dance** is held in the temple grounds at sunset; tickets cost 35,000Rp. Although the performance obviously caters for tourists, the gorgeous setting makes it one of the more delightful on the island.

Sleeping

There's a whole string of cheap and very basic surfing dives on the main road from Pecatu. If you're not picky you can count on being able to find accommodation of some sort near the surf break of your choice. Expect to pay about 50,000Rp for a room with cold water, a fan and a shared bathroom. Many surfers choose to stay in Kuta and make the commute of less than an hour.

Thomas Homestay (Map p128; ☎ 0813-3813 0583; r 60,000-70,000Rp) A bare-bones four-room place on cliffs overlooking a lonely beach of people fishing and seaweed growers. The cold-water bathrooms are shared. Look for the crushed coral road just west of the Padang Padang surf break.

Padang Padang Inn (Map p128; ☎ 0812 391 3617; Jl Melasti 432; r 70,000Rp) A better than average budget place, this place has 24 clean rooms with private cold-water bathrooms and a nice little café.

Gong (Map p128; ☎ 081-5578 4754; thegongacc@yahoo .com; Jl Pantai Suluban; r 175,000Rp) You can't go wrong at the Gong. Eight tidy rooms with good ventilation and hot water face a small compound and have distant ocean views. There's also a café and surf shop.

Rocky Bungalows (Map p128; ☎ 0817 346 209; off Jl Ulu Watu; r 250,000-450,000Rp; ✵ ☚) There's nothing ostentatious about this low-key place just west of the Padang Padang surf break. It has 10 rooms with views out to sea from the balconies and pool and is a three-minute walk to the water.

Uluwatu Resort (Map p128; ☎ 7420610; www.uluwa turesort.com; Jl Pantai Suluban; villas US$70-100; ✵ ☐ ☚) On the cliff top across the river from Pantai Suluban, this stylish place has the kind of ocean views you go on holiday for. It's laidback and a good place to soak up the sea.

Blue Point Bay Villas & Spa (Map p128; ☎ 7441077; www.bluepointbayvillas.com; Jl Labuansait; villas from US$230; ✵ ☚) A 31-unit resort with attitude – and altitude – above the Pantai Suluban break, it

DETOUR: THE SOUTH COAST

The south coast of the Bukit Peninsula has high wind-blown cliffs and big swells. Development choked off after the 1990s and, as you gaze out to the whitecaps of the Indian Ocean, you know you're at the edge of things.

Lots of little tracks lead to the cliffs from the southern roads linking Nusa Dua with Pecatu via Kuluh. Try exploring some. From the west, look for a steep track down to the beach and the **Green Ball** surf break about 4km from the little village of Ulu Watu. Other roads lead down to the coast to small beaches and sea temples such as **Pura Gunung Payung** (Map p128), which is near the invasive Nikko Bali Resort, a Soeharto-era leftover. Diminutive **Pura Mas Suka** (Map p128) is reached by a twisting narrow road through a barren, red-rock landscape, but the views are divine. See p79 for details of the area's surf breaks.

has a lovely pool where you can float while the sun goes down. Service and the restaurant are both high calibre.

Eating

Most of the hotels and inns have restaurants and any beach where there's surfers will have a few warung selling necessities like beer. There are cafés on the road looping around from Pecatu, with several nice ones near Pura Luhur Ulu Watu.

Jiwa Juice (Map p128; ☎ 7424196; Jl Melasti; sandwiches 15,000-20,000Rp;) Jiwa means 'soul', and the juices and fresh, light food here are good for the same. This popular stop has internet access.

Yeye's Warung (Map p128; Jl Labuan Sait; dishes 18,000-25,000Rp) A gathering point away from the cliffs, there's an easy-going ambience, cheapish beers and tasty Western, Indonesian and vegetarian food. Many gather for the pizza.

Getting There & Away

The best way to see the west coast is with your own vehicle or by chartering a taxi. Note that the cops often set up traps near Pecatu Indah for motorcycle-riding Westerners. While you pay a fine for a 'loose' chin strap, helmet-less locals wiz by laughing.

Public bemo to Ulu Watu are infrequent and stop running by mid-afternoon. Some of the dark-blue bemo from Kuta serve Jimbaran and Ulu Watu – it's best to catch one west of Tuban (on Jl Raya Kuta, outside the Supernova shopping centre) or Jimbaran (on Jl Ulu Watu).

You may see offers in Kuta or Sanur to see the sunset or the Kecak dance at the temple. These cost from about 80,000Rp and sometimes include a side trip to a beach or to Jimbaran.

NUSA DUA

Nusa Dua translates literally as 'Two Islands' – although they are actually small raised headlands, each with a little temple. But Nusa Dua is much better known as Bali's gated compound of resort hotels. It's a vast and manicured place where you leave the rest of the island as you pass the guard. Gone are the street vendors, hustle, bustle and engaging chaos of the rest of the island. Here you even talk more quietly.

Built in the 1970s, Nusa Dua was designed to compete with international beach resorts the world over. The goal was to attract free-spending holiday-makers while keeping them isolated from the rest of the island. Balinese 'culture' in the form of attenuated dances and other performances was literally trucked in for the masses nightly.

With thousands of hotel rooms Nusa Dua took on a definite life when it was full. But these days occupancy is down, with many people who want an anonymous beach holiday going elsewhere. The Bali Collection, a shopping centre that is continually rebuilt in an effort to give it a spark, is more desolate walled camp than festive retail centre.

Still, the hotel grounds are as well groomed as the staff and there is a huge range of services at these places. Just outside the gates, the village of Bualu is a real Balinese town. It has shops with decent prices and tourist restaurants that would not be out of place in Kuta.

Orientation & Information

Nusa Dua is very spread out. You enter the enclave through one of the big guarded gateways, and inside there are expansive lawns, manicured gardens and sweeping driveways leading to the lobbies of large resort hotels. It can be surprisingly confusing to walk anywhere as streets curve this way and that.

In the middle of the resort, the **Bali Collection** (Map p135; ☎ 771662) shopping centre has some chain stores and an ATM. For most supplies, try the Tragia Shopping Centre (see p136). A **post office** (Map p135; Jl Ngurah Rai) is nearby.

All of the hotels have doctors on call.

Activities

BEACH PROMENADE

One of the nicest features of Nusa Dua is the five-kilometre-long beach promenade that stretches the length of the resort and continues north along much of the beach in Tanjung Benoa. Not only is it a good stroll at any time but it also makes it easy to sample the pleasures of the other beachside resorts. The walk is paved for most of its length.

SURFING & BEACHES

The reef-protected beach at Nusa Dua is shallow at low tide, and the wave action is pretty limp. The surf breaks at Nusa Dua are way out on reefs to the north and south of the two 'islands'. They work best with a big swell during the wet season. **Sri Lanka** is a right-hander in front of Club Med. The so-called **Nusa Dua** breaks are peaks, reached by boat from the beach south of the Hilton – go past the golf course and turn left on a dirt road. Nonsurfers from all over southern Bali also flock to this pretty beach, which now has a dozen warung.

The beach between the two peaks behind the Galleria Nusa Dua is also nice and has a large shady and paved parking area that makes it a good stop for day-trippers, especially families, who will enjoy the calm atmosphere.

GOLF

Designed by well-known architects Nelson & Wright, the **Bali Golf & Country Club** (Map p135; ☎ 771791; green fees US$150) is an 18-hole course with all the amenities one would expect from a course at a major resort. Lots of condos are going up along the fairways.

SPAS

All the resort hotels have pricey spas that provide a broad range of therapies, treatments and just plain, simple relaxation. The most lauded of the spas are at the Amanusa, Westin and Grand Hyatt in Nusa Dua (see right) and at the Conrad in Tanjung Benoa (see p138). All are open to non-guests, which means you could just go on a tour!

Sleeping

The Nusa Dua hotels are similar in several ways: they are all big (although some are just plain huge) and they have long beachfronts. Each has several restaurants and bars, as well as various pools and other resort amenities. But what's most important is in the detail as that's where the real differences lie. Some hotels, such as the Westin and Grand Hyatt, have invested heavily in property, adding loads of amenities (such as the elaborate pools and day camps for kids) demanded by travellers today. Other hotels seem little changed from when they were built during the heyday of the Soeharto era in the 1970s.

While some will revel in the resort experience here – scores of restaurants and bars, lots of activities and numerous over-priced shops (all of which can be paid for with the flick of a pen)– others won't make it past the gates.

If you're considering a stay at Nusa Dua, prowl the internet looking for deals. During slack periods, you can get excellent deals that bring nightly rates down towards US$100. The international chains all have wi-fi and broadband in the rooms.

Grand Hyatt Bali (Map p135; ☎ 771234; www.bali.grand.hyatt.com; r from US$200; ☒ ❄ 🖳 🏊) Sort of a little city, the Hyatt has directional signs – which have up to 21 arrows – scattered across the grounds. Like any city, some neighbourhoods are better than others. Some in the West Village (there are four; the East and South Villages are best located) face the taxi parking lot. The river-like pool (one of six) is huge and has a fun slide. The children's club will keep the little joys busy for days. All 648 rooms were recently refurbished.

Westin Resort (Map p135; ☎ 771906; www.westin.com/bali; r from US$200; ☒ ❄ 🖳 🏊) Attached to a large convention centre, the Westin has an air-conditioned lobby (one of only three in Bali) and vast public spaces. Guests in the 355 rooms enjoy the best pools in Nusa. There are waterfalls and more in this aquatic playground. The Kids Club has extensive activities and facilities.

Sheraton Laguna (Map p135; ☎ 771327; www.starwood.com/bali; r from US$240; ☒ ❄ 🖳 🏊) The lobby sets the tone for this 270-room resort: understated with a few royal touches accenting the comfortable rattan furniture. The swimming pools (called 'swimmable lagoons') are vast with sandy beaches, landscaped islands and cascading waterfalls. Room renovations have added slick details such as plasma TVs.

TANJUNG BENOA & NUSA DUA

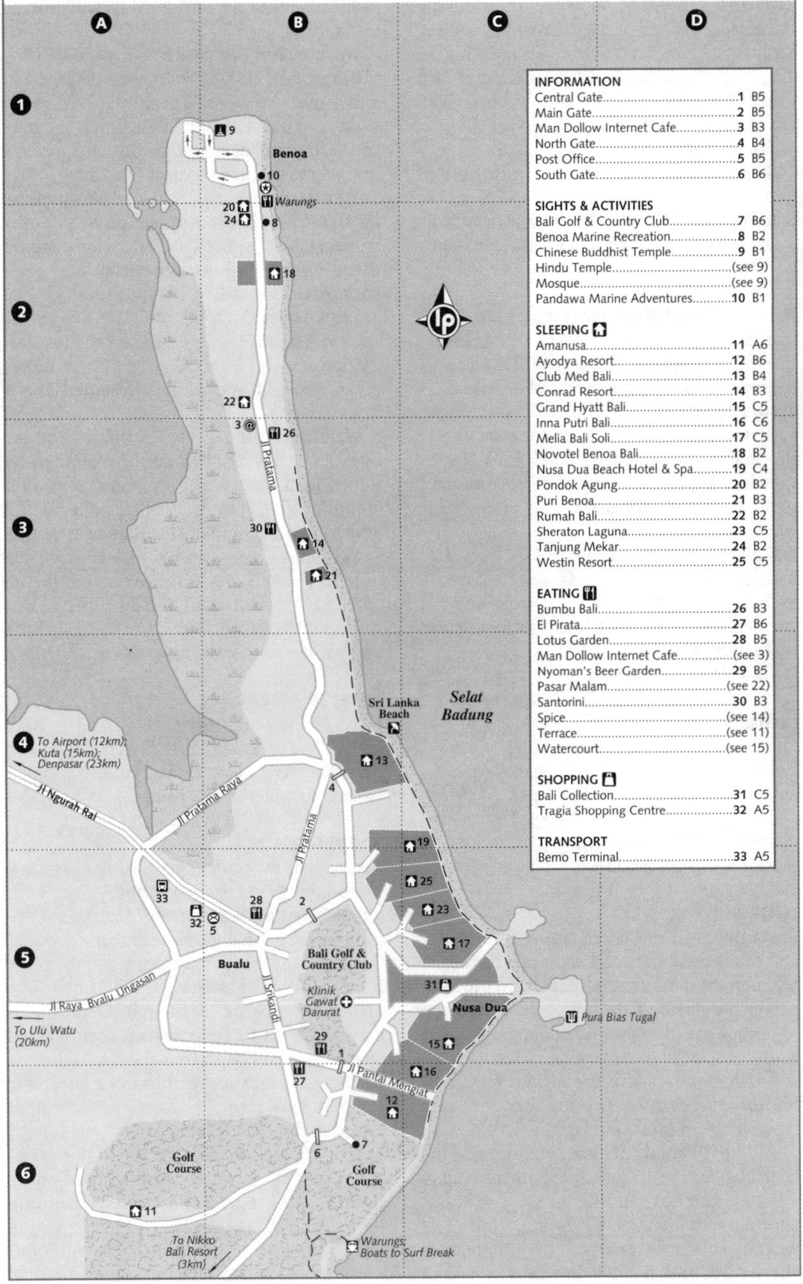
0 1 km
0 0.5 miles
A
B
C
D
1
2
3
4
5
6
INFORMATION
Central Gate....1 B5
Main Gate....2 B5
Man Dollow Internet Cafe....3 B3
North Gate....4 B4
Post Office....5 B5
South Gate....6 B6
SIGHTS & ACTIVITIES
Bali Golf & Country Club....7 B6
Benoa Marine Recreation....8 B2
Chinese Buddhist Temple....9 B1
Hindu Temple....(see 9)
Mosque....(see 9)
Pandawa Marine Adventures....10 B1
SLEEPING
Amanusa....11 A6
Ayodya Resort....12 B6
Club Med Bali....13 B4
Conrad Resort....14 B3
Grand Hyatt Bali....15 C5
Inna Putri Bali....16 C6
Melia Bali Soli....17 C5
Novotel Benoa Bali....18 B2
Nusa Dua Beach Hotel & Spa....19 C4
Pondok Agung....20 B2
Puri Benoa....21 B3
Rumah Bali....22 B2
Sheraton Laguna....23 C5
Tanjung Mekar....24 B2
Westin Resort....25 C5
EATING
Bumbu Bali....26 B3
El Pirata....27 B6
Lotus Garden....28 B5
Man Dollow Internet Cafe....(see 3)
Nyoman's Beer Garden....29 B5
Pasar Malam....(see 22)
Santorini....30 B3
Spice....(see 14)
Terrace....(see 11)
Watercourt....(see 15)
SHOPPING
Bali Collection....31 C5
Tragia Shopping Centre....32 A5
TRANSPORT
Bemo Terminal....33 A5
Benoa
Warungs
Jl Pratama
Sri Lanka Beach
Selat Badung
To Airport (12km); Kuta (15km); Denpasar (23km)
Jl Ngurah Rai
Jl Pratama Raya
Bualu
Bali Golf & Country Club
Klinik Gawat Darurat
Nusa Dua
Pura Bias Tugal
Jl Raya Bvalu Ungasan
To Ulu Watu (20km)
Jl Srikandi
Jl Pantai Mengiat
Golf Course
Golf Course
To Nikko Bali Resort (3km)
Warungs, Boats to Surf Break

Amanusa (Map p135; ☎ 772333; www.amanresorts.com; villas from US$650;) Overlooking the golf course and beyond across the Badung Strait, the Amanusa is one of Bali's best hotels. The elegant, understated architecture, rich decorations, superb service and brilliant views are the province of just 35 individual villas. Guests enjoy a private beach club.

The other major Nusa Dua resorts are as follows:

Inna Putri Bali (Map p135; ☎ 771020; www.putribali.com; r from US$120;) This 384-room resort lacks the spark of other places. It's popular with value-conscious tour groups.

Nusa Dua Beach Hotel & Spa (Map p135; ☎ 771210; www.nusaduahotel.com; r from US$150;) The design of many of the 381 plush rooms has a curious preponderance of walls where there could be windows.

Ayodya Resort (Map p135; ☎ 771102; www.balihilton.com; r from US$160;) An enormous place with 537 rooms (although it actually feels bigger) in six-storey blocks, the Ayodya dropped the Hilton name in 2006. Lagoons covering the grounds are all for show – for swimming use the okay pool.

Nikko Bali Resort (Map p128; ☎ 773377; www.nikkobali.com; r from US$150;) About 3km south of the enclave, the 16-storey, 390-room Nikko is dramatically built down the side of an otherwise unspoiled cliff facing the sea.

Melia Bali Soli (Map p135; ☎ 771510; www.meliabali.com; r from US$170;) The resort has 489 contemporary rooms with a 'Bali Style' look. The large, naturalistic pool is good and there is shade by the beach.

Club Med Bali (Map p135; ☎ 771521; www.clubmed.com; 1-week all-inclusive from US$1000;) A walled enclave within the Nusa Dua walled enclave, the Club Med has oodles of activities to keep guests entertained and mere mortals out.

Eating

Restaurants in the hotels are in abundance and many are quite good, although the prices are high even by top-end Bali standards. For people not staying at the hotels, the best reason to venture in is if you want a bounteous Sunday brunch at one of the international chains.

South of the enclave, the various warung at the surfers' beach serve some very good and typically fresh local standards.

Along Jl Pantai Mengiat, just outside the central gate, South Gate, there are a string of open-air eateries offering an unpretentious alternative to Nusa Dua dining. None will win any culinary awards but they are relaxed alternatives and, if you pause long enough in front of any, the staff will offer you escalating inducements to step inside. Most will provide transport.

Nyoman's Beer Garden (Map p135; ☎ 775746; Jl Pantai Mengiat; dishes 25,000-50,000Rp) Some tables are in and some are out at this lively place with a big U-shaped bar. The handy menu has pictures of the myriad of menu choices from pizza mafioso to schnitzel to beef rendang.

El Pirata (Map p135; ☎ 776644; Jl Pantai Mengiat; dishes 25,000-60,000Rp) The place to get a pirate's favourite vegetable: caRRRRots. The wide-ranging menu at this simple joint means you can even get mARRRRmalade with your toast.

Lotus Garden (Map p135; ☎ 773378; Jl Ngurah Rai; dishes 25,000-70,000Rp) One of the higher quality options, this Lotus Garden branch serves pizza, seafood and nicely presented Indonesian dishes.

Watercourt (Map p135; ☎ 771234; Grand Hyatt Bali; dishes 80,000-200,000Rp; dinner) Surrounded by ponds with lily pads, it is a romantic vision at night with its hundreds of tea light candles and twinkling lights. The Balinese food is exquisite.

Terrace (Map p135; ☎ 772333; Amanusa; dishes 80,000-200,000Rp; lunch & dinner) You'll be torn at this restaurant between looking at the sweeping view or the excellent Thai cuisine.

Entertainment

Most of the hotels offer Kecak and Legong dances one or more nights. Hotel lounges also often have live music, from crooners crooning ballads to mellow rock bands.

Shopping

Just outside the resort, Bualu village has some reasonably priced tourist shops.

Bali Collection (Map p135; ☎ 771662) This shopping centre has had numerous name changes. The latest incarnation is mostly empty except for the dozens of assistants in the small Sogo Department Store. Although its problems can be traced to the rigorous security and closed nature of Nusa Dua, the isolation from Balinese life means that it hasn't enjoyed the boom in local shoppers experienced by other island malls.

Tragia Shopping Centre (Map p135; ☎ 772170; Jl Ngurah Rai) Has a variety store with an entire floor devoted to souvenirs, several fast-food outlets and ATMs. A sign in the main store has the following unintentionally ominous message: 'After checking out from your hotel come spend your last hours with your friends at Tragia.'

Getting There & Away

The fixed taxi fare from the airport is 85,000Rp; a metered taxi *to* the airport will be much cheaper. Public bemo travel between Denpasar's Tegal terminal and the terminal at Bualu (10,000Rp). From Bualu, it's at least a kilometre to the hotels – not that anyone we know paying US$200 per night has ever taken a bemo to Nusa Dua. Bemo run less frequently from Denpasar's Batubulan terminal (10,000Rp).

Getting Around

Find out what shuttle bus services your hotel provides before you start calling taxis. A free **shuttle bus** (☎ 771662; 🕑 9am-10pm) connects all Nusa Dua and Tanjung Benoa resort hotels with the Bali Collection shopping centre about every hour.

TANJUNG BENOA

The peninsula of Tanjung Benoa extends about 4km north from Nusa Dua to Benoa village. It's flat and lined with resort hotels, most of midrange calibre. The downturn in Bali visitors has hit this area hard, with many places now closed. However, it does have one restaurant that makes the trip worthwhile.

Like beaches at Sanur and Nusa Dua, those here are protected from waves by an offshore reef. However, that has allowed a local beach activities industry to flourish in the placid waters. Overall Tanjung Benoa is a fairly sedate place, especially at night.

Orientation & Information

Restaurants and hotels are really strung out along Jl Pratama, which runs the length of the peninsula. It may be one of the most perilous streets in South Bali for a stroll. From the Nusa Dua north gate north to the Conrad Hotel, there are no sidewalks and in many places nowhere to walk but on the narrow road, which also has blind curves. Fortunately, the delightful beach promenade is a lovely alternative.

The police station is easy to find and hotels have doctors on call. There's middling internet access at **Man Dollow Internet Cafe** (Map p135; ☎ 748 3887; Jl Pratama). Other services can be found south in the Nusa Dua area.

Sights

Benoa is one of Bali's multi-denominational corners, with an interesting **Chinese Buddhist temple** (Map p135), a **mosque** (Map p135) and a **Hindu temple** (Map p135) within 100m. It's an interesting little fishing town that makes for a good stroll. On the dark side, however, it is also the centre of Bali's illegal trade in turtles (p70).

Activities

Quite a few water-sports centres along Jl Pratama offer daytime diving, cruises, windsurfing and water-skiing. Check equipment and credentials before you sign up. Most have a thatched-roof bar and restaurant attached to their premises. Each morning convoys of buses arrive from all over South Bali bringing day-trippers to enjoy the calm waters and various activities. By 10am parasailers float over the water like a flock of egrets looking for a place to land.

Among the established water sports operators are **Pandawa Marine Adventures** (Map p135; ☎ 778585; Jl Pratama) and **Benoa Marine Recreation** (BMR; Map p135; ☎ 771757; Jl Pratama). As if by magic, all operators have similar prices.

Water sports include the following:

Banana-boat rides (per 15min US$25) Wild rides for two as you try to maintain your grasp of the inflatable fruit over the waves.

Diving With the operators mentioned, diving costs US$80/100 for one or two dives around Tanjung Benoa, including equipment rental; US$120 for two dives in Tulamben; and about US$380 for a three-day Professional Association of Diving Instructors (PADI) open-water course. A minimum of two people is required for most dive trips and courses.

Glass-bottomed boat trips (90-min tour with snack US$35) The non-wet way to see the denizens of the shallow.

Jet-skiing (per 15min US$25) Big with people who like to go fast and belch smoke.

Parasailing (per round US$25) Popular; you float above the water while towed by a speedboat.

Snorkelling (per hr per person US$25) These trips include equipment and a boat ride to a reef (minimum two people).

Sleeping

The Conrad Resort is the notable high-end and high-profile hotel amid what are mostly midrange places aimed at groups. Unfortunately several of the places that were full of character have closed.

BUDGET

A few places close to Benoa village offer no-frills accommodation across the road from the beach.

Pondok Agung (Map p135; ☎ 771143; roland@eksadata.com; Jl Pratama; r 100,000-250,000Rp;) The 11 cheery rooms in a large house-like building are good value. Higher priced rooms come with air-con and TV.

Tanjung Mekar (Map p135; ☎ 081-2363 1374; Jl Pratama; r from 90,000Rp) Set in a little garden, this small guesthouse has four simple, pleasant rooms.

MIDRANGE

Rumah Bali (Map p135; ☎ 771256; www.balifoods.com; Jl Pratama; r US$60-100;) Rumah Bali is a luxurious interpretation of a Balinese village by Heinz von Holzen of Bumbu Bali fame (right. Guests have large family rooms or individual villas (some with three bedrooms) with their own plunge pools. There's a 'village centre' with a delectable warung (Pasar Malam, see right). Besides a large communal pool, there's also a tennis court. The beach is a short walk away.

Novotel Benoa Bali (Map p135; ☎ 772239; www.novotelbali.com; Jl Pratama; r from US$70;) The Novotel straddles both sides of the busy road, so you know which side to get a room (hint: think sand). The 175 rooms and facilities are tasteful with whimsical touches like a huge pineapple sculpture. The beach here beats the pool.

Puri Benoa (Map p135; ☎ 771634; www.puribenoa.com; Jl Pratama; r from US$75;) It feels a bit like a boutique hotel on the beach, with only 18 bungalow-style rooms. Some of the décor of Puri Benoa has a dated feel, but the outdoor bathrooms in the rooms are airy delights. More money gets you a villa on the beach.

TOP END

Some top-end resorts are really time-share properties renting out rooms, while others are used almost exclusively by people on package tours.

Conrad Resort (Map p135; ☎ 778788; www.conradhotels.com; Jl Pratama; r from US$150;) Tajung Benoa's best hotel is from the luxury branch of the Hilton chain. It combines Bali modern styling with a refreshing, casual style. The 314 rooms are large and thoughtfully designed. Some units have patios with steps right down into the lake-sized pool, easing the morning dip. Bungalows have their own private lagoon and there is a large kids' club.

Eating & Drinking

Each hotel has several restaurants. There are also several tourist restaurants in or near Tajung Benoa. On the border with Nusa Dua, some warung cater to hotel guests and offer good value for money, while several busy local warung are clustered around the police station in Benoa.

Man Dollow Internet Cafe (Map p135; ☎ 748 3887; Jl Pratama; meals 10,000-20,000Rp;) There's middling internet access here and simple dishes served under a thatched roof.

Santorini (Map p135; ☎ 777942; Jl Pratama; meals 30,000-60,000Rp) A vision of white, this taverna brings the Greek Islands to the island of Bali. One of the more fun places on this street, the food is authentic – the wine too (not that that is a plus…).

Pasar Malam (Map p135; ☎ 771256; Jl Pratama; dishes 20,000-70,000Rp) Inside Rumah Bali (left), this warung fulfils the role of the village market eatery. There are local coffees, and exhibits and dishes celebrate the many forms of Balinese rice. The food is of the same high standard as that at Bumbu Bali.

our pick Bumbu Bali (Map p135; ☎ 774502; Jl Pratama; dishes 45,000-70,000Rp; noon-9pm) One of the finest restaurants on the island, Bumbu Bali serves the best Balinese food you'll have during your visit. Long-time resident and cookbook author Heinz von Holzen, his wife Puji and an enthusiastic staff serve exquisitely flavoured dishes beautifully. Many diners opt for one of several set menus (185,000Rp). The rijstaffel shows the range of cooking in the kitchen from satays served on their own little coconut husk grill to the tender *be celeng base manis* (pork in sweet soy sauce) to the amazingly tasty and different *jaja batun bedil* (sticky dumpling rice in palm sugar) with a dozen more courses in between.

The frenetic von Holzen can be seen everywhere during opening hours, one minute adjusting the artful presentation of a dish, the next checking the seasoning of another and stopping for a moment to help with a backlog of dishes. The staff takes these cues and is both skilled and engaging. The tables are set under the stars and in small pavilions. The sound of frogs can be heard from the fish ponds. There's complimentary transport in the area. It's wise to book.

Von Holzen also runs a cooking school on many days. It starts with a 6am visit to Jimbaran's fish and village markets to buy goods and finishes with lunch (US$75). And the empire extends to Rumah Bali (opposite) and Pasar Malam (opposite).

Spice (Map p135; ☎ 778788; Conrad Resort, Jl Pratama; dishes 80,000-200,000Rp; ⏲ dinner) Has a grand setting atop the hotel with tables inside and out. Nusa Lembongan twinkles in the distance. Service is excellent; the wine list voluminous.

Getting There & Around

Taxis from the airport cost 100,000Rp. Take a bemo to Bualu (see p137), then take one of the infrequent green bemo that shuttle up and down Jl Pratama (3000Rp) – after about 3pm bemo become really scarce on both routes. A metered taxi will be much easier and quicker. Or walk the beach promenade.

SANUR

☎ **0361**

Sanur is often saddled with the moniker 'Snore' and while it's true that the relaxed pace locally can take some people a while to appreciate, it's also true that this has long been the locale for people who prefer things simple and unhurried.

It's a very relaxed alternative to Kuta, with a fraction of the hassles – and some would say a fraction of the fun. But that really depends on who you are. True, if you want a foam party in Sanur you'll need a bar of soap and bathtub. But if you'd rather not be hectored by cries of 'transport?', get stuck in hot, sweaty traffic or just plain tire of lanes teaming with chaos, then Sanur is perfect.

In keeping with the local demeanour, the white-sand beach is sheltered by a reef and the surf is sedate, making it popular with some parents. At low tide the beach is wide, but the water is shallow and you have to pick your way out over rocks and coral through knee-deep water. At high tide the swimming is fine, but the beach is narrow and almost nonexistent in places.

A walk on the delightful beachside walkway (try that in Kuta) reveals views of Nusa Penida and East Bali and brings you past numerous cafés. Offshore you'll see gnarled fishermen in woven bamboo hats standing in the shallows rod-fishing for a living and, at the northern end of the beach, elderly men convivially gather at sunrise and beyond for *meditasi* – swimming and baking in the black volcanic sand found only at that end of the beach.

HISTORY

Inscriptions on a stone pillar found near modern Sanur tell of King Sri Kesari Varma, who came to Bali to teach Buddhism in AD 913.

Sanur was one of the places favoured by Westerners during their pre-war discovery of Bali. Artists Miguel Covarrubias, Adrien Jean Le Mayeur and Walter Spies, anthropologist Jane Belo and choreographer Katharane Mershon all spent time here. The first simple tourist bungalows appeared in Sanur in the 1940s and 1950s, and more artists, including Australian Donald Friend and Scotsman Ian Fairweather, made their homes in Sanur. This early popularity made Sanur a likely locale for Bali's first big tourist hotel, the Soekarno-era Inna Grand Bali Beach Hotel.

Over this period, Sanur was ruled by insightful priests and scholars, who recognised both the opportunities and the threats presented by the expanding tourism. Properly horrified at the high-rise Bali Beach Hotel, they imposed the famous rule that no building could be higher than a coconut palm. They also established village cooperatives that owned land and ran tourist businesses, ensuring that a good share of the economic benefits remained in the community.

The priestly influence remains strong, and Sanur is one of the few communities still ruled by members of the Brahmana caste. It is known as a home of sorcerers and healers, and a centre for both black and white magic. The black-and-white chequered cloth known as *kain poleng* – which symbolises the balance of good and evil – is emblematic of Sanur.

ORIENTATION

Sanur stretches for about 5km along an east-facing coastline, with the lush and green landscaped grounds of resorts fronting right onto the sandy beach. The monstrous Grand Bali Beach Hotel, located at the northern end of the strip, fronts the best stretch of beach. West of the beachfront hotels is the noisy main drag, Jl Danau Tamblingan, with hotel entrances, oodles of tourist shops, restaurants and cafés.

Jl Ngurah Rai, commonly called Bypass Rd, skirts the western side of the resort area, and is the main link to Kuta and the airport.

INFORMATION

Bookshops

Other than a few used book exchanges in hotels that will allow you to complete your Dan Brown collection, Sanur lacks a good bookshop.

Hardy's Supermarket (Map p140; ☎ 285806; Jl Danau Tamblingan 136; 🕑 8am-10pm) Sells newspapers and magazines.

Emergency

Police station (Map p140; ☎ 288597; Bypass Rd)

Internet Access

Cybergate (Map p140; ☎ 287274; Jl Danau Tamblingan; per hr 15,000Rp; 🕑 8am-10pm) Broadband; burns CDs.

Star Café Bali (Map p140; ☎ 7439766; Jl Danau Tamblingan 91; per min 500RP) Has fast internet access.

Zoo Restaurant & Bar (Map p140; ☎ 288807; Jl Danau Tamblingan 82) Also has fast internet access.

Medical Services

Guardian Pharmacy (Map p140; ☎ 284343; Jl Danau Tamblingan 134) The chain pharmacy also has a doctor on call.

Money

Moneychangers here have a dubious reputation. There are numerous ATMs along Jl Danau Tamblingan and several banks.

Post

There are convenient postal agencies on Jl Danau Tamblingan.

Post office (Map p140; ☎ 754012; Jl Danau Buyan; 🕑 8am-7pm Mon-Sat) Located west of Jl Ngurah Rai.

SIGHTS

Museum Le Mayeur

The Belgian artist Adrien Jean Le Mayeur de Merpes (1880–1958) arrived in Bali in 1932. Three years later, he met and married the beautiful Legong dancer Ni Polok when she was just 15. They lived in this compound, which houses the museum, when Sanur was still a quiet fishing village. The main house must have been delightful – a peaceful and elegant home filled with art and antiques right by the tranquil beach. After his death, Ni Polok lived in the house until she died in 1985. The house is an interesting example of Balinese-style architecture – notice the beautifully carved window shutters that recount the story of Rama and Sita from the *Ramayana*.

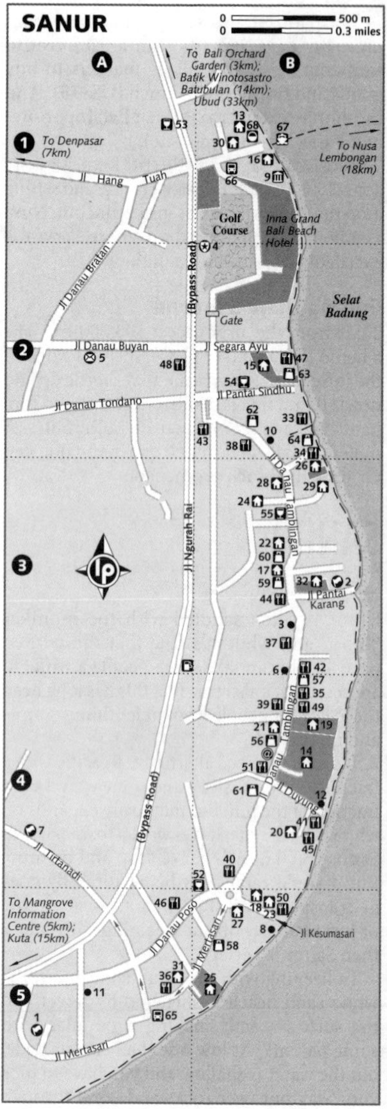

Almost 90 Le Mayeur paintings are displayed inside the **museum** (Map p140; ☎ 286201; adult/child 2000/1000Rp; 🕑 7.30am-3.30pm Mon-Thu, 7.30am-1pm Fri) in a naturalistic Balinese interior of woven fibres. A useful guidebook in English is available. Some of Le Mayer's early works are interesting, Impressionist-style paintings from his travels in Africa, India, Italy, France

and the South Pacific. Paintings from his early period in Bali are romantic depictions of daily life and beautiful Balinese women – often Ni Polok. The works from the 1950s are in much better condition and show less signs of wear and tear, with the vibrant colours that later became popular with young Balinese artists. There are beautiful black-and-white photos of Ni Polok.

Bali Orchid Garden

Given Bali's warm weather and rich volcanic soil, no-one should be surprised that orchids thrive in abundance here. At this **garden** (Map p128; ☎ 466010; Jl Bypass Tohpati; admission 50,000Rp; 8am-6pm) you can see thousands of orchids in a variety of settings. Fans of the beautiful plant will love everything, others will enjoy the back areas, which have a wild tropical feel. The gift shop sells orchid plants as well as books about the gorgeous flowers. It's 3km north of Sanur along Jl Ngurah Rai just past the major intersection with the coast road, Jl Bypass Tohpati.

Stone Pillar

The pillar (Map p140), behind Pura Belangjong, is Bali's oldest dated artefact and has ancient inscriptions recounting military victories of more than 1000 years ago. These inscriptions are in Sanskrit and are evidence of Hindu influence 300 years before the arrival of the Majapahit court.

ACTIVITIES

Surfing

Sanur's fickle breaks (tide conditions often don't produce waves) are offshore along the reef. The best area is called **Sanur Reef**, a right break in front of the Inna Grand Bali Beach Hotel. Another good spot is known as the **Hyatt Reef,** in front of, you guessed it, the Bali Hyatt. However, this break is easily blown out, so only try this one on calm days. See p79 for details on these surf breaks.

Diving

The diving near Sanur is not great, but the reef has a good variety of fish and offers quite good snorkelling. Sanur is the best departure point for dive trips to Nusa Lembongan. A recommended local operator is **Global Aquatic Diving Center** (Map p140; ☎ 282434; www.globalaquatic.com; Jl Kesumasari No 9; local half-day trip €60), which is located right on the beach. Besides trips out to the Sanur Reef, which is known for its lion fish, Global can arrange trips throughout Bali.

Water Sports

Various water sports are offered at kiosks along the beach: close to Museum Le Mayeur; near Sanur Beach Market; and at **Surya Water Sports** (Map p140; ☎ 287956; Jl Duyung). Prices at all three places are similar, and are based on a minimum of two people. You can go parasailing (US$20 per go), jet-skiing (US$25, 15 minutes), water-skiing (US$25, 15 minutes), snorkelling by boat (US$30, two hours), windsurfing (US$30, one hour), or be towed with a pal on an inflatable banana (US$15, 15 minutes).

Spas

Natural Spa (Map p140; ☎ 283677; Jl Danau Tamblingan 23; 2hr massage 450,000Rp; 9am-11pm) is a huge operation, which offers various massages, reflexology and body treatments, including an after-sun treatment.

Most of the large beachside hotels also have spas.

SLEEPING

Usually the best places to stay are right on the beach; however, that isn't always the case here. A few of the properties have been coasting for decades. But in general you shouldn't have a problem finding a place you'll enjoy. Modest budgets will find fiscal succour on the nonbeach side of Jl Danau Tambligan, although overall Sanur is a top-end town.

In case you find yourself at the mercy of a travel agent, don't let them book you into either the Inna Grand Bali Beach Hotel or the Inna Sindhu Beach. Both are well past their prime.

Budget

Watering Hole I (Map p140; ☎ 288289; wateringhole_sanurbali@yahoo.com; Jl Hang Tuah 37; r 60,000-100,000Rp;) In the northern part of Sanur, the Hole is a busy, friendly place close to the Nusa Lembongan boats. There are 25 pleasant, clean rooms with the cheapest having fan cooling and cold water.

Watering Hole II (Map p140; ☎ 270545; wateringhole_sanurbali@yahoo.com; Jl Mertasari; r 80,000-125,000Rp;) The southern branch of the Hole group has 14 rooms and a pool with a little waterfall. All rooms have hot water; the cheaper ones have fans.

Yulia 2 Homestay (Map p140; ☎ 287495; kf_billy@indo.net.id; Jl Danau Tamblingan; s/d 80,000/90,000Rp) Yulia 2 has seven clean, pleasant rooms in a somewhat cramped compound. All have hot water and fans, and there's a fun little café.

> **SANUR'S ENVIRONMENTAL HUB**
>
> **PPLH Bali** (Pusat Pendidikan Lingkungan Hidup; Map p140; ☎ 281684; www.pplhbali.or.id; Jl Danau Tamblingan 168) organises a broad range of environmental and educational programmes. Located in the Hotel Santai (see left), the PPLH has a large library and resource centre. Volunteers and employees are understandably passionate about Bali, its land, the sea and the environmental challenges faced across the island.
>
> Just dropping by to peruse some of the wealth of information on issues such as fair trade or have a chat is an illuminating break. Donations and possibly volunteer services are welcome. With the hotel, the adjacent Café Tali Jiwa helps fund the centre.

Keke Homestay (Map p140; ☎ 287282; Jl Danau Tamblingan 96; s/d 60,000/75,000Rp, with air-con 100,000/150,000Rp;) Set back a little from the noisy main road, Keke welcomes travellers and has seven quiet, clean rooms. All have cold water and fans.

Ananda Beach Hotel (Map p140; ☎ 288327; Jl Hang Tuah 143; s/d US$12/15;) Right on the beach, the Ananda has slightly dark rooms that are jumble of antiques and furniture that's simply old. Deluxe room no 7 has a nice balcony with sea views.

Hotel Santai (Map p140; ☎ 287314; santai@indosat.net.id; Jl Danau Tamblingan 148; s/d 130,000/150,000Rp;) The Santai has 17 clean rooms facing a large pool (nonguests can take the plunge for 5000Rp). It's home to PPLH Bali, see above.

Jati Homestay (Map p140; ☎ 281730; www.balivision.com/hotels/jatihomestay; Jl Danau Tamblingan; r 150,000-200,000Rp) Situated in pretty grounds, the delightful Jati has 15 pleasant and clean bungalows, with small but well-organised kitchen facilities and hot water.

Kesumasari (Map p140; ☎ 287824; Jl Kesumasari 6; r 150,000-200,000Rp;) The only thing between you and the beach is a small shrine. Beyond the comfy lounging porches, the polychromatic carved Balinese doors don't prepare you for the riot of colour inside. No two linens match.

Midrange

Flashbacks (Map p140; ☎ 281682; www.flashbacks-chb.com; Jl Danau Tamblingan 106; r 110,000-340,000Rp;) This welcoming place has nine rooms that vary greatly. The nicer ones are bungalows while more modest ones share kitchens and have cold water. The design takes a lot of cues from traditional Balinese style; the bathrooms are works of stone. There is also a new café.

Hotel Palm Gardens (Taman Palm; Map p140; ☎ 287041; www.palmgarden-bali.com; Jl Kesumasari 3; r from 275,000Rp;) Everything is peaceful here, from the 17 large and comfy rooms to the relaxed service and pretty grounds. It's close to the beach and there is a nice medium-sized pool with a small waterfall.

Hotel Segara Agung (Map p140; ☎ 288446; www.segaraagung.com; Jl Duyung 43; r US$20-35, f US$50;) Down a quiet, unpaved residential street, the hotel is only a two-minute walk to the beach. The 16 rooms are clean and pleasant, staff are friendly and there's a big swimming pool.

Stana Puri Gopa Hotel (Map p140; ☎ 289948; www.purigopabali.com; Jl Kesumasari 4; r US$30-45;) This 24-room hotel has traditional Balinese architecture, large bathrooms, and a small pool. It's a short walk to the beach, which you can see from some rooms.

Diwangkara Beach Hotel (Map p140; ☎ 288577; dhvbali@indosat.net.id; Jl Hang Tuah 54; r from US$40;) Facing the beach near the end of Jl Hang Tuah, this 38-room hotel is a tad old-fashioned (especially the pool), but the smaller bungalows are right by the beach.

Tamu Kami Hotel (Map p140; ☎ 282510; www.tamukami.com; Jl Danau Tamblingan 64X; r US$35-70;) There are 20 large, modern rooms and bungalows, finished with Indonesian touches, overlooking a swimming pool. It is also home to Alise's Restaurant, p145.

Respati Bali (Map p140; ☎ 288427; brespati@indo.net.id; Jl Danau Tamblingan 33; r US$40-60;) Despite its narrow site, the Respati's 32 contemporary bungalow-style rooms don't feel cramped. The beach frontage is a plus and the pool is decent-sized.

SOUTH BALI

A CLASSIC BALINESE DANCER

Besides its cultural importance, Balinese dance just may be a fountain of youth as well. Ask Nyoman Supadmi when she started teaching the art and she says '1970'. A little quick mental calculation confirms that she looks at most half her age.

Lithe and lively, Nyoman has taught thousands of women the precise moves and elaborate choreography demanded by classic Balinese dances such as Legong. And the key word is classic as she has become a major force against the dilution of the island's great dances by what she dismisses as 'modernity'.

And just what is this aberration that brings such a frown to her otherwise serene face. Well, she demonstrates. 'The basic moves of classic dance require enormous discipline,' she says as she slips into the rigid pose with splayed arms and wide eyes that is immediately recognisable to anyone who has seen a performance.

Continuing, she says, 'Modern is like this,' and slumps into a slouch that would do any slacker proud. Still, she understands the allure of the modern. 'It's much easier to learn and people have so many distractions that they can't find the time to learn the old ways.

'My teachers emphasised the basics,' says Nyoman – whose dancer mother provided her with a private tutor. 'Your hand went here and your bottom here,' a statement backed up by a seemingly simple shift of position in her chair that leaves no doubt of her meaning.

'Today people just approximate the position.'

In order to preserve classic Balinese dance, Nyoman promotes dance courses in the schools for students from age five. She keeps an eye out for promising pupils, who can then be guided for the years needed to master the art. A niece is one of these stars and is now much in demand for temple ceremonies and other occasions where sponsors demand the best.

'But the best is expensive,' she admits. There are the fees for large gamelan orchestras, the dances, actors, transport, food and 'just getting people to commit the time needed to be the best.'

Besides local women, Nyoman also teaches visitors, although the coursework is not for those looking for a quick lesson: learning the basics of one dance requires at least 36 two-hour lessons spread over three months – and that doesn't include the extensive homework. Still, at US$10 a lesson, it's a remarkable deal for those with the time to invest. Not only do you learn one of the world's great art forms but one look at Nyoman will confirm other benefits as well.

Nyoman Supadmi offers dance lessons through the Tandjung Sari (see p144).

Hotel Paneeda View (Map p140; ☎ 288425; www.paneedaview.com; Jl Danau Tamblingan 89; r from US$55;) Right on the beach, this hotel has three small pools and 55 rooms. Much attention to detail is devoted to the attractively redecorated rooms; each has a patio.

Desa Segara (Map p140; ☎ 288407; www.segara-village.com; s/d from US$65/75, bungalows US$130;) Two pools and beach access ensure fun at the Desa Segara. The 144 rooms are a bit faded but come in a variety of flavours, from blocks to bungalows. At the café, Le Pirate, you can debate the eternal question: why did the pirate eat? (Answer: he didn't want to staRRRRve.)

Top End

Bali Hyatt (Map p140; ☎ 281234; www.bali.resort.hyatt.com; Jl Danau Tamblingan; r US$120-400;) The Made Wijaya–designed gardens are an attraction themselves at this 390-room beachfront resort. Hibiscus, wild ginger, lotus and more than 600 species of plants and animals can be found here. Rooms are comfortable and the resort is regularly updated. Regency Club rooms come with free drinks and food in a lovely pavilion. The two pools are vast, and one has a waterfall-shrouded cave perfect for romantic encounters.

Puri Santrian (Map p140; ☎ 288009; www.santrian.com; Jl Mertasari; r US$120-350;) Lush gardens, three large pools, a tennis court and beach frontage, as well as 184 comfortable, well-equipped rooms make this a good choice. Many rooms are in older-style bungalows, others in two- and three-storey blocks.

ourpick **Tandjung Sari** (Map p140; ☎ 288441; www.tandjungsari.com; Jl Danau Tamblingan 29; bungalows US$150-265;) The mature trees along the shaded driveway set the gracious tone at this Sanur veteran, which was one of the first Balinese boutique hotels. Like a good tree, it has flourished since its start in 1967 and continues to be lauded by people across the island for its artful design inside and out. The 26 gorgeous traditional-style bungalows are superbly decorated with crafts and antiques. Four-poster beds repose under traditional thatched roofs that soar to a peak, and fabrics reflect the pattern in the stone floors. At night, lights in the trees above the pool are magical. The gracious staff are a delight. You can take superb classes here in Balinese dance (see p143).

Pavilions Bali (Map p140; ☎ 288381; www.balipavilions.com; Jl Danau Tamblingan 76; villas from US$150;) Down a shady walk under a beautiful canopy of bamboo, you'll find this compound of villas where lovely little touches abound, such as tiny glittering tea light candles floating in the pool at night. The units are large with comfortable furnishings like nice wicker loungers.

EATING

There's great eating in Sanur at every budget level and at some places you can dine on the sand. Many of the drinking places listed are also great for a casual meal. And always check with higher-end places to see if they'll provide transport.

For groceries and personal items, there's a large **Hardy's Supermarket** (Map p140; ☎ 285806; Jl Danau Tamblingan 136), which has all manner of local and imported food items and periodicals. Nearby is Café Batu Jimbar's gourmet market (opposite).

On Sundays, there's an amazing **organic market** (Map p140; Jl Danau Tamblingan; 10am-2pm) in Gudang Keramic parking lot.

The **Pasar Sindhu night market** (Map p140; off Jl Danau Tamblingan; 6am-midnight) sells fresh vegetables, dried fish, pungent spices and various household goods.

Jl Ngurah Rai

West of the main Sanur strip, the fast-moving Jl Ngurah Rai Bypass is mostly home to fast-food chains.

Splash Bakery (Map p140; ☎ 288186; Jl Ngurah Rai; snacks from 4000Rp; 8am-8pm) Makes a good selection of bread, cakes, pastries and meat pies. It has a small eat-in area.

Northern Sanur

There are numerous little cafés and warung down by the beach.

Watering Hole (Agung & Sue) Restaurant (Map p140; ☎ 288289; Jl Hang Tuah; dishes 10,000-40,000Rp) Popular for tourist classics (pizza, Chinese, burgers…) that are served at decent prices. This is a good travellers' hang-out at this end of town.

Beach

The beach path offers restaurants, warung and bars where you can catch a meal, a drink or a sea breeze. There are several places near the end of each road that lead to the beach. Many places have sunset drinks specials (though the beach faces east, so you'll need to enjoy the reflected glow off Nuda Penida).

Stiff Chili (Map p140; Jl Kesumasari; dishes 8000-20,000Rp) Besides the evocative name, this beach-side hut with great views features good sandwiches, pizza and gelato.

New Banjar Club (Map p140; ☎ 287359; near Jl Duyung; dishes 20,000-40,000Rp) A nice beachfront restaurant, look for a typical menu of pizza, seafood and Indo classics.

Sanur Bay (Map p140; ☎ 288153; Jl Duyung; 25,000-40,000Rp) Tables right on the sand let you hear the surf and see the moonlight reflecting on the water at this classic beachside seafood grill.

Benno's Restaurant (Map p140; Shindu Beach Market 42; dishes 20,000-60,000Rp) Looks over the water and has a long seafood menu. Try the chilli crab.

Spirit Café (Map p140; ☎ 746 4407; Paradise Plaza; dishes 20,000-60,000Rp) This vaguely new-agey place is set back from the beach in a little retail courtyard. Smoothies, teas and veggie sandwiches highlight the small but creative menu.

Bonsai Cafe (Map p140; ☎ 282908; Jl Danau Tambligan 27; dishes 20,000-60,000Rp) Although the menu is all beachside standards, the real reason to seek this place out is that back off the beach is proof that the name is not notional: here are hundreds of bonsai trees in myriad sizes – all small. You can get here from street and beach.

Jl Danau Tamblingan

Café Tali Jiwa (Map p140; ☎ 287314; Jl Danau Tamblingan 148; dishes 10,000-32,000Rp) Adjoining the Hotel Santai, this wholesome place has an appetising choice of dishes, from fruit smoothies to veggie burgers. Many of the ingredients are organic. Expect fair-trade coffee – this is the home of PPLH Bali (see p142).

Randy's Café Bar & Restaurant (Map p140; ☎ 288962; Jl Danau Tamblingan 17; dishes 12,000-35,000Rp) Randy's hypes its Canadian theme, although the 'Canadian' items on the menu, such as chilli con carne over mashed potatoes, will dishearten Cannuck gourmets. There's good people-watching over breakfast at this corner spot.

Star Café Bali (Map p140; ☎ 7439766; Jl Danau Tamblingan 91; dishes 20,000-40,000Rp; 💻) English breakfasts and an array of teas give way to creative Indonesian and Western standards. The wicker chairs are good for lounging. There's internet access in an air-con room.

Zoo Restaurant & Bar (Map p140; ☎ 288807; Jl Danau Tamblingan 82; dishes 20,000-50,000Rp) A cool and stylish café with fast internet access (400Rp per min) and comfy places to people-watch out front.

Retro Café & Gallery (Map p140; ☎ 282472; Jl Danau Tamblingan 126; dishes 25,000-50,000Rp) All the classics are on the menu and there's a relaxed back section here, well away from the traffic noise, with walls filled with paintings.

Lumut (Map p140; ☎ 270009; Jl Danau Tamblingan; dishes 15,000-80,000Rp; 🕙 10am-10pm) This gracious 2nd-floor café is set back from the road. The emphasis is on fresh seafood (lots of lobster) and dishes from around Indonesia. It's also good for a coffee or juice during the day.

Café Batu Jimbar (Map p140; ☎ 287374; Jl Danau Tamblingan 152; dishes 30,000-60,000Rp) Beloved locally for its fine food, this gem of a café has a large wooden patio in front of an airy dining room. The baked goods on display are beyond enticing. Besides the best banana smoothie on Bali, the menu has Indonesian classics as well as smattering of other items. Next door it has a gourmet grocery.

Alise's Restaurant (Map p140; ☎ 282510; Tamu Kami Hotel, Jl Danau Tamblingan 64X; dishes 20,000-70,000Rp; 🕙 7.30-10pm) Character-filled Alise's has a romantic, lantern-lit outdoor dining area by the pool and serves a melange of international food. Unintentionally camp local musicians perform classic ballads to doe-eyed diners.

Palay Restaurant (Map p140; ☎ 288335; Jl Danau Tamblingan 81; dishes 20,000-80,000Rp; 🕙 noon-10pm) Like an upscale surfers joint, look for fine versions of pasta, burgers, pizza and local faves here. It's all served under a soaring thatched roof.

Telaga Naga (Map p140; ☎ 281234; Jl Danau Tamblingan 180; dishes 30,000-100,000Rp; 🕙 5pm-10pm) Torches light the pathway to this jewel-like restaurant where bright red lanterns glow over the tables. Offerings on the Chinese Szechwan menu are complex, such as *abalone masak jamur hitan* (abalone with black mushrooms). You may need to book.

Lotus Pond Restaurant (Map p140; ☎ 289398; Jl Danau Tamblingan 30; dishes 35,000-105,000Rp) The Sanur branch of the Lotus empire is in a high-thatched building surrounded by lotus ponds (of course). The menu features pasta, wood-fired oven pizza, seafood and Indonesian dishes. At night it glows and there are cultural displays.

Massimo (Map p140; ☎ 288942; Jl Danau Tamblingan 206; dishes 30,000-125,000Rp) The interior here is like an open-air Milan café, the outside is like a Balinese garden – a perfect combo. The menu boasts highly authentic pasta, pizza and more.

South Sanur

Sari Bundo (Map p140; ☎ 281389; Jl Danau Poso; dishes 5,000-10,000Rp; 24hr) This spotless padang-style joint is one of many down here. Choose from arrays of fresh and very spicy food. The curry chicken is the best in Sanur.

Cat & Fiddle (Map p140; ☎ 282218; Jl Cemara 36; dishes 25,000-50,000Rp) Look for Brit standards like fish and chips on the menu at this open-air place that's not surprisingly popular with expats. Traditional breakfasts in the morning balance live music many nights.

DRINKING

Many of Sanur's drinking establishments cater to retired expats and are, thankfully for them, air-conditioned. This is not a town where things go late. Also note that many of the eating places we've listed are good just for a drink.

Café Billiard (Map p140; ☎ 281215; Jl Danau Poso; noon-1am) This new place draws a well-lubricated expat crowd who dominate the billiards tables and toss down cheap drafts of Heineken. It's the sort of merry place where you lose your hat on the way home and wake up wishing to be asleep.

Circle K (Map p140; 24hr) Don't laugh. The reliable chain of convenience stores has an outlet right here on the beach where you can get a 7000Rp Bintang inside and sit at the provided tables outside. And there's no shortage of salty snacks for purchase.

Jazz Bar & Grille (Map p140; ☎ 285892; Kompleks Sanur 15, Jl Ngurah Rai; dishes 30,000-80,000Rp; 10am-2am;) There's live jazz and/or pop most nights. The international menu features Mexican and Mediterranean dishes.

Kalimantan (Map p140; ☎ 289291; Jl Pantai Sindhu 11; dishes 15,000-55,000Rp) Also known as Borneo Bob's, this veteran boozer is one of many joints on this street popular with expats. It's a relaxed place with a palm-tree shaded expanse and offers cheap drinks. For food, enjoy Mexican and Indonesian classics and steaks.

Lazer Sport Bar (Map p140; ☎ 288807; Jl Danau Tamblingan 82; noon-midnight) Adjoining the Zoo Restaurant & Bar (p145), there are tables under two big trees and live rock many nights (sweaty stuff on TV too).

SHOPPING

Arts & Crafts

Sanur is in easy reach of much of the good arts and crafts shopping around Ubud. Locally, there are several painting studios/shops, with a wide selection of paintings on offer, on the main street and around Jl Pantai Sindhu. Batik cloth is also easy to find. Sanur has a plenty of tailors on the main strip if you want something special made up.

Nogo (Map p140; ☎ 288765; Jl Danau Tamblingan 100) Look for the wooden loom out front of this classy store, which bills itself as the 'Bali Ikat Centre'. The goods are gorgeous and easy to savour in the air-con comfort.

Rare Angon (Map p140; ☎ 288962; Jl Danau Tamblingan 17) A gallery with works from over a dozen local artists. Many are often working right in the shop.

Clothing & Housewares

Ardana (Map p140; ☎ 282360; Jl Danau Tamblingan) Beautiful custom-made wicker furniture fills a shady pavilion open to the road. Obviously you'll want to try the merchandise out for an extended period. If only they served gin and tonics…

Gudang Keramik (Map p140; ☎ 289363; Jl Danau Tamblingan) The outlet store for Jenggala Keramik Bali in Jimbaran (see p130) has a amazing prices on the firm's gorgeous tableware and decorator items. What's called 'seconds' here would be firsts everywhere else.

Mama + Leon (Map p140; ☎ 288044; Jl Danau Tamblingan 99A) An upmarket women's fashion shop specialising in cool, classic cuts and colours, much of it made in Bali.

Putih Pino (Map p140; ☎ 287889; Jl Danau Tamblingan) For homewares try Putih Pino – it sells a range of natural textiles and knick-knacks in an exquisite setting.

Souvenirs

For souvenirs, try the numerous shops on the main street, or one of the various 'art markets'. **Sanur Beach Market** (Map p140; off Jl Segara Ayu) has a wide selection. **Pasar Sindhu Art Market** (Map p140; off Jl Danau Tamblingan), the maze-like **Shindu Beach Market** (Map p140; south of Jl Pantai Sindhu) and **Jaya Kesuma Art Market** (Map p140; Jl Mertasani) have numerous stalls selling T-shirts, sarongs, woodcarvings and other dubious items.

Hardy's (p140) has a range of goods on its second floor at very good prices.

GETTING THERE & AWAY

Bemo

The public bemo stops are at the southern end of Sanur on Jl Mertasari, and just outside the main entrance to the Inna Grand Bali Beach

Hotel on Jl Hang Tuah. You can hail a bemo anywhere along Jl Danau Tamblingan and Jl Danau Poso.

Green bemo go along Jl Hang Tuah and up Jl Hayam Wuruk to the Kereneng terminal in Denpasar (5000Rp).

Boat

Public boats to Nusa Lembongan as well as the Perama boat and the fast Scoot boat leave from the northern end of Sanur beach. See p152 for details.

Tourist Shuttle Bus

The **Perama office** (Map p140; ☎ 285592, Jl Hang Tuah 39; 🕑 7am-10pm) is at Warung Pojok at the northern end of town. It runs shuttles to the following destinations, most only once daily.

Destination	Fare
Candidasa	40,000Rp
Kuta	15,000Rp
Lovina	70,000Rp
Padangbai	40,000Rp
Ubud	30,000Rp

GETTING AROUND

Bemo go up and down Jl Danau Tamblingan and Jl Danau Poso for 3000Rp. Metered taxis can be flagged down in the street, or call **Bali Taxi** (☎ 701111).

SOUTH OF SANUR

PULAU SERANGAN

Only about 250m offshore, south of Sanur, Pulau Serangan (Turtle Island) is connected to the mainland by a causeway and bridge. This link, and a large area of landfill on the eastern and southern sides of the island, were part of a massive, abortive development project associated with Soeharto's infamous son Tommy. The earthworks obliterated the island's sandy beaches and other features. The island was named for the turtles that used to lay eggs here, but no beach means no turtles.

The island has two villages, Ponjok and Dukuh, and an important temple, **Pura Sakenan**, just east of the causeway. Architecturally, the temple is insignificant, but it's one of the holiest in Bali, and major festivals attract huge crowds of devotees, especially during the Kuningan festival.

The only other reason to come here is for the irregular **surf break** at the southern end of the landfill area, where a row of warung has appeared to provide food, drinks and souvenirs (see p79 for details on surfing). The wide road to the island branches off Jl Ngurah Rai just east of the Benoa Harbour turn-off – a booth at the end of the causeway collects a 1000Rp fee.

MANGROVE INFORMATION CENTRE

West of Sanur are vast mangroves that stretch almost to Kuta. Learn about this vital yet abused resource at the **Mangrove Information Centre** (Map p128; ☎ 726969; admission free; 🕑 8am-4pm Mon-Thu, 8am-2pm Fri), a joint Indonesian–Japanese project. The centre studies ways to preserve the health of mangroves, which are vital to filtering much of the island's ever-growing run-off.

Although you get a sense of the money behind the project, it already feels a bit sleepy. Some of the exhibits are in little better shape than the mangroves. Still there's a range of interesting activities you can sign on for here. A 1.5km boardwalk to the beach is sign-posted with information. You can also engage a guide and rent a four-person canoe (40,000Rp per hour) or go on a boat ride (four people for 100,000Rp per hour) through the mangroves.

Look for the centre's signs 5km west of Sanur. It's 1.5km south of Jl Ngurah Rai Bypass.

BENOA HARBOUR

Bali's main port is at the entrance of Teluk Benoa (Benoa Bay), the wide but shallow bay east of the airport runway. Benoa Harbour is on the northern side of the bay – a square of docks and port buildings on reclaimed land, linked to mainland Bali by a 2km causeway. It's referred to as Benoa port or Benoa Harbour to distinguish it from Benoa village, on the southern side of the bay.

Benoa Harbour is the port for tourist day-trip boats to Nusa Lembongan and for Pelni ships to other parts of Indonesia.

Visitors must pay a toll to go on the causeway (1000Rp per vehicle). Public bemo (5000Rp) leave from Sanglah terminal in Denpasar. A taxi from Kuta or Sanur should cost around 25,000Rp one way, plus the toll.

For more information on cruises to Nusa Lembongan from Benoa Harbour see p150.

NUSA LEMBONGAN & ISLANDS

One of three islands just off the southern coast of East Bali, Nusa Lembongan is overshadowed by its much larger sibling Nusa Penida, but it is foremost in terms of traveller popularity thanks to its enjoyable beach scene and great diving, and because it's the destination of choice for aquatic sports day trips.

Glimpsed from across south and east Bali, the islands beckon many a traveller – as well they should. Lembongan is the main destination and, even though other parts of Bali are begging for visitors, an increasing crowd just keeps making the voyage. Certainly they are well rewarded. Lembongan has a mellow travellers vibe and great surfing and diving and is made for casual exploration.

Nusa Penida, the giant of the trio, is seldom visited and that's a shame. It's got dramatic vistas right the way around, a wild and unpopulated interior and delightful residents who are very interested that you've decided to drop by. It's the closest place to Bali where you can fall right off the beaten path and be glad you did.

Tiny Nusa Ceningan is very sparsely populated and makes a good little jaunt from Lembongan.

The islands have been a poor region for many years. Thin soils and a lack of fresh water do not permit the cultivation of rice, but other crops such as maize, cassava and beans are staples grown here. The main cash crop, however, is seaweed (see Seaweed Sundae p150).

NUSA LEMBONGAN

☎ 0366

Lembongan is a wonderful place. Low-budget bungalows are ideal for extended stays by the seaside, while more upmarket hotels offer comfort and quiet. It's free of cars, motorcycle noise and hassles. It has a local population of about 7000 people, mostly living in two small villages, Jungutbatu and Lembongan.

For a short visit, take a convenient cruise boat, stopping to snorkel or bask on a beach, or do a more specialised diving or surf trip.

Orientation

Most surfers, divers and budget travellers stay at Jungutbatu beach in the island's northwest, while more upmarket accommodation is further south towards Mushroom Bay, where many of the day-trip cruise boats stop.

About 4km southwest along the sealed road from Jungutbatu is Lembongan village, the island's other town. Leaving Jungutbatu you climb up a steep knoll that offers a wonderful view back over the beach. You can go right around the island, following the rough track that eventually comes back to Jungutbatu, but the roads are challenging for cyclists and walkers.

There's no jetty at Jungutbatu – the boats usually beach in the shallows by the village. The Perama boat stops outside Mandara Beach Bungalows, while the public shuttle boat and Scoot boat stops further south. This part of the beach is the only bit that's truly dirty.

Information

It's vital that you bring sufficient cash for your stay as there's no ATM. **Bank BPD** (🕑 8am-3pm Mon-Thu, 8am-1pm Fri) can exchange travellers cheques and cash but rates are bad and hours short. **Mainski Inn** (☎ 24481r from 70,000Rp; 💻) can process Visa and Mastercard cash advances. Sometimes there's a line.

Mainski Inn also has a **wartel** (public telephone office; per min 1000Rp) and it offers fast broadband and wi-fi, as does Pondok Baruna.

Small markets can be found on the main street with the bank, but unless you're on a diet of bottled water and Ritz crackers, selection is small.

Offerings of thanks are still being given for 24-hour electricity, which was introduced in 2005.

The medical clinic in the village is well versed in minor surfing injuries and ear ailments.

Boats from Bali are met by men offering to carry your luggage or lead you to a hotel. If your hotel is far you may wish to carefully negotiate for their luggage services. But there's no need for the latter.

Sights

JUNGUTBATU

The beach here, a mostly lovely arc of white sand with clear blue water, has superb views across to Gunung Agung on Bali. The village itself is pleasant, with quiet lanes, no cars and lots of seaweed production. **Pura Segara** and its enormous banyan tree are the site of frequent ceremonies.

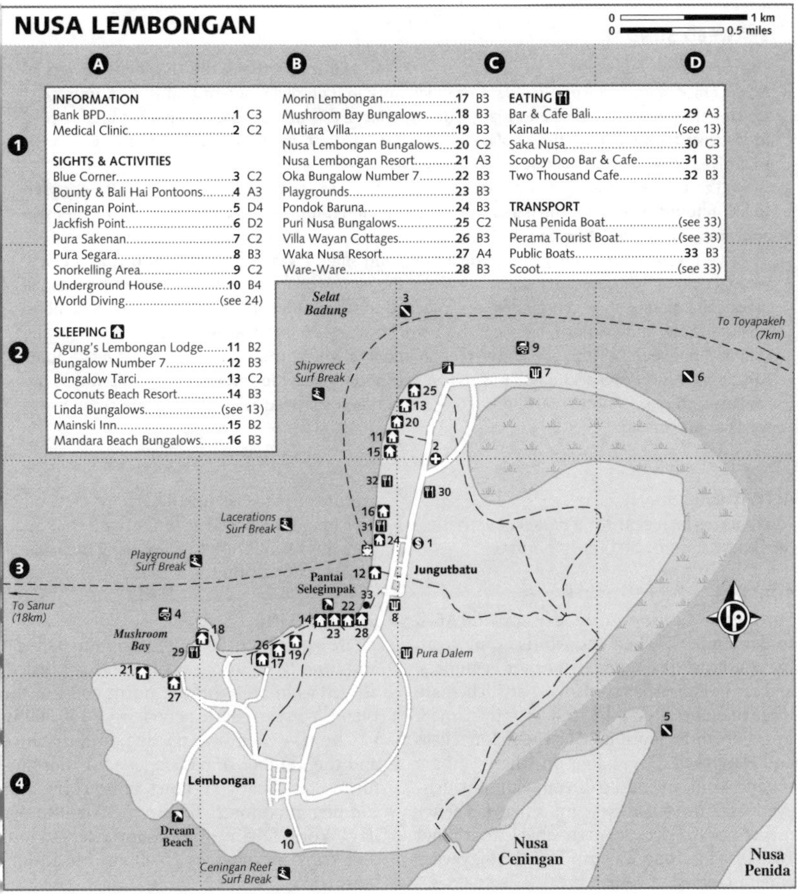

At the north end of town is a somewhat rickety metal **lighthouse**. Follow the path around east to **Pura Sakenan**.

MUSHROOM BAY

This gorgeous little bay, unofficially named for the mushroom corals offshore, has a perfect crescent of white-sand beach. During the day, the tranquillity may be disturbed by banana-boat rides or parasailing. In the morning and the evening, it's always a delightful place to spend some time.

The most pleasant way to get here from Jungutbatu is to walk along the trail that starts from the southern end of the main beach and follows the coastline for a kilometre or so, past a couple of smaller beaches (see 'Traversing Lembongan' p151). Alternatively, get a boat from Jungutbatu.

DREAM BEACH

Down a little track, on the south side of the island, this 150m crescent of white sand has pounding surf and a cute little café.

LEMBONGAN

The other main town on the island looks across the seaweed farm-filled channel to Nusa Ceningan. It's a beautiful scene of clear water and green hills. You may get some hype for the **underground house**. Ignore it; it's a diversion for day-trippers and amounts to little more than a couple of holes in the ground.

SEAWEED SUNDAE

The next time you enjoy some creamy ice cream, you might thank the seaweed growers of Nusa Lembongan and Nusa Penida. Carrageenan is an emulsifying agent that is used to thicken ice cream as well as cheese and many other products. It is also used as a fat substitute in 'diet' foods (just look for it on the endless ingredients label). In nature it turns seawater into a gel that gives seaweed its structure.

On Lembongan 85% of the population work at farming seaweed for carrageenan (as opposed to 5% in tourism) and it is the major industry. Although returns are OK, the work is very intensive and time-consuming. Women are the main labourers.

As you walk around the villages you'll see – and smell – vast areas used for drying the seaweed. Looking down into the water, you'll see the patchwork of cultivated seaweed plots. Small pieces of a marine algae *(Eucheuma)* are attached to strings that are stretched between bamboo poles – these underwater fences can be seen off many of the beaches, and especially in the shallows between Lembongan and Ceningan and at low tide. Growth is so fast that new shoots can be harvested every 45 days. This region is especially good for production as the waters are shallow and rich in nutrients. The dried red and green seaweed is exported around the world for final processing.

Activities

Most places rent gear for a passel of activities. Surfboards go for 50,000Rp per day.

SURFING

Surfing here is best in the dry season (April to September), when the winds come from the southeast. It's definitely not for beginners, and can be dangerous even for experts. There are three main breaks on the reef, all aptly named. From north to south are **Shipwreck**, **Lacerations** and **Playground**. Depending on where you are staying, you can paddle directly out to whichever of the three is closest; for others it's better to hire a boat. Prices are negotiable – from about 10,000Rp for a one-way trip. You tell the owner when to return. A fourth break – **Racecourses** – sometimes emerges south of Shipwreck.

The surf can be crowded here even when the island isn't – charter boats from Bali sometimes bring groups of surfers for day trips from the mainland, or as part of a longer surfing trip between Bali and Sumbawa. For day trips to Nusa Lembongan boats can be chartered from Sanur Beach for a minimum of 600,000Rp.

For more on surfing here, see p79.

DIVING

The excellent **World Diving** (☎ 081 2390 0686; www.world-diving.com), based at Pondok Baruna on Jungutbatu Beach, is highly regarded. It offers a complete range of courses, including five-day PADI open-water courses for US$345, and dive trips for US$27 to US$35 per dive to sites around all three islands. There are a few other dive operators based at Jungutbatu that operate from various hotels. See Diving the Islands, p155 for details on the area's dive sites.

SNORKELLING

There's good snorkelling just off the Bali Hai and Bounty pontoons off Jungutbatu Beach, as well as in areas off the north coast of the island. You can charter a boat from 150,000Rp per hour, depending on demand, distance and the number of passengers; for more information ask at your hotel. Snorkelling gear can be rented for 20,000Rp to 30,000Rp per day. World Diving allows snorkellers to join dive trips and charges 75,000Rp for a four-hour trip.

There's good drift snorkelling along the mangrove-filled channel west of Cenigan Point between Lembongan and Ceningan.

CRUISES

A number of cruise boats offer day trips to Nusa Lembongan from Benoa Harbour in South Bali. Trips include hotel transfer from South Bali, basic water sports, snorkelling, banana-boat rides, island tours and a buffet lunch. Note that with hotel transfers, the following day trips can make for a very long day.

Bali Hai (☎ 0361-720331; www.balihaicruises.com; reef cruises adult/child US$85/42.50, catamaran cruises adult/child US$85/57) This also has an unsightly offshore pontoon for snorkelling and water play.

Bounty Cruises (☎ 0361-726666; www.balibountycruises.com; cruises adult/child US$85/42.50) This group has an offshore pontoon only slightly less ugly than Bali Hai and offers similar cruises.

Island Explorer Cruises (☎ 0361-728088; www.bali-activities.com; per adult/child US$55/27.50) This has three ways to get to Lembongan, which all get you back to Bali around 5pm: relaxing and slow-sailing yacht, party boat and fast, stomach-churning boat. These trips include use of the outfit's Coconuts Beach Resort pool.

Sleeping

JUNGUTBATU

Most places to stay in Jungutbatu are basic and many of the following places have beachfront restaurants serving typical travellers' fare. The strip of beachfront joints is going through the classic Bali development cycle: each year more rooms are added and old ones are spruced up. Unless noted otherwise, amenities are limited to cold water and fans.

More upmarket establishments are spreading like weeds across the hillside to the south.

Budget

Agung's Lembongan Lodge (☎ 24483; r 50,000-150,000Rp) The simple rooms are mostly in colourful bungalows. The restaurant has hanging bird cages, ocean views, a pool table and a much nicer atmosphere than many others.

Nusa Lembongan Bungalows (☎ 24484; nusalembongan@hotmail.com; bungalows 60,000-150,000Rp) Of the five nice units here, the front one is a duplex with great views from the 2nd-floor patio.

Linda Bungalows (☎ 24495; r 70,000-90,000Rp) Of the 12 very clean cold-water rooms in this two-level place with bright blue roof, one offers an ocean view. Everything is well run, although the concrete mushrooms out front are a bit odd.

Pondok Baruna (☎ 0812 3900 686; www.world-diving.com; r 75,000-100,000Rp, dishes 10,000-18,000Rp; 💻) Associated with World Diving, this is one of the best places to stay. Staff, led by the manager Putu, are friendly, the seven rooms are pleasant and porches face the ocean. The restaurant serves excellent meals.

Bungalow Number 7 (☎ 24497; r 70,000-100,000Rp) This good, clean and friendly place has 14 rooms, with three on the beach with great views. The grounds are attractive and it is a little apart from the rest of the strip. It has a beachfront restaurant serving simple but good dishes (costing 7000Rp to 20,000Rp).

Bungalow Tarci (☎ 24494; r from 100,000Rp) The front units upstairs at this two-level place have excellent views of the water. It's got a popular bar.

Mandara Beach Bungalows (☎ 24470; www.mandara-lembongan.com; r 100,000-160,000Rp, with air-con 250,000Rp; ❄) Eight large bungalow-style rooms are set around a popular café. There's a nascent garden away from the water.

Puri Nusa Bungalows (☎ 24482; r 70,000-200,000Rp) The 17 rooms here are clean and comfortable, the two upstairs have excellent views and there's a good café (dishes 7000Rp to 25,000Rp).

Ware-Ware (☎ 0812 397 0572; r 120,000-200,000Rp;) The nine units at this hillside place are a mix of traditional square and groovy circular numbers with thatched roofs. Rooms are large with rattan couches and big bathrooms. The café has spectacular, breezy views and dishes cost between 20,000Rp and 50,000Rp.

Oka Bungalow Number 7 (☎ 24497; r from 250,000Rp; ❄) This good, clean and friendly place has three rooms, each with a good veranda and views down to the water. Units are spacious.

TRAVERSING LEMBONGAN

You can walk around the entire island in a day. It's a fascinating journey with good views all around. Or you can just cover the major sites in a few hours. To do this follow the hillside trail from **Jungutbatu** past the Mutiara Villa and on to **Pantai Selegimpak**. Here it becomes a little tricky to reach **Mushroom Bay**, but with a little Tarzan spirit, you can stay with the faint trail and be rewarded by refreshments.

From Mushroom Bay, head over to dreamy **Dream Beach**. You can easily do this on foot or hail a passing vehicle: 5000Rp will get you there.

Next go to **Lembongan** village. From here it is a gentle uphill walk along the sealed road to the killer hill that leads *down* to Jungutbatu. Note: you want to do this walk counter-clockwise to avoid having to climb this hill.

To explore the rest of the island, stick to the trails that follow the coast. Note that motorbikes won't be able to navigate most trails; you're better off walking.

Midrange

Playgrounds (☎ 24524; www.playgroundslembongan.com; r 400,000-500,000Rp;) On the hillside, Playgrounds' six rooms have good views, satellite TV and fridges. The cheaper rooms don't have air-con but do have better views from their long porch. There's also an adjoining private house for 700,000Rp a night.

Coconuts Beach Resort (☎ 0361-728088; www.bali-activities.com; d US$70, with air-con US$90;) Coconuts has unusual, spacious, circular bungalows staggered up the hillside overlooking a lovely pool and the sea. It's part of Island Explorer Cruises (see p151) so look for package deals.

PANTAI SELEGIMPAK

Reaching these places is a bit more of a challenge along the hillside trail. Without backpacks, you may want to avail yourself of the boat-greeting luggage carriers. It's a 15-minute up-and-down walk from Jungutbatu.

Villa Wayan Cottages (☎ 0361-745 2527, 0811-386540; www.lembonganislands.com; r US$20-35) Villa Wayan Cottages has six varied and unusually decorated rooms; some are suitable for families or groups. Trees give the grounds nice shade and there's a good café. Ask about boat transfer from Sanur.

Mutiara Villa (☎ 0361-745 3857; www.mutiara-villa.com; r US$50-60;) There are four units at this hillside place, two with views. The medium-sized pool disappears over the horizon and there's a telescope in the common area. Rooms have a stark, stylish design.

Morin Lembongan (☎ 081-2385 8396; wayman40@hotmail.com; US$25-30) More lushly planted than many of the hillside places, Morin has six comfy rooms with views over the water from their verandas. It's fan-only; be sure to bargain.

MUSHROOM BAY

A nice collection of more upscale places surround this pretty bay. You can get here by vehicle from Jungutbatu for 9000Rp.

Mushroom Bay Bungalows (☎ 24515; www.mushroom-lembongan.com; r US$25-50; dishes 10,000-20,000Rp;) Perched on a tiny knoll at the east end of Mushroom Bay, this family-run place has 11 rooms, one with air-con. There are good-sized bathtubs and a popular café for viewing sunsets.

Waka Nusa Resort (☎ 0361-723629; www.wakaexperience.com; bungalows from US$100;) This pretty little place has 10 thatch-roofed bungalows set in sandy grounds. The beachside restaurant and bar is delightfully located under coconut palms. Transfers from Bali are aboard a sailing boat.

Nusa Lembongan Resort (☎ 0361-725864; www.nusa-lembongan.com; villas from US$175;) Twelve secluded and stylish villas overlooking a gorgeous sweep of ocean are the draw here. The pool and grounds are lovely. The resort has a creative restaurant (meals US$10 to US$25) with patio views over the bay.

Eating & Drinking

JUNGUTBATU

The usual menu of Indonesian and Western dishes is omnipresent here. The restaurants at Oka Bungalow Number 7, Pondok Baruna, Puri Nusa Bungalows and Ware-Ware are especially good. The bar at Bungalow Tarci is usually hopping (unless the surf has been great, in which case everyone is snoozing).

Scooby Doo Bar & Cafe (dishes 7500-15,000Rp) Although probably not licensed to use the name of the popular pooch, Scooby's serves up a long list of snacks and drinks right on the sand to a big crowd every night. There are sofas for lounging.

Two Thousand Cafe (☎ 0812 394 1273; dishes 15,000-30,000Rp) This pleasant café-bar is right on the sand and is a good sunset spot.

Kainalu (dishes 12,000-30,000Rp) Spread over two levels right on the sand, it has a pool table, serves up surfer classics and has chairs for sunbathing.

Saka Nusa (dishes 10,000-20,000Rp; 6-10pm) Take a break from the beach at this warung set back among the palm and fruit trees.

MUSHROOM BAY

Bar & Cafe Bali (☎ 24536; dishes 20,000-50,000Rp) Right in the centre of the beach, enjoy pizza, pasta, seafood and the Indo-usuals with your feet in the sand. The bar is lively and you can arrange from transport from Jungutbatu.

Getting There & Away

Getting to or from Nusa Lembongan offers numerous choices. In descending order of speed are the Scoot boat, the Perama boat and the public boats. Getting between the boats and shore and getting around once on land is not especially easy, so this is the time to travel very light.

SANUR & SOUTH BALI

Public boats to Nusa Lembongan leave from the northern end of Sanur beach at 7.45am

(35,000Rp, 1½ to two hours). This is the boat used by locals and you may have to share space with a live chicken.

The **Perama tourist boat** (which is more reliable) leaves at 10.30am (70,000Rp, 1½ hours). The ride is often rough and you're likely to get wet. The Lembongan office is in the Mandara Beach Bungalows.

New to the scene is **Scoot**, a super-fast boat that makes the journey (US$25) in about 40 minutes. While four huge outboards roar at the back, passengers cling to their wicker seats as the boat flies over waves before crashing into troughs. It's really an adventure in itself. The boat goes twice daily, and bookings are a must.

From Nusa Lembongan to Sanur, public boats leave Jungutbatu beach at 7.45am. The Perama boat to Sanur leaves at 8.30am and connects with the through service to Kuta (85,000Rp) and Ubud (90,000Rp).

BENOA HARBOUR

The day-tripping cruise boats to Nusa Lembongan from Benoa Harbour (see p150) will usually take people for passage only for about US$20 to US$30 round-trip. Call to confirm. Alternatively if you go on the full day trip and then decide you want to stay, you can return on a boat another day.

NUSA PENIDA

Boats take locals between Jungutbatu and Toyapakeh (one hour) between 5.30am and 6am for 10,000Rp. Otherwise, charter a boat for 150,000Rp one way.

Getting Around

The island is fairly small and you can easily walk around it in a few hours; however, the roads across the middle of the island are quite steep. Bicycles (30,000Rp per day) and motorbikes (25,000Rp per hour) are widely available for rent.

NUSA PENIDA

☎ 0366

Largely overlooked by tourists, Nusa Penida is awaiting discovery. It's an untrammelled place that answers the question: what would Bali be like if tourists never came? There's not a lot of formal activities or sights; rather you go to Nusa Penida to explore and relax, to adapt to the slow rhythm of life here and learn to enjoy subtle pleasures such as the changing colour of the clouds and the sea. Life is simple; you'll still see topless older women carrying huge loads on their heads.

The island is a limestone plateau with white-sand beaches on its north coast, and views over the water to the volcanoes on Bali. The beaches are not great for swimming as most of the shallows are filled with bamboo frames used for seaweed farming. The south coast has 300m-high limestone cliffs dropping straight down to the sea and a row of offshore islets – it's rugged and spectacular scenery. The interior is hilly, with sparse-looking crops and old-fashioned villages. Rainfall is low and parts are arid.

The population of around 50,000 is predominantly Hindu, although there are some Muslims in Toyapakeh. The culture is distinct from that of Bali: the language is an old form of Balinese no longer heard on the mainland, and there is also local dance, architecture and craft, including a unique type of red ikat weaving (cloth in which the pattern is produced by dyeing individual threads before weaving). Nusa Penida was once used as a place of banishment for criminals and other undesirables from the kingdom of Klungkung, and still has a somewhat sinister reputation.

Services are limited to small shops in the main towns. Bring cash and anything else you'll need.

PENIDA'S DEMON

Nusa Penida is the legendary home of Jero Gede Macaling, the demon who inspired the Barong Landung dance. Many Balinese believe the island is a place of enchantment and *angker* (evil power) – paradoxically, this is an attraction. Although few foreigners visit, thousands of Balinese come every year for religious observances aimed at placating the evil spirits.

The island has a number of interesting temples dedicated to Jero Gede Macaling, including Pura Dalem Penetaran Ped, near Toyapakeh. It houses a shrine, which is a source of power for practitioners of black magic, and a place of pilgrimage for those seeking protection from sickness and evil.

Activities

Nusa Penida has amazing **diving**; see 'Diving the Islands' p155. There's a dive shop in Toyapakeh; see p154. Alternatively, make

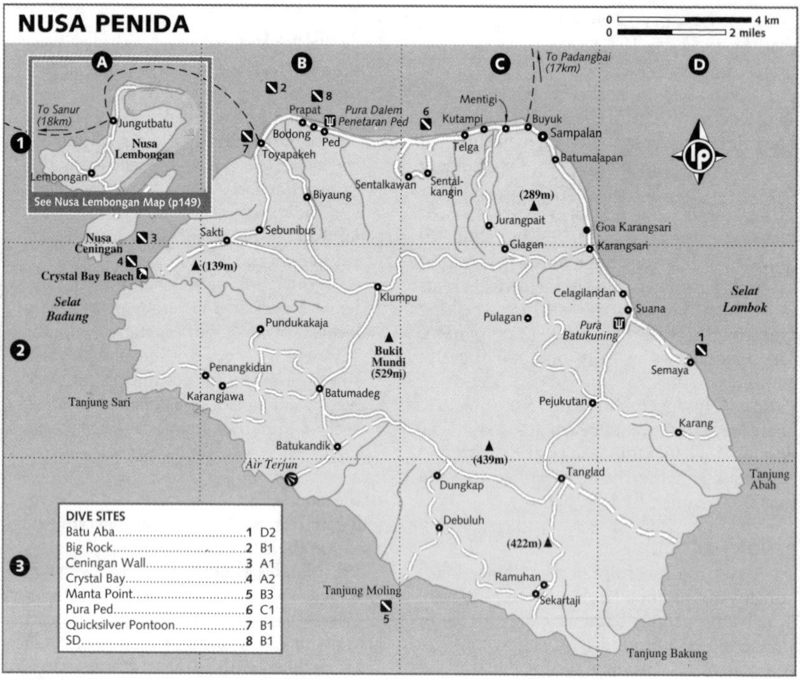

arrangements through **World Diving** (☎ 081 2390 0686; www.world-diving.com) on Nusa Lembongan. If you plan to go **snorkelling**, bring your own gear or rent it from **MM Diving** (☎ 081-3370 77590, 081-3370 22676; www.mmdiving.cz) in Toyapakeh.

Between Toyapakeh and Sampalan there is excellent **cycling** on the beautiful, flat coast road. The hitch is you need to bring a *good* bike with you to Penida. If you really want to explore, bring a mountain bike and camping equipment from the mainland (but remember, Nusa Penida is hilly). Alternatively, plan to do some serious **hiking**, but come well prepared.

Sampalan

Sampalan, the main town on Penida, is quiet and pleasant, with a market, schools and shops strung out along the curving coast road. The **market area**, where the bemo congregate, is in the middle of town. It's a good place to absorb village life.

SLEEPING & EATING

Not many people stay here, although there's plenty of rooms, so you can just show up. For meals you'll need to try one of the small warung in town – no more than 10 minutes by foot from any of the inns.

Made's Homestay (☎ 0852-3764 3649; r 70,000-80,000Rp) A friendly place with four small, clean rooms and a pleasant garden. Breakfast is included. A small side road between the market and the harbour leads here.

Bungalow Pemda (☎ 0813-3852 9435, 23580; r 25,000-120,000Rp) Opposite the police station, 200 metres east of the market, is this government rest-house. There are 14 very basic rooms here; the best have toilets and no mosquito nets but great sea views.

Nusa Garden Bungalows (☎ 0813-3855 7595; r 60,000-70,000Rp) Crushed coral pathways running between animal statuary link the 10 rooms here. Rates include a small breakfast. Turn on Jl Nusa Indah just east of the centre.

Toyapakeh

If you come by boat from Lembongan, you'll probably be dropped at the beach at Toyapakeh, a pretty town with lots of shady trees. The beach has clean white sand, clear blue water, a neat line of boats, and Gunung Agung as a

DIVING THE ISLANDS

There are great diving possibilities around the islands, from shallow and sheltered reefs, mainly on the northern side of Lembongan and Penida, to very demanding drift dives in the channel between Penida and the other two islands. Vigilant locals have protected their waters from dynamite bombing by renegade fishing boats, so the reefs are mostly still intact. And a side benefit of seaweed farming is that locals no longer rely so much on fishing.

The best local dive operation, based at Nusa Lembongan, is **World Diving** (Map p149; ☎ 081 2390 0686; www.world-diving.com), which runs trips to 20 different dive sites. There is also now a dive shop on Penida; see p153.

If you arrange a dive trip from Candidasa or South Bali, stick with the most reputable operators, as conditions here can be tricky and local knowledge is essential. A particular attraction is the large marine animals, including turtles, sharks and manta rays. The large (3m fin to fin) and unusual *mola mola* (sunfish) is sometimes seen around the islands between mid-July and October, while manta rays are often seen south of Nusa Penida.

The best dive sites include **Blue Corner** (Map p149) and **Jackfish Point** (Map p149) off Nusa Lembongan and **Ceningan Point** (Map p149) at the tip of that island. The channel between Ceningan and Penida is renowned for drift diving but it is essential that you have a good operator who can judge fast-changing currents and other conditions. Upswells can bring cold water from the open ocean to sites such as **Ceningan Wall** (Map p154). This is one of the world's deepest natural channels and attracts all manner and sizes of fish.

Sites close to Nusa Penida include **Big Rock**, **Crystal Bay**, **SD**, **Pura Ped** and **Manta Point** (Map p154). Of these, Crystal Bay, SD and Pura Ped are suitable for novice divers and are good for snorkelling. For more on diving on Bali, see p74.

backdrop. Step up from the beach and you're at the road where bemo can take you to Ped or Sampalan (4000Rp).

Offshore, the big grey thing that looks like a tuna-processing plant is the **Quicksilver pontoon** (☎ 0361-7425161; www.quicksilver-bali.com). Day-trips (adult/child US$40/20) from Benoa Harbour include a buffet lunch, snorkelling, banana board rides and an excursion ashore to an extremely unattractive 'tourist village' of limpid souvenir sellers and slightly roasted trees.

The one place to stay in town is also a good choice to stay. **MM Diving Resort & Mutiara Bungalows** (☎ 081-3370 77590, 081-3370 22676; www.mmdiving.cz; r 90,000-150,000Rp;) has eight good rooms back off the beach and behind the Quicksilver 'village'. The bungalow-style rooms are comfortable and some have aircon. There's a good café and a common area with a library.

Run by enthusiastic Czechs, the dive operation specialises in Nusa Penida. Two-dive trips are US$40 to US$50. You can rent snorkelling equipment for US$4 a day.

Around the Island

A trip around the island, following the north and east coasts, and crossing the hilly interior, can be completed in half a day by motorcycle. You could spend much longer, lingering at the temples and the small villages, and walking to less accessible areas, but there's no accommodation outside the two main towns. The following description goes clockwise from Sampalan.

The coastal road from Sampalan curves and dips past bays with rows of fishing boats and offshore seaweed gardens. After about 6km, just before the village of Karangsari, steps go up on the right side of the road to the narrow entrance of **Goa Karangsari** caves. There are usually people who can provide a lantern and guide you through the cave for a small negotiable fee of around 20,000Rp each. The limestone cave is over 15m tall in some sections. It extends more than 200m through the hill and emerges on the other side to overlook a verdant valley.

Continue south past a naval station and several charming **temples** to Suana. Here the main road swings inland and climbs up into the hills, while a very rough side track goes southeast, past more interesting temples to **Semaya**, a fishing village with a sheltered beach and one of Bali's best dive sites offshore, **Batu Aba**.

About 9km southwest of Suana, **Tanglad** is a very old-fashioned village and a centre for traditional weaving. Rough roads south and east lead to isolated parts of the coast.

GETTING AWAY FROM IT ALL

You've already gotten away from most of it by coming to Nusa Penida, but you can go further still. South of Toyapakeh, a 10km road through the village of Sakti leads to gorgeous and almost untouched **Crystal Bay Beach**, which fronts the popular dive spot. The sand here is the whitest around Bali and you'll likely have it to yourself. Should you somehow have the gear, this would be a fine place to camp.

A scenic ridge-top road goes northwest from Tanglad. At Batukandik, a rough road leads to a spectacular **air terjun** (waterfall). There's a temple here and it's a short walk from the road.

Limestone cliffs drop hundreds of feet into the sea, surrounded by crashing surf. At their base, underground streams discharge fresh water into the sea – a pipeline was made to bring the water up to the top. You can follow the pipeline down the cliff face on an alarmingly exposed metal stairway. From it, you can see the remains of the rickety old wooden scaffolding women used to clamber down, returning with large pots of water on their heads.

Back on the main road, continue to Batumadeg, past **Bukit Mundi** (the highest point on the island at 529m; on a clear day you can see Lombok), through Klumpu to Sakti, which has traditional stone buildings. Return to the north coast at Toyapakeh, about one hour after Bukit Mundi.

The important temple of **Pura Dalem Penetaran Ped** is near the beach at Ped, a few kilometres east of Toyapakeh. It houses a shrine for the demon Jero Gede Macaling (see Penida's Demon, p153). The temple structure is sprawling and you will see many people making offerings for safe sea voyages from Nusa Penida; you may wish to join them.

Across from the temple, the spotless and simple **Depot Anda** (meals 3000-10,000Rp; 6am-9pm) is the eating choice on the island with tasty local standards.

The road between Sampalan and Toyapakeh follows the craggy and lush coast.

Getting There & Away

The strait between Nusa Penida and southern Bali is very deep and subject to heavy swells – if there is a strong tide, boats often have to wait. You may also have to wait a while for the public boat to fill up with passengers. Boats to and from Kusamba are not recommended.

PADANGBAI

On the beach just east of the car park in Padangbai, you'll find the twin-engine fibreglass boats that run across the strait to Buyuk, 1km west of Sampalan on Nusa Penida (25,000Rp, 45 minutes, four daily). The boats run between 7am and noon. Boats back to Padangbai cost 18,000Rp.

NUSA LEMBONGAN

Boats take locals between Toyapakeh and Jungutbatu (one hour) between 5.30am and 6am for 10,000Rp. Enjoy the mangrove views on the way. Otherwise, charter a boat for 150,000Rp one way.

Getting Around

Bemo regularly travel along the sealed road between Toyapakeh and Sampalan, and sometimes on to Suana and up to Klumpu, but beyond these areas the roads are rough and transport is limited. You should be able to charter your own bemo or private vehicle with driver for about 10,000Rp per hour.

You may also be able to negotiate an *ojek* (motorcycle with passengers) for about 30,000Rp per hour.

NUSA CENINGAN

There is a narrow suspension bridge crossing the lagoon between Nusa Lembongan and Nusa Ceningan, which makes it quite easy to explore the network of tracks on foot or by bicycle. The lagoon is filled with frames for seaweed farming and there's also a fishing village and several small agricultural plots. Although the island is quite hilly, if you're up for it, you'll get glimpses of great scenery as you wander or cycle around the rough tracks.

To really savour Nusa Ceningan, take a tour of the island with **JED** (Village Ecotourism Network; ☎ 0361-735320; www.jed.or.id), the cultural organisation that gives people an in-depth look at village and cultural life. For US$60 to US$120 (depending on number of people), you spend the night in a village, eat local meals, get a fascinating tour and receive transport from Bali.

There's also a **surf break** at Ceningan reef, but it's very exposed and only surfable when it's too small for the other breaks.

(Continued on page 165)

ANDERS BLOMQVIST

Pura Tanah Lot (p272)

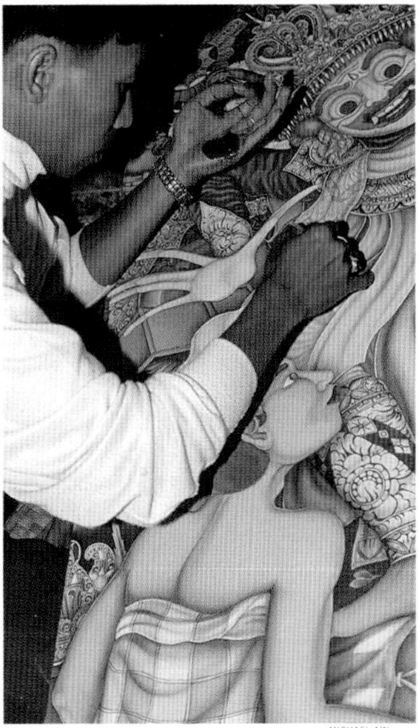

MICHAEL AW

Local artist at work (p51)

Lebih (p209), Bali

GREGORY ADAMS

PAUL BE

Sunbathing on Kuta Beach (p101)

Surfboards, Kuta (p102)

RICHARD I'A

PAUL BEINSSEN

Motorbikes, Denpasar (p165)

Beachside hotel, Legian (p104)

STEPHANE VICTOR

Kuningan festival (p336), Seminyak

PAUL BEINSSEN

RICHARD I'ANSON

Taman Kertha Gosa (p213), Semarapura

Ramayana ballet, Ubud Palace (p175)

RICHARD I'ANSON

JERRY ALEXANDER

Vegetarian meal, Ubud (p193)

Procession through rice paddies, Tampaksiring (p203)

BILL WAS

TOM COCKREM

Rice harvesting, Sangeh (p274)

JERRY ALEXANDER

Rice terraces, Tabanan (p275)

Waterfalls, Gitgit (p252)

ANDERS BLOMQVIST

PETER PTSCHELINZEW
Danau Bratan (p249) near Bedugul

Fresh produce at a local market
JERRY ALEXANDER

Danau Batur (p246)
JERRY ALE

JAMES LYON

Danau Segara Anak and Gunung Baru (p315), Lombok

PHIL WEYMOUTH

Garlic fields, Sembalun Valley (p313)

Baskets of freshly caught fish

RICHARD I'ANSON

ANDREW

Gilli Trawangan (p305), Lombok

BERNARD NAPTHINE

Cidomo, Tetebatu (p317)

Hawksbill turtle, Gili Trawangan (p305)

(Continued from page 156)

DENPASAR

Sprawling, hectic and ever-growing, Bali's capital has been the focus of a lot of the island's growth and wealth over the last five decades. There are still tree-lined streets and some pleasant gardens, but the traffic, noise and pollution challenge the casual visitor.

Denpasar might not be a tropical paradise, but it's as much a part of 'the real Bali' as the rice paddies and cliff-top temples. This is the hub of the island for locals and here you will find the shopping malls, restaurants and parks enjoyed by the people who actually live on Bali. Unless you're content to skip over the surface of the island, you'll want to sample Denpasar's markets, its one excellent museum and its purely modern Balinese vibe. Most visitors stay in the tourist towns of the south and visit Denpasar as a day trip. Others may pass through while changing bemo or catching a bus to Java.

HISTORY

Denpasar, which means 'next to the market', was an important trading centre and the seat of local rajahs (lord or prince) before the colonial period. The Dutch gained control of northern Bali in the mid-19th century, but their takeover of the south didn't start until 1906. After the three Balinese princes destroyed their own palaces in Denpasar and made a suicidal last stand – a ritual *puputan* – the Dutch made Denpasar an important colonial centre. And as Bali's tourism industry expanded in the 1930s, most visitors stayed at one or two government hotels in the city of Denpasar.

The northern town of Singaraja remained the Dutch administrative capital, but a new airport was built in the south. This made Denpasar a strategic asset in WWII, and when the Japanese invaded, they used it as a springboard to attack Java. After the war the Dutch moved their headquarters to Denpasar, and in 1958, some years after Indonesian independence, the city became the official capital of the province of Bali. Denpasar is a self-governing municipality that includes Sanur and Benoa Harbour.

Many of Denpasar's residents descended from immigrant groups such as Bugis mercenaries and Chinese, Arab and Indian traders. Recent immigrants, including civil servants, artisans, business people and labourers, have come from Java and all over Indonesia, attracted by opportunities in schools, factories and businesses in the growing Balinese capital. Much of the business infrastructure that supports Balinese tourism is based here.

Although non-Balinese tend to live in detached houses or small apartments, Balinese communities still maintain their traditions and family compounds, even as their villages are engulfed by growth. In fact, Denpasar's southern reaches have collided with northern expansion from Kerobokan.

ORIENTATION

The main road, Jl Gunung Agung, starts at the western side of town. It changes first to Jl Gajah Mada, then Jl Surapati and finally Jl Hayam Wuruk. This name changing is common in Denpasar, and can be confusing.

In contrast to the rest of Denpasar, the Renon area, southeast of the town centre, is laid out on a grand scale, with wide streets, large car parks and huge landscaped blocks of land. You'll find the government offices here, many of which are impressive structures, built with huge budgets in modern Balinese style.

INFORMATION

Emergency

Police Office (Map pp166-7; ☎ 424346; Jl Pattimura) The place for any general problems.

Tourist Police (Map pp166-7; ☎ 224111)

Medical Services

Rumah Sakit Umum Propinsi Sanglah (RSUP Sanglah; Map pp166-7; ☎ 227911; Sanglah; 24hr) The city's general hospital has English-speaking staff and a casualty room. It's the best hospital on the island.

Money

All major Indonesian banks have offices in Denpasar, and most have ATMs. Several are on Jl Gajah Mada, near the corner of Jl Arjuna, and there are also plenty of ATMs in the shopping malls.

Post

Main post office (Map pp166-7; ☎ 223565; Jl Panjaitan; 8am-8pm) Has poste restante service, but is inconveniently located in Renon.

Tourist Information

Denpasar tourist office (Map pp166-7; ☎ 234569; Jl Surapati 7; 7.30am-3.30pm Mon-Thu, 8am-1pm Fri) Deals with tourism in the Denpasar municipality (including

DENPASAR

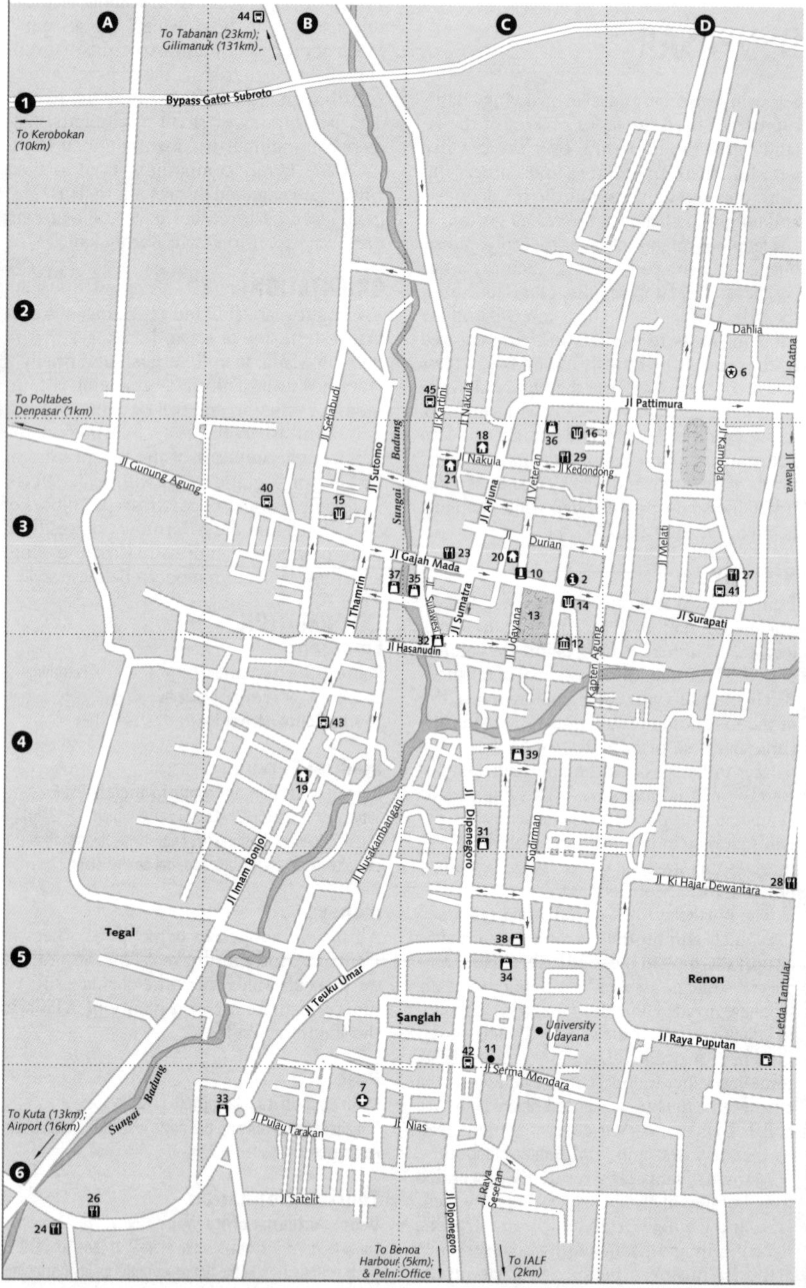
A
B
C
D
1
2
3
4
5
6
To Tabanan (23km); Gilimanuk (131km)
Bypass Gatot Subroto
To Kerobokan (10km)
To Poltabes Denpasar (1km)
Jl Gunung Agung
Jl Setiabudi
Jl Sutomo
Sungai Badung
Jl Kartini
Jl Nakula
Jl Arjuna
Jl Veteran
Jl Kedondong
Jl Pattimura
Jl Dahlia
Jl Ratna
Jl Kamboja
Jl Plawa
Jl Melati
Jl Durian
Jl Gajah Mada
Jl Thamrin
Jl Sulawesi
Jl Sumatra
Jl Udayana
Jl Kapten Agung
Jl Surapati
Jl Hasanudin
Jl Imam Bonjol
Jl Nusakambangan
Jl Dipenegoro
Jl Sudirman
Jl Ki Hajar Dewantara
Tegal
Jl Teuku Umar
Sanglah
Renon
Letda Tantular
University Udayana
Jl Raya Puputan
Jl Serma Mendara
Jl Pulau Tarakan
Jl Nias
Jl Raya Seseten
Jl Satelit
Jl Dipenegoro
To Kuta (13km); Airport (16km)
Sungai Badung
To Benoa Harbour (5km); & Pelni Office
To IALF (2km)
2
6
7
10
11
12
13
14
15
16
18
19
20
21
23
24
26
27
28
29
31
32
33
34
35
36
37
38
39
40
41
42
43
44
45

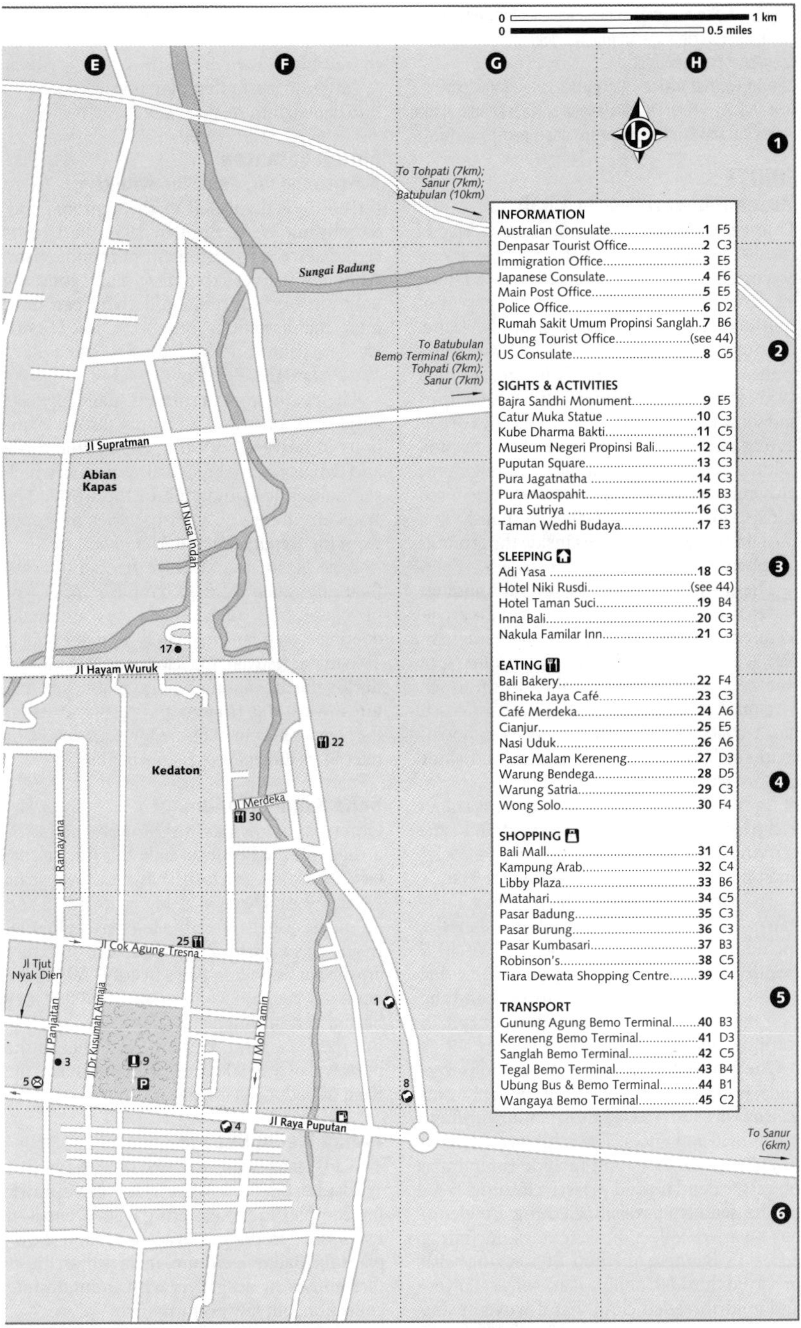
0 1 km
0 0.5 miles
E
F
G
H
1
2
3
4
5
6
To Tohpati (7km); Sanur (7km); Batubulan (10km)
Sungai Badung
To Batubulan Bemo Terminal (6km); Tohpati (7km); Sanur (7km)
Jl Supratman
Abian Kapas
Jl Nusa Indah
Jl Hayam Wuruk
Kedaton
Jl Merdeka
Jl Ramayana
Jl Cok Agung Tresna
Jl Tjut Nyak Dien
Jl Panjaitan
Jl Dr Kusumah Atmaja
Jl Moh Yamin
Jl Raya Puputan
To Sanur (6km)
INFORMATION
Australian Consulate....1 F5
Denpasar Tourist Office....2 C3
Immigration Office....3 E5
Japanese Consulate....4 F6
Main Post Office....5 E5
Police Office....6 D2
Rumah Sakit Umum Propinsi Sanglah.7 B6
Ubung Tourist Office....(see 44)
US Consulate....8 G5
SIGHTS & ACTIVITIES
Bajra Sandhi Monument....9 E5
Catur Muka Statue....10 C3
Kube Dharma Bakti....11 C5
Museum Negeri Propinsi Bali....12 C4
Puputan Square....13 C3
Pura Jagatnatha....14 C3
Pura Maospahit....15 B3
Pura Sutriya....16 C3
Taman Wedhi Budaya....17 E3
SLEEPING
Adi Yasa....18 C3
Hotel Niki Rusdi....(see 44)
Hotel Taman Suci....19 B4
Inna Bali....20 C3
Nakula Familar Inn....21 C3
EATING
Bali Bakery....22 F4
Bhineka Jaya Café....23 C3
Café Merdeka....24 A6
Cianjur....25 E5
Nasi Uduk....26 A6
Pasar Malam Kereneng....27 D3
Warung Bendega....28 D5
Warung Satria....29 C3
Wong Solo....30 F4
SHOPPING
Bali Mall....31 C4
Kampung Arab....32 C4
Libby Plaza....33 B6
Matahari....34 C5
Pasar Badung....35 C3
Pasar Burung....36 C3
Pasar Kumbasari....37 B3
Robinson's....38 C5
Tiara Dewata Shopping Centre....39 C4
TRANSPORT
Gunung Agung Bemo Terminal....40 B3
Kereneng Bemo Terminal....41 D3
Sanglah Bemo Terminal....42 C5
Tegal Bemo Terminal....43 B4
Ubung Bus & Bemo Terminal....44 B1
Wangaya Bemo Terminal....45 C2

Sanur), but also has some information about the rest of Bali. It's not worth a special trip, but does offer the useful *Calendar of Events* booklet.

Ubung Tourist office (Map pp166-7; 🕑 8am-2pm Mon-Thu, 8am-noon Fri) This helpful office is located at the Ubung Bus and Bemo Terminal and offers transport advice.

SIGHTS

Museum Negeri Propinsi Bali

This **museum** (Map pp166-7; ☎ 222680; adult/child 2000/1000Rp; 🕑 8am-12.30pm Mon-Fri, 8am-3pm Sun) was originally established in 1910 by a Dutch resident who was concerned by the export of culturally significant artefacts from the island. Destroyed in a 1917 earthquake, it was rebuilt in the 1920s, but used mainly for storage until 1932. At that time, German artist Walter Spies and some Dutch officials revived the idea of collecting and preserving Balinese antiquities and cultural objects, and creating an ethnographic museum. Today the museum is well organised and most displays are labelled in English. You can climb one of the towers inside the grounds for a better view of the whole complex.

The museum comprises several buildings and pavilions, including examples of the architecture of both the *puri* (palace) and *pura* (temple), with features such as a *candi bentar* (split gateway) and a *kulkul* (warning drum) tower. The main building, to the back as you enter, has a collection of prehistoric pieces downstairs, including stone sarcophagi, and stone and bronze implements. Upstairs are examples of traditional artefacts, including items still in everyday use. Look for the fine wood-and-cane carrying cases for transporting fighting cocks, and tiny carrying cases for fighting crickets.

The **northern pavilion**, in the style of a Tabanan palace, houses dance costumes and masks, including a sinister Rangda (widow-witch), a healthy-looking Barong (mythical lion-dog creature) and a towering Barong Landung (tall Barong) figure. See the Glossary (p380) for more about these mythical figures.

The **central pavilion**, with its spacious veranda, is like the palace pavilions of the Karangasem kingdom (based in Amlapura), where rajahs held audiences. The exhibits are related to Balinese religion, and include ceremonial objects, calendars and priests' clothing.

The **southern pavilion** (Gedung Buleleng) has a varied collection of textiles, including *endek* (a Balinese method of weaving with pre-dyed threads), double ikat, *songket* (silver- and gold-threaded cloth, hand-woven using a floating weft technique) and *prada* (the application of gold leaf or gold or silver thread in traditional Balinese clothes).

Museum staff often play music on a bamboo gamelan to magical effect.

Pura Jagatnatha

Next to the museum, the **state temple** (Map pp166–7) is dedicated to the supreme god, Sanghyang Widi. Built in 1953, part of its significance is its statement of monotheism. Although Balinese recognise many gods, the belief in one supreme god (who can have many manifestations) brings Balinese Hinduism into conformity with the first principle of Pancasila – the 'Belief in One God'.

The *padmasana* (shrine) is made of white coral, and consists of an empty throne (symbolic of heaven) on top of the cosmic turtle and two *naga* (mythological serpents), which symbolise the foundation of the world. The walls are decorated with carvings of scenes from the *Ramayana* and *Mahabharata*.

Pura Jagatnatha is more frequently used than any other Balinese temple – local people come every afternoon to pray and make offerings – so it can often be closed to the public. Two major festivals are held here every month, during the full moon and new moon, and feature *wayang kulit* (shadow puppet plays). Ask at the Denpasar Tourist Office for exact details, or refer to its *Calendar of Events* booklet.

Bajra Sandhi Monument

Otherwise known as the Monument to the Struggle of the People of Bali, this huge **monument** (Map pp166-7; ☎ 264517; Jl Raya Puputan; admission 2000Rp; 🕑 9am-4.30pm) is as big as its name and dominates what's already a big park in Renon. Inside this vaguely Borobodur-like structure are dioramas tracing Bali's history. Taking the name as a cue, you won't be surprised that they have a certain jingoistic soap-opera quality. But they're a fun diversion. Note that in the portrayal of the 1906 battle with the Dutch, the King of Badung is literally a sitting target.

Taman Wedhi Budaya

This **arts centre** (Map pp166-7; ☎ 222776; admission free; 🕑 8am-3pm Mon-Thu, 8am-1pm Fri-Sun) is a sprawling complex in the eastern part of Denpasar. Established in 1973 as an academy and showplace for Balinese culture, its lavish architecture houses an art gallery with an interesting collection, but few performances.

From mid-June to mid-July, the centre hosts the Bali Arts Festival (see p170), with dances, music and craft displays from all over Bali. You may need to book tickets at the centre for more popular events.

WALKING TOUR

This walk includes most of the attractions in the middle of town and a few vestiges of when Denpasar – and Bali – was a much slower place. Allow extra time for visiting the museum or shopping.

Start the walk at **Museum Negeri Propinsi Bali** (**1**; p168). Opposite is **Puputan Sq** (**2**), a park that commemorates the heroic but suicidal stand of the rajahs of Badung against the invading Dutch in 1906. A monument depicts a Balinese family in heroic pose, brandishing the weapons that were so ineffective against the Dutch guns. The woman also has jewels in her left hand, as the women of the Badung court reputedly flung their jewellery at the Dutch soldiers to taunt them. The park is popular with locals at lunch time and with families near sunset.

Back on the corner of Jl Surapati and Jl Veteran is the towering **Catur Muka statue** (**3**), which represents Batara Guru, Lord of the Four Directions. The four-faced, eight-armed figure keeps a close eye (or is it eight eyes?) on the traffic swirling around him. Head 100m north on Jl Veteran to the **Inna Bali** (**4;** Jl Veteran 3; p170). It dates from 1927 and was once the main tourist hotel on the island. It makes a nostalgic place for a refreshment.

Return to the Catur Muka statue and head west on Jl Gajah Mada (named after the 14th-century Majapahit prime minister). Go past banks, shops and a café towards the bridge over the grubby Sungai Badung (Badung River). Just before the bridge, on the left, is the renovated **Pasar Badung** (**5; p171**), the main produce market. This is one of the better places to see the fertile fruit of Bali. On the left, just after the bridge, **Pasar Kumbasari** (**6; p171**) is a handicraft and textiles market.

At the next main intersection, detour north up Jl Sutomo, and turn left along a small *gang* (lane) leading to the **Pura Maospahit** (**7**) temple. Established in the 14th century, at the time the Majapahit arrived from Java, the temple was damaged in a 1917 earthquake and has been heavily restored since. The oldest structures are at the back of the temple, but the most interesting features are the large statues of Garuda and the giant Batara Bayu.

Turn back, and continue south along Jl Thamrin, to the junction of Jl Hasanudin. On this corner is the **Puri Pemecutan** (**8**), a palace destroyed during the 1906 invasion. It's now long since been rebuilt and you can look inside the compound but don't expect anything palatial.

Go east on Jl Hasanudin, then north onto Jl Sulawesi, and you'll be in the area of the gold shops, known as Kampung Arab for the many people there of Middle Eastern or Indian descent. Continue north past Pasar Badung market to return to Jl Gajah Mada.

WALK FACTS

Start	Denpasar Tourist Office
Finish	Tiara Dewata Shopping Centre
Distance	2km
Duration	2-3hr

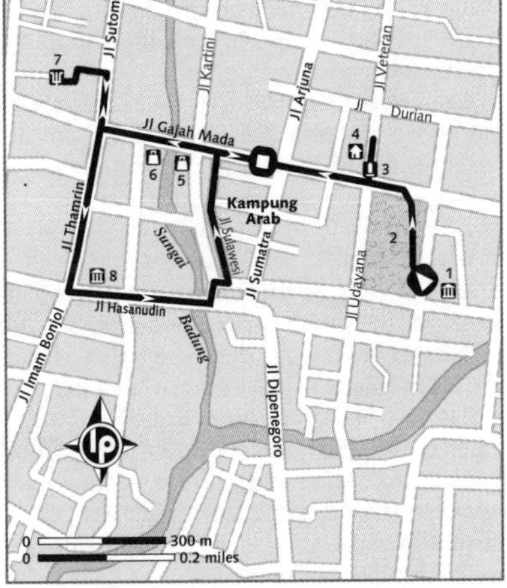

ACTIVITIES

Many Balinese wouldn't think of having a massage from anyone but a blind person. Government-sponsored schools offer lengthy courses to certify blind people in reflexology, shiatsu massage, anatomy and much more. Usually graduates work together in group locations such as **Kube Dharma Bakti** (☎ 749 9440; Jl Serma Mendara 3; massage per hr 30,000Rp; 9am-9pm). In this airy building redolent with liniments, you can choose from a range of therapies and contribute to a very good cause at the same time.

SOUTH BALI

SOUTH BALI

COURSES

The best place for courses in Bahasa Indonesia is the **Indonesia Australia Language Foundation** (IALF; Map p128; ☎ 225243; www.ialf.edu; Jl Raya Sesetan 190), which has a language lab, library, and well-run four-week 40-hour course (two hours per day Monday to Friday, costing 1,250,000Rp). Courses are available in six levels, from beginner to advanced.

FESTIVALS & EVENTS

The annual **Bali Arts Festival** (www.baliartsfestival.com), based at the Taman Wedhi Budaya arts centre (p168) in Denpasar, lasts for about a month starting in mid-June. It's a great time to visit Bali, and the festival is an easy way to see a wide variety of traditional dance, music and crafts from the island. The productions of the *Ramayana* and *Mahabharata* ballets are grand, and the opening ceremony and parade in Denpasar are particularly colourful.

The festival is the main event of the year for scores of village dance and musical groups. Competition is fierce with local pride on the line at each performance. To do well here sets a village on a good course for the year. Some events are held in a 6000-seat amphitheatre, a venue that allows you to realise the mass appeal of traditional Balinese culture. Tickets are usually available before performances and schedules are available throughout South Bali, Ubud and at the Denpasar tourist office.

SLEEPING

Denpasar has several hotels, but it's hard to think of a compelling reason to stay here unless you want to be close to the bus stations or have some other business here. At times when many Indonesians travel (July, August, around Christmas and Idul Fitri – November/December), it may be wise to book a room.

Budget

Adi Yasa (Map pp166-7; ☎ 222679; Jl Nakula 23B; s/d 40,000/60,000Rp) Budget travellers have crashed here since the 1970s. It's centrally located and friendly; the nine rooms are very basic.

Nakula Familar Inn (Map pp166-7; ☎ 226446; Jl Nakula 4; s/d 50,000/80,000Rp) Across the road and 100m west from the Adi Yasa, the eight rooms here are decent (cold-water showers only) and clean, and all have a small balcony area. The traffic noise isn't too bad and there is a nice little enclave in the middle. Tegal-Kereneng bemo go along Jl Nakula.

Hotel Niki Rusdi (Map pp166-7; ☎ 416397; Jl Pidada XIV; r 80,000-200,000Rp; ❄) This simple place is located right behind the Ubung Bus Terminal and is a good choice if you have an early or late bus. Rooms are very clean. There are other options nearby if this one is full.

Midrange

Most midrange places cater to Indonesian business travellers. There are no hotels in the top-end category.

Hotel Taman Suci (Map pp166-7; ☎ 484445; www.tamansuci.com; Jl Imam Bonjol 45; r from 225,000-275,000Rp; ❄ 💻) A good choice for business travellers, this modern, multifloor 45-room hotel insulates you from the hubbub outside from the minute you enter its air-con lobby.

Inna Bali (Map pp166-7; ☎ 225681; www.innabali.com; Jl Veteran 3; s from 375,000-415,000Rp; ❄ 🏊) A government-owned hotel, the Inna Bali has simple gardens and retains a certain nostalgic charm from its early days as a Dutch outpost built in 1927. Room interiors are standard, but many make up for this with deeply shaded verandas. The hotel is a good base for the *Ngrupuk* parades that take place the day before Nyepi (see the boxed text, p338), as they pass right by the front of the hotel.

EATING

You can eat very well in Denpasar. Most places cater to locals and Indonesian visitors, so they offer tasty authentic food at good prices. At the **Pasar Malam Kereneng** (Kereneng Night Market; Map pp166–7) dozens of vendors dish up food till dawn. A number of places along Jl Teuku Umar and in Renon cater to more affluent locals while all the shopping malls have food-court options.

Café Merdeka (Map pp166-7; ☎ 244784; Jl Teuku Umar 240; baked goods from 500Rp) Delightful Balinese bakery with a wide range of sweet and savoury baked goods you choose yourself and can take away or enjoy at the outside tables.

Warung Satria (Map pp166-7; Jl Kedondong; dishes 4000-10,000Rp) A long-running warung on a quiet street; try the wonderful seafood satay served with a shallot sambal. Otherwise, choose from the immaculate displays of what's fresh.

Nasi Uduk (Map pp166-7; Jl Teuku Umar; 5000-12,000Rp) Open to the street, this spotless little stall has a few chairs and serves up treats such as *nasi uduk* (sweetly scented coconut rice with fresh peanut sauce) and *lalapan* (a simple salad of fresh lemon basil leaves).

Bhineka Jaya Café (Map pp166-7; ☎ 224016; Jl Gajah Mada 80; coffee 3000Rp; 9am-4pm) Home to Bali's Coffee Co, this storefront sells locally grown beans and makes a mean espresso, which you can enjoy at the two tiny tables while watching the bustle of Denpasar's old main drag.

Bali Bakery (Map pp166-7; ☎ 243147; Jl Hayam Wuruk; dishes 5000-30,000Rp;) Small branch of the Kuta favourite. Great baked goods and small café. Free wi-fi.

Wong Solo (Map pp166-7; ☎ 231191; Jl Merdeka 18; 8000-20,000Rp) Part of small local chain; chicken in myriad forms is the specialty here. Sit at an open-air table and have it spicy and grilled or try the *ikan lele* (grilled catfish).

Warung Bendega (Map pp166-7; ☎ 225112; Jl Cok Agung Tresna 37A; dishes 7000-25,000Rp) Walled off from street noise, this lovely and stylish open-air oasis hums to the rhythm of Balinese pop music at dinner. Creatively spiced seafood is the specialty.

Cianjur (Map pp166-7; ☎ 230015; Jl Cok Agung Tresna; dishes 8000-25,000Rp;) Big, airy and cool, this upmarket place has Balinese seafood in an array of preparations (crispy, grilled, steamed or wrapped in a banana leaf). Hugely popular with families and groups of bureaucrats.

SHOPPING

Local goods can be found in the markets and at the large shopping malls south of the centre, which are all the rage locally.

Markets

The **Pasar Badung** (Map pp166–7) is busy in the morning and evening, and is a great place to browse and bargain. You'll find produce and food from all over the island as well as easy-to-assemble temple offerings that are popular with working women. Deals include a half-kilo of saffron for 250,000Rp. Ignore guides who may offer their services.

Across the river, **Pasar Kumbasari** (Map pp166–7) has handicrafts, a plethora of vibrant fabrics and costumes decorated with gold. It's a modern, multi-level building of shops and stalls and you should just plunge at random into the canyons of colour.

Kampung Arab (Map pp166–7) has jewellery and precious metal stores. North on Jl Veteran, **Pasar Burung** (Map pp166–7) is a bird market with hundreds of caged birds and small animals, such as guinea pigs, rabbits and monkeys, for sale. There are also gaudy and colourful birdcages. You wonder how many endangered species are traded behind the scenes.

An impromptu dog market also operates directly opposite the bird market. While you're here, have a look at the elaborate **Pura Sutriya** (Map pp166–7), just east of the market.

Shopping Malls

Western-style shopping malls are very fashionable and jammed on Sundays with locals shopping and teens flirting. The brand-name goods are genuine.

Most malls have a food court with stalls serving fresh Asian fare, as well as fast-food joints (which have pleased more than one homesick holidaying tourist tot). Some have video arcades for kids and all offer plenty of parking.

Bali Mall (Map pp166-7; Jl Dipenegoro) Has the top-end Ramayana Department Store and an A&W restaurant.

Libby Plaza (Map pp166-7; Jl Teuku Umar) Has a huge Hero Supermarket.

Matahari (Map pp166-7; Jl Teuku Umar) Main branch of the department store, with numerous other stores and a Swenson's Ice Cream café.

Robinson's (Map pp166-7; Jl Teuku Umar or Jl Sudirman) Arch-competitor of Matahari has large selection of midrange and top-end goods.

Tiara Dewata Shopping Centre (Map pp166-7; Jl Udayan) Low-rise place with a good food court and a Dunkin' Donuts.

GETTING THERE & AWAY

Denpasar is *the* hub of road transport on Bali – you'll find buses and minibuses bound for all corners of the island.

Air

Sometimes called 'Denpasar' in airline schedules, Bali's Ngurah Rai international airport is south of Kuta. See p350 for details.

Bemo

The city has several bemo terminals – if you're travelling independently around Bali you'll often have to go via Denpasar, and transfer from one terminal to another. The terminals for transport around Bali are Ubung, Batubulan and Tegal, while the Gunung Agung, Kereneng and Sanglah terminals serve destinations in and around Denpasar. Each terminal has regular bemo connections to the other terminals in Denpasar for 5000Rp.

Bemo and minibuses cover shorter routes between towns and villages, while full-size buses are often used on longer, more heavily travelled routes. Buses are quicker and more comfortable, but they're less frequent.

UBUNG

Well north of the town, on the road to Gilimanuk, Ubung is the terminal for northern and western Bali and most long-distance bus service. In the complex, there is a helpful **tourist office** (see p165) to provide help with fares and schedules. Arriving here by taxi guarantees a reception by baggage and ticket touts.

Destination	Fare
Gilimanuk (for the ferry to Java)	25,000Rp
Kediri (for Tanah Lot)	6000Rp
Mengwi	6000Rp
Negara	20,000Rp
Pancasari (for Danau Bratan)	15,000Rp
Singaraja (via Pupuan or Bedugul)	28,000Rp
Tabanan	6000Rp

BATUBULAN

Located a very inconvenient 6km northeast of Denpasar on a road to Ubud, this terminal is for destinations in eastern and central Bali.

Destination	Fare
Amlapura	20,000Rp
Bangli	10,000Rp
Gianyar	8000Rp
Kintamani (via Tampaksiring)	15,000Rp
Nusa Dua (via Sanur)	6000Rp
Padangbai (for the Lombok ferry)	15,000Rp
Sanur	6000Rp
Semarapura	15,000Rp
Singaraja (via Kintamani)	25,000Rp
Singaraja (via Semarapura & Amlapura)	25,000Rp
Ubud	6000Rp

TEGAL

On the western side of town on Jl Iman Bonjol, Tegal is the terminal for Kuta and the Bukit Peninsula.

Destination	Fare
Airport	8000Rp
Jimbaran	10,000Rp
Kuta	8000Rp
Legian	8000Rp
Nusa Dua	10,000Rp
Ulu Watu	15,000Rp

GUNUNG AGUNG

This terminal, at the northwestern corner of town (look for orange bemo), is on Jl Gunung Agung, and has bemo to Kerobokan and Canggu (6000Rp).

KERENENG

East of the town centre, Kereneng has bemo to Sanur (5000Rp).

SANGLAH

In Jl Diponegoro, near the general hospital in the south of the city, Sanglah has bemo to Suwung and Benoa Harbour (5000Rp).

Bus

The usual route to Java is a bus from Denpasar's Ubung Terminal to Surabaya (120,000Rp, 10 hours), which includes the short ferry trip across the Bali Strait. Other buses go as far as Yogyakarta (180,000Rp, 16 hours) and Jakarta (275,000Rp, 24 hours), usually travelling overnight.

Book directly at offices in the Ubung terminal, 3km north of the city centre. To Surabaya or even Jakarta, you may get on a bus within an hour of arriving at Ubung, but at busy times you should buy your ticket at least one day ahead.

There are no tourist shuttle buses to/from Denpasar.

GETTING AROUND

Bemo

Bemo take various circuitous routes from and between the many bus/bemo terminals around. They line up for various destinations at each terminal, or you can try and hail them from anywhere along the main roads – look for the destination sign above the driver's window. The Tegal–Nusa Dua bemo (dark blue) is handy for Renon; and the Kereneng–Ubung bemo (turquoise) travels along Jl Gajah Mada, past the museum.

Taxi

If you're looking for a taxi, you're in luck – you'll find them prowling the streets of Denpasar looking for fares. As always, the blue cabs of **Bali Taxi** (☎ 701111) are the most reliable choice.

Ubud & Around

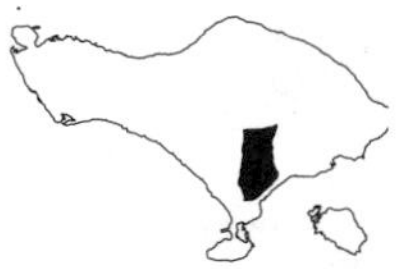

Ubud takes a Balinese holiday and makes it sublime. In one easy package you plunge into the incomparably rich culture of Bali while making certain that you never want for pleasure.

Compared to other parts of Bali where you might spend a day at the beach or on a tour or otherwise idling away, Ubud fills your time with walks, performances, art museums, fine food and much more. And it's all there ready for you. Generations of visitors haven't dimmed the natural openness of the locals, who are generally thrilled that you are interested in their beautiful temples, intriguing cultural ceremonies and beautiful land.

Set on the gentle slopes leading to Bali's highlands, Ubud enjoys weather that while tropical – and often wet! – during the day, cools off with gentle mountain breezes at night. Its fabric is striated with one surging river, stream and rice field channel after another. You're never more than a few steps away from fast-flowing clear water. Walks in the countryside and river valleys are journeys into natural beauty, where you will run out of words for 'green'.

When you're ready to see others do the work, attend any of the myriad cultural shows staged nightly in and around town. These reveal the rich artistry of Balinese dance and music. The settings are simple, which enhances the authenticity.

When you're feeling consumptive, you can choose from an array of creative and inviting cafés, restaurants and shops. For rest, select from family-run guesthouses to world-class resorts, and revive yourself in a spa.

Ubud is the kind of place where a stay of days turns into weeks.

HIGHLIGHTS

- Becoming entranced by a traditional **dance** performance in and around Ubud (p197)
- Tasting the many delights in Ubud, capital of Balinese **cuisine** (p193)
- Walking through fabulous scenery of the gorgeous **Sungai Ayung valley** (p182)
- Indulging your health and yourself at world-class **spas** (p181)
- Exploring ancient wonders such as **Yeh Pulu** (p201), the home of 14th-century stone carvings depicting everyday life

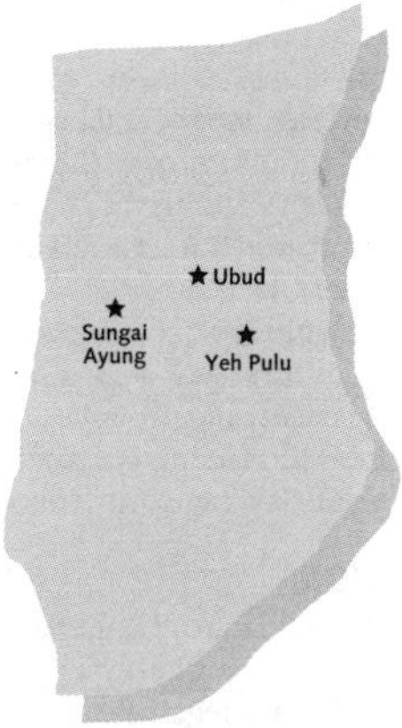

UBUD

☎ 0361

Ubud is culture, yes. It's also home to some of Bali's best restaurants, cafés and streets of shops, many selling goods from the region's artisans and craftmakers. There's somewhere to stay for every budget, and no matter what the price you can enjoy lodgings that reflect the local *zeitgeist*: artful, creative and serene.

The weather is slightly cooler but much wetter than the south; expect it to rain at any time. At night mountain breezes obviate a slumberer's need for air-con.

Spend a few days in Ubud to appreciate it properly. It's one of those places where days can become weeks and weeks become months, as the noticeable expatriate community demonstrates.

For details on routes and sights to Ubud from South Bali, see the section South of Ubud, p204.

HISTORY

Late in the 19th century, Cokorda Gede Sukawati established a branch of the Sukawati royal family in Ubud and began a series of alliances and confrontations with neighbouring kingdoms. In 1900, with the kingdom of Gianyar, Ubud became (at its own request) a Dutch protectorate and was able to concentrate on its religious and cultural life.

The Cokorda's descendants encouraged Western artists and intellectuals to visit the area in the 1930s, most notably Walter Spies, Colin McPhee and Rudolf Bonnet (see Western Visitors in the 1930s, p52). They provided an enormous stimulus to local art, introduced new ideas and techniques, and began a process of displaying and promoting Balinese culture worldwide. As mass tourism arrived on Bali, Ubud became an attraction not for beaches or bars, but for the arts.

For an in-depth look at Ubud's history and present-day culture, seek a copy of *Ubud Is A Mood*. This lavishly illustrated book includes photos by local Rio Helmi (see p180) and is far superior to your average tourist book.

ORIENTATION

The once small village of Ubud has expanded to encompass its neighbours – Campuan, Penestanan, Padangtegal, Peliatan and Pengosekan are all part of what we see as Ubud today. The centre of town is the junction of Monkey Forest Rd and Jl Raya Ubud, where the bustling market and crowded *bemo* (small minibus) stops are found, as well as Ubud Palace and the main temple, Pura Desa Ubud. Monkey Forest Rd (officially Jl Wanara Wana, but always known by its unofficial name) runs south to Sacred Monkey Forest Sanctuary and is lined with shops, hotels and restaurants.

Jl Raya Ubud ('Ubud Main Rd' – often Jl Raya for short) is the main east–west road. In the east, a mix of cheap accommodation, idiosyncratic shops and little cafés gives Jl Goutama a feel of Ubud 25 years ago. West of Ubud, the road drops steeply down to the ravine at Campuan, where an old suspension bridge, next to the new one, hangs over the Sungai Wos. West of Campuan, the pretty village of Penestanan is famous for its painters and bead-work. East and south of Ubud proper, the 'villages' of Peliatan, Nyuhkuning and Pengosekan and are known variously for painting, woodcarving and traditional dance. The latter has been the focus of recent development, with rice paddies giving way to new hotels. The area north of Ubud is less densely settled, with picturesque paddy fields interspersed with small villages, many of which specialise in a local craft.

Maps

The maps in this guidebook will be sufficient for most visitors, but if you want to explore the surrounding villages on foot or by bicycle, the locally sold *Bali Pathfinder* map is useful.

INFORMATION

Along the main roads, you'll find most services you need including travel agents and *wartel* (public telephone offices).

Ubud is home to many non-profit and volunteer groups; see p348 for details.

Bookshops

Ubud is the best place on Bali for book shopping. Selections are wide and varied and you can get numerous books about Balinese art and culture. Many carry titles by small and obscure publishers. Shops typically carry newspapers such as the *International Herald Tribune*.

ARMA (p178) Large selection of cultural titles.

Ary's Bookshop (Map p188; ☎ 978203; Jl Raya Ubud) Good for art books and maps.

Cinta Bookshop (Map p188; ☎ 973295; Jl Dewi Sita) Nice assortment of used novels and vintage books about Bali.
Ganesha Bookshop (Map pp176-7; ☎ 970320; www.ganeshabooksbali.com; Jl Raya Ubud) Ubud's best bookshop has an amazing amount of stock jammed into the small space. Excellent selection of titles on Indonesian studies, travel, arts and music, fiction (including used titles) and maps. Good recommendations and mail-order service.
Neka Art Museum (p178) Good range of art books.
Periplus (Map p188; ☎ 975178; Monkey Forest Rd) A typically glossy branch of the Bali chain. Also a new location in Campuan (Map pp176-7; ☎ 976149; Bintang Centre, Jl Raya Campuan) Large store with small café.
Pondok Pecak Library & Learning Centre (below) Regularly thins its collection and has some excellent fiction for sale.
Rendezvousdoux (Map p188; ☎ 747 0163; Jl Raya Ubud 14;) Small selection of books, many French titles.

Emergency

Police station (Map pp176-7; ☎ 975316; Jl Raya Andong; 24hr) Located east, at Andong.

Internet Access

The following two neighbouring places are a cut above average with fast broadband connections and large screens.
@Highway (Map pp176-7; ☎ 972107; Jl Raya Ubud; per min 500Rp; 24hr;) Full-service and very fast.
Bali 3000 (Map pp176-7; ☎ 978538; Jl Raya Ubud; per hr 16,000Rp; 8am-11pm;) Fashionable internet café with a full range of computing services and good sandwiches, coffees and juices.

Watch for Ubud's many cafés to adopt the trend to install wi-fi access. One already equipped is Coffee & Silver; see p194.

Libraries

Pondok Pecak Library & Learning Centre (Map p188; ☎ 976194; Monkey Forest Rd, on the far side of the football field; 9am-5pm Mon-Sat, 1-5pm Sun) A relaxed place, with a children's book section. Charges membership fees for library use. Small café and a pleasant reading area on the roof. See p185 for information on cultural courses.

Medical Services

See Health (p366) for details on international clinics and hospitals in Bali.
Mua Pharmacy (Map p188; ☎ 974674; Monkey Forest Rd; 8am-9pm)
Ubud Clinic (Map pp176-7; ☎ 974911; www.ubudclinic.com; Jl Raya Campuan 36; 24hr) Best medical centre in Ubud. Charges range from 200,000Rp for a clinical consultation.

Money

Ubud has numerous banks, ATMs and moneychangers along Jl Raya Ubud and Monkey Forest Rd.

Post

Main post office (Map pp176-7; Jl Jembawan; 8am-6pm) Has a sort-it-yourself poste restante system – address poste restante mail to Kantor Pos, Ubud 80571, Bali, Indonesia.

Tourist Information

Ubud Tourist Information (Yaysan Bina Wisata; Map p188; ☎ 973285; Jl Raya Ubud; 8am-8pm) The one really useful tourist office on Bali. It has a good range of information and a notice board listing current happenings and activities. The staff can answer most regional questions and have up-to-date information on ceremonies and traditional dances held in the area; dance tickets are sold here.

SIGHTS

Palaces & Temples

Ubud Palace and **Puri Saren Agung** (Map p188; cnr Jl Raya Ubud & Jl Suweta) share space in the heart of Ubud. The compound has many ornate corners and was mostly built after the 1917 earthquake. The local royal family still lives here and you can wander around most of the large compound exploring the many traditional and not excessively ornate buildings. If you really like it, you can stay the night (p190).

Just north, **Pura Marajan Agung** (Map p188; Jl Suweta) has one of the finest gates you'll find and is the private temple for Ubud's royal family.

Pura Desa Ubud (Map p188; Jl Raya Ubud) is the main temple for the Ubud community. Just a bit west is the very picturesque **Pura Taman Saraswati** (Ubud Water Palace; Map p188; Jl Raya Ubud). Waters from the temple at the rear of the site feed the pond in the front, which overflows with pretty lotus blossoms. There are carvings that honour Dewi Saraswati, the goddess of wisdom and the arts, who has clearly given her blessing to Ubud. There are weekly dance performances.

Museums

MUSEUM PURI LUKISAN

The **Museum of Fine Arts** (Map p188; ☎ 975136; off Jl Raya Ubud; www.mpl-ubud.com; admission 20,000Rp; 9am-5pm) displays fine examples of all schools of Balinese art. Just look at the lush

UBUD AREA

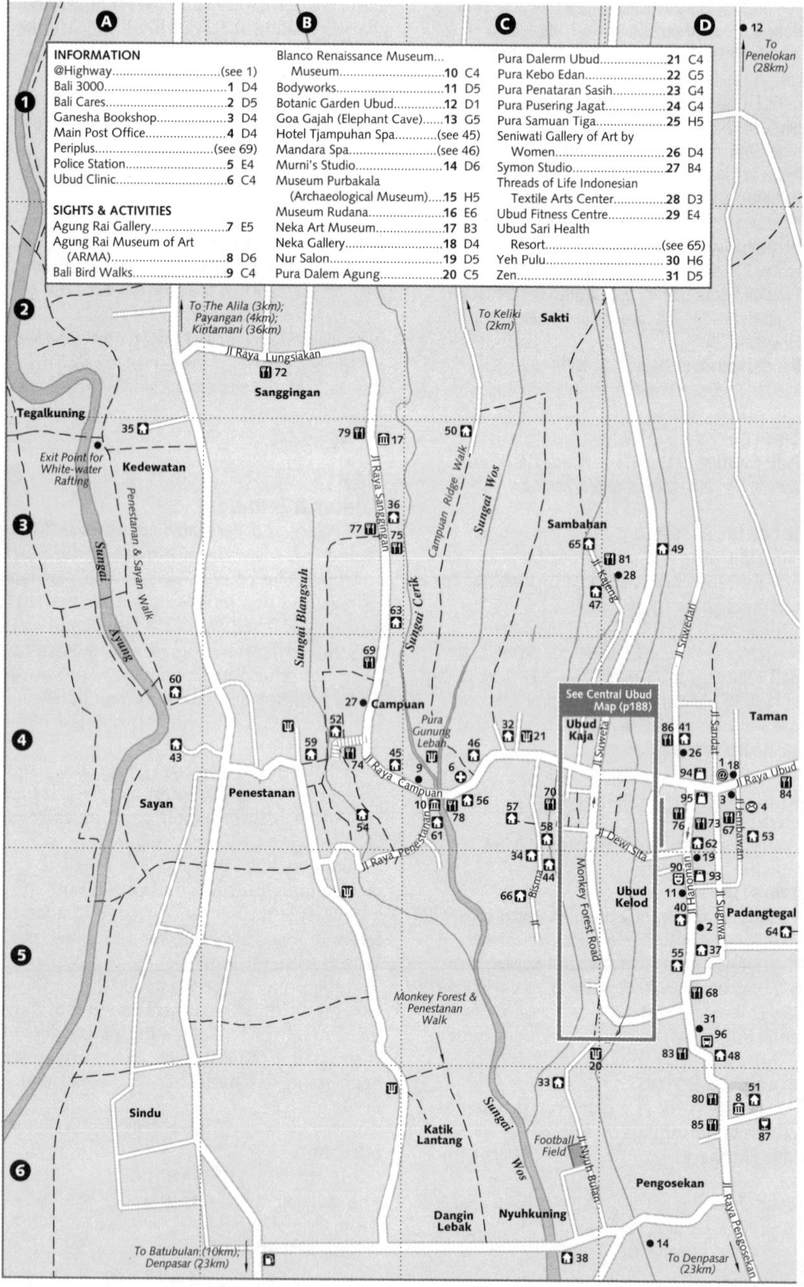
A
B
C
D
1
2
3
4
5
6
INFORMATION
@Highway....(see 1)
Bali 3000....1 D4
Bali Cares....2 D5
Ganesha Bookshop....3 D4
Main Post Office....4 D4
Periplus....(see 69)
Police Station....5 E4
Ubud Clinic....6 C4
SIGHTS & ACTIVITIES
Agung Rai Gallery....7 E5
Agung Rai Museum of Art (ARMA)....8 D6
Bali Bird Walks....9 C4
Blanco Renaissance Museum... Museum....10 C4
Bodyworks....11 D5
Botanic Garden Ubud....12 D1
Goa Gajah (Elephant Cave)....13 G5
Hotel Tjampuhan Spa....(see 45)
Mandara Spa....(see 46)
Murni's Studio....14 D6
Museum Purbakala (Archaeological Museum)....15 H5
Museum Rudana....16 E6
Neka Art Museum....17 B3
Neka Gallery....18 D4
Nur Salon....19 D5
Pura Dalem Agung....20 C5
Pura Dalerm Ubud....21 C4
Pura Kebo Edan....22 G5
Pura Penataran Sasih....23 G4
Pura Pusering Jagat....24 G4
Pura Samuan Tiga....25 H5
Seniwati Gallery of Art by Women....26 D4
Symon Studio....27 B4
Threads of Life Indonesian Textile Arts Center....28 D3
Ubud Fitness Centre....29 E4
Ubud Sari Health Resort....(see 65)
Yeh Pulu....30 H6
Zen....31 D5
To Penelokan (28km)
To The Alila (3km); Payangan (4km); Kintamani (36km)
To Keliki (2km)
Sakti
Jl Raya Lungsiakan
Sanggingan
Tegalkuning
Exit Point for White-water Rafting
Kedewatan
Penestanan & Sayan Walk
Sungai Ayung
Jl Raya Sanggingan
Campuan Ridge Walk
Sungai Wos
Sungai Cerik
Sungai Blangsuh
Sambahan
Jl Kajeng
Jl Sriwedari
Campuan
Pura Gunung Lebah
See Central Ubud Map (p188)
Ubud Kaja
Jl Suweta
Taman
Jl Sandat
Jl Raya Ubud
Jl Raya Campuan
Penestanan
Sayan
Jl Raya Penestanan
Jl Dewi Sita
Jl Jembawan
Jl Bisma
Monkey Forest Road
Ubud Kelod
Jl Hanoman
Jl Sugriwa
Padangtegal
Monkey Forest & Penestanan Walk
Sindu
Katik Lantang
Sungai Wos
Football Field
Jl Nyuh Bulan
Pengosekan
Jl Raya Pengosekan
Dangin Lebak
Nyuhkuning
To Batubulan (10km); Denpasar (23km)
To Denpasar (23km)

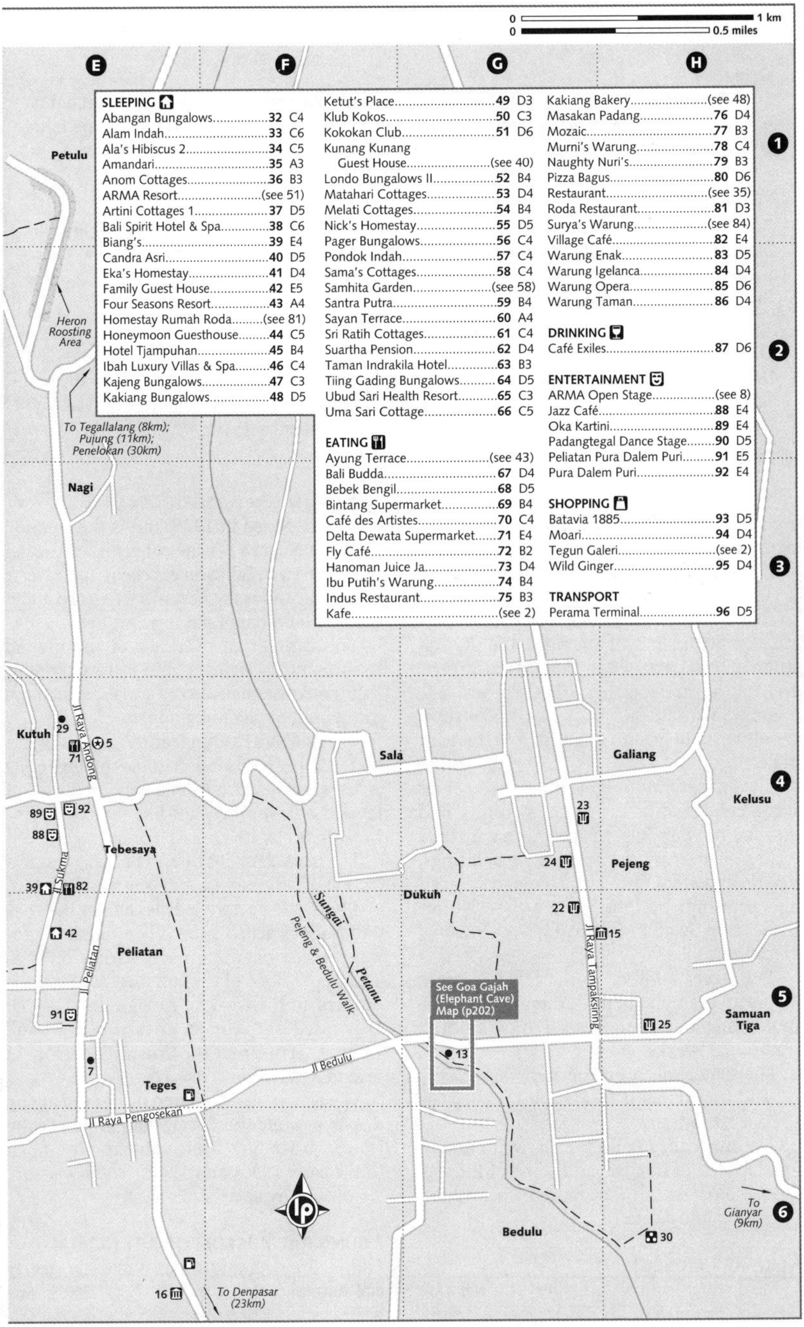

SLEEPING

Abangan Bungalows....................32 C4
Alam Indah....................33 C6
Ala's Hibiscus 2....................34 C5
Amandari....................35 A3
Anom Cottages....................36 B3
ARMA Resort....................(see 51)
Artini Cottages 1....................37 D5
Bali Spirit Hotel & Spa....................38 C6
Biang's....................39 E4
Candra Asri....................40 D5
Eka's Homestay....................41 D4
Family Guest House....................42 E5
Four Seasons Resort....................43 A4
Homestay Rumah Roda....................(see 81)
Honeymoon Guesthouse....................44 C5
Hotel Tjampuhan....................45 B4
Ibah Luxury Villas & Spa....................46 C4
Kajeng Bungalows....................47 C3
Kakiang Bungalows....................48 D5
Ketut's Place....................49 D3
Klub Kokos....................50 C3
Kokokan Club....................51 D6
Kunang Kunang Guest House....................(see 40)
Londo Bungalows II....................52 B4
Matahari Cottages....................53 D4
Melati Cottages....................54 B4
Nick's Homestay....................55 D5
Pager Bungalows....................56 C4
Pondok Indah....................57 C4
Sama's Cottages....................58 C4
Samhita Garden....................(see 58)
Santra Putra....................59 B4
Sayan Terrace....................60 A4
Sri Ratih Cottages....................61 C4
Suartha Pension....................62 D4
Taman Indrakila Hotel....................63 B3
Tiing Gading Bungalows....................64 D5
Ubud Sari Health Resort....................65 C3
Uma Sari Cottage....................66 C5

EATING

Ayung Terrace....................(see 43)
Bali Budda....................67 D4
Bebek Bengil....................68 D5
Bintang Supermarket....................69 B4
Café des Artistes....................70 C4
Delta Dewata Supermarket....................71 E4
Fly Café....................72 B2
Hanoman Juice Ja....................73 D4
Ibu Putih's Warung....................74 B4
Indus Restaurant....................75 B3
Kafe....................(see 2)
Kakiang Bakery....................(see 48)
Masakan Padang....................76 D4
Mozaic....................77 B3
Murni's Warung....................78 C4
Naughty Nuri's....................79 B3
Pizza Bagus....................80 D6
Restaurant....................(see 35)
Roda Restaurant....................81 D3
Surya's Warung....................(see 84)
Village Café....................82 E4
Warung Enak....................83 D5
Warung Igelanca....................84 D4
Warung Opera....................85 D6
Warung Taman....................86 D4

DRINKING

Café Exiles....................87 D6

ENTERTAINMENT

ARMA Open Stage....................(see 8)
Jazz Café....................88 E4
Oka Kartini....................89 E4
Padangtegal Dance Stage....................90 D5
Peliatan Pura Dalem Puri....................91 E5
Pura Dalem Puri....................92 E4

SHOPPING

Batavia 1885....................93 D5
Moari....................94 D4
Tegun Galeri....................(see 2)
Wild Ginger....................95 D4

TRANSPORT

Perama Terminal....................96 D5

UBUD IN...

One Day

Stroll the streets of Ubud, enjoying the galleries and sampling the fine cuisine. Try to get out on one of the short nearby walks through the verdant rice fields. Go to an evening dance performance at the Ubud Palace.

Three Days

Take longer walks in the countryside, especially the Campuan Ridge and Satan Valley. Visit the Museum Puri Lukisan, Neka Art Museum and ARMA (Agung Rai Museum of Art). Attend dance performances not just in Ubud, but also in the nearby villages. Indulge at a local spa. Drop by the market in the morning.

One Week or More

Do everything we've listed but take time to simply chill out. Get in tune with Ubud's rhythm. Take naps, read books, wander about. Think about a course in Balinese culture. Compare and choose your favourite café, get out to craft villages and ancient sites.

composition of 'Balinese Market' by Anak Agung Gde Sobrat to see the vibrancy of local painting.

It was in Ubud that the modern Balinese art movement started; where artists first began to abandon purely religious themes and court subjects for scenes of everyday life. Rudolf Bonnet was part of the Pita Maha artists' cooperative, and together with Cokorda Gede Agung Sukawati (a prince of Ubud's royal family) they helped to establish a permanent collection.

The **first pavilion** straight ahead as you enter has a collection of early works from Ubud and the surrounding villages. These include examples of classical *wayang*-style paintings, fine ink drawings by I Gusti Nyoman Lempad and paintings by Pita Maha artists. Notice the level of detail in Lempad's *The Dream of Dharmawangsa*.

The **second pavilion** on the left has some colourful examples of the 'Young Artist' style of painting and a good selection of 'modern traditional' works.

The **third pavilion** on the right has classical and traditional paintings and is used for special exhibitions.

The museum's collection is well curated and labelled in English, and some of the artwork is often for sale. The museum has a good bookshop and a café.

NEKA ART MUSEUM

Quite distinct from Neka Gallery, the **Neka Art Museum** (Map pp176-7; ☎ 975074; www.museumneka.com; Jl Raya Sanggingan; adult/child 20,000Rp/free; 🕑 9am-5pm) was opened in 1976, and is the creation of Suteja Neka, a private collector and dealer in Balinese art. It has an excellent and diverse collection and is the best place to learn about the development of painting on Bali.

You can get an overview of the myriad local painting styles in the **Balinese Painting Hall**. Look for the *wayang* works, which are influenced by shadow puppets.

The **Arie Smit Pavilion** features Smit's works on the upper level, and examples of the Young Artist school, which he inspired, on the lower level. Look for Bruegel-like *The Wedding Ceremony*', by I Nyoman Tjarka.

The **Lempad Pavilion** houses Bali's largest collection of works by I Gusti Nyoman Lempad.

The **Contemporary Indonesian Art Hall** has paintings by artists from other parts of Indonesia, many of whom have worked on Bali. The upper floor of the **East-West Art Annexe** is devoted to the work of foreign artists, such as Louise Koke, Miguel Covarrubias, Rudolf Bonnet, Han Snel, the Australian Donald Friend and Antonio Blanco.

The temporary exhibition hall has changing displays, while the **Photography Archive Centre** features black-and-white photography of Bali in the early 1930s and 1940s. The bookstore is noteworthy and there's a café.

AGUNG RAI MUSEUM OF ART (ARMA)

Founded by Agung Rai as a **museum, gallery and cultural centre** (Map pp176-7; ☎ 976659; www.armamuseum.com; Jl Raya Pengosekan; admission 25,000Rp;

9am-6pm), the impressive ARMA is the only place in Bali to see the haunting works by the influential German artist Walter Spies.

The museum is housed in several traditional buildings set in gardens with water coursing through channels. It features work by 19th-century Javanese artist Raden Saleh. It exhibits classical Kamasan paintings, Batuan-style work from the 1930s and '40s, and works by Lempad, Affandi, Sadali, Hofker, Bonnet and Le Mayeur. The collection is well labelled in English.

Look for the enigmatic *Portrait of a Javanese Nobleman and his Wife* by Raden Saleh, which predates the similar *American Gothic* by decades.

It's interesting to visit ARMA when local children practise **Balinese dancing** (3-5pm Mon-Fri, 10.30am-noon Sun) and during **gamelan practice** (hours vary). See p186 for details on regular Legong and Kecak (types of classic Balinese dance) dance performances. See p185 for details on the myriad of cultural courses offered here.

You can enter the museum grounds from the southern end of Jl Raya Pengosekan (there's parking near Kafe ARMA) or around the corner on Jl Pengosekan at the the Kafe ARMA. The Ubud–Gianyar bemo will drop you here.

THREADS OF LIFE INDONESIAN TEXTILE ARTS CENTER

This small, professional **textile gallery and educational studio** (Map pp176-7; 972187; www.threadsoflife.com; Jl Kajeng 24; 10am-6pm Mon-Sat) sponsors the production of naturally dyed, handmade ritual textiles, helping to recover skills in danger of being lost to modern dyeing and weaving methods. Commissioned pieces are displayed in the gallery, which has good explanatory material. It also runs regular textile appreciation courses (see p185) and has a good shop.

MUSEUM RUDANA

This large, imposing **museum** (Map pp176-7; 975779; www.museumrudana.com; admission 20,000Rp; 9am-5pm) is the creation of local politician and art-lover Nyoman Rudana and his wife Ni Wayan Olasthini. The three floors contain over 400 traditional paintings, including a calendar dated to the 1840s, some Lempad drawings, and more modern pieces. The museum is beside the Rudana Gallery, which has a large selection of paintings for sale.

BLANCO RENAISSANCE MUSEUM

The picture of Antonio Blanco mugging with Michael Jackson says it all. His namesake **Blanco Renaissance Museum** (Map pp176-7; 975502; Jl Raya Campuan; adult/child 20,000/10,000Rp; 9am-5pm) captures the artist's theatrical spirit. Blanco came to Bali from Spain via the Philippines. He specialised in erotic art, illustrated poetry and playing the role of an eccentric artist à la Dali. He died in Bali in 1999, and his flamboyant home is now this museum. The design of the compound is a pastiche of elaborate styles from around the world.

Galleries

Ubud is dotted with galleries – every street and lane seems to have a place exhibiting artwork for sale. They vary enormously in the choice and quality of items on display. Several major galleries display a huge variety of work, generally of a very high quality.

Often you will find local artists in the most unusual places, including your place to stay. A good example is **Nyoman Sudiarsa**, a painter who has a studio in the grounds of his family's Padma Accommodation (see p188).

NEKA GALLERY

Operated by Suteja Neka, the **Neka Gallery** (Map pp176-7; 975034; Jl Raya Ubud; 9am-5pm) is separate entity from the Neka Art Museum. It has an extensive selection from all the schools of Balinese art, as well as works by European residents such as the renowned Arie Smit.

SENIWATI GALLERY OF ART BY WOMEN

This **gallery** (Map pp176-7; 975485; www.seniwatigallery.com; Jl Sriwedari 2B; 9am-5pm Tue-Sun) exhibits works by over 70 Balinese, Indonesian and resident foreign women artists. The information on many of the artists makes for fascinating reading. The gallery and workshop aims to publicise Balinese women artists and to encourage the next generation. The works span all media and this place is an excellent example of the kind of cultural and artistic organisation that can thrive in Ubud.

SYMON STUDIO

Danger! Art! screams the sign in Campuan. With this you know you've found the **gallery/studio** (Map pp176-7; 974721; www.symonbali.com; Jl Raya Campuan; 9am-6pm) of the irrepressible

American artist Symon. The gallery is a spacious and airy place full of huge, colourful and exotic portraits. The work ranges from the sublime to the profane.

KOMANEKA ART GALLERY

Exhibiting works from established Balinese artists, the **gallery** (Map p188; ☎ 976090; Monkey Forest Rd) is a good place to see high-profile art. The space is large and lofty, making a good place for viewing.

AGUNG RAI GALLERY

In Peliatan, the **gallery** (Map pp176-7; ☎ 975449; Jl Peliatan; 9am-6pm) is in a pretty compound and its collection covers the full range of Balinese styles. It works as a cooperative, with the work priced by the artist and the gallery adding a percentage.

RIO HELMI GALLERY

Noted photographer and Ubud resident Rio Helmi has a small **gallery** (Map p188; ☎ 972304; www.riohelmi.com; Jl Suweta 5; 10am-8pm) where you can see examples of journalistic and artistic work. Photos change often and show Helmi's travels worldwide. You can also see his work in many coffee-table books about Bali.

LEMPAD'S HOUSE

I Gusti Nyoman Lempad's **home** (Map p188; Jl Raya Ubud; admission free; daylight) is open to the public, but it's mainly used as a gallery for a group of artists, which includes Lempad's grandchildren. There are only a few of Lempad's own paintings and drawings here. The Puri Lukisan (p175) and Neka (p178) museums have more extensive collections of Lempad's drawings. The family compound itself is a good example

A LUST FOR PAINT

Only 40 years old when she died in 2006, I Gusti Ayu Kadek Murniasih's life was short but intense. Her influence on the lives of Balinese women will be felt for a long time to come.

At her studio in Pengosekan, Murni (everyone called her that) painted works that earned her street cred as Bali's most innovative contemporary painter. Breaking taboos, she explored her own sexuality, not through depictions of herself, but through distorted images of male and female genitalia.

Of the act itself, her canvases showed penises and vaginas and all sorts of acts you won't find painted by a man, let alone a woman, in the galleries of Bali. 'She broke every taboo while maintaining her very sincere and devout Balinese persona,' says Mary Northmore-Aziz, founder and director of the Seniwati Gallery of Art By Women in Ubud (see p179).

'She set new standards of personal honesty in a culture that prefers to idealise the role and life of women.'

Sexually abused as a child by her father, a farmer, Murni used paint to exorcise this lasting nightmare. Her first shows in the early 1990s shocked many. 'I recall fences, knives, headless women, it was very disturbing to a number of people,' says Northmore-Aziz.

'But over the years her work developed and a lovely sense of humour also emerged, she could laugh at herself and at human sexuality and invent weird and wonderful images.'

Murni was always most comfortable in her Ubud studio. As her work became better known, she found relative fame in the art world and her work was displayed worldwide, often in solo shows. In person, Murni was a witty, cheery and engaging person. It was quite a considerable transformation for a woman who as a child had sought refuge from abuse and poverty by drawing everything around her.

In 1993, Murni made another statement that will impact the lives of Balinese women for years to come. She was granted what is thought to be Bali's first legally issued divorce to a woman. Her husband had taken up with someone else and she wasn't going to have it.

Always a compulsive painter, Murni kept working, even after she was diagnosed with cancer. She told Carla Bianpoen, an author and journalist who writes about Indonesian culture, 'I paint for the feeling that I exist.'

'Her frankness and courage has certainly inspired more Balinese young women to come forward as an artist,' says Bianpoen, 'though none so far has come near what Murni has dared to do.'

of traditional Balinese architecture and layout – Lempad was also an architect and sculptor. It's also home to many animals in cages.

PHO

You never know what you'll find at **Pho** (Map p188; ☎ 0813-3866 9382; Jl Goutama), an enigmatic and enthusiastic open-air gallery right beside the road. From performance art to wild installations it could be here.

Artists' Homes

The home of Walter Spies is now part of **Hotel Tjampuhan** (p182). Aficionados can stay in the 'Spies house' if they book well in advance. Dutch-born artist Han Snel lived in Ubud from the 1950s until his death in early 1999, and his family runs his namesake bungalows on Jl Kajeng (p191).

Music scholar Colin McPhee is well known thanks to his perennial favourite *A House in Bali*. Although the actual 1930s house is long gone, you can visit the riverside site (which shows up in photographs in the book) at the **Sayan Terrace** (p192). Sayan Terrace employee Wayan Ruma, whose mother was McPhee's cook, is good for a few stories. For more, see Western Visitors to Bali in the 1930s, p52.

Arie Smit (1916-) is the best-known and the longest surviving Western artist in Ubud. He worked in the Dutch colonial administration in the 1930s, was imprisoned during WWII, and came to Bali in 1956. In the 1960s, his influence sparked the Young Artists school of painting in Penestanan, earning him an enduring place in the history of Balinese art. His home is not open to the public.

Sacred Monkey Forest Sanctuary

This cool and dense swathe of jungle, officially called **Mandala Wisata Wanara Wana** (Map p188; ☎ 971304; Monkey Forest Rd; adult/child 10,000/5000Rp; ⌚ 8.30am-6pm), houses three holy temples. The sanctuary is inhabited by a band of grey-haired and greedy long-tailed Balinese macaques who are nothing like the innocent-looking doe-eyed monkeys on the brochures. They are ever vigilant for passing tourists who just might have peanuts and ripe bananas available for a quick hand-out. Don't hand food directly to these creatures.

The interesting **Pura Dalem Agung** (Temple of the Dead) is in the forest and has a real Indiana Jones feel to it. Look for the Rangda figures devouring children at the entrance to the inner temple.

You can enter through one of the three gates: at the southern end of Monkey Forest Rd; 100m further east, near the car park; or from the southern side, on the lane from Nyuhkuning.

Botanic Garden Ubud

Care to feed a pitcher plant? A huge collection of these Sumatran meat-eaters is but one part of the amazing new **Botanic Garden Ubud** (Map pp176-7; ☎ 970951; www.botanicgardenbali.com; admission 50,000Rp; ⌚ 8am-6pm) Spread over more than six hectares, the gardens – there are many – are devoted to various themes such as orchids (in greenhouses), Bali-grown plants like cinnamon and vanilla, flowering butterfly-friendly gardens, an enormous lotus pond and much more. The work of Stefan Reisner, this is a welcome addition to the Ubud scene. Get lost in the maze and when you finally escape, take comfort from Bali's medicinal plants. The exhibit about the cacti of East Bali is worth the cost of admission alone.

Petulu

Every evening at around 6 o'clock, thousands of big **herons** and **egrets** fly in to Petulu (Map pp176–7), squabbling over the prime perching places before settling into the trees beside the road, and becoming a minor tourist attraction. The herons, mainly the striped Java pond species, started their visits to Petulu in 1965 for no apparent reason. Villagers believe they bring good luck (as well as tourists), despite the smell and the mess. A few *warung* (food stalls) have been set up in the paddy fields, where you can have a drink while enjoying the spectacle. Walk quickly under the trees if the herons are already roosting – the copious droppings on the road will indicate if it's unwise to hang around.

A bemo from Ubud to Pujung will drop you off at the turn-off just south of Petulu (the trip should take about 10 to 15 minutes), but it's more convenient with your own transport. It would make a pleasant walk or bicycle ride on any of several routes north of Ubud, but if you stay for the birds you'll be heading back in the dark.

ACTIVITIES

Massage, Spas & Salons

Ubud has several salons and spas where you can seriously pamper yourself. In fact visiting a spa is at the top of many visitors' itinerary.

For more on the joys of spas on Bali, see Ahhh, A Spa, p84.

For a basic workout, Ubud has a gym, **Ubud Fitness Centre** (Map pp176-7; ☎ 974804; Jl Jero Gading; visitor/monthly 40,000/150,000Rp; 🕑 7am-9pm), which offers weight training and aerobics.

Bodyworks (Map pp176-7; ☎ 975720; Jl Hanoman; 1hr massage 90,000Rp; 🕑 9am-9pm) is set in a traditional Balinese compound and treatment rooms are light-filled, although traffic noise competes with the gurgling fountains. A facial is 75,000Rp while a spice, salt, milk or seaweed bath costs from 125,000Rp to 150,000Rp.

Cendana Resort & Spa (Map p188; ☎ 971927; Monkey Forest Rd; 1hr massage US$15; 🕑 9am-7pm) has a nice setup, including an open-air Jacuzzi. The couples' massage room is particularly pleasant. One-day use of the hotel's pool, sauna and steam room is available for US$5. You can have a bath of mud or milk with your massage or try one Hawaiian-style, which involves lots of aromatic oils.

Eve Spa (Map p188; ☎ 747 0910; Monkey Forest Rd; 1hr massage 75,000Rp; 🕑 9am-9pm) will cleanse you of toxins from eating an apple or other dubious substances. The menu is straight-forward and affordable, and you can go on something of a spa orgy: an all-day festival of treatments is 325,000Rp.

Komaneka Resort & Spa (Map p188; ☎ 976090; Monkey Forest Rd; 1hr massage US$40; 🕑 9am-7pm) offers open-air treatments for singles and couples in lush surrounds.

Ibah Spa (Map pp176-7; ☎ 974466; Ibah Luxury Villas & Spa, off Jl Raya Campuan; 1hr massage US$40; 🕑 8am-8pm) looks to nature for calming inspiration. It has a very calm wooden interior and a Jacuzzi; treatments come with evocative names such as Mountain Ritual and Ibah Foot Fetish.

Milano Salon (Map p188; ☎ 973448; Monkey Forest Rd; 1hr massage 60,000Rp; 🕑 9am-8pm) offers facials and massages in a simple setting.

Nur Salon (Map pp176-7; ☎ 975352; Jl Hanoman 28; 1hr massage 90,000Rp; 🕑 9am-8pm) is in a traditional Balinese compound. It offers a long menu of spa and salon services including a traditional Javanese massage that takes two hours and starts with a body scrub (245,000Rp).

Hotel Tjampuhan Spa (Map pp176-7; ☎ 975368; Jl Raya Campuan; 1hr massage US$25; 🕑 9am-7pm) is in a unique grotto setting, overlooking the river, and features organic carved stone reliefs. Use of all the facilities for a day for non-guests is US$50.

Ubud Sari Health Resort (Map pp176-7; ☎ 974393; Jl Kajeng; 1hr massage US$15; 🕑 8am-8pm) is a spa and hotel in one. Besides a long list of one-day spa and salon services, there are a vast range of packages that include stays at the hotel (see p191).

Zen (Map pp176-7; ☎ 970976; Jl Hanoman; 1hr massage 75,000Rp; 🕑 9am-8pm) has a good reputation. It offers body scrubs, 90-minute *mandi lulur* (Javanese body scrub) and massage treatments (90,000Rp).

Cycling

Many shops, agencies and hotels in central Ubud, especially on Monkey Forest Rd, rent mountain bikes.

Mutiara Corner (Map p188; ☎ 80571; Jl Raya Ubud; per day 25,000Rp) Look for the bikes on display along the street in front of the store.

In general, the land is dissected by rivers running south, so any east–west route will involve a lot of ups and downs as you cross the river valleys. North–south routes run between the rivers, and are much easier going, but can have heavy traffic. Some of the walking routes (below) described are also suitable for cycling, especially southwest to Nyuhkuning and Penestanan, and southeast to Pejeng and Bedulu.

Riding a bike would be an excellent way to visit the many museums and cultural sites described in the Around Ubud section; see p192.

Rafting

The nearby Sungai Ayung is the most popular river in Bali for white-water rafting, so Ubud is a convenient base for rafting trips. You start north of Ubud and end near the Amandari hotel in the west. Note that depending on rainfall, the run can range from sedate to thrilling. See p77 for names of operators.

WALKS AROUND UBUD

For information on guided walks see p186. The growth of Ubud has engulfed a number of nearby villages, although they have still managed to retain distinct identities. There are lots of interesting walks in the area, to surrounding villages or through the paddy fields. You'll frequently see artists at work in open rooms and on verandas, and the timeless tasks of rice cultivation continue alongside luxury villas.

In most places there are plenty of warung or small shops selling snack foods and drinks, but bring your own water anyway. Also bring a good hat, decent shoes and wet-weather gear for the afternoon showers; long pants are better for walking through thick vegetation.

It's good to start walks at daybreak, before it gets too hot. In the walks below, distances are approximate and are measured with the Ubud Palace as the start and end point. Walking times do not include any stops so you need to factor in your own eating, shopping and rest stops.

Monkey Forest & Penestanan

This walk features a good range of rice paddy and rural Ubud scenery.

Take your time strolling through the Sacred Monkey Forest Sanctuary at the bottom of Monkey Forest Rd, then take the sealed road at the southwestern corner of the forest near the temple. Continue south on the lane to the village of **Nyuhkuning**, and turn west along the south end of the football field, then turn south down the narrow road. At the southern end of the village, turn right and follow the paved road across the bridge over Sungai Wos to Dangin Lebak (this busy road is the most unpleasant part of the trip but should only take around 15 minutes). Take the track to the right just after the large Bale Banjar Dangin Lebak (Dangin Lebak Community Hall). From here follow paths due north through the paddy fields, and veer left, westwards through the rice paddies to a paved road to reach **Katik Lantang**, where you join a paved road that continues north to **Penestanan**. Many artists live here, and you can stop at their homes/studios/galleries and see paintings for sale at places like I Wayan Karja's Santra Putra gallery and lodging (see p185). Follow the rice field paths north to reach these places, then descend the steep concrete stairs to Campuan and on to Ubud.

WALK FACTS
Distance: 8km
Duration: 3hr

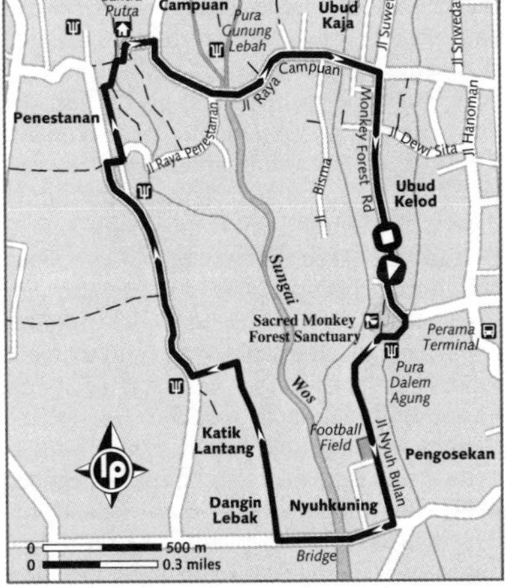

Campuan Ridge

This walk passes over the lush river valley of the Sungai Wos, offering views of Gunung Agung and glimpses of small village communities and rice fields.

At the confluence of the Sungai Wos and Sungai Cerik is **Campuan**, which means 'Where Two Rivers Meet'. The walk leaves Jl Raya Campuan here at the Ibah Luxury Villas. Enter the hotel driveway and take the path to

WALK FACTS
Distance: 7km
Duration: 2½hr

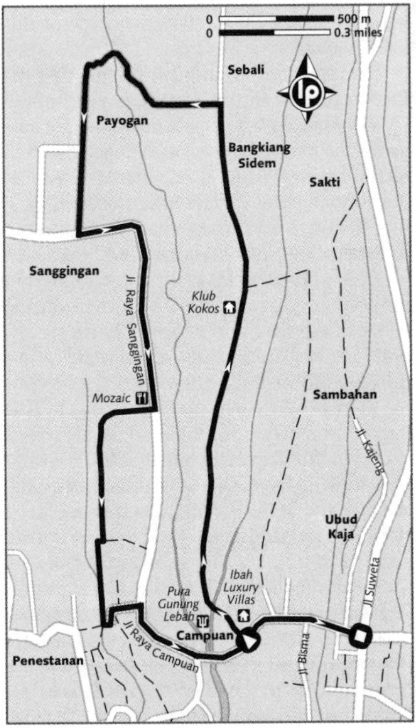

the left, where a walkway crosses the river to Pura Gunung Lebah. From there follow the concrete path north, climbing up onto the ridge between the two rivers. Fields of elephant grass, traditionally used for thatched roofs, slope away on either side.

Continuing north along the Campuan ridge past the Klub Kokos lodging (a convenient drink stop; see p191), the road improves as it passes through paddy fields and the small village of **Bangkiang Sidem**. On the outskirts of the village, an unsigned road heads west, winding down to Sungai Cerik (the west branch of Sungai Wos), then climbing steeply up to **Payogan**. From here you can walk south to the main road, and continue along Jl Raya Sanggingan to the restaurant Mozaic (see p197). Here, veer to the west onto trails that stay level with the rice fields as the main road drops away. It's a fantasyland of coursing waterways and good views among the rice and villas. When you come to the steep concrete steps, take them down to Campuan and back to Ubud.

Penestanan & Sayan

The wonders of Sungai Ayung are the focus of this outing, where you will walk below the luxury hotels built to take advantage of this lush, tropical river valley.

Just west of the Campuan bridge, past the Blanco Renaissance Museum, a steep uphill road, Jl Raya Penestanan, bends left and winds across the forested gully of the Sungai Blangsuh to the artists village of Penestanan. West of Penestanan, take a small road north (it's before the busy main road) that curves around to **Sayan**. The Sayan Terrace hotel was Colin McPhee's home in the 1930s, as chronicled in his book *A House in Bali*. The views over the valley of the magnificent **Sungai Ayung** are superb. The best place to get to the riverside is just north of Sayan Terrace hotel (p192) – follow the increasingly narrower tracks down. (This part can be tricky but there are locals who'll show you for a tip of about 2000Rp.)

Following the rough trails north, along the eastern side of the Ayung, you traverse steep slopes, cross paddy fields and pass irrigation canals and tunnels. But for many people, it's a highlight of their walk as we're talking about serious tropical jungle here. After about 1.5km you'll reach the finishing point for many white-water rafting trips – a good but steep trail goes from there up to the main road at **Kedewatan**, where you can walk back to Ubud. Alternatively, cross the river on the nearby bridge and climb up to the very untouristy village of **Tegal Kuning** on the other side. There and back will add about 1km to your walk.

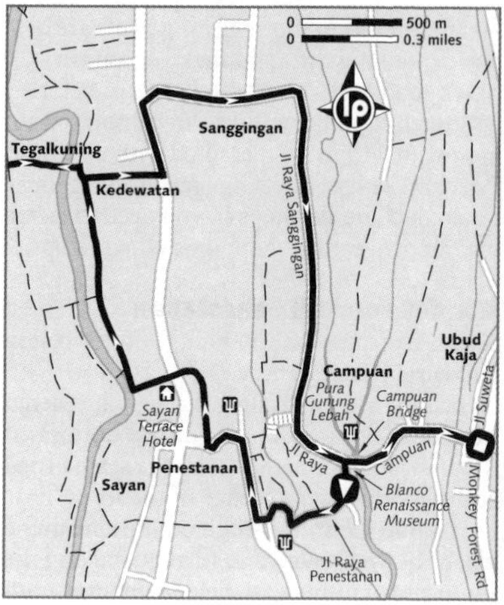

WALK FACTS

Distance: 6.5km
Duration: 4hr

Pejeng & Bedulu

The beautiful temples of Pejeng and archaeological sites of Bedulu can be visited in a day's outing. As most of the attractions are on sealed roads, you can also go by bicycle. Looking at the map, you'll see several places where you can shorten the route if your energies wane. Note that bemo to Ubud abound on Jl Bedulu.

If you have the time and energy, do the entire loop by going to the far eastern end of Jl Raya Ubud, and taking the small road that continues east from there. It passes the dump, descends steeply to cross the shady Sungai Petanu valley, then climbs to the village of Sala. Some back roads will take you east through Pejeng to the main road, where you turn south to pass several important temples and archaeological sites such as Pura Pusering Jagat and its ancient bronze bell (see p203).

Keep walking south down through Bedulu to the 14th-century carved cliffs of **Yeh Pulu** (see p201). From there follow Sungai Petanu upstream to **Goa Gajah** (Elephant Cave; see p200), but finding the right trail through the paddy

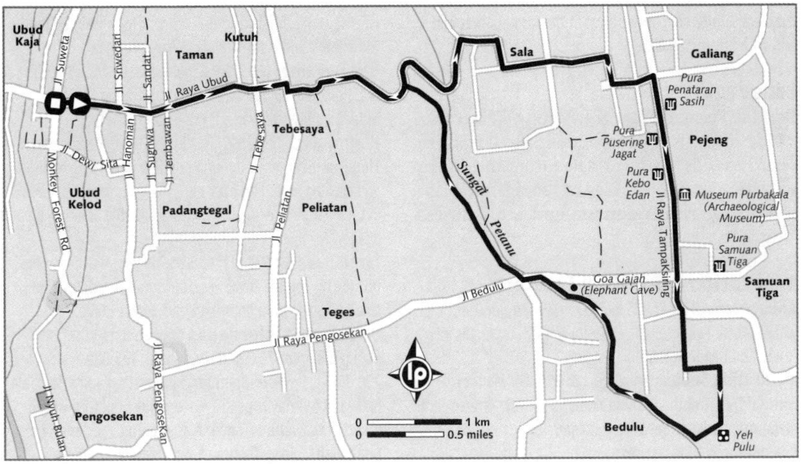

WALK FACTS

Distance: 10km
Duration: 3hr

fields can be tricky so don't hesitate to ask anyone you see. Follow the trail by Sungai Petanu back to the small road by the dump – most of it is pretty, despite this landmark.

COURSES

Ubud is a natural place to spend a few weeks developing your artistic or language skills, or learning about Balinese culture and cuisine. Two organisations, ARMA and the Pondok Pecak Library & Learning Centre, offer a wide range of cultural courses.

Arts & Crafts

The Ubud area is the best place for art courses. A wide range of courses is available including batik, jewellery making and painting.

ARMA (Map pp176-7; ☎ 976659; www.armamuseum.com; Jl Raya Pengosekan; 🕒 9am-6pm) A cultural powerhouse offering classes in painting, woodcarving and batik. Other courses include Balinese history, Hinduism and architecture. Classes cost US$25 to US$50.

Nirvana Batik Course (Map p188; ☎ 975415; www.nirvanaku.com; Nirvana Pension & Gallery, Jl Goutama 10; 🕒 classes 10am-3pm Mon, Wed & Sat) Nyoman Suradnya teaches the highly regarded batik courses. Classes cost US$35 to US$125 depending on duration (one to five days).

Pondok Pecak Library & Learning Centre (Map p188; ☎ 976194; Monkey Forest Rd, on the far side of the football field; 🕒 9am-5pm Mon-Sat, 1-5pm Sun) Painting and mask carving classes. Sessions cost from 50,000Rp for one hour. This is also a good place to find out about other courses being offered locally.

Santra Putra (Map pp176-7; ☎ 977810; Penestan; classes per hr 100,000Rp) Intensive painting and drawing classes are run by abstract artist I Wayan Karja, whose studio is on site. Accommodation is also available; see p190.

Studio Perak (Map p188; ☎ 945749; www.studioperak.com; Jl Goutama) This studio has a friendly atmosphere and it specialises in Balinese-style silversmithing courses. A three-hour lesson, where you'll make a finished piece, costs 150,000Rp.

Taman Harum Cottages (Map p201; ☎ 975567; www.tamanharumcottages.com; Mas; lessons per hr from US$7) In the centre of Bali's woodcarving district, this place offers carving and painting courses. You can also learn how to make the temple offerings found just about everywhere. See p207 for details on accommodation.

Threads of Life Indonesian Textile Arts Center (Map pp176-7; ☎ 972187; www.threadsoflife.com; Jl Kajeng 24) Textile appreciation courses in the gallery and educational studio start at 150,000Rp. The range of classes includes ones that involve extensive travel around Bali.

Cooking

Balinese Cooking Courses (Map pp176-7; ☎ 973283; www.casalunabali.com; Honeymoon Guesthouse, Jl Bisma) Janet de Neefe runs regular cooking courses at her guesthouse. Half-day courses (250,000Rp) are held five days per week and cover ingredients, cooking techniques and the cultural background of the Balinese kitchen. Sunday gourmet tours cover sea salt and palm sugar production (300,000Rp).

Bumbu Bali 2 Restaurant (Map p188; ☎ 976698; Monkey Forest Rd) Balinese cooking course, with Indian cuisine also offered. Courses start at the local market and end with lunch; 150,000Rp.

Language

Pondok Pecak Library & Learning Centre (see p175) offers inexpensive courses. Its notice board has ads for the private tutors and teachers who provide courses on an ad hoc basis in both Bahasa Indonesia and the Balinese language.

Meditation & Spiritual Interests

ARMA (Map pp176-7; ☎ 976659; www.armamuseum.com; Jl Raya Pengosekan; 9am-6pm) Has classes in Hindu and Balinese astrology.

Meditation Shop (Map p188; ☎ 976206; Monkey Forest Rd) Part of the Brahma Kumaris Society; offers silent meditation practice between 6pm and 7pm daily, and five-day meditation courses.

Ubud Sari Health Resort (Map pp176-7; ☎ 974393; Jl Kajeng; 8am-8pm) Offers meditation and yoga classes.

Music & Dance

The most visitor-friendly courses are in Ubud, where private teachers advertise instruction in various Balinese/Indonesian instruments. A well-recommended teacher of Balinese music is **Wayan Pasek Sucipta** (Map pp176-7; Eka's Homestay; ☎ 970550; Jl Sriwedari 8) who charges 50,000Rp for one hour, or lower rates for longer lessons.

Noted gamelan musician **Nyoman Warsa** (Map p188; ☎ 974807; Pondok Bamboo, Monkey Forest Rd;) offers courses in that most basic of Balinese instruments. Simple mastery can take six months or more.

ARMA, Pondok Pecak Library & Learning Centre and Taman Harum Cottages also have courses in Balinese dance and music.

TOURS

Taking a tour or two is a good idea as many of the attractions around Ubud are quite difficult to reach by public transport, and finding your way around this part of Bali can be a challenge – even with your own vehicle.

Specialised tours include thematic walks and cultural adventures.

Bali Bird Walks (Map pp176-7; ☎ 975009; US$33; Tue, Fri, Sat & Sun 9am-12.30pm from the former Beggar's Bush Bar) For the keen bird-watcher, this tour started by Victor Mason is still going strong. A gentle morning's walk will give you the opportunity to see maybe 30 of the 100 or so local species.

Bali Eco and Educational Cycling Tour (Bali Budaya Tours; ☎ 975557, 081 833 6580; per person 360,000Rp) For the active, offers a combination of mountain biking (downhill!) and cultural and culinary activities.

Bali Trekking (☎ 975162; guided walks US$30-125) Huge range of guided walks and treks around Ubud, including hills, river valleys, rice fields and villages.

Herb Walks (☎ 975051; walks US$18; 8.30am Mon-Thu) Four-hour walks through lush Bali landscape; medicinal and cooking herbs and plants are identified and explained in their natural environment; includes herbal drinks. A great deal.

Jaran Bali (☎ 977121; ubudstable@yahoo.com; rides US$16-38) See the Ubud area, including rice fields and small villages, from horseback and with a guide.

Ubud Tourist Information (Yaysan Bina Wisata; Map p188; ☎ 973285; Jl Raya Ubud; 125,000-200,000Rp; 8am-8pm) Runs interesting and affordable half- and full-day trips to a huge range of places, not to mention Uluwatu, Mengwi, Alas Kedaton and Tanah Lot, or Goa Gajah, Pejeng, Gunung Kawi and Kintamani.

FESTIVALS & EVENTS

One of the best places in Bali to see the many religious and cultural events celebrated on the island each year is in the Ubud area. See p337 for details of the events.

The **Ubud Writers & Readers Festival** (www.ubudwritersfestival.com) brings together scores of writers and readers from around the world in a celebration of writing – especially that which touches on Bali. It is usually held in October.

SLEEPING

Ubud has hundreds of places to stay. Choices range from simple little losmen (basic accommodation) to luxurious retreats that are among the best in the world. Generally, Ubud offers good value for money at any price level. A simple, clean room within a family home compound is the least expensive option.

Midrange hotels generally offer swimming pools and other amenities, while the top-end hotels are often perched on the edges of the deep river valleys, with superb views and service (although even some cheap places have amazing views that urge you to curl up with a book and simply contemplate). Neighbourhood descriptions in the Budget category apply to all price levels.

Addresses in Ubud can be imprecise – but signage at the end of a road will often list the names of all the places to stay. Away from the main roads there are no streetlights and it can be very difficult to find your way after dark. If walking you will definitely need a torch (flashlight).

Rentals

There are many houses you can rent or share in the Ubud area. For information about options, check the notice boards at Pondok Pecak Library (see p175), Ubud Tourist Information (see p175) and Bali Buddha (see p195). Also look in the free *Bali Advertiser* (www.baliadvertiser.biz) newspaper.

Budget

Many inexpensive family lodgings are very small, often with just two, three or four rooms. They tend to operate in clusters so you can easily look at a few before making your choice.

CENTRAL UBUD

This was the first place developed for tourists in Ubud and there are many good-value places.

Monkey Forest Rd

Jungut Inn (Map p188; ☎ 978237; Jl Arjuna; r 40,000-60,000Rp) The torch-bearer for value on thrift-seeker-friendly Jl Arjuna just off Monkey Forest Rd, Jungut's three rooms are bare bones but very cheap. The family is often sitting in the compound making offerings.

Frog Pond Inn (Map p188; Monkey Forest Rd; r 40,000-60,000Rp) It's quiet, ultra-basic, friendly and has seven rooms with open-air bathrooms and cold water. The breakfast is tasty.

Nyuh Gading Accommodation (Map p188; ☎ 973410; Monkey Forest Rd; s/d 50,000/70,000Rp) In a quiet garden enclosure opposite the football field, this place has seven clean, simple rooms with hot water in bungalow-style units.

Pramesti (Map p188; ☎ 970843; uni_pramesti@hotmail.com; Monkey Forest Rd; s/d 70,000/80,000Rp) Linens with vibrant tropical scenes brighten the bungalow-style rooms with hot water. Enjoy the simple but groomed garden from your porch.

Puri Muwa Bungalows (Map p188; ☎ 976441; Monkey Forest Rd; r 75,000-125,000Rp) Near the top of Monkey Forest Rd in a thicket of basic places is this quiet family-run place. The cheaper rooms are cold-water only.

Loka House (Map p188; ☎ 973326; off Monkey Forest Rd; s/d 90,000/100,000Rp) Once through the lush entrance, Loka is a peaceful place, where the two-storey main building overlooks a small carp pond in the garden. The three rooms have hot water and fans.

Ubud Terrace Bungalows (Map p188; ☎ 975690; Monkey Forest Rd; r 120,000Rp; 🏊) There's good value here, as the basic rooms come with a pool and hot water.

White House Bali (Map p188 ☎ 974855; purietak@yahoo.com; Monkey Forest Rd; s/d 150,000/200,000Rp; 🏊) Rejoice! A Bush-free White House (although this one does have the odd shrub in the garden). Back of the street amid rice fields, 17 hot-water rooms are scattered in one- and two-storey blocks. Statues spout into the pool.

Gayatri Bungalows 2 (Map p188; ☎ 979129; meggy292003@yahoo.com; off Monkey Forest Rd; r 150,000-200,000Rp; 🏊) The 12 large rooms have hot water and fans. It's a nice jaunt over coursing water and past rice paddies.

Kubuku (Map p188; ☎ 971552; Monkey Forest Rd; r 200,000Rp) Kubuku has a small vegetarian café with lounging *bale* (open-sided pavilion with a steeply pitched thatched roof). The two bungalows here are way back amid rice fields.

East of Monkey Forest Rd

Small streets east of Monkey Forest Rd, including Jl Karna, have numerous, family-style homestays, which are secluded but still handy to the centre.

Gandra House (Map p188; ☎ 976529; Jl Karna; r 40,000-70,000Rp) Modern bathrooms and spacious gardens are the highlights of this cold-water 10-room place. One of several on this street.

Sayong House (Map p188; ☎ 973305; Jl Maruti; r 100,000-140,000Rp; 🏊) At the northern end of this quiet lane, Sayong has seven basic hot-water rooms. Cross the lane and dive into the azure pool.

Sania's House (Map p188; ☎ 975535; sania_house@yahoo.com; Jl Karna 7; r 150,000-250,000Rp; 🏊) Pets wander about this family-run place, where the pool with fountains, huge terrace and large rooms will have even you wagging your tail.

Jl Goutama

This charming street has several cheap, quiet and accessible places to stay.

Donald Homestay (Map p188; ☎ 977156; Jl Goutama; r 50,000-80,000Rp) The four rooms – some with hot water – are in a nice back corner of the family compound. Like many family-compound places, the chickens running around have satay in their future.

North of Jl Raya Ubud

Both Jl Kajeng and Jl Suweta, leading north from Jl Raya, offer an excellent choice of budget lodgings, some quite close to the entre of town.

Roja's Bungalows (Map p188; ☎ 975107; Jl Kajeng 1; r 50,000-90,000Rp) One of several cheap clean places on Jl Kajeng, Roja's is a classic family compound where you can observe the patterns of day-to-day life.

Padma Accommodation (Map p188; ☎ 977247; aswatama@hotmail.com; Jl Kajeng 13; r 120,000Rp) A very friendly place, Padma has only two adjoining, very private bungalows in a tropical garden. Rooms are decorated with local crafts and the modern outdoor bathroom has hot water. Nyoman Sudiarsa, a painter and family member, has a studio here and offers classes (see p185).

NORTH OF THE CENTRE

Things get quiet as you head uphill from Jl Raya Ubud, but note that some places are almost a kilometre to the north.

Homestay Rumah Roda (Map pp176-7; ☎ 975487; rumahroda@indo.net.id; Jl Kajeng 24; r 60,000-80,000Rp) Next door to the Threads of Life gallery on peaceful Jl Kajeng, Rumah Roda is a typically friendly homestay. The five bungalows have hot water and there's a good breakfast from the popular Roda Restaurant (see p195).

Kajeng Bungalows (Map pp176-7; ☎ 975018; Jl Kajeng; r 60,000-150,000Rp; pool) Enjoy two classic Ubud amenities here: a pool and a stunning setting overlooking a lush valley. The most expensive rooms have hot-water, large bathtubs and the best views.

EAST OF THE CENTRE

You can get to the heart of Ubud in less than 15 minutes by foot from this snoozy part of town.

Jl Sriwedan

Eka's Homestay (Map pp176-7; ☎ 970550; Jl Sriwedari 8; r 50,000Rp) Follow your ears to this nice little family compound with six basic cold-water rooms. Eka's is the home of Wayan Pasek Sucipta, a teacher of Balinese music (see p186).

Jl Hanoman

East of central Ubud, but still conveniently located, this area has several budget lodgings along Jl Hanoman.

Suartha Pension (Map pp176-7; ☎ 974244; Jl Hanoman 17; r 50,000-150,000Rp) There's a charming, traditional family setting here. Ikat furnishings and decorative features like fresh flowers strewn about make for a welcoming setting. More expensive rooms have hot water.

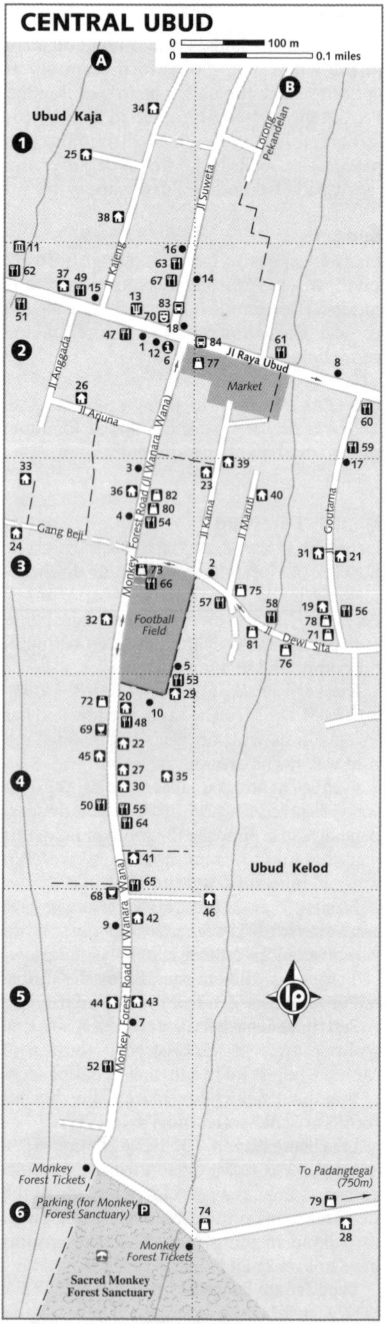

INFORMATION
- Ary's Bookshop....1 A2
- Cinta Bookshop....2 B3
- Mua Pharmacy....3 A3
- Periplus....4 A3
- Pondok Pecak Library & Learning Centre....5 A3
- Ubud Tourist Information....6 A2

SIGHTS & ACTIVITIES
- Eve Spa....7 A5
- Komaneka Art Gallery....(see 27)
- Lempad's House....8 B2
- Meditation Shop....9 A5
- Milano Salon....10 A4
- Museum Puri Lukisan....11 A2
- Mutiara Corner....12 A2
- Pura Desa Ubud....13 A2
- Pura Marajan Agung....14 B2
- Pura Taman Saraswati....15 A2
- Puri Saren Agung....(see 18)
- Rio Helmi Gallery....16 A2
- Studio Perak....17 B3
- Ubud Palace....18 A2

SLEEPING
- Agung Cottages....19 B3
- Cendana Resort & Spa....20 A4
- Donald Homestay....21 B3
- Frog Pond Inn....22 A4
- Gandra House....23 B3
- Gayatari Bungalows 2....24 A3
- Han Snel Bungalow....25 A1
- Jungut Inn....26 A2
- Komaneka Resort & Spa....27 A4
- Kubuku....28 B6
- Loka House....29 A4
- Lumbung Sari....30 A4
- Nirvana Pension & Gallery....31 B3
- Nyuh Gading Accommodation....32 A3
- Oka Wati Hotel....33 A3
- Padma Accommodation....34 A1
- Pramesti....35 A4
- Puri Muwa Bungalows....36 A3
- Puri Saraswati Bungalows....37 A2
- Puri Saren Agung....(see 18)
- Roja's Bungalows....38 A1
- Sania's House....39 B3
- Sayong House....40 B3
- Sri Bungalows....41 A4
- Ubud Bungalows....42 A5
- Ubud Inn....43 A5
- Ubud Terrace Bungalows....44 A5
- Ubud Village Hotel....45 A4
- White House Bali....46 B5

EATING
- Ary's Warung....47 A2
- Bumbu Bali 2....48 A4
- Bumbu Bali Restaurant....(see 67)
- Café Lotus....49 A2
- Café Wayan & Bakery....50 A4
- Casa Luna....51 A2
- Coffee & Silver....52 A5
- Deli Cat....53 A4
- Delta Mart....54 A3
- Delta Mart....55 A4
- Dewa Warung....56 B3
- Dragonfly....57 B3
- Kafé Batan Waru....58 B3
- Kintarou....59 B2
- Lamak....(see 48)
- Nomad....60 B2
- Rendezvousdoux....61 B2
- Ryoshi....62 A2
- Terazo....63 A2
- The Waroeng....64 A4
- Three Monkeys....65 A4
- Toko Tako....(see 31)
- Tutmak Café....66 A3
- Warung Ibu Oka....67 A2

DRINKING
- AngKaSa....(see 63)
- Napi Orti....68 A5
- Putra Bar....69 A4

ENTERTAINMENT
- Ubud Wantilan....70 A2

SHOPPING
- Alamkara....71 B3
- Alamkara....72 A4
- Kertis Gingsir....73 A3
- Kites Centre....74 B6
- Kou....75 B3
- Masery....76 B3
- Pasar Seni (Art Market)....77 B2
- Pho....78 B3
- Pondok Bamboo....79 B6
- Pusaka....80 A3
- Thebb....81 B3
- Toko East....(see 12)
- Zarong....82 A3

TRANSPORT
- Bemo Stop....83 A2
- Bemo Stop....84 B2

Candra Asri (Map pp176-7; ☎ 970517; Jl Hanoman 43; r 50,000-150,000Rp) Orchids dapple the attractive grounds here. The wide range of rooms add hot water as you climb the price scale. At the top – literally – are 3rd-floor rooms with fine paddy views.

Nick's Homestay (Map pp176-7; ☎ 975526; www.nickshotels-ubud.com; Jl Hanoman 57; US$10) Toss Polly a cracker as you check in at this nice little place that likes pet birds. Six rooms boasting hot water are set in spacious grounds amid carp ponds.

Artini Cottages 1 (Map pp176-7; ☎ 975348; www.artinicottage.com; Jl Hanoman; r 150,000Rp) The Artini family runs a small empire of good-value guesthouses on Jl Hanoman. This is the original one and was the maternal home. The three bungalows have hot water and large bathtubs. The more upscale No 2 with rice field views is opposite.

Kunang Kunang Guest House (Map pp176-7; ☎ 976052; Jl Hanoman; r 90,000-160,000Rp) More money buys you starchy rice paddy views from rooms on the second floor. All nine rooms in this quiet retreat have hot water.

Tebesaya

A little further east, this quiet village comprises little more than its main street, Jl Sukma, which runs between two streams.

Biangs (Map pp176-7; ☎ 976520; Jl Sukma 28; r 50,000-100,000Rp) In a little garden, Biangs – mama – has six well-maintained rooms, with hot water. The views expand as you rise up the price chart.

Family Guest House (Map pp176-7; ☎ 974054; Jl Sukma; familyhouse@telkom.net; r 80,000-350,000Rp) This justifiably popular place is set in a pleasant garden. Healthy breakfasts featuring brown bread from Café Wayan are served. Some of the 12 rooms have hot water.

WEST OF THE CENTRE

Jl Bisma

Paved with cement blocks inscribed by the local donors, Jl Bisma goes into rice field country. It is south of Jl Raya Ubud, just west of the centre, and is handy to town.

Ala's Hibiscus 2 (Map pp176-7; ☎/fax 970476; off Jl Bisma; r 80,000-100,000Rp) Smack bang in the middle of rice paddies, this good place is about 150m through the fields off Jl Bisma. The clean rooms have exceptional views and hot water, and are decorated with local handicrafts.

Pondok Indah (Map pp176-7; ☎ 966323; off Jl Bisma; s/d 80,000/100,000Rp) Follow the swift-flowing paddy waterways for 150m off the road, to this peaceful place where the top-floor terraces look over paddy fields. All five rooms have hot water.

Sama's Cottages (Map pp176-7; ☎ 973481; Jl Bisma; s/d 100,000/150,000Rp;) This lovely little hideaway is terraced down a hill. It also has a well maintained pool and for companionship you can befriend the cocks pecking about.

Campuan & Penestanan

West of Ubud but still within walking distance, places in the paddy fields are pitched at those seeking low-priced, longer-term lodgings. Most will offer discounted weekly rates, and some bigger bungalows are quite economical if you can share with a group of people. There are many signs for rooms and villas in the area; walk around and see what you find.

Note that these places are a steep climb up a set of concrete stairs off Jl Raya Campuan. (You can avoid this by approaching from the west.)

Londo Bungalows II (Map pp176-7; ☎ 976764; londobungalows@hotmail.com; off Jl Raya Campuan; bungalows 60,000Rp) It's great value. The three simple hot-water bungalows have gorgeous paddy views and morning views of Gunung Batukau.

Santra Putra (Map pp176-7; ☎ 977810; karjabali@yahoo.com; off Jl Raya Campuan; Penestan; r US$12-15) Run by internationally exhibited abstract artist I Wayan Karja whose studio/gallery is also on site, this place has five big, open airy rooms with hot water. Enjoy paddy field views from all vantage points. Painting and drawing classes are offered by the artist; see p185.

Midrange

Choices are many in this price range. Expect a pool, hot water, good service and some or more amenities such as river views, satellite TV, fridge, air-con and perhaps breakfast.

CENTRAL UBUD

Jl Raya Ubud

Look for a place on Ubud's main street that is protected from road noise.

Puri Saren Agung (Map p188; ☎ 975057; fax 975137; Jl Raya Ubud; r US$50-65;) Part of the Ubud royal family's historic palace (see p175), this place is tucked behind the courtyard where the regular dance performances are held. Accommodation is in traditional Balinese pavilions, with big verandas, four-poster beds, antique furnishings and hot water. There's lots of over-stuffed chairs about.

Puri Saraswati Bungalows (Map p188; ☎ 975164; www.purisaraswati.com; Jl Raya Ubud; r US$50-90;) Very central and pleasant with lovely gardens that open onto the Ubud Water Palace. The 18 rooms are well back from Jl Raya Ubud, so it's quiet. Cheaper rooms have fans.

Monkey Forest Rd

Ubud Bungalows (Map p188; ☎ 975537; www.ubudbungalow.com; Monkey Forest Rd; r US$20-40;) Back from the road, there are 18 spacious rooms in bungalow-style units. Five have air-com. The pool and gardens are inviting.

Sri Bungalows (Map p188; ☎ 975394; sribungalows@hotmail.com; Monkey Forest Rd; r US$35;) Some 50m off the busy street, look for a traditional Balinese entrance sheltering 16 bright bungalow-style rooms. The pool is large and there's an internet café.

Ubud Inn (Map p188; ☎ 975071; www.ubudinn.com; Monkey Forest Rd; r US$18-60;) In a town where even the simplest place has a riot of plants and flowers, the Ubud Inn seems to have more than most. Rooms span several budgets: basic are fan-only; the size swells as you add cash and you get extras like fridges and air-con. The angular pool has a children's area.

Oka Wati Hotel (Map p188; ☎ 973386; www.okawatihotel.com; off Monkey Forest Rd; r US$25-60;) Oki Wati (the owner) is an unassuming veteran with an old-Ubud style. The 19 rooms have large verandas where the delightful staff will deliver your choice of breakfast. The décor features vintage details like four-poster beds. The pool is commodious.

Lumbung Sari (Map p188; ☎ 976396; www.lumbungsari.com; Monkey Forest Rd; r US$45-85;) Artwork decorates the walls at the smartish Sari, which has a nice breakfast *bale* by the pool. The eight rooms have tubs; cheaper ones have fans.

Cendana Resort & Spa (Map p188; ☎ 973242; www.cendanaresort-spa.com; Monkey Forest Rd; r US$45-95;) Rooms have TV and face a lone paddy field. Higher priced rooms have modern bathrooms and both face pools that are surrounded by classical statuary. The water appears to cascade over the rice paddies. See p182 for details of the spa.

Jl Goutama

These three places have more style than the cheaper options on this street.

Nirvana Pension & Gallery (Map p188; 975415; www.nirvanaku.com; Jl Goutama 10; s/d 150,000/200,000Rp) There's *alang alang* (woven thatch) roofs, a plethora of paintings, ornate doorways and modern bathrooms with hot water here. Batik courses are also held (p185).

Agung Cottages (Map p188; 975414; Jl Goutama; r 150,000-250,000Rp, villa 300,000Rp;) Follow a short path to reach this slightly rural-feeling retreat with friendly staff. The six huge, spotless rooms (some fan-only) front lovely gardens, and local art hangs on the walls.

North of Jl Raya Ubud

Han Snel Bungalow (Map p188; 975699; www.hansnelbungalow.com; Jl Kajeng 3; bungalows US$30-60;) Owned by the family of the late Han Snel, a well-known Ubud painter, this quiet compound has eight bungalows with interesting stone designs. Some rooms are perched right on the edge of the river gorge; the pool is part way down.

NORTH OF THE CENTRE

Ubud Sari Health Resort (Map pp176-7; 974393; www.ubudsari.com; Jl Kajeng; r US$45-75;) There's 10 back-to-nature rooms *and* colonic irrigation for all guests here. See p182 for details of the spa. The plants in the gardens are labelled for their medicinal qualities and the café serves organic, vegetarian fare. Week-long intensive health packages are available from US$1450.

Ketut's Place (Map pp176-7; 975304; www.indo.com/hotels/ketut-place; Jl Suweta 40; r US$21-46;) The nine simply elegant rooms range from basic with fans to deluxe versions with air-con and bathtub. All enjoy the stunning pool glittering down the hillside and river valley views. See p195 for details of the popular Balinese feasts.

Klub Kokos (Map pp176-7; 978270; www.klubkokos.com; r from US$45;) A beautiful 1.5km walk north along the Campuan ridge (see p183 for details), Klub Kokos is a secluded place with a big pool and seven spotless sizeable rooms. It's reachable by car from the north; call for directions. Among the amenities for guests are a massive selection of jigsaw puzzles.

Abangan Bungalows (Map pp176-7; 975977; abanganbungalows@yahoo.com; off Jl Raya Ubud; r from US$25;) Up a steep driveway, Abangan has a lovely setting with views over the lush rice fields and distant palms. Some of the 15 *lumbung*-style rooms are fan-only.

EAST OF THE CENTRE

Matahari Cottages (Map pp176-7; 975459; www.matahariubud.com; Jl Jembawan; r US$25-60;) This wild place has flamboyant, themed rooms, including the 'Batavia Princess' and the 'Indian Pasha'. The Library is a vision out of a 1920s fantasy. You can wash those men right outa your hair in the South Pacific suite.

Tiing Gading Bungalows (Map pp176-7; 973228; tiing@indosat.net.id; Jl Sukma; r from US$50;) Overlooking a rainforest valley, the 11 bungalow-style rooms have lush, tropical views. Groves of bamboo provide shelter for the kidney-shaped pool and restaurant.

SOUTH OF THE CENTRE

Jl Raya has quick access to the centre; other locales are more isolated.

Kakiang Bungalows (Map pp176-7; 978984; www.kakiang.com; Jl Raya Pengosekan; r US$50-80;) This elegant place has 10 bungalows with a rural design but modern conveniences. All have nice verandas. The pool area is attractive and a study in cut stone. There's also a good bakery.

Alam Indah (Map pp176-7; 974629; www.alamindahbali.com; Jl Nyuh Bulan; r US$50-95;) Just south of the Monkey Forest in Nyuhkuning, this isolated and spacious resort has 10 rooms that are beautifully finished in natural materials to traditional designs. The Wos river valley views are entrancing. The 'commute' to Ubud through the forest is a bonus.

WEST OF THE CENTRE

Jl Bisma

Close to town, this area maintains rural charm while moving upmarket.

Uma Sari Cottage (Map pp176-7; 981538; www.umasari.com; Jl Bisma; r $35-40;) While ducks patrol the rice in the surrounding fields, you can patrol the jade-green pool here looking for fun. Most of the eight large rooms are fan-only; go for the upper floor as the verandas have the best views.

Honeymoon Guesthouse (Map pp176-7; 973282; www.casalunabali.com; Jl Bisma; r 350,000-600,000Rp;) Run by the Casa Luna (p194) clan and set in a family compound, there's a high rate of return visitors so it's recommended to book ahead. The 16 rooms have terraces, fans and tubs; it's worth paying extra to avoid a dark room. See p185 for details about the cooking classes held here.

Campuan & Penestanan

Just west of the Campuan bridge, steep Jl Raya Penestanan branches off to the left, and climbs up and around to Penestanan. Stay on the east side going uphill for valley views.

Taman Indrakila Hotel (Map pp176-7; ☎/fax 975017; Jl Raya Sanggingan; r US$15-35; ☒) One of Ubud's best deals; eight airy rooms tumble down the Sungai Cerik valley. Views from the bedrooms and verandas are sweeping. The ovoid pool is an oasis, the staff gracious.

Pager Bungalows (Map pp176-7; ☎ 975433; Jl Raya Campuan; r 150,000-300,000Rp, family villas 500,000Rp) Run by painter Nyoman Pageh and his family, this cute homestay hugs a hillside location back from the main road. Cheapest are two large bungalows that face the compound. Five more rooms are comfortable and look into the recesses of the dense river valley. The family villa is a fully appointed apartment.

Anom Cottages (Map pp176-7; ☎ 977234; www.anom cottage.com; Jl Raya Sanggingan; r 300,000-350,000Rp; ☒) Six art-filled bungalows are scattered around this hillside compound. Upstairs rooms have sweeping views of the river valley. Amenities include fridges and satellite TV.

Sri Ratih Cottages (Map pp176-7; ☎ 975638; sriratih@ dps.centrin.net.id; Jl Raya Penestanan; r US$20-40; ☒ ☒) There's a pool with a view of the lotus flower-inspired roof of Antonio Blanco's house, spacious grounds and 26 clean if simply designed rooms here, some fan-only. Breakfasts are bounteous and fruitful.

Melati Cottages (Map pp176-7; ☎ 974650; melati cottages@hotmail.com; off Jl Raya Penestanan; r US$25-35; ☒) Quack like a classic Ubud rice-field duck as you stroll out to these traditional-style rooms set around a café by a pool. You can walk in from the north or south. After dark, listen to nature's night music wafting in from the fields.

Hotel Tjampuhan (Map pp176-7; ☎ 975368; www.indo .com/hotels/tjampuhan; Jl Raya Campuan; r US$70, with air-con US$115; ☒ ☒) This venerable place overlooks the confluence of Sungai Wos and Campuan. The influential German artist Walter Spies lived here in the 1930s, and his former home, which sleeps four people (US$175), is now part of the hotel. There are shared garden bungalows that spill down the hill. The two swimming pools have verdant views in all directions. See p182 for details of the spa.

Sayan & Ayung Valley

ourpick **Sayan Terrace** (Map pp176-7; ☎ 974384; www .sayanterraceresort.com; Jl Raya Sayan; r US$60-150; ☒ ☒)

With a jaw-dropping view of the Sungai Ayung Valley below and the tops of palm trees stretching west, the Sayan Terrace is the place to gaze off into space. Many of the hotels built along here are luxury properties where rooms start at well over US$300. Here you can enjoy the verdant views for a fraction of the price. The 11 rooms are large and open onto terraces; the cheapest are best value. Don't expect décor out of books like *Bali Style*, but that doesn't matter when you sink back on the lounging chairs and wonder at the panorama in front of you. This is the site of Colin McPhee's *A House in Bali*; see p181 for details. Once here, you'll understand why he built his house here.

Top End

At this price range you have your choice of prime properties in the area. The big decision: close to town or not. Look for views, expansive pools, rooms with architectural features such as marble and/or outdoor bathrooms and a full range of amenities. Many hotels provide shuttle service around the Ubud area.

CENTRAL UBUD

Ubud Village Hotel & Resort (Map p188; ☎ 975571; www.theubudvillage.com; Monkey Forest Rd; r US$80-150, villas from US$350; ☒ ☒) Close to Ubud's urban action – such as it is – the Village features a big pool, lush garden and 28 tasteful, fully equipped rooms and 25 posh new villas with rice field views and small private pools.

Barong Resort (Map p188; ☎ 971759; www.barong -resort.com; Monkey Forest Rd; villas from US$150; ☒ ☒ ☒) Eleven walled villas are hidden away in this discreet compound in central Ubud. The design is contemporary with Balinese flair in the use of natural materials. The marble bathrooms are large and roomy.

Komaneka Resort & Spa (Map p188; ☎ 976090; www.komaneka.com; Monkey Forest Rd; r from US$200; ☒ ☒ ☒) Set back behind a burbling fountain, this 20-unit resort exudes contemporary, minimalist elegance. Rooms are beautifully decorated in rough-hewn furniture and feature sunken marble tubs. The Komaneka Art Gallery (p180) is at the front of the hotel. See p182 for details of the spa.

SOUTH OF THE CENTRE

ARMA Resort (Map pp176-7; ☎ 976659; www.armaresort .com; Jl Raya Pengosekan; r US$80-175, villas from US$375; ☒ ☒) Revel in Balinese culture at the hotel enclave of the ARMA compound (see p178 for details about the excellent museum and p185 for details of the range of courses offered). The resort features fine views, imaginative architecture and attractive décor. Villas come with private pools.

Bali Spirit Hotel & Spa (Map pp176-7; ☎ 974013; www .balispirithotel.com; Nyuh Kuning Village; r US$100-160; ❌ 🖳 ♨) Overlooking the Wos Valley, the Bali Spirit has stylish rooms and stunning views. The 19 rooms tumble down the hillside and feature Balinese artworks and antiques. The spring-fed pool sits in a tropical bowl down by the rapids. There's complimentary transport.

WEST OF THE CENTRE
Properties generally go from posh to posher as you near the fabled Ayung Valley.

Jl Bisma
Samhita Garden (Map pp176-7; ☎ 975443; www.samhita garden.com; Jl Bisma; r US$85, villa US$250; ❌ ♨) From the moment you step through the traditional entrance this small boutique hotel charms. There are 11 rooms and two villas, the latter with private plunge pools. All have traditional *alang alang* (woven thatch) ceilings and the balconies are draped in white bougainvillea. The mosaic-tiled pool is spectacular.

Campuan
Ibah Luxury Villas & Spa (Map pp176-7; ☎ 974466; www .ibahbali.com; off Jl Raya Campuan; suites US$150-500; ❌ 🖳 ♨) Overlooking the lush Wos Valley, the Ibah offers an elegant environment, superb spa facilities (see p182), and 15 spacious, stylish individual suites and villas which combine rustic and modern details. The swimming pool is set into the hillside beneath an ancient-looking stone wall.

Sayan & Ayung Valley
Two kilometres west of Ubud, the fast flowing Sungai Ayung has carved out a deep valley, its sides sculpted into terraced paddy fields and draped in thick rainforest. Overlooking this verdant valley are some of the most stylish, luxurious and expensive hotels on Bali.

Four Seasons Resort (Map pp176-7; ☎ 977577; www .fourseasons.com; ste from US$550, villa from US$575; ❌ ❌ 🖳 ♨) Set slightly into the valley, the curved open-air reception area looks like a Cinerama screen of verdant Ubud landscape. Electric carts ferry guests around the secluded

rooms and villas. Many have private pools and all share the same amazing views. At night you hear just the water rushing below.

Amandari (Map pp176-7; ☎ 975333; www.amanresorts .com; ste from US$675; ❌ ❌ 🖳 ♨) In Kedewatan village, the Amandari is unquestionably classy with superb views over the paddies and down to the river – the 30m green-tiled swimming pool seems to drop right over the edge. The 30 private pavilions have stone gateways and private gardens. They are spacious and exquisitely decorated. Some have their own private swimming pool.

NORTHWEST OF UBUD
Alila Ubud (Map p201; ☎ 975963; www.alilahotels.com; r from US$250, villa US$450; ❌ ❌ 🖳 ♨) Near Payangan, the Alila offers great views and modern luxury amid rural tranquillity. It has a stunning ebony pool that rises out of the green like a stark vision. Rooms are lined with natural wood and entire sides open up so guests can savour the views (which are better in some than others).

EATING
Ubud's restaurants are some of the best on Bali. It's a good place to try authentic Balinese dishes, as well as a range of other Asian and international cuisine. The quintessential Ubud restaurant has fresh ingredients, a delightful ambience and an eclectic menu, with dishes fusing inspiration from around the world.

Many make beautiful use of natural design elements and some offer serene settings with views out over the rice fields. Cafés where you can sip an excellent coffee or juice are all the rage – some people never seem to leave. There are also many inexpensive warung serving Indonesian dishes. Many of the places listed under Drinking (p197) also serve food. And don't wait past 9pm to eat or you won't.

The small local chain of convenience stores, **Delta Mart**, is useful for snacks and sundries. Among the many are two central locations (Both: Map p188; Monkey Forest Rd; ☽ 24hr). For organic foods, try **Bali Buddha** (see p195).

The new **Bintang Supermarket** (Map pp176-7; Bintang Centre, Jl Raya Campuan) is well located and has a large range of food and other essentials. The older **Delta Dewata Supermarket** (Map pp176-7; ☎ 973049; Jl Raya Andong) has a vast range of goods.

Central Ubud

JL RAYA UBUD

There are broad choices on Ubud's main street.

Rendezvousdoux (Map p188; ☎ 747 0163; Jl Raya Ubud 14; dishes 20,000-35,000Rp;) This cute place is a fusion of French-accented forms: café, library and bookshop. There's a light menu, global music (at times live) and historic films on Ubud on loop.

Casa Luna (Map p188; ☎ 977409; Jl Raya Ubud; dishes 10,000-50,000Rp) One of Ubud's top choices has a creative Indonesian-focused menu and a delicious range of bread, pastries, cakes and more from its well-known bakery. The bamboo skewers on the addictive seafood satay will skewer your heart. The owner, Janet de Neefe, runs regular Balinese cooking courses (see p185).

Nomad (Map p188; ☎ 977169; Jl Raya Ubud; dishes 15,000-60,000Rp) There's a daily barbeque and often a gamelan player as well. Balinese food is served in tapas-sized portions. It's a good central spot for a drink, especially back in the dark corners.

Café Lotus (Map p188; ☎ 975357; Jl Raya Ubud; dishes 25,000-55,000Rp) A leisurely meal at this Ubud classic overlooking the lotus pond is a relaxing treat for many when they first arrive in Ubud. The menu features Western and Indonesian fare that's well prepared. For 50,000Rp you can book front-row seats for dance performances at Pura Taman Saraswati (see p175).

Ryoshi (Map p188; ☎ 972192; Jl Raya Ubud; dishes 25,000-60,000Rp; 11am-midnight) The Ubud branch of the local chain of good Japanese sushi restaurants is attractively perched off the road.

Ary's Warung (Map p188; ☎ 978359; Jl Raya Ubud; mains 30,000-90,000Rp) The name Ary's Warung is something of a misnomer – crisp table linen, architectural food presentation, well-trained waiters and high prices won't be found in any other warung. The spare design opens the ground floor to the street. Alluring bar.

MONKEY FOREST RD

Lamak (Map p188; ☎ 974668; Monkey Forest Rd; dishes 40,000-155,000Rp; 11am-midnight) Artful presentations from the eclectic menu set the mood at this excellent eatery. The large kitchen is open and each day there are specials of Indonesian food that are not found on your average menu. Long wine list.

Three Monkeys (Map p188; ☎ 974830; Monkey Forest Rd; mains 20,000-70,000Rp) A top choice, the dining room opens onto rice fields at the back. Add the glow of tiki torches for a magical effect. By day there are sandwiches, salads and gelato. At night there's a fusion menu of Asian classics, pasta and steaks. Local children's art decorates the walls.

Coffee & Silver (Map p188; ☎ 975354; Monkey Forest Rd; dishes 20,000-70,000Rp; 10am-midnight;) Tapas and more substantial items make up the menu at this comfortable place with seating inside and out. Vintage photos of Ubud line the walls. Good coffee drinks and free wi-fi.

The Waroeng (Map p188; ☎ 970928; Monkey Forest Rd; dishes from 15,000Rp) A small and artful upmarket warung with wooden benches and music befitting its owners (they're behind the Jazz Cafe – see p197). Create your own *nasi campur* (steamed rice with meat and vegetable side dishes) from an array of fresh items.

Bumbu Bali 2 (Map p188; ☎ 976698; Monkey Forest Rd; dishes 15,000-45,000Rp) Unlike the varied Asian cuisine at the original a few hundred metres north, the menu here is almost entirely Balinese featuring items such as *lawar* (green bean salad), *bebek betutu* (smoked duck) and *sate lilit* (minced meat and grated coconut skewers). It's a large and attractive place.

Café Wayan & Bakery (Map p188; ☎ 975447; Monkey Forest Rd; mains 20,000-50,000Rp) Another old Ubud favourite, Café Wayan has relaxed a garden-setting ambience. Its food and baked goods draw many repeat customers, especially upscale locals. Sunday night Balinese buffets (120,000Rp) are a festive treat.

EAST OF MONKEY FOREST RD

Deli Cat (Map p188; ☎ 971284; off Monkey Forest Rd; dishes 15,000-35,000Rp; 10am-midnight) A character-filled place filled with characters, Deli Cat is like a little tropical bodega. Wine – some delightfully cheap – is sold along with snacks, cheese and meaty mains. Try the little grilled sausages outside at the tables right on the football field. Many people end their Ubud evenings with a nightcap here.

Tutmak Café (Map p188; ☎ 975754; Jl Dewi Sita; dishes 15,000-35,000Rp) The multi-level location here facing both Jl Dewi Sita and the football field makes this a breezy stop on a hot day. Try one of the artful sandwiches, burgers, juices or coffees.

Dragonfly (Map p188; ☎ 972973; Jl Dewi Sita; dishes 20,000-60,000Rp) Large and small plates feature foods from east and west at this popular café. Treats from India, Mexico, Vietnam, Italy and many more, including Bali, showcase the range of the kitchen. The wine list by the glass is long and welcome.

Kafe Batan Waru (Map p188; ☎ 977528; Jl Dewi Sita; dishes 20,000-70,000Rp) This café serves consistently excellent Indonesian food. Tired of tired *mie gorengs* made from instant noodles? With noodles made fresh daily, this version celebrates a lost art. Western dishes include sandwiches and salads. Smoked duck (*bebek betutu*) and suckling pig (*babi guling*) can be ordered in advance. Patio tables are a pleasure.

JL GOUTAMA

Toko Tako (Map p188; Jl Goutama; tea 3000Rp) This tiny outdoor Japanese teashop is an ethereal vision at night when scores of tiny lanterns cast their glow. Enjoy chai, coffee and juices.

Kintarou (Map p188; ☎ 746 2550; Jl Goutama; dishes 5000-25,000Rp) A cute little juice and Balinese food café run by engaging guys. A bonus for all customers is the free sample of their house-made glycerine soaps.

Dewa Warung (Map p188; Jl Goutama; dishes 5000-10,000Rp) You feel like you're at a rural warung with its shady position elevated above the street. Enjoy fresh and authentic local standards under the tin roof.

NORTH OF JL RAYA UBUD

Warung Ibu Oka (Map p188; Jl Suweta; dishes 7000-10,000Rp; 11am-4pm) You'll see lunchtime crowds opposite Ubud Palace waiting for one thing: the eponymous Balinese-style roast suckling pig. Line up and find a place under the shelter for one of the best meals you'll have in Ubud. Order a *spesial* to get the best cut.

Bumbu Bali Restaurant (Map p188; ☎ 974217; Jl Suweta 1; dishes 20,000-50,000Rp) Balinese, Indian and vegetarian influences combine at this excellent restaurant where many of its candle-lit tables face Ubud Palace. Dishes are inventive and the flavours complex.

Terazo (Map p188; ☎ 978941; Jl Suweta; dishes 30,000-80,000Rp) A popular place serving stylish, eclectic Balinese fusion cuisine. The wine list is long and features numerous French, Italian and Australian choices. The spare interior is accented by evocative vintage travel posters and bold flower arrangements.

North of the Centre

Roda Restaurant (Map pp176-7; ☎ 975487; Jl Kajeng 24; dishes 7000-18,000Rp) Above Threads of Life (see p179), Roda serves Balinese dishes with wonderful overlay of local culture. Dishes include hard-to-find Balinese desserts, such as the Moorish *jaja Bali* (sticky rice, coconut, palm sugar and fruit steamed in banana leaves). You can book a traditional meal (30,000Rp per person; minimum five people) in advance.

our pick **Ketut's Place** (Map pp176-7; ☎ 975304; Jl Suweta 40; feast 100,000Rp; Sun, Wed & Fri night) Ketut's famous traditional Balinese feast is an excellent introduction to Balinese life and customs. The range of tasty dishes covers just about everything from *bebek betutu* (smoked duck) to various bamboo-skewer satays made from minced meats – a classic Balinese style of satay that varies from the little chunks of meat elsewhere in Indonesia and Asia. Other dishes include a piquant *jukut ares* (banana tree curry), a delightful something we call 'tapioca surprise' and unusual palm sugar desserts. It's very sociable and you'll have fun just comparing some of the fruits not found at any supermarket at home. Call to confirm times and book; see p191 for details of accommodation.

East of the Centre

Masakan Padang (Map pp176-7; Jl Hanoman; dishes 6000-12,000Rp; noon-1am) This Padang-style eatery – where you choose from the plates on display – has some of the freshest, tastiest eats in town. Food is fresh and much of it is spicy.

Warung Igelanca (Map pp176-7; ☎ 974153; Jl Raya Ubud; dishes 8000-15,000Rp) Noodle fans rejoice; this orzo-sized street side den has 'em in everything, from a Jakarta chicken noodle soup to North Sumatra fried rice noodles.

Surya's Warung (Map pp176-7; ☎ 0813-3805 2998; Jl Raya Ubud; dishes 15,000-20,000Rp) A simple street side place with a menu of Thai and Indonesian food with one twist: organic baby food. Carrot and banana goop? Yum!

Warung Taman (Map pp176-7; Jl Sriwedari; dishes 10,000-30,000Rp; lunch & dinner Mon-Sat) The woks are busy at this neighbourhood warung, which serves consistently good Indonesian and Chinese food. Rough-hewn tables and friendly staff make it a relaxed choice.

Bali Buddha (Map pp176-7; ☎ 976324; Jl Jembawan 1; dishes 12,000-35,000Rp) This breezy upper-floor place offers a full range of vegetarian *jamu* (health tonics), salads, tofu curries, savoury crepes, pizza and gelato. It has a comfy lounging area and is candle-lit in the evening. The café also doubles as an exhibition space for local artists. On the ground floor, a market sells fresh organic fruit and vegetables, home baked date bars, breads and cookies. The bulletin board is a community resource.

Matahari Cottages (Map pp176-7; ☎ 975459; Jl Jembawan; high tea 60,000Rp; 2-5pm) This flamboyant inn serves extravagant high tea in open-air pavilions. Call to confirm. See p191 for details of accommodation.

JL HANOMAN

Hanoman Juice Ja (Map pp176-7; ☎ 971056; Jl Hanoman 12; dishes 6000-18,000Rp) Cleanse your system at this appropriately fruit-coloured café serving health juices, including wheat germ grass and ginseng shots. Non-liquid items include salads and sandwiches.

Kafe (Map pp176-7; ☎ 970992; www.balispirit.com; Jl Hanoman 44; dishes 15,000-40,000Rp) Part of Bali Spirit, an umbrella organisation for a number of Ubud-based charitable organisations (see p348, Kafe's menu is great for veggie grazing or just having a coffee or juice.

Bebek Bengil (Map pp176-7; Dirty Duck Diner; ☎ 975489; Jl Hanoman; dishes 20,000-50,000Rp; 11am-10pm) This rambling place does a special line in crispy deep-fried duck dishes and has a wide-open dining area. Views of rice fields include ducks who should be worried…

TEBESAYA

Village Café (Map pp176-7; ☎ 973229; Jl Sukma; dishes 7500-20,000Rp;) You gotta love a place where the owner calls himself 'Mr Chicken'. You can find his namesake on the menu as well as juice concoctions. There's also internet access.

South of Ubud

In recent years many highly regarded restaurants have opened on Jl Raya Pengosekan. It's always worth seeing what's new.

Kokokan Club (Map pp176-7; ☎ 973495; ARMA, Jl Raya Pengosekan; mains 35,000-65,000Rp; noon-10pm) On the grounds of the ARMA Resort, this elegant restaurant serves superb southern Thai and seafood dishes such as *hor mok goong* (prawns steamed in banana leaf). The open-sided, upstairs dining area defines understated elegance. Phone for transport.

Warung Opera (Map pp176-7; ☎ 977564; Jl Raya Pengosekan; dishes 15,000-45,000Rp) This big, open place is popular for its diverse menu of snacks, steaks, sandwiches and local fare. The chicken salad and crispy duck are two favourites. Many come for the sophisticated entertainment that includes live jazz and blues many nights; free transport.

Warung Enak (Map pp176-7; ☎ 972911; Jl Raya Pengosekan; dishes 15,000-150,000Rp) There are peaceful rice paddy views from the breezy upper level of this brightly coloured place that specialises in Indonesian food. The *rijstaffel* is always an excellent choice and you can wash it down with imported wine from a long list.

Kakiang Bakery (Map pp176-7; ☎ 978984; Jl Raya Pengosekan; dishes 8000-20,000Rp;) This modern little café is a good place for a coffee, a snack or sandwich. You could even share a tart.

Pizza Bagus (Map pp176-7; ☎ 978520; Jl Raya Pengosekan; dishes 18,000-30,000Rp) Ubud's best pizza bakes up with a crispy thin crust at this small place. Besides the long list of pizza options, there's pasta and sandwiches. They deliver.

West of Ubud

The restaurants and cafés in this section are all pretty spread out.

JL BISMA

Café des Artistes (Map pp176-7; ☎ 972706; Jl Bisma 9X; dishes 22,000-90,000Rp; 10am-midnight) In a quiet and cultured perch up off Jl Raya Ubud, the popular Café des Artistes brings Belgian-accented food to Ubud. But the menu strays into France and Indonesia as well, with a foray or two to other places for sandwiches and salads. Local art is on display and the bar is refreshingly cultured. Enjoy the sinfully pleasant wicker seating.

CAMPUAN

Murni's Warung (Map pp176-7; ☎ 975233; Jl Raya Campuan; dishes 16,000-50,000Rp) Since 1977, Murni's has been an Ubud favourite. The riverside setting is beautiful and a four-level dining room and bar overlooks the lush valley. The menu has good versions of Indo and Western classics. You may find the sizeable gift shop not unlike fly paper.

SANGGINGAN

Fly Café (Map pp176-7; ☎ 975440; Jl Raya Lungsiakan; 17,000-55,000Rp) Buzz in to this popular place with a silly name for good meals of Western and Indonesian food. A good coffee bar and very comfortable wicker seats pull in loungers and talkers.

Naughty Nuri's (Map pp176-7; ☎ 977547; Jl Raya Sanggingan; dishes 15,000-60,000Rp) This legendary expat hangout packs 'em in for grilled steaks, ribs and burgers. Thursday night grilled tuna specials are wildly popular and something of a scene.

UBUD & AROUND

Indus Restaurant (Map pp176-7; ☎ 977684; Jl Raya Sanggingan; dishes 20,000-70,000Rp) Perched on a ridge above the Sungai Cerik Valley, this branch of the Casa Luna (p194) empire combines excellent river and rice terrace views with creative Indonesian fare.

Mozaic (Map pp176-7; ☎ 975768; www.mozaic-bali.com; Jl Raya Sanggingan; meals 150,000-300,000Rp; 6-10pm Tue-Sun) Chef Chris Salans has created a much-lauded restaurant that brings fine French fusion cuisine to Ubud. Dine in an elegant garden or ornate pavilion. One of Bali's finest, Mozaic is consistently popular for its high standards. Tasting menus are very popular.

PENESTANAN

Ibu Putih's Warung (Map pp176-7; ☎ 976146; off Jl Raya Campuan; dishes 6000-15,000Rp) This shady place on the Everest-like cement stairs leading to Penestanan serves simple and tasty food. There's always a few funky folks hanging around and you may end up hanging out for a while – especially if the stairs have caused you to seize up.

SAYAN & AYUNG VALLEY

The top-end resorts have excellent restaurants that can make for a special night out from Ubud.

Restaurant (Map pp176-7; ☎ 975333; Amandari; dinner per person US$25-50) Thanks to the name you won't end up in, you guessed it, Bar asking for food. A vision in teak, the Amandari's (see p193) place to eat is perched over the valley below. The changing menu draws from Western and Asian influences. The wine selection befits a celebration.

Ayung Terrace (Map pp176-7; ☎ 977577; Four Seasons Resort; dinner per person US$25-50) The same stunning view that makes the Four Seasons (see p193) such a dramatic place to stay awaits diners here. During the day it's casual, but at night it's fine Pan-Asian fusion fare. Menus change almost nightly.

DRINKING

Ubud. Bacchanalia. Mutually exclusive. No-one comes to Ubud for wild nightlife. A few bars get lively around sunset and later into the night, but the venues certainly don't aspire to the extremes of beer-swilling debauchery and club partying found in Kuta and Seminyak.

Bars close early in Ubud, often by 11pm. Many eating places listed above are also good just for a drink, including Ary's Warung, Deli Cat, Nomad, Terazo, Waring Opera, Café des Artistes, Murni's Warung and Naughty Nuri's.

Napi Orti (Map p188; ☎ 970982; Monkey Forest Rd; drinks from 12,000Rp; noon-late) This upstairs place is your best bet for a late night drink. Get boozy under the hazy gaze of Jim Morrison and Sid Vicious.

Jazz Café (Map pp176-7; ☎ 976594; Jl Sukma 2; dishes 35,000-60,000Rp; 5pm-midnight) An expat meeting place, Jazz Café has a relaxed atmosphere in a garden of coconut palms and ferns, good Asian fusion food and live music Tuesday to Saturday from 7.30pm. The cocktail list is long. It provides transport around Ubud.

Putra Bar (Map p188; Monkey Forest Rd; draught beer 14,000Rp; 11am-11pm) Ubud's rasta wannabes hang out at this Kuta-wannabe place where the happy hour motto is 'Get yourself drunk'.

AngKaSa (Map p188; ☎ 977395; Jl Suweta; drinks from 12,000Rp) This cute little bar-café with a Japanese accent has papaya-coloured walls to go with papaya drinks on the menu.

Café Exiles (Map p188; ☎ 974812; Jl Raya Pengosekan; dishes 19,000-28,000Rp; 11am-midnight) You'll feel exiled at Exiles, an open-air café-bar with a grassy outlook south of town. There's live music most nights.

ENTERTAINMENT

The joy of Ubud – and what keeps people coming back – is the cultural entertainment. It's a good base not only for the nightly array of performances, but also for keeping up with news of scheduled events in surrounding villages.

Dance

If you're in the right place at the right time you may see dances performed in temple ceremonies for an essentially local audience. These dances are often quite long and not as accessible to the uninitiated.

Dances performed for visitors are usually adapted and abbreviated to some extent to make them more enjoyable, but most are done with a high degree of skill and commitment, and usually have appreciative locals in the audience (or peering over the screen!). It's also common to combine the features of more than one traditional dance in a single performance. For the perspective on the state of dance on Bali today from one of its top dancers, see A Classic Balinese Dancer, p143.

In a week in Ubud, you can see Kecak, Legong and Barong dances, *Mahabharata* and

Ramayana ballets, *wayang kulit* puppets and gamelan orchestras. The main venues are:

ARMA Open Stage (Map pp176-7; ☎ 976659; Jl Raya Pengosekan) See also p178.
Padangtegal Dance Stage (Map pp176-7; Jl Hanoman)
Peliatan Pura Dalem Puri (Map pp176-7; Jl Peliatan)
Pura Dalem Puri (Map pp176-7; Jl Raya Ubud)
Pura Dalem Ubud (Map pp176-7; Jl Raya Ubud)
Pura Taman Saraswati (Water Palace; Map p188; Jl Raya Ubud) See p175.
Ubud Palace (Map p188; Jl Raya Ubud) Nightly performances in a beautiful setting; see p175.
Ubud Wantilan (Map p188; Jl Raya Ubud) Large meeting *bale* across from Ubud Palace.

Other performances can be found in nearby towns like Batuan, Mawang and Kutuh.

Ubud Tourist Information (see p175) has performance information and sells tickets (usually 50,000Rp). For performances outside Ubud, transport is often included in the price. Tickets are also sold at many hotels, and by street vendors who hang around outside Ubud Palace – all charge the same price as the tourist office.

Vendors sell drinks at the performances, which typically last about one to 1½ hours. Before the show, you might notice the musicians checking out the size of the crowd – ticket sales fund the troupes. Also watch for potential members of the next generation of performers: local children avidly watch from under the screens, behind stage and from a musician's lap or two.

One word to the wise about a problem unimaginable just a few of years ago: turn off your mobile phone! Nobody wants to hear it.

Shadow Puppets

You can also find shadow puppet shows – although these are greatly attenuated from traditional performances that often last the entire night. Regular performances are held at **Oka Kartini** (Map pp176-7; ☎ 975193; Jl Raya Ubud; tickets 50,000Rp), which has bungalows and a gallery.

SHOPPING

Ubud has a huge variety of quality art shops, boutiques and galleries. Many places have clever and unique items made in and around the area. You can use Ubud as a base to explore craft and antique shops all the way down to Batubulan (see p204).

The euphemistically named **Pasar Seni** (Art Market; Map p188) is a busy two-storey place that sells a wide range of clothing, sarongs, footwear and souvenirs of variable quality at negotiable prices. Decent souvenirs include leather goods, batiks, baskets and silverware.

More interesting is Ubud's colourful **produce market**, which operates to a greater or lesser extent every day and is buried within Pasar Seni. It starts early in the morning and winds up by lunch time.

You can spend days in and around Ubud shopping. Jl Raya Ubud, Monkey Forest Rd, Jl Hanoman and Jl Dewi Sita should be the focus of your expeditions.

Arts & Crafts

You'll find paintings for sale everywhere. Check the gallery listings (p179) for recommendations. Prices in galleries range from cheap to collector-level depending on the artist. Prices often are lower if you buy directly from the artist's workshop.

Small shops at Pasar Seni and by Monkey Forest Rd often have good woodcarvings, particularly masks. There are other good woodcarving places along Jl Bedulu east of Teges, and along the road between Nyuhkuning and the southern entrance to Monkey Forest Sanctuary.

Surrounding villages also specialise in different styles or subjects of masks. Along the road from Teges to Mas (see p206), look for masks and some of the most original carved pieces with natural wood finishes. North of Ubud, look for carved Garudas in Junjungan, and painted flowers and fruit in Tegallalang.

Just southeast of Ubud, Peliatan produces shadow puppets and statuary that is serious, artistic and profane.

Bali Cares (Map pp176-7; ☎ 981504; www.idepfoundation.org; Jl Hanoman 44) This lovely shop sells goods to benefit several local charities including IDEP (see p348). Items range from wood-carvings made from sustainable woods to paintings, handicrafts and other items produced by local people. It adjoins Kafe (p196) and the shop is an excellent resource for information on charitable and non-profit groups.

Moari (Map pp176-7; ☎ 977367; Jl Raya Ubud) New and restored Balinese musical instruments are sold here.

Pondok Bamboo (Map p188; ☎ 974807; Monkey Forest Rd) Hear the music of a thousand bamboo wind chimes at this store owned by noted gamelan musician Nyoman Warsa (see p186 for details of his music lessons).

Tegun Galeri (Map pp176-7; ☎ 973361; Jl Hanoman 44) Everything the souvenir stores are not; beautiful handmade items from around the island. Next to Bali Cares.

Threads of Life Indonesian Textile Arts Center (Map pp176-7; ☎ 972187; Jl Kajeng 24) This center stocks exquisite handmade traditional fabrics. See p185 for information about the courses in weaving.

Clothes

For fashion and fabrics, the most interesting shops are found on Monkey Forest Rd, Jl Dewi Siti and Jl Hanoman. Many will make or alter to order.

Pusaka (Map p188; ☎ 978619; Monkey Forest 71) 'Modern ethnic clothing' is the motto here, which translates into cool, comfy yet stylish cottons. Need a gift for somebody small (or not so small)? Adorable house-made plush toys are only 5000Rp. Look for the fountain out front.

Wild Ginger (Map pp176-7; ☎ 979248; Jl Hanoman 1) This small air-con boutique has gorgeous displays of unique Bali-made hand-painted gauzy women's wear.

Zarong (Map p188; ☎ 977601; Monkey Forest Rd) A slightly offbeat, hippy chic fashion store. There's lots of cool cottons here that will be at home in any Balinese situation. Among the local lines sold here is Aryti, which makes boldly patterned sarongs.

Housewares

Batavia 1885 (Map pp176-7; ☎ 972885; Jl Hanoman 32) It's not a shop, it's an adventure. Who knows what you'll find in this musty, dusty lit by just a couple of lights. Urns, bowls, forlorn puppets, statues and a lot more. You'll be asking 'Is this a Ming original of a Balinese knock-off?'. Look for the plates embedded in the wall outside.

Masery (Map p188; ☎ 744 3175; Jl Dewi Sita) Large air-con shop with boldly coloured Asian-influenced interiors and clothes. Cushions to bags to housewares, it could be called 'World of Accents'.

Thebb (Map p188; ☎ 975880; Jl Dewi Sita) Smart and hip housewares in distinctive designs made in Bali.

Toko East (Map p188; ☎ 978306; Jl Raya Ubud; 🕑) High-end Balinese-made housewares and handicrafts; quite stylish and some, like the exquisite small picture frames, might just fit into your already full luggage.

Jewellery

Alamkara Monkey Forest Rd (Map p188; ☎ 972213); Jl Dewi Sita (Map p188; ☎ 971004) One of the best jewellery galleries in Ubud. On display are unusual but very wearable designs in gold and silver, featuring black pearls and gems, some made locally.

Other Items

For concentrated souvenir shopping besides Pasar Seni, go Jl Hanoman and Monkey Forest Rd. Shops are stocked to the brim with baskets, textiles, paintings, mirrors, mosaics, bags, kites, drums, umbrellas – and much more.

Places with DVDs of dubious origin have proliferated. Most also have large selections of CDs both legitimate and pirated.

Kou (Map p188; ☎ 971905; Jl Dewi Sita) Luscious handmade organic soaps made locally. Breathe deep on the way in.

Kertas Gingsir (Map p188; ☎ 973030 Jl Dewi Sita) Specialises in interesting paper handmade from banana, pineapple and taro plants. If you're a real fan, ask about factory visits.

Kites Centre (Map p188; ☎ 970924; Monkey Forest Rd) There are colourful wind-born creations such as dragons and sailing ships. A sweet little frog goes for 25,000Rp.

GETTING THERE & AWAY

To/From the Airport

Official taxis from the airport to Ubud cost 175,000Rp. A taxi or car with driver to the airport will cost about half.

Bemo

Ubud is on two bemo routes. Orange bemo travel from Gianyar to Ubud (8000Rp) and larger brown bemo from Batubulan terminal in Denpasar to Ubud (6000Rp), and then head to Kintamani via Payangan. Ubud doesn't have a bemo terminal; **bemo stops** (Map p188) are near the market in the centre of town.

Taxi

There are very few taxis in Ubud – those that honk their horns at you have usually dropped off passengers from southern Bali in Ubud and are hoping for a fare back. Instead, use one of the drivers with private vehicles hanging around on the street corners. From Central Ubud to, say, Sanggingan should cost about 10,000-15,000Rp.

Tourist Shuttle Bus

Perama (Map pp176-7; ☎ 973316; Jl Hanoman; ⏰ 9am-9pm) is the major tourist shuttle operator, but its terminal is inconveniently located in Padangtegal; to get to your final destination in Ubud will cost another 5000Rp.

Destination	Fare
Candidasa	40,000Rp
Kuta	30,000Rp
Lovina	70,000Rp
Padangbai	40,000Rp
Sanur	20,000Rp

GETTING AROUND

Bemo

Bemo don't directly link Ubud with nearby villages; you'll have to catch one going to Denpasar, Gianyar, Pujung or Kintamani and get off where you need to. Bemo to Gianyar travel along eastern Jl Raya, down Jl Peliatan and east to Bedulu. To Pujung, bemo head east along Jl Raya and then north through Andong and past the turn-off to Petulu.

To Payangan, they travel west along Jl Raya Ubud, go up past the many places on Jl Raya Campuan and Jl Raya Sanggingan and turn north at the junction after Sanggingan. Larger brown bemo to Batubulan terminal go east along Jl Raya and down Jl Hanoman.

The fare for a ride within the Ubud area shouldn't be more than 4000Rp.

Bicycle

See bike rental information under Activities, p182.

Car & Motorcycle

With numerous nearby attractions, many of which are difficult to reach by bemo, renting a vehicle is sensible. Ask at your accommodation or hire a car and driver. See p356 for details.

AROUND UBUD

The region east and north of Ubud has many of the most ancient monuments and relics on Bali. Some of them predate the Majapahit era and raise as-yet-unanswered questions about Bali's history. Others are more recent, and in other instances, newer structures have been built on and around the ancient remains. They're interesting to history and archaeology buffs, but not that spectacular to look at – with the exception of Gunung Kawi. Perhaps the best approach is to plan a whole day walking or cycling around the area, stopping at the places that interest you, but not treating any one as a destination in itself.

If you're travelling by public transport, start early and take a bemo to the Bedulu intersection southeast of Ubud, and another due north to Tirta Empul, about 15km from Ubud. From the temple of Tirta Empul, follow the path beside the river down to Gunung Kawi, then return to the main road and walk south for about 8km to Pejeng, or flag down a bemo going towards Gianyar.

BEDULU

Bedulu was once the capital of a great kingdom. The legendary Dalem Bedaulu (see the Legend of Dalem Bedaulu, p203) ruled the Pejeng dynasty from here, and was the last Balinese king to withstand the onslaught of the powerful Majapahit from Java. He was defeated by Gajah Mada in 1343. The capital shifted several times after this, to Gelgel and then later to Semarapura (Klungkung). For a walking tour around this area see p184.

Sights

GOA GAJAH

Two kilometres southeast of Ubud on the road to Bedulu, a large car park and a few of souvenir shops indicate that you've reached a big tourist attraction – **Goa Gajah** (Elephant Cave; Map pp176-7; adult/child 4100/2100Rp, car parking 1000Rp, motorbike parking 300Rp; ⏰ 8am-6pm). There were never any elephants on Bali; the cave probably takes its name from the nearby Sungai Petanu, which at one time was known as Elephant River, or perhaps because the face over the cave entrance might resemble an elephant.

The origins of the cave are uncertain – one tale relates that it was created by the fingernail of the legendary giant Kebo Iwa. It probably dates to the 11th century, and was certainly in existence during the Majapahit takeover of Bali. The cave was rediscovered by Dutch archaeologists in 1923, but the fountains and pool were not found until 1954.

The cave is carved into a rock face and you enter through the cavernous mouth of a demon. The gigantic fingertips pressed beside the face of the demon push back a riotous jungle of surrounding stone carvings.

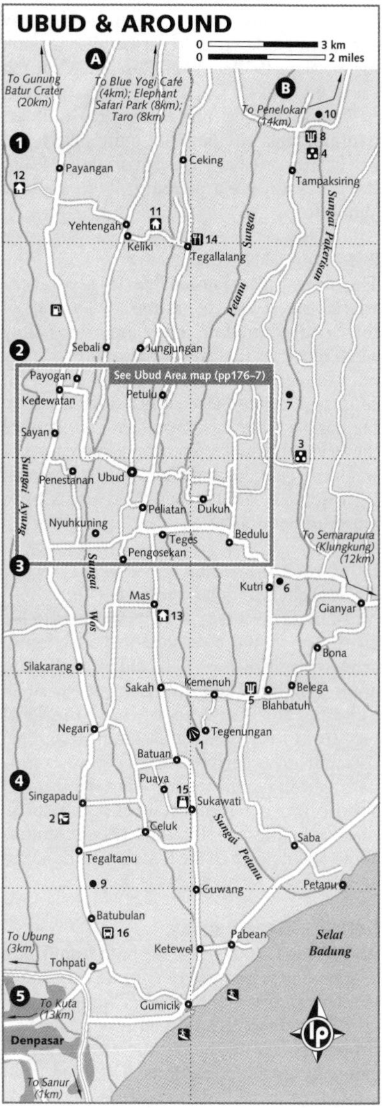

SIGHTS & ACTIVITIES
Air Terjun Tegenungan.......1 B4
Bali Bird Park & Rimba Reptil Park.......2 A4
Goa Garba.......3 B2
Gunung Kawi.......4 B1
Pura Gaduh.......5 B4
Pura Kedarman.......6 B3
Pura Krobokan.......7 B2
Pura Mengening.......8 B1
Pura Puseh.......9 A4
Tirta Empul.......10 B1

SLEEPING
Alam Sari.......11 A1
Alila Ubud.......12 A1
Taman Harum Cottages.......13 A3

EATING
Cafe Kampung.......14 B1

SHOPPING
Pasar Seni (Craft Market).......15 A4

TRANSPORT
Batubulan Bus/Bemo Terminal.......16 A5

Inside the T-shaped cave you can see fragmentary remains of the *lingam*, the phallic symbol of the Hindu god Shiva, and its female counterpart the *yoni*, plus a statue of Shiva's son, the elephant-headed god Ganesha. In the courtyard in front of the cave are two square bathing pools with water trickling into them from waterspouts held by six female figures.

To the left of the cave entrance, in a small pavilion, is a statue of Hariti, surrounded by children. In Buddhist lore, Hariti was an evil woman who devoured children, but under the influence of Buddhism she reformed completely to become a protector of children and a symbol of fertility.

From Goa Gajah you can clamber down through the rice paddies to Sungai Petanu, where there are crumbling **rock carvings** of *stupas* (domes for housing Buddhist relics) on a cliff face, and a small **cave**.

Try to get here before 10am, when the big tourist buses start to arrive.

YEH PULU

This 25m-long **carved cliff face** (Map pp176-7; adult/child 4100/2100Rp) is believed to be a hermitage dating from the late 14th century. Apart from the figure of elephant-headed Ganesha, the son of Shiva, there are no obvious religious scenes here. The energetic frenzy includes various scenes of everyday life, although the position and movement of the figures suggests that it could be read from left to right as a story. One theory is that they are events from the life of Krishna, the Hindu god.

One of the first recognisable images is of a man carrying a shoulder pole with two jugs, possibly full of *tuak* (palm wine). He is following a woman whose jewellery suggests wealth and power. There's a whimsical figure peering round a doorway, who seems to have armour on his front and a weapon on his back. The

GOA GAJAH (ELEPHANT CAVE)

Bale (Pavilion)	1	A3
Bathing Pools	2	A3
Buddha Statues	3	B4
Buddhist Antiquities	4	B4
Goa Gajah	5	B2
Hariti Statue	6	B2
Meditation Niche	7	A3
Pura Taman	8	B3
Ticket Office	9	B2

thoughtful seated figure wears a turban, which suggests he is a priest.

The hunting scene starts with a horseman and a man throwing a spear. Another man seems to be thrusting a weapon into the mouth of a large beast, while a frog imitates him by disposing of a snake in the same manner. Above the frog, two figures kneel over a smoking pot, while to the right, two men carry off a slain animal on a pole. Then there's the depiction of the woman holding the horse's tail – is she begging the rider to stay or being dragged off as his captive?

The Ganesha figures of Yeh Pulu and Goa Gajah are quite similar, indicating a close relationship between them. You can walk between the sites, following small paths through

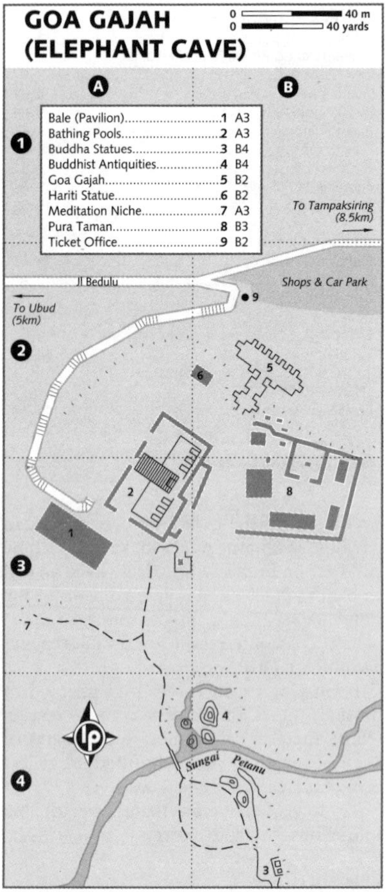

the paddy fields, but you might need to pay a local to guide you. By car or bicycle, look for the signs to 'Relief Yeh Pulu' or 'Villa Yeh Pulu', east of Goa Gajah.

Even if your interest in carved Hindu art is minor, this site is really quite lovely and rarely will you have much company. From the entrance, it's a pleasant 300m walk to Yeh Pulu.

PURA SAMUAN TIGA
The majestic **Pura Samuan Tiga** (Temple of the Meeting of the Three; Map pp176-7) is about 200m east of the Bedulu junction. The name is possibly a reference to the Hindu trinity, or it may refer to meetings held here in the early 11th century. Despite these early associations, all the temple buildings have been rebuilt since the 1917 earthquake. The imposing main gate was designed and built by I Gusti Nyoman Lempad, one of Bali's renowned artists and a native of Bedulu.

MUSEUM PURBAKALA
This archaeological **museum** (Map pp176-7; ☎ 942354; admission by donation; ☀ 8am-3pm Mon-Thu, 8am-12.30pm Fri) has a reasonable collection of artefacts from all over Bali, and most displays are in English. The exhibits in several small buildings include some of Bali's first pottery from near Gilimanuk, and sarcophagi dating from as early as 300 BC – some originating from Bangli are carved in the shape of a turtle, which has important cosmic associations in Balinese mythology. The museum is about 500m north of the Bedulu junction, and easy to reach by bemo or by bicycle.

Getting There & Away
About 3km east of Teges, the road from Ubud reaches a junction where you can turn south to Gianyar or north to Pejeng, Tampaksiring and Penelokan. Ubud–Gianyar bemo will drop you off at this junction, from where you can walk to the attractions. The road from Ubud is reasonably flat, so coming by bicycle is a good option.

PEJENG
Continuing up the road towards Tampaksiring you soon come to Pejeng and its famous temples. Like Bedulu, this was once an important seat of power, as it was the capital of the Pejeng kingdom, which fell to the Majapahit invaders in 1343.

Sights

PURA KEBO EDAN

Also called the **Crazy Buffalo Temple** (Map pp176-7), this is not an imposing structure, but it is famous for its 3m-high statue, known as the **Giant of Pejeng**, thought to be approximately 700 years old. Details are sketchy, but it may represent Bima, a hero of the *Mahabharata*, dancing on a dead body, as in a myth related to the Hindu Shiva cult. There is some conjecture about the giant's giant genitalia – it has what appear to be pins on the side. Some claim this was to give the woman more pleasure – an early version of what is often sold by vending machines in men's toilets.

PURA PUSERING JAGAT

The large **Pura Pusering Jagat** (Navel of the World Temple; Map pp176-7) is said to be the centre of the old Pejeng kingdom. Dating from 1329, this temple is visited by young couples who pray at the stone *lingam* and *yoni*. Further back is a large stone urn, with elaborate but worn carvings of gods and demons searching for the elixir of life in a depiction of the *Mahabharata* tale 'Churning the Sea of Milk'. The temple is on a small track running west of the main road.

PURA PENATARAN SASIH

This was once the state **temple** (Map pp176-7; Jl Raya Tampaksiring) of the Pejeng kingdom. In the inner courtyard, high up in a pavilion and difficult to see, is the huge bronze drum known as the **Fallen Moon of Pejeng**. The hourglass-shaped drum is 186cm-long, the largest single-piece cast drum in the world. Estimates of its age vary from 1000 to 2000 years, and it is not certain whether it was made locally or imported – the intricate geometric decorations are said to resemble patterns from as far apart as Irian Jaya and Vietnam. Even in its inaccessible position, you can make out these patterns and the distinctive heart-shaped face designs.

Balinese legend relates that the drum came to earth as a fallen moon, landing in a tree and shining so brightly that it prevented a band of thieves from going about their unlawful purpose. One of the thieves decided to put the light out by urinating on it, but the moon exploded and fell to earth as a drum, with a crack across its base as a result of the fall.

Although the big noise here is all about the drum, be sure to notice the **statuary** in the temple courtyard that dates from the 10th to the 12th century.

> **THE LEGEND OF DALEM BEDAULU**
>
> A legend relates how Dalem Bedaulu possessed magical powers that allowed him to have his head chopped off and then replaced. Performing this unique party trick one day, the servant entrusted with lopping off his head and then replacing it unfortunately dropped it in a river and, to his horror, watched it float away. Looking around in panic for a replacement, he grabbed a pig, cut off its head and popped it upon the king's shoulders. Thereafter, the king was forced to sit on a high throne and forbade his subjects to look up at him; Bedaulu means 'he who changed heads'.

TAMPAKSIRING

Tampaksiring is a small town about 18km northeast of Ubud with a large and important temple and the most impressive ancient monument in Bali.

Sights

GUNUNG KAWI

On the southern outskirts of town, a sign points east off the main road to Gunung Kawi and its **ancient monuments** (Map p201; adult/child 4100/2100Rp; 7am-5pm). From the end of the access road, a steep, stone stairway leads down to the river, at one point making a cutting through an embankment of solid rock. There, in the bottom of this lush green valley, is one of Bali's oldest and largest ancient monuments.

Gunung Kawi consists of 10 rock-cut *candi* (shrines) – memorials cut out of the rock face in imitation of actual statues. They stand in awe-inspiring 7m-high sheltered niches cut into the sheer cliff face. A solitary *candi* stands about a kilometre further down the valley to the south; this is reached by a trek through the rice paddies on the western side of the river.

Each *candi* is believed to be a memorial to a member of the 11th-century Balinese royalty, but little is known for certain. Legends relate that the whole group of memorials was carved out of the rock face in one hard-working night by the mighty fingernails of Kebo Iwa.

The five monuments on the eastern bank are probably dedicated to King Udayana, Queen Mahendradatta, their son Airlangga and his brothers Anak Wungsu and Marakata. While Airlangga ruled eastern Java, Anak Wungsu ruled Bali. The four monuments on the western side are, by this theory, to Anak Wungsu's chief concubines. Another theory is that the whole complex is dedicated to Anak Wungsu, his wives, concubines and, in the case of the remote 10th *candi*, to a royal minister.

TIRTA EMPUL

A well-signposted fork in the road north of Tampaksiring leads to the popular holy springs at **Tirta Empul** (Map p201; adult/child 4100/2100Rp; 8am-6pm), discovered in AD 962 and believed to have magical powers. The springs bubble up into a large, crystal-clear tank within the temple and gush out through waterspouts into a bathing pool – they're the main source of Sungai Pakerisan, the river that rushes by Gunung Kawi only 1km or so away. Next to the springs, **Pura Tirta Empul** is one of Bali's most important temples.

You'll need a sarong or long pants, and maybe a scarf. Come in the early morning or late afternoon to avoid the tourist buses. You can also use the clean, segregated and free public baths in the grounds.

OTHER SITES

There are other groups of *candi* and monks' cells in the area encompassed by the ancient Pejeng kingdom, notably **Pura Krobokan** (Map p201) and **Goa Garba** (Map p201), but none so grand as Gunung Kawi. Between Gunung Kawi and Tirta Empul, **Pura Mengening** (Map p201) temple has a freestanding *candi*, similar in design to those at Gunung Kawi.

NORTH OF UBUD

Abused and abandoned logging elephants from Sumatra have been given refuge on Bali at the **Elephant Safari Park** (Map p201; ☎ 721480; www.baliadventuretours.com; adult/child US$16/8; 9am-5pm). Located in the cool, wet highlands of **Taro** (12km north of Ubud), the park is home to almost 30 elephants. Besides a full complement of exhibits about elephants, most people will probably want to *ride* an elephant (adult/child including admission US$68/47). The park has received praise for its conservation efforts; however, be careful you don't end up at one of the rogue parks, designed to divert the unwary to unsanctioned displays of elephants.

A good lunch stop near the park, with picturesque paddy-field views is **Blue Yogi Cafe** (Map p201; ☎ 901368; dishes 15,000-40,000Rp; 8am-5pm). After lunch, walk things off with a stroll among the rice.

A smaller road goes north through **Keliki**, where you'll find **Alam Sari** (☎ 240308; www.alamsari.com; r from US$55;), a fine, small hotel in a wonderfully isolated location. There are 12 luxurious yet rustic rooms, a pool and a great view. The hotel is one of the few on the island that treats its own wastewater.

SOUTH OF UBUD

The road between South Bali and Ubud is lined with places making and selling handicrafts. Many visitors shop along the route as they head to Ubud, sometimes by the busload, but much of the craftwork is actually done in small workshops and family compounds on quiet back roads. You may enjoy these places more after visiting Ubud, where you'll see some of the best Balinese arts and develop some appreciation of the styles and themes.

For serious shopping and real flexibility in exploring these villages, it's worth renting or chartering your own transport, so you can explore the back roads and carry your purchases without any hassles. If you decide to charter a vehicle, the driver may receive a commission from any place you spend your money – this can add 10% or more to the cost of purchases. Also, a driver may steer you to workshops or artisans that he favours, rather than those of most interest to you.

From the **Batubulan Bus/Bemo terminal** (Map p201; see p171), bemo to Ubud stop at the craft villages along the main road through Negari. The following places are presented in the order you'll encounter them on the way to Ubud from the south.

Batubulan

The start of the road from South Bali is lined with outlets for stone sculptures – **stone carving** is the main craft of Batubulan (moonstone), and workshops are found right along the road to Tegaltamu, with another batch further north around Silakarang. Batubulan is the source of the stunning temple-gate guardians seen all over Bali. The stone used for these sculptures is a porous grey volcanic rock called *paras*, which resembles pumice; it's soft and surprisingly light.

The temples around Batubulan are, naturally, noted for their fine stonework. Just 200m to the east of the busy main road, **Pura Puseh** (Map p201) is worth a visit for its unusual decorations. The statues draw on ancient Hindu and Buddhist iconography and Balinese mythology; however, they are not old – many are based on illustrations from books on Javanese archaeology.

Batubulan is also a centre for making 'antiques', textiles and woodwork, and has numerous craft and antique shops. Several venues offer regular performances of traditional Barong (mythical lion-dog creature) and Rangda (widow-witch who represents evil in Balinese theatre and dance) dances, often during the day, and commonly included in tours from southern Bali.

Bali Bird Park & Rimba Reptil Park

Just north of Tegaltama, the **bird park** (Map p201; ☎ 299352; www.bali-bird-park.com; adult/child US$8/4; ⏲ 8am-6pm) boasts more than 1000 birds from over 250 different species, including rare *cendrawasih (*birds of paradise) from Irian Jaya and highly endangered Bali starlings (see On a Wing and a Prayer, p282) – many of these birds are housed in special walk-through aviaries. In one of them you follow a walk at tree-level – or what some with feathers might say is bird-level. The two hectares of landscaped gardens feature a fine collection of tropical plants.

Next door, **Rimba Reptil Park** (☎ 299344; adult/child US$8/4; ⏲ 8am-6pm) has about 20 species of creatures from Indonesia and Africa, as well as turtles, crocodiles, a python and yet more Komodo dragons.

Both places are popular with kids. You can buy a combination ticket to both parks (adult/child US$15/7.50). Allow at least two hours for the bird park alone, which also has a good restaurant.

Many tours stop at the parks, or you can take a Batubulan–Ubud bemo, get off at the junction at Tegaltamu, and follow the signs north for about 600m. There is a large parking lot.

> **DETOUR**
>
> The usual road from Ubud to Batur is through Tampaksiring, but there are other lesser roads up the gentle mountain slope. One of the most attractive goes north from Peliatan, past Petulu and its birds (see p181), and through Tegallalang and Ceking, to bring you out on the crater rim between Penelokan and Batur. It's a sealed road all the way and you pass through woodcarving towns like **Jati** and **Pujung**.
>
> In **Tegallalang** you can pause at **Cafe Kampung** (Map p201; ☎ 901201; dishes 20,000-50,000Rp, r from US$85), a remote and rustic warung and upscale guesthouse. The design makes great use of natural rock and the views are excellent.

Singapadu

Singapadu is largely uncommercial and preserves a traditional appearance, with walled family compounds and shady trees. The area has a strong history of music and dance, specifically the *gong gede* (large orchestra) gamelan, the older, but smaller *gong saron* gamelan and the Barong dance. Local artisans specialise in producing **masks** for Topeng and Barong dances.

Singapadu's dancers now perform mostly at large venues in the tourist areas – there are no regular public performances. There are not many obvious places in the town to buy locally produced crafts, as most of the better products are sold directly to dance troupes or quality art shops. Ask around to find some of the workshops, but even at the source, the best quality masks will still be rather expensive. If you are relying on public transport wait for a bemo at the junction at Tegaltamu.

Celuk

Celuk is the **silver** and **gold** centre of Bali. The bigger showrooms are on the main road, and have marked prices that are quite high, although negotiation is possible. The variety and quality of the designs on display is not as good as those in the shops of Ubud, and the prices are no cheaper, except for commercial buyers.

Hundreds of silversmiths and goldsmiths work in their homes on the backstreets north and east of the main road. Most of these artisans are from *pande* families, members of a sub-caste of blacksmiths whose knowledge of fire and metal has traditionally put them outside the usual caste hierarchy. Their small workshops are interesting to visit, and have the lowest prices, but they don't keep a large stock of finished work. They will make something to order if you bring a sample or sketch.

Sukawati & Puaya

Once a royal capital, Sukawati is now known for a number of specialised crafts and for the daily **Pasar Seni** (Art Market; Map p201), a two-storey **craft market** where every type of quality craftwork and touristy trinket is on sale. One group of artisans, the *tukang prada,* make temple umbrellas, beautifully decorated with stencilled gold paint, which can be seen at roadside shops. The *tukang wadah* make cremation towers, which you're less likely to see. Other craft products include intricate patterned *lontar* (specially prepared palm leaves) baskets and wind chimes.

The craft market is on the western side of the main road – public bemo stop right outside. Across the road is the colourful morning **produce market**, which also sells sarongs and temple ceremony paraphernalia.

Sukawati is also renowned for its traditional dances and *wayang kulit* (shadow puppet) performances.

Puaya, about 1km northwest of Sukawati, specialises in high-quality **leather shadow puppets** and Topeng masks.

Batuan

Batuan's recorded history goes back 1000 years, and in the 17th century its royal family controlled most of southern Bali. The decline of its power is attributed to a priest's curse, which scattered the royal family to different parts of the island.

In the 1930s two local artists began experimenting with a new style of **painting** using black ink on white paper. Their dynamic drawings featured all sorts of scenes from daily life – markets, paddy fields, animals and people crowded onto each painting – while the black-and-white technique evoked the Balinese view of the supernatural.

Today, this distinct Batuan style of painting is noted for its inclusion of modern elements. Sea scenes often include a windsurfer, while tourists with gadgets or riding motorcycles pop up in the otherwise traditional Balinese scenery. There are good examples in galleries along, or just off, the main road in Batuan, and in Ubud's Museum Puri Lukisan (p175).

Batuan is also noted for its traditional dance, and is a centre for carved wooden relief panels and screens. The ancient Gambuh dance is performed in Batuan's Pura Puseh every full moon.

Mas

Mas means 'gold' in Bahasa Indonesia, but **woodcarving** is the principal craft in this village. The great Majapahit priest Nirartha once lived here, and **Pura Taman Pule** is said to be built on the site of his home. During the three-day Kuningan festival (see p336), a performance of *wayang wong* (an older version of the *Ramayana* ballet) is held in the temple's courtyard.

Carving was a traditional art of the priestly Brahmana caste, and the skills are said to have been a gift of the gods. Historically, carving was limited to temple decorations, dance masks and musical instruments, but in the 1930s carvers began to depict people and animals in a naturalistic way, and the growth of tourism provided a market for woodcarving, which has become a major cottage industry.

Generally the carving for sale in Mas is priced quite high – you should see items for less elsewhere as you shop around. Although this is the place to come if you want something custom-made in sandalwood – just be

DETOUR

An alternative route between Denpasar and Ubud goes through the coastal village of **Gumicik**, which has a broad, black deserted **beach**. This bypasses the congested roads of Batubulan and Celuk, and is part of the new east coast road going via Lebih to Kusamba.

The coast around here has some good wet-season surfing: **Padang Galak**, a right-hand beach break at low- to mid-tide; and **Ketewel**, a barrelling right-hander at high tide.

The beach at **Pabean** is a site for irregular religious purification ceremonies, and cremated ashes are ritually scattered here, near the mouth of the Sungai Wos (Wos River). Just north of Ketewel town, **Guwang** is another small woodcarving centre.

From Gumicik, head north through Ketewel and Guwang to **Sukawati** and the tourist mobs at the Pasar Seni (see above).

prepared to pony up. Mas is also the centre of Bali's booming furniture industry, producing chairs, tables and reproduction antiques, mainly from teak imported from other Indonesian islands.

Along the main road in Mas are the **Taman Harum Cottages** (Map p201; ☎ 975567; www.tamanharumcottages.com; r from US$35, villas US$50-75;). There are 17 rooms and villas – some quite large. By all means get one overlooking the rice fields. It's behind a gallery, which is also a venue for a huge range of art and cultural courses (see p185). Airport pickups and Ubud shuttles are free.

North of Mas, woodcarving shops make way for art galleries, cafés and hotels, and you soon know that you're approaching Ubud.

Alternative Routes

From Sakah, along the road between Batuan and Ubud, you can continue east for a few kilometres to the turn-off to Blahbatuh and continue to Ubud via Kutri and Bedulu.

In Blahbatuh, **Pura Gaduh** (Map p201) has a one-metre-high stone head, believed to be a portrait of Kebo Iwa, the legendary strongman and minister to the last king of the Bedulu kingdom. Gajah Mada – the Majapahit strongman – realised that it wouldn't be possible to conquer Bedulu (Bali's strongest kingdom) while Kebo Iwa was there. So Gajah Mada lured him away to Java (with promises of women and song) and had him murdered. The stone head possibly predates the Javanese influence in Bali, but the temple is simply a reconstruction of an earlier one destroyed in the earthquake of 1917.

About 2km southwest of Blahbatuh, along Sungai Petanu, is **Air Terjun Tegenungan** (Tegenungan Waterfall; also known as Srog Srogan). Follow the signs from Kemenuh village for the best view of the falls, from the western side of the river.

THE STATUE OF KUTRI

This statue on the hilltop shrine at Kutri is thought to date from the 11th century and shows strong Indian influences.

One theory is that the image is of Airlangga's mother, Mahendradatta, who married King Udayana, Bali's 10th-century ruler. When her son succeeded to the throne she hatched a plot against him and unleashed *leyak* (evil spirits) upon his kingdom. She was defeated, but this led to the legend of Rangda, the widow-witch and ruler of evil spirits.

The temple at the base of the hill has images of Durga, and the body of a *Barong,* the mythical lion-dog creature, can be seen in one of the pavilions (the sacred head of the Barong is kept elsewhere).

KUTRI

Heading north from Blahbatuh, Kutri has the interesting **Pura Kedarman** (aka Pura Bukit Dharma; Map p201). If you climb up Bukit Dharma behind the temple, there's a great panoramic **view** and a **hilltop shrine**, with a stone statue of the six-armed goddess of death and destruction, Durga, killing a demon-possessed water buffalo.

BONA & BELEGA

On the back road between Blahbatuh and Gianyar, Bona is a **basket-weaving** centre and features many articles made from *lontar* leaves. (Note: most road signs in the area read 'Bone' instead of Bona, so if you end up getting lost, you'll have to ask: 'Do you know the way to Bone?') Nearby, the village of Belega is a centre for **bamboo furniture** production.

East Bali

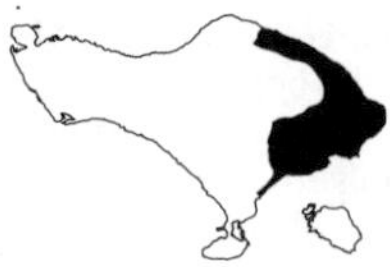

East and West Bali vie for the title of the 'real' Bali. Certainly it has many good arguments: it's home to Gunung Agung, the 3142m-high volcano known as the 'navel of the world' and 'Mother Mountain'; its rice terraces are beautiful, pervasive and appreciated on myriad back road drives. It's also home to Bali's holiest temple.

But maybe it is the water that sets East Bali apart. Temples line the shore, some meant to protect the island from the demons said to lurk in places such as Nusa Penida offshore. Towns such as Padangbai and Candidasa delight visitors with their relaxed pace and seaside vibe. Amed and nearby the little coastal villages revel in the kind of mellow charm that travellers have always sought. And Tulamben adds another dimension when people venture below the waves for amazing diving.

With the completion of a new coastal road, all of East Bali is more accessible than ever. Getting to Padangbai and other points is now an hour quicker. Better yet, the road makes possible all sorts of circle tours from South Bali and Ubud. Now you can take in seaside temples, beaches, the royal city of Semarapura, the awesome Sidemen Road, the mountain scenery near Muncan and the towns of Bangli and Gianyar, all in an easy day with plenty of stops.

Tourism aside though, East Bali also remains a traditional place. Starting with mountain towns Isuch as Tirta Gangga or Sidemen, you can take walks that put you in touch with the rhythm of day-to-day life. Follow the ducks across a rice field, avert your eyes from bathers in a river and seek out a hidden temple on a peak.

One way or another, you're sure to find your own real Bali.

HIGHLIGHTS

- Enjoying the new, easy access on the coast road to beaches like **Saba Beach** (opposite)
- Climbing the often cloud-shrouded **Gunung Agung** (p219)
- Hearing the echoes at Semarapura's **Kertha Gosa** (p214)
- Diving the WWII wreck off **Tulamben** (p238)
- Following the rice terrace of your dreams at **Sidemen** (p215)

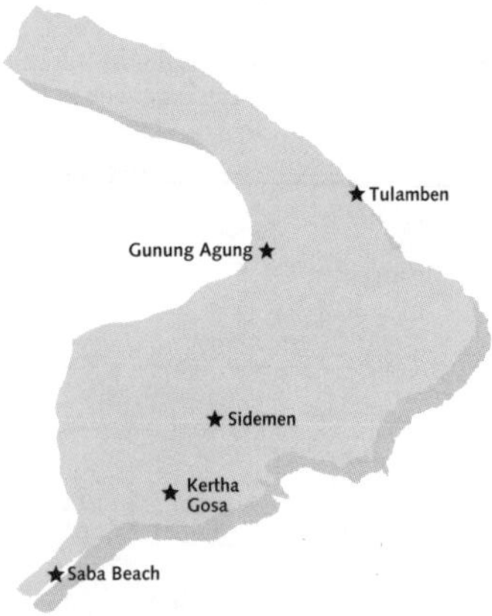

BALI'S 'NEW' BEACHES

The new coast road from Sanur east has made it easy to get to large stretches of shore that were until recently pretty inaccessible. Here are some beaches we believe are worth exploring, starting in the west and heading east. Swimming is generally dangerous. **Ketewel** (Map p128) and **Lebih** are good spots for surfing; see p79 for details.

- **Saba Beach** has a small temple, covered shelters, a shady parking area and a pretty tropical drive from the coast road; it's about 12km east of Sanur.
- **Pura Masceti Beach** has an architecturally significant temple with gaudy statuary and a few drink vendors.
- **Lebih** has a beach made of mica that sparkles with a billion points of light. There's a couple of cafés.
- **Tegal Basar Beach** is a turtle sanctuary with no shade but with a good view of Nusa Lembongan.
- **Pantai Beach** is oxymoronic using two languages (*pantai* means beach). There's a tiny café and a long row of dunes at this picture-perfect spot.
- **Pura Klotek Beach** has a small temple and some very fine black sand.

Note that swimming in the often pounding surf is dangerous. You'll need your own transport to reach surfing areas and you'll find services are few, so bring your own drinking water and towels.

COAST ROAD TO KUSAMBA

☎ 0361

After several years of construction and staged openings, the new coast road (for now called the Sanur–Kusamba Bypass, but these things change so we'll just say Coast Road) serving East Bali opened in 2006.

It promises to revolutionise the way people travel in the region. For one it means that places such as Padangbai, Candidasa and points east are now one to two hours closer by road to South Bali. No longer is all traffic funnelled onto the choked and meandering route through Gianyar and Semarapura. Now it's a straight shot a few hundred metres inland from the coast, which also means that the many beaches along here are now easily accessible (see above).

Inland, towns like Semarapura will finally have a chance to breathe, now that traffic is greatly reduced. Given its royal sights, this could help the city add lustre to its charms.

The coast east of Sanur is striking, with seaside temples, black-sand beaches and pounding waves. The entire coast has great religious significance, and there are many temples. At the many small coastal village beaches, cremation formalities reach their conclusion when the ashes are consigned to the sea. Ritual purification ceremonies for temple artefacts are also held on these beaches.

Pura Masceti, 15km east of Sanur, is one of Bali's nine directional temples (see p63). It is right on the beach. The large Sungai Pakerisan (Pakerisan River), which starts near Tampaksiring, reaches the sea near **Lebih**.

The impressive **Pura Segara** looks across the strait to Nusa Penida, home of Jero Gede Macaling – the temple helps protect Bali from his evil influence.

At **Pura Batu Kolok**, it's difficult without your own transport. It's quiet and of great significance. Sacred statues are brought here from Pura Besakih (see p218) for ritual cleansing.

Sleeping

With the ease of access and increased traffic, expect a boom in places to stay. Already rental and expat villas are popping up among the rice fields and tropical palms.

About 11km east of Sanur near Saba Beach, **Lor-In Villa Resort** (☎ 297070; www.lorinresortsababai.com; villas US$120-300; ❄ 🏊) is a modern and impressive beachside resort. The 32 villas are set in gardens of grand proportions. The best ones have private plunge pools and sea breezes from their upper-levels. Service is very good at this luxurious 'escape'.

GIANYAR

☎ 0361

This is the affluent administrative capital and main market town of the Gianyar district, which also includes Ubud. The town has a number of factories producing batik and ikat

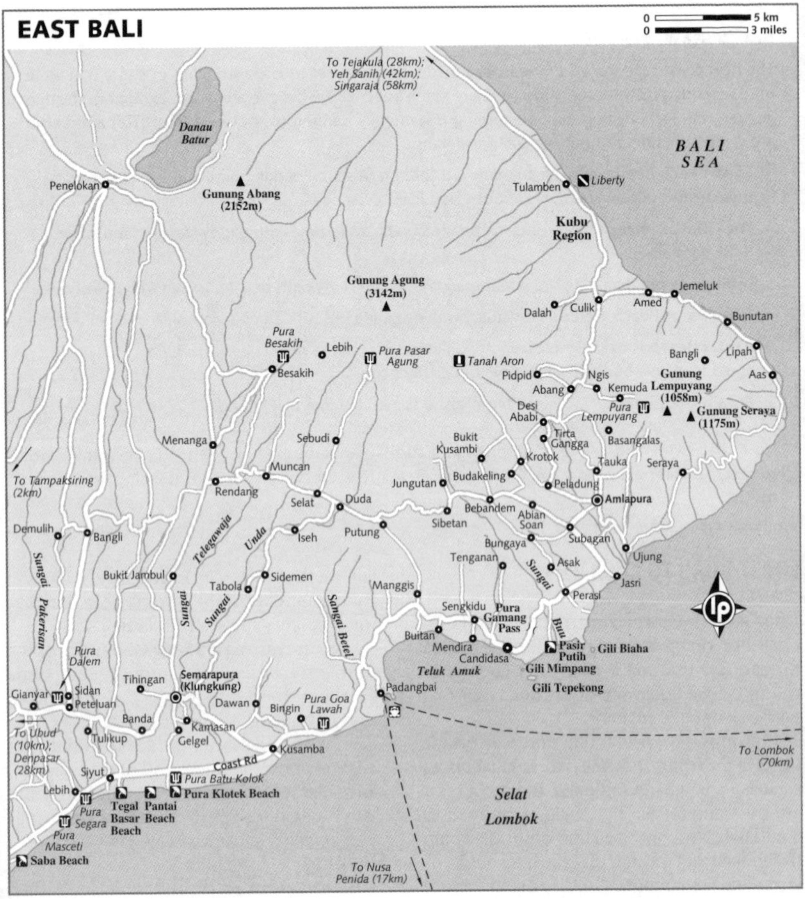

fabrics, and a compact centre with some good food.

Sights

It dates from 1771, but **Puri Gianyar** (Jl Ngurah Rai) was destroyed in a conflict with the neighbouring kingdom of Klungkung in the mid-1880s and rebuilt. Under threat from its aggressive neighbours, the Gianyar kingdom requested Dutch protection. A 1900 agreement let the ruling family retain its status and its palace, though it lost all political power. The *puri* (palace) was damaged in the 1917 earthquake, but restored soon after and appears little changed from the time the Dutch arrived. It's a fine example of traditional palace architecture. While tourists are not usually allowed inside, if you report to the guard inside, you may be given a quick look around, or you can see some of it through the gates.

Eating

People come to Gianyar to sample the market food, like *babi guling* (spit-roast pig stuffed with chilli, turmeric, garlic and ginger – delicious) for which the town is noted. The descriptively named **Gianyar Babi Guleng** (meals 5000-8000Rp; 7am-4pm) is favoured by locals among many competitors. (There are lots of cops and *bemo* (small minibus) drivers here – they know.) It's in a tiny side street at the west end of the centre. Look for the large sign.

Nearby are numerous stands selling fresh food including delectable *piseng goreng* (fried banana). Also worth sampling for *babi guling* and other local treats are the food stalls in the **food market** (11am-2pm) and the **main market** (6-9pm). All of these places line both sides of the main section of Jl Ngurah Rai.

Shopping

A must for any fashionista or lover of hand woven fabrics. There are a few textile factories at the western end of town on the main Ubud road, including **Tenun Ikat Setia Cili** (943409; Jl Astina Utara; 9am-5pm) and the adjacent **Cap Bakti** (Jl Astina Utara), as well as **Cap Togog** (943046; Jl Astina Utara 11; 8am-5pm). These places have showrooms where you can buy material by the metre, or have it tailored. You can at times see weavers at work and see how the thread is dyed before weaving to produce the vibrantly patterned weft ikat, which is called *endek* on Bali. Prices are 50,000Rp to 75,000Rp per metre for cotton fabric, depending on how fine the weaving is – costs will rise if it contains silk. Handmade batik is also for sale here.

Getting There & Away

There are regular bemo between Batubulan terminal near Denpasar and Gianyar's main terminal (8000Rp), which is behind the main market. Bemo from Gianyar's main terminal also serve Semarapura (8000Rp) and Amlapura (16,000Rp). Bemo to and from Ubud (8000Rp) use the bemo stop across the road from the main market.

SIDAN

When driving east from Gianyar you come to the turn-off to Bangli about 2km out of Peteluan. Follow this road for about 1km until you reach a sharp bend, where you'll find Sidan's **Pura Dalem**. This good example of a temple of the dead has very fine carvings. In particular, note the sculptures of Durga with children by the gate and the separate enclosure in one corner of the temple – this is dedicated to Merajapati, the guardian spirit of the dead.

BANGLI

0366

Halfway up the slope to Penelokan, Bangli, once the capital of a kingdom, is said to have the best climate on Bali.

It has an interesting temple, **Pura Kehen**, and the town makes for a good rest stop during a day of exploring.

HISTORY

Bangli dates from the early 13th century. In the Majapahit era it broke away from Gelgel to become a separate kingdom, even though it was landlocked, poor and involved in long-running conflicts with neighbouring states.

In 1849 Bangli made a treaty with the Dutch. The treaty gave Bangli control over the defeated north coast kingdom of Buleleng, but Buleleng then rebelled and the Dutch imposed direct rule there. In 1909 the rajah (lord or prince) of Bangli chose to become a Dutch protectorate rather than face suicidal *puputan* (a warrior's fight to the death) or complete conquest by the neighbouring kingdoms or the colonial power.

Information

The compact and well-organised centre has a Bank BRI with international ATM, and there is a nearby hospital. There's also a police station and post office. The **market** is worth a stroll.

Sights & Activities

PURA KEHEN

The state temple of the Bangli kingdom, **Pura Kehen** (admission 4100Rp; 9am-5pm) is one of the finest temples in eastern Bali – it's a miniature version of Pura Besakih (p216). It is terraced up the hillside, with a flight of steps leading to the beautifully decorated entrance. The first courtyard has a huge banyan tree with a *kulkul* (hollow tree-trunk warning drum) entwined in its branches. The Chinese porcelain plates were set into the walls as decoration, but most of the originals have been damaged or lost. The inner courtyard has an 11-roof *meru* (multi-roofed shrine), and there are other shrines with thrones for the Hindu trinity – Brahma, Shiva and Vishnu. The carvings are particularly intricate.

There's a counter opposite the temple entrance where you pay your admission. Sarong and/or sash rental costs 2000Rp (see Avoiding Offence, p42).

PURA DALEM PENUNGGEKAN

The exterior wall of this fascinating 'temple of the dead' features vivid relief carvings of wrong-doers getting their just desserts in the afterlife. One panel addresses the lurid fate of adulterers (men in particular may find the viewing uncomfortable). Other panels portray sinners as monkeys, while another is a good

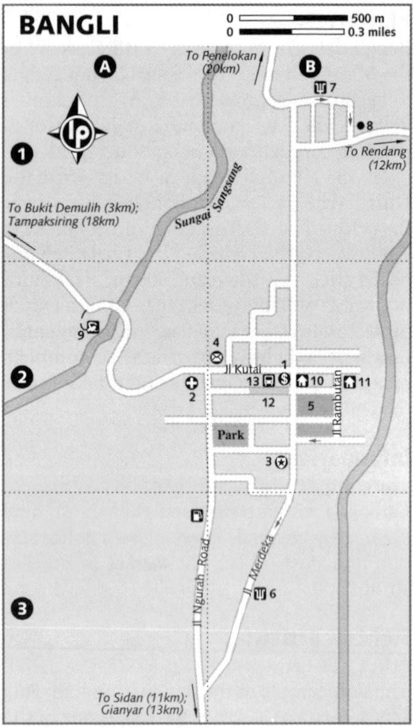

INFORMATION
Bank BRI 1 B2
Hospital 2 A2
Police Station 3 B2
Post Office 4 B2

SIGHTS & ACTIVITIES
Market 5 B2
Pura Dalem Penunggekan 6 B3
Pura Kehen 7 B1
Sasana Budaya Giri Kusuma 8 B1
Tirta Buana 9 A2

SLEEPING
Artha Sastra Inn 10 B2
Bangli Inn 11 B2

EATING
Pasar Malam 12 B2

TRANSPORT
Bemo Terminal 13 B2

representation of evil-doers begging to be spared the fires of hell. It's just to the south of Pura Kehen.

SASANA BUDAYA GIRI KUSUMA

Supposedly a showplace for Balinese dance, drama, gamelan (Balinese orchestra) and the visual arts, this large arts centre rarely has anything on. But it's well maintained, so it's always worth asking if something *will* be on.

BUKIT DEMULIH

Three kilometres west of Bangli is the village of Demulih, and a hill called Bukit Demulih. If you can't find the sign pointing to it, ask local children to direct you. After a short climb to the top, you'll see a small temple and good views over South Bali.

On the way to Bukit Demulih, a steep side road leads down to Tirta Buana, a **public swimming pool** in a lovely location deep in the valley, visible through the trees from the road above. You can take a vehicle most of the way down, but the track peters out and you'll need to walk the last 100m or so.

Sleeping & Eating

A *pasar malam* (night market), on the street beside the bemo terminal, has some good *warung* (food stalls), and you'll also find some in the market area during the day.

Artha Sastra Inn (☎ 91179; Jl Merdeka; s/d 35,000/50,000Rp) Still run by descendants of the last royal family, this bare-bones former royal residence is cheap and friendly.

Bangli Inn (☎ 91419; Jl Rambutan 1; r 120,000Rp) Somewhat modern, but just as friendly as the Artha Sastra, the 10 cold-water rooms are clean and include breakfast.

Getting There & Away

Bangli is located on the main road between Denpasar's Batubulan terminal (10,000Rp) and Gunung Batur, via Penelokan.

SEMARAPURA (KLUNGKUNG)

☎ 0366

Once the centre of Bali's most important kingdom, Semarapura is today a great artistic and cultural focal point on the island. Now the capital of Klungkung district, with its distinctly Chinese character, is coming to terms with the sudden decrease in traffic thanks to the new coast road. Many people predict that it will find new appeal as relaxed country town.

Officially named Semarapura, it is still often commonly called Klungkung. The Kertha Gosa complex is a 'must-see' site and is definitely worth a detour from the new coast road, or as part of a circle tour from the south or Ubud.

History

Successors to the Majapahit conquerors of Bali established themselves at Gelgel (just south of modern Semarapura) in around 1400, the Gelgel dynasty strengthening the growing Majapahit presence on the island. During the 17th century, the successors of the Gelgel line established separate kingdoms and the dominance of the Gelgel court was lost. The court moved to Klungkung in 1710, but never regained a pre-eminent position.

In 1849 the rulers of Klungkung and Gianyar defeated a Dutch invasion force at Kusamba. Before the Dutch could launch a counter attack, a force from Tabanan had arrived and the trader Mads Lange was able to broker a peace settlement.

For the next 50 years, the South Bali kingdoms squabbled, until the rajah of Gianyar petitioned the Dutch for support. When the Dutch finally invaded the south, the king of Klungkung had a choice between a suicidal *puputan*), like the rajah of Denpasar, or an ignominious surrender, as Tabanan's rajah had done. He chose the former. In April 1908, as the Dutch surrounded his palace, the Dewa Agung and hundreds of his relatives and followers marched out to certain death from Dutch gunfire, or the blades of their own kris (traditional dagger). It was the last Balinese kingdom to succumb and the sacrifice is commemorated in the large **Puputan Monument**.

Information

Jl Nakula and the main street, Jl Diponegoro, have several banks with international ATMs. The post office and wartel are further west.

District tourist office (☎ 21448; 🕑 8am-2pm Mon-Fri) The small office is in the Museum Semarajaya building of Taman Kertha Gosa. It means well.

Police station (☎ 21115)

Sights

TAMAN KERTHA GOSA

When the Dewa Agung dynasty moved here in 1710, the Semara Pura was established. The palace was laid out as a large square, believed to be in the form of a mandala, with courtyards, gardens, pavilions and moats. The complex is sometimes referred to as Taman Gili (Island Garden). Most of the original

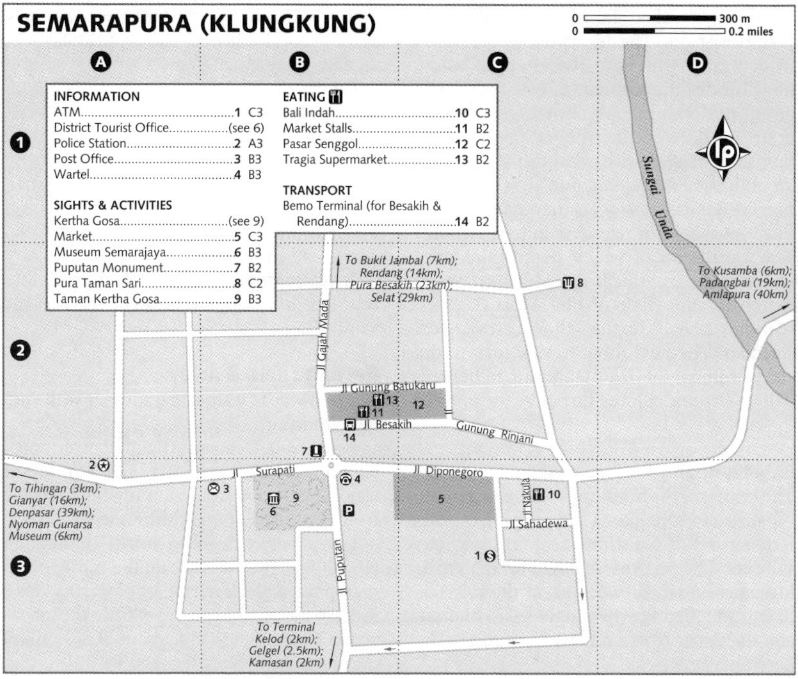

palace and grounds were destroyed by Dutch attacks in 1908 – the Pemedal Agung, the gateway on the south side of the square, is all that remains of the palace itself (but it's worth a close look to see the carvings). Two important buildings are preserved in a restored section of the grounds, and with a museum, they comprise the **Taman Kertha Gosa complex** (adult/child 5000/2000Rp, parking 1000Rp; 7am-6pm). Parking is easy, and vendors are persistent.

Kertha Gosa

In the northeastern corner of the complex, the 'Hall of Justice' was effectively the supreme court of the Klungkung kingdom, where disputes and cases that could not be settled at the village level were eventually brought. This open-sided pavilion is a superb example of Klungkung architecture. The ceiling is completely covered with fine paintings in the Klungkung style. The paintings, done on asbestos sheeting, were installed in the 1940s, replacing cloth paintings, which had deteriorated.

The rows of ceiling panels depict several themes. The lowest level illustrates five tales from Bali's answer to the *Arabian Nights,* where a girl called Tantri spins a different yarn every night. The next two rows are scenes from Bima's travels in the afterlife, where he witnesses the torment of evil-doers. The gruesome tortures are shown clearly, but there are different interpretations of which punishment goes with what crime. (There's an authoritative explanation in *The Epic of Life – A Balinese Journey of the Soul* by Idanna Pucci, available for reference in the pavilion.) The fourth row of panels depicts the story of Garuda's (mythical man-bird creature) search for the elixir of life, while the fifth row shows events on the Balinese astrological calendar. The next three rows return to the story of Bima, this time travelling in heaven, with doves and a lotus flower at the apex of the ceiling.

Bale Kambang

The ceiling of the beautiful 'Floating Pavilion' is painted in Klungkung style. Again, the different rows of paintings deal with various subjects. The first row is based on the astrological calendar, the second on the folk tale of Pan and Men Brayut and their 18 children, and the upper rows on the adventures of the hero Sutasona.

Museum Semarajaya

This recently renovated museum has an interesting collection of archaeological and other pieces. There are exhibits of *songket* weaving and palm toddy (palm wine) and palm sugar extraction. Be sure not to miss out on the moving display about the 1908 *puputan,* along with some interesting old photos. The exhibit on salt-making gives you a good idea of the hard work involved (see Working in the Salt Brine, p237).

MARKET

Semarapura's sprawling market is one of the best in East Bali. It's a vibrant hub of commerce and a meeting place for people of the region. You can easily spend an hour wandering about the warren of stalls as well as shops on nearby streets.

PURA TAMAN SARI

The quiet lawns and ponds around this temple make it a relaxing stop. The towering 11-roofed *meru* indicates that this was a temple built for royalty.

Eating

Snack stalls line the parking area. The best bet for food locally are the **market stalls** with all manner of lunch items.

Bali Indah (☎ 21056; Jl Nakula 1; dishes 10,000-20,000Rp) A veteran Chinese sit-down place with simple meals. Sumba Rosa almost next door is similar.

Pasar Senggol (4pm-midnight) A night market, this is by far the best spot to eat if you're in town late. It's the usual flurry of woks, customers and noise.

Tragia supermarket (☎ 21997; Jl Gunung Batukaru) This has a large choice of groceries and sundries.

Getting There & Away

The best way to visit Semarapura is with your own transport.

Bemo from Denpasar (Batubulan terminal) pass through Semarapura (15,000Rp) on the way to points further east. They can be hailed from near the Puputan Monument.

For a bemo heading north to Besakih (10,000Rp), they leave from the centre of Semarapura, a block northeast of Kertha Gosa. Most of the other bemo leave from the inconvenient Terminal Kelod, about 2km south of the city centre.

AROUND SEMARAPURA

East of Semarapura, the main road crosses Sungai Unda, then swings south towards Kusamba and the sea. Lava from the 1963 eruption of Gunung Agung destroyed villages and cut the road here, but the lava flows are now overgrown.

Gelgel

Situated about 2.5km south of Semarapura, Gelgel was once the seat of Bali's most powerful dynasty. The town's decline started in 1710, when the court moved to present-day Semarapura, and finished when the Dutch bombarded the place in 1908.

Today the wide streets and the surviving temples are only faintly evocative of past grandeur. The **Pura Dasar** is not particularly attractive, but its vast courtyards are a real clue to its former importance, and festivals here attract large numbers of people from all over Bali.

A little to the east, the **Masjid Gelgel** is Bali's oldest mosque. It was established in the late 16th century for the benefit of Muslim missionaries from Java, unwilling to return home after failing to make any converts.

Kamasan

This quiet, traditional village is the place where the classical Kamasan painting style originated, and several artists still practise this art. You can see their workshops and small showrooms along the main street. The work is often a family affair, with one person inking the outlines, while another mixes the paints and yet another applies the colours. The paintings depict traditional stories or Balinese calendars, and although they are sold in souvenir shops all over Bali, the quality is better here. Look for smooth and distinct line-work, evenly applied colours and balance in the overall composition. The village is also home to families of *bokor* artisans, who produce the silver bowls used in traditional ceremonies.

To reach Kamasan, go about 2km south of Semarapura and look for the turn-off to the east.

Bukit Jambal

The road north of Semarapura climbs steeply into the hills, via Bukit Jambal, which is understandably popular for its magnificent views. There are several restaurants here that provide buffet lunches for tour groups. This road continues to Rendang and Pura Besakih.

Sungai Unda & Sungai Telagawaja

East of Semarapura, the main road crosses the dammed-up Sungai Unda. Further upstream, the Telagawaja is used for white-water rafting trips (see p77).

Tihingan

Several workshops in Tihingan are dedicated to producing gamelan instruments. Small foundries make the resonating bronze bars and bowl-shaped gongs, which are then carefully filed and polished until they produce the correct tone. Some pieces are on sale, but most of the instruments are produced for musical groups all over Bali. It's not really set up for tourists, but the workshops with signs out the front will receive visitors (albeit sometimes grudgingly); the work is usually done very early in the morning when it's cool. From Semarapura, head west along Jl Diponegoro and look for the signs.

Nyoman Gunarsa Museum

Dedicated to classical and contemporary Balinese painting, this beautiful **museum complex** (☎ 22255; adult/child 20,000Rp/free; 🕐 10am-5pm) was established by Nyoman Gunarsa, one of the most respected and successful modern artists in Indonesia. The vast three-storey building exhibits an impressive variety of well-displayed older pieces, including stone- and woodcarvings, architectural antiques, masks, ceramics and textiles.

Many of the classical paintings are on bark paper and are some of the oldest surviving examples. Check out the many old puppets, still seemingly animated – even in retirement. The top floor is devoted to Gunarsa's own bold, expressionistic depictions of traditional life. Look for *Offering*.

There's a large performance space nearby and some fine examples of traditional architecture just outside in the compound.

The museum is about 5km west from Semarapura, near a bend on the road to Gianyar – look for the dummy policemen at the base of a large statue nearby.

SIDEMEN ROAD

☎ 0366

A less-travelled route to Pura Besakih goes northeast from Semarapura, via Sidemen and Iseh, to the Rendang–Amlapura road. The area offers marvellous paddy field scenery, a delightful rural character and exciting views of Gunung Agung (when the clouds permit).

Sidemen has a spectacular location and is a centre for culture and arts, particularly *endek* (ikat) cloth and *songket*, which is woven with threads of silver and gold. German artist Walter Spies lived in Iseh for some time from 1932 in order to escape the perpetual party of his own making in Ubud. Later, the Swiss painter, Theo Meier, nearly as famous as Spies for his influence on Balinese art, lived in the same house.

There are many **walks** through the rice fields and streams in the multihued green valley. One involves a climb up to **Pura Bukit Tageh**, a small temple with big views.

Sidemen Road can be a beautiful part of any day-trip from South Bali or Ubud. It connects in the north with the Rendang to Amlapura Rd just west of Duda. The road is in good shape and regular bemo shuttle up and down from Semarapura.

Sleeping & Eating

Views throughout the area are often spectacular, from terraced green hills to Gunung Agung. Places to stay always have restaurants and can give advice or set you up for walking tours.

Near the centre of Sidemen, a small road heads west for 500m to a fork and a signpost with the names of several places to stay.

Lihat Sawah (☎/fax 24183; r 150,000-250,000Rp; dishes 12,500-25,000Rp) Take the right fork in the road to this very friendly place with great gardens. All nine rooms (the cheapest have cold water) have views of the valley and mountain. The surrounding rice fields course with water.

Tanto Villa (☎ 081-2395 0271; r US$20-40) Views of the Luwah Valley are the appeal at this modern place, which has four large and comfortable rooms with hot water. Two upstairs rooms have the best views of the surrounding chilli, bean and peanut fields.

Subak Tabola Inn (☎ 23015; r from US$25; 🏊) Set in a shockingly green amphitheatre of rice terraces, the 11 rooms here have a bit of style and open-air bathrooms. Verandas have amazing views down the valley to the ocean. The grounds are spacious and there's a cool pool with frog fountains. It's near the 2km hotel signpost.

Nirarta (Centre for Living Awareness; ☎ 24122; www.awareness-bali.com; Br Tabola; r US$25-60) Guests here partake in serious programmes for personal and spiritual development, including meditation intensives and yoga. The eight comfortable bungalows have hot water and some are well suited to families and groups.

Sacred Mountain Sanctuary (☎ 24330; www.sacredmountainresort.com; villas US$90-140; 💻 🏊) Close to the river, this remote and rusticated resort has a new age vibe and a huge spring-fed swimming pool. The 19 bamboo villas have open-air bathrooms and many artistic touches. The resort can arrange treks of Gunung Agung (from US$55), as well as a range of courses. Massage is available. The restaurant, where dishes range from 20,000Rp to 35,000Rp, features Thai and vegetarian cuisine.

Elsewhere on the Sidemen Road are these two good choices.

Pondok Wisata Sidemen (☎ 23009; r 200,000-400,000Rp) At the south end of Sidemen, this place has four clean, simple rooms with four-poster beds and great views. Accommodation includes a fine breakfast and dinner of traditional Balinese foods. You can arrange courses in local art and music.

Patal Kikian (☎/fax 23005; villas US$50-70; 🏊) Two kilometres north of Sidemen, look for a steep driveway on the eastern side of the road. This retreat has four spacious, stylishly furnished villas with vast verandas overlooking terraced hillsides – one of the best views in East Bali. Rates include all meals, which are served as private banquets on your own veranda. Rooms have hot water and there is a soaking pool.

PURA BESAKIH

Perched nearly 1000m up the side of Gunung Agung is Bali's most important temple, Pura Besakih. In fact, it is an extensive complex of 23 separate-but-related temples, with the largest and most important being Pura Penataran Agung. Unfortunately, many people find it a deeply disappointing experience due to the avarice of numerous local characters. See An Unholy Experience on p219 for the details, which may well help you to decide whether to skip it. Another disincentive to visit is that tourists are usually barred from entering the temples.

Besakih, as it is known, is at its most impressive during one of the frequent festivals, when hundreds, perhaps thousands, of gorgeously dressed devotees turn up with beautifully arranged offerings. The panoramic view and the mountain backdrop are impressive too.

History

The precise origins of Pura Besakih are not totally clear, but it almost certainly dates from prehistoric times. The stone bases of Pura Penataran Agung and several other temples resemble megalithic stepped pyramids, which date back at least 2000 years. There are legendary accounts of Sri Dangkyang Markendaya conducting meditation and ceremonies here in the 8th century AD, while stone inscriptions record a Hindu ritual on the site in AD 1007. There are some indications of Buddhist activity, but it was certainly used as a Hindu place of worship from 1284, when the first Javanese conquerors settled on Bali, and this is confirmed by accounts from the time of the Majapahit conquest in 1343. By the 15th century, Besakih had become a state temple of the Gelgel dynasty.

The central temple was added to over the years, and additional temples were built for specific family, occupational and regional groups. The complex was neglected during the colonial period, perhaps because of lack of royal patronage, and was virtually destroyed in the 1917 earthquake. The Dutch assisted with its reconstruction, and the dependent rajahs were encouraged to support the maintenance of the temples.

Orientation

The main entrance, the Tourist Fee Office, is 2km south of the complex on the road from Menanga and the south. The fees are as follows: adult/child 7500/6000Rp, still camera 1000Rp, video camera 2500Rp and car park 1000Rp. The fact that you may well be charged for a video camera whether you have one or not gives you a taste of things to come.

About 200m past the ticket office, there is a fork in the road with a sign indicating Besakih to the right and Kintamani to the left. Go left because going to the right puts you in the main parking area at the bottom of a hill some 300m from the complex. Going past the road to Kintamani, where there is the small West Ticket Office, puts you in the north parking area only 20m from the complex. Snack stands and warung are found along the trash-strewn approaches and at both parking lots.

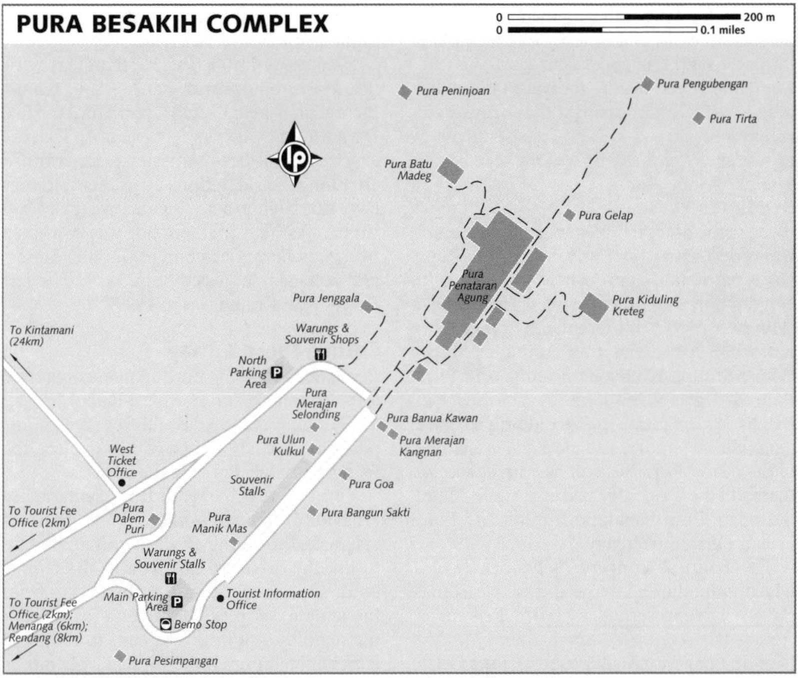

Sights & Activities

PURA PENATARAN AGUNG

This is the central temple of the complex – in significance, if not exactly in position. It is built on six levels, terraced up the slope, with the entrance approached from below, up a flight of steps. This entrance is an imposing *candi bentar* (split gateway), and beyond it, the even more impressive *kori agung* is the gateway to the second courtyard.

Tourists are not permitted inside, so for the best view, climb the steps to the left of the main entrance and follow the path around the western side. From here, you can just see over the wall into the second courtyard (do not climb up on the wall), where the *padmasana* (temple shrine resembling a vacant chair) is. In most modern temples this is a single throne for the supreme god, but Besakih stresses the Hindu trinity, and therefore it has a triple throne called *padmasana tiga* (*padmasana trisakti*), with separate seats for Brahma, Vishnu and Shiva. This point is the spiritual centre of the temple and, indeed, of the whole Besakih complex.

Continuing on the footpath around the temple, you can see quite a few imposing *meru*, the multi-roofed towers through which gods can descend to earth, but otherwise the temple is unspectacular. The upper courtyards are usually empty, even during festivals. One of the best views is from the path at the northeastern end, where you can look down past the many towers and over the temple to the sea.

OTHER TEMPLES

None of the other temples are striking, except when decorated for festivals, but each one has a particular significance, sometimes in conjunction with other temples. The *trimurti* (Hindu trinity) is represented by the combination of Pura Penataran Agung as Shiva, Pura Kiduling Kreteg as Brahma and Pura Batu Madeg as Vishnu. Just as each village in Bali has a *pura puseh* (temple of origin), *pura desa* (village temple) and *pura dalem* (temple of the dead), Pura Besakih has three temples that fulfil these roles for Bali as a whole – Pura Basukian, Pura Penataran Agung and Pura Dalem Puri, respectively.

The Balinese concept of *panca dewata*, which embodies a centre and four cardinal points, is represented by Pura Penataran Agung (the centre), Pura Kiduling Kreteg (south), Pura Batu Madeg (north), Pura Gelap (east) and Pura Ulun Kulkul (west). Each district of Bali is associated with a specific temple at Besakih, and the main temples of Bali are also represented by specific shrines here. Some temples are associated with families descended from the original Gelgel dynasty, and there are shrines and memorials going back many generations. Various craft guilds also have their own temples, notably the metal-workers, whose Pura Ratu Pande is built onto the side of the main temple.

FESTIVALS

Besakih is at its best when a festival is on, and with so many temples and gods represented here, there seems to be one every week or so. Ask at a tourist office anywhere on Bali, and try to identify which part of the Besakih complex will be the focus of attention. The founding of Besakih itself is celebrated at Bhatara Turun Kabeh around the full moon of the 10th lunar month (usually in March and April), when all the gods descend at once. The annual rites at Pura Dalem Puri, usually in January, attract thousands who make offerings for the dead. In addition, each individual temple has its own *odalan* (Balinese temple 'birthday festival'), held annually according to the 210-day *wuku* calendar.

Even more important are the great purification ceremonies of Panca Wali Krama, theoretically held every 10 years, and the Eka Dasa Rudra held every 100 years. In fact, the exact dates of these festivals are determined after long considerations by priests, and they have not been exactly regular. An Eka Dasa Rudra was held in 1963, but was disrupted by the disastrous eruption of Gunung Agung, and restaged successfully in 1979. The last Panca Wali Krama was in 1999.

Getting There & Away

Besakih is a major feature on many organised tours of eastern and northern Bali.

The best way to visit is with your own transportation, which allows you to explore the many gorgeous drives in the area.

You can visit by bemo from Semarapura (10,000Rp) but from other parts of Bali this can make the outing an all-day affair. Be sure to ask the driver to take you to the temple entrance, not to the village about 1km from the temple complex. Make certain you leave the temple by 3pm if you want to return to either Semarapura or South Bali by bemo.

AN UNHOLY EXPERIENCE

So intrusive are the scams and irritations faced by visitors to Besakih that many wish they had skipped the complex altogether. What follows are some of the ploys you should be aware of before a visit.

- Near the main parking area is a building labelled Tourist Information Office. Guides here may emphatically tell you that you need their services. You don't; you may always walk among the temples. No 'guide' can get you into a closed temple.
- Other 'guides' may foist their services on you throughout your visit. There have been reports of people agreeing to a guide's services only to be hit with a huge fee at the end.
- It will require an endless repetition of 'no thank you' and 'please leave' to get the 'guides' to go away, but this is essential as there have been reports of people giving in and allowing the guide to tag along without negotiating a price. Later they are intimidated into paying a fee of 200,000Rp or more.
- Touts on scooters may follow you on your walk up the hill from the main parking area demanding that you pay 8000Rp for a ride. This is another good reason to use the north parking area close to the complex.
- Once inside the complex, you may receive offers to 'come pray with me'. Visitors who seize on this chance to get into a forbidden temple can face demands of 50,000Rp or more.

It should be noted that guides or drivers who accompany you from other parts of Bali are generally not allowed into the temples by the local 'guides'.

GUNUNG AGUNG

Bali's highest and most revered mountain, Gunung Agung is an imposing peak seen from most of South and East Bali, although it's often obscured by cloud and mist. Many references give its height as 3142m, but some say it lost its top in the 1963 eruption and opinion varies as to the real height. The summit is an oval crater, about 700m across, with its highest point on the western edge above Besakih.

Climbing Gunung Agung

It's possible to climb Agung from various directions. The two shortest and most popular routes are from Pura Besakih, on the southwest side of the mountain, and from Pura Pasar Agung, on the southern slopes. The latter route goes to the lower edge of the crater rim (2900m), but you can't make your way from there around to the very highest point. You'll have great views of the south and east, but you won't be able to see central Bali.

To have the best chance of seeing the view before the clouds form, get to the top before 8am. You'll have to start at night, so plan your climb when there will be some moonlight. Take a strong torch (flashlight), extra batteries, plenty of water (2L per person), snack food, waterproof clothing and a warm jumper (sweater). The descent is especially hard on your feet, so you'll appreciate strong shoes or boots and manicured toes.

You should take a guide for either route. Early in the climb the guide will stop at a shrine to make an offering and say some prayers. This is a holy mountain and you should show respect.

It's best to climb during the dry season (April to September), although July to September are the most reliable months. At other times, the paths can be slippery and dangerous and the views are clouded over. Climbing Gunung Agung is not permitted when major religious events are being held at Pura Besakih, which generally includes most of April. No guide will take you up at these times.

GUIDES

Trips with guides on either of the following routes up Gunung Agung generally include breakfast and other meals and a place to stay, but be sure to confirm all details in advance. They can also arrange transportation.

Most of the places to stay in the region, including those at Selat (see p220), along the Sidemen Road (see p216) and Tirta Gangga (see p233) will recommend guides for

Gunung Agung climbs. Expect to pay a negotiable 250,000R to 600,000Rp per person for your climb.

Recommended guides include:

Gung Bawa Trekking (☎ 0366-24379; gbtrekk@yahoo.com; Selat) A reliable trekking operation near the market.

Ketut Uriada (☎ 081-2364 6426; Muncan) This experienced guide can arrange transport for an extra fee (look for his small sign on the road east of the village).

FROM PURA BESAKIH

This climb is much tougher than from the southern approach and is only for the very physically fit. For the best chance of a clear view before the clouds close in, you should start at midnight. Allow at least six hours for the climb, and four to five hours for the descent. The starting point is Pura Pengubengan, northeast of the main temple complex, but it's easy to get lost on the lower trails, so definitely hire a guide.

FROM PURA PASAR AGUNG

This route involves the least walking, because Pura Pasar Agung (Agung Market Temple) is high on the southern slopes of the mountain (around 1500m) and can be reached by a good road north from Selat. From the temple you can climb to the top in three or four hours, but it's a pretty demanding trek. With or without a guide, you must report to the police station at Selat before you start. If you don't have a guide the police will strongly encourage you to take one.

It is much better to stay the night near Muncan or Selat so that you can drive up early in the morning to Pura Pasar Agung. This temple has been greatly enlarged and improved, in part as a monument to the 1963 eruption that devastated this area.

Start climbing from the temple at around 3am. There are numerous trails through the pine forest but after an hour or so you'll climb above the tree line. Then you're climbing on solidified lava, which can be loose and broken in places, but a good guide will keep you on solid ground. At the top, you can gawk into the crater, watch the sun rise over Lombok and see the shadow of Agung in the morning haze over southern Bali.

Allow at least two hours to get back down to the temple. If you don't have a car waiting for you, walk down to Sebudi, from where there are public bemo down to Selat.

RENDANG TO AMLAPURA ROAD

☎ 0366

A scenic road goes around the southern slopes of Gunung Agung from Rendang to near Amlapura. It runs through some superb countryside, descending more or less gradually as it goes further east. If you have your own wheels, you'll find it very scenic, with some interesting places to stop. Water flows everywhere and you can easily exhaust your film, tape or memory card.

Cyclists enjoy the route and find going east to be an easier ride.

You can get to the start of the road in Rendang from Bangli in the west on a very pretty road through rice terraces and thick jungle vegetation. **Rendang** itself is an attractive mountain village. After going east for about 3km, you'll come into a beautiful small valley of rice terraces. At the bottom is the **Sungai Telegawaja**, a popular river for white-water rafting. Some companies (see p77) have their facilities near here.

The old-fashioned village of **Muncan** has quaint shingle roofs. It's approximately 4km along the winding road. Nearby are scores of open-air factories where the soft lava rock is carved into temple decorations.

The road then passes through some of the most attractive rice country in Bali before reaching **Selat**, where you turn north to get to Pura Pasar Agung, a starting point for climbing Gunung Agung. **Puri Agung Inn** (☎ 23037; r 125,000-175,000Rp) has 10 clean and comfortable rooms with rice field views. You can arrange rice field walks here or climbs up Gunung Agung (p219).

Just before **Duda**, the very scenic Sidemen Road (see p216) branches southwest via Sidemen to Semarapura (see p213). Further east, a side road (about 800m) leads to **Putung**. This area is superb for hiking: there's an easy-to-follow track from Putung to **Manggis**, about 8km down the hill.

Continuing east, **Sibetan** is famous for growing *salak*, the delicious fruit with a curious 'snakeskin' covering, which you can buy from roadside stalls. This is one of the villages you can visit on tours and homestays organised by **JED** (Village Ecotourism Network; ☎ 0361-735320; www.jed.or.id; tours US$25-100), the non-profit group that organises rural tourism (see p348).

Near Sibetan, a poorly signposted road leads north to Jungutan, with its **Tirta Telaga Tista** – a decorative pool and garden complex built for the water-loving old rajah of Karangasem.

The scenic road finishes at **Bebandem**, where there's a cattle market every three days, and plenty of other stuff for sale as well. Bebandem and several nearby villages are home to members of the traditional metal-workers caste, which includes silversmiths as well as blacksmiths.

KUSAMBA TO PADANGBAI

The new coast road from Sanur joins the traditional route to the east at the fishing town of Kusamba.

Kusamba

A side road leaves the main road and goes south to the fishing and salt-making village of Kusamba, where you will see rows of colourful fishing *prahu* (outriggers) lined up all along the beach. The fishing is usually done at night and the 'eyes' on the front of the boats help navigate through the darkness. The fish market in Kusamba is really excellent.

Local boats travel to the islands of Nusa Penida and Nusa Lembongan, which are clearly visible from Kusamba (but you can get faster and safer boats from Padangbai; see p355). Both east and west of Kusamba, there are small salt-making huts lined up in rows along the beach – see Working in the Salt Brine, p222.

Pura Goa Lawah

Three kilometres east of Kusamba is **Pura Goa Lawah** (Bat Cave Temple; admission 4100Rp, car park 1000Rp, sash rental 1000Rp; 8am-6pm), which is one of nine directional temples in Bali. The cave in the cliff face is packed, crammed and jammed full of bats, and the complex is equally overcrowded with tour groups. There is a distinctly batty stench emanating from the cave, and the roofs of the temple shrines, which are in front of the cave, are liberally coated with bat droppings. Superficially, the temple is small and unimpressive, but it is very old and of great significance to the Balinese.

It is said that the cave leads all the way to Pura Besakih, some 19km away, but it's unlikely that you'd want to try this route. The bats provide sustenance for the legendary giant snake, the deity Naga Basuki, which is also believed to live in the cave.

> **DETOUR**
>
> East of Kusamba and 300m west of Pura Goa Lawah (above), **Merta Sari** (10am-3pm) serves up a meal for 10,000Rp that's hard to beat. Their renowned *nasi campur* includes juicy, pounded fish satay, a slightly sour, fragrant fish broth, fish steamed in banana leaves, snake beans in a fragrant tomato-peanut sauce and a fire red sambal. The open-air pavilion is 300m north of the coast road in the village of Bingin. Look for the Merta Sari signs.

PADANGBAI

☎ 0363

Reflecting the odd patterns of tourism that has some places ascending while others are declining, Padangbai is definitely on the upswing. Nominally the port for Bali–Lombok ferries and passenger boats to Nusa Penida, Padangbai sits on a small bay and has a nice little curve of a beach. It has a whole compact seaside travellers scene with cheap places to stay and some very funky and fun cafés. A recent town beautification drive has spiffed things up, albeit at the cost of losing some of the colourful food and drink stands that used to line the beach. An esplanade is planned for Jl Silayukti.

The pace is slow, but if you want to pick up your own, there's good snorkelling and diving nearby plus some easy walks and a couple of great beaches. Meanwhile you can soak up the languid vibe punctuated by the occasional arrival and departure of a ferry.

Information

Moneychangers at hotels and along Jl Pelabuhan offer okay rates. The **Bank BRI** (Jl Pelabuhan) also exchanges money and has an international ATM.

You can find slow internet access (per min 300Rp) at numerous places including Kerti Bungalows and Made's Homestay (see p223).

Sights

Padangbai is interesting for a little walk. At the west end of town near the post office there's a small **mosque** and a temple, **Pura Desa**. Towards the middle, there are two more temples, **Pura Dalem** and **Pura Segara**, and a new **market** that is home to numerous stalls and various vendors displaced from the beach.

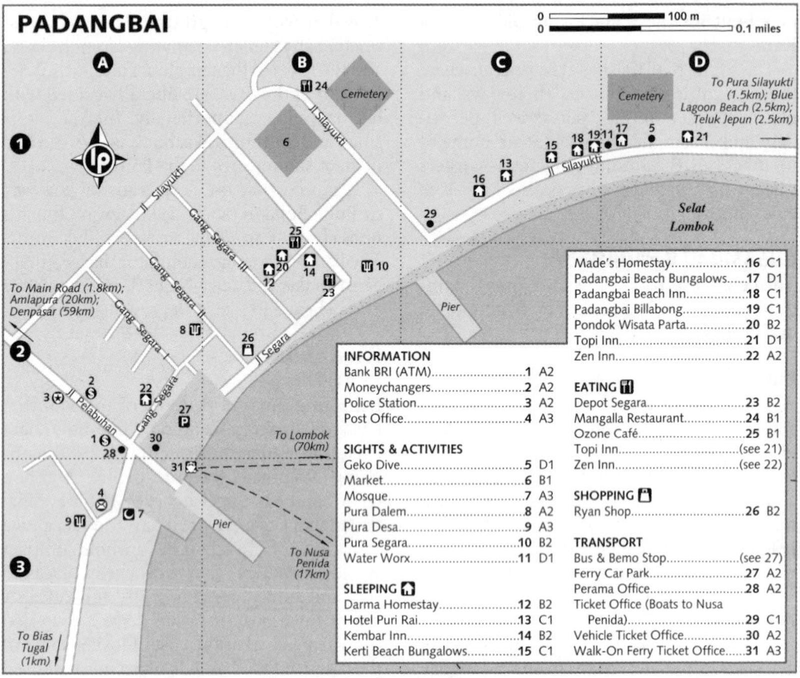

With its protected bay, Padangbai has a good beach right in front. Others are nearby; walk southwest from the ferry terminal and follow the trail up the hill to idyllic **Bias Tugal**, also known as Pantai Kecil (Little Beach), on the exposed coast outside the bay. Be careful in the water as it is subject to strong currents. There are a couple of daytime warung here.

On a headland at the northeast corner of the bay, a path leads uphill to three temples, including **Pura Silayukti**, where Empu Kuturan – who introduced the caste system to Bali in the 11th century – is said to have lived. On the other side of this headland is the small, light-sand **Blue Lagoon Beach**.

Activities

The Topi Inn (see opposite) arranges a huge variety of cultural workshops for guests and non-guests. The fee is 100,000Rp for a course of two to four hours.

DIVING

There's some pretty good diving on the coral reefs around Padangbai, but the water can be a little cold and visibility is not always ideal. The most popular local dives are **Blue Lagoon** and **Teluk Jepun** (Jepun Bay), both in Teluk Amuk, the bay just east of Padangbai. There's a good variety of soft and hard corals and varied marine life, including sharks, turtles and wrasse, and a 40m wall at the Blue Lagoon.

Several good local outfits offer diving trips in the area, including to Gili Tepekong and Gili Biaha, and on to Tulamben and Nusa Penida. All dive prices are competitive, costing US$40 to US$90 for two boat dives, depending on the site. Dive courses are available.

Recommended operators include the following:

Geko Dive (☎ 41516; www.gekodive.com; Jl Silayukti) The longest-established operator; nice café across from the beach.

Water Worx (☎ 41220; www.waterworxbali.com; Jl Silayukti) Another good dive operator, which should have a new diving pool.

SNORKELLING

One of the best and most accessible walk-in snorkel sites is off Blue Lagoon Beach. Note that it is subject to strong currents when the tide is out. Other sites such as Teluk Jepun can be reached by local boat (or check with the dive operators to see if they have any room on their dive boats). Snorkel sets cost about 20,000Rp per day.

Local *jukung* (boats) offer snorkelling trips (bring your own snorkelling gear) around Padangbai (140,000Rp), and as far away as Nusa Lembongan (300,000Rp) for two passengers.

Sleeping

Accommodation in Padangbai – like the town – is pretty laid-back. Prices are fairly cheap and it's pleasant enough here that there's no need to hurry through to or from Lombok if you want to hang out on the beach and in cafés with other travellers.

VILLAGE

In the village, there are several tiny places in the alleys, some with a choice of small, cheap downstairs rooms or bigger, brighter upstairs rooms.

Pondok Wisata Parta (☎ 41475; off Gang Segara III; r 40,000-150,000Rp;) The pick of the 10 rooms in this nice place is the 'honeymoon room', which has a harbour view and good breezes. The most expensive rooms have air-con.

Darma Homestay (☎ 41394; Gang Segara III; r 50,000-80,000Rp) The more expensive rooms of the 12 have hot showers. Go for the private room on the top floor.

Kembar Inn (☎ 41364; kembarinn@hotmail.com; r 50,000-150,000Rp;) There are six rooms at this inn linked by a steep and narrow staircase. The best awaits at the top and has a nice private terrace.

Zen Inn (☎ 41418; www.zeninn.com; Gang Segara; r 50,000-150,000Rp;) Close to the ferry terminal, Zen's four rooms are eclectically decorated with bamboo and rattan interiors and both indoor and outdoor showers. Extra money gets hot water and air-con. The café is a treat.

JALAN SILAYUKTI

This little strip of beach places a mere two minutes east of the village makes for a mellow hangout.

Made's Homestay (☎ 41441; Jl Silayukti; s/d 50,000/60,000Rp;) Clean simple rooms and internet access are the draws here.

Kerti Beach Bungalows (☎ 41391; Jl Silayukti; r 50,000-80,000Rp;) Go for the 18 rooms in pretty bungalows rather than the stuffy rice barns.

Padangbai Bilabong (☎ 0813-3831 2607; Jl Silayukti; r 50,000-100,000Rp) Go for the bungalows right up front at this scrupulously tidy place, which has found a way to create garden features out of used plastic water bottles.

Topi Inn (☎ 41424; www.topiinn.com; Jl Silayukti; r 50,000Rp, f 150,000Rp) Sitting at the end of the bay in a serene location, Topi has six pleasant rooms. The enthusiastic owners offer cultural courses among other diversions. The café is excellent.

Padangbai Beach Inn (☎ 41439; Jl Silayukti; r 60,000-100,000Rp) Go with the pleasant bungalows and avoid the rice-barn style two-storey cottages, which can get hot and stuffy.

Padangbai Beach Bungalows (☎ 41417; Jl Silayukti; r 75,000-100,000Rp, with air-con 200,000Rp;) The bungalows are attractive, with open-air bathrooms, and set in a classic Balinese garden setting.

Hotel Puri Rai (☎ 41385; purirai_hotel@yahoo.com; Jl Silayukti 3; r 250,000Rp, with air-con 300,000Rp;) The most upmarket option in town, the Puri Rai has 30 rooms, some with fans in a two-storey stone building, pleasantly facing the pool. Others with air-con enjoy harbour views or overlook a parking area.

Eating & Drinking

Beach fare and backpackers' staples are what's on offer in Padangbai – lots of fresh seafood, Indonesian classics, pizza and, yes, banana pancakes. Most of the places to stay have a café. You can easily laze away a few hours soaking up the scene at the places along Jl Segara and Jl Silayukti, which have harbour views during the day and cool breezes in the evening.

Depot Segara (☎ 41443; Jl Segara; dishes 10,000-20,000Rp) Fresh seafood is prepared in a variety of ways at this popular café with a touch of style. Ponder the murals while you gobble down one of their good breakfasts.

Mangalla Restaurant (☎ 0813-3850 3618; Jl Silayukti; 15,000-30,000Rp) Well-priced seafood, pizza and fresh local fare are popular here. Relax on the comfy rattan chairs.

Zen Inn (☎ 41418; Gang Segara; dishes 18,000-30,000Rp) Burgers and other meaty mains with a Dutch accent are served in this dark café with movies at night and a good bar.

Ozone Café (☎ 41501; dishes 15,000-35,000Rp) This popular travellers' gathering spot has more character than every other place in East Bali combined. Incomprehensible slogans painted on the wall (example: Acting like a monkey when you see a nice girl is so important for you.) set the tone. There's pizza and live music, sometimes by patrons.

Topi Inn (☎ 41424; Jl Silayukti; mains 18,000-40,000Rp) Juices, shakes and good coffees served up throughout the day. Big breakfasts and at night fresh seafood from the boats right across the street.

Shopping
Ryan Shop (☎ 41215; Jl Segara 38) A name you can trust for quality. It has a fair selection of second-hand paperbacks, some maps and sundries.

Getting There & Away
BEMO
Padangbai is 2km south of the main Semarapura–Amlapura road. Bemo leave from the car park in front of the port; orange bemo go east through Candidasa to Amlapura (7000Rp); blue or white bemo go to Semarapura (8000Rp).

BOAT
Lombok
Public ferries (adult/child 21,000/14,000Rp;) travel non-stop between Padangbai and Lembar on Lombok. Motorcycles cost 155,000Rp and cars cost 330,000Rp – go through the weighbridge at the west corner of the Padangbai car park. Depending on conditions the trip can take three to five hours. Boats run 24 hours and leave about every 90 minutes; food and drink is sold on board. Passenger tickets are sold near the pier.

Anyone who carries your luggage on or off the ferries at both ports will expect to be paid, so agree on the price first or carry your own stuff. Also, watch out for scams whereby the porter may try to sell you a ticket you've already bought.

Perama has a 40-passenger boat (200,000Rp, four hours), which usually leaves at 9am for Senggigi, where you can connect to the Gilis.

Nusa Penida
On the beach just east of the car park, you'll find the twin-engine fibreglass boats that run across the strait to Buyuk, 1km west of Sampalan on Nusa Penida (25,000Rp, 45 min, four daily). The boats run between 7am and noon. Boats back to Padangbai cost 18,000Rp.

BUS
To connect with Denpasar, catch a bemo out to the main road and hail a bus to the Batubulan terminal (15,000Rp).

TOURIST SHUTTLE BUS
Perama (☎ 41419; Café Dona, Jl Pelabuhan; ☷ 7am-8pm) has a stop here for its services around the east coast.

Destination	Fare
Candidasa	15,000Rp
Kuta	40,000Rp
Lovina	100,000Rp
Sanur	40,000Rp
Ubud	40,000Rp

PADANGBAI TO CANDIDASA
☎ 0363
It's worth prowling some of the beachside lanes off the main road for little places to stay. It's 11km along the main road from the Padangbai turn-off to the resort town of Candidasa, and there are bemo or buses every few minutes. Between the two is an attractive stretch of coast, which has some tourist development, and a large oil-storage depot in Teluk Amuk.

Buitan & Manggis
Balina Beach is the name bestowed on the small tourist development at the village of Buitan. It's an attractive area on a quiet coastal stretch, though the beach is being lost to erosion and what's left is black sand and stones. To find the turn-off, look for the small yellow sign 'Balina' from the main road. Nearby is the pretty village of Manggis.

SLEEPING & EATING
Two of Bali's best hotels are off the main road along here.

One of Bali's best resorts, the **Amankila** (☎ 41333; www.amankila.com; villa from US$650; ☒ ☒ ☐ ☒), is hidden along the jutting cliffs. About 5.6km beyond the Padangbai turn-off and 500m past the road to Manggis, a discreetly marked side road leads to the hotel. It features an isolated seaside location with views to Nusa Penida and even Lombok. The renowned architecture features classically simple rectangular structures with thatched roofs and lots of natural wood and stone. The three main swimming pools step down into the sea, in matching shades of blue. The **Beachclub pool** (150,000Rp) is on a stretch of sand and is open to non-guests. It has a café and water sports. The restaurants at the Amankila are open to non-guests. The superb **Terrace** (lunch 80,000-200,000Rp) is more casual and has creative and varied cuisine. The **Restaurant** (mains 140,000-210,000Rp) has complex fusion and Balinese dishes.

Somewhat more accessible to the masses on everyday budgets, the **Alila Manggis** (☎ 41011; www.alilahotels.com; r US$180-250;) has elegant, white, thatch-roofed buildings in spacious lawn gardens facing a beautiful stretch of secluded beach. The 55 rooms are very comfortable, with smart modern interiors; the best are the deluxe ones on the top floor with balconies. The restaurant features excellent *nouvelle* Balinese cuisine and you can be served at tables in your room or at the beach. Activities include a kids' camp, a spa and cooking courses. The latter may well tempt you after you enjoy the superb pan-Asian cuisine in the restaurant **Seasalt**.

Mendira & Sengkidu

Coming from the west, there are hotels and losmen (basic accommodation) off the main road at Mendira and Sengkidu, before you reach Candidasa. Although the beach has suffered from erosion and unsightly sea walls have been constructed, it's a good place for a getaway if you have your own transport.

SLEEPING & EATING

All of the following are on small tracks between the main road and the water; none are far from Candidasa.

The three places listed here are reached down narrow roads from a single turn off the main road 1km west of Candidasa. Look for a large sign listing places to stay.

Amarta Beach Inn Bungalows (☎ 41230; r 100,000-200,000Rp) In a panoramic seaside setting, the 10 units here are right on the water and are great value. The more expensive ones have hot water and spiffy open-air bathrooms. At low tide there is a tiny beach; at other times you can sit and watch the bananas grow.

Candi Beach Cottage (☎ 41234; www.candibeachbali.com; r US$70-90, bungalow US$80-120;) This low-key resort-style hotel has two pools and lovely grounds right at the waves. There are 32 rooms and 32 bungalows, all with satellite TV.

Pondok Pisang (☎ 41065; www.pondokpisang.com; r 200,000-350,000Rp) The name here means 'banana hut', and there's plenty of appeal. The six, spacious bungalows are widely spaced facing the sea. Each bungalow has a unique interior, including mosaic-tiled bathrooms. Yoga intensives are held at various times and you can often find women sewing cushions and bags.

The next two places are an easy walk to Candidasa.

Nirwana (☎ 41136; nirwana-cottages@telkom.net; r US$35-60;) This older resort has 12 bungalow-style rooms that are a little dowdy but well maintained. The best units are near the seawall with the pool and café. It's 300m down a forested dirt track from the main road.

Lotus Bungalows (☎ 41104; www.lotusbungalows.com; r US$20-45;) The 20 rooms here (some with air-con, all with hot water) are in well-spaced bungalow-style units. Four (numbers 1, 2, 13 and 14) are right on the ocean, with the last being the top pick. The décor is bright and airy, and there is a large and stylish pool area.

Tenganan

Tenganan is a village of Bali Aga people, the descendants of the original Balinese who inhabited Bali before the Majapahit arrival. The village is surrounded by a wall, and consists basically of two rows of identical houses stretching up the gentle slope of the hill.

The Bali Aga are reputed to be exceptionally conservative and resistant to change with much being made of the fact that things have changed little since the 11th century. Well that's only partially true: TVs and other modern conveniences are hidden away in the traditional houses. But it is fair to say that the village has a much more traditional feel than most other villages on Bali. Cars and motorcycles are forbidden from entering.

The most striking feature of Tenganan is its postcard-like beauty, with the hills providing a photogenic backdrop. As you enter the village you may be greeted by a guide who will take you on a tour of the village – and generally lead you back to their family compound to look at textiles and *lontar* (specially prepared palm leaves) strips. Unlike Besakih, however, there's no pressure to buy anything, so you won't need your own armed guards. For more on *lontar* books see p234.

A peculiar, old-fashioned version of the gamelan known as the *gamelan selunding* is

A HORSE WALKS INTO A TOWN...

There's a smelly legend about how the villagers of Tenganan came to acquire their land. The story relates how Dalem Bedaulu lost a valuable horse. When the villagers of Tenganan found the carcass, the king offered them a reward. They asked that they be given the land where the horse was found – that is, the entire area where the dead horse could be smelled.

The king sent a man with a keen nose who set off with the village chief and walked an enormous distance without ever managing to get away from the foul odour. Eventually accepting that enough was enough, the official headed back to Bedaulu, scratching his head. Once out of sight, the village chief pulled a large hunk of dead horse out from under his clothes.

still played here, and girls dance an equally ancient dance known as the Rejang. There are other Bali Aga villages nearby, including Tenganan Dauh Tenkad, 1.5km west off the Tenganan road, with a charming old-fashioned ambience, and several weaving workshops. At Asak, southeast of Tenganan, another ancient instrument, the *gamelan gambang*, is still played.

FESTIVALS

Tenganan is full of unusual customs, festivals and practices. At the month-long **Usaba Sambah Festival**, which usually starts in May or June, men fight with sticks wrapped in thorny pandanus leaves. At this same festival, small, hand-powered ferris wheels are brought out and the village girls are ceremonially twirled around.

TOURS

To really experience the ambience and culture of the village, consider one of the tours offered by **JED** (Village Ecotourism Network; ☎ 0361-735320; www.jed.or.id; tours US$25-50). These highly regarded tours include local guides who explain the culture in detail and show how local goods are produced. Tours include transport from South Bali and Ubud.

SHOPPING

A magical cloth known as *kamben gringsing* is woven here – a person wearing it is said to be protected against black magic. Traditionally this is made using the 'double ikat' technique, in which both the warp and weft threads are 'resist dyed' before being woven. MBAs would thrill to studying the integrated production of the cloth: everything, from growing the cotton to producing the dyes from local plants to the actual production, is accomplished here. It's very time-consuming, and the exquisite pieces of double ikat available for sale are quite expensive (from about 600,000Rp). You'll see cheaper cloth for sale but it usually comes from elsewhere on Bali.

Many baskets from across the region, made from *ata* palm, are on sale. Another local craft is traditional Balinese calligraphy, with the script inscribed onto *lontar* palm strips, in the same way that the ancient *lontar* books were created. Most of these books are Balinese calendars or depictions of the *Ramayana* (one of the great Hindu holy books). They cost 150,000Rp to 300,000Rp, depending on quality.

GETTING THERE & AWAY

Tenganan is 4km up a side road just west of Candidasa. At the turn-off where bemo stop, motorcycle riders offer *ojek* (motorcycle that carries pillion passengers) rides to the village for about 5000Rp. A nice option is to take an *ojek* up to Tenganan, and enjoy a shady downhill walk back to the main road.

CANDIDASA

☎ 0363

Candidasa is a relaxed pause on the route east. It has several noted hotels and some excellent restaurants. However, it also has problems stemming from decisions made three decades ago that should serve as cautionary notes to any undiscovered place that suddenly finds itself on the map.

Until the 1970s, Candidasa was just a quiet little fishing village, then beachside losmen and restaurants sprang up and suddenly it was *the* new beach place on Bali. As the facilities developed, the beach eroded – unthinkingly, offshore barrier-reef corals were harvested to produce lime for cement for the orgy of construction that took place – and by the late 1980s Candidasa was a beach resort with no beach.

Mining stopped in 1991, and concrete sea walls and groynes have limited the erosion and now provide some sandy swimming spots, but it's not your typical, tropical stretch of golden-sand beach.

Still, the relaxed seaside ambience and sweeping views from the hotels built right on the water appeal to a more mature crowd of visitors. Candidasa is a good base from which to explore the interior of East Bali and the east coast's famous diving and snorkelling sites.

Information

Foto Asri (☎ 41098; Jl Raya Candidasa) sells groceries and sundries and has a postal agency. A **moneychanger** and a bank are nearby but, in something of a blow locally, the ATM has gone (the closest ones are in Padangbai and Amlapura). The **police station** is at the west end of town; the **post office** the east.

There are a few not-very-fast internet options including the suitably amiable **Happy's Internet** (☎ 41019; Jl Raya Candidasa; per min 500Rp). **Nilwati** (☎ 41272; Jl Raya Candidasa 45) has used books.

Sights

Candidasa's temple, **Pura Candidasa** (admission by donation), is on the hillside across from the lagoon at the eastern end of the village strip. It has twin temples devoted to the male-female gods Shiva and Hariti. The fishing village, just east of the lagoon, has colourful *prahu* drawn up on what's left of the beach. In the early morning you can watch the boats coasting in after a night's fishing. The owners canvass visitors for snorkelling trips to the reef and the nearby islets.

Apart from the Bali Aga village of Tenganan (see p225), there are several traditional villages inland from Candidasa and attractive countryside for walking.

Ashram Gandhi Chandi (☎ 41108; Jl Raya Candidasa), a community by the lagoon, follows the pacifist teachings of Mahatma Gandhi. Guests may stay for short or extended periods, but are expected to participate in community life, including waking early for daily yoga practice. There are simple guest cottages by the ocean and payment is by donation.

Activities

Diving and snorkelling are popular activities in Candidasa. Gili Tepekong, which has a series of coral heads at the top of a sheer drop-off, is perhaps the best dive site. It offers the chance to see lots of fish, including some larger marine life. Other features include an underwater canyon, which can be dived in good conditions, but is always potentially hazardous. The currents here are strong and unpredictable, the water is cold and visibility is variable – it's recommended for experienced divers only.

Other dive sites are beside Gili Mimpang, further east at Gili Biaha, and Nusa Penida. A recommended and popular dive operator is **Dive Lite** (☎ 41660; www.divelite.com; Jl Raya Candidasa; 2 dives US$60-95), which dives Tulamben, Amed, Nusa Penida/Lembongan and Menjangan. A four-day PADI open water course is US$400. Snorkelling tours are US$25.

Hotels and shops along the main road rent snorkel sets for about 20,000Rp per day. For the best snorkelling, take a boat to offshore sites or to Gili Mimpang (a one-hour boat trip should cost about 100,000Rp for up to three people).

On shore, you can catch up on your beauty treatments at **Dewi Spa** (☎ 41042; Jl Raya Candidasa; massage from US$7; 🕑 9am-7pm). Waxing, steaming, rubbing, manicuring and more are on offer.

Sleeping

Candidasa's main drag is well supplied with seaside accommodation, as well as restaurants and other tourist facilities. On the small roads branching off Forest Rd east of the lagoon several places are hidden among the palm trees near the original fishing village. These are nicely relaxed and often have a sliver of beach. You might also consider some of the places west of town; many are close.

BUDGET

Rama Bungalows (☎ 41778; r 50,000-60,000Rp) On a little road near the lagoon and ocean, the eight rooms are in a two-storey stone structure with temple design and bungalows. Upstairs rooms have views of the lagoon.

Seaside Cottages (☎ 41629; www.bali-seafront-bungalows.com; Jl Raya Candidasa; cottages 30,000-230,000Rp; ❄) The choice of rooms here is like *nasi campur* – quite variable. Basic rooms have cold water and fan. As you move up the rate card you add hot water, air-con, open-air garden bathrooms, kitchens and delightful views. The Temple Café is a fun place.

Bali Santi Bungalows (☎ 41611; www.balisanti.com; r 75,000-200,000Rp; ❄) Among a few places scattered in the palm trees west of the centre, Bali Santi is right on the water and is the sort of

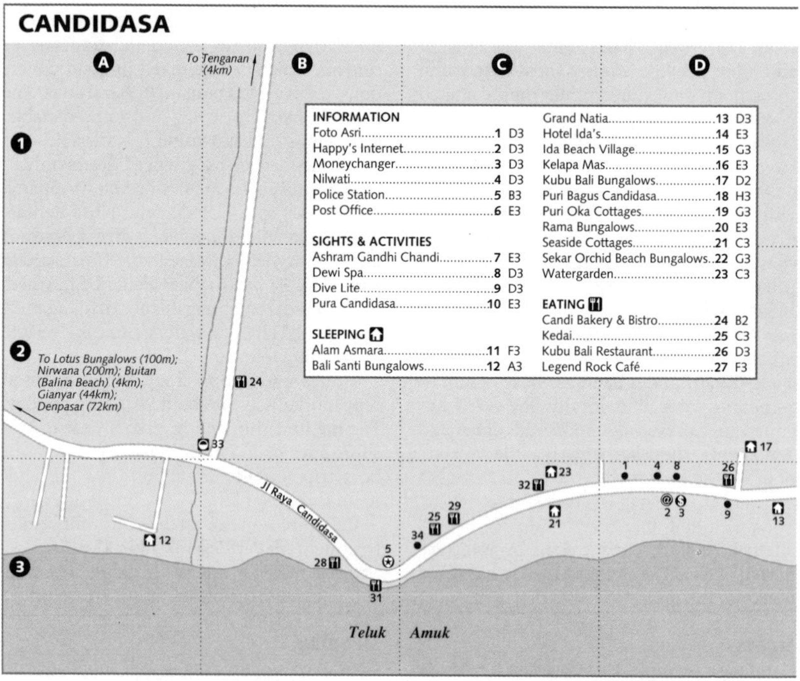

place where you'll want to finish a book. The 10 rooms (one with air-con) are comfortable bungalow-style units.

Hotel Ida's (☎ 41096; jsidas1@aol.com; Jl Raya Candidasa; bungalows 80,000-120,000Rp) Set in a rambling seaside garden shaded by coconut trees, Ida's has six thatched bungalows with open-air bathrooms. Rustic balcony furniture, including a day bed, ensures you'll chill right out.

Puri Oka Cottages (☎ 41092; puri_oka@hotmail.com; Jl Pantai Indah; r 100,000-250,000Rp;) Hidden by a banana grove east of town, the cheapest of the 24 rooms here are small, while the better ones have water views. The pool is medium-sized and at low tide there's a small beach out front.

Sekar Orchid Beach Bungalows (☎ 41086; www.sekar-orchid.com; Jl Pantai Indah 26; bungalows 120,000-150,000Rp) The grounds here live up to the name with orchids growing in profusion. There's a small beach and the seven large rooms are very good value with nice views from the 2nd floor. The site is nicely isolated.

Kelapa Mas (☎ 41369; www.kelapamas.com; Jl Raya Candidasa; r 150,000-250,000Rp;) This relaxing rustic compound deserves its name – the grounds are filled with tall coconut palms. Bamboo-clad rooms with lounging verandas are set in lush gardens; there's even a little sand at low tide. Some rooms have views; others have hot water and air-con.

MIDRANGE

Ida Beach Village (☎ 41118; fax 41041; Jl Pantai Indah; bungalow US$45-60;) The 17 units range from Balinese rice-barn-style bungalows with private gardens to more modest cottages. The seaside swimming pool is a highlight; the location is very quiet.

Kubu Bali Bungalows (☎ 41532; www.kububali.com; s/d US$50/55, ste US$60-65;) Behind Kubu Bali restaurant (p230) and up a lane, this garden spot has streams, ponds and a swimming pool landscaped into the steep hillside. The 20 units have views over palm trees, the coast and the sea; you'll have to climb a bit to get to your room.

Grand Natia (☎ 42007; hotelnatia@yahoo.com; Jl Raya Candidasa; r US$50-85;) This hotel resembles a modern water palace – narrow pathways are lined with carp-filled waterways. Each of the 12 rooms has an open-air bathroom. The

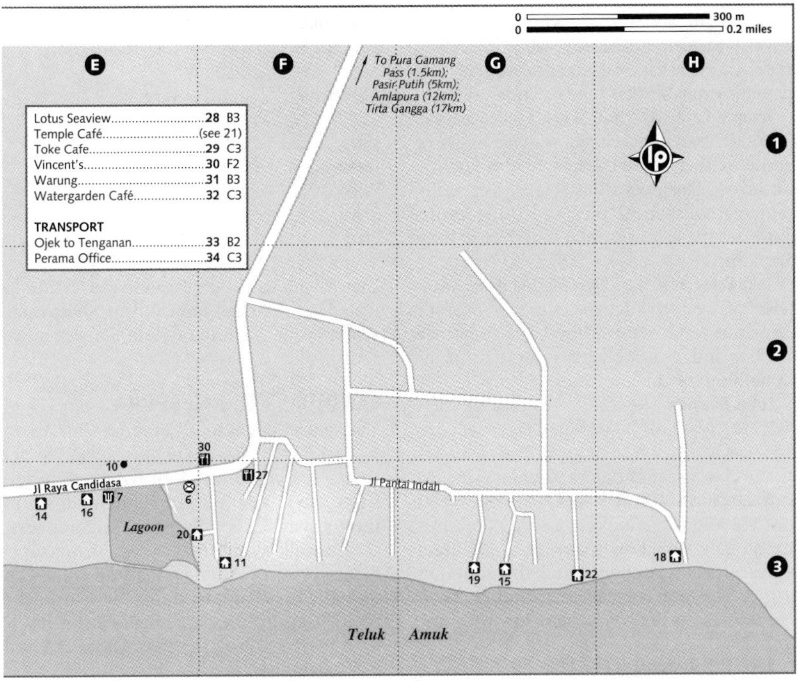

small pool drops away to the ocean, although the two 'ocean-view' rooms aren't worth the premium.

Alam Asmara (☎ 41929; www.asamarabali.com; r US$55-95;) Walk through little waterways to the 12 units at this private new place. The pool is on the ocean; rooms have a traditional yet stylish design with lots of room and details such as stone tubs and satellite TV.

Puri Bagus Candidasa (☎ 41131; www.bagus-discovery.com; Jl Pantai Indah; r US$50-160;) At the eastern end of the beach near an outcropping of outriggers, this well-run beachfront resort is hidden away in the palm trees. A sandy beach area with cabanas is by the pool and restaurant. The 46 rooms have open-air bathrooms; they're a great deal when prices are low.

TOP END

Watergarden (☎ 41540; www.watergardenhotel.com; Jl Raya Candidasa; r from US$85, 2-bedroom ste US$180;) The Watergarden lives up to its name with a swimming pool and fish-filled ponds that wind around the buildings and through the lovely garden. The design has a Japanese influence and each of the 14 rooms has a veranda projecting over the lily ponds. The décor is minimalist. The café is a treat (p230).

Eating

There's a good range of eating options in Candidasa. Many of the hotels have seafront restaurants and cafés that are lovely at lunch time and great for sea breezes and moonlight at night.

At restaurants along Jl Raya Candidasa, beware of traffic noise, although it improves after dark. Among the cheapest and tastiest eateries are the warung and *kaki lima* (food carts) that spring up every evening (and to a lesser extent during the day) at the western end of town where the main road broadsides the sea.

Where noted, many of these places are also good for a drink. If you're out of town, the better places will provide transport; call.

Legend Rock Café (Jl Raya Candidasa; dishes 9000-25,000Rp) A bar that also serves Western and Indonesian meals, it has live music many nights each week. It's a well-mannered bar, about as wild as things get in Candidasa.

Candi Bakery & Bistro (☎ 41883; Jl Tenganan; dishes 10,000-35,000Rp) About 100m up from the

Tenganan turn-off west of town, this smart café is worth the detour. The tiny bakery specialises in delicious pastries, cakes and croissants. You can enjoy meals out on the veranda.

Temple Café (☎ 41629; Jl Raya Candidasa; dishes 15,000-30,000Rp) Global citizens can get a taste of home at this café attached to the Seaside Cottages. The menu has wraps, Vegemite, cabbage rolls, meat pies and other mundane treats. The popular bar has a long drink list.

Toke Café (☎ 41991; Jl Raya Candidasa; dishes 20,000-50,000Rp) The open kitchen at this mellow place turns out some good seafood. It's got a nice old bar and is a good place for a drink or something for the munchies.

Lotus Seaview (☎ 41257; Jl Raya Candidasa; dishes 20,000-60,000Rp) This Lotus branch is smack dab on the ocean, just west of town. The menu has all the classics from Italian to Indonesian.

Watergarden Café (☎ 41540; Jl Raya Candidasa; dishes 15,000-50,000Rp) Overlooking a carp pond, this stylish café somehow manages to maintain a peaceful atmosphere amid the zooming trucks. The food is excellent, including Asian specialities. Its breakfasts hang low with ripe fruit.

Kubu Bali Restaurant (☎ 41532; Jl Raya Candidasa; dishes 20,000-60,000Rp) This big place has an open kitchen out the front (the woks drown out the trucks), where Indonesian and Chinese dishes – including excellent seafood – are turned out with great energy and panache. The bar exudes: 'gin & tonic.'

Vincent's (☎ 41368; Jl Raya Candidasa; dishes 25,000-80,000Rp) A deep and open place with several distinct rooms and a lovely rear garden with rattan lounge furniture. There's a plethora of artfully prepared Thai and veggie options but the real stars are the local dishes. It has a refined bar.

Kedai (☎ 42020; Jl Raya Candidasa; mains 25,000-90,000Rp; ⌚ noon-2pm, 5-9pm) Set in a stately open-air pavilion under a high conical thatched roof, Kedai offers a refined dining experience. The menu of Balinese specialties changes with the seasons and includes many organic and vegetarian options.

Getting There & Away

Candidasa is on the main road between Amlapura and South Bali, but there's no terminal, so hail bemo (buses probably won't stop). You'll need to change in either Padangbai or Semarapura.

Perama (☎ 41114; Jl Raya Candidasa; ⌚ 7am-7pm) is at the western end of the strip.

Destination	Fare
Kuta	40,000Rp
Lovina	100,000Rp
Padangbai	15,000Rp
Sanur	40,000Rp
Ubud	40,000Rp

Two or more people can charter a ride to Amed in the far east for about 60,000Rp each. Ask at your accommodation about vehicle rental.

CANDIDASA TO AMLAPURA

The main road east of Candidasa curves up to **Pura Gamang Pass** (*gamang* means 'to get dizzy' – something of an overstatement), from where you'll find fine views down to the coast and lots of greedy-faced monkeys. If you walk along the coastline from Candidasa towards Amlapura, a trail climbs up over the headland, with fine views over the rocky islets off the coast. Beyond this headland there's a long sweep of wide, exposed black-sand beach.

Although Candidasa lacks good beaches, about 5km east is **Pasir Putih**, an idyllic white-sand beach. When you see crude signs with either 'Virgin Beach Club' or 'Jl Pasir Puteh', turn off the main road and follow a paved track for about 1km to a bridge where locals will collect a fee (5000Rp). Another 1km brings you to a small temple that has good parking. You can drive a further 600m directly to the beach but the road is a fiasco and the walk instead is quite pretty.

The beach is almost a cliché: a long crescent of white sand backed by coconut trees. At one end cliffs provide shade; at the other is a little line of fishing boats. At times stands sell drinks and snacks. The surf is often mellow; bring your own snorkelling gear to explore the waters.

AMLAPURA

☎ 0363

Amlapura is the capital of Karangasem district, and the main town and transport junction in eastern Bali. The smallest of Bali's district capitals, it's a multicultural place with Chinese shophouses, several mosques and confusing one-way streets (which are the

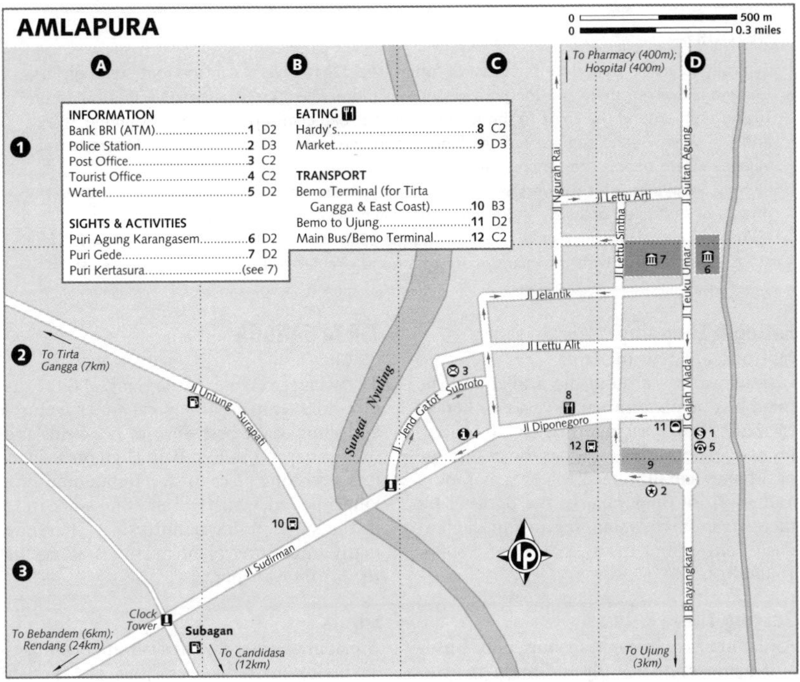

tidiest on Bali). It's worth a stop to see the royal palaces but a lack of choice means you'll want to spend the night elsewhere, such as near-by Tirta Gangga.

Information

The friendly staff at the **tourist office** (☎ 21196; Jl Diponegoro; ⏰ 7am-3pm Mon-Thu, 7am-noon Fri) will snap to attention if any traveller walks in requesting information, but it's not worth a special stop. **Bank BRI** (Jl Gajah Mada) will change money. It has an international ATM as does **Hardy's**. There is a **pharmacy** (Apotik; Jl Ngurah Rai 47) and a small hospital across the street.

Sights

Amlapura's three palaces, on Jl Teuk Umar, are decaying reminders of Karangasem's period as a kingdom at its most important when supported by Dutch colonial power in the late 19th and early 20th centuries.

Outside the **Puri Agung Karangasem** (Jl Teuku Umar; admission 5000Rp; ⏰ 8am-6pm), there is an impressive three-tiered entry gate and beautifully sculpted panels. After you pass through the entry courtyard, a left turn takes you to the main building, known as the Maskerdam (Amsterdam), because it was the Karangasem kingdom's acquiescence to Dutch rule that allowed it to hang on long after the demise of the other Balinese kingdoms. Inside you'll be able to see several rooms, including the royal bedroom and a living room with furniture that was a gift from the Dutch royal family. The Maskerdam faces the ornately decorated Bale Pemandesan, which was used for the royal tooth-filing ceremonies. Beyond this, surrounded by a pond, is the Bale Kambang, still used for family meetings and for dance practice.

Across the street, **Puri Gede** (Jl Teuku Umar; admission free; ⏰ 8am-6pm) has ongoing renovations. The rambling palace grounds feature many brick buildings dating from the Dutch colonial period. Look for stone and wood carvings from the 19th century. The Rangki has been returned to its glory and is surrounded by fish ponds. Look for the stern portrait of the late king AA Gede Putu; his wife still lives in one of the buildings.

The other royal palace building, **Puri Kertasura**, is not open to visitors.

DETOUR

Typically travellers bound for the coast of **Amed** (see p234) travel the inland route through Tirta Gangga. However, there is a longer, twistier and more adventurous alternative that runs from **Ujung** right around the coast to the Amed area. The road climbs up the side of Gunung Seraya, and the views out to sea are breathtaking. Along the way it passes through numerous small villages where people are carving fishing boats.

Near **Seraya** look for weavers and cotton-fabric-makers. Lots of the time, you'll just be in the middle of fruit-filled orchards and jungle. About 4km south of **Aas** there's a lighthouse.

The road is narrow but paved, and covering the 35km to Aas will take about one hour without stops. Combine this with the inland road for a good circular visit to Amed from the west.

Eating & Shopping

Options are few in Amlapura; there are various warung around the **market** and the main bus/bemo terminal. A vast new **Hardy's** (☎ 22363; Jl Diponegoro) supermarket has groceries and lots of sundries. It has the best range of supplies like sunscreen east of Semarapura and south of Singaraja. In the parking lot there are numerous stalls serving up all manner of cheap and fresh Asian foods (5000-10,000Rp).

Getting There & Away

Amlapura is a major transport hub. Buses and bemo regularly ply the main road to Denpasar's Batubulan terminal (20,000Rp; roughly three hours), via Candidasa, Padangbai and Ginayar (16,000Rp). Plenty of buses also go around the north coast to Singaraja (about 15,000Rp), via Tirta Gangga, Amed and Tulamben.

If you are driving to Amed and beyond, fill up at the petrol station on the road to Tirta Gangga. It's the last one until Yeh Sanih in the north.

AROUND AMLAPURA

Five kilometres south of Amlapura, **Taman Ujung** is a major complex that may leave you slack-jawed – and not necessarily with wonder. The last king of Karangasem completed the construction of a grand water palace here in 1921, which was extensively damaged by an earthquake in 1979. A tiny vestige of the old palace is surrounded by vast modern ponds and terraces built for untold billions of rupiah. Today, the wind-swept grounds are seldom trod by visitors. It's a bit sad really and you can see all that you'd want to from the road. Just a bit further on is the interesting fishing village of **Ujung** and the alternative road to Amed.

TIRTA GANGGA

☎ 0363

Tirta Gangga (Water of the Ganges) is the site of a holy temple, some great water features and some of the best views of rice fields and the sea beyond in East Bali. High on a ridge, it is a relaxing place to stop for an hour or a longer period, which will allow for some treks in the surrounding countryside. There are many interesting plant nurseries along the road from Amlapura.

Sights

Amlapura's water-loving rajah, after completing his lost masterpiece at Ujung, had another go at building the water palace of his dreams. He succeeded at **Taman Tirta Gangga** (adult/child 5100/3100Rp, parking 1000Rp; site 24hr, ticket office 6am-6pm), which has a stunning crescent of rice terrace-lined hills for a backdrop.

Originally built in 1948, the water palace was damaged in the 1963 eruption of Gunung Agung and again during the political events that rocked Indonesia two years later. The palace has several swimming pools and ornamental ponds, which serve as a fascinating reminder of the old days of the Balinese rajahs. 'Pool A' (adult/child 6000/4000Rp) is the cleanest and is in the top part of the complex. 'Pool B' (adult/child 4000Rp/free) is pond-like. Look for the 11-tiered fountain and plop down under the huge old banyans.

Hiking in the surrounding hills is recommended. The rice terraces around Tirta Gangga are some of the most beautiful on Bali. Back roads and walking paths take you to many picturesque traditional villages. Or you can ascend the side of Gunung Agung. Guides are a good idea. Ask at any of the accommodation we've listed. One local guide who comes with good marks is **Komang Gede Sutama** (☎ 0813-38770893).

Sleeping & Eating

Most places to stay have cafés and there's another cluster by the sedate shops at the parking area.

Genta Bali (☎ 22436; dishes 10,000-12,000Rp) Across the road from the parking area, you can find a fine yoghurt drink here, as well as pasta and Indonesian food. It has an impressive list of puddings, including ones with banana, jackfruit and taro. All are served with coconut milk, brown sugar and coconut.

Dhangin Taman (☎ 22059; r 40,000-80,000Rp) Adjacent to the water palace, this fascinating place features elaborate tiled artworks in a garden. It has a range of 14 simple rooms – the cheapest ones facing the rice paddies are the best – and a restaurant with tables overlooking the palace. Dishes range from 5000Rp to 8000Rp. You leave your breakfast order hanging on the door, just like at the Hilton.

Pondok Lembah Dukah (r 50,000-100,000Rp) Down the path to the right of Good Karma, follow the signs for 300m along the rice field and then up a steep set of steps. Three very simple bungalows are clean and have fans, cold water and incredible views over bougainvillea from their porches.

Puri Prima (☎ /fax 21316; r 50,000-100,000Rp) About 1km north of Tirta Gangga along the main road, this slightly modern place offers outstanding views and nine pleasant rooms. It has a small restaurant, with dishes ranging from 10,000Rp to 16,000Rp. Staff can also organise trekking to Gunung Agung (from 600,000Rp for two people).

Homestay Rijasa (☎ 21873; r 65,000-125,000Rp) With elaborately planted grounds, this family-run place is a good choice opposite the water palace entrance. Two of the seven rooms have hot water, good for the large soaking tubs. The owner, I Ketut Sarjana, is an experienced trekking guide.

Good Karma (☎ 22445; r 70,000-100,000Rp) Good Karma has four very clean and simple bungalows and a good vibe derived from the surrounding pastoral rice field. The restaurant serves up excellent food in a comfortable setting right off the main parking lot. Expect to pay around 10,000Rp to 16,000Rp for dishes.

Puri Sawah Bungalows (☎ 21847; fax 21939; bungalows 100,000-200,000Rp) Just up the road from the palace, Puri Sawah has four comfortable and spacious rooms with great views of the airy compound. Family bungalows sleep six (with hot water). The restaurant has rice paddy views and serves sandwiches and local classics; dishes range from 16,000Rp to 22,000Rp.

Tirta Ayu Homestay (☎ 22697; fax 21383; r 150,000-250,000Rp, villas US$50-150; 🏊) Right in the palace compound, this has four pleasant bungalows (cold water only) and three spacious villas with nice outdoor bathrooms. Free use of the palace swimming pool is included. A café overlooks the palace grounds; dishes range from 10,00Rp to 25,000Rp. One of the villas is huge and has its own plunge pool.

Getting There & Away

Bemo and minibuses making the east coast haul between Amlapura and Singaraja stop at Tirta Gangga, right outside the water palace or any hotel further north. The fare to Amlapura should be 3000Rp.

AROUND TIRTA GANGGA

The main road running from Amlapura through Tirta Gangga and on to Amed and the coast doesn't do the local attractions justice – although it is an attractive road. To appreciate things, you need to get off the main road or go hiking.

Throughout the area the *rontal* palms all look like new arrivals at army boot camp, as they are shorn of their leaves as fast as they grow them in order to meet the demand for inscribed *lontar* books.

Pura Lempuyang

One of Bali's nine directional temples, it is perched on a hilltop at 768m. To get here, turn south off the Amlapura–Tulamben road to Ngis (2km), a palm sugar and coffee- growing area, and follow the signs another 2km to Kemuda (ask for directions if the signs confuse you). From Kemuda, climb 1700 steps to Pura Lempuyang (allow at least two hours, one way). If you want to continue to the peaks of Lempuyang (1058m) or Seraya (1175m), you should take a guide.

Bukit Kusambi

This small hill has a big view – at sunrise Lombok's Gunung Rinjani throws a shadow on Gunung Agung. It is easy to reach from Abian Soan – look for the obvious large hill to the northwest, and follow the tiny canals through the rice fields. On the western side of the hill, a set of steps leads to the top.

Budakeling & Krotok

Budakeling, home to several Buddhist communities, is on the back road to Bebandem, a few kilometres southeast of Tirta Gangga. It's a short drive, or a pleasant three-hour walk through rice fields, via Krotok, home of traditional blacksmiths and silversmiths.

Tanah Aron

This imposing monument to the post-WWII Dutch resistance is gloriously situated on the southeastern slopes of Gunung Agung. The road is quite good, or you can walk up and back in about six hours from Tirta Gangga.

AMED & THE FAR EAST COAST

☎ 0363

This popular region has grown immeasurably since the 1990s. Stretching from Amed to Bali's far eastern tip, this once-remote stretch of coast draws visitors to a succession of small scalloped black-sand beaches, relaxed atmosphere and excellent diving and snorkelling.

Often called simply 'Amed', this is a misnomer as the coast here is a series of seaside *dusun* (small villages) that start with the actual Amed in the north and then run southeast to Aas. If you're looking to get away from crowds, this is the place to come. Everything is very spread out, so you never feel like you're in the middle anything much except maybe one of the small fishing villages.

Traditionally, this area has been quite poor, with thin soils, low rainfall and very limited infrastructure. Salt production is still carried out on the beach at Amed; see Working in the Salt Brine. Villages further east rely on fishing, and colourful *jukung* line up on every available piece of beach. Inland, the steep hillsides are generally too dry for rice – corn, peanuts and vegetables are the main crops.

Orientation

As noted, this entire 10km stretch of coast is often called 'Amed' by both tourists and marketing-minded locals. Most development at first was around two bays, Jemeluk, which has cafés and a few shops, and Lipah, which has warung, shops and a few services. 'Progress' has marched onwards through Lehan, Selang and Aas. To really appreciate the coast, stop at the viewpoint at Jemeluk; besides the sweep of land, you can see fishing boats lined up like polychromatic sardines on the beach.

Information

There's no tourist office or post office, but you may be charged a tourist tax. Enforcement of a 5000Rp per person fee at a tollbooth on the outskirts of Amed is sporadic. When collected, the funds go in part to develop the infrastructure at the beaches.

Telephone services have not kept pace with development and land lines have been strung only a little past Lipah. **Aurora Internet & Wartel** (☎ 23519; Lipah; 🕑 8am-9pm) has dial-up internet service as does Apa Kabar in Jemeluk. Both charge 500Rp per minute.

Pondok Kebun Wayan (☎ 23473; east of Amed) changes US dollar travellers cheques and has a small market with groceries and sundries. There are moneychangers in Lipah but there are no ATMs or banks.

Activities

DIVING & SNORKELLING

Snorkelling is excellent at several places along the coast. Jemeluk is a protected area where you can admire live coral and plentiful fish within 100m of the beach. There's a **wreck** of a Japanese fishing boat near Aas – just offshore from Eka Purnama bungalows – and coral gardens and colourful marine life at Selang.

LONTAR BOOKS

Lontar is made from the fan-shaped leaves of the *rontal* palm. The leaf is dried, soaked in water, cleaned, steamed, dried again, then flattened, dyed and eventually cut into strips. The strips are inscribed with words and pictures using a very sharp blade or point, then coated with a black stain which is wiped off – the black colour stays in the inscription. A hole in the middle of each *lontar* strip is threaded onto a string, with a carved bamboo 'cover' at each end to protect the 'pages', and the string is secured with a couple of pierced Chinese coins, or *kepeng*.

The Gedong Kirtya Library in Singaraja has the world's largest collection of works inscribed on *lontar* (specially prepared palm leaves). Some 4000 historic Balinese manuscripts cover everything from literary to mythological and historical to religious themes. They are written in fine Sanskrit calligraphy, and some are elaborately decorated.

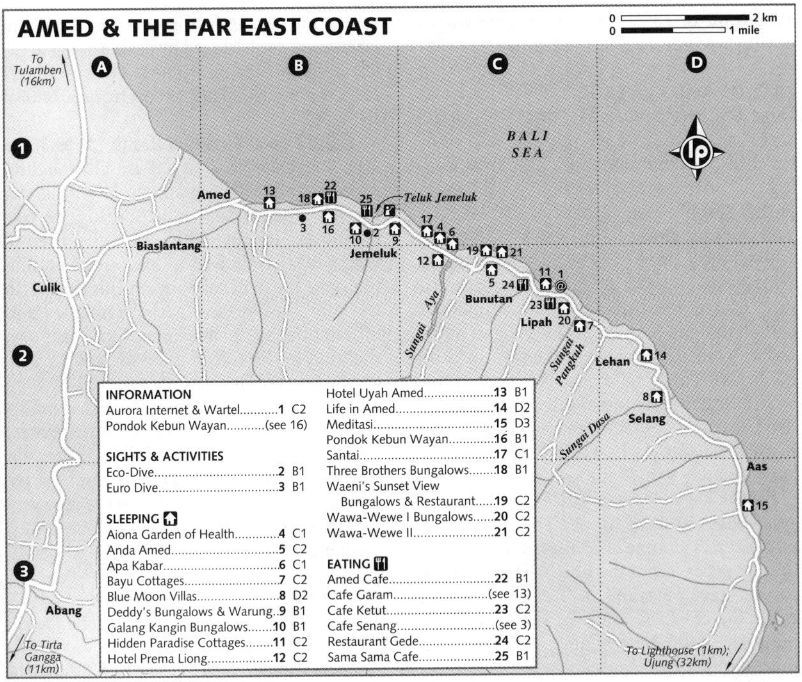

Almost every hotel rents snorkelling equipment for about 20,000Rp per day.

Scuba diving is also excellent, with dive sites off Jemeluk, Lipah and Selang featuring coral slopes and drop-offs with soft and hard corals, and abundant fish. Some are accessible from the beach, while others require a short boat ride. The *Liberty* wreck at Tulamben is only a 20-minute drive away.

Two good dive operators have shown a real commitment to the communities by organising regular beach clean-ups and educating locals on the need for conservation. Both have similar prices for a long list of offerings (eg local dives from about US$50, open-water dive course about US$350).

Eco-dive (☎ 081 658 1935; www.ecodivebali.com; Jemeluk; dives from US$45) Full service shop with simple accommodation for clients.

Euro Dive (☎ 23469; www.eurodivebali.com; east of Amed; dives from US$45) Has a long list of services.

TREKKING

Quite a few trails go inland from the coast, up the slopes of Gunung Seraya (1175m) and to some little-visited villages. The countryside is sparsely vegetated and most trails are well defined, so you won't need a guide for shorter walks – if you get lost, just follow a ridge top back down to the coast road. Allow a good three hours to get to the top of Seraya, starting from the rocky ridge just east of Jemeluk Bay, near Prem Liong Art Bungalows. To reach the top for sunrise you'll need to start in the dark, so a guide is probably a good idea – ask at your hotel.

Sleeping

The entire area is very spread out, so take this into consideration when choosing accommodation. If you want to venture to restaurants beyond your hotel's own, for example, you'll have to either walk or find transport.

You will also get to choose between places to stay in the little beachside villages or places on the sunny and dry headlands connecting the inlets. The former puts you right on the sand and offers a small amount of life while the latter gives you broad, sweeping vistas and isolation.

Accommodation can be found in every price category; almost every place has a restaurant or café. Places with noteworthy dining are indicated in the listings.

EAST OF AMED VILLAGE

Three Brothers Bungalows (☎ 23472; r 80,000-120,000Rp) The boys have popular and basic beachfront accommodation, plus an adjoining café with a few tables right on the sand. Dishes cost between 10,000Rp and 25,000Rp. You can't get closer to the water.

Hotel Uyah Amed (☎ 23462; hoteluyah@natrebali.com; r 270,000-330,000Rp;) This cute place features four-poster beds set in stylish interiors bathed in light. Some units have views of the water; from all you can see the saltworks on the beach. The hotel makes the most of this by offering fascinating and free salt-making demonstrations (see Working in the Salt Brine, opposite). The tasty Café Garam is appropriately named for salt.

Pondok Kebun Wayan (☎ 23473; www.amedcafé.com; r 100,000-300,000Rp;) This Amed empire features a range of 25 rooms mostly on a hillside across from the beach. The most expensive have views and amenities like air-con while the cheapest are two small beachside huts. The good Amed Café is separate from the lodging area.

JEMELUK

Deddy's Bungalows & Warung (☎ 23510; warung_deddys@hotmail.com; s/d 35,000/50,000Rp) On the hillside above the bay, Deddy's has three clean, pleasant rooms.

Galang Kangin Bungalows (s/d from 50,000/80,000Rp) One of several budget places in this area, this hillside place has clean, basic cold-water rooms.

Hotel Prema Liong (☎ 23486; www.bali-amed.com; r 150,000-400,000Rp) Javanese-style two-storey bungalows are terraced up the hillside and have a new age ethos. The cold-water, open-air bathrooms are lush and almost double as a garden, while the balconies have comfy cushions and day beds.

Apa Kabar (☎ 23492; www.apakabarvillas.com; bungalows US$60-95, villas US$90-150;) Right in front of fishing boats on the beach, Apa Kabar has six stylish and spacious unites overlooking a swimming pool that gurgles with a small waterfall. Some units have ocean views.

Santai (☎ 23487; www.santaibali.com; r US$40-80;) This lovely option is on a slight hill down to the beach. The 10 rooms have four-poster beds, timber floors, open-air bathrooms and big comfy balcony sofas. A snaking swimming pool, fringed by purple bougainvillea, adds to the atmosphere. The restaurant faces the beach and dishes cost from 20,000Rp to 52,000Rp.

our pick **Aiona Garden of Health** (☎ 0813-3816 1730; aiona_bali@hotmail.com; €18-25) This slightly eccentric place takes pains to let you know that no animals were killed during the collecting for its cute little seashell museum. Like a bivalve allowed to live out its natural life, you too will take joy in life thanks to the many interesting herbal remedies and other potions available here. Needless to say, the food in the café is good for you as well; the Swiss and German owners will ply you with organic muesli, fibery breads, yoghurt and other goodies all made in house. Expect to pay 20,000Rp to 40,000Rp for dishes. Of course all this wholesomeness might drive you to drink. That's why they serve aloe vera cocktails. The two bungalows here are shaded by mango trees.

BUNUTAN

These places are on a sun-drenched, arid stretch of highland.

Waeni's Sunset View Bungalows & Restaurant (☎ 23515; madesani@hotmail.com; r 80,000-100,000Rp) Waeni's is a hillside place with unusual rustic stone cottages that have gorgeous views of the mountains behind and the bay below. The café is a good place for a sunset drink. Prices for dishes range from 15,000Rp to 30,000Rp.

Wawa-Wewe II (☎ 23521; wawawewevillas@yahoo.com; r 200,000-250,000Rp;) On the headlands, this nice and peaceful place has eight bungalows on shady grounds that go down to the water. The infinity pool is shaped like a Buddha and is set far from the road. The café is mellow as is the price range of 18,000Rp to 23,000Rp.

Anda Amed (☎ 23498; www.andaamedresort.com; villa US$55-85;) This hillside place feels Grecian. The infinity pool has sweeping views of the sea well above the road. The four villas are a good deal; they have one or two bedrooms and lots of posh details like deep, soaking tubs.

LIPAH

This village is just large enough for you to go wandering.

Wawa-Wewe I Bungalows (☎ 23506; wawawewevillas@yahoo.com; r 50,000Rp) The first Wawa-Wewe

WORKING IN THE SALT BRINE

For a real day at the beach, try making some salt. You start by carrying, say, 500L of ocean water across the sand to bamboo and wood funnels, which filter the water after it is poured in. Next the water goes into *palungan* (shallow trough), made of palm tree trunks split in half and hollowed out, or cement canisters where it evaporates leaving salt behind. And that's just the start and just what you might see on the beach in Amed.

In the volcanic areas around the east coast between Sanur and Yeh Sanih in the north a range of salt-making methods is used. What is universal is that the work is hard, very hard, but is also an essential source of income for many families.

In some places the first step is drying sand that has been saturated with sea water. It's then taken inside a hut, where more sea water is strained through it to wash out the salt. This very salty water is then poured into a *palungan*. Hundreds of these troughs are lined up in rows along the beaches during the salt-making season (the dry season), and as the hot sun evaporates the water, the almost-dry salt is scraped out and put in baskets. There are good exhibits on this method at the Museum Semarajaya in Semarapura (p214).

Most salt produced on the coast of Bali is used for processing dried fish. And that's where Amed has an advantage: although its method of making salt results in a lower yield than that using sand, its salt is prized for its flavour. In fact there is a fast-growing market for this 'artisan salt' worldwide. The grey and cloudy crystals are finding their way into many top-end kitchens.

Visitors to the Amed area can learn all about this fascinating process at the adjoining Hotel Uyah Amed (see opposite) and Café Garam (see p238). Many of the staff here also work in salt production. Tours are offered, and you can buy big bags of the precious stuff (per kilo 10,000Rp) for a tiny fraction of the cost once it's gone through many hands and made its way to your local gourmet market.

has two simple rooms equipped with outdoor bathrooms set back from the bay. On Saturday nights the café hosts local reggae and blues bands. Dishes range from 15,000Rp to 30,000Rp.

Bayu Cottages (☎ 23495; www.bayucottages.com; r US$22-28;) The good-value Bayu has rooms with balconies overlooking the coast from the hillside. There's a small pool and many amenities including open-air marble bathrooms.

Hidden Paradise Cottages (☎ 23514; www.hiddenparadise-bali.com; r US$30-50;) The 16 simply decorated rooms at this older beachside place have patios and open-air bathrooms. The pool is the classic kidney shape; the bar shows movies at night.

LEHAN

Life in Amed (☎ 0813-3850 1555; www.lifebali.com; r US$65-75, villa US$90-150;) If you can get past the pretentious name, life at Life in Amed is pretty posh although a bit urban. The six bungalow-style units are in a slightly cramped compound along with two villas on the beach. The café has a fairly complex menu of Asian fusion dishes, ranging from 30,000Rp to 70,000Rp.

SELANG

Blue Moon Villas (☎ 0817 4738 100; www.bluemoonvilla.com; r from US$70, villa US$120-185;) On the hillside across the road from the cliffs, Blue Moon is a small and upmarket place, complete with a little pool. The five rooms set in three villas have open-air stone bathrooms. The café takes usual fare and gives it a dash of panache, with dishes costing from 20,000Rp to 50,000Rp.

AAS

The Aas end of the Amed coast is sparsely developed.

Meditasi (fax 22166; r 150,000-200,000Rp) Rooms are close to good swimming and snorkelling at this chilled-out yet tidy place where the bamboo bungalows have balconies overlooking the beach.

Eating & Drinking

As already noted, many places to stay have good cafés. Ones that are especially notable are listed here.

Amed Café (☎ 23473; Pondok Kebun Wayan, east of Amed; dishes 15,000-40,000Rp) Set right on the beach, this refined café with very comfy chairs has an extensive seafood menu, as well as the usual Chinese and Indonesian dishes.

Café Garam (☎ 23462; Hotel Uyah Amed, east of Amed; dishes 14,000-40,000Rp) There's a polished ambience here with pool tables and Balinese food plus live Genjek music at 8pm on Wednesday and Saturday. *Garam* means salt and the café honours the local salt-making industry .

Cafe Senang (East of Amed; dishes 9000-20,000Rp) At Euro Dive, this small, sleek café is popular with travellers.

Sama Sama Cafe (Jemeluk; dishes 15,000-35,000Rp) Prawns, barracuda, mackerel and other fish almost jump from the boats onto the grill at this five-table beachside joint with a lovely view of the minute bay.

Restaurant Gede (☎ 23517; Bunutan; dishes 16,000-35,000Rp) The huge menu focuses on Chinese dishes. Artwork by the owner decorates the walls.

Cafe Ketut (Lipah; dishes 7000-15,000Rp) A dash of style here goes well with the burgers and Indo classics. There's a couple other cafés nearby.

Getting There & Around

Most people drive here via the main highway from Amlapura and Culik. The spectacular road going all the way around the headlands from Aas to Ujung is in good shape; it's possible to do the journey as a circle. See p232 for details.

All the places east of Culik are difficult to reach by public transport. Minibuses and bemo from Singaraja and Amlapura pass through Culik, the turn-off for Amed. Infrequent public bemo go from Culik to Amed (3.5km), and some continue to Seraya until 1pm. A public bemo should cost around 7000Rp from Culik to Lipah.

You can also charter transport from Culik for a negotiable 40,000Rp (by *ojek* is less than half). Be careful to specify which hotel you wish to go to – if you agree on a price to 'Amed', you may be taken only to Amed village, far short of your destination.

Perama offers charter tourist-bus services from Candidasa (see p226); the cost is 75,000Rp each for a minimum of two people. This is competitive with the cost of hiring a car and driver.

Many hotels rent bicycles for about 35,000Rp per day.

KUBU REGION

Driving along the main road you will pass through vast old lava flows from Gunung Agung down to the sea. The landscape is strewn with lava and boulders, and is nothing like the lush rice paddies elsewhere.

TULAMBEN

☎ 0363

The big attraction here sunk over 60 years ago. The wreck of the US cargo ship *Liberty* is among the best and most popular dive sites on Bali and this has given rise to an entire town based on scuba diving. Other great dive sites are nearby, and even snorkellers can easily swim out and enjoy the wreck and the coral.

But if you don't plan to explore the briny waves, don't expect to hang out on the beach either. The shore is made up of rather beautiful, large washed stones, the kind you pay a small fortune for at a DIY store and which are good for your garden and bad for your back.

Orientation & Information

The town is a quiet place, and is essentially built around the wreck – the hotels, all with cafés, and many with dive shops, are spread along a 3km stretch either side of the main road.

You can change cash at a few signposted places at the eastern end of the main road; otherwise services are sparse.

For dial-up-only internet access, try **Tulamben Wreck Divers Resort** (per min 500Rp).

Activities

DIVING & SNORKELLING

The wreck of the *Liberty* is about 50m directly offshore from Puri Madha Bungalows (there's also a shady car park here; 1000Rp). Swim straight out and you'll see the stern rearing up from the depths, heavily encrusted with coral, and swarming with dozens of species of colourful fish – and with scuba divers most of the day. The ship is more than 100m

THE WRECK OF THE LIBERTY

In January 1942 the US Navy cargo ship USAT *Liberty* was torpedoed by a Japanese submarine near Lombok. Taken in tow, it was beached at Tulamben so that its cargo of rubber and railway parts could be saved. The Japanese invasion prevented this and the ship sat on the beach until the 1963 eruption of Gunung Agung broke it in two and left it just off the shoreline, much to the delight of scores of divers.

THE 1963 ERUPTION

The most disastrous volcanic eruption on Bali in 100 years took place in 1963, when Gunung Agung blew its top in no uncertain manner at a time of considerable prophetic and political importance.

Eka Dasa Rudra, the greatest of all Balinese sacrifices and an event that takes place only every 100 years on the Balinese calendar, was to culminate on 8 March 1963. It had been well over 100 Balinese years since the last Eka Dasa Rudra, but there was dispute among the priests as to the correct and most favourable date.

Naturally, Pura Besakih was a focal point for the festival, but Gunung Agung was acting strangely as final preparations were made in late February. The date of the ceremony was looking decidedly unpropitious, but President Soekarno had already scheduled an international conference of travel agents to witness the great occasion as a highlight of their visit to the country, and he would not allow it to be postponed. By the time the sacrifices began, the mountain was glowing, belching smoke and ash, and rumbling ominously, but Gunung Agung contained itself until the travel agents had flown home.

On 17 March, Gunung Agung exploded. The catastrophic eruption killed more than 1000 people (some estimate 2000) and destroyed entire villages – 100,000 people lost their homes. Streams of lava and hot volcanic mud poured right down to the sea at several places, completely covering roads and isolating the eastern end of Bali for some time. The entire island was covered in ash, and crops were wiped out everywhere.

Although Pura Besakih is high on the slopes of Gunung Agung, only about 6km from the crater, the temple suffered little damage from the eruption. In contrast, the inhabitants of the village of Lebih, also high up on Gunung Agung's slopes, were all but wiped out. Agung erupted again on 16 May, with serious loss of life, although not on the same scale as the March eruption.

long, but the hull is broken into sections and it's easy for divers to get inside. The bow is in quite good shape, the midships region is badly mangled and the stern is almost intact – the best parts are between 15m and 30m deep. You will want at least two dives to really explore the wreck.

Many divers commute to Tulamben from Candidasa or Lovina, and in busy times it can get quite crowded between 11am and 4pm, with up to 50 divers around the wreck at a time. Stay the night in Tulamben or – better – in nearby Amed and get an early start.

Most hotels have their own diving centre, and some will give a discount on accommodation if you dive with their centre. If you are an inexperienced diver, see Sink or Swim: Diving Safely, p75 for tips on choosing a dive operation.

Among the many dive operators, **Tauch Terminal** is one of longest-established. A four-day PADI open-water certificate course costs about US$400.

Expect to pay as little as US$25/40 for one/two dives at Tulamben, and a little more for a night dive or dives around Amed.

Most hotels and dive centres rent out snorkelling gear for a negotiable 20,000Rp.

Sleeping & Eating

At high tide even the rocky shore vanishes but places situated on the water still have great views of the surf. All places to stay are on the main road or right off it.

Puri Aries (☎ 23402; r 50,000-70,000Rp) On the inland side of the road, there are eight small, clean cold-water bungalows in a really lush, green garden setting.

Puri Madha Bungalows (☎ 22921; r 70,000Rp) This is the first hotel you approach from the northwest; it faces the wreck and the day-use parking area. There are nine small, clean cold-water rooms on the water.

Bali Coral Bungalows (☎ /fax 22909; r 100,000Rp, with air-con 200,000Rp;) Ten pleasant, clean bungalows with modern bathrooms huddle here, some with sea views.

Matahari Tulamben Resort (☎ 22916; www.divetulamben.com; r 100,000-200,000Rp;) On a long, narrow site, this simple, cheery place has 14 decent rooms ranging from those with cold-water to pricier ones with hot water and air-con. There's a restaurant, dishes range from 8000Rp to 15,000Rp, and the pool's on the water.

Tulamben Wreck Divers Resort (☎ 23400; r 200,000-400,000Rp;) There's seven rooms at this homey place on the inland side of the road.

The top ones are just that: on top of the building and with good views.

Tauch Terminal Resort (☎ 0361-730200, 22911; www.tauch-terminal.com; r US$40-80; ❄ 🏊) Down a side road, this is the pick of Tulamben accommodation. Rooms have large terraces; the cheaper ones in bungalows are actually more atmospheric and better value. The restaurant is right at the waves with a menu that spans Europe and Asia. Service is efficient if a tad curt.

Getting There & Away

Plenty of buses and bemo travel between Amlapura and Singaraja and will stop anywhere along the Tulamben road, but they're infrequent after 2pm. Expect to pay 8000Rp to either town.

Perama offers charter tourist-bus services from Candidasa; the cost is 75,000Rp each for a minimum of two people. This is competitive with the cost of hiring a car and driver.

If you are driving to Lovina for the night, be sure to leave by about 3pm so you will still have a little light when you get there.

TULAMBEN TO YEH SANIH

North of Tulamben, the road continues to skirt the slopes of Gunung Agung, with frequent evidence of lava flows from the 1963 eruption. Further around, the outer crater of Gunung Batur slopes steeply down to the sea. The rainfall is low and you can generally count on sunny weather. The scenery is very stark in the dry season and it's thinly populated. The route has public transport, but it's easier to make stops and detours with your own vehicle.

At **Les**, a road goes inland to lovely **Air Terjun Yeh Mampeh** (Yeh Mampeh Waterfall), at 40m one of Bali's highest. Look for a large sign on the main road and then turn inland for about 1km. Walk the last 2km or so on an obvious path by the stream, shaded by rambutan trees. A 2000Rp donation is requested; there's no need for a guide.

The next main town is **Tejakula**, famous for its stream-fed public bathing area, said to have been built for washing horses, and often called the 'horse bath'. The renovated bathing areas (separate for men and women) are behind walls topped by rows of elaborately decorated arches, and are regarded as a sacred area. The baths are 100m inland on a narrow road with lots of small shops – it's a quaint village, with some finely carved *kulkul* towers. Take a stroll above the baths, past irrigation channels flowing in all directions.

At Pacung, about 10km before Yeh Sanih, you can turn inland 4km to **Sembiran**, which is a Bali Aga village, although it doesn't promote itself as such. The most striking thing about the place is its hillside location and brilliant coastal views.

Sleeping

Alam Anda (☎ 0361-750444; www.alamanda.de; bungalow from €65; ❄ 🏊) Near Sambirenteng, this is a delightful resort on the beach, with a fine coral reef just offshore. It boasts its own diving centre. The 10 ocean-facing bungalows are set in a spacious garden and are built from stone, bamboo and thatch. Designed by the German architect owner, Alam Anda has a lush tropical feel. The waterfront restaurant, with dishes ranging from €3 to €8 (has daily buffets and fresh seafood). There's also some simple economy rooms (from €35).

Central Mountains

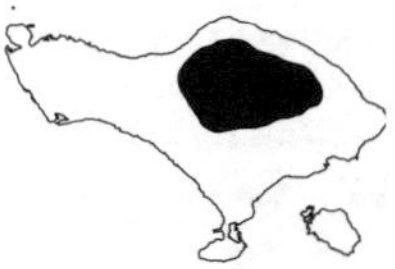

Volcanoes are the spine of Bali and for many they are the soul. As you climb up any of the many roads that traverse Bali's mountains, at a certain point you'll notice that palm trees have been replaced by pines and you'll realise that yes, you are entering another world. They divide the broad plains of the south from the narrower strip of the north. Starting as an outcrop in the east near Amlapura, the volcanoes march west. The island's 'Mother Mountain' Gunung Agung (3142m) is in the east and northwest is Gunung Batur (Mt Batur; 1717m), with its lunarlike double caldera, lake and numerous smaller craters.

In the Danau Bratan (Lake Bratan) area, vegetation covers a complex of long dormant volcanic craters, interspersed with several lakes. After Gunung Batukau, the second-highest mountain (2276m), a string of smaller mountains stretch off into the sparsely inhabited western region.

Opportunities for visitors abound. Amid too many hassles, there are stunning geologic spectacles around Gunung Batur, especially at sunrise. Much more relaxed hikes exist aplenty in the lakes and hills around Danau Bratan.

At Munduk in the west, a dense landscape of waterfalls, jungle and coffee plantations draws ever-more visitors for hikes and stays at some beautiful and culturally aware hotels.

To the south, Gunung Batukau shelters a beautiful and important temple while some of the island's most stunning ancient rice terraces grow their stuff around Jatiluwih.

You can visit the mountains as part of day trips or on longer, circular itineraries. One look at the trees tells you, it's like no place else in Bali.

HIGHLIGHTS

- Enjoying the superb views and lush waterfall-filled landscape in and around **Munduk** (p252)
- Finding your favourite rice terrace at **Jatiluwih** (p254)
- Feeling the energy at one of Bali's holiest temples, **Pura Luhur Batukau** (p253)
- Hiking around **Danau Buyan** (p252) and **Danau Tamblingan** (p252)
- Surviving the vast double caldera, crater lake, lava flows, smoking cones and touts of **Gunung Batur** (p242)

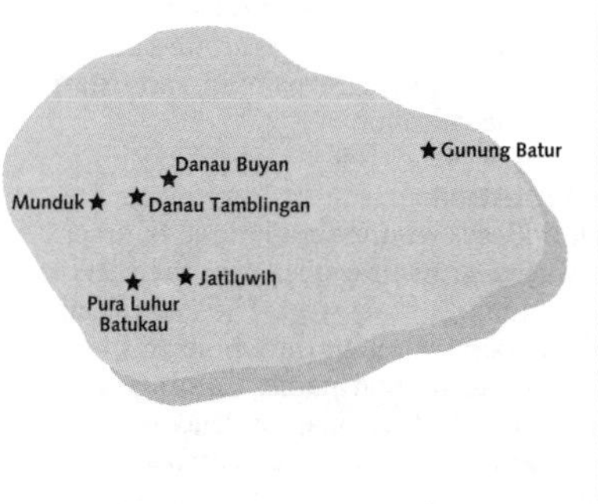

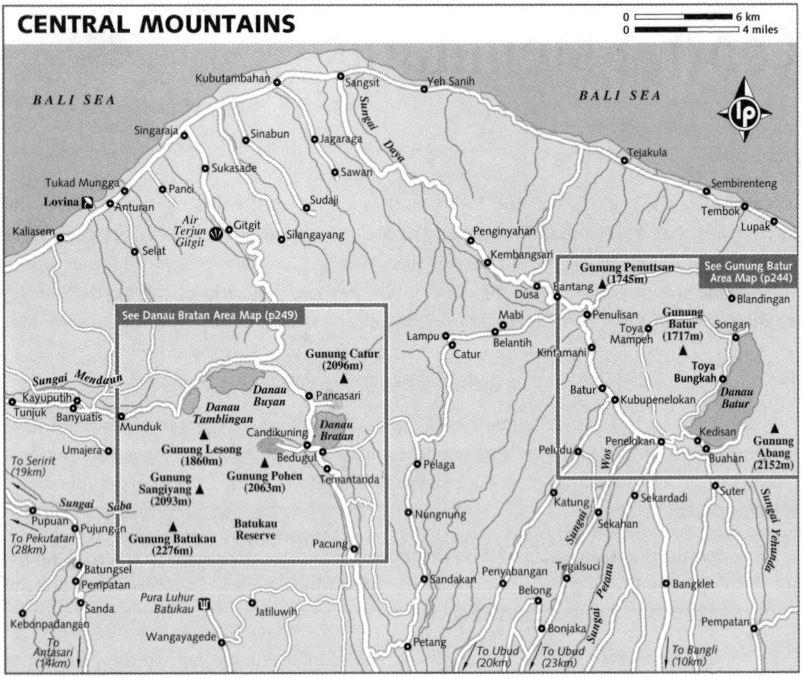

GUNUNG BATUR AREA

☎ 0366

This area is like a giant dish, with the bottom half covered with water and a set of volcanic cones growing in the middle. Sounds a bit spectacular? It is. The road around the southwestern rim of the Gunung Batur crater is one of Bali's most important north–south routes and has one of Bali's most popular vistas. Most people intending to do some trekking stay in the pleasant villages around the shores of Danau Batur, and plan an early start to climb the volcano.

Orientation

The villages around the Gunung Batur crater rim have grown together over the years in a continuous, untidy strip. The main village is Kintamani, although the whole area is often referred to by that name. Coming up from the south, the first village is Penelokan, where tour-group busloads stop to gasp at the view, eat a buffet lunch and are hassled by the ever-present souvenir sellers.

Penlokan is also where you can take a short road down into the crater. From here, a road loosely follows the shore of Danau Batur, linking the villages of Kedisan and Toya Bungkah.

Entry Tickets

If you arrive by private vehicle, you will be stopped at ticket offices at Penelokan or Kubupenelokan; to save any hassle, you should stop and buy a ticket. Entry is 4000/2000Rp per adult/child. Bicycles are free (and should be, given the climb needed to get here). This ticket is for the whole Gunung Batur area; you shouldn't be charged any more down at the lakeside.

Information

Services are few in the Gunung Batur area. There is an international ATM in the car parking area for the Lakeview Hotel. In Kubupenelokan there is a post office and in Kintamani there is a Bank BPD. There are no services in the villages around Danau Batur. The moral here is: bring lots of cash from the lowlands.

Getting There & Around

From Batubulan terminal in Denpasar, *bemo* (small minibus) travel regularly to Kintamani (15,000Rp). You can also get a bus on the busy Denapsar (Batabulan)–Singaraja route which will stop in Penelokan and Kintamani (about 15,000Rp). Alternatively, you can just hire a car or use a driver. From South Bali expect to pay at least 400,000Rp.

Orange bemo regularly shuttle back and forth around the crater rim, between Penelokan and Kintamani (7000Rp for tourists). Public bemo from Penelokan down to the lakeside villages go mostly in the morning (tourist price is about 6000Rp to Toya Bungkah). Later in the day, you may have to charter transport (40,000Rp or more).

TREKKING GUNUNG BATUR

Vulcanologists describe Gunung Batur as a 'double caldera', ie one crater inside another. The outer crater is an oval about 14km long, with its western rim about 1500m above sea level. The inner crater is a classic volcano-shaped peak that reaches 1717m. Activity over the last decade has spawned several smaller cones on its western flank, unimaginatively named Batur I, II, III and IV. More than 20 minor eruptions were recorded between 1824 and 1994, and there were major eruptions in 1917, 1926 and 1963. Geological activity and tremors have continued to occur regularly.

Statistics aside, you really have to see it to believe it. One look at this otherworldly spectacle and you'll understand why people want to go through the many hassles and expenses of taking a trek. But is it worthwhile? You'll get some amazing pictures and come close to volcanic action not easily seen anywhere. But the flip side is that it's costly, you have to deal with various characters and at some point you may just say, 'I could have enjoyed all this from the parking lot viewpoint in Penelokan'.

> **WARNING**
>
> The Gunung Batur area has a reputation as a money-grubbing place. Keep an eye on your gear and don't leave any valuables in your car, especially at the start of any trail up the volcano. Break-ins are common.
>
> Also be wary of touts on motorcycles who will attempt to steer you to a hotel of *their* choice as you descend into the Danau Batur area from the village of Penelokan. Finally, some of the vendors in the area can be highly aggressive and irritating. Guide services are controlled by the HPPGB (Mt Batur Tour Guides Association; see right).

HPPGB

The notorious **HPPGB** (Mt Batur Tour Guides Association; ☎ 52362; Toya Bungkah office **Map p247**; 5am-9pm; Pura Jati office **Map p244**; 3am-noon) has a monopoly on guided climbs up Gunung Batur. The HPPGB requires that all trekking agencies that operate on the mountain hire at least one of its guides for trips up the mountain. In addition, it has developed an unsavoury reputation for intimidation in requiring climbers to use its guides and during negotiations for its services.

Reported tactics have ranged from dire warnings given to people who inquired at its offices to outright physical threats against people attempting to climb without a guide. There have also been reports of guides stationing themselves outside of hotels to intercept climbers.

Pinning these guys down on rates can be enough to send you back to South Bali, but expect to pay the following:

Trek	Duration	Cost
Batur Sunrise	4-8am	200,000-300,000Rp
Gunung Batur Main Crater	4-10am	200,000-300,000Rp

Trekking Agencies

Even reputable and highly competent adventure tour operators from elsewhere in Bali cannot take their customers up Gunung Batur without paying the HPPGB (see above) and using one of its guides, so these tours are relatively expensive.

Pretty much all the accommodation in the area can help you put a trek together. They can recommend alternatives to the classic Batur climb such as the outer rim of the crater, or treks to other mountains such as Gunung Agung.

Trekking agencies can also arrange other treks in the area, to Gunung Abang or the outer rim of the crater, or to other mountains such as Gunung Agung. All of the agencies listed here can get you up Gunung Batur

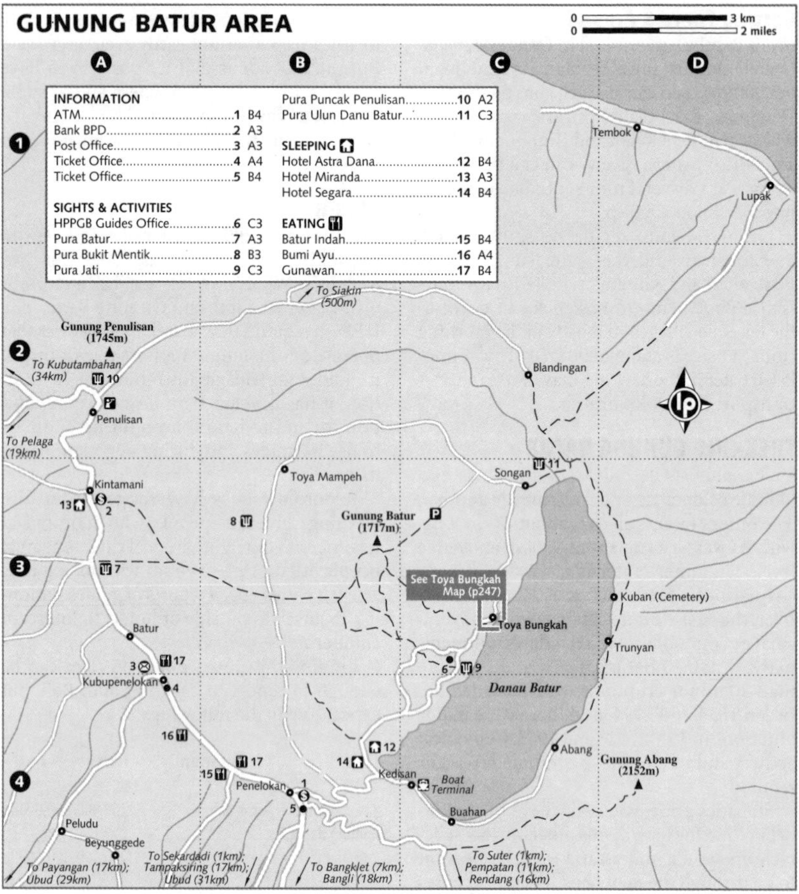

for rates from about US$20 (not including HPPGB fees); everything is negotiable.

Arlina's Trekking Agency (Map p247; ☎ 51165; Arlina's Bungalows, Toya Bungkah) Offers a range of treks.

Hotel Astra Dana (Map p244; ☎ 52091; Kedisan) Another recommended place.

Hotel Miranda (Map p244; ☎ 52022; Jl Raya Kintamani, Kintamani) One of the few agencies that will take solo climbers.

Hotel Segara (Map p244; ☎ 51136; hotelsegara@plasa.com; Kedisan) Popular with larger groups.

Jero Wijaya Tourist Service (Map p247; ☎ 51249; jero_wijaya@hotmail.com; Lakeside Cottages, Toya Bungkah) Well-regarded, offers treks up Gunung Agung (US$75) and in Taman Nasional Bali Barat (US$90).

Volcano Breeze (Map p247; ☎ 51824; Toya Bungkah) Located in the café of the same name, offers many treks.

Equipment

If you're climbing before sunrise, take a torch (flashlight) or be absolutely sure that your guide provides you with one. You'll need good strong footwear, a hat, a jumper (sweater) and drinking water.

Trekking Routes

The climb to see the sunrise from Gunung Batur is still the most popular trek, even with the high fees charged by, not to mention the dodgy reputation of, the HPPGB; see p243.

Ideally, trekkers should get to the top for sunrise (about 6am), before mist and cloud obscure the view. It is a magnificent sight, although hardly a wilderness experience – as it's not uncommon to have 100 people on

WHEN TO TREK

The volcanically active area west of the main peak can be deadly, with explosions of steam and hot lava, unstable ground and sulphurous gases. To find out about current conditions, ask at the trekking agencies (see p243), or alternatively look at the website of the **Directorate of Volcanology & Geographical Hazard Mitigation** (www.vsi.esdm.go.id).

The active areas are sometimes closed to visitors for safety reasons – if this is the case, don't try it alone, and don't pay extra for an extended main crater trek that you won't be able to do.

Think twice about trekking in the wet season (October to March), because the trails can be muddy and slippery, and clouds often block the views. Note that monsoonal rains often cause landslides in some mountain areas.

top for sunrise in the tourist season. Neither is it necessary to be at the top for sunrise – a halfway point is fine. If you start at 5am, you'll avoid the crowds.

Guides will provide breakfast on the summit for a fee (50,000Rp), and this often includes the novelty of cooking an egg or banana in the steaming holes at the top of the volcano. There are several refreshment stops along the way, but bottled beverages can be pricey. Water sources may be dubious.

FROM TOYA BUNGKAH

The basic trek is to start climbing from Toya Bungkah at about 3am, reach the summit for sunrise, and possibly walk right around the main cone, then return to Toya Bungkah. The route is pretty straightforward – walk out of the village towards Kedisan and turn right just after the car park. After about 30 minutes you'll be on a ridge with a well-defined track; keep going up. It gets pretty steep towards the top and it can be hard walking over the loose volcanic sand. Allow about two hours to reach the top, which is at the northern edge of the inner crater.

Climbers have reported that they've easily made the journey without a HPPGB guide, though it shouldn't be tried while dark. The major obstacle is actually avoiding any hassle from the guides themselves.

You can follow the rim to the western side, with a view of the area of the most recent volcanic activity, continue to the southern edge, and then return to Toya Bungkah by the route you climbed up.

Longer trips go around the recent volcanic cones southwest of the summit. This has the most exciting volcanic activity, with smoking craters, bright-yellow sulphur deposits, and steep slopes of fine black sand. If the activity is *too* exciting, the area may be closed for trekking, although the summit can still be OK (see the boxed text, above).

Climbing up Gunung Batur, spending a reasonable time on the top and then strolling back down takes four or five hours; for the longer treks around the newer cones, allow around eight hours.

FROM PURA JATI

A huge parking lot near Pura Jati makes this the main entrance for groups and day-trippers. The shortest trek is basically across the lava fields, then straight up (allow about two hours to the top). If you want to see the newer cones west of the peak (assuming the area is safe to visit), go to the summit first – do not go walking around the active area before sunrise.

FROM THE NORTHEAST

The easiest route is from the northeast – that's if you can get transport to the trailhead at 4am. From Toya Bungkah take the road northeast towards Songan and take the left fork after about 3.5km. Follow this small road for another 1.7km to a badly signposted track on the left – this climbs another kilometre or so to a parking area. From here, the walking track is easy to follow to the top, and should take less than an hour.

FROM KINTAMANI

From the western edge of the outer crater, trails go from Batur and Kintamani down into the main crater, then up Gunung Batur from the west side. This route passes close to the rather exciting volcanically active area and may be closed for safety reasons. Check the current status with the guide at Hotel Miranda (p246).

THE OUTER CRATER

A popular place to see the sunrise is on the outer crater rim northeast of Songan. You'll need transport to Pura Ulun Danu Batur, near the northern end of the lake. From there you can climb to the top of the outer crater rim in under 30 minutes, and see Bali's northeast coast, about 5km away. At sunrise, the silhouette of Lombok looms across the water, and the first rays strike the great volcanoes of Batur and Agung. If you can reconnoitre this route in daylight, you'll be able to do it without a guide.

VILLAGES AROUND GUNUNG BATUR CRATER

☎ 0366

There are several small villages on the ridge around Gunung Batur crater. The Penelokan area is filled with bus-tour restaurants, although some are good. Generally places on the west side of the road enjoy views down to South Bali while those on the east side look into the double caldera.

Penelokan

Penelokan means 'Place to Look' – and you will be stunned by the view across to Gunung Batur and down to the lake at the bottom of the crater. Apart from the vista (check out the large lava flow on Gunung Batur), there's not much here – a large bus-tour hotel, several ugly monolithic restaurants peering over the crater and numerous desperate souvenir sellers.

The road around the rim has several huge, overpriced buffet-style restaurants geared to busloads of tour groups. They all have fine views, and provide lunches from 60,000Rp to 80,000Rp or more.

But amid this there are some decent choices, including many humble places where you can sit on a plastic chair and have a simple meal while enjoying a priceless view. **Batur Indah** (☎ 51020; meals 30,000-60,000Rp; 🕑 8am-5pm) has South Bali views as does **Bumi Ayu** (☎ 52345; meals 30,000-70,000Rp; 🕑 8am-5pm). For views into the crater, consider **Gunawan** (☎ 51404; meals 30,000-80,000Rp; 🕑 8am-5pm).

Batur & Kintamani

The villages of Batur and Kintamani now virtually run together. Kintamani is famed for its large and colourful **market** held every three days. It starts early and by 11am it's all over. If you don't want to go on a trek, the sunrise view from the road here is pretty good.

The original village of Batur was in the crater, but was wiped out by a violent eruption in 1917. It killed thousands of people before the lava flow stopped at the entrance to the village's main temple.

Taking this as a good omen, the village was rebuilt, but Gunung Batur erupted again in 1926. This time, the lava flow covered everything except for the loftiest temple shrine. Fortunately, there were evacuations and few lives were lost. The village was relocated up on the crater rim, and the surviving shrine was also moved up there and placed in the new temple, **Pura Batur** (sarong & sash rental 1000Rp, admission donation 4100Rp).

Spiritually, Gunung Batur is the second most important mountain in Bali (only Gunung Agung outranks it) so this temple is of considerable importance. It's a great stop as there are always a few colourful mountain characters hanging around. Within the complex is a Taoist shrine.

The **Hotel Miranda** (☎ 52022; Jl Raya Kintamani, Kintamani; s/d 25,000/50,000Rp) is the only accommodation here. The six rooms are clean and very basic with squat toilets. It has good food and a congenial open fire at night. The informative owner can also act as a trekking guide (see p243).

Penulisan

The road gradually climbs along the crater rim beyond Kintamani, and is often shrouded in clouds, mist or rain. Penulisan is where the road bends sharply and heads down towards the north coast. A viewpoint about 400m south from here offers an amazing panorama over three mountains: Gunung Batur, Gunung Abang and Gunung Agung. If you're coming from the north, this is where you'll first see what all the tourism fuss is about.

Near the road junction, several steep flights of steps lead to Bali's highest temple, **Pura Puncak Penulisan** (1745m). Inside the highest courtyard are rows of old statues and fragments of sculptures in the open *bale* (pavilions). Some of the sculptures date back to the 11th century. The temple views are superb: facing north you can see over the rice terraces clear to the Singaraja coast (weather permitting).

VILLAGES AROUND DANAU BATUR

☎ 0366

The little villages around Danau Batur have a crisp lakeside setting and views up to the surrounding peaks. There's a lot of fish-farming here and the air is redolent with the smell of onions from the many farms. You'll also see chillies, cabbage and garlic growing. Yum!

A hairpin-bend road winds its way down from Penelokan to the shore of Danau Batur. At the lakeside you can go left along the good road that winds its way through lava fields to Toya Bungkah, the usual base for climbing Gunung Batur.

Kedisan & Buahan

The villages around the southern end of the lake have a few places available to stay in a fairly isolated setting. Buahan is a pleasant 15-minute stroll from Kedisan, and has market gardens going right down to the lakeshore.

Beware of the motorcycle touts who will follow you down the hill from Penelokan, trying out the various guide and hotel scams. Local hotels ask that you try to call ahead and reserve so that they can have your name on record and thus avoid paying a bounty to the touts.

SLEEPING & EATING

Both of these places have basic cafés.

Hotel Astra Dana (☎ 52091; r 50,000-100,000Rp) The more expensive of the 12 rooms have hot water and views to the lake across onion and cabbage fields. This is the home of the always delightful Dizzy, local guide extraordinaire. See p243 for details on the trekking agency based here.

Hotel Segara (☎ 51136; hotelsegara@plasa.com; r 60,000-100,000Rp; 🖳) Next door to Hotel Surya, the Segara has bungalows set around a courtyard. The more expensive rooms have hot water. It's clean and comfortable enough for a night. The restaurant is a good place to sample the local fish. See p243 for details on the trekking agency based here.

Trunyan & Kuban

The village of Trunyan is squeezed between the lake and the outer crater rim. It is inhabited by Bali Aga people. But unlike Tenganan (see p225) it is not a welcoming place.

Trunyan is known for the **Pura Pancering Jagat**, with its 4m-high statue of the village's guardian spirit, but tourists are not allowed to go inside. There are also several traditional Bali Aga–style dwellings, and a large banyan tree, said to be more than 1100 years old. Touts and guides, however, hang about soliciting tips. Don't.

A little beyond Trunyan, and accessible only by boat is the **cemetery** at Kuban. The people of Trunyan do not cremate or bury their dead – they lie them out in bamboo cages to decompose. A collection of skulls and bones lies on a stone platform. This is a tourist trap for those with macabre tastes.

Boats leave from a jetty near the middle of Kedisan, where there is a ticket office and a car park (1000Rp) with a few pushy vendors. Tourists are not allowed to catch the public boat. The price for a four-hour return trip – Kedisan–Trunyan–Kuban–Toya Bungkah–Kedisan – depends on the number of passengers, with a maximum of seven (200,000Rp to 220,000Rp).

Toya Bungkah

The main tourist centre is Toya Bungkah (also known as Tirta), with its hot springs (*tirta* and *toya* both mean water). Toya Bungkah is a simple village, but travellers stay here so they can climb Gunung Batur early in the morning. And if you take a moment to smell the onions (and take in the view of the placid lake) you may just decide

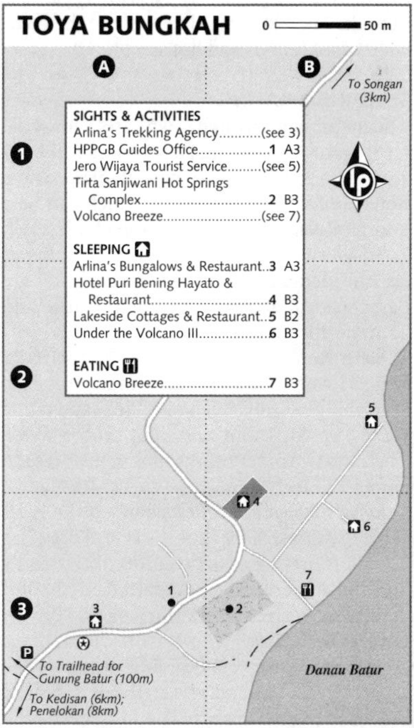

DETOUR

A turn-off in Songan takes you on a rough but passable road around the crater floor. Much of the area is very fertile, with bright patches of market garden and quite strange landforms. On the northwestern side of the volcano, **Toya Mampeh** village (Yeh Mampeh) is surrounded by a vast field of chunky black lava – a legacy of the 1974 eruption. Further on, **Pura Bukit Mentik** was completely surrounded by molten lava from this eruption, but the temple itself, and its impressive banyan tree, were quite untouched – it's called the 'Lucky Temple'.

you want to stay for a while, even if you don't go up the mountain.

ACTIVITIES

Hot springs bubble in a couple of spots, and have long been used for bathing pools. Beside the lake, with a wonderful mountain backdrop, **Tirta Sanjiwani Hot Springs Complex** (☎ 51204; adult/child US$5/2.50; 8am-8pm) has lovely gardens near the lake. Entry includes use of the cold-water pool (20°C) and hot spa (40°C).

SLEEPING & EATING

The main road through town can be noisy, so try to get rooms at the back of hotels. Better still, get one with a lake view. Unless noted, hotels only have cold water, which can be a boon for waking up for a sunset climb.

Small, sweet lake fish known as *ikan mujair* are the delicious local speciality. They are barbecued to a crisp with onion, garlic and bamboo sprouts.

Under the Volcano III (☎ 081 3386 0081; r 70,000Rp) With a lovely, quiet lakeside location opposite vegetable plots, this inn has six clean and pretty rooms; go for room one right on the water. There are two other nearby inns in the Volcano empire, all run by the same cheery family.

Arlina's Bungalows & Restaurant (☎ 51165; s/d 50,000/80,000Rp, with hot water 70,000/100,000Rp) Has 11 rooms that are clean, comfortable, friendly and above the average standard. See p243 for details on the trekking agency based here.

Lakeside Cottages & Restaurant (☎ 51249; jero_wijaya@hotmail.com; r US$10-35;) At the end of the track on the water's edge, this is definitely one of the better places. The top-end rooms have hot water and satellite TV. The restaurant (dishes 12,000-25,000Rp) serves home-style Japanese dishes, such as *oyako-don* (rice topped with egg and chicken). See p243 for details on the trekking agency based here.

Hotel Puri Bening Hayato & Restaurant (☎ 51234; www.indo.com/hotels/puribeninghayato; bungalow US$14-20, r US$42-50;) An incongruously modern place, it has a few quaint water-view bungalows and oversized 'deluxe' rooms all with hot water and lake views. The pool is small but there's also a hot-spring-fed whirlpool. The restaurant (dishes 12,000-30,000Rp) is slightly formal.

Volcano Breeze (☎ 51824; dishes 15,000-25,000Rp) A delightful and sociable travellers' café. Fresh lake fish in many forms is the speciality here. It's also a good place to just hang out. See p243 for details on the trekking agency based here.

Songan

Two kilometres around the lake from Toya Bungkah, Songan is a large and interesting village with market gardens extending to the lake's edge. At the lakeside road end is the temple **Pura Ulun Danu Batur**, under the edge of the crater rim.

DANAU BRATAN AREA

Approaching from the south, you gradually leave the rice terraces behind and ascend into the cool, often misty mountain country around Danau Bratan. Candikuning is the main village in the area, and has an important and picturesque temple. Bedugul is at the south end of the lake, with the most touristy attractions. About 4km north of the lake, Pancasari has the local market, the main bemo terminal and a golf course. Danau Buyan and Danau Tamblingan are pristine lakes northwest of Danau Bratan which offer good trekking possibilities. Beyond this are some interesting villages. To the south and west there are other beautiful highland areas, little visited by tourists.

While the choice of accommodation near the lake is limited, much of the area is geared towards domestic, not foreign, tourists. On Sundays and public holidays, the lakeside can be crowded with courting couples and Kijangs bursting with day-tripping families.

Wherever you go, you are likely to see the blissfully sweet local strawberries on offer. Note that it is often misty and can get chilly up here.

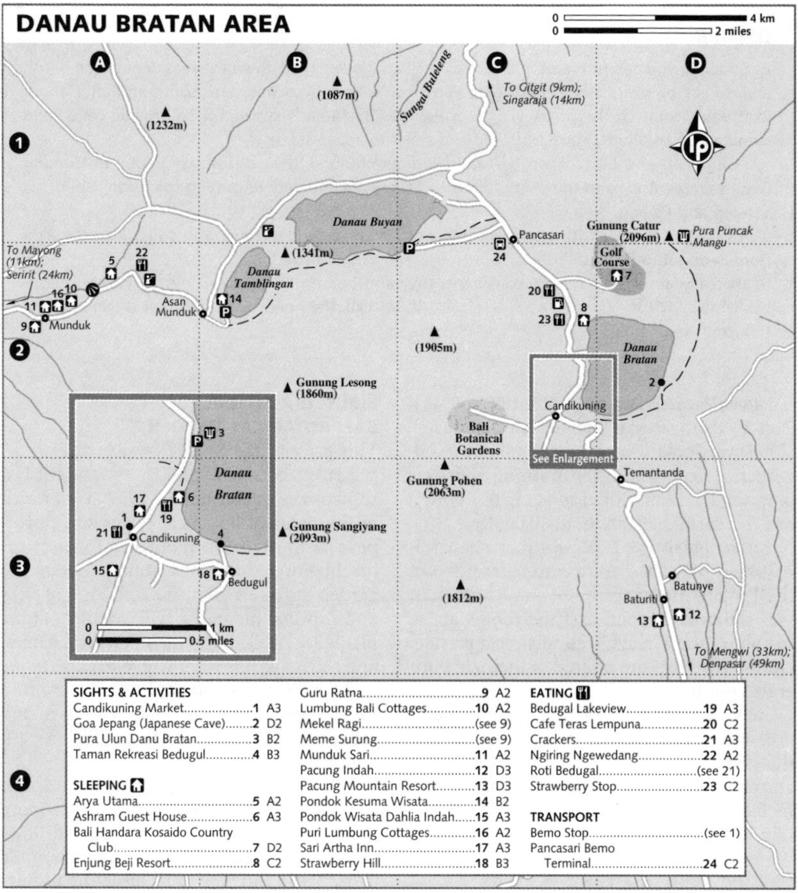

BEDUGUL

☎ 0368

'Bedugul' is sometimes used to refer to the whole lakeside area, but strictly speaking, it's just the first place you reach at the top of the hill when coming from South Bali. At the large billboard, take a right to the southern edge of the lake for the harmless tourist trap.

Activities

TAMAN REKREASI BEDUGUL

Lakeside eateries, a souvenir market and a selection of water sports – parasailing, water- and jet-skiing plus speedboats – are the features at this tacky and noisy **recreation park** (☎ 21197; admission 5000Rp, parking 1500Rp), which attracts many tour buses filled with locals.

TREKKING

From the water sports area, a trail around the south side of the lake goes to the mundane **Goa Jepang** (Japanese Cave), which was dug during WWII. From there, a difficult path ascends to the top of Gunung Catur (2096m), where the old **Pura Puncak Mangu** temple is popular with monkeys. Allow about four hours to go up and back from Taman Rekreasi Bedugul.

Sleeping & Eating

Upmarket hotels on the slope 9km south of Bedugul offer outstanding views to the south. And they are good choices for a snack or a refreshment if you're just passing by. Beware of a string of run-down places up at the ridge around Bedugul.

DETOUR

At Bedugul, you can turn east and take a small and lovely road down the hillside into some lush ravines cut by rivers. After about 6km you'll come to a T-junction, turn south and after about 2km you'll come to the pretty village of **Pelaga**. This area is known for its organic coffee and cinnamon plantations. You'll both see and smell them.

Pelaga can also be reached by road from Penulisan at the northwestern edge of Gunung Batur's crater. And from the south, there's a little-used and very rewarding road from Ubud, via Sangeh and Petang.

It's best to do this with your own transport. With some directions, you could hike the 8km from Bedugul to Pelaga.

To really appreciate Pelaga, consider a tour and homestay organised by **JED** (Village Ecotourism Network; ☎ 0361-735320; www.jed.or.id; tours US$25-100), the nonprofit group that organises rural tourism (see p348).

Pacung Mountain Resort (☎ 21038; r US$40-70;) This 39-room resort is built on a steep terraced slope over-looking an exquisite valley carved with rice fields and early morning views of Gunung Batukau. Buffet lunch is 65,000Rp, and à la carte is 20,000Rp to 80,000Rp

Pacung Indah (☎ 21020; www.pacungbali.com; r 200,000-500,000Rp;) Across the street from the Pacung Mountain Resort, this hotel has views almost as good and the rooms are a cut above the average – all include a private courtyard. Treks are offered in the rich, emerald countryside.

Strawberry Hill (Bukit Stroberi; ☎ 21265; dishes 10,000-25,000Rp) Opposite the Taman Rekreasi turn-off, this good restaurant has polished floorboards and on a clear day you can see Kuta. The menu includes burgers and soul-healing *soto ayam* (chicken soup). There's a good bar.

Getting There & Away

Any minibus or bemo between South Bali and Singaraja will stop at Bedugul on request (see opposite for details).

CANDIKUNING

☎ 0368

Spread out along the western side of the lake, Candikuning is the horticultural focus of central Bali. Its daily market was once the main supplier of vegetables, fruit and flowers for the southern hotels, but now its patrons are mostly tourists, with a smattering of locals shopping for herbs, spices and potted plants.

Several places to stay and eat can be found around the market. Down a gentle hill you'll find Pura Ulun Danu Bratan, an important local holy site.

Sights & Activities

BALI BOTANICAL GARDENS

This **garden** (Kebun Raya Eka Karya Bali; ☎ 21273; admission 3500Rp, car parking 1500Rp; 7am-6pm) is a showplace. Established in 1959 as a branch of the national botanical gardens at Bogor, near Jakarta, it covers more than 154 hectares on the lower slopes of Gunung Pohen. The garden boasts an extensive collection of trees and flowers, including wild orchids. Some plants are labelled with their botanical names, and the booklet *Six Self Guided Walks in the Bali Botanical Gardens*, sold at the ticket office for 20,000Rp, is helpful. The gorgeous orchid area is often locked to foil flower filchers; ask that it be unlocked.

Within the park there's a new attraction sure to delight anyone who wants to do more than just walk around and look at pretty flowers: the **Bali Treetop Adventure Park** (adult/child US$18/11) lets you play like a bird – or a squirrel. Winches, ropes, nets and more let you explore the forest well above the ground. And it's not passive, you hoist, jump, balance and otherwise circumnavigate the ark. Special programmes are geared to different ages.

Coming north from Bedugul, at a junction conspicuously marked with a large, phallic corncob sculpture, a small side road goes 600m west to the garden. Although normally cool, shady, scenic and uncrowded, on Sunday and public holidays it's very popular with Balinese families.

PURA ULUN DANU BRATAN

This very important Hindu–Buddhist **temple** (adult/child 3300/1800Rp, parking 2000Rp; tickets 7am-5pm, site 24hr) was founded in the 17th century. It is dedicated to Dewi Danu, the goddess of the waters, and is actually built on small islands, which means it is completely surrounded by the lake. Both pilgrimages and ceremonies are held here to ensure that there is a supply of water for farmers all over Bali.

It is truly beautiful, with a classical Hindu thatch-roofed *meru* (multi-roofed shrines) reflected in the water and silhouetted against the often cloudy mountain backdrop – one of the most common photographic images of Bali. A large banyan tree shades the entrance, and you walk through manicured gardens and past an impressive Buddhist stupa to reach the lakeside.

An unfortunate aspect is the small animal zoo, left of the main entrance, where tourists are encouraged to be photographed alongside snakes, bats and iguanas, all of which appear to be kept in less than humane conditions.

WATER SPORTS

At the temple gardens, you can hire a four-passenger speedboat with a driver (125,000Rp per 30 minutes), a five-person boat with boatman (80,000Rp per 30 minutes), or, a two-person pedal boat (35,000Rp per 30 minutes).

For an almost surreal experience, take a quiet paddle across the lake and see Pura Ulun Danu Bratan at sunrise – arrange it with a boatman the night before.

Sleeping

Sari Artha Inn (☎ 21011; r 60,000Rp) Although close to the market and lacking views, this basic place does have hot-water rooms.

Pondok Wisata Dahlia Indah (☎ 21233; r 50,000Rp, with hot water 80,000-125,000Rp) In the village along a lane near the road to the botanical garden, this is a decent budget option with 17 comfortable, clean rooms.

Ashram Guest House (☎ 21450; fax 21101; r 60,000-175,000Rp) Overlooking the lake, Ashram has a range of rooms. Prices start with shared bathroom and no hot water, then increase for a private bathroom, more still for hot water (much welcome on a chilly, misty day) and top price for everything, plus a view of the lake.

Enjung Beji Resort (☎ 21490; fax 21022; cottages 250,000-500,000Rp) Just north of the temple and overlooking the lake, this 23-room place is a peaceful, pleasant option. The superior cottages are excellent quality and have outdoor showers and sunken baths. All have hot water, good on cool misty days.

Eating

Food stalls at Candikuning's market offer cheap eats. Also in this part of the market is a very worthwhile T-shirt shop Smile For Life run by widows of the 2002 Kuta bombings.

Roti Bedugal (☎ 0815 5857 5355; snacks 5000Rp; 8am-6pm), Follow your nose to this place in a far corner of the market which has a continuous stream of fragrant freshly baked treats emerging all day. Nearby, you can feel like a grand potentate at the 'Deluxe Western Toilets' (5000Rp), the cleanest facility on the island.

Crackers (☎ 08-1138 8697; snacks 5000Rp) Back from Roti Bedugal, Crackers serves baked treats from roti and has a long drinks list (possibly to drive business to the toilets).

At the entrance to Pura Ulun Danu Bratan are several Padang warung (food stalls), and there's a café with a view on the grounds.

Bedugul Lakeview (dishes 8000-20,000Rp) Between the temple and the market, this place is big, clean and fresh (and we're not talking about the tasty chicken) and has a fine Indo menu.

Strawberry Stop (☎ 21060; dishes 7000-20,000Rp; 8am-6pm) North of Candikuning, they make good use of locally grown strawberries in milk shakes, juices and a myriad of different pancakes. Bananas sub when berries are out of season (which might drive you to drink the strawberry wine, 80,000Rp).

Cafe Teras Lempuna (☎ 0362-29312; dishes 15,000-40,000Rp) A welcome new addition to the dining scene, this cafe is modern, with a good menu ranging from burgers to Japanese. The coffees and teas are just the thing on cool days. When it's sunny, enjoy the inviting covered patio.

Getting There & Away

Danau Bratan is beside the main north–south road, so it's easy to reach from South Bali or Singaraja.

Although the main terminal is in Pancasari, most minibuses and bemo will stop along the road in Bedugul and Candikuning. There are frequent connections from Denpasar's Ubung terminal (15,000Rp) and Singaraja's Sukasada terminal (15,000Rp). For Gunung Batur, you have to connect through Singaraja or hire transport.

PANCASARI

The broad, green valley northwest of Danau Bratan is actually the crater of an extinct volcano. In the middle of the valley, on the main road, Pancasari is a nontourist town with a bustling market and the main terminal for public bemo.

Just south of Pancasari, you will see the entrance to **Bali Handara Kosaido Country Club** (☎ 22646; www.indo.com/hotels/balihandara; r from US$70), a well-situated (there's plenty of water here for the grass!), top-flight 18-hole golf course which offers comfortable accommodation in the sterile atmosphere of a 1970s resort, that somehow seems like the villain's grand lair in an old James Bond movie.

DANAU BUYAN & DANAU TAMBLINGAN

Also northwest of Danau Bratan are two more lakes, Danau Buyan and Danau Tamblingan – neither has been heavily developed for tourism, which is an advantage. There are several tiny villages and abandoned temples along the shores of both lakes, and although the frequently swampy ground makes it unpleasant in parts to explore, this is still a good place for a walk.

Sights & Activities

Danau Buyan (admission 2000Rp, parking 1000Rp) has parking right at the lake, a delightful 1.5km drive off the main road. The entire area is home to market gardens growing produce such as strawberries.

A 4km **hiking** trail goes around the southern side of Danau Buyan from the car park, then over the saddle to Danau Tamblingan, and on to Asan Munduk. It combines forest and lake views.

Danau Tamblingan (adult/child 3000/1500Rp, parking 1000Rp) also has a parking lot at the end of the road from the village of Asan Munduk. The lake is a 400m walk and this is where you can catch the trail to Danau Buyan. If you have a driver, you could always walk this path in one direction and be met at the other end. There are usually a couple of guides hanging around the car park (you don't need them for the lake path) who will gladly take you up and around **Gunung Lesong** (per 6hr 320,000Rp).

Sleeping & Eating

Pondok Kesuma Wisata (☎ 0817-472 8826; r 200,000Rp) This cute little guesthouse featuring rooms with hot water has a nice café (dishes 8000 Rp to 20,000Rp) and is just up from the Danau Tamblingan parking lot – you will get a surprise or two: you may be greeted by a monkey.

MUNDUK & AROUND

☎ 0362

The simple mountain village of Munduk may be one of Bali's most interesting places right now. It has a cool mountain ambience set among lush hillsides covered with jungle, rice, fruit trees and pretty much anything else that grows on the island. Waterfalls tumble off the precipices by the dozen. There are hikes and treks galore and a number of really nice places to stay, from old Dutch summer homes to retreats where you can plunge full on into local culture. Many people come for a day and stay for week.

Archaeological evidence suggests there was a developed community in the Munduk region between the 10th and 14th centuries. When the Dutch took control of North Bali in the 1890s, they experimented with commercial crops, establishing plantations for coffee, vanilla, cloves and cocoa. Quite a few Dutch buildings are still intact along the road in Munduk and further west.

Sights & Activities

Heading to Munduk from Pancasari, the main road climbs steeply up the rim of the old volcanic crater. It's worth stopping to enjoy the **views** back over the valley and lakes – watch out for monkey business from the simians on the road. Turning right (east) at the top will take you on a scenic descent to the coastal town of Singaraja, via the Gitgit waterfalls (p261). Taking a sharp left turn (west), you follow a ridge-top road with Danau Buyan on one side and a slope to the sea on the other; coffee is a big crop in the area.

If you turn left at this junction, a trail leads to near Danau Tamblingan, among forest and market gardens. Turning right takes you along beautiful winding roads to the main village of Munduk. Watch for superb panoramas of North Bali and the ocean and consider a stop at **Ngiring Ngewedang** (☎ 0828 365 146; dishes 15,000-40,000Rp; 🕙 10am-4pm), a coffee house 5km east of Munduk that has views of the ocean. You can buy coffee grown on the surrounding slopes and staff are happy to show you the coffee-production process.

About 2km east of Munduk look for signs indicating parking for a 15m **waterfall** near the road. This is the most accessible of many in the immediate area.

Almost everything in the Munduk area is at an elevation of at least 1000m. Numerous trails are suitable for two-hour or much longer

treks to coffee plantations, rice paddies, waterfalls, villages, and around both Danau Tamblingan and Danau Buyan. You will be able to arrange a guide through your lodgings.

Sleeping & Eating

There's a range of sleeping choices around Munduk. Enjoy simple old Dutch houses in the village or more naturalistic places in the countryside. Your accommodation will have a café, usually serving food from the region. There's a couple of cute warung along the road down to Seririt and North Bali.

Arya Utama (bungalow 100,000Rp) There are two simple cold-water bungalows here in the middle of coffee trees. The big activity: sit on your porch, gaze out and just listen. There's no food, says the young couple who own it, 'just sleep'. It's 2.8km east of Munduk.

Guru Ratna (☎ 92182; r 100,000-200,000Rp) The cheapest place in the village, it has five comfortable cold-water rooms in an old Dutch house. The best rooms have some style and nice porches.

Meme Surung & Mekel Ragi (☎ 92811; r 200,000Rp) These atmospheric old Dutch houses adjoin each other in the village and are run by the same owner. The former – Meme Surung – has excellent views down the valleys.

Munduk Sari (☎ 0361-297123; munduksari@yahoo.com; s/d 300,000/400,000Rp) Five gleaming rooms at this mainstream-feeling new place have the classic views of the area and big tubs with hot water. It's just east of the village.

Lumbung Bali Cottages (☎ 92818; r from US$40) About 800m east of Munduk, this place has villas overlooking the lush local terrain. The open-air bathrooms are as refreshing as the porches are relaxing. Like all local places, there is a wide range of hikes on offer here.

our pick **Puri Lumbung Cottages** (☎ 92810; www.purilumbung.com; cottage s/d US$67/75, cottage US$95-149; 💻) Founded by Nyoman Bagiarta to develop sustainable tourism, this great hotel has bright two-storey cottages with stunning views (units three, eight, 10 and 11 have the best) right down to the coast from their upstairs balconies. Rice grows outside each unit. Dozens of trekking options and courses, including dance and cooking, are offered. The hotel's restaurant (dishes 15,000Rp to 30,000Rp), Warung Kopi Bali, has a great outlook onto the lush valleys and also serves excellent food, including the local dish *timbungan bi siap* (chicken soup with sliced cassava and fried shallots). The hotel is on the right-hand side of the road 700m before Munduk from Bedugul.

Getting There & Away

Bemo leave Ubung terminal in Denpasar for Munduk frequently (20,000Rp). Morning bemo from Candikuning also stop in Munduk (12,000Rp). If you're driving to or from the north coast, a decent road west of Munduk goes through a number of picturesque villages to Mayong, then down to the sea at Seririt.

GUNUNG BATUKAU AREA

Often over-looked – probably a good thing given what the rapacious hordes have done to Gunung Agung – Gunung Batukau is Bali's second-highest mountain (2276m), the third of Bali's three major mountains and the holy peak of the island's western end.

You can climb its slippery slopes from one of the island's most holy and most underrated temples, Pura Luhur Batukau, or just revel in the ancient rice terrace greenery around Jatiliuweh that could be a fantasy if it wasn't real.

ORIENTATION

There are two main approaches to the Gunung Batur area, the easiest is to go via Tabanan (see p275) and take the Pura Luhur Batukau road north 9km to a fork in the road. Take the one on the left (towards the temple) and go a further 5km to a junction near a school in Wangayagede village. Here you can continue straight to the temple or turn right (east) for the rice fields of Jatiluwih.

The other way is to approach from the east. On the main Denpasar–Singaraja road, look for a small road to the west, just south of the Pacung Mountain Resort (p250). Here you follow a series of small, paved roads west until you reach the Jatiluweh rice fields. You'll get lost, but locals will quickly set you right and the scenery is superb anyway.

SIGHTS & ACTIVITIES

Pura Luhur Batukau

On the slopes of Gunung Batukau, **Pura Luhur Batukau** (donation 5000Rp) was the state temple when Tabanan was an independent kingdom. It has a seven-roofed *meru* dedicated to Maha

GROWING MONEY

The rich volcanic soil, regular rain mixed with sun and temperate nights mean that large swathes of the slopes leading up the central mountains of Bali are extremely fertile. Driving any of the roads, you'll certainly see this.

The produce and goods grown can be found in all of Bali's markets – from diet staples such aa tomatoes and carrots to cash crops including coffee and vanilla. But until recently, there's been no added value, as a marketer would say. Enter a bunch of American hippies, old- and post-. John Hardy came to Bali in 1975 and in three decades has created an international jewellery empire (www.johnhardy.com). But still remembering his hippy roots even as the millions rolled in and his pony tail got cut off, Hardy wanted an organic farm to supply wholesome food to his workers at his jewellery factory north of Denpasar.

Enter Ben and Blair Ripple. Fleeing a rainy and muddy organic farm near Seattle, these post-hippy hippies found themselves warming up and warming to Bali. One thing led to another, they met Hardy, he hired them for his dream farm, and the rest is, well, history.

The Ripples proved to have a talent for more than just growing pesticide-free foods, it turns out they are genius marketers who don't just sell food, but rather an entire cuisine concept. From their farm near Jatiluweh (see below) they have cornered the market for the kinds of unusual, boutique produce craved by Bali's best chefs. French Chantenay carrots, Italian Chiogga beets and more flow forth. And now it's not just produce, but products. Under the brand **Big Tree Farms Bali** (www.bigtreebali.com), the Ripples are selling Balinese sea salt (see the boxed text, p237), Balinese long peppers and other boutique flavourings in gourmet markets in the USA with plans to extend to Britain and Australia.

And who benefits? Well the Ripples obviously, but also the many farmers who grow crops for them at much more than commodity prices, the families making salt in the east and the dozens of people working behind the scenes. 'We called it Big Tree because we like the idea of it dropping seeds in a big sustainable forest,' says Ben.

Meanwhile, the Ripples are trying to stay close to what bought them to Bali. On several nights during the dry season (April to September), they host dinners at the torch-lit tables of **Big Tree Farm** (☎ 0361-461978; farm@bigtreebali.com). If you can elbow aside a celebrity or two, you might be able to join them. The cost is about US$70 for a multicourse tasting of their amazing cooking – which takes lots of inspiration from Balinese foods.

Dewa, the mountain's guardian spirit, as well as shrines for Bratan, Buyan and Tamblingan lakes. Surrounded by forest, it's often damp and misty. Sarongs can be rented and a donation to the temple is requested.

This is certainly the most spiritual temple you can easily visit on Bali. The main pagoda-like structures have little doors shielding small ceremonial items. There's a general lack of touts and other characters – including hordes of tourists. The atmosphere is cool and misty. Facing the temple, take a short walk around to the left to see a small white-water stream. The air vibrates with the tumbling water.

Gunung Batukau

At Pura Luhur Batukau you are fairly well up the side of **Gunung Batukau**, and you may wish to go for a climb. But to **trek** to the top of the 2276m peak, you'll need a guide which can be arranged at the temple ticket booth. Expect to pay at least 800,000Rp for a muddy and arduous journey that will take at least seven hours in one direction. The rewards are amazing views alternating with thick, dripping jungle and the knowledge that you've taken the trail that is much less travelled compared with the peaks in the east.

Rice Fields

At **Jatiluwih** you will be rewarded with vistas of centuries-old rice terraces that exhaust your ability to describe green. The locals will also be rewarded with your 'green', as there's a road toll (per person 3300Rp, plus 1500Rp per car). This is a good place for a **rice field walk**. After all, Jatiluwih means 'Truly Marvellous', and the view truly is – it takes in a huge chunk of South Bali.

Any road heading south will eventually take you back to the main Tabanan–Denpasar road.

SLEEPING & EATING

Prana Dewi Mountain Resort (☎ 732032; www.balipranaresort.com; bungalows from US$40) Just past the village of Wangayagede and signposted to the left off the main Pura Luhur Batukau road, this resort is set among rice paddies and coursing waterways. The eight rustic, beautifully furnished bungalows have thick slab timber floors and hot water. The restaurant (dishes 15,000Rp to 35,000Rp), surrounded by low, terraced red-rice fields and a bamboo forest, has a lush vista. Most of the vegetables used in the creative dishes are grown organically in the surrounding fields.

There are a couple of simple cafés around Jatiluweh.

GETTING THERE & AWAY

The only realistic way to explore the Gunung Batukau area is with a car. Either rent one for a day or get a driver; see p359 for details on costs.

North Bali

In many respects, North Bali seems so far away from the rest of the island. And in a literal sense it is. To get here from the south you either take one of many routes up and over the mountains or traverse the thinly populated coasts in the west and the east.

In North Bali's case, getting there can be half the fun. The various routes over and through the volcanoes and lakes are lush, amazing and surprising. The coastal routes take you through tiny villages unchanged for decades, and give you access to numerous under-appreciated cultural and religious sites.

And, as fun as it is to get to North Bali, it's also plenty fun once you're there. Lovina is a beach town that defines relaxed. Uncrowded and definitely unhurried, it has a huge range of mellow places to stay right near its reef-protected simple beach. Toss in dining that's both good and fun and you've got a fine escape from the mania of the south.

The north's charms extend beyond Lovina. The region, known as Buleleng, has a deep history that is a vital part of Bali as a whole. It was the centre of Dutch influence until WWII and for generations of early visitors, the port of Singaraja was their first glimpse of the island. Today, Bali's second city is still a local cultural haven.

In the northwest, Pemuteran is both a dive mecca and a leader in ecologically sound development – just one more reason to explore the 'far' coast of Bali.

HIGHLIGHTS

- Diving and snorkelling at **Pemuteran** (p269)
- Chilling at **Lovina** (p262), the north's alternative to Kuta
- Heading for the breathtaking hills on the road from **Seririt** (p268)
- Bobbing in the spring-fed pools at **Yeh Sanih** (p257)
- Experiencing Buleleng's rich culture at the museums of **Singaraja** (p257)

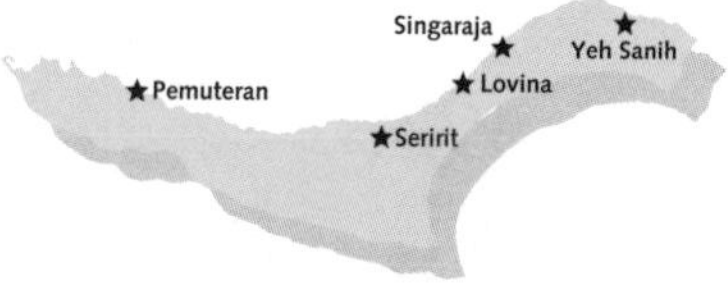

YEH SANIH

☎ 0362

On the road to the beach towns of East Bali, about 15km east of Singaraja, Yeh Sanih (also called Air Sanih) is a hassle-free seaside spot with a few guesthouses on the beachfront. It's named for its fresh-water springs, **Air Sanih** (adult/child 2000/1000Rp; ☻ 8am-6pm), which are channelled into large swimming pools before flowing into the sea. The pools are particularly picturesque at sunset, when throngs of locals bathe under blooming frangipani trees – most of the time they're alive with frolicking kids.

Pura Ponjok Batu has a commanding location between the sea and the road, some 7km east of Yeh Sanih. It has some very fine limestone carvings in the central temple area. Legend has it that it was built to provide some balance for Bali, what with all the temples in the south.

Between the springs and the temple, the road is often close to the sea. It's probably Bali's best stretch of coast driving, with water crashing onto the breakwater that's built all along here, and great views out to sea.

Completely out of character for the area is **Art Zoo** (☻ 8am-6pm), 5.7km east of Yeh Sanih on the Singaraja road. The American artist Symon (who also has a gallery in Ubud, see p179) has a gallery bursting with vibrant, exotic and often homoerotic paintings and sculpture. You can chat up his models and even the man himself if he's in residence.

Sleeping & Eating

If you're doing the North Bali to East Bali shuffle along the coast road, you may wish to break your journey around here rather than push too far in either direction.

Pondok Wisata Cleopatra (☎ 0812 362 2232; r 50,000Rp) This new budget place has nine nice, cold-water rooms with showers and tubs – go ahead and stick your toe in. The big, flowery grounds are about 1.5km west of the springs.

Pondok Sembiran (☎ 24437; r 200,000-350,000Rp; ☒ ☒) There are two facilities here, one with a pool 20m from the beach and one right on the beach. The 10 pleasant bungalows are large, good for families and have kitchens and hot water. The hotel is off the main road in Alassari, 1km east of the temple and 8.3km east of Yeh Sanih. It's popular with the Dutch, so be sure to get your Ver's and Van's right.

Cilik's Beach Garden (☎ 26561; www.ciliksbeachgarden .com; s/d €40/60, villas €75-110; ☐) Coming here is like visiting your rich friends, albeit ones with good taste. These villas, 3km east of Yeh Sanih, are large and have vast private gardens. Other accommodation is in stylish *lumbung* (rice barns with round roofs) set in a delightful garden facing the ocean. Meals (dishes from 20,000Rp to 40,000Rp) are served in a pavilion.

Puri Rena (☎ 26581; dishes 10,000-20,000Rp) Across from Air Sanih and up a flight of stairs, Puri Rena has a well-priced menu of local standards aimed at parents needing sustenance while the kids make like Flipper. Good views.

Puri Bagus Ponjok Batu (☎ 21430; dishes 15,000-30,000Rp) This lovely spot 6.8km east of Yeh Sanih is next to Pura Ponjok Batu and overlooks the water. It serves good grilled seafood in covered pavilions. Call to confirm hours before making a special trip.

Getting There & Away

Yeh Sanih is on the main road along the north coast. Frequent bemo (small minibuses) and buses from Singaraja stop outside the springs (7000Rp).

If you are driving the coast road to Amed and beyond, be sure to fill up at the petrol station 9km east of Yeh Sanih as there isn't another until almost Amlapura.

SINGARAJA

☎ 0362

With a population of more than 100,000 people, Singaraja (which means 'Lion King' – evidently Disney has yet to threaten to sue for trademark infringement) is Bali's second-largest city. With its tree-lined streets, Dutch colonial buildings and charmingly moribund waterfront area north of Jl Erlangga, it's worth wandering around for a few hours. Most people, however, prefer to stay in nearby Lovina.

Singaraja was the centre of Dutch power in Bali and remained the administrative centre for the Lesser Sunda Islands (Bali through to Timor) until 1953. It is one of the few places in Bali where there are visible traces of the Dutch period, as well as Chinese and Muslim influences. Today Singaraja is a major educational and cultural centre, and its two university campuses provide the city with a substantial, and sometimes vocal, student population.

The 'suburb' of Beratan, to the south of Singaraja, is the silverwork centre of northern Bali. You'll find a few traditional pieces, such as *cucuk* (gold headpieces) on display, but it mostly has uninspiring tourist jewellery. A few workshops in and around Singaraja

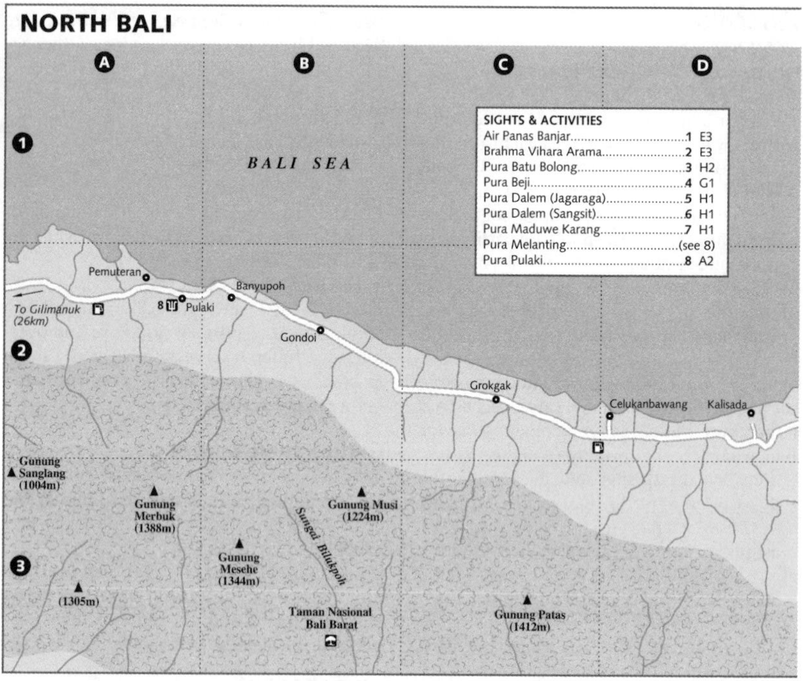

produce hand-woven sarongs – especially *songket* (cloth woven with silver or gold threads).

Orientation

The main commercial areas are in the northeastern part of town, south of the old harbour. Most hotels, restaurants and bus company offices are found along Jl Jen Achmed Yani. The traffic does a few complicated one-way loops around town, but it's easy enough to get around on foot or by bemo.

Information

EMERGENCY

Police station (☎ 41510; Jl Pramuka)

INTERNET ACCESS & TELEPHONE

There are several wartel (public telephone offices) along the main streets and there is **Internet access** (per min 400Rp) at the rear of the post office.

MEDICAL SERVICES

RSUP Hospital (☎ 22046; Jl Ngurah Rai; 🕑 24hr) Singaraja's hospital is the largest in northern Bali.

MONEY

There are numerous banks that will change money and have ATMs.

Bank BCA (Jl Jen Achmed Yani)

Bank Danamon (Jl Jen Achmed Yani)

POST OFFICE

Post office (Jl Imam Bonjol)

TOURIST INFORMATION

Diparda (☎ 25141; cnr Jl Veteran & Jl Gajah Mada; 🕑 7.30am-3.30pm Mon-Fri) The regional tourist office loves visitors and has some pamphlets. Ask about dance and other cultural events.

Sights & Activities

OLD HARBOUR & WATERFRONT

The conspicuous **Yudha Mandala Tama monument** commemorates a freedom fighter killed by gunfire from a Dutch warship early in the struggle for independence. Close by, there's the colourful Chinese temple, **Ling Gwan Kiong**. There are a few old canals here as well and you can still get a little feel of the old colonial port. Walk up Jl Imam Bonjol and you'll see the art deco lines of late-colonial Dutch buildings.

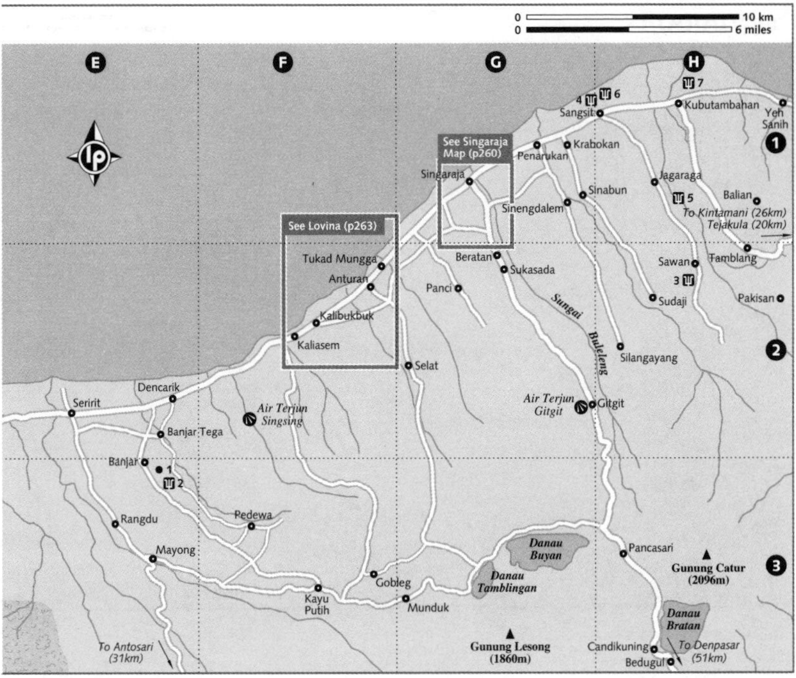

GEDONG KIRTYA LIBRARY & MUSEUM BULELENG

This small historical **library** (☎ 22645; admission 5000Rp; 8am-4pm Mon-Thu, 8am-1pm Fri) was established in 1928 by Dutch colonialists and named after the Sanskrit word 'to try'. It has a collection of *lontar* (dried palm leaves) books (see p234), as well as some even older written works, in the form of inscribed copper plates called *prasasti*. Dutch publications, dating back to 1901, may interest students of the colonial period.

The nearby **museum** (donation 5000Rp; 9am-3.30pm) recalls the life of the last Radja (rajah; prince) of Buleleng, Pandji Tisna, who is credited with developing Lovina's tourism. Among the items here is the Royal (brand) typewriter he used during his career as a travel writer (obviously, the rajah was a smart, if poorly remunerated guy) before his death in 1978. It also traces the history of the region back to when there was no history.

PURA JAGAT NATHA

Singaraja's main temple, the largest in northern Bali, is not usually open to foreigners. You can appreciate its size and admire the carved stone decorations from the outside.

Festivals & Events

Every May or June, Singaraja is host to the **Bali Art Festival of Buleleng**. Over one week dancers and musicians from some of the region's most renowned village troupes, such as those of Jagaraga, perform. In August, the **North Bali Festival** thrills locals with events such as the tongue-twisting 'Miss & Master Beauty & Brains Contest'. Consult with the Diparda tourist office (opposite) for details on both.

Sleeping & Eating

There are slim accommodation pickings in Singaraja, and there's no real reason to stay here as it's just a short drive from Lovina.

Hotel Wijaya (☎ 21915; fax 25817; Jl Sudiman 74; r 60,000-120,000Rp;) This is the most comfortable place in town; economy fan rooms have an outside bathroom. It also has a restaurant. The bus terminal is a three-minute walk away.

Café Lima Lima (☎ 21769; Jl Jen Achmed Yani; dishes 4000-10,000Rp) This is a cheap place with fresh food and simple open-air tables.

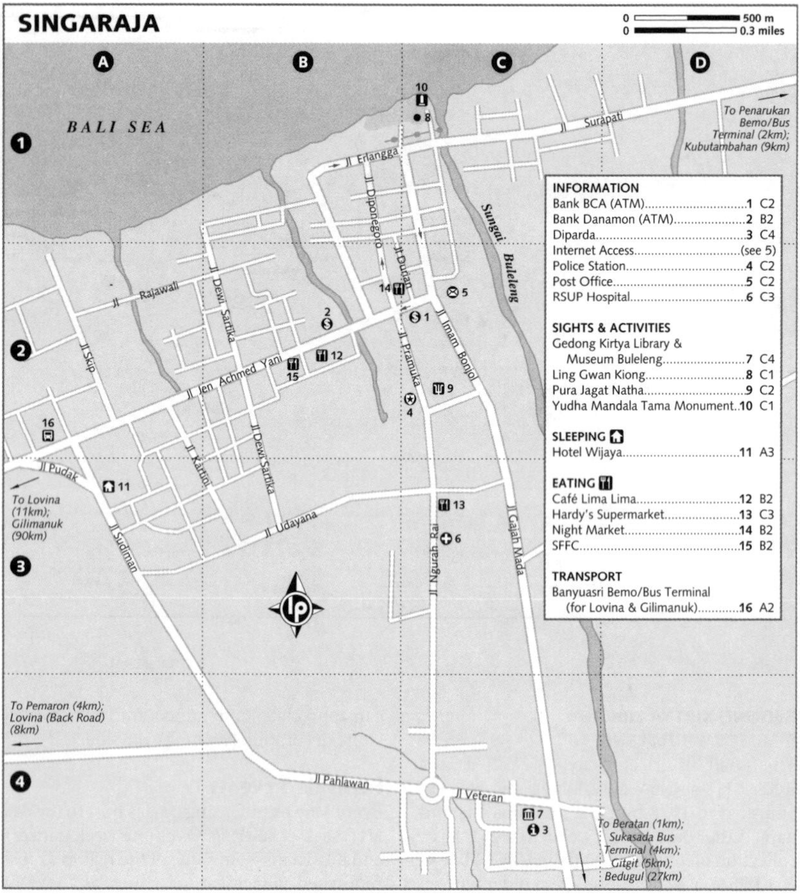

SFFC (☎ 24474; Jl Jen Achmed Yani 57; dishes 4000-10,000Rp) Fortunately the food is a lot better than the name – although it is descriptive – it means 'Special Fish & Fried Chicken'. And that's just what's served in this cheery place.

For supplies and sundries, head to **Hardy's Supermarket** (Jl Pramuka; 6am-10pm). In the evening, there are food stalls in the night market on Jl Durian.

Getting There & Away

BEMO & BUS

Singaraja is the main transport hub for the northern coast, with three bemo/bus terminals. From the Sukasada terminal, 3km south of town, minibuses go to Denpasar (Ubung terminal, 28,000Rp) via Bedugul/Pancasari (13,000Rp) about every 30 minutes from 6am to 4pm.

The Banyuasri terminal, on the western side of town, has buses heading to Gilimanuk (15,000Rp, two hours) and Java, and plenty of blue bemo to Lovina (6000Rp).

The Penarukan terminal, 2km east of town, has bemo to Yeh Sanih (7000Rp) and Amlapura (15,000Rp, three hours) via the coastal road; and also minibuses to Denpasar (Batubulan terminal, 25,000Rp) via Kintamani.

To Java

From Singaraja, several companies have overnight services to Surabaya (110,000Rp, 13 hours), which include the short ferry trip across the Bali Strait. Other buses go as far as Yogyakarta (170,000Rp, 16 hours) and Jakarta (250,000Rp, 24 hours), usually travelling overnight – book at Banyuasri terminal a day before.

TOURIST SHUTTLE BUS

All of the Perama shuttle buses going to Lovina (p267) from South Bali via Bedugul can drop you off in Singaraja.

Getting Around

Plenty of bemo link the three main bemo/bus terminals, and zip along all main roads in between. The bemo are all well signed and colour-coded and cost about 4000Rp for a ride anywhere around town. The green Banyuasri–Sukasada bemo goes along Jl Gajah Mada to the tourist office; this bemo, and the brown one between Penarukan and Banyuasri terminals, also goes along Jl Jen Achmed Yani.

AROUND SINGARAJA

The interesting sites around Singaraja include some of Bali's most important temples. See p43 for background information.

Sangsit

A few kilometres northeast of Singaraja, you can see an excellent example of the colourful architectural style of North Bali. Sangsit's **Pura Beji** is a *subak* (village association for rice-growers) temple, dedicated to the goddess Dewi Sri, who looks after irrigated rice fields. The sculptured panels along the front wall set the tone with their cartoonlike demons and amazing *naga* (mythical snakelike creatures). The inside also has a variety of sculptures covering every available space. It's about 500m off the main road towards the coast.

The **Pura Dalem** shows scenes of punishment in the afterlife, and other humorous, sometimes erotic, pictures. You'll find it in the rice fields, about 500m northeast of Pura Beji.

Buses and bemo going east from Singaraja's Penarukan terminal will stop at Sangsit.

Jagaraga

It was the capture of the local rajah's stronghold at Jagaraga that marked the arrival of Dutch power in Bali in 1849. The village, a few kilometres south of the main road, also has a **Pura Dalem**. The small, interesting temple has delightful sculptured panels along its front wall, inside and out. On the outer wall, look for a vintage car driving sedately past, a steamer at sea and even an aerial dogfight between early aircraft. Jagaraga is also famous for its Legong troupe, said to be the best in North Bali, but performances are irregular.

Bemo from the Penarukan terminal in Singaraja stop at Jagaraga on the way to Sawan.

Sawan

Several kilometres inland from Jagaraga, Sawan is a centre for the manufacture of gamelan gongs and instruments. You can see them being cast and the intricately carved gamelan frames being made. **Pura Batu Bolong** (Temple of the Hollow Stone) and its baths are also worth a look. Around Sawan there are cold water springs that are believed to cure all sorts of illnesses.

Regular bemo to Sawan leave from Penarukan terminal in Singaraja.

Kubutambahan

About a kilometre east of the turn-off to Kintamani is **Pura Maduwe Karang** (Temple of the Land Owner). Like Pura Beji at Sangsit, this temple of dark stone is dedicated to agricultural spirits, but this one looks after nonirrigated land.

This is one of the most delightful temples in North Bali and is particularly noted for its sculptured panels, including the famous bicycle stone-carved relief that depicts a gentleman riding a bicycle with flowers for wheels. It's on the base of the main plinth in the inner enclosure. The cyclist may be WOJ Nieuwenkamp, a Dutch artist who, in 1904, brought probably the first bicycle to Bali.

The temple is easy to find in the village. Kubutambahan is on the road between Singaraja and Amlapura, and there are regular bemo and buses.

Gitgit

About 11km south of Singaraja, the well-signposted path goes 800m west from the main road to the touristy waterfall, **Air Terjun Gitgit** (adult/child 4000/2000Rp). The path is lined with souvenir stalls and guides to nowhere. The 40m waterfalls pound away and you'll feel cool just looking at them.

About 2km further up the hill, there's a multitiered **waterfall** (donation 5000Rp) about 600m off the western side of the main road. The path crosses a narrow bridge and follows he river up past several small sets of waterfalls, through verdant jungle.

GETTING THERE & AWAY

Regular bemo and minibuses between Denpasar (Ubung terminal) and Singaraja (Sukasada terminal) stop at Gitgit. Gitgit is also a major stop on organised tours of central and North Bali.

LOVINA

☎ 0362

Relaxed is how people most often describe Lovina and they are correct. This low-key, low-rise beach resort has a mellow vibe that many travellers enjoy after the frenetic go-go of South Bali. The waves are calm, the people are calm, the bars are calm, it's all, well, very calm.

This is where you catch up on your journal, finish a book or make new friends at a laid-back beachside café. If you're feeling more active you can start with a wander on the delightful beach walk. There's also some good diving in the area, and if you really want to get you motor revving – literally – there's early morning dolphin watching.

While not arid, Lovina is also not a tropical jungle. It's sunny and there are palm trees about. It is definitely spread out though – don't plan on walking from one end to the other.

Lovina is a convenient base for trips around the north coast or the central mountains. The beaches are made up of washed-out grey and black volcanic sand, and they are mostly clean near the hotel areas but not spectacular. Reefs protect the shore, calming the waves and keeping that water clear.

A highlight every afternoon at fishing villages like Anturan, is watching *prahu* (traditional outrigger canoes) being prepared for the night's fishing; as sunset reddens the sky, the lights of the fishing boats appear as bright dots across the horizon.

Orientation

The Lovina tourist area stretches over 8km, and consists of a string of coastal villages – Kaliasem, Kalibukbuk, Anturan, Tukad Mungga – collectively known as Lovina. The main focus is Kalibukbuk, 10.5km west of Singaraja and often thought of as the heart of Lovina. The main street is also the main east–west road. It goes by various names, including Jl Raya Lovina and Jl Raya Kaliasem. Traffic in the daytime can be loud and constant.

For trips to Singaraja, the back road is a bucolic alternative.

Information

If you are planning a reading holiday in Lovina, come prepared. Other than some used book stalls, there's no good source for books or newspapers (if only the urchins selling over-priced papers in the south came here, they'd clean up).

EMERGENCY

Police station (Jl Raya Lovina) Near the tourist office.

INTERNET ACCESS

Spice Cyber (☎ 41305; Jl Bina Ria; per min 300Rp; 8am-midnight;) The best place for internet access, and it's reasonably fast.

MEDICAL SERVICES

Apotek Rahayu (☎ 41314; Jl Raya Lovina; 24hr) Pharmacy with a doctor on call.

MONEY

There are moneychangers around Lovina, especially in Kalibukbuk. There is a Bank BCA ATM at the corner of Jl Bina Ria and Jl Raya Lovina.

POST

The main post office is 1km west of central Kalibukbuk.

Sights & Activities

BEACHES

A paved beach path runs along the sand in Kalibukbuk. It greatly eases a beach stroll – even if it is popular with scooters. Enjoy the postcard view to the east of the mountainous North Bali coast.

Otherwise, the best beach areas include the main beach east of the **Dolphin Monument** as well as the curving stretch a bit west. The cluster of cheap hotels in Anturan also enjoy fun in the sand.

DOLPHIN WATCHING

Sunrise boat trips to see dolphins are Lovina's much-hyped tourist attraction – so much so that a large concrete-crowned monument has been erected in honour of the over-touted cetaceans. Some days, no dolphins are sighted, but most of the time at least a few surface.

Expect constant hassle from your hotel and touts selling dolphin trips – and if you want to go, it's best to buy a ticket the day before. The price is fixed at 40,000Rp per person by the boat owners' cartel. Trips start at a non-

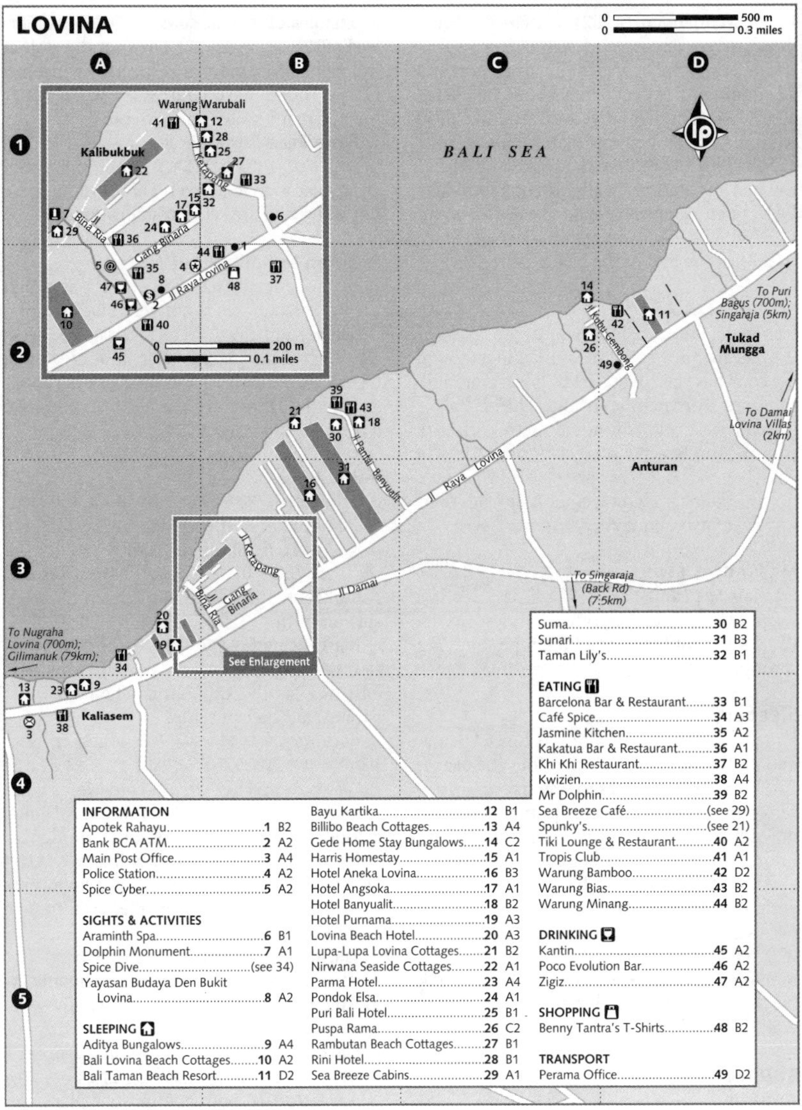

holiday-like 6am and last about two hours. Note that the ocean can get pretty crowded with loud, roaring power boats.

There's great debate about what all this means to the dolphins. Do they like being chased by boats? If not, why do they keep coming back? Maybe it's the fish, of which there are plenty off Lovina. For a dolphin, maybe the buzzing boats are on par with someone yakking on a cell phone at dinner. Or maybe not.

DIVING

Scuba diving on the local reef is better at lower depths and night diving is particularly recommended. Many people stay here to dive

Pulau Menjangan (p282), a two- to three-hour drive west.

For a two-dive trip, including transport and all equipment, expect to pay about US$35 for a Lovina reef or night dive; and around US$50 to Amed, Tulamben or Pulau Menjangan.

Spice Dive (☎ 41509; www.balispicedive.com) has the best reputation locally. It runs four-dive PADI open-water certificate courses for about US$250. It is based at the pleasant Café Spice (p267), at the end of the beach path.

SNORKELLING

Generally, the water is clear and some parts of the reef are quite good for snorkelling, though the coral has been damaged by 'bleaching' and, in places, by dynamite fishing. The best place is to the west, a few-hundred metres offshore from Billibo Beach Cottages. A boat trip will cost about 40,000Rp per person for two people for two hours, including equipment. Snorkelling gear costs about 20,000Rp per day.

MASSAGE & SPAS

Araminth Spa (☎ 0812 384 4655; Jl Ketapang; massage from 80,000Rp; 🕑 10am-7pm) offers Balinese, Ayurveda, and foot massage in a simple but cute setting.

Sleeping

Hotels are spread out along Jl Raya Lovina, and on the side roads going off to the beach. There are decent places to stay in every price range and while Bali visitor numbers remain down, bargains are commonplace and many midrange places are rather cheap.

Anturan is largely a backpackers' beach with a mellow charm. There are some nice places grouped from Anturan to Kalibukbuk – which is jammed with all manner of accommodation and services. West of Kalibukbuk the hotel density again diminishes right along with the beach.

BUDGET

Anturan

A few tiny side tracks and one proper sealed road, Jl Kubu Gembong, lead to this lively little fishing village, busy with swimming locals and moored fishing boats. It's a real travellers' hang-out. It's a long way from Lovina's evening delights though – expect to pay around 20,000Rp for transport back to Anturan from Kalibukbuk after 6pm when the bemo stop operating.

Gede Home Stay Bungalows (☎ 41526; Jl Kubu Gembong; r 50,000-120,000Rp; ❄) The friendly staff at this eight-room place are especially winsome. Cheap rooms have cold water while better ones have hot water and air-con.

Puspa Rama (☎ 42070; Jl Kubu Gembong; s/d incl breakfast 60,000/70,000Rp) This is one of several cheap places on this street. The six rooms have hot water and are set in lush grounds.

Anturan to Kalibukbuk

Jl Pantai Banyualit has many hotels, although the beachfront area is not very inspiring.

Suma (☎ 41566; Jl Pantai Banyualit; r US$10-35; ❄ 🏊) In a mannered stone building, Suma has views of the sea from its upstairs rooms. The pool is large and naturalistic; there's also a pleasant café.

Kalibukbuk

A little over 10km from Singaraja, the 'centre' of Lovina is the village of Kalibukbuk. Jl Ketapang is marginally quieter and more pleasant than Jl Bina Ria. There are small *gangs* (footpaths) lined with cheap places to stay off both.

Harris Homestay (☎ 41152; Gang Binaria; s/d incl breakfast 40,000-50,000Rp) This cosy little place is part of a family compound. The cold-water rooms have nice porches.

Hotel Angsoka (☎ 41841; www.angsoka.com; Gang Binaria; r 40,000-200,000Rp; ❄ 🏊) There's a large range of rooms here, from cold-water basic to large with air-con and hot water. All enjoy a good-sized pool, café and quiet gardens.

Pondok Elsa (☎ 41186; Gang Binaria; r 50,000-120,000Rp; ❄) This two-storey heavily ornate building has seven clean, pleasant rooms; three with air-con and hot water.

Taman Lily's (☎ 41307; gervanleenen@hotmail.com; Jl Ketapang; r from 75,000Rp) This has a friendly atmosphere and six good-value bungalow-style rooms on a grassy, walled compound.

Puri Bali Hotel (☎ 41485; www.puribalilovina.com; Jl Ketapang; r 80,000-180,000Rp; ❄ 🏊) The pool area is very attractive, with mature, lush plantings. The better rooms, with hot water and air-con, are simple but comfortable.

Rini Hotel (☎ /fax 41386; rinihotel@telkom.net; Jl Ketapang; r 80,000-300,000Rp; ❄ 🏊) This tidy 30-room place has a large saltwater pool. Cheaper rooms are basic but the more expensive ones are huge, with air-con and hot water. A new grand entrance welcomes the many loyal customers.

West of Kalibukbuk

Parma Hotel (☎ 41555; Jl Raya Lovina; r 30,000-50,000Rp) Maintenance here is as relaxed as the staff but the six bungalow-style rooms are clean and reasonably well protected from traffic noise. Rooms that face the sandy beachfront are great value.

Hotel Purnama (☎ 41043; Jl Raya Lovina; s/d 40,000/50,000Rp) One of the best deals on this stretch has seven clean rooms with cold water. The beach is a two-minute walk away.

Lovina Beach Hotel (☎ 41005; www.lovinabeachhotel .com; Jl Raya Lovina; r 75,000-250,000Rp, bungalows 250,000Rp; ☒ ☻) Clean rooms in heavily detailed Balinese bungalows are set in pleasant grounds on the beach. Better ones come with hot water; private bungalows have air-con and views.

Billibo Beach Cottages (☎ 41355; Jl Raya Lovina; r 125,000-200,000Rp; ☒) Located near one of the best spots for snorkelling, the cottages here are clean and comfortable with hot water and good access to the beach.

MIDRANGE
Anturan

Bali Taman Beach Resort (☎ 41126; www.indo.com /hotels/bali_taman; Jl Raya Lovina; r US$35-85; ☒ ☻) Facing the busy road, but extending down to the beach, the Bali Taman has 30 rooms that vary greatly. The best ones are bungalows with ocean views and satellite TV. The pool faces the ocean and is surrounded by leafy gardens. There's also a small spa.

Anturan to Kalibukbuk

This quiet area has several midrange choices on little parallel lanes running to the beach.

Lupa-Lupa Lovina Cottages (☎ 41698; Jl Pantai; r US$15-30) The name of the lane here is Beach Rd and that says it. There are two rooms in a two-storey bungalow and another large unit on its own. The water is just a few metres from your door. There's a quiet café nearby.

Hotel Banyualit (☎ 41789; www.banyualit.com; Jl Pan- tai Banyualit; r 150,000-450,000Rp; ☒ ☻) Back from the beach, the Banyualit has a lush garden of snaking vines, flowers, statues and a large pool. The 22 rooms offer great choice and better ones come with satellite TV and other amenities. There are also a couple of fan-only economy rooms.

Hotel Aneka Lovina (☎ 41121; www.anekahotels .com; Jl Raya Lovina; s/d US$45/50, villa US$60/70; ☒ ☻) On a long, narrow site extending all the way to the beach, the Aneka is a enjoyable place.

The 24 rooms and 35 bungalow-style villas have minibars and modern bathrooms. The grounds are spacious and units are well sepa- rated. The large pool area has good views.

Kalibukbuk

Nirwana Seaside Cottages (☎ 41288; www.nirwana seaside.com; bungalows 100,000-125,000Rp, deluxe r 210,000- 300,000Rp; ☒ ☻) On large and lovely beach- front grounds, the 58-unit Nirwana sprawls over a large site. The bungalows are a bit funky and have hot water. Those with beach views are a great deal. A newer wing has hotel-style air-con rooms with satellite TV.

Bayu Kartika (☎ 41219; www.bayukartikaresort.com; Jl Ketepang; r 100,000-300,000Rp; ☒ ☻) There is a range of 27 light and airy rooms here. The best ones have air-con and ocean or pool views. The sprawling grounds feature a small creek.

Sea Breeze Cabins (☎ 41138; r US$15, bungalows US$35-40; ☒ ☻) An excellent choice in the heart of Kalibukbuk, off Jl Bina Ria, the Sea Breeze has three appealing bungalows right on the beach, some with sensational views from their verandas. The two rooms have cold water.

Bali Lovina Beach Cottages (☎ 41285; www.bali lovinahotel.com; Jl Raya Lovina; r US$25-35; ☒ ☻) The 26 rooms here are in mixed two-storey and bungalow-style units. As always, the best ones face the beach. The pool has an iconic dolphin fountain and parts are shaded by large trees.

Rambutan Beach Cottages (☎ 41388; www.rambutan .org; Jl Ketepang; r 300,000-500,000Rp; ☒ ☻) The hotel, on a large area of land, features two swimming pools and charming gardens. The 33 rooms and villas are tasteful with lashings of Balinese style. There are a few cold-water economy rooms for 100,000Rp. Diversions include a playground for kids and darts for adults.

West of Kalibukbuk

Aditya Bungalows (☎ 41059; www.adityalovina.com; r 300,000-600,000Rp; ☒ ☻) There are 65 rooms at this big place on a sandy beach. The best ones have views of the ocean and all have a good range of amenities and attractive bathrooms. The large pool vies with the ocean for your affections.

Nugraha Lovina (☎ 41601; Jl Raya Lovina; r 450,000- 500,000Rp; ☒ ☻) This modern oceanfront hotel features lashings of Balinese detailing inside and out. The rooms have showers and either patios or balconies facing the ocean. It's a pleasant location at the west edge of the Lovina strip.

TOP END

Singaraja to Anturan

Puri Bagus (☎ 21430; www.lovina.puribagus.net; villa US$95-155;) Well off the main road, Puri Bagus has 40 private villas set on immaculate grounds along a stone beach. The stylish units have large bathrooms with outdoor showers and nice verandas for enjoying the tropical views and thatched roofs. The pool is large and free-form and the hotel is surrounded by rice paddies.

Anturan to Kalibukbuk

Sunari (☎ 41775; www.sunari.com; r US$85-130, villas US$240-360;) Off Jl Raya Lovina, the imposing entrance to this place leads to a large beachfront resort with redecorated rooms and good services. Various villas come with private plunge pools, whirlpools and ocean views. Grounds are verdant with banana trees and a profusion of posies.

South of Lovina

Damai Lovina Villas (☎ 41008; www.damai.com; villa from US$150;) There are views across Lovina at this boutique hotel renowned for its organic cuisine. It has eight luxury bungalows furnished with beautiful fabrics and antiques. The pool seemingly spills onto a landscape of peanut fields, rice paddies and coconut palms. The restaurant, on a raised pavilion fringed by cerise bougainvillea, focuses on fusion cuisine. Call for transport, or at the main junction in Kalibukbuk, go south on Jl Damai and follow the road for about 3km.

Eating & Drinking

Just about every hotel has a café or restaurant. Close to the centre of Lovina you can find several places that go beyond the usual travellers' establishment. Most places are good for just a drink and some have sunset happy hours.

ANTURAN

Warung Bamboo (dishes 7000-30,000Rp) A small, open-fronted place, Bamboo fronts a lively section of beach; watch fishers prepping boats, travellers making out (or planning to…) etc. One of several here, it serves classic fare and cheap beer. To find it, walk east along the beach from the end of Jl Kubu Gembong.

ANTURAN TO KALIBUKBUK

Mr Dolphin (☎ 0813-3848 7612; Jl Banyualit; dishes 5000-10,000Rp) Right on the beach, the fresh juices are good at this place, which, not surprisingly given the name, is a hang-out for dolphin tour skippers.

Warung Bias (☎ 411692; Jl Pantai Banyualit; dishes 10,000-40,000Rp; 4.30-9pm) Worth a trip, Bias serves homemade baked goods, as well as Indian curries, European dishes like wiener schnitzel, pastas and pizzas. It's in a simple open-air setting surrounded by a carp pond.

Spunky's (☎ 41134; Jl Pantai; dishes 20,000-50,000Rp; 11am-4pm) A real comer in the lunch department, Spunky's serves Indo classics right on the beach. Take a dip, take a drink.

KALIBUKBUK

This is ground zero for nightlife. There's a good range of restaurants, beachside cafés, bars where you can get a burger and maybe hear music or fun places that defy description.

Warung Minang (☎ 0812 393 0792; Jl Raya Lovina; dishes 6000-8000Rp) This stylish Pedang-style café is a find. Choose from lots of fresh dishes on display and savour the local art on the walls.

Kantin (☎ 0812 460 7791; Jl Raya Lovina; dishes 6000-12,000Rp; 11am-2am) Funky open-air place where you can watch traffic by day and groove to acoustic guitar by night. There's a long drinks list, fresh juices and coffee and a few local snacks.

Kakatua Bar & Restaurant (☎ 41344; Jl Bina Ria; dishes 7000-35,000Rp) A squawking sulphur-crested cockatoo at the front of the restaurant beckons you in (or tells you to get lost; who speaks cockatoo after all?). The menu merges Mexican, Thai, Indian and Balinese (and let's not forget pizza) – all of which is decent.

Khi Khi Restaurant (☎ 41548; dishes 8000-100,000Rp) Well off Jl Raya Lovina, this barn of a place is filled with fishy aromas. It specialises in Chinese food and grilled seafood, including lobster. It's always popular.

Zigiz (Jl Bina Ria; snacks from 10,000Rp; 6pm-1am) This small place has walls covered in artwork and live music some nights.

Tiki Lounge & Restaurant (☎ 41191; Jl Raya Lovina; dishes 10,000-20,000Rp) The name lets you know this place takes its tropical motif seriously, right down to the bamboo detailing everywhere. The long Indonesian menu has pictures to help you choose, or you may just drop by for a beer.

Barcelona Bar & Restaurant (☎ 41894; Jl Ketapang; dishes 10,000-35,000Rp) This restaurant has a shady garden area out the back. The well-prepared food includes *sate pelecing* (fish satay with Balinese spices) and *pepesan babi guling* (suckling pig slices wrapped in banana leaf).

Poco Evolution Bar (☎ 41535; Jl Bina Ria; dishes 12,000-25,000Rp; ⏰ 11am-1am) At various times movies are shown and cover bands perform at this popular bar-café. Classic travellers' fare is served.

Sea Breeze Café (☎ 41138; dishes 12,000-45,000Rp) Right by the beach off Jl Bina Ria and blessed with sweeping views, this cafe has a range of Indonesian and Western dishes and good breakfasts. It's a good spot for sunset drinks.

Tropis Club (☎ 42090; Jl Ketepang; dishes 15,000-30,000Rp) The long menu at this beachside place includes wood-fired pizza which may not transport you to Italy, but may get you as far as Oman. It's an attractive place with a soaring roof and good sunset views.

Jasmine Kitchen (☎ 41565; Gang Binaria; dishes 15,000-30,000Rp) Enjoy excellent Thai fare in this elegant two-level restaurant. The menu is long and authentic and the help gracious. While soft jazz plays, try the homemade ice cream for dessert.

WEST OF KALIBUKBUK

Café Spice (☎ 41509; dishes 24,000-45,000Rp) Part of Spice Dive, this delightful beachside place is right at the western end of the beach path. The walls are covered in artwork and the menu is interesting and good. Besides the dive vibe you can sometimes hear the squeals of local kids learning English at the shop's free school upstairs.

Kwizien (☎ 42031; Jl Raya Lovina; dishes 24,000-75,000Rp; ⏰ 11am-midnight) The big news in Lovina dining is this excellent place run by the folks behind the much-lauded Café des Artistes in Ubud (p196). The location back from the road has a relaxed elegance, which sets the mood for a perusal of the long wine list (bottles from 120,000Rp). Grilled seafood tops the menu highlighted by creative Indonesian fare. The tuna is a treat.

SOUTH OF LOVINA

Damai Lovina Villas (☎ 41008; www.damai.com; lunch US$4-10, 5-course dinner US$40) Enjoy the renowned restaurant at this boutique hotel (opposite).

Entertainment

Some of the joints on Jl Bina Raya have live music.

Yayasan Budaya Den Bukit Lovina (Lovina Culture Foundation; ☎ 41293; Jl Raya Lovina) Organises Kecak dances on Tuesday nights from good local troupes as well as Legong and bull races (see p278) other days.

Shopping

Shops on the main streets of Kalibukbuk sell a range of souvenirs, sundries and groceries.

Benny Tantra's T-Shirts (Jl Raya Lovina) For something different, check out the amusing range of T-shirts and postcards, portraying to an uncanny degree the life of a tourist in Lovina.

Getting There & Away

BUS & BEMO

To reach Lovina from South Bali by public transport, you'll need to change in Singaraja (see p257). Regular blue bemo go from Singaraja's Banyuasri terminal to Kalibukbuk (about 6000Rp) – you can flag them down anywhere on the main road.

If you are coming by long-distance bus from the west you can ask to be dropped off anywhere along the main road.

TOURIST SHUTTLE BUS

Perama buses stop at its office, in front of **Hotel Perama** (☎ 41161) on Jl Raya Lovina in Anturan. Passengers are then ferried to other points on the Lovina strip (5000Rp).

Destination	Fare
Candidasa	100,000Rp
Kuta	70,000Rp
Padangbai	100,000Rp
Sanur	70,000Rp
Ubud	30,000Rp

Getting Around

The Lovina strip is *very* spread out, but you can easily travel back and forth on bemo (2000Rp). Bikes are easily rented around town for about 30,000Rp per day.

WEST OF LOVINA

The main road west of Lovina passes many interesting attractions and follows the mostly undeveloped coast, where a few resorts and diving centres take advantage of the secluded beaches and coral reefs. The road continues to the Taman Nasional Bali Barat (p280) and the port of Gilimanuk (p283).

Air Terjun Singsing

About 5km west of Kalibukbuk, a sign points to **Air Terjun Singsing** (Daybreak Waterfall).

About 1km from the main road, there is a warung (food stall) on the left and a car park on the right. Walk past the warung and along the path for about 200m to the lower falls. The waterfall is not huge, but the pool underneath is ideal for swimming. The water isn't crystal clear, but it's cooler than the sea and very refreshing.

Clamber further up the hill to another waterfall, **Singsing Dua**, which is slightly bigger and has a mud bath which is supposedly good for the skin (maybe if you're a worm?). This one also cascades into a deep swimming pool.

The area is thick with tropical forest and makes a nice day trip from Lovina. The falls are more spectacular in the wet season, and may be just a trickle in the dry season.

Brahma Vihara Arama

Bali's single Buddhist monastery, only vaguely Buddhist in appearance, with colourful decorations, a bright orange roof and statues of Buddha, has very Balinese decorative carvings and door guardians. It is quite a handsome structure in a commanding location, with views that reach down into the valley and across the rice fields to the sea. You should wear long pants or a sarong (which can be hired for a small donation; see the boxed text, p42). The monastery does not advertise any regular courses or programmes, but visitors are more than welcome to meditate in special rooms.

The temple is 3.3km off the main road – take the obvious turn-off in Dencarik. If you don't have your own transport, arrange it with an *ojek* (motorcycle) driver at the turn-off (10,000Rp). The road continues past the monastery, winding further up into the hills to Pedewa, a Bali Aga village.

Air Panas Banjar

☎ 0362

Not far from Brahma Vihara Arama, these **hot springs** (adult/child 4100/2000Rp, parking 1000Rp; 🕑 8am-6pm) percolate amid lush tropical plants. You can relax here for a few hours and have lunch at the restaurant, or even stay the night.

Eight fierce-faced carved stone *naga* pour water from a natural hot spring into the first bath, which then overflows (via the mouths of five more *naga*), into a second, larger pool. In a third pool, water pours from 3m-high spouts to give you a pummelling massage. The water is slightly sulphurous and pleasantly hot, so you might enjoy it more in the morning or the evening than in the heat of the Balinese day. You must wear a swimsuit and you shouldn't use soap in the pools, but you can do so under an adjacent outdoor shower.

In a verdant setting on a hillside very close to the baths, the rooms at **Pondok Wisata Grya Sari** (☎ 92903; fax 92966; r 90,000-150,000Rp, ste 200,000Rp) are clean and have outdoor bathrooms. Treks into the surrounding densely grown countryside can be organised from here.

Overlooking the baths, **Restoran Komala Tirta** (dishes 8000-16,000Rp) has the usual Indonesian menu and an unpretentious mood.

It's only about 3km from the monastery to the hot springs if you take the short cut – go down to Banjar Tega, turn left in the centre of the village and follow the small road west, then south to Banjar village. From there it's a short distance uphill before you see the 'Air Panas 1km' sign on the left (on the corner by the police station). From the bemo stop on the main road to the hot springs you can take an *ojek;* going back is a 2.4km downhill stroll.

Seririt

This town is a junction for roads that run south over the mountains to Munduk and the central mountains (p252) or to Papuan and West Bali (see the boxed text, p277). These are very scenic drives.

The road continuing west along the coast towards Gilimanuk is in good shape. In Seririt, there's a Bank BCA ATM at the Lovina end of town. There are many warung in the market area, just north of the bemo stop and you can find petrol stations on the main road. Temple offering stalls here are bold visions of orange flowers.

Celukanbawang

Celukanbawang is the main cargo port for North Bali, and has a large wharf. Bugis schooners – the magnificent sailing ships that take their name from the seafaring Bugis people of Sulawesi – can sometimes be seen anchoring here.

Pulaki

Pulaki is famous for its many grape vines and for **Pura Pulaki**, a coastal temple that was completely rebuilt in the early 1980s, and is home to a large troop of monkeys.

A few hundred metres east of the temple, a well-signposted 3km paved road leads to **Pura Melanting**. This temple has a dramatic setting in the foothills, and is gloriously devoid of tourists and hawkers. It is dedicated to good fortune in business. A donation is expected as entry to the complex, although you're not permitted in the main worship area. Look for the dragon statue with the lotus blossom on its back near the entrance.

PEMUTERAN

☎ 0362

This resort enclave on the far northwest corner of Bali is something of an oasis among little else. The once impoverished villagers have realized that healthy reefs and sea life draw visitors, so they've found relative prosperity as good stewards to the local environment.

This is the place to come for a real beach getaway. Most people do some diving or snorkelling while here.

Sights & Activities

The extensive coral reefs are about 3km offshore. Coral that's closer in is being restored as part of a unique project (see the boxed text, below). Diving and snorkelling on the local reefs is universally popular. Many people also do one or the other at the fabled dive sites at Pulau Menjangan to the west (p282).

Pemuteran is home to the Reef Seen Turtle Project, run by the Australian-owned **Reef Seen Aquatics** (☎ 93001; www.reefseen.com). Turtle eggs and small turtles purchased from locals are looked after here until they're ready for ocean release. More than 6000 turtles have been released since 1994. You can visit the small hatchery and see Boomer, the turtle who wouldn't leave, and make a donation to sponsor and release a tiny turtle. It's just off the main road east of Pondok Sari.

Reef Seen also offers diving, boat cruises and horse riding. A PADI introductory dive costs US$60 and dives at Pemuteran/Pulau Menjangan are US$60/70 for two dives. Sunset and sunrise cruises and glass-bottomed boat trips (per person 160,000Rp) are offered. Horse-riding treks pass through the local villages and beaches (290,000Rp for two hours). Simple accommodation is available (p270).

Easy Divers (☎ 94736; www.easy-divers.eu) comes well recommended and offers a worthwhile five-day PADI open-water course for US$350. Dive trips to Tulamben and Menjangan cost US$65.

Pemuteran's hotels all have their own dive operations.

WANT A NEW REEF? CHARGE IT!

Pemuteran is set among a fairly arid part of Bali where people have always had a hard-scrabble existence. In the early 1990s, tourism development began to take advantage of the excellent diving in the area.

Locals who'd previously been scrambling to grow or catch something to eat began getting language and other training to welcome people to what would become a slightly upscale collection of resorts.

But there was one big problem: the reefs that were meant to bring people in had their clocks fast running out. Dynamite and cyanide fishing was rampant but after a few fits and starts, the community managed to control this. Then came the late 1990s and the El Niño warming of the water, which bleached and damaged large parts of the reef.

A group of local hotel and dive-shop owners and community leaders hit upon a novel solution: charge a new reef! Not with plastic, of course, but with electricity. The idea had already been floated by scientists internationally, but Pemuteran was the first place to implement it on a wide – and hugely successful – scale.

Using local materials, the community built dozens of large metal cages which were placed out among the threatened reef. Then they were literally hooked to *very* low-wattage generators on land (you can see the cables running ashore near the Taman Sari Bali Cottages). What had been a theory proved a reality. The low current stimulated limestone formation on the cages which in turn quickly grew new coral. All told, Pemuteran's small bay is getting new coral at five to six times the rate it would take to grow naturally.

The results are win-win all around. Locals and visitors are happy and so are the reefs.

For much more on Pemuteran's reef project follow the links at www.balitamansari.com.

Sleeping & Eating

Pemuteran is an unpretentious and relaxed place to stay with many midrange and top-end choices. There are several small warung along the main drag, otherwise all the hotels have good, mostly modestly-priced, restaurants.

Many of the hotels are located on a small bay with a semicircle of beach that's good for swimming.

Jubawa Home Stay (☎ 94745; r 150,000-200,000Rp;) Not far from the Matahari on the south side of the road, this cheery place is a good budget choice. The best rooms have hot water and air-con and guests have free internet access. The café serves Balinese and Thai food and there is a long list of cocktails. It's on the mountain side of the road.

Reef Seen (☎ 93001; www.reefseen.com; r 200,000-275,000Rp;) Five new, solid Balinese-style brick bungalows join two older ones. All have open-air bathrooms, one has air-con. This is a well-regarded dive centre (see p269) and it's located on the small bay.

Taman Sari Bali Cottages (☎ 288096; www.balitamansari.com; bungalows US$35-150;) Thirty-one rooms are set in gorgeous bungalows (some quite grand) which feature intricate carvings and other traditional artwork. The open-air bathrooms are delightful places for that wake-up shower. It's located on a long stretch of quiet beach on the small bay. It's also part of the reef restoration project (see the boxed text, p269).

Pondok Sari (☎ 92337; www.pondoksari.com; r US$38-45;) There are pleasant bungalows here, on the small bay, with traditional rooms and lovely flower-filled open-air bathrooms. The restaurant features Western and Indo classics.

Taman Selini Beach Bungalows (☎ 94746; www.tamanselini.com; r US$55-85;) The 11 bungalows here have quaint thatched roofs that lure you in from the road. Rooms, which open onto a small garden area, have four-poster beds and big outdoor bathrooms. The restaurant, Caffe Selini, is a picturesque, relaxed spot featuring Indonesian and Mediterranean cuisine. It's on the small bay.

Matahari Beach Resort & Spa (☎ 92312; www.matahari-beach-resort.com; r US$150-400;) One of Bali's best hotels, the Matahari is an elegant place in an isolated location on the eastern outskirts of Pemuteran. Beautiful and traditionally furnished bungalows take their design cues from Balinese family compounds and are set in attractive gardens. The large pool overlooks a black-sand beach. Perhaps the best part of the resort however is the spa, which is like a grand water palace and is open to nonguests.

Menjangan Resort (☎ 94700; www.menjangan.net; Monsoon Forest Resort r US$150-350, Cliff Villas US$400-950;) There are two separate properties here: the Monsoon Forest Resort and Cliff Villas. The former is set in slightly dry forest and features rustic buildings around a pool. The latter has posh stylish rooms perched right above an ocean cove. Service at both places is quite good. Activities include a full range of water sports as well as horse riding. The resort is right at the west end of North Bali.

Getting There & Away

Pemuteran is served by any of the buses and bemo on the Gilimanuk–Lovina run. Labuhan Lalang (p283) and Taman Nasional Bali Barat are 12km west.

West Bali

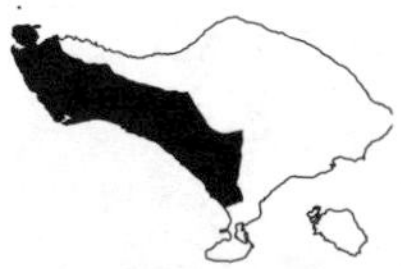

West Bali is the sinuous bit of the island that runs in the shadow of the central string of volcanoes. It is the least densely populated part of the island; much of the land is given over to agriculture.

Many visitors hurtle through the region on their way to or from Java or to the incredible dive locations in the Taman Nasional Bali Barat (West Bali National Park). This too is a shame as West Bali has deep cultural significance. Near the wild beaches north of Seminyak, Pura Tanah Lot is hugely popular for its clichéd role as a postcard-perfect temple at the sea. Yet journey further west and you find the wonderful temple Pura Rambut Siwi, a vision in limestone that honours the place where Nirartha landed in the 16th century. (He was rather important; he shaped the Balinese faith.)

Make your own discoveries all along the coast. Untouched beaches uncurl like a ribbon from horizon to horizon. Here and there surfers have staked their claims, but follow almost any road to the sea and you'll find your own private sandy refuge. You'll know from the waves that you can't swim but you can soak up the wild ambience while you gaze out into the distance.

In fact, take just about any road at random in West Bali and see what you find. From incredible rice terraces to tropical forest dropping fruit over the road, you'll luxuriate in green.

HIGHLIGHTS

- Discovering the serene sea temple of **Pura Rambut Siwi** (p278)
- Viewing the rice terraces at **Pupuan** (p277)
- Exploring Bali's national park, **Taman Nasional Bali Barat** (p280), by foot or boat
- Diving at the spectacular **Pulau Menjangan** (p282)
- Driving through a huge acacia tree near **Manggissari** (p277)

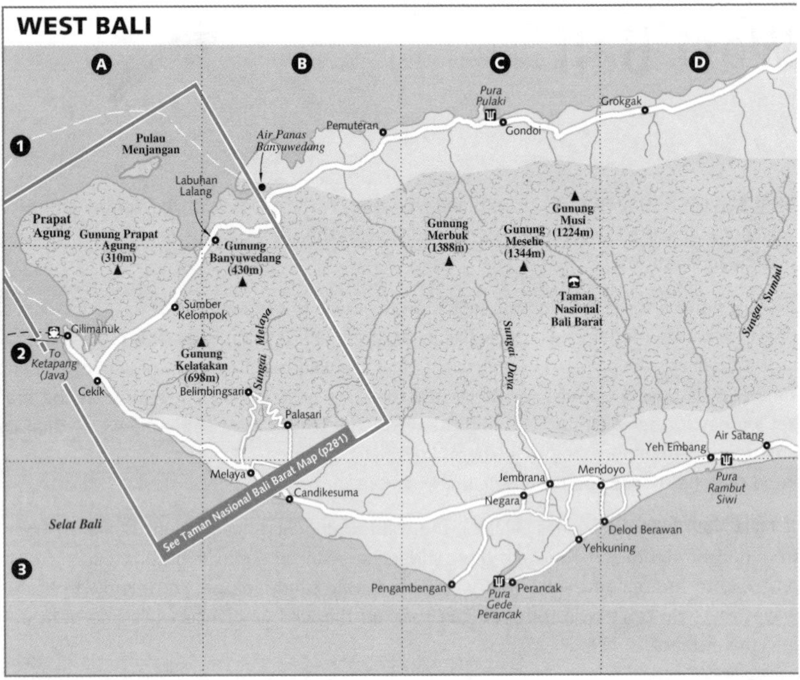

PURA TANAH LOT

☎ 0361

The subject of a zillion pixels, **Pura Tanah Lot** (adult/child 3300/1800Rp, car park 1500Rp) is the most popular and most photographed temple in Bali. It's an obligatory stop on many tours from South Bali, very commercialised, and especially crowded at sunset. It has all the authenticity of a stage set – even the tower of rock that the temple sits upon is an artful reconstruction (the entire structure was crumbling). Over one-third of the rock you see is artificial.

For the Balinese, Pura Tanah Lot is one of the most important and venerated sea temples. Like Pura Luhur Ulu Watu, at the tip of the southern Bukit Peninsula, and Pura Rambut Siwi to the west, it is closely associated with the Majapahit priest, Nirartha. It's said that each of the 'sea temples' was intended to be within sight of the next, so they formed a chain along Bali's southwestern coast – from Pura Tanah Lot you can usually see the clifftop site of Pura Ulu Watu far to the south, and the long sweep of sea shore west to Perancak, near Negara.

But at Tanah Lot itself you may just see from one vendor to the next. To reach the temple, a walkway runs through a sort of carnival alley with dozens of souvenir shops down to the sea. To ease the task of making purchases, there is an ATM.

To visit the temple you should pick the correct time – everybody shows up for sunset and the mobs obliterate any spiritual feeling the place has. If you visit before noon, crowds are few and the vendors are all but asleep.

You can walk over to the temple itself at low tide, but non-Balinese people are not allowed to enter. One other thing: local legend has it that if you bring a partner to Tanah Lot before marriage, you will end up as split as the temple. Let that be a warning – or an inducement.

Sleeping & Eating

If you want to join the sunset spectacle and also avoid traffic afterwards, you can stay near Tanah Lot. Cheap warung (food stalls) line the car park, and more expensive restaurants are inside the grounds and on the clifftops facing the temple.

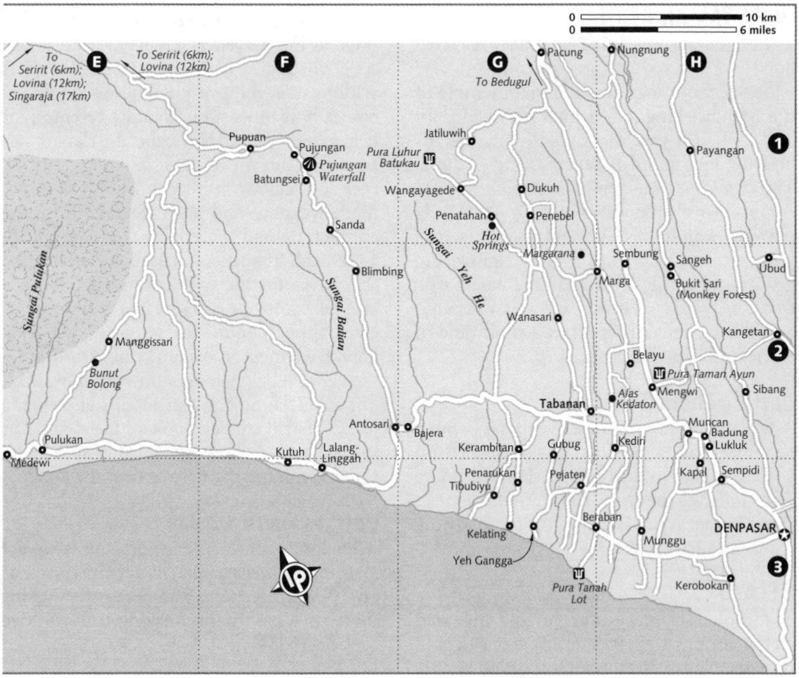

Dewi Sinta Restaurant & Villa (☎ 812933; www.indo.com/hotels/dewisinta; r US$18-40;) Off a souvenir-shop gang, not far from the ticket office lies this midrange hotel. The 27 rooms are comfortable and modern. Some have views across the pool and beyond to rice fields, Others see a different green: the nearby golf course. The restaurant offers buffet lunches, with meals ranging from 18,000Rp to 60,000Rp.

Le Meridien Nirwana Golf Spa & Resort (☎ 815900; www.starwoodhotels.com; r from US$120;) Occupying a swathe of black-sand beach, this large resort has 278 luxurious rooms and an 18-hole golf course. Traditional stone designs are used throughout and the resort is attractive. There's a view of Tanah Lot, albeit from a disrespectful viewpoint (it's set higher than the temple).

Getting There & Away

Coming from South Bali with your own transport, take the coastal road west from Kerobokan, north of Seminyak, and follow the signs or the traffic. From other parts of Bali, turn off the Denpasar–Gilimanuk road near Kediri and follow the signs. During the pre- and postsunset rush, traffic is predictably bad.

By bemo (small minibus), go from Denpasar's Ubung terminal to Tanah Lot (6000Rp) via Kediri, noting that bemo stop running by nightfall. Alternatively, take an organised tour which includes many other sights as well.

KAPAL

About 10km north of Denpasar, Kapal is the garden feature and temple doo-dad centre of Bali. If you need a polychromatic tiger or other decorative critter rendered in colours not found in nature, then this your place! (Although shipping might be a bitch.) This is on the main road to the west, so it might be worth getting out of traffic just to walk with the animals.

The most important temple in the area is **Pura Sadat**. It was possibly built in the 12th century, then damaged in an earthquake early in the 20th century and subsequently restored after WWII.

Throughout this part of Bali you will see peanuts and corn growing in rotation with rice. Bananas and other fruits grow wild alongside the roads.

PURA TAMAN AYUN

The huge state temple of **Pura Taman Ayun** (adult/child 4100/2100Rp; 8am-6pm), surrounded by a wide, elegant moat, was the main temple of the Mengwi kingdom, which survived until 1891, when it was conquered by the neighbouring kingdoms of Tabanan and Badung. The large, spacious temple was built in 1634 and extensively renovated in 1937. It's a lovely place to wander around and its size means you can get away from rapidly sightseeing group-tour hordes ('Back on the bus!'). The first courtyard is a large, open, grassy expanse and the inner courtyard has a multitude of *meru* (multiroofed shrines).

Getting There & Away

Any bemo running between Denpasar (Ubung terminal) and Bedugul or Singaraja can drop you off at the roundabout in Mengwi, where signs indicate the road (250m) to the temple. Pura Taman Ayun is a stop-off on many organised tourist tours.

BELAYU

Traditional *songket* (silver- or gold-threaded cloth) sarongs are intricately woven with gold threads. These are for ceremonial use only and not for everyday wear. You'll find them in the small village of Belayu (or Blayu), 3km north of Mengwi.

To get there, take any bemo or bus between Denpasar (Ubung terminal) and Bedugul or Singaraja, get off at the turn-off to Belayu and walk about 1km west; alternatively bemo go directly from Ubung terminal to Belayu (4000Rp).

MARGA

Between the walls of traditional family compounds in Marga, there are some beautifully shaded roads – but this town wasn't always so peaceful. On 20 November 1946, a much larger and better-armed Dutch force, fighting to regain Bali as a colony after the departure of the Japanese, surrounded a force of 96 independence fighters. The outcome was similar to the *puputan* (warrior's fight to the death) of 40 years earlier – Ngurah Rai (later of airport-name fame), who lead the resistance against the Dutch, and every one of his men was killed. There was, however, one important difference – this time the Dutch suffered heavy casualties as well, and this may have helped weaken their resolve to hang onto the rebellious colony.

The independence struggle is commemorated at the **Margarana** (admission 3000Rp; 9am-5pm), northwest of Marga village. Tourists seldom visit, but every Balinese schoolchild comes here at least once, and a ceremony is held annually on 20 November. In a large compound stands a 17m-high pillar, and nearby there's a **museum**, with a few photos, homemade weapons and other artefacts from the conflict. Behind is a smaller compound with 1372 small stone memorials to those who gave their lives for the cause of independence – they're headstone markers in a military cemetery, though bodies are not actually buried here. Each memorial has a symbol indicating the hero's religion, mostly the Hindu swastika, but also Islamic crescent moons and even a few Christian crosses. Look for the memorials to 11 Japanese who stayed on after WWII and fought with the Balinese against the Dutch.

Getting There & Away

Even with your own transport it's easy to get lost finding Marga and the memorial, so, as always, ask directions. You can easily combine this with a tour of the amazing Jatiluwih rice terraces (p254).

SANGEH

If you love monkeys, you'll love the 14-hectare monkey forest of **Bukit Sari**. But if you are put off by the thieving, copulating little buggers, than perhaps you should give it a miss. Actually we're among the former and the monkeys here are all rather workmanlike: they eat three squares a day (breakfast is bananas, lunch is cassava and dinner is rice, a very Balinese diet in fact) and when tourists leave they relax after a day of high-jinks ('Hey did you see the hat I stole off that bald guy?').

Also noteworthy, but not as exciting, are a rare grove of nutmeg trees in the monkey forest and a **temple**, Pura Bukit Sari, with an interesting old Garuda (mythical man-bird creature) statue. This place is definitely touristy, but the forest is cool, green and shady. The souvenir sellers are restricted to certain areas and are easy to avoid.

Getting There & Away

You can reach Sangeh and Bukit Sari by any bemo heading to Plaga from Wangaya terminal in Denpasar (6000Rp). Most people visit on an organised tour or drive themselves; it's about 20km north of Denpasar.

TABANAN

☎ 0361

A renowned centre for dancing and gamelan (traditional Balinese orchestra) playing, Tabanan, like most regional capitals in Bali, is a large, well-organised place. Mario, the renowned dancer of the prewar period, hailed from Tabanan. His greatest achievement was to perfect the Kebyar dance. He is featured in Miguel Covarrubias' classic book, *Island of Bali*. Nowadays it's hard for visitors to find performances here on a regular basis but you can enjoy the vibrant rice fields and related museum.

Orientation & Information

The main road thankfully bypasses the centre, where you'll find ATMs, wartel (public telephone office) with internet access, a hospital, a **police station** (☎ 91210) and a post office in Tabanan. The road to Pura Luhur Batukau and the rice terraces of Jaliluwih (see p254) heads north from the centre.

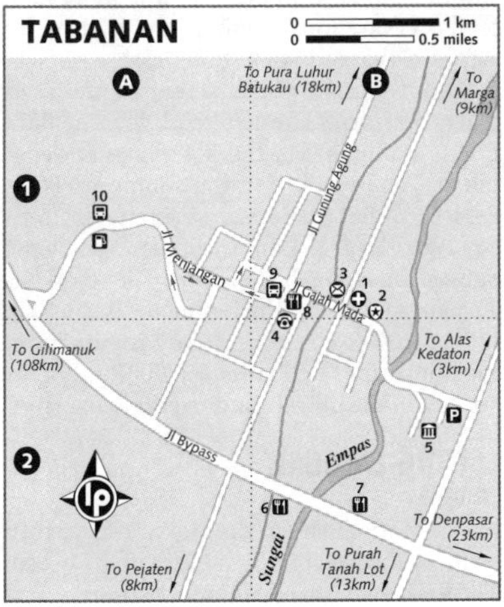

INFORMATION
- Hospital 1 B1
- Police Station 2 B1
- Post Office 3 B1
- Wartel & Internet 4 B2

SIGHTS & ACTIVITIES
- Mandala Mathika Subak 5 B2

EATING
- Babi Guling Stall 6 B2
- Hardy's 7 B2
- Market 8 B1

TRANSPORT
- Bemo Terminal 9 B1
- Bus Terminal 10 A1

Sights

Playing a critical role in rural Bali life, the *subak* is a village association that deals with water, water rights and irrigation. The **Mandala Mathika Subak** (☎ 810315; Jl Raya Kediri; admission 5000Rp; 7am-4.30pm) is quite a large complex devoted to Tabanan's *subak* organisations. Within this is the somewhat forlorn **Subak Museum** with displays about the irrigation and cultivation of rice, and the intricate social systems that govern it.

With water passing through many, many scores of rice fields before it drains away for good, there is always the chance that growers near the source would be water-rich while those at the bottom would be selling carved wooden critters at Tanah Lot. Regulating a system that apportions a fair share to everyone is a model of mutual cooperation and an insight into the Balinese character. (One of the strategies used is to put the last guy on the water channel in control.)

Exhibits are housed in a large building with water coursing by right out front. The genial staffers will turn on lights so you can see the displays, many of which are decently labelled.

Eating

There are plenty of basic warung in the town centre as well as at the bustling regional market; a night market sets up on the south side.

Babi Guling Stall (dishes 5000-10,000Rp; 7am-7pm) Out on the main road, this stall has new batches of fresh-roasted seasoned young pork throughout the day. It's a treat Balinese love.

Hardy's (☎ 819850) Also on the main road, mundane, yet practical, you can stock up on supplies at this supermarket if you're heading to one of the surf sites in the west.

Getting There & Away

All bemo and buses between Denpasar (Ubung terminal) and Gilimanuk stop at the terminal at the western end of Tabanan (6000Rp). The bemo terminal in the town centre only has transport to nearby villages. If you're driving, note that most main streets are one way, with traffic moving in a clockwise direction around the central blocks.

SOUTH OF TABANAN

Driving in the southern part of Tabanan district takes you though many charming villages and past a lot of vigorously growing rice.

Just south of Tabanan, **Kediri** has Pasar Hewan, one of Bali's busiest cattle markets. About 10km south of Tabanan is **Pejaten**, a centre for the production of traditional pottery, including elaborate ornamental roof tiles. Porcelain clay objects, which are made purely for decorative use, can be seen in a few workshops in the village. Check out the small showroom of **CV Keramik Pejaten** (☎ 831997), which is a prominent local producer. The trademark pale-green pieces are lovely and when you see the prices, you'll at least buy a frog.

A little west of Tabanan, a road goes 8km south via Gubug to the secluded coast at **Yeh Gangga**, where there's some good accommodation choices and **Island Horse** (☎ 0361-730218; www.baliislandhorse.com; rides from US$50), which offers horse rides along the long flat beach.

The next road west from Tabanan turns down to the coast via **Kerambitan**, a village noted for its beautiful old buildings (including two 17th-century palaces); a tradition of *wayang*-style painting; and its own styles of music and dance, especially *tektekan*, a ceremonial procession.

South of Kerambitan, you will pass through **Penarukan**, known for its stone- and woodcarvers, and also its dancers. Continue to the coast, where you'll find the beach at **Kelating** wide, black and usually deserted.

About 4km from southern Kerambitan is **Tibubiyu**. For a gorgeous drive through huge bamboo, fruit trees, rice paddies and more, take the scenic road northwest from Kerambitan to the main road.

Sleeping

Bali Wisata Bungalows (☎ 0361-7443561; www.baliwisatabungalows.com; Yeh Gangga; bungalows 180,000-350,000Rp;) West of Tabanan and on the coast at Yeh Gangga, this attractive accommodation has excellent views in a superb setting on 15km of black-sand beach. The ocean-view rooms are definitely worth it.

Puri Anyar Kerambitan (☎ 0361-812668; wiryana2000@yahoo.com; r from 250,000Rp) One of Kerambitan's two palaces accepts guest bookings in spacious, traditional accommodation in the lively and welcoming palace compound. The prince lives in the palace and you can watch him at work on paintings. The simple rooms are decorated with carved teak and unrestored antiques. Balinese feasts and dancing can be arranged. Even if you're not shacking up with the prince, the compound makes for a good stop.

Waka Gangga (☎ 0361-416257; www.wakagangga.com; Yeh Gangga; r from US$100;) Ten circular bungalows with views in three directions are scattered about rice fields at this remote boutique resort. The beach is out front, the design is rustic yet elegant and the trappings luxurious.

NORTH OF TABANAN

The area north of Tabanan is good to travel around with your own transport. There are some strictly B-level attractions; the real appeal here is just driving the fecund back roads.

Yet another monkey forest, **Alas Kedaton** (adult/child 5000/2500Rp; 7.30am-6.30pm) is a stop-off on many organised tours. Your ticket includes a guide, who may do little more than fend off avaricious monkeys and lead you to a cousin's carved-stick shop nearby.

About 9km north of Tabanan the road reaches a fork. The left road goes to Pura Luhur Batukau, via the **hot springs** at Penatahan. Here you'll find the simple **Yeh Panas Resort** (☎ 0361-262356; espa_yehpanes@telkom.net; r from 250,000Rp;), 4km from the fork, by the Sungai Yeh Ho (Yeh Ho River). The resort has a small, cool pool, which nonguests can soak in for 30,000Rp. Another pool has water from the hot springs and costs 150,000Rp. Rooms are set on the hillside and overlook the river.

LALANG-LINGGAH

☎ 0361

At Antosari, the main road takes a sharp turn south to the welcoming breezes of the ocean. The first town you encounter continuing west another 10km is Lalang-Linggah. Here a road leads to the surf breaks near the mouth of Sungai Balian (Balian River). The entire area has deep spiritual significance and caves along the river are the scene of ceremonies.

Sleeping & Eating

You'll find warung scattered about the area with both funky and swank accommodation.

Sacred River Retreat (☎ 814993; www.sacred-river.com; r US$40-60) Just east of town, Sacred River Retreat is a new-agey place with suitably hippyesque décor and activities that include yoga and spiritual retreats. The 11 airy two-level bungalows are suitably restive (No 1 has the best view). Meditate upon the hotel's motto: 'A conscious resort' and wonder about the alternative.

Gajah Mina (☎ 081-23811630; www.gajahminaresort.com; ste from US$85;) Designed by the French architect-owner, the ocean is close to this eight-suite boutique hotel. The stylishly furnished bungalows all have outdoor and indoor bathrooms, and addictive loungers on the balcony. The turn-off from the main road is near the village market and there is a gate where 1000Rp is collected before you make the scenic 1km-drive.

JEMBRANA COAST

About 34km west of Tabanan you cross into Bali's most sparsely populated district, Jembrana. The main road follows the south coast most of the way to Negara. There's some beautiful scenery, but little tourist development along the way, with the exception of the surf break action at Medewi.

Medewi

☎ 0365

The surf scene at Medewi is centred on one short lane from the road down to the waves. There are a couple of places aimed at surfers (and their parents) and not much else.

Along the main road, a large sign points down the paved road (200m) to the surfing mecca of Pantai Medewi. The 'beach' is a stretch of huge, smooth grey rocks interspersed among round black pebbles. Think of it as a reflexology course. It's a placid place where cattle graze by the beach. Medewi is noted not for its beach but for its *long* left-hand wave – and there is little else here.

SLEEPING & EATING

Some places for the Medewi surf break are right on the one main lane. Others are along the coast to the east and west. For a casual meal, some of the finest fare is freshly stir-fried and served up at a cart right by the beach.

Homestay CSB (Pulukan; r 70,000Rp) Some 2km east of the Medewi surf break at Pulukan, Homestay, signposted from the highway on the ocean side, has nice bungalows with rice-paddy views and sea views in the near distance.

Gede Bungalow (☎ 081-23976668; Pulukan; r 70,000Rp) Only 100m from the beach, Gede Bungalow has rice-barn style cottages set amid rice paddies. To reach it, go past Homestay CSBabove and take the first right. It's the first building on the left.

Mai Malu Restaurant & Guesthouse (☎ 43897; s/d 60,000/80,000Rp) Near the highway on the

WEST BALI

SCENIC ROUTES TO THE NORTH COAST

You can cross between Bali's south and north coasts via **Pupuan**, well west of the two main cross-island routes (via Kintamani and Bedugul in the central mountains). From the Denpasar–Gilimanuk road, one road goes north from **Antosari** and another road goes north from **Pulukan**; the two roads meet at Pupuan then drop down to Seririt, west of Lovina.

The road from Antosari starts through rice paddies, climbs into the fragrant spice-growing country via **Sanda** and then descends through the coffee plantations to Pupuan. From Pupuan, if you continue 12km or so towards the north coast you reach Mayong, where you can turn east to Munduk and on to Danau Bratan.

The Pulukan–Pupuan road climbs steeply up from the coast providing fine views back down to the sea. The route also runs through spice-growing country – you'll see (and smell) spices laid out on mats by the road to dry. After about 10km and just before Manggissari, the narrow and winding road actually runs right through **Bunut Bolong** – an enormous tree that forms a complete tunnel (the *bunut* is a type of ficus; *bolong* means 'hole').

Further on, the road spirals down to Pupuan through some of Bali's most beautiful rice terraces.

It is worth stopping off for a walk to the magnificent **waterfalls** near Pujungan, a few kilometres south of Pupuan. Follow signs down a narrow, rough road and then walk 1.5km to the first waterfall, it's nice but before you say 'is that all there is?' follow your ears to a second that's 50m high.

Wind up the exhilarating day with a stay at **Sanda Bukit Villas & Restaurant** (☎ 0828 369 137; www.sandavillas.com; bungalows from US$100;) In the foothills of Gunung Batukau, 8km south of Pupuan at Sanda, this showplace of a boutique hotel has a large infinity pool that seems to disappear into the rice terraces. The engaging owners will recommend many walks in this beautiful area.

Medewi side road, Mai Malu is a popular hang-out, serving crowd-pleasing pizza, burgers and Indonesian meals in its modern, breezy upstairs eating area. Dishes range from 10,000Rp to 35,000Rp. The three rooms have cold water and fans. Other cheapies huddle nearby.

Medewi Beach Cottages (☎ 40029; r US$10-60;) There's a lively two-storey building on the western side of the road with seven second-rate cold-water rooms aimed at surfers and a posher wing on the other side that might be the choice of their parents (no matter how old the surfer). The spiffy side features satellite TV and lush grounds, but security measures have obstructed what should be a good view.

Puri Dajuma Cottages (☎ 43955; www.dajuma.com; r US$70-90;) Coming from the east, you won't be able to miss this seaside resort, thanks to its prolific signage. Happily, the 18 large rooms actually live up to the billing. Bathrooms are both inside and out, and its location on a pounding bodysurfing break is dramatic. Pantai Medewi is a 2km walk west. Ask for a deal on the listed rates.

Pura Rambut Siwi

Picturesquely situated on a clifftop overlooking a long, wide stretch of black-sand beach, this superb temple shaded by flowering frangipani trees is one of the important sea temples of West Bali. Like Pura Tanah Lot and Pura Ulu Watu, it was established in the 16th century by the priest **Nirartha**, who had a good eye for ocean scenery. Legend has it that when Nirartha first came here, he donated some of his hair to the local villagers. The hair is now kept in a box buried in this temple, the name of which means 'Worship of the Hair'. Unlike Tanah Lot, it remains a peaceful and little-visited place (which means you should put a change to that).

The caretaker rents sarongs for 2000Rp (see the boxed text, p42) and is happy to show you around the temple and down to the beach. He then opens the guest book and requests a donation – about 10,000Rp is a suitable amount (regardless of the much higher amounts attributed to previous visitors).

GETTING THERE & AWAY

The temple is between Air Satang and Yeh Embang, at the end of a 300m side road. You'll find it's well signposted, but look for the turn-off near a cluster of warung on the main road. Any of the regular bemo and buses between Denpasar (Ubung terminal) and Gilimanuk will stop at the turn-off.

NEGARA

☎ 0365

Set amid the broad and fertile flatlands between the mountains and ocean, Negara is a prosperous little town, and useful for a pit stop. Although it's a district capital, there's not much to see. The town springs to life when the famous bull races (below) are held nearby. There's a hospital, police station, post office and a wartel. Most banks change money and have international ATMs.

Sleeping & Eating

The main road bypasses the town to the north – you'll need to turn in to the main drag, Jl Ngurah Rai. There are assorted warung in the market area.

Hotel Wira Pada (☎ 41161; Jl Ngurah Rai 107; r with fan/air-con 85,000/125,000Rp;) There are 10 basic rooms around a nice little plant-filled courtyard. The best rooms have little terraces.

BULL RACES

This part of Bali is famous for the bull races, known as *mekepung*, which culminate in the Bupati Cup in Negara in early August. The racing animals are actually the normally docile water buffalo, which charge down a 2km-long stretch of road or beach pulling tiny chariots. Gaily-clad riders stand or kneel on top of the chariots forcing the bullocks on, sometimes by twisting their tails to make them follow the curve of the makeshift racetrack. The winner, however, is not necessarily first past the post. Style also plays a part and points are awarded for the most elegant runner. Gambling is not legal in Bali, but…

Important races are held during the dry season, from July to October. Occasional races are set up for tourist groups at a park in Perancak on the coast, and minor races and practices are held at several Perancak and other sites on Sunday mornings, including Delod Berawan and Yeh Embang. Check with your hotel or the **Jembrana Government Tourist Office** (☎ 41210, ext 224) for details.

INFORMATION			SLEEPING 🏠	
Bank BCA ATM	...1	C2	Hotel Wira Pada	...7 C2
Bank Danamon ATM	...2	C2		
Hospital	...3	A2	EATING 🍴	
Police Station	...4	B2	Depot Natalia	(see 7)
Post Office	...5	D2	Hardy's Supermarket	...8 C2
Wartel	...6	A2		
			TRANSPORT	
			Bus/Bemo Terminal	...9 B2

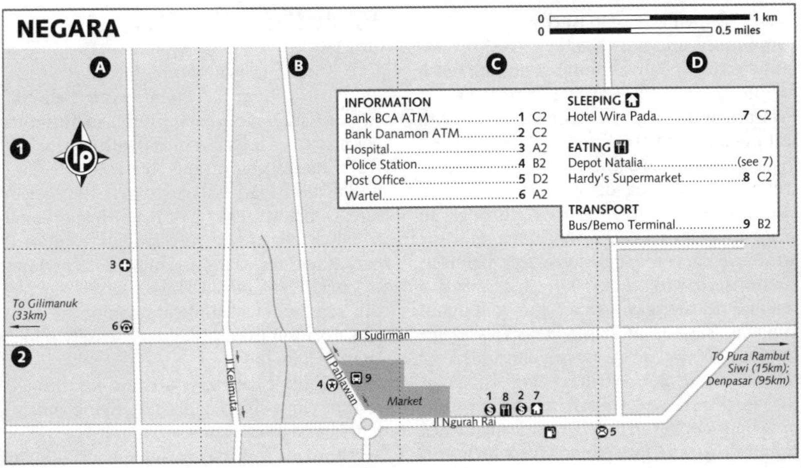

Depot Natalia (☎ 42669; Jl Ngurah Rai 107; dishes 5000-20,000Rp) In front of Hotel Wira Pada, the Depot is bright and clean, and has a large, tasty Indonesian menu.

Hardy's Supermarket (☎ 40709; Jl Ngurah Rai; ☒) Hardy's has a popular indoor food court with several stands wok-ing up all manner of fresh, cheap chow. Dishes are generally under 4000Rp. This large supermarket has the best selection of goods in western Bali.

Getting There & Away

Most bemo and minibuses from Denpasar (Ubung terminal) to Gilimanuk drop you in Negara (20,000Rp).

AROUND NEGARA

At the southern fringe of Negara, Loloan Timur is the largely Bugis community (originally from Sulawesi) that retains 300-year-old traditions. Look for the distinctive houses on stilts, some decorated with wooden fretwork.

To reach **Delod Berawan**, turn off the main Gilimanuk–Denpasar road at Mendoyo and go south to the coast, which has a black-sand beach and irregular surf. You can see bull-race practices Sunday mornings at the nearby football field.

Perancak is the site of Nirartha's arrival on Bali in 1546, commemorated by a dignified limestone temple, **Pura Gede Perancak**. Bull races are run at **Taman Wisata Perancak** (☎ 0365-42173), and Balinese buffets are sometimes staged for organised tours from South Bali. If you're

travelling independently, give the park a ring before you go there. In Perancak, ignore the sad little zoo and go for a walk along the picturesque fishing harbour.

Once capital of the region, **Jembrana** is the centre of the *gamelan jegog,* a gamelan using huge bamboo instruments that produce a very low-pitched, resonant sound. Performances often feature a number of gamelan groups engaging in musical contest. To see and hear them in action, time your arrival with a local festival, or ask in Negara where you might find a group practising.

BELIMBINGSARI & PALASARI

Two fascinating religious towns north of the main road are reason enough for a detour.

Christian evangelism on Bali was discouraged by the Dutch, but sporadic missionary activity resulted in a number of converts, many of whom were rejected by their own communities. In 1939 they were encouraged to resettle in Christian communities in the wilds of West Bali.

Palasari is home to a Catholic community which boasts a huge church largely made from white stone. From the right angle it blots out the sun and is set on a large town square. It is really rather peaceful and with the gently waving palms, it feels like old missionary Hawaii rather than Hindu Bali. The church does show Balinese touches in the spires, which resemble the *meru* in a Hindu temple, and features a façade with the same shape as a temple gate.

Belimbingsari was established as a Protestant community, and now has the largest Protestant church in Bali, although it doesn't reach for the heavens the way the church does in Palasari. Still, it's an amazing structure, with features rendered in a distinctly Balinese style – in place of a church bell there's a *kulkul* (hollow tree-trunk warning drum) like those in a Hindu temple. The entrance is through an *aling aling*-style (guard wall) gate, and the attractive carved angels look very Balinese. Go on Sunday to see inside.

For a near religious experience you might consider staying at **Taman Wana Villas & Spa** (☎ 0365-40970; www.bali-tamanwana-villas.com; Palasari; r from US$150;), a striking 2km-drive past the Palasari church. This architecturally stunning boutique resort has 27 rooms in unusual round structures. Everything is very luxurious and you really are away from it all. Views are panoramic, get one of the rice fields.

These villages are north of the main road, and the best way to see them is on a loop with your own transport. About 17km from Negara, look for signs for the Taman Wana Villas. Follow these for 6.1km to Palasari. From the west, look for a turn for Belimbingsari, some 20km southeast of Cekik. A good road leads to the village. Between the two towns, tackle the thicket of little but passable lanes. You'll get lost but soon get set straight by anyone you see.

CEKIK

At this junction one road continues west to Gilimanuk and another heads northeast towards Lovina. All buses and bemo to and from Gilimanuk pass through Cekik.

Archaeological excavations here during the 1960s yielded the oldest evidence of human life in Bali. Finds include burial mounds with funerary offerings, bronze jewellery, axes, adzes and earthenware vessels from around 1000 BC, give or take a few centuries. Look for some of this in the **Museum Situs Purbakala Gilimanuk** (p283).

On the southern side of the junction, the pagoda-like structure with a spiral stairway around the outside is a **war memorial**. The memorial commemorates the landing of independence forces in Bali to oppose the Dutch, who were trying to reassert control of Indonesia after WWII.

Cekik is home to the park headquarters of the Taman Nasional Bali Baratright.

TAMAN NASIONAL BALI BARAT

☎ 0365

Call it nature's symphony. Most visitors to Taman Nasional Bali Barat (West Bali National Park) are struck by the mellifluous sounds from myriad birds with a nice riff from the rustling various trees.

Bali's only national park covers 19,000 hectares of the western tip of Bali. An additional 55,000 hectares are protected in the national park extension, as well as almost 7000 hectares of coral reef and coastal waters. Together this represents a significant commitment to conservation on an island as densely populated as Bali.

It's a place where you can hike through forests, enjoy the island's best diving and explore coastal mangroves.

Although you may imagine dense jungle, most of the natural vegetation in the park is not tropical rainforest, which requires rain year-round, but coastal savannah, with deciduous trees that become bare in the dry season. The southern slopes receive more regular rainfall, and so have more tropical vegetation, while the coastal lowlands have extensive mangroves.

There are more than 200 species of plant growing in the park. Local fauna includes black monkeys, leaf monkeys and macaques (seen in the afternoon along the main road near Sumber Kelompok); rusa, barking, sambar, Java and mouse deer *(muncak);* and some wild pigs, squirrels, buffaloes, iguanas, pythons and green snakes. There were once tigers, but the last confirmed sighting was in 1937 – and that one was shot. The bird life is prolific, with many of Bali's 300 species found here, including the very rare Bali starling.

Just getting off the road a bit on one of the many trails (see opposite, transports you into the heart of nature. One discordant note: hikes in fuel prices mean that there are lots of people selling firewood snatched from the forest along the road.

Information

The **park headquarters** (☎ 61060; 7am-5pm) at Cekik displays a topographic model of the park area, and has a little information about plants and wildlife.

The small **Labuhan Lalang visitors centre** (8am-3pm) is located on the northern coast, where boats leave for Pulau Menjangan.

You can arrange trekking guides and permits at either place, however there are always a few characters hanging around and determining who is an actual park official can be like finding a Bali starling: difficult.

The main roads to Gilimanuk go through the national park, but you don't have to pay an entrance fee just to drive through. If you want to stop and visit any of the sites within the park, you must buy a ticket (2500Rp).

Sights & Activities

By land, by boat or by water, the park awaits exploration.

TREKKING

All trekkers must be accompanied by an authorised guide. It's best to arrive the day before you want to trek, and make inquiries at the park offices in Cekik or Labuhan Lalang.

The set rates for guides in the park depend on the size of the group and the length of the trek – with one or two people it's 150,000Rp for one or two hours, 200,000Rp for three or four hours, and 400,000Rp for five to seven hours; with three to five people it's 250,000Rp, 300,000Rp or 500,000Rp. Transport and food are extra and all the prices are negotiable. Early morning, say 6am, is the best time to start – it's cooler and you're more likely to see some wildlife.

Although you can try to customise your hike, the guides are most familiar with the four listed here. If once you're out you have a good rapport with your guide, you might consider getting creative.

Gunung Kelatakan (Mt Kelatakan) From Sumber Kelompok, go up the mountain (698m), then down to the main road near Kelatakan village (six to seven hours). You may be able to get permission from park headquarters to stay overnight in the forest – if you don't have a tent, your guide can make a shelter from branches and leaves which will be an adventure in itself. Clear streams abound in the dense woods.

Kelatakan Starting at the village, climb to the microwave tower, go down to Ambyasari and get transport back to Cekik (four hours). This takes you through the forested southern sector of the park. From the tower you get a feel for what much of Bali looked like centuries ago.

Prapat Agung From Sumber Kelompok, you can trek around here, via the Bali Starling Pre-Release Centre and Batu Lucin – but only from about June to September, when the sensitive Bali starlings move further inland (allow at least five hours). It's easier and quicker to access the peninsula by chartered boat from Gilimanuk where you will see the mangroves and drier savannah landscape.

Teluk Terima (Terima Bay) From a trail west of Labuhan Lalang, hike around the mangroves here. Then partially follow the Sungai Terima into the hills and walk back down to the road along the steps at Makam Jayaprana. You might see grey macaques, deer and black monkeys (allow two to three hours).

TAMAN NASIONAL BALI BARAT

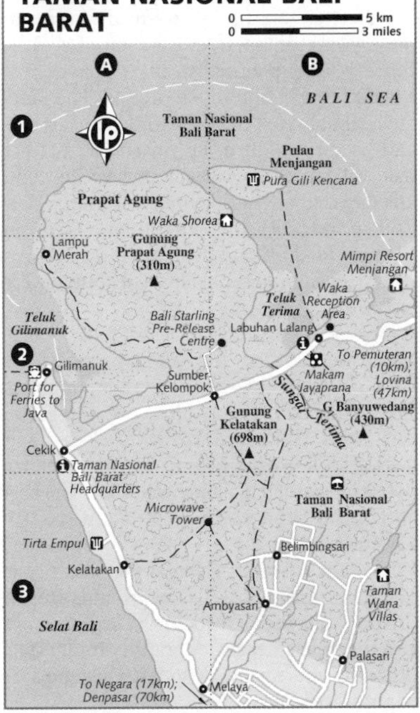

BOAT TRIPS

The best way to explore the mangroves of Teluk Gilimanuk or the west side of Prapat Agung is by chartering a boat (maximum of two people) for about 150,000Rp per boat per hour. You can arrange this at either of the park offices. A guide will cost another 150,000Rp. This is the ideal way to see bird life, including kingfishers, Javanese herons and, very, very rarely, Bali starlings.

DIVING

Pulau Menjangan is Bali's best-known dive area, with a dozen distinct dive sites. The diving is excellent – there's lots of tropical fish (including clown fish, parrot fish, sharks and barracuda), soft corals, great visibility (usually), caves and a spectacular drop-off.

ON A WING & A PRAYER

Also known as the Bali myna, Rothschild's mynah, or locally as *jalak putih,* the Bali starling is perhaps Bali's only endemic bird (opinions differ – as other places are so close, who can tell?). It is striking white in colour, with black tips to the wings and tail, and a distinctive bright blue mask. These natural good looks have proven to be a major problem as the bird has been poached into virtual extinction. On the black market, Bali starlings command US$7000 or more.

The wild population has been estimated to be a dozen or none – well below the number needed for sustainable reproduction if that's even possible. In captivity, however, there are hundreds if not thousands. Unfortunately the bird is so docile that a mass escape seems unlikely.

The internationally supported Bali Starling Project attempted to rebuild the population by re-introducing captive birds to the wild. At the Bali Starling Pre-Release Centre, formerly caged birds were introduced to the food sources of the natural environment and encouraged to nest in native trees, before being released around Taman Nasional Bali Barat (West Bali National Park). This proved impossible. Despite heroic efforts by some staff members, birds were often killed by predatory falcons, while countless others were stolen from the centre by armed thieves.

Today international support for the project has faded. There is talk among scientists of starting another at a double-secret location on Nusa Penida but plans haven't jelled.

It's possible to visit the **Pre-Release Centre** (8am-3pm). Some 6km off the main road through the park, the compound is supposedly closed to visitors, but with great sincerity – and possibly 100,000Rp – you might talk your way in to see the remaining birds. Whatever you do, don't fall for suggestions that you need to go through the guides at the park information offices. Should this happen you'll feel like a Bali starling (or an egg): poached.

Near Ubud, the Bali Bird Park (p205) has large aviaries where you can see Bali starlings. The park was one of the major supporters of efforts to reintroduce the birds into the wild.

Unfortunately, the coral has suffered somewhat from coral bleaching (caused by warm water during the 1998 El Niño event) but it is recovering.

Divers who like wall diving will love it here. Most of the dive sites are suitable for all experience levels except for Anker Wreck, a mysterious sunken ship that challenges even experts. The closest and most convenient dive operators are found at Pemuteran (p269) and Lovina (p263).

PULAU MENJANGAN

This uninhabited island boasts what is thought to be Bali's oldest temple, **Pura Gili Kencana**, dating from the Majapahit period in Java. You can walk around the island in about an hour, but the attractions are mainly underwater. Snorkellers can find some decent spots not far from the jetty – ask the boatman where to go. Dive sites are dotted all around the island, so it's worth discussing the possibilities with the dive master when you arrange the trip.

MAKAM JAYAPRANA

A 20-minute walk up some stone stairs from the southern side of the road, a little west of Labuhan Lalang, will bring you to Jayaprana's grave. There are fine views to the north at the top. Jayaprana, the foster son of a 17th-century king, planned to marry Leyonsari, a beautiful girl of humble origins. The king, however, also fell in love with Leyonsari and had Jayaprana killed. Leyonsari learned the truth of Jayaprana's death in a dream, and killed herself rather than marry the king. This Romeo and Juliet story is a common theme in Balinese folklore, and the grave is regarded as sacred, even though the ill-fated couple were not deities.

Sleeping

Park visitors will want to spend the night as close to the park as possible in order to get an early start. Gilimanuk (p284) is closest and has basic choices. Much nicer are the luxury hotels in Labuhan Lalang (opposite). The best all-around choice is in Pemuteran (p270), 12km further east.

There is a free camping at the park headquarters in Cekik (p280). The grounds are not pristine, but the bathroom is clean enough and the toilets decent. A gratuity to the staff is greatly appreciated. You'll need some sort of gear, however.

Getting There & Away

The national park is too far away for a comfortable day trip from Ubud or South Bali, though many dive operators do it. You'll want to stay at one of the places suggested under Sleeping, opposite).

If you don't have transport, any Gilimanuk-bound bus or bemo from North or West Bali can drop you at park headquarters at Cekik (those from North Bali can also drop you at the Labuhan Lalang visitors centre).

LABUHAN LALANG

To catch a boat to Pulau Menjangan, head to the jetty at this small harbour in the national park (opposite). There's also a small park visitors centre (p280), warung and a pleasant beach 200m to the east. Some of the warung rent snorkelling gear (50,000Rp for four hours) and can point out the best sites.

Local boat owners have a strict cartel and fixed prices: it costs 250,000Rp for a four-hour trip to Menjangan, and 20,000Rp for each subsequent hour, in a boat holding 10 people (or five scuba divers with equipment). A guide costs an additional 60,000Rp.

Sleeping

The choices are quite luxurious. All have dive operations.

Mimpi Resort Menjangan (☎ 0362-94497, 0361-701070; www.mimpi.com; r US$95, villas US$195-355;) At isolated Banyuwedang, this 24-unit resort has a large site extending down to a small, mangrove-fringed, white-sand beach. The rooms have a stark, simple design with open-air bathrooms. Villas have a hot-spring tub and their own private courtyard; some have a pool.

Waka Shorea (☎ 0362-94666; www.wakaexperience.com; units from US$165;) Located in splendid isolation in the park, Waka Shorea is a 10-minute boat ride from the hotel's reception area 100m east of Labuhan Lalang. It's a boutique resort, with units built on stilts among forest. The emphasis here is on nature, whether through diving, trekking or bird-watching.

GILIMANUK

☎ **0365**

Gilimanuk is the terminus for ferries that shuttle back and forth across the narrow strait to Java. Most travellers to or from Java can get an onward ferry or bus straight away,

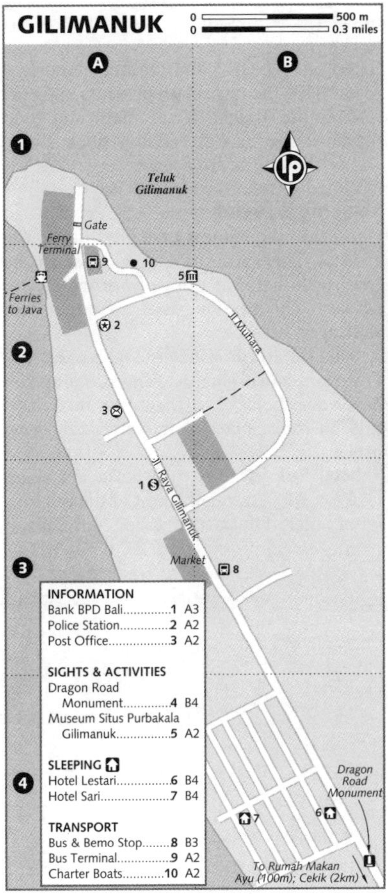

and won't need to stop in Gilimanuk. The museum is the only attraction – the town is really a place one passes through quickly. It has the closest accommodation to the national park if you want to start a trek early.

Information

There is a Bank BDP Bali (without ATM) on Jl Raya, a post office, a police station and wartel, but not many shops or other services.

Sights

This part of Bali has been occupied for thousands of years. The **Museum Situs Purbakala Gilimanuk** (☎ 61328; donation 5000Rp; 8am-4pm Mon-Fri) is centred on a family of skeletons thought to be 4000 years old, which were found locally in 2004. The museum is 500m south of the ferry port.

Stop anywhere along the north shore of town to see the huge clash of waves and currents in the straight. It's dramatic and good reason *not* to have that dodgy duck dish if you're about to board a ferry.

Sleeping & Eating

Good sleeping choices here are thin on the ground. There's nothing good close to the ferry terminal, but things improve as you go west. The best food is at the bus station warung.

Hotel Lestari (☎ 61504; r 65,000-325,000Rp;) From fan-cooled singles to air-con suites you have your choice of basic accommodation at this 25-room place that feels oddly suburban.

Hotel Sari (☎ 61264; r 100,000Rp, with air-con 175,000Rp;) Among the best of the dubious lot of hotels. On the ocean side of Jl Raya, it has basic rooms, although the karaoke bar next door can be invasive.

Warung Men Tempeh (10am-4pm) Known for its succulent and spicy *ayam betutu* (chicken in spices).

Getting There & Away

Frequent buses hurtle along the main road between Gilimanuk's huge bus depot and Denpasar's Ubung terminal (25,000Rp), or along the north-coast road to Singaraja (20,000Rp).

To get to and from Ketapang on Java (30 minutes), **car ferries** (adult/child 4300/2900Rp, car & driver 81,500Rp; 24hr) are the main reason method of transport.

Getting Around

At the ferry, bemo and bus terminals, you can get an *ojek* (motorcycle that takes passengers), charter car or even a *dokar* (pony cart) for a negotiable 8000Rp.

WEST BALI

Lombok

Just a short hop east of Bali, Lombok is an incredibly diverse island of abundant natural and cultural interest. Physically, it's dominated by the mighty presence of Gunung Rinjani (Mt Rinjani), a volcano which towers over the entire northern half of the island. Rivers spilling down its fissured slopes water the island's crops (chiefly rice, soya beans, coffee and tobacco), while its summit – complete with a dazzling crater lake – lures both trekkers and local pilgrims, for whom Rinjani is a sacred peak.

Lombok's other key attractions are the fabled Gili Islands – three exquisite tropical islets of white-sand beaches, coconut palms and coral reefs teeming with marine life. Accommodation here runs the full gamut: from no-frills beach huts to uber chic air-conditioned contemporary hotels; and you can feast on everything from a humble *nasi campur* to zenlike arrangements of sushi and sashimi. While most visitors spend their days here diving, snorkelling or simply chilling by the sea, Gili Trawangan also offers plenty of after-dark action including a lively bar scene and vibrant nightlife.

Lombok's dramatic south coast, characterised by a chain of headlands dividing a series of wonderful sandy beaches, offers big breaks that are a magnet for surfers. Here the mellow village of Kuta (no relation to its Bali namesake) is a good base, with an array of attractive hotels and no crowds.

In contrast to Bali, most people on Lombok (around 90% of the population) are Sasaks, a Muslim people with a culture and language unique to the island. There's also a significant Hindu Balinese minority – a legacy of the time when Bali controlled Lombok.

HIGHLIGHTS

- Trekking the lush slopes of **Gunung Rinjani** (p314), Lombok's emblematic volcanic cone
- Plunging into the big blue off the **Gili Islands** (p299), where the prolific reef life offers terrific snorkelling and scuba diving
- Grooving to the funky beat under the coconut palms in party central **Gili Trawangan** (p305)
- Exploring the beautiful sandy coves and spectacular coastline east and west of **Kuta** (p322), a region that has some of Lombok's best surf
- Searching for the perfect beach in the thinly populated **Southwestern peninsula** (p292), a rugged region that includes the lovely offshore islands of Gili Nanggu and Gili Gede

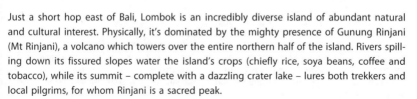

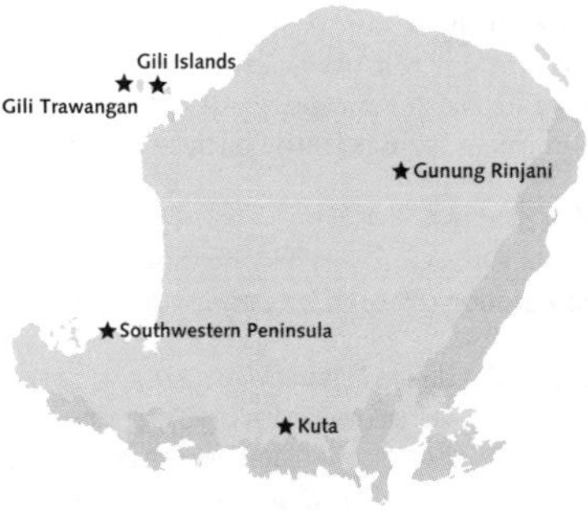

WESTERN LOMBOK

☎ 0370

Most travellers who visit Lombok spend some time in the western part of the island, if only because the airport (Mataram) and the main port (Lembar) for ferries to and from Bali are here. It's the most populous part of Lombok, with the largest urban area centred on the Mataram conurbation, as well as the biggest tourist resort: the Senggigi beach strip. There are a number of attractive villages around Mataram, as well as some stunning coastal areas on the southwest peninsula.

MATARAM

pop 321,000

The capital, and main city on Lombok, is Mataram, although it's actually a conglomeration of several separate towns – Ampenan (the port); Mataram (administrative centre); Cakranegara (business centre), which is often shortened to Cakra; and Bertais-Sweta to the east, home to the bus terminal. This urban area contains over a million people and stretches more than 10km from east to west. It's not an unattractive place, and has some broad tree-lined avenues, but as sights are slim on the ground, and as there are beaches close by at Senggigi, very few visitors choose to stay here.

Orientation

The four towns are spread along one main road – it starts as Jl Pabean in Ampenan, becomes Jl Yos Sudarso, then changes to Jl Langko, Jl Pejanggik and travels from Sweta to Bertais as Jl Selaparang. It's one-way all the way, running west to east. A parallel one-way road, running east to west, Jl Tumpang Sari–Jl Panca Usaha–Jl Pancawarga–Jl Caturwarga–Jl Pendidikan, brings traffic back to the coast.

Information

EMERGENCY

Police station (☎ 631225; Jl Langko) In an emergency, dial ☎ 110.

Rumah Sakit Umum Mataram (☎ 622254; Jl Pejanggik 6) The best hospital on Lombok; has English-speaking doctors and a special tourist service from 8am to noon.

INTERNET ACCESS

Most cybercafés are in the streets around the Mataram Mall (p290).

Deddy's (Mataram Mall Lt 1; per hr 6000Rp; 🕒 9am-9pm)

MONEY

You'll find plenty of banks with ATMs scattered along Cakra's main drag, particularly Jl Penanggik; most of them will also change cash as well as travellers cheques. Mataram Mall and the airport also have ATMs and moneychangers (which open longer than the banks).

POST

Main post office (Jl Sriwijaya 37; 🕒 8am-5pm Mon-Thu, 8-11am Fri, 8am-1pm Sat) Inconveniently located, but has internet and poste-restante services.

Sub-post office (Jl Langko, Ampenan; 🕒 8am-4.30pm Mon-Thu, 8-11am Fri, 8am-1pm Sat) Near the Nitour Hotel.

TELEPHONE

There are wartel (public telephone offices) on Jl Pejanggik and at the airport.

Telkom (☎ 633333; Jl Pendidikan 23, Mataram; 🕒 24hr) Offers phone and fax services.

TOURIST INFORMATION

West Lombok tourist office (☎ 621658; Jl Suprato 20; 🕒 7.30am-2pm Mon-Thu, 7.30-11am Fri, 8am-1pm Sat) Has some maps and leaflets but is not a particularly informative office.

West Nusa Tenggara tourist office (☎ 634800; Jl Singosari 2; 🕒 8am-2pm Mon-Thu, 8-11am Fri, 8am-12.30pm Sat) Offers limited information about Lombok but staff are friendly enough.

Sights

MUSEUM NEGERI NUSA TENGGARA BARAT

This modern **museum** (☎ 632519; Jl Panji Tilar Negara 6; admission 1500Rp; 🕒 8am-2pm Tue-Thu & Sat-Sun, 8-11am Fri) has exhibits on the geology, history and culture of Lombok and Sumbawa. If you intend on buying antiques or handicrafts, take a look at the kris (traditional daggers), *songket* (silver- or gold-threaded cloth), basketware and masks for comparison.

MAYURA WATER PALACE

This **palace** (Jl Selaparang; admission 1000Rp if requested; 🕒 7am-7.30pm) was built in 1744, and was once part of the Balinese kingdom's royal court on Lombok. It's a pleasant retreat now, popular with fishermen and families, but in 1894 it was the site of bloody battles between the Dutch and Balinese. The complex contains a large artificial lake, with a modest replica of a *bale kambang* (floating pavilion) in its centre, connected to the shoreline by a raised

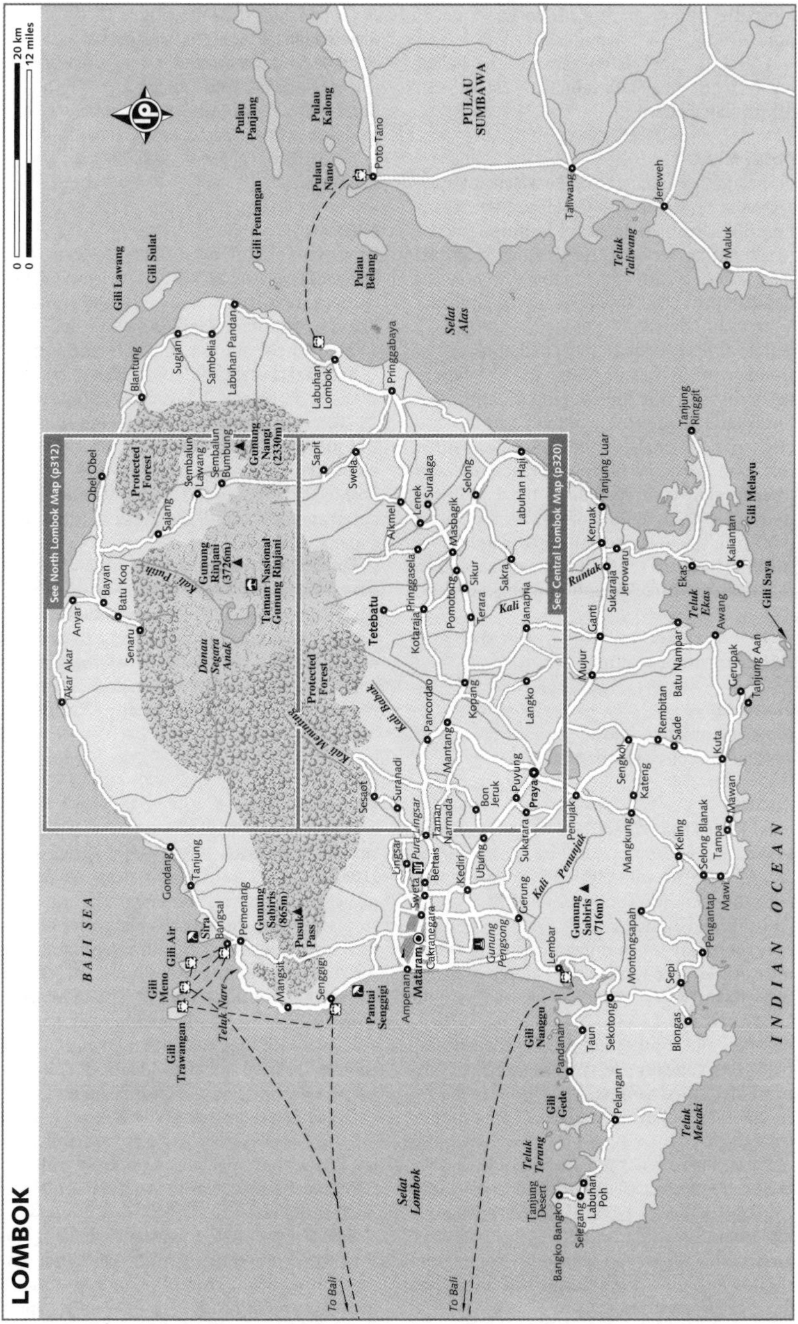
LOMBOK
0 20 km
0 12 miles
BALI SEA
INDIAN OCEAN
Selat Lombok
Selat Alas
PULAU SUMBAWA
See North Lombok Map (p312)
See Central Lombok Map (p320)
Gili Lawang
Gili Sulat
Gili Pentangan
Pulau Panjang
Pulau Kalong
Pulau Nano
Pulau Belang
Poto Tano
Taliwang
Jereweh
Maluk
Teluk Taliwang
Blantung
Sugian
Sambelia
Labuhan Pandan
Labuhan Lombok
Pringgabaya
Obel Obel
Protected Forest
Sembalun Lawang
Sembalun Bumbung
Gunung Nangi (2330m)
Sajang
Bayan
Batu Koq
Anyar
Senaru
Akar Akar
Kali Putih
Gunung Rinjani (3726m)
Taman Nasional Gunung Rinjani
Danau Segara Anak
Sapit
Swela
Alkmel
Lenek
Suralaga
Selong
Labuhan Haji
Masbagik
Pringgasela
Pomotong
Sikur
Sakra
Terara
Tetebatu
Kotaraja
Kali Jangkok
Janapria
Kopang
Pancordao
Mantang
Langko
Kali Babak
Kali Meninting
Sesaot
Suranadi
Bon Jeruk
Puyung
Praya
Taman Narmada
Pura Lingsar
Lingsar
Sweta
Bertais
Kediri
Ubung
Sukarara
Penujak
Kali Penunjak
Tanjung Luar
Keruak
Jerowaru
Sukaraja
Runtak
Ganti
Mujur
Tanjung Ringgit
Gili Melayu
Kaliantan
Ekas
Teluk Ekas
Awang
Gili Saya
Tanjung Aan
Gerupak
Batu Nampar
Rembitan
Sade
Sengkol
Kateng
Kuta
Mawan
Mangkung
Keling
Selong Blanak
Tampa
Mawi
Pengantap
Montongsapah
Sepi
Blongas
Gunung Sabiris (716m)
Gerung
Lembar
Gunung Pengsong
Sekotong
Taun
Pandanan
Gili Nanggu
Gili Gede
Pelangan
Teluk Mekaki
Teluk Terang
Tanjung Desert
Labuhan Poh
Selegang
Bangko Bangko
Gondang
Tanjung
Bangsal
Sira
Pemenang
Gunung Sabiris (865m)
Pusuk Pass
Gili Air
Gili Meno
Gili Trawangan
Teluk Nare
Mangsit
Senggigi
Pantai Senggigi
Ampenan
Mataram
Cakranegara
To Bali
To Bali

LOMBOK

footpath. The original pavilion was a court of justice.

You'll find that the entrance to the walled enclosure of the palace is on the western side, off Jl Selaparang.

PURA MERU

Opposite the water palace, **Pura Meru** (admission by donation; 8am-5pm), is the largest temple on Lombok. Built in 1720 by Balinese prince Anak Agung Made Karang of the Singosari kingdom in an attempt to unite Lombok, it's dedicated to the Hindu trinity of Brahma, Vishnu and Shiva.

The outer courtyard has a hall housing the wooden drums that are beaten to call believers to ceremonies (the June full moon is the most important of these). The inner court has one large and 33 small shrines, as well as three *meru* (multiroofed shrines), which are in a line: the central *meru*, with 11 tiers, is Shiva's house; the *meru* to the north, with nine tiers, is Vishnu's; and the seven-tiered *meru* to the south is Brahma's. The *meru* are also said to represent the three great mountains, Rinjani, Agung and Bromo.

The caretaker will lend you a sash and sarong if you need one.

Sleeping

Most visitors find Cakranegara the most convenient and pleasant place to stay.

BUDGET

Hotel Herta Yoga (621775; Jl Pejanggik 64; s/d incl breakfast 40,000/50,000Rp, with air-con 80,000/85,000Rp;) A new place with pleasant, spotless rooms with air-con, good mattresses, clothes rails and private shower/mandi (bath). The fan-only rooms are much rougher and a last resort only. It's located next to the Perama office.

Karthika II Hotel (641776; Jl Subak 1, Cakra; r with fan/air-con 70,000/90,000Rp;) Built like a Balinese temple compound, this excellent-value place has squeaky clean, if slightly garishly presented tiled rooms with modern bathrooms that all have verandas. There's ample parking.

Hotel Handika (633578; fax 635049; Jl Panca Usaha 3; s/d with fan 55,000/60,000Rp, s with air-con 85,000-130,000Rp, d with air-con 95,000-145,000Rp, all incl breakfast;) Behind the Mataram Mall, this hotel has an array of idiosyncratic rooms, some with slightly alarming carved-eagle bed frames, in five price categories.

Or consider the following:

Ganesha Inn (624878; Jl Subak 2; s/d 30,000/40,000Rp) Guesthouse with well-presented, good-value rooms and cold water bathrooms.

Hotel Melati Viktor (633830; Jl Abimanyu 1; s/d 45,000/50,000Rp, with hot water & air-con 75,000/100,000Rp;) Smart, clean, tiled rooms and bathrooms.

MIDRANGE

Nitour Hotel (623780; fax 625328; Jl Yos Sudarso 4; s/d incl breakfast from 200,000/250,000Rp) Welcoming, but the accommodation, scattered among random patches of garden, is looking a bit jaded, with an assortment of mismatched furnishings.

Hotel Sahid Legi (636282; sahid@mataram.wasantara.net.id; Jl Sriwijaya 81; r/deluxe 365,000/580,000Rp;) Swish hotel that marries modern and Indonesian design influences. It offers the most comfortable base in town with well appointed rooms, three restaurants and a circular pool surrounded by lush gardens and expansive lawns.

Hotel Lombok Raya (632305; lora@mataram.wasantara.net.id; Jl Panca Usaha 11; s/d from 390,000/525,000Rp, plus 21% tax;) This centrally-situated hotel has spacious, comfortable rooms. Its decor is on the bland side of beige but all rooms have balconies and mod cons including multi-channelled TV. Escape the city heat in the large pool or spa.

Eating

You'll find plenty of Western fast-food outlets and Indonesian staples in the Mataram Mall.

Seafood Alfa (660-0088; Jl Pejanggik 34; dishes 8000-25,000Rp; 9am-11pm) A bright, clean welcoming place; perch yourself on one of the coloured stools and tuck into dishes like *gurami asam manis* (freshwater fish with sweet sauce) or the rice and noodles dishes under 10,000Rp.

Rumah Makan Dirgahayu (637559; Jl Cilinaya 19; mains 8000-30,000Rp;) Huge, popular Makassar place with long menu that takes in veggie choices like fried spinach and tofu, or delicious *karper goreng* (fried carp) for 20,000Rp.

Denny Bersaudra (633619; Jl Pelikan 6; dishes 10,000-27,000Rp) Agreeable, airy and welcoming place that specialises in Sasak cuisine. Look for the sign near the roundabout along western Jl Pejanggik.

Dua M (622914; Jl Transisto 99; dishes 12,500-20,000Rp; 8am-10pm Mon-Sat; 9am-9.30pm Sun) Authentic Sasak food, including terrific *ayam goreng taliwang* (Sumbawa-style spicy

MATARAM

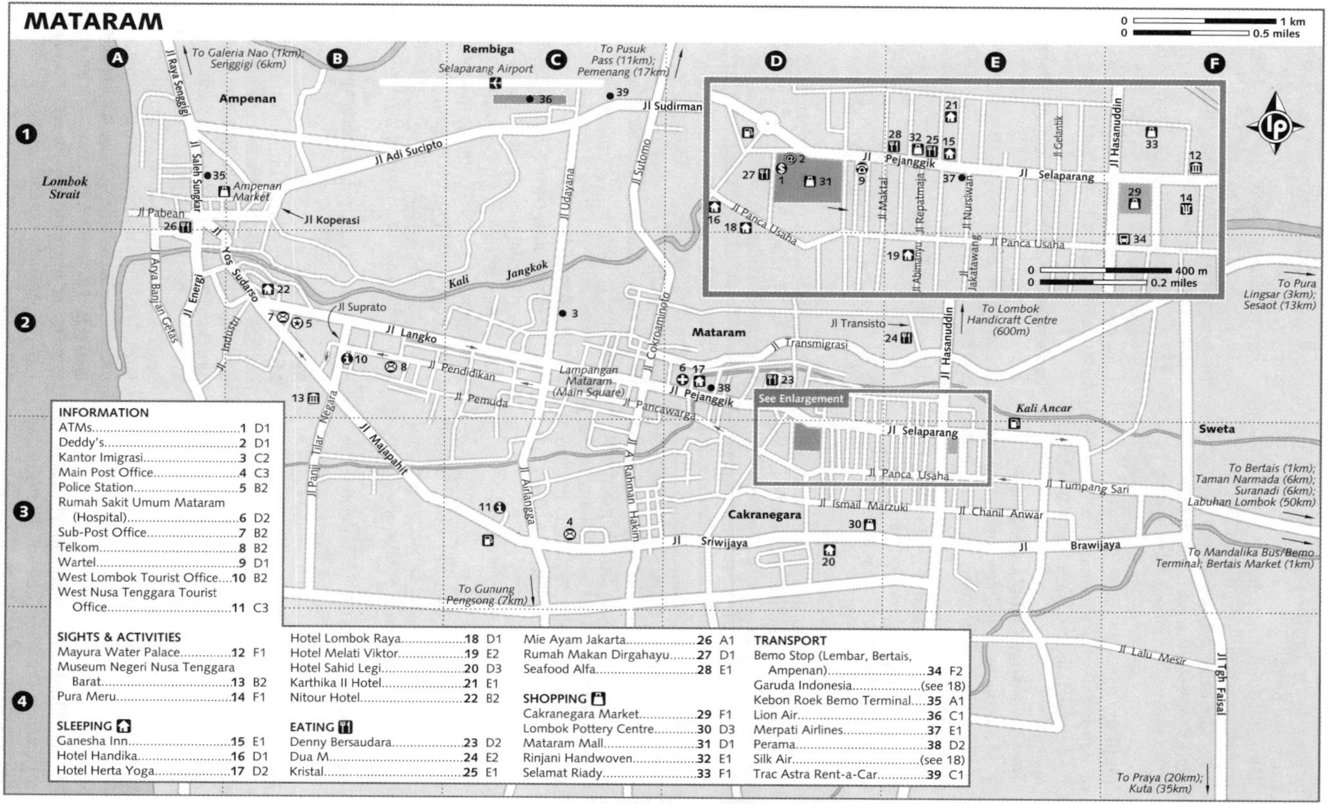

INFORMATION

ATMs	1	D1
Deddy's	2	D1
Kantor Imigrasi	3	C2
Main Post Office	4	C3
Police Station	5	B2
Rumah Sakit Umum Mataram (Hospital)	6	D2
Sub-Post Office	7	B2
Telkom	8	B2
Wartel	9	D1
West Lombok Tourist Office	10	B2
West Nusa Tenggara Tourist Office	11	C3

SIGHTS & ACTIVITIES

Mayura Water Palace	12	F1
Museum Negeri Nusa Tenggara Barat	13	B2
Pura Meru	14	F1

SLEEPING

Ganesha Inn	15	E1
Hotel Handika	16	D1
Hotel Herta Yoga	17	D2
Hotel Lombok Raya	18	D1
Hotel Melati Viktor	19	E2
Hotel Sahid Legi	20	D3
Karthika II Hotel	21	E1
Nitour Hotel	22	B2

EATING

Denny Bersaudara	23	D2
Dua M	24	E2
Kristal	25	E1
Mie Ayam Jakarta	26	A1
Rumah Makan Dirgahayu	27	D1
Seafood Alfa	28	E1

SHOPPING

Cakranegara Market	29	F1
Lombok Pottery Centre	30	D3
Mataram Mall	31	D1
Rinjani Handwoven	32	E1
Selamat Riady	33	F1

TRANSPORT

Bemo Stop (Lembar, Bertais, Ampenan)	34	F2
Garuda Indonesia	(see 18)	
Kebon Roek Bemo Terminal	35	A1
Lion Air	36	C1
Merpati Airlines	37	E1
Perama	38	D2
Silk Air	(see 18)	
Trac Astra Rent-a-Car	39	C1

chicken). Try to bag the low table facing the garden and pond.

Other recommendations:

Mie Ayam Jakarta (Jl Pabean; dishes 5000-12,000Rp) Scores for tasty, inexpensive Javanese food.

Kristal (☎ 627564; Jl Pejanggik 22; dishes 6000-20,000Rp) Head here for Chinese cuisine and seafood.

Shopping

For handicrafts try the many stores on Jl Raya Senggigi, the road heading north from Ampenan.

Lombok Handicraft Centre (Jl Hasanuddin; 8am-6pm) At Sayang Sayang (2km north of Cakra) this place has a wide range of crafts from across Lombok and eastern Indonesia.

Mataram Mall (Jl Selaparang; 7am-7pm) This multistorey shopping mall contains a supermarket, electrical goods and clothes stores as well as food stalls.

Galeria Nao (☎ 626835; Jl Raya Senggigi 234, Menintimg; 8.30am-6pm) Beautifully finished contemporary wooden furniture and artefacts that wouldn't look out of place in *Wallpaper**.

Lombok Pottery Centre (☎ 640351; Jl Sriwijaya 111) Offers a vast range of Lombok pottery, and prices are reasonably competitive.

Rinjani Handwoven (☎ 633169; Jl Pejanggik 44; 8am-6pm Mon-Sat) You can see weavers in action at this workshop and buy their handiwork.

Selamat Riady (☎ 631196; www.lombokpottery.com; Jl Tanun 10) Offers textiles, including ikat from Lombok, Flores and Sumba, and other crafts.

Getting There & Away

AIR

See p350 for airlines serving Lombok and details on the airport and departure tax. Note that fares from Bali are often quite cheap – under US$30.

Garuda Indonesia (☎ 638259; www.garuda-indonesia.com; Hotel Lombok Raya, Mataram) Jakarta, Surabaya and Bali.

Lion Air (☎ 629111, 692222; www.lionair.co.id; Hotel Sahid Legi, Mataram) Surabaya.

Merpati Airlines (☎ 621111; www.merpati.co.id; Jl Pejanggik 69, Mataram) Flies to Bali and Sumbawa.

Silk Air (☎ 628254; www.silkair.com; Hotel Lombok Raya, Mataram) Serves Singapore direct.

Wings Air (see Lion Air, above)

BUS

The sprawling, dusty Mandalika bus station in Bertais is the main bus and bemo (small minibus) terminal for the entire island and also for long-distance buses to Sumbawa, Bali and Java (p353).

The terminal is fairly chaotic, so be sure to keep a level head to avoid the 'help' of the commission-happy touts. Long-distance buses leave from behind the main terminal building, while bemo and smaller buses leave from one of two car parks on either side.

Some distances and fares for buses and bemo from Mandalika terminal:

Destination	Distance	Price (Rp)	Duration
Labuhan Lombok	69km	15,000	2hr
Lembar	22km	7500	30min
Praya	27km	6000	30min
Kuta (via Praya & Sengkol)	54km	6000 (+6000)	90min
Pemenang (for Bangsal)	30km	5000	40min

Kebon Roek terminal in Ampenan has the bemo to Bertais (1500Rp) and services to Senggigi (3000Rp).

TOURIST SHUTTLE BUS

Perama (☎ 635928; www.peramatour.com; Jl Pejanggik 66) operates shuttle buses to popular destinations in Lombok (including Bangsal, Senggigi and Kuta) and to Bali.

Getting Around

TO/FROM THE AIRPORT

Lombok's Selaparang airport is on the north side of the city, 5km from Cakra. A taxi desk sells prepaid tickets: 17,500Rp to anywhere in Mataram; 44,000Rp to Senggigi; 98,000Rp to Bangsal and Lembar; 145,000Rp to Kuta; 210,000Rp to Senaru. Alternatively, walk out of the airport to Jl Adi Sucipto and take one of the No 7 bemo that run frequently to Ampenan.

BEMO

Mataram is *very* spread out, so don't plan on walking. Yellow bemo shuttle back and forth between Kebon Roek terminal in Ampenan and Mandalika terminal in Bertais (10km away). Some make slight detours, but they generally travel along the two main thoroughfares. The bemo terminals are good places to organise a charter trip. Outside the **Cakranegara market** (cnr Jl Hasanuddin & Jl Selaparang; 6am-5.30pm) there is a handy bemo stop for services to Bertais, Ampenan, Sweta and Lembar. The standard fare is 1500Rp, regardless of distance.

LOMBOK

AVOIDING OFFENCE

Most of Lombok is culturally conservative, and immodest dress and public displays of affection between couples can cause offence. Both men and women should dress appropriately away from Senggigi and the Gilis. Nude or topless bathing anywhere is very offensive.

Islamic law forbids drinking alcohol and, although booze is widely available on Lombok, public drunkenness is quite definitely frowned upon. It's particularly offensive to drink alcohol near a mosque. Ramadan is a time to be particularly sensitive about local cultural sensibilities – most locals fast during daylight hours during this month, and there are no parties on Gili Trawangan.

CAR & MOTORCYCLE

Most hotels can arrange car hire, but you'll almost certainly find a much better deal in Senggigi. If you'd rather someone else did the driving, contact **Ido Ado Dalmin** (☎ 0813 3956 2129) a reliable driver-guide who speaks fair English. He charges around 350,000Rp per day for a car and his services. For care hire, try **Trac Astra Rent-a-Car** (☎ 626363; www.trac.astra.co.id; Jl Adi Sucipto 5, Rembiga Mataram; Kijang with driver per 6hr 425,000Rp, self-drive per day 385,000Rp).

TAXI

For a metered taxi, call **Lombok Taksi** (☎ 627000).

AROUND MATARAM

East from Mataram there are some gorgeous areas with villages, rice fields and temples, reminiscent of some of the best landscapes and scenery that Bali has to offer. You can easily visit all the following places in half a day if you have your own transport.

Taman Narmada

Apparently designed as a scaled down version of the summit of Gunung Rinjani and its crater lake, **Taman Narmada** (Narmada Park; admission 5000Rp; 7am-6pm) was built in 1805. Though the rectangular main pool and manicured terraced gardens hardly look like a volcanic cone, the extensive grounds of the park are a pleasant enough place to spend an hour or two (except perhaps on Sundays when it's packed).

The temple, **Pura Kalasa**, is still in use, and the Balinese Pujawali celebration is held here every year (in November or December) in honour of the god Batara, who is said to dwell on Gunung Rinjani. There's also a large swimming pool (2000Rp extra) in the grounds.

Narmada is 6km east of Bertais, and then 100m south of Lombok's main east–west highway. Frequent bemo from Mandalika run to Narmada market, which is directly opposite the entrance to the gardens.

Pura Lingsar

This large **temple compound** (admission by donation; 7am-6pm), built in 1714 by King Anak Agung Ngurah, is the holiest in Lombok. It combines the Bali Hindu and Wektu Telu (p316) religions in one complex. Designed with two separate sections and built on two different levels, the Hindu temple (Pura Gaduh) in the northern half is higher than the Wektu Telu temple in the southern section. Pura Gaduh has four shrines: one orientated to Gunung Rinjani (seat of the gods on Lombok), one to Gunung Agung (seat of the gods in Bali) and a double shrine representing the union between the two islands.

The Wektu Telu temple is noted for its small enclosed pond devoted to Lord Vishnu, and the holy eels which can be enticed from their hiding places with hard-boiled eggs (available at stalls outside). You will be expected to rent a sash and/or sarong (or bring your own) to enter the temple, but not to enter the outer buildings.

A huge ritual battle, Perang Topat, is held here every year here in November or December (the exact date depends on the lunar month). After a costumed parade, Hindus and Wektu pelt each other with *ketupat* (sticky rice in coconut leaves).

Pura Lingsar is 9km northeast of Mandalika. First take a bemo from the terminal to Narmada, and another to Lingsar. Ask to be dropped off near the entrance to the temple complex, which is 300m down a well-marked path from the main road.

Suranadi

Suranadi is a pleasant little village surrounded by picturesque countryside. It has a temple, a small pocket of forest and a swimming pool, making it a popular spot for locals on weekends.

SIGHTS

Set amid gorgeous countryside, **Pura Suranadi** (admission by donation; 7.30am-6pm) is one of the holiest Hindu temples on Lombok. It's worth a visit for its lovely gardens which have a bubbling, icy cold natural spring and restored baths with ornate Balinese carvings (plus the obligatory holy eels).

Just opposite the village market, an entrance leads to **Hutan Wisata Suranadi** (admission 1000Rp; 8am-5pm), a small forest sanctuary which is a shady and quiet area good for short hikes and bird-watching. There's a **Sumatran elephant** (rides through the forest 15/25min 40,000/60,000Rp) here too.

SLEEPING & EATING

Just above the temple, **Losmen Jati** (☎ 6606437; r 30,000Rp) is a friendly and well-kept place, while the once-wonderful colonial atmosphere of the **Suranadi Hotel** (☎ 636411; fax 635630; r from 195,000Rp;) still has some faded charm, as well as a pool and tennis courts.

Several smart restaurants are dotted along the main road close to the temple and there are plenty of cheap warung (food stalls) in the neighbouring village of Surandi.

The temple is 6km northwest of Narmada and served by frequent public bemo. Failing that, charter one.

Sesaot & Around

Some 4km northeast of Suranadi is Sesaot, a charming market town on the edge of a forest. There are some gorgeous picnic spots and you can swim in the river. The water is very cool and is considered holy as it comes straight from Gunung Rinjani. Regular transport connects Narmada with Sesaot, and bites are available at the warung along the main street.

Further east, **Air Nyet** is another pretty village with more options for swimming and picnics. Ask for directions to the unsigned turn-off in the middle of Sesaot. The bridge and road to Air Nyet are rough, but it's a lovely stroll (about 3km) from Sesaot; otherwise charter a vehicle from Sesaot or Narmada.

Gunung Pengsong

This Balinese hilltop **temple** (admission by donation; 7am-6pm), 9km south of Mataram, has spectacular views across a green ocean of rice fields towards distant volcanoes and the sea. Japanese soldiers hid here towards the end of WWII, and remnants of cannons can be found, as well as plenty of pesky monkeys.

Once a year, generally in March or April, a buffalo is taken up the steep 100m slope and sacrificed to give thanks for a good harvest. The **Desa Bersih festival** (p337) also occurs here at harvest time – houses and gardens are cleaned, fences whitewashed, and roads and paths repaired. Once part of a ritual to rid the village of evil spirits, it's now held in honour of the rice goddess Dewi Sri.

It's a 15-minute walk up to the temple top from the entrance. Very little direct public transport comes here – it's best visited with your own wheels.

Banyumulek

This is one of the main **pottery centres** on Lombok, specialising in decorated pots and pots with a woven fibre covering, as well as more traditional urns and water flasks. It's close to the city – head south of Sweta on the main road to Lembar, and after 6km take a turnoff on the right to Banyumulek, a couple of kilometres to the west.

LEMBAR

Lembar is Lombok's main port for liners coming in from Bali and Pelni. Though the harbour itself, with azure inlets ringed by soaring green hills, has to be one of Indonesia's most beautiful, there's no reason to stay the night given the derth of facilities and excellent transport connections with Mataram and Senggigi. But if you do somehow get stuck, or need a bite to eat, the clean and very hospitable **Losmen Tidar** (☎ 681444; Jl Raya Pelabuhan; s/d with bathroom 40,000Rp, cottages 75,000Rp, all incl breakfast) 1km north of the ferry port is an excellent deal. It offers neat rooms and cottages, all with cable TV and one with its very own fish pond. Very hearty Indonesian meals (8000Rp to 17,000Rp) are also served by the family owners.

Plenty of bemo shuttle back and forth between Lembar and the Mandalika terminal in Bertais (3500Rp), or you can catch one at the market stop in Cakra. See p350 for details on the ferries and boats between Bali and Lembar, including the public ferries from Padangbai (p221).

SOUTHWESTERN PENINSULA

The corrugated, beach-blessed coastline and tiny offshore islands west of Sekotong has long been hyped as Lombok's next big tourist destination, but while the odd pocket of development is ongoing here, for now it remains a tranquil, highly scenic region. The hump-shaped inland hills form rich pastureland in the rainy season; visit the area at this time and you'll hear cow bells clanking. The road which hugs the coast, passing white-sand cove after cove, is narrow but paved until Selegang. A track continues to the west past Bangko Bangko to Tanjung Desert (Desert Point), one of Asia's legendary surf breaks, but there's no accommodation here, so you'll need to bring camping gear.

Only a few of the beautiful offshore islands, fringed with coconut palm–studded sandy beaches and offering fine snorkelling, are inhabited. Currently, Gili Nanggu and Gili Gede have accommodation. The latter island has some Bugis villages where locals make a living from boat building, and also some offshore pearl farms.

Sleeping & Eating

Places to stay and restaurants are slim on the ground in this region, and some close in the rainy season. **Sundancer** (www.sundancerresort.com), a huge new hotel and resort complex, with a PADI scuba diving centre is due to open in late 2006 just west of Pandanan.

MAINLAND

Putri Doyang (☎ 0812 375 2459; Jl Raya Pelangangi, Tembowong; s/d 25,000/50,000Rp) Simple clean rooms and hospitable owners make this losmen (basic accommodation), 2km north of Pelangan, a budget option worth considering.

Sekotong Indah Beach Cottages (☎ 6601921; r without/with air-con 55,000/85,000Rp; ❄) Offers basic tiled, nearly clean rooms with bamboo furniture that would benefit from a little more TLC. However, the location opposite a slim sandy beach 2km west of Taun is great. Meals are 5000 Rp to 20,000Rp.

Bola Bola Paradis (☎ 623783; batuapi99@hotmail.com; Jl Raya Bangko-Bangko; r 160,000-280,000Rp; ❄) Just west of Pelangan, this attractive place set on a fine stretch of sand has funky octagonal bungalows, comfortable air-con rooms, and a restaurant (mains 20,000Rp to 55,000Rp) and chic lounge area.

Nirvana Roemah Air (☎ 640107; www.floatingvilla.com; Jl Raya Medang, Sekotong Barat; villas incl airport transfers US$150-250 ; ❄) Billing itself as a floating island resort, this luxurious place, 2km west of Sekotong, in a secluded mangrove-fringed location, has stylish wood-panelled villas. Book via the internet for substantial discounts in the low season.

ISLANDS

Gili Nanggu Cottages (☎ 623783; www.gilinangu.com; cottages s/d 100,000/120,000Rp, s/d bungalows 225,000/275,000Rp; ❄) A great choice, this island resort has a beachfront location and rustic two-storey *lumbung* (rice barn) cottages, plus less attractive but comfortable air-con bungalows. Lifts from Lembar can be organised. Meals are 16,000Rp to 38,000Rp.

Secret Island Resort (☎ 661-3579; www.secretislandresort.com; r 200,000Rp, bungalow 250,000Rp, two bed villa 1,000,000Rp; ❄) This new resort on Gili Gede offers beautiful accommodation, all with fine sea or mountain views and terraces. The double-deck bar-restaurant rustles up great seafood and barbecued meats. Check out the hot tub – spa, plunge pool and swimming pool are planned. Kayak, snorkel and dive trips can be arranged here.

Getting There & Away

Bemo buzz between Lembar and Pelangan (one hour, 45 minutes, every 30 minutes) via Sekotong (25 minutes). West of Pelangan, transport is less regular, but the route is still served by infrequent bemo services until Selegang.

To reach Gili Nanggu, a return charter on a *prahu* (outrigger fishing boat) from Taun costs 150,000Rp. Public boats connect Tembowong with the islands of Gili Gede and Gili Ringit (both 8000Rp one way), leaving from Putri Doyong losmen, 2km north of Pelangan. Alternatively, you can charter your own boats here for about 60,000Rp one way or arrange a day trip around the islands for about 225,000Rp.

SENGGIGI

Superbly positioned along a stretch of sweeping bays, Senggigi is Lombok's principal beach resort. Accommodation here is generally excellent value for money, as luxury hotels have slashed rates in an attempt to draw in tourists following several tough years. Unless you visit in peak season, expect quiet restaurants and empty shopping malls, but plenty of attention from the street hawkers.

Senggigi has fine sandy beaches, and as the sun sinks, all eyes turn west to take in the blood-red sunsets over Bali that can be enjoyed from one of the seafront restaurants. As it gets dark, the fishing fleet lines up offshore, the bright lanterns glinting like a floating village against the night sky.

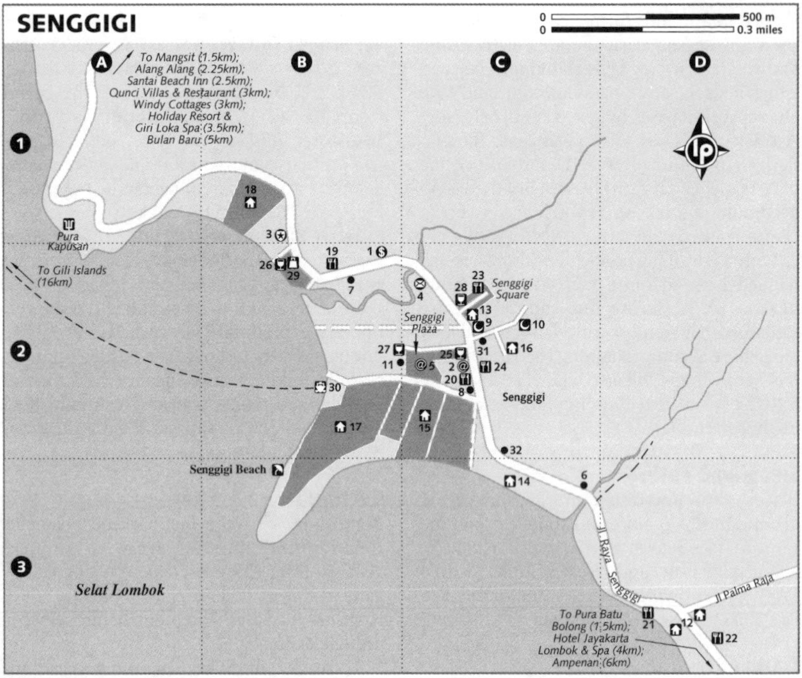

Orientation

The Senggigi area spans about 10km of coastal road. Most of the shops and other facilities, and a fair concentration of hotels, are on the main road, Jl Raya Senggigi, which starts about 6km north of Ampenan. Street numbers are not used in Senggigi.

Information

EMERGENCY

The nearest hospitals are in Mataram.

Police station (☎ 110) Next to the Pasar Seni.

Senggigi Medical Clinic (☎ 693856; 8am-7pm) Based at the Senggigi Beach Hotel.

Tourist Police (☎ 632733)

INTERNET ACCESS & TELEPHONES

Most internet cafés on the main strip also double as wartel.

Millennium Internet (☎ 693860; Jl Raya Senggigi; per min 300Rp; 24hr)

Superstar (Senggigi Plaza A2; per min 300Rp; 24hr)

MONEY

There are several ATMs in central Senggigi. The Bank Central Asia (BCA) and Bank Negara Indonesia (BNI) on Jl Raya Senggigi both have ATMs and will exchange cash and travellers cheques.

POST

Post office (Jl Raya Senggigi; 8am-6pm)

Sights

PURA BATU BOLONG

The small pagodas of this modest Balinese **temple** (admission by donation; 7am-7pm) cling to a rocky volcanic outcrop that juts into the sea about 2km south of central Senggigi. Crabs scuttle over statues and families come here to snack and cool off at the beach directly below. The temple is orientated towards Gunung Agung, Bali's holiest mountain, and is a favoured spot to watch the sunset. The rock underneath the temple has a natural hole that gives it its name – *batu bolong* (literally, 'rock with hole').

Activities

SNORKELLING & DIVING

There's reasonable snorkelling off the point in Senggigi, in the sheltered bay around the

INFORMATION
- BCA ATM (see 13)
- BNI ATM 1 B2
- Millennium Internet 2 C2
- Police Station 3 B1
- Post Office 4 C2
- Senggigi Medical Clinic (see 17)
- Superstar 5 C2

SIGHTS & ACTIVITIES
- Blue Marlin 6 C3
- Dive Indonesia 7 B2
- Dream Divers 8 C2
- Laguna Beach Spa (see 18)
- Lombok Biking Tours (see 8)
- Mandara Spa (see 17)
- Mesjid 9 C2
- Mesjid Baru 10 C2
- Rinjani Trek Club (see 20)
- Stylish Salon 11 B2

SLEEPING
- Batu Bolong Cottages 12 D3
- Café Wayan (see 22)
- Hotel Elen 13 C2
- Lina Cottages 14 C3
- Mascot Cottages 15 C2
- Raja's Bungalows 16 C2
- Senggigi Beach Hotel 17 B2
- Sheraton Senggigi Beach Resort 18 B1

EATING
- Asmara 19 B2
- Bumbu 20 C2
- Café Alberto 21 D3
- Café Wayan 22 D3
- English Tea Room 23 C2
- Papaya Café 24 C2
- Rumah Makan Padang (see 9)
- Sugar Café (see 27)

DRINKING
- Happy Café 25 C2
- Office 26 B2
- Papaya Café (see 24)
- Sugar Café 27 B2
- Tropicana 28 C2

SHOPPING
- Asmara Collection (see 19)
- Pasar Seni (Art Market) 29 B2

TRANSPORT
- Departure point for Perama boats 30 B2
- Kotasi 31 C2
- Perama 32 C2

headland, and in front of Windy Cottages, a few kilometres north of the town. You can rent snorkelling gear (25,000Rp per day) from several spots along the beach near Senggigi Beach Hotel.

Diving trips from Senggigi normally visit the Gili Islands, so you may want to consider basing yourself there. Professional dive centres include the following:

Blue Marlin (☎ 692003; www.dive-indo.com; Jl Raya Senggigi & Holiday Resort Lombok)

Dive Indonesia (☎ 639367; www.diveindonesiaonline.com; Galeria Mall, Jl Raya Senggigi)

Dream Divers (☎ 692047; www.dreamdivers.com; Jl Raya Senggigi)

BIKING & HIKING

Guided mountain bike rides are offered by **Lombok Biking Tours** (☎ 6605792; Jl Raya Senggigi; day excursions per person from 200,000Rp) through rural areas of Lombok including the Sekotong region and the countryside around Lingsar and Surandi.

If you're thinking of hiking Gunung Rinjani, you could drop by the local office of the **Rinjani Trek Club** (☎ 693202; rtc.senggigi@gmail.com; Jl Raya Senggigi) for information about routes and conditions.

MASSAGES, SPAS & SALONS

Several local masseurs armed with mats and oils tout for business on Senggigi Beach – you won't have to wait long before someone approaches you. Expect to pay about 40,000Rp for one hour after bargaining. Almost all hotels can also arrange for a masseur to come to your room; rates start at about 60,000Rp.

For a really indulgent experience, visit one the many spas in the Senggigi area, most are hotel-based. **Giri Loka Spa** (☎ 693444; Holiday Resort; ⌚ 8am-9pm) offers fabulous warm stone massages (one hour; US$45). First rosemary and orange oils are applied to your body then a masseur rubs the heated stones over your 'chakra' points, stimulating the lymph nodes, blood and muscles.

Laguna Beach Spa (☎ 693333; Sheraton Senggigi Beach Resort; ⌚ 9am-9pm) has Balinese milk-and-honey body scrub treatments (1½ hours; US$50) and massages (one hour; US$28). The **Mandara Spa** (☎ 693210; Senggigi Beach Hotel; ⌚ 10am-9pm) offers a comprehensive range of treatments and massages (from US$26) including Balinese aromatherapy massages and reflexology. Rates at the **Jayakarta Spa** (☎ 693048; Hotel Jayakarta Lombok; ⌚ 8am-11pm) are competitive at 120,000Rp for a traditional massage and 255,000Rp for a Lulu Indonesian exfoliation and 'body polishing' treatment.

For a manicure, pedicure or other beauty treatments in simple surrounds, **Stylish Salon** (☎ 6194240; Senggigi Plaza Blok 1 No 4; treatments & massages from 40,000Rp; ⌚ 8.30am-7.30pm) fits the bill.

Sleeping

Senggigi has an excellent choice of accommodation spread up and down the coastal road; if you want to stay close to the action, chose a place on the main strip – virtually everything listed below is located on or just off the main drag JI Raya Sengiggi. Many of the places north of here in Mangsit have more character and wonderful gardens, and some offer free transport into central Senggigi.

Virtually all the top-end places have special promotional rates outside peak times, when discounts of up to 50% are common.

BUDGET

Senggigi

Hotel Elen (☎ 693014; r without/with air-con 50,000/75,000Rp;) This hotel offers a quadrangle of smallish, cheap, if not very cheerful rooms; those with air-con are a little better presented. Prepare yourself for a double-barrelled early morning wake-up call from the two local mosques, Mesjid (Mosque) and Mesjid Baru (New Mosque).

Raja's Bungalows (☎ 0812 3770 138; rajas22@yahoo.com; s/d 60,000/75,000Rp) A welcoming, bohemian guesthouse that's popular with travellers, Raja's has inviting, spotless rooms with high ceilings, bamboo furniture and zany outdoor bathrooms with mandi and showers. There's plenty of communal chilling space, a few books to browse and veggie meals (9000Rp to 14,000Rp) are offered.

Lina Cottages (☎ 693237; r with fan/air-con/sea view 60,000/75,000/150,000Rp;) Occupying pole position right on the beach, Lina is a good choice with a variety of rooms, the cheapies on the small side and fan-only; all have verandas. There's an adjoining Indo-Chinese restaurant.

Café Wayan (☎ 693098; s/d incl breakfast 100,000/150,000Rp) At the rear of the café, these four stylish rooms, tastefully furnished with beautiful ikat fabrics and Balinese artefacts and with large bathtubs, enjoy a peaceful location overlooking a blossoming garden.

Mangsit

Santai Beach Inn (☎ 693038; www.santaibeachinn.com; lumbung s/d 70,000/80,000Rp, bungalows 95,000-200,000Rp) Set in a lush garden by the beach this unusual place has a selection of rustic *lumbung* and spacious bungalows, constructed from local wood and bamboo. Inexpensive, veggie and fish dishes are eaten communally in a pleasant pavilion (lunch/dinner 15,000/25,000Rp) and there's a book exchange.

Windy Cottages (☎ 693191; lidya@mataram.wasantara.net.id; cottages with cold/hot water 110,000/150,000Rp, r 140,000Rp;) Charming, popular beachside place with decent snorkelling offshore and attractive thatched cottages, many with sea-view verandas. Also has air-con rooms and hot-water bathrooms; local and Western meals are offered (dishes 14,000Rp to 30,000Rp).

Bulan Baru (☎ 693786; r 200,000Rp;) Set in a lovely garden and a short walk from a fine sandy beach, this welcoming hotel has spacious, well-furnished rooms, all with minibars, air-con and hot water bathrooms. The friendly Australian owners, and staff, are a mine of information about Lombok and local culture. No children are allowed.

MIDRANGE

Senggigi

Batu Bolong Cottages (☎ 693065; bbcresort_lombok@yahoo.com; r incl breakfast inland/beachside 125,000/260,000Rp;) This place, located south of central Senggigi, has good-value, spacious rooms with fridges and Balinese artefacts facing a lawned beachfront plot, with the waves just beyond. Its cheaper digs facing a garden on the other side of the road are looking a little tired however.

Hotel Jayakarta Lombok (☎ 693048; www.indo.com/hotels/jayakartalombok; r US$38-43, ste from US$63;) This Indonesian chain hotel, 5km south of central Sengpi offers competitive rates on its comfortable air-con rooms with bathtubs, minibars and sea views. There's a beachfront setting, extensive grounds, a spa (p295), and a large pool.

Mascot Cottages (☎ 693365; fax 693236; s/d bungalows 200,000/275,000Rp;) Undergoing renovation at the time of research, this place has air-con bungalows set in a garden that extends towards the beach.

Mangsit

Holiday Resort (☎ 693444; www.holidayresort-lombok.com; Jl Raya Senggigi; r from US$68, bungalows from US$140;) A well-designed luxury hotel with extensive gardens plotted with coconut trees and the full gamut of accommodation options, from rooms to private villas. Also offers a fine spa, tennis courts, a scuba school and a playground and day nursery for children aged two to 11.

TOP END

Senggigi has an excess of luxury hotels, so discounts on the rack rates listed here are usually available.

Senggigi

Senggigi Beach Hotel (☎ 693210; www.senggigibeach.aerowisata.com; r US$80, beach bungalows US$100-160 plus 21% tax;) These classy detached bungalows enjoy a beautiful setting in lush gardens set back from the beach, though only Nos 105 and 106 have direct sea views. There's a large pool that's well situated close to the shore, a spa and tennis courts in the complex.

Sheraton Senggigi Beach Resort (☎ 693333; www.sheraton.com; r from US$178;) Just north of the centre this fine hotel has commodious rooms, all with terraces or balconies. There's a palm-fringed swimming pool and a kids' pool, two restaurants and a well-regarded spa (p295) and health club. Discounts can drop rates to around US$80 a night at quiet times.

Mangsit

Qunci Villas (☎ 693800; www.quncivillas.com; r garden/ocean view US$70/90 plus 21% tax;) Lombok's hippest hotel, combining textbook minimalist style with Balinese and Japanese design influence. The rooms are undeniably gorgeous (book No 8 for the best sea view) and popular with moneyed Europeans and rich kids from Jakarta. There's a small pool at the ocean's edge and a very fine restaurant (p298). You'll find the staff is extremely well trained and welcoming. For groups or the seriously solvent, there are two private villas (from US$325 a night) up in the hills behind the hotel, each with private pool and butler service that come close to defining Lombok luxe.

Alang Alang (☎ 693518; www.alang-alang-villas.com; s/d bungalows US$80/110;) Stylish bungalows set in lush gardens, most are semidetached with commodious beds and Balinese wood furniture. Only Nos 101 to 110 have decent sea views. The beach here consists of a slimline stretch of sand and the pool is small.

Eating

Central Senggigi is an excellent place to eat out, with a cosmopolitan glut of restaurants. Many offer free transport for evening diners – phone for a ride.

For authentic Indonesian street food, head to the hillside warung on the route north to Mangsit where *sate* (satay) sizzles and pots of noodles bubble.

SENGGIGI

Rumah Makan Padang (☎ 693026; meals 8000-14,000Rp) Come here for real local atmosphere and authentically fiery Padang food, including a filling *rendang* (beef coconut curry).

Café Wayan (☎ 693098; dishes 9000-45,000Rp) A highly enjoyable place to eat, this stylish Balinese-run café has an extensive menu of soups and salads, pizza, pasta dishes, pancakes, seafood and yummy freshly baked breads and cakes.

Bumbu (☎ 692236; mains 18,000-30,000Rp) Deservedly popular little restaurant on the main strip, come here for inexpensive Thai curries and Indo cooking served up on a slim streetside terrace. Some Western dishes are also served, and there's always a daily special.

Asmara (☎ 693619; www.asmara-group.com; mains 18,000-75,000Rp;) Consistently recommended by expats, this is a comfortable, spacious and airy two-storey thatched restaurant offering fine European cuisine – try the *frikadellen* (meatballs with mustard gravy and sautéed potatoes) – plus Indonesian and international favourites. Children are well catered for from a special menu, and there's a small pool and play area too.

English Tea Room (☎ 692085; Blok A4, Senggigi Square; dishes 21,000-65,000Rp; 9am-9pm;) A civilised air-con retreat, this delightful place, located in a shopping plaza, offers a wide choice of salads and sandwiches as well as terrific cakes. The teas include Ceylon and Indonesian green and you'll find some interesting coffees too. There's a terrace table upstairs.

Sugar Café (☎ 6194000; Plaza Senggigi; mains 22,000-44,000Rp; 6-11.30pm;) Perhaps the most modern place in town, this chic little lounge bar-restaurant is highly atmospheric, with candlelit tables and creative, beautifully presented Indonesian and Asian fusion cuisine. Eat in the air-conditioned interior or outside on the terrace.

Papaya Café (☎ 693616; mains 28,000-50,000Rp; 8am-11.30pm;) Invitingly decorated with rattan sofas and exposed stone walls, this enjoyable place has a tempting menu of Indonesian, Chinese and Japanese dishes and some of the best cocktails in town.

Café Alberto (☎ 693039; mains 30,000-85,000Rp; 11.30am-11pm) Occupying a large beachfront plot well away from the road, feast on Italian (pizza and pasta) or Indonesian (the usual suspects in generous portions) cuisine at this enjoyable restaurant. Lunch at a table on the sand and then snooze it off on one of Alberto's loungers. There's also a small kids' playground here with slides and a sandpit.

MANGSIT

Bulan Baru (☎ 693786; mains 24,000-48,000Rp) Head to this hotel restaurant for Western comfort food – think meaty bangers and creamy mash, or maybe a juicy imported steak. You'll also find snacks such as spring rolls and burgers.

our pick **Qunci restaurant** (☎ 693800; www.quncivillas.com; mains 46,000-64,000Rp) Abutting the beach in Mangsit, this terrific, hip hotel-restaurant (p297) has a modern menu with both Asian and European – think tuna balsamico and seafood risotto – dishes. The well-trained staff will guide you through the menu and make suggestions, while low-key electronica music adds atmosphere to the dining experience. Arrive before sunset and get the party started properly with two-for-one cocktails during happy hour (4pm to 7pm).

Drinking & Entertainment

Senggigi's after-dark action is pretty middle-of-the-road by nature, revolving around a handful of bars and a disco or two. All bars are on Jl Raya Senggigi except one, and may close early if it's very quiet.

Happy Café (☎ 693984; 8am-2am) This slightly staid but always popular bar has a resident cover band playing reggae or pop tunes every night.

Papaya Café (☎ 693616; 8am-1am) It's hardly cutting edge, but the Papaya also has live music of the Muzak variety and is fine for a relaxed drink. Happy hour is from 4pm to 8pm.

Office (☎ 693162; 9am-2am) Beachside bar with fine sunset views, a pool table and live sports events on the TV. It's popular with middle-aged expats and there are regular pool competitions on Tuesday.

Sugar Café (☎ 0812 3962 206; Plaza Senggigi) Tiny, hip place with electronica and lounge music and a mixed gay and straight clientele. Also serves fine food (p297).

Tropicana (☎ 693432; www.tropicanalombok.com; admission 25,000Rp; 11pm-3am) Old skool–style disco with slightly cheesy DJs spinning Western pop, rock and a few Indo hits plus live acts and bands. Expect 'Mr & Miss Tropicana' contests and the like.

Shopping

Senggigi's shopping malls are woefully under-occupied. The **Pasar Seni** (Art Market; Jl Raya Senggigi) has some handicraft stalls and you'll find **Asmara Collection** (☎ 693619; Jl Raya Senggigi; 9am-9.30pm), in front of the restaurant of the same name, has some fine weavings, tribal art and furniture.

The warehouses and craft shops along the main road to Ampenan are also worth stopping for a browse.

DETOUR

North of Senggigi is a succession of wonderful, near-deserted sandy coves where you can pretty much guarantee to have a beach to yourself, bar the odd fishermen and his net. Just west of the Bulan Baru hotel, about 7km from central Senggigi, there are some beautiful beaches, Pantai Setangi being just one fine example. The coastal road from Mangsit to Pemenang is a spectacular drive in itself, slaloming around the coastal contours, serving up sweeping views of the waves below.

Getting There & Away

BOAT

Perama (☎ 693007; Jl Raya Senggigi) operates a daily boat service from Padangbai in Bali to Senggigi (p224; 200,000Rp, four hours). There's also a daily Perama boat from Senggigi to the Gili Islands (70,000Rp, 30 to 60 minutes) at 9am, which means you avoid having to deal with Bangsal. The dive schools (p294) also operate speed-boat shuttles (from 120,000Rp per person) to the Gilis most days – contact them in advance.

BUS

Regular bemo travel to Senggigi from the Kebon Roek terminal in Ampenan (3000Rp), some continuing north as far as Pemenang or Bayan. Overcharging tourists is common on this route.

The Perama company has a few tourist shuttle bus/boat services daily between Senggigi and Bali; Kuta (Bali) and Bali airport (160,000Rp), Ubud (160,000Rp); and other places on Lombok including Kuta (80,000Rp).

Getting Around

A prepaid taxi from the airport to Senggigi costs 48,000Rp. The very efficient and prompt **Bluebird taxis** (☎ 627000) will whisk you around the Senggigi area and beyond. Remember that many restaurants offer free lifts for diners – call for a ride.

Cars and motorbikes are readily available for hire in Senggigi; ask at any hotel or travel agent. **Kotasi** (☎ 693804; Jl Raya Senggigi) has bikes from 40,000Rp per day and jeeps from 175,000Rp per day (its insurance covers you for a maximum charge of US$500 in case of damage). You could also hire a car and guide-driver

GILI ISLANDS

☎ 0370

Just off the northwest coast of Lombok is a vision of tropical paradise – a trio of tiny coral-fringed islands, each with white sandy beaches and pellucid water teeming with a kaleidoscopic array of reef fish. For years the islands of Gili Air, Gili Meno and Gili Trawangan were a budget-priced stopover for travellers on the Asian trail, but recently, accommodation options have diversified and now there are luxury villas and rustic chic bungalows dotted between the simple bamboo-and-thatch huts for rent.

Delightfully free of cars and motorcycles, the only traffic on the Gilis is the tinkling *cidomo* (pony cart) and the odd bicycle. All three islands have professional scuba diving centres, and the snorkelling is excellent too.

Each Gili has its own character and charm: Trawangan has a big party scene and Meno is very mellow, with Gili Air falling somewhere between the two in terms of atmosphere.

Information

INTERNET & TELEPHONE

All the islands have wartel and internet cafés, but surfing (around 400Rp per minute) is woefully slow in most places.

MONEY

There are no banks on the Gilis and moneychanger exchange rates at the shops and hotels are dire. Credit card cash advances are available through many dive operators, although a 7% commission is charged. It's better to change money in Mataram or Senggigi or use the ATMs there. Try to bring as many small-denomination notes as possible, as there's often a problem changing the bigger notes.

Dangers & Annoyances

There are no police on any of the Gilis, so report any theft to the island *kepala desa* (village head) – if you need help locating them, or need someone to help you translate, the dive schools are a good point of contact. If you are on Gili Trawangan, notify Satgas, the community organisation that runs island affairs, via your hotel or dive centre. Satgas uses its community contacts to resolve problems or track down stolen property with a minimum of fuss.

Touts often meet boats as they land, and they can be quick to take your luggage, plus you, to the place of *their* choice. If you want to stay in a particular place, don't let a tout convince you that it's full, expensive, closed, or doesn't exist.

Incidents are rare, but several foreign women have experienced sexual harassment and even assault while on the Gilis – it's best to walk home in pairs to the quieter parts of the islands. Each island has a gaggle of local Kuta cowboy–style gigolos who compete to impress and seduce visiting Western women, and can get very territorial with other males that they see as competition.

SURVIVING BANGSAL

Bangsal, a squalid little port, is the gateway for public boats to the Gilis. Frankly, it's a hole and has become so overrun with persistent small-time hustlers and would-be scammers that it's best to completely ignore anything that you're told here about boats being cancelled, or other tall tales.

Public bemo to Bangsal actually stop in Pemenang on the main road, 1km or so from the port. Hiring a *cidomo* (pony cart; around 3000Rp) to the port is money well spent as it'll save you an ear-bending from the hustlers on your way to the terminal.

Keep calm, and head straight for the ramshackle Koperasi harbour office on the left, as you approach the sea. Here you can buy inexpensive, fixed-price, public boat tickets (as well as shuttle and charter tickets) to the three Gili islands – there are printed price lists available. The harbour office has a scruffy waiting area where they'll announce when the public boats have enough passengers to depart.

It's quite possible to avoid Bangsal completely by using the Perama boat service between Senggigi and the Gilis, or by booking a speedboat transfer (from US$12, 15 minutes) to/from Lombok using the Gili dive schools – these operate from the serene little bay of Teluk Nare to the south.

Jellyfish are common when strong winds blow from the mainland, and they can leave a painful rash. See p370.

Getting There & Away

From Bali, most people either use the Perama tourist bus and boat service via Padangbai (see p224) and Senggigi; or, fly to Mataram and travel on from there.

Coming from other parts of Lombok you can travel via Senggigi (there are direct Perama boats to the Gilis from here); via Bangsal (the cheapest route) or book a shuttle bus/speed boat. Blue Marlin and Manta Dive (p306) on Gili Trawangan can arrange transfers (125,000 to 250,000Rp per person, depending on destination and passenger numbers). All the above use the idyllic harbour of Teluk Nare, south of Bangsal.

Coming by public transport, catch a bus or bemo to Pemenang, from where it's about 1km by *cidomo* (3000Rp) to Bangsal harbour. Bangsal is a headache, see p299 for tips on dealing with the inevitable hassle there. Boat tickets are sold at the Koperasi harbour office, where the prices are displayed – the public boats (roughly 8am to 5pm) don't leave until full (about 18 people). While it can take hours for the boat to Gili Meno to fill up, you shouldn't have to wait more than an hour for the other two islands. The one-way fares at the time of research were 5500Rp to Gili Air, 6800Rp to Gili Meno and 8800Rp to Gili Trawangan, though expect steep price rises because of escalating fuel costs. Special charters can also be organised in Bangsal.

All boats pull up on the beach when they get to the Gilis, so you'll have to wade ashore with your luggage.

Getting Around

CIDOMO

Hiring a *cidomo* for a clip-clop around an island is a great way to explore the terrain; a short trip costs around 7000Rp, or you can pay about 20,000Rp for a two-hour jaunt.

ISLAND-HOPPING

There's a twice-daily boat service that loops between all three islands, meaning that you can spend the day snorkelling and exploring Meno and get back to Air or Trawangan for a sunset drink. The morning boat leaves Air at 8.30am, stopping on Meno at 8.45am, Trawangan at 9.30am, Meno again at 9.45am and returning to Air at 9.45am. In the afternoons the boat leaves Air at 3pm, Meno at 3.15pm, Trawangan at 3.30pm, Meno at 4.15pm and gets back to Air at 4.30pm. Check the latest timetable at the islands' dock.

WALKING

The Gilis are flat and easy enough to get around by foot (or bicycle, opposite). A torch (flashlight) is useful at night –you can buy one at local shops for around 25,000Rp.

GILI AIR

Closest to the mainland, Gili Air's easy-going appeal contrasts with party-boy Gili T and sedate Gili Meno. The island retains a distinctly rural character, its coconut grove–filled, flat landscape juxtaposed with dramatic views of Gunung Rinjani and, on a clear day, Gunung Agung in Bali. The slim white-sand beaches, turquoise water and laid-back atmosphere are the main draw, but in high season the bar scene can get quite lively. Gili Air is the most heavily populated of the three islands, yet this still amounts to just 1800 or so inhabitants.

Orientation

Boats stop at the southern end of the island, near the jetty; the **Koperasi** (🕒 8am-5.30pm) has a hut here with prices marked clearly outside. Virtually all accommodation and restaurants are on the east and south coasts, which have the best beaches for swimming. The network of dirt tracks that crisscrosses the island can get quite confusing at times. To explore Air it's simplest to follow the coastal path around the island – it's a lovely walk that takes about an hour and a half.

Information

There's a small **Perama** (☎ 637816) office next to the Gili Indah Hotel. **Ozzy's Shop** (☎ 622179; per min 400Rp; 🕒 8am-8pm) about halfway up the east coast has pedestrian-paced, internet access, a wartel and will change money, as will Hotel Gili Air, but exchange rates are poor. Blue Marlin charge 7% for cash advances on credit cards. There's a **clinic** (🕒 8am-6pm) in the village for medical services.

Activities

SNORKELLING & DIVING

You'll find diverse marine life and great **snorkelling** all along the east coast. Beach access is

LOMBOK

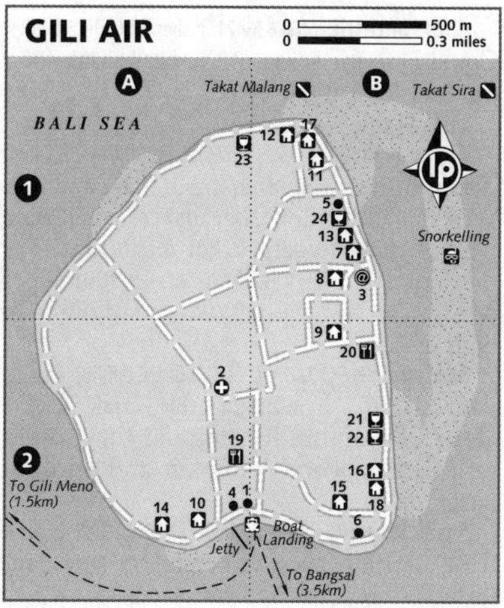

INFORMATION
Koperasi/Public Boat Office....1 A2
Medical Clinic....2 A2
Ozzy's Shop....3 B1
Perama....4 A2

SIGHTS & ACTIVITIES
Blue Marlin Dive Centre....5 B1
Dream Divers....6 B2

SLEEPING
Abdi Fantastik....7 B1
Coconut Cottages....8 B1
Gili Air Santay....9 B2
Gili Indah Hotel....10 A2
Gusung Indah....11 B1
Hotel Gili Air....12 B1
Kira Kira....13 B1
Lucky's....14 A2
Nusa Tiga Bungalows....15 B2
Pino Cottages....16 B2
Pondok Sandi....17 B1
Sunrise Cottages & Restaurant....18 B2

EATING
Abdi Fantastik....(see 7)
Blue Marlin....(see 5)
Coconut Cottages....(see 8)
Gecko Café....19 A2
Gusung Indah....(see 11)
Hotel Gili Air....(see 12)
Munchies....20 B2
Santay....(see 9)

DRINKING
Chill Out Bar....21 B2
Gita Gili....22 B2
Hallelujah Bar....(see 11)
Legend Pub....23 A1
Star Bar....24 B1

easy and gear can be hired from Ozzy's Shop for 15,000Rp a day. Check with dive centres first about currents, as sometimes they can be extremely strong. Ozzy's Shop also operates **glass-bottomed boat tours** (per person 40,000Rp, minimum 4 people) around all three islands.

There are several good **scuba diving** sites a short boat ride away. See p306 for more information. Gili Air has two dive schools, **Blue Marlin Dive Centre** (☎ 634387; www.diveindo.com) and **Dream Divers** (☎ 634547; www.dreamdivers.com).

SURFING

Directly off the southern tip of the island there's a long, peeling right-hand break. To rent a board, ask around in the dive schools.

CYCLING

Ozzy's Shop has bikes for hire for 20,000Rp a day. Exploring the island by bike is a delight, though sandy tracks can make the going a bit tough, and you're sure to end up in someone's back yard at times due to the unmarked trails.

Sleeping

Most places are spread up and down the east coast, where the best swimming is. Prices quoted are high-season rates – expect about a 25% discount in low season. Breakfast is included in all (except one) of the hotels listed.

BUDGET

Gili Air Santay (☎ 641022; giliair_santay@yahoo.com; s/d 40,000/50,000Rp) Set back from the beach in a quiet coconut grove, these spacious bamboo-and-timber huts are just above the bog standard category, all coming with hammocks, fans and fairly modern bathrooms. There's also a little shoreside restaurant here, see p302.

Abdi Fantastik (☎ 636421; r 75,000-80,000Rp) Enjoying unobstructed sea vistas, these neat – rather than 'fantastik' – thatched bungalows are just a few metres from the shore and come equipped with verandas and a hammock to swing in.

Sunrise Cottages & Restaurant (☎ 642370; s 50,000-75,000Rp, d 80,000-100,000Rp) A class above the real cheapies, this efficiently run place has rustic two-storey *lumbung*-style bungalows with bathroom and separate living area (with day bed and hammock). The accommodation is well spaced and sits at the rear of a pretty garden. There's a safe for valuables and a great beachside café-restaurant.

Kira Kira (☎ 641021; kirakira@mataram.wasantara.net.id; s 70,000-110,000Rp, d 80,000-125,000Rp) Stylish, well-presented thatched cottages with rattan furniture, large ceiling fans, decent beds and hammocks overlooking a small garden. The bathrooms are cold water while the restaurant, open from 7am to 9pm, offers Japanese dishes such as tempura.

Coconut Cottages (☎ 635365; www.coconuts-giliair.com; r 110,000-180,000Rp) A delightful, welcoming Indo-Scottish–owned place with a selection of atmospheric accommodation spread around a fecund, well-tended garden. Some of the well-maintained cottages have shell-inlaid decorative detailing, all have good quality mattresses, bamboo furniture and bedside reading lights. There's a fine restaurant here too, right, and books for sale or rent.

Also worth considering:

Nusa Tiga Bungalows (r 40,000-50,000Rp) Basic bamboo bungalows set in a coconut grove, inland from the east coast.

Lucky's (☎ 0812 378 2156; 45,000Rp) Run by a friendly family, these simple bungalows enjoy a quiet location. No breakfast is included.

Pondok Sandi (s/d 50,000/100,000Rp) Facing the sea, these are spacious huts with bathrooms.

Pino Cottages (☎ 639304; r 60,000-80,000Rp) Situated back from the beach, Pino has well-maintained, clean thatched cottages with hammocks.

Gusung Indah (☎ 0812 3789 054; r 70,000-100,000Rp) Facing a good stretch of beach, these simple beach bungalows with verandas are decent value. You pay more for a sea view.

LOMBOK

MIDRANGE

Gili Indah Hotel (☎ 637328; gili_indah@mataram.wasantara.net.id; bungalows 200,000-350,000Rp; ❄) Conveniently close to the jetty, this well-run hotel has a variety of good, well-constructed bungalows, all with hot-water bathrooms. The best also have air-con and huge front decks with expansive sea views.

Hotel Gili Air (☎ 634435; www.hotelgiliair.com; r US$17, with hot water US$33, with hot water & TV US$43-63; ❄ 🏊) Setting itself up as the island's 'proper' hotel, this place offers four classes of digs – from rustic-but-comfy huts to international hotel-chain-style rooms with marble bathrooms, attractive wood furniture and laminate floors. The pool is small and the gardens look neglected however.

Eating

Dining out in Gili Air is a treat, with an array of simple places serving Indonesian and Western dishes, many located right by the sea – there's nothing fancy though. Beware – service can be slow.

Abdi Fantastik (☎ 636421; dishes 10,000-25,000Rp) Come here for some of the best Sasak food on the island at fair prices; try the *kangkung pelecing* (spicy water spinach).

Coconut Cottages (☎ 635365; dishes 10,000-28,000Rp) An inventively prepared menu that combines Western and Indonesian dishes, you'll dine well in this pleasant hotel restaurant. Try the fantastic Sasak buffet, at 40,000Rp per person, served every Wednesday night in high season.

Santay (☎ 641022; dishes 12,000-20,000Rp) Perch yourself on a beachside table, soak up the views of Gunung Rinjani and tuck into a sandwich, a good pumpkin and coconut curry, or satay.

Sasak Warung (mains 12,000-28,000Rp) Dine well here, by the waves, under pretty shell lanterns. It's one of the best places to eat fish and seafood.

Blue Marlin (☎ 634387; dishes 15,000-35,000Rp) The best bet for Western food, the kitchen here serves up a mean burger as well as pasta, sandwiches, stick-to-yer-ribs breakfasts, and some Indonesian dishes.

Hotel Gili Air (☎ 634435; dishes 15,000-56,000Rp) Recommended by resident foreigners as the best venue for pizza and pasta on the island, the service is prompt. Also serves Indonesian dishes and steaks.

Gecko Café (☎ 641014; dishes 10,000-25,000Rp; 🕒 11am-3pm & 6.30-8.30pm) This friendly caff is good for sandwiches, cake and coffee, or Indonesian snacks. Its Wednesday-night dinners, from 35,000Rp – such as roast beef followed by apple crumble – are an island institution for homesick Divemaster candidates.

Or try one of the following:

Munchies (dishes 7500-26,000Rp; 🕒 noon-11pm) Serves fine curries, fish and overflowing sandwiches.

Gusung Indah (☎ 0812 3789 054; dishes 10,000-30,000Rp; 🕒 8am-10.30pm) Sit under a beachfront *beruga* (open-sided pavilion) & feast on local food such as *opor ayam* (braised chicken in coconut milk), and sandwiches or pasta.

Drinking

Except for the odd party, Gili Air is generally pretty quiet at night.

Star Bar (🕒 3pm-late Thu-Tue) Next to the Blue Marlin, this little bar's trump card is Azam, the resident trickster barman.

Chill Out Bar (🕒 11-2am) Popular with visitors and locals, it has a good selection of spirits and cocktails.

Gita Gili (11-1am) A friendly bar where you can request a DVD to watch while you sink a cold one.

Hallelujah Bar (8am-11pm) Offers a beachside location and a well-stocked bar including plenty of spirits.

Legend Pub (10am-11.30pm Thu-Tue, happy hour 5-7pm, party 10pm-2am Wed) Wednesday night is the big one here, especially in high season, with speakers bumpin' to (mainly) reggae bass lines.

GILI MENO

Gili Meno is the quietest of the three islands, and has the best beaches. With a permanent population of just 300, it's not hard to play Robinson Crusoe along Meno's isolated shores should you so desire. Most of the accommodation is strung out along the eastern coast, near the widest and most picturesque beach. Inland you'll find scattered homesteads, coconut plantations and a shallow lake that produces salt in the dry season.

Information

There are a couple of minimarkets by the boat landing, so you will be able to locate most basic supplies. **Internet access** (per min 500Rp) and a wartel are available near the boat landing. Money can be exchanged at the Gazebo Meno and Kontiki Meno hotels, as well as at others, at poor rates. For tours and shuttle bus/boat tickets, the travel agent **Perama** (☎ 632824) is based at Kontiki Meno bungalows. The **medical clinic** near the bird park is attended by a resident nurse. Doctors are also on call in Mataram.

Sights & Activities

TAMAN BURUNG

About 300m inland from the boat landing, this **bird park** (☎ 642321; admission 30,000Rp; 9am-5pm) has an impressive and well-cared-for collection of 300 or so exotic species from Asia and Australasia, as well as three kangaroos and a baby Komodo dragon. The birds are let out of their cages for three hours a day, when they fly around a large expanse covered by a net. Interactive feeding times are also held. There's also a bar and accommodation (p304).

SNORKELLING & DIVING

Snorkelling trips (per person 40,000Rp, minimum four people), sometimes using glass-bottomed boats, leave from the jetty. There's good snorkelling off the northeast coast near Amber House huts, on the west coast near Good Heart and also around the former jetty of the (abandoned) Bounty resort – gear is available for 20,000Rp per day from several places on the eastern strip. Always ask about the state of the currents. For more on snorkelling and diving, see the boxed text p306.

GILI ISLANDS CURRENTS: WARNING

Currents between the Gili Islands are very strong. Take care when snorkelling offshore and do not attempt to swim between islands – this goes double after a night on the ale.

Blue Marlin Dive Centre (☎ 639979; www.diveindo.com) offers fun dives and courses from Discover Scuba to Divemaster.

Sleeping

The basic places are generally more expensive than equivalent lodgings on the other Gilis, and don't usually include breakfast. Prices quoted are high-season rates – reductions of up to 25% are possible the rest of the year.

BUDGET

Biru Meno (☎ 0813 3657 322; r 80,000-100,000Rp) A very welcoming place, located in a tranquil spot south of the main strip with a selection of spacious sea-facing bungalows – the most expensive have big windows and coral walls. There's also a simple restaurant.

Tao Kombo (☎ 0812 3722 174; tao_kombo@yahoo.com; platforms/bungalows 25,000/90,000Rp) About 200m inland, this mellow place has attractive, individually decorated bungalows scattered around a large garden, and some bamboo sleeping platforms (with mattresses, mosquito nets and safety boxes). There's 24-hour power, a chillout lounge and a bar-restaurant.

Kontiki Meno (☎ 632824; r with fan/air-con 90,000/150,000Rp;) Clean, breeze-block bungalows, some with elaborately carved doorways. Book No 1 or 2 for a direct sea view.

Malia's Child (☎ 622007; www.gilimeno-mallias.com; r 150,000Rp) Facing the sea, these attractive, orderly bamboo-and-thatch bungalows with fans, nets and Western toilets sit pretty on a well-raked stretch of sandy beach.

Good Heart (☎ 0813 3955 6976; bungalows 150,000Rp) Excellent, friendly Balinese-owned place with a row of superb, newly constructed twin-deck

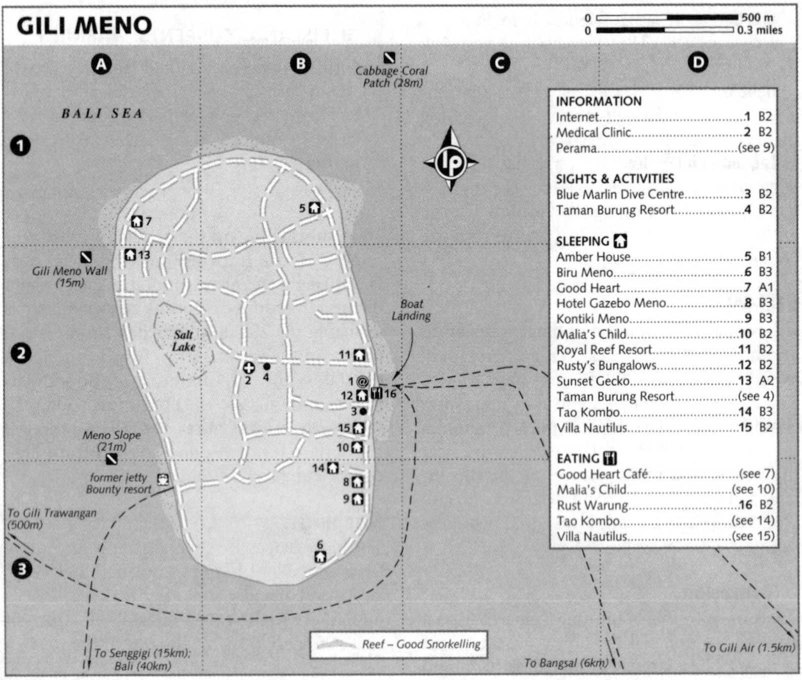

lumbung-like bungalows with coconut- wood roofs and beautiful open-air fresh-water bathrooms. It's opposite a slim stretch of beach that faces Gili Trawangan and there's also a book exchange and a good restaurant. Discounts of around 40% are offered in low season.

Sunset Gecko (081 576 6418; firefrog11@hotmail.com; bungalows/house 150,000/350,000Rp) This new place, built by a multinational team to high eco-standards, offers gorgeous shared bathroom, A-frame bungalows and a stunning two-bed timber house with the best views on the island from its upper deck. All accommodation has excellent ventilation and plenty of natural light. It's in an isolated spot, but next to a tranquil beach with some snorkelling. A restaurant serving Japanese, Indonesian and Western food is planned. Rates drop substantially at quiet times.

Other recommendations:

Amber House (☎ 643676; amber_house02@hotmail.com; s/d from 30,000/40,000Rp) Attractive bamboo bungalows in a flourishing garden with sea aspects.

Rusty's Bungalows (Pondok Wisata; ☎ 642324; s/d 50,000/60,000Rp) Bog standard but acceptable huts behind the boat landing.

Royal Reef Resort (☎ 642340; r 150,000Rp) Large, orderly bungalows overlooking the sea.

MIDRANGE

Taman Burung Resort (Bird Park Resort; ☎ 642321; www.balipvbgroup.com; dm/deluxe r 30,000/300,000Rp; ❄) Offers four comfortable air-con rooms with TV/DVD player and basic self-catering equipment, as well as a funky dormitory with three bunk beds. Check out the restaurant and Beatles-themed bar too.

Hotel Gazebo Meno (☎/fax 635795; r with fan/air con US$30/65; ❄ 🏊) Classy, spacious and stylish bungalows, those with air-con adopting a distinctly colonial feel with parquet floors, desks and chaise lounges, set in a coconut grove just off the beach. There's a small saltwater swimming pool.

TOP END

Villa Nautilus (☎ 642143; www.villanautilus.com; r US$75; ❄) Deluxe detached villas, beautifully finished in contemporary style with natural wood, marble and limestone. The design allows plenty of natural light to flood the lounge level, which has doors opening to a decked terrace – book No 1, 2 or 3 for sea views. Steps lead up to the bedroom/dressing room and down to the shower.

Eating & Drinking

The beachfront restaurants near the boat landing all offer fine views for your meal, which is just as well as service can be slow.

Rust Warung (☎ 642324; mains 6000-28,000Rp) Simple *beruga* with low tables and a menu of Indonesian and Western favourites.

Good Heart Café (mains 7500-20,000Rp) Perfectly primed for the sunset, Good Heart has a relaxed atmosphere aided by bamboo wind chimes and shells decorating the trees. There are regular BBQs, happy hour from 6pm to 8pm, and the bar has a variety of cocktails.

Tao Kombo (☎ 0812 3722 174; mains 9000-24,000Rp) Popular bar run by French Bob with a chilled vibe, lounge tunes, cocktails and a pool table. Tuck into fine Italian and Indonesian cuisine here too.

Villa Nautilus (☎ 642143; mains 15,000-27,000Rp) Come here for breakfast, a sandwich, pasta, or a pizza from a wood-fired oven.

Malia's Child (☎ 622007; dishes 15,000-28,000Rp) You'll eat well here, with tasty Indonesian food and pizza served either on an upper terrace with fine views or on one of the seaside *beruga*.

GILI TRAWANGAN

Trawangan has a reputation as a party island, a Shangri La for backpackers and hedonistic Indonesians, awash with budget-priced digs and dive centres. Shoestring ravers do still flood here, but the island's increasingly upmarket facilities – a mushrooming luxe-fest of lounge bars, sushi restaurants and boutique hotels – has meant that Jakartan hipsters and weekending Singaporeans are almost as common as rupiah-light gap-year students. It's the one corner of Lombok where tourism is really vibrant, and while there are still plenty of tranquil corners, the island's main strip buzzes every night until the early hours.

Unfortunately, environmental management has yet to catch up with the pace of development, and discarded garbage blots the landscape, particularly in the village just inland from the beach.

Diving is so critical to the local economy that the island's fishermen are paid by the scuba schools not to fish on Trawangan's reefs, a pioneering initiative that has resulted in greatly increased diversity, with turtles and top predators such as reef sharks frequently spotted here. Culturally, this moratorium is not without its difficulties however, as the islanders are descended from Bugis fishermen who arrived in Trawangan 55 years ago.

Orientation & Information

Boats dock on the eastern side of the island, which is also home to virtually all of Trawangan's accommodation, restaurants, stores and facilities. The best stretch of beach is just north of the jetty. There are a few places to stay at other points around the coast (and one inland) but they're quiet and away from the action.

Several stores will change cash or travellers cheques, but rates are poor. Dive shops give cash advances on credit cards for a hefty 7% commission.

There is no post office, but stamps and postcards are sold in the wartel and Pasar Seni (Art Market).

EMERGENCIES

Satgas (a community organisation which controls security on the island) Contact Satgas via your hotel or dive school.

Clinic (🕑 9am-5pm) Just south of Villa Ombak Hotel.

INTERNET ACCESS & TELEPHONE

Also offering a wartel, the owner of **Lightening** (internet access per min 400Rp) was installing a satellite link for broadband when we visited. Other places are spread along the eastern waterfront.

TRAVEL AGENCIES

Located just north of the jetty, **Perama** (☎ 638514; www.peramatour.com) offers boat tickets to Pandangbai in Bali and Senggigi as well as ongoing destinations by shuttle buses. Trips to Komodo can also be arranged here (see the boxed text, p361).

Sights

TURTLE HATCHERY

At the southern end of the beach, there's a glass aquarium housing the hatchery, where green and hawksbill turtle hatchlings are raised until they are around nine months' old (around 25cm in length). It's a small scheme set up by a local restaurant owner that releases several hundred turtles into local waters each year. The turtles are fed three times a day on chunks of fresh tuna; if you want to support this conservation project there's a donation box beside the tank.

UNDERWATER GILIS

The Gili Islands are a terrific dive destination. Though coral life above 18m is not generally in good condition – years of fish bombing and the El Niño phenomenon, which caused 'heatstroke' damage to the temperature-sensitive reefs back in the 1990s, have taken their toll – you'll find marine life is plentiful and varied. Turtles and black- and white-tip reef sharks are common, and the macro life (small stuff) is excellent with seahorses, pipefish and lots of crustaceans. Around full moon, large schools of bumphead parrot fish appear to feast on coral spawns, while at other times of the year manta rays glide by dive sites.

Safety standards are high in the Gilis despite the modest dive costs – there are no dodgy dive schools, and instructors and training are professional. Rates are fixed (no matter who you dive with) at US$25 a dive, with discounts for a package of 10 dives. A PADI Open Water course costs US$300, the Advanced course is US$225, Divemaster starts at US$650, and Nitrox and Trimex dives are offered by some schools. For contact details of dive schools, see individual island entries.

The Gili Eco Trust, a partnership between dive operators and the local community, aims to improve the condition of the reefs. All divers help fund the trust by paying a one-off fee of 30,000Rp with their first dive. Another initiative has seen the establishment of several reef growth accelerators, called **Biorock**. They use electrical currents to stimulate coral development. Two Biorock installations are located directly opposite the Vila Ombak hotel on Gili Trawangan at a depth of 8m. For more information, consult www.biorock.net.

Surrounded by coral reefs and with easy beach access, the Gilis are superb for snorkelling too. Masks, snorkels and fins can be hired for as little as 20,000Rp per day. On Trawangan, try snorkelling the area right off the beach where turtles are often seen. Around Gili Meno, the pier by the (closed) Bounty resort has prolific marine life, while over on Air the walls off the east coast are good.

Some of the best dive sites include the following:

Deep Halik The canyon-like profile of this site is ideally suited to drift diving. Black- and white-tip sharks can often be seen at 28m to 30m.

Deep Turbo At around 30m, this site is ideally suited to Nitrox diving. It has impressive sea fans and catches the prevailing currents so anything can come out of the big blue (including, very occasionally, mantas or even whale sharks).

Hans Reef Off the northeast coast of Gili Air, this reef is great for macro life including frogfish, ghostfish, seahorses and pipefish.

Japanese Wreck For experienced divers only (as it lies at 45m) this shipwreck of a Japanese patrol boat is another site ideal for Nitrox divers. Prolific soft coral, lots of nudibranches – look out for lionfish and frogfish.

Shark Point Perhaps the most exhilarating dive in the Gilis: reef sharks and turtles are very regularly encountered, as well as schools of bumphead parrotfish and mantas. Look out too for cuttlefish and octopi. At shallow depths there can be a strong surge.

Simon's Reef The reef here is in excellent condition; you can see schools of trevally, and occasionally, great barracuda and leopard sharks.

Sunset (Manta Point) The sloping profile of the reef here has good coral growth below 18m, including some impressive table coral. Large pelagics are frequently encountered and strong currents are rarely an issue.

Activities

DIVING

Trawangan is a veritable diver's delight with seven established scuba schools, no cowboy outfits and inexpensive prices (see the boxed text, above)

Big Bubble (☎ 625020; www.bigbubblediving.com)
Blue Marlin Dive Centre (☎ 632424; www.diveindo.com)
Dive Indonesia (☎ 642289; www.diveindonesianonline.com)
Dream Divers (☎ 634496; www.dreamdivers.com)
Manta Dive (☎ 643649; www.manta-dive.com)
Trawangan Diving (☎ 649220; www.trawangadive.com)
Villa Ombak Diving Academy (☎ 638531; gilidive@mataram.wasantara.net.id)

BOAT TRIPS & SNORKELLING

Glass-bottomed boat trips (40,000Rp per person, including snorkelling equipment) to coral reefs can be booked at many stores on the main strip.

There's fair snorkelling off the beach north of the jetty, though there's plenty of coral damage in evidence here and strong currents

MANDI SAFAR

Many of Trawangan's locals do not visit the island's beach frequently, partly because many cannot swim and have no interest in sunbathing, but also because Sasak Muslim attitudes towards modesty mean that most prefer to avoid seeing half-naked Western bodies roasting in the sun.

But in an annual ceremony held at the end of the second month of the Islamic calendar, a ritual purification, Safar, takes place as hundreds of villagers enjoy a day on the beach and take a dip in the ocean in a tradition said to symbolise the last bath of the Prophet Muhammad. The ceremony begins with the construction of a *pondok pisang* (banana house), a square structure which is loaded with fruit. Drumming, seated dancing and reading from the *Koran* follows. Prayers are then written on mango leaves before the participants take to the sea, taking their prayers with them.

Later everyone returns to shore to pin up the prayer leaves beside a local well (it's believed this action will maintain the well's water purity) and munch on the fruit from the *pondok pisang*. Later, everyone tucks into a huge rice-table-style buffet donated by Trawangan's restaurants.

Anyone is welcome to attend the event, but make sure you're well covered so as not to offend local customs.

further out from the shoreline. The reef is in better shape close to the lighthouse off the northwest coast, but you'll have to scramble over some low coral to access it.

Snorkelling gear can be hired for around 20,000Rp per day from shacks near the jetty.

SURFING & WATER SPORTS

Trawangan has a fast right-hand wave that breaks over a coral outcrop that is not sharp. It's best at high tide and can be surfed all year long. You'll find it just south of Vila Ombak.

Fun Ferrari (☎ 0812 3756 138; Horizontal; watersports per 15min incl tuition 150,000Rp, fishing per person US$50) offers water-skiing, parasailing, wakeboarding and sports fishing.

WALKING & CYCLING

Trawangan is perfect for exploring on foot or by bike. You can walk around the whole island in a couple of hours – if you finish at the hill on the southwestern corner (which has the remains of an old Japanese gun placement) at sunset you'll have terrific views of Bali's Gunung Agung.

Bikes can be hired from 15,000Rp a day from just south of the jetty.

Sleeping

There are approaching a hundred places to stay in Gili T, from simple beach huts to air-conditioned private villas with private pools. Most of the very cheapest accommodation is in the village – you'll pay more for a beach-side address. Perhaps the hottest real estate is the area north of the jetty, where you can stumble out of your bungalow and flop on the beach, neutralising those (perhaps inevitable) hangovers with a morning dip.

In all but the most expensive places, the tap water is quite saline. Rates quoted are high-season prices, they drop about 30% off-peak. Breakfast is included unless stated otherwise.

BUDGET

Main Strip

Pak Majid (r 60,000Rp) In the thick of the action, this place has clean concrete bungalows with plain furnishings. Breakfast is not included.

Creatif Satu (☎ 634861; r with fan/air-con 75,000/125,000Rp; ❄) Close to the jetty, the large rooms here are clean and quite acceptable.

Trawangan Cottages (☎ 623582; r without/with air-con 100,000/140,000Rp; ❄) Well-kept rooms with private bathrooms and verandas with nice seating.

Village

If the following places are full you'll find a dozen or so comparable alternatives in the village.

Pandian Wangi Cottages (s/d 40,000/75,000Rp) Friendly place with simple clean rooms with fans and mozzie nets.

Pondok Sederhana (☎ 0813 3860 9964; r 60,000Rp) Run by a house-proud and friendly Balinese lady, the spotless rooms here face a neat little garden.

Lisa Homestay (☎ 0813 3952 3364; 75,000Rp) Very friendly little place with airy and light tiled rooms that look out over a garden.

GILI TRAWANGAN

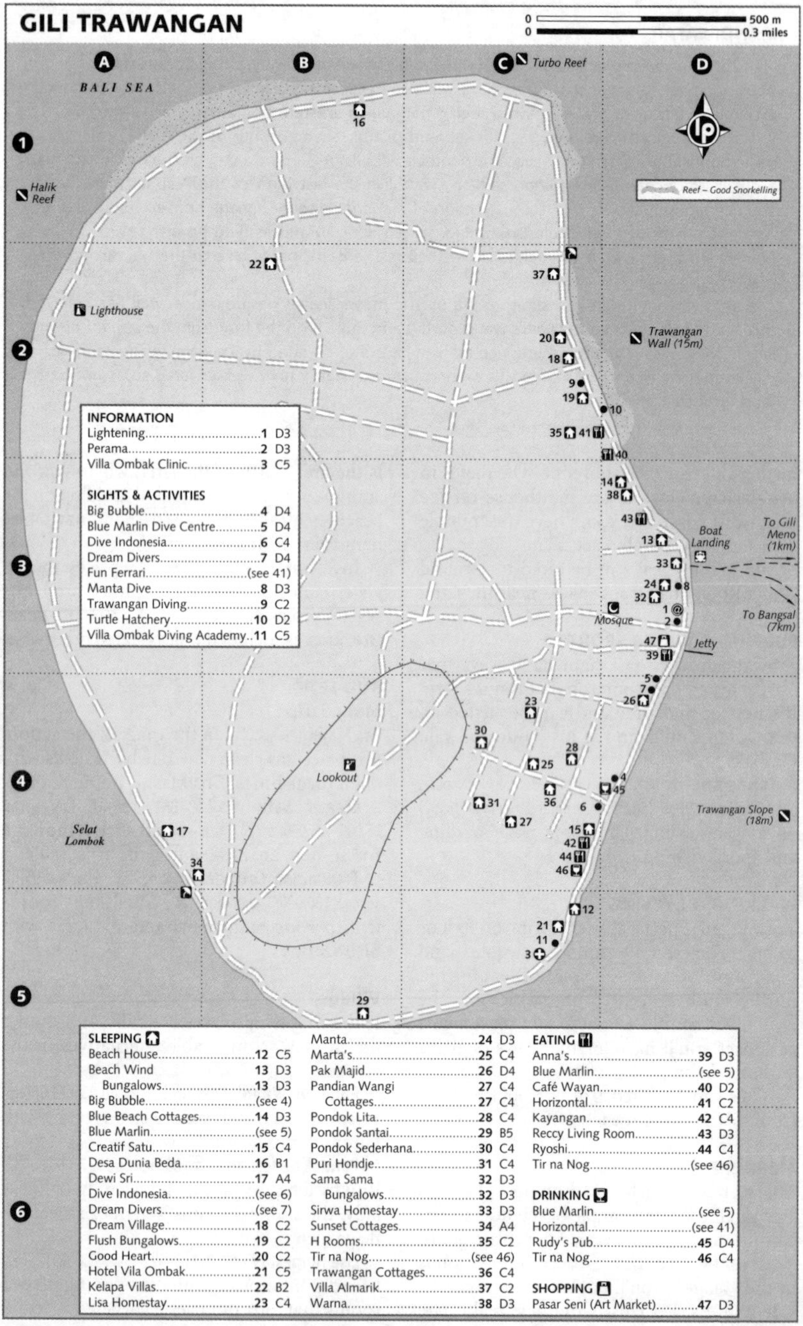

INFORMATION
- Lightening.....1 D3
- Perama.....2 D3
- Villa Ombak Clinic.....3 C5

SIGHTS & ACTIVITIES
- Big Bubble.....4 D4
- Blue Marlin Dive Centre.....5 D4
- Dive Indonesia.....6 C4
- Dream Divers.....7 D4
- Fun Ferrari.....(see 41)
- Manta Dive.....8 D3
- Trawangan Diving.....9 C2
- Turtle Hatchery.....10 D2
- Villa Ombak Diving Academy..11 C5

SLEEPING
- Beach House.....12 C5
- Beach Wind Bungalows.....13 D3
- Big Bubble.....(see 4)
- Blue Beach Cottages.....14 D3
- Blue Marlin.....(see 5)
- Creatif Satu.....15 C4
- Desa Dunia Beda.....16 B1
- Dewi Sri.....17 A4
- Dive Indonesia.....(see 6)
- Dream Divers.....(see 7)
- Dream Village.....18 C2
- Flush Bungalows.....19 C2
- Good Heart.....20 C2
- Hotel Vila Ombak.....21 C5
- Kelapa Villas.....22 B2
- Lisa Homestay.....23 C4
- Manta.....24 D3
- Marta's.....25 C4
- Pak Majid.....26 D4
- Pandian Wangi Cottages.....27 C4
- Pondok Lita.....28 C4
- Pondok Santai.....29 B5
- Pondok Sederhana.....30 C4
- Puri Hondje.....31 C4
- Sama Sama Bungalows.....32 D3
- Sirwa Homestay.....33 D3
- Sunset Cottages.....34 A4
- H Rooms.....35 C2
- Tir na Nog.....(see 46)
- Trawangan Cottages.....36 C4
- Villa Almarik.....37 C2
- Warna.....38 D3

EATING
- Anna's.....39 D3
- Blue Marlin.....(see 5)
- Café Wayan.....40 D2
- Horizontal.....41 C2
- Kayangan.....42 C4
- Reccy Living Room.....43 D3
- Ryoshi.....44 C4
- Tir na Nog.....(see 46)

DRINKING
- Blue Marlin.....(see 5)
- Horizontal.....(see 41)
- Rudy's Pub.....45 D4
- Tir na Nog.....46 C4

SHOPPING
- Pasar Seni (Art Market).....47 D3

Pondok Lita (r 80,000-100,000Rp) Nine good rooms with tiled floors, set around a garden. All rooms have two beds and a clean bathroom. Also has a book exchange and laundry service.

Puri Hondje (r 150,000Rp; air-con) Tucked away down a quiet village lane, these very stylish rooms overlook a small fish pond surrounded by bougainvillea and palms.

Beachside

Sirwa Homestay (s/d 40,000/45,000Rp) Spacious rooms – some have two double beds – with prices to suit those on a strict budget. There's a simple restaurant up front.

Beach Wind Bungalows (☎ 0812 3764 347; s/d with fan 75,000/85,000Rp, with air-con 120,000/150,000Rp; air-con) Excellent-value, stylish, spacious rooms in a row just off the beach, all with handsome bamboo-framed beds and a veranda; those with air-con have two beds. There's also table tennis, a book exchange and snorkelling gear available for hire.

Flush Bungalows (r 120,000-150,000Rp) This small, rustic place is just off the shore, and has one room with a glorious sea-facing balcony. Initial rates asked are a little pricey, so be sure to bargain. Free water, mozzie nets and fans are provided.

Warna (☎ 623859; r 140,000Rp) Four well-priced, tasteful bungalows with large beds, reading lights and attractive wooden furniture set off a gorgeous slim garden, just off the beach. Rates are seriously slashed during quiet times.

Blue Beach Cottages (☎ 623538; bbc@indo.net.18; r with fan/air-con 170,000/250,000Rp; air-con) Representing good value for money, these attractive huts have high ceilings, rattan furniture, ikat wall hangings, hot water and lovely verandas set off a blossoming garden. But best off all, the beach is a few steps away.

Southwest Coast

Sunset Cottages (☎ 0812 3785 290; s/d 50,000/60,000Rp) Friendly place, opposite a small beach offering traditional-style huts with fans, and verandas that catch the afternoon breeze.

Pondok Santai (s/d 60,000/70,000Rp) On the south coast, yet only a five-minute walk from the main strip; these simple, secluded thatched huts all have two beds and attached mandi.

Dewi Sri (☎ 0819 3314 5164; r 60,000Rp & 100,000Rp) Family-owned place with two classes of well-built bungalows set around a beachside plot. There's good home cooking available and a slim beach area with loungers opposite.

MIDRANGE

Main Strip

Big Bubble (☎ 625020; www.bigbubblediving.com; r fan/air-con US$22/30; air-con pool) A row of very stylish modern rooms, built from natural materials and each with hammocks and front terraces, face a beautiful slender garden. Out the front there's a wonderful pool and decked area.

Dive Indonesia (☎ 642289; www.diveindonesianonline.com; r US$25; non-smoking air-con pool) At the rear of the dive shop are seven really attractive bungalows, each with a bathtub, tropical-chic bamboo furniture and front patios.

Blue Marlin (☎ 632424; www.diveindo.com; r US$25; air-con pool) Decent air-con rooms, all with wardrobes and desks, hot water, bathrooms and TV. Guests also have access to a fully-equipped gym.

Tir na Nog (☎ 639463; tirnanog@mataram.wasantara.net.id; r US$25, villa US$125; air-con) At the rear of the bar, these huge rooms with air-con have been thoughtfully designed and decorated; most have spacious private terraces and swanky modern bathrooms. For real luxury book the private villa which even comes with its own chef and plunge pool.

Beach House (☎ 642352; www.beachhousegilit.com; r 320,000-525,000Rp, villa 2.5 million rupiah; air-con pool) Competitive pricing and the simple elegance of these understated modern rooms, in three price categories, means that this place is busy all year round. There's a freshwater plunge pool at the rear (and an amazing four-bedroom villa with modish furnishings and its own pool, but no sea views).

Village

Marta's (☎ 0812 3722 777; martas_trawangan@yahoo.com; bungalow/family bungalow 250,000/400,000Rp; air-con) Representing exceptional value for money, these sumptuous detached two-storey air-con bungalows, owned by a helpful and welcoming English-Indonesian couple, are grouped around a lush garden. Decorated mainly in calming creams and beige, the attention to detail is excellent and the beds are absolutely sumo-sized. If you're in a group, consider the super-spacious family rooms, which sleep four.

Beachside

Good Heart (☎ 0812 2395 170; r 100,000Rp, bungalows 350,000-500,000Rp; air-con) A great choice with superb-value budget rooms (each with large beds) and a couple of very stylish thatched A-frame bungalows – these have all the mod cons you could need, and pebble-floored open-air bathrooms.

Sama Sama Bungalows (☎ 0812 3763 650; r with fan/air-con 250,000/350,000Rp;) Combining natural materials – logwood bed frames, timber flooring and coconut wood – with mod cons including TV/DVD players, these rooms make a comfortable base. It's set back a little from the beach.

Manta (☎ 643649; www.manta-dive.com; r 380,000Rp;) Eight delightful modern *lumbung*-style bungalows, each with twin or king-sized beds, polished timber floorboards, a fridge, security box, and wonderful screened outdoor bathrooms with volcanic stone floor tiles. Prices are flexible during low season and there are discounts for Manta Dive school customers.

Dream Village (☎ 0818 546 591; www.dreamvillagetrawangan.com; bungalows 400,000-500,000Rp;) A wonderful new place offering a contemporary take on *lumbung*-style chic, each cottage is well finished with teak floors and rattan chairs, fridge, TV, security box and gorgeous freshwater outdoor bathrooms. An Italian restaurant, spa and small pool are planned.

Villa Almarik (☎ 638520; www.almarik-lombok.com; r US$70-75;) Huge, light and airy, high-ceilinged bungalows with dining/living-room area and modern bathroom, TV and minibar. The swimming pool is modestly sized though.

LOMBOK

TOP END

Hotel Vila Ombak (☎ 642336; www.hotelombak.com; r US$75-135 plus 21% tax;) Just south of the main drag, this highly attractive resort occupies a leafy garden plot partly shaded by yuccas and palms. The faux-traditional two-storey A-frame bungalows are not that large for the price, but do have real character. The stunning superior rooms are more minimalist in design. Has a great pool, spa, diving academy, restaurant and beach bar too.

our pick **H Rooms** (☎ 639248; somersguy@yahoo.com; villas US$100;) Redefining the mod-Asian look that is so prevalent in Bali, these remarkable modernist villas to the rear of the Horizontal bar can sleep four comfortably, with dividing walls separating sleek interiors replete with Japanese-style tatami matting, distressed coconut-wood walls and decked floors. Home cinema equipment, huge Jacuzzis and gorgeous open-air bathrooms are all standard, while butler and personal DJ services can also be arranged.

Desa Dunia Beda (☎ 641575; www.desaduniabeda.com; bungalows US$110 plus 21% tax;) Out on their own in the north of the island, these absolutely astonishing Javanese Joglo bungalows command the biggest wow factor on the island. Each has been decorated with classy furniture and boasts a four-poster bed, writing desk, sofas and back-to-nature open-air bathrooms. Smallish pool though, and it is isolated up here.

Kelapa Villas (☎ 632424; www.kelapavillas.com; villas US$150-410 plus 21% tax;) Between the coasts, surrounded by coconut groves, these beautifully finished luxury villas boast full catering facilities, private pools and all the comforts of home including TV/DVD and fresh-water bathrooms.

Eating

It's easy to munch your way around the world in Trawangan, which belies its size and offers everything from sushi to Irish stew. In the evenings several places display fresh fish and seafood on the main strip.

Anna's (dishes 5000-8000Rp) Tiny, friendly warung with a very short menu. It serves up a mean *nasi campur* and *soto ayam* (chicken soup).

Kayangan (dishes 7500-15,000Rp) It may look a bit grubby, but the inexpensive Chinese and Indonesian dishes here are executed well.

Café Wayan (dishes 17,000-35,000Rp) Hygiene standards are high, so it's a great venue for salads (try the papaya and chicken) as well as pasta, Thai and Indo faves like prawns *a la ketut* (served with cashews). Leave room for cake, including death-by-chocolate and carrot.

Beach House (☎ 642352; dishes 17,000-50,000Rp) Boasts a great beachside terrace and a menu that takes in everything from tasty baguettes through the usual Indonesian suspects to chargrilled sirloin steaks. It sells wine and there's also a fine choice of juices – try the pineapple, guava and mint.

Ryoshi (☎ 639463; dishes 17,000-48,000Rp, set menus from 37,000Rp) Authentic, superfresh sushi, teriyaki chicken and other Japanese treats at moderate prices served on Nippon-style low tables (though you can also eat your Eastern treats next door in the Irish bar, Tir na Nog, too).

Tir na Nog (☎ 639463; dishes 21,000-37,000Rp) Ideal for enormous portions of comfort food such as Irish stew and fish 'n' chips, and puds like *banoffi* (banana and condensed milk) pie.

our pick **Horizontal** (☎ 639248; dishes 25,000-65,000Rp) With more than a nod to Seminyak style, this lounge-bar-restaurant boasts sleek contemporary seating including luxe scarlet lounges, sculptured white 'escape pods' and lots of hip design details. The extensive, eclectic menu fuses pan-Asian and mod-European food, with bar snacks like hot 'n' spicy quesadillas to munch on, mains including salt-and-pepper squid with lime and lemon dip to savour, and desserts to die for. The bizarre looking white globe with a chimney by the entrance is actually a wood-fired pizza oven (not a mosque for cats as one local mused). Homesick Brits should check out the 7pm Sunday roast, with all the trimmings of course.

Other recommendations:

Blue Marlin (mains 9000-35,000Rp) Offering mainly Western food, this place serves up some of the finest fish and seafood on Trawangan – choose yours from the iced streetside display.

Reccy Living Room (dishes 12,000-23,000Rp) Friendly place with *beruga* overlooking the beach that offers decent Western food including lasagne. Order the house special 'rice table' a day in advance.

Drinking & Entertainment

Despite its diminutive size, Trawangan punches way above its weight in the party stakes. Its rotating parties fire up around 11pm and go on until 4am or so (except during Ramadan when the action is completely curtailed out of respect for local culture). At the time of research the party schedule shifted between Dive Indonesia (Saturday), Blue Marlin (Monday), Tir na Nog (Tuesday), Horizontal (Thursday) and Rudy's (Friday).

Imported DJs from Bali and beyond mix techno, trance and House music while Rudy's has a more eclectic musical policy.

Blue Marlin (8am-midnight Tue-Sun, 8am-3am Mon) Of all the party bars, this upper-level venue has the largest dance floor and the meanest sound system – which pumps out trance and tribal sounds on Monday. There's also a great outdoor terrace with views across the ocean to Lombok.

Tir na Nog (7am-2am Wed-Mon, 7am-4am Tue) Known to one and all as the 'Irish bar', it combines a sociable barnlike main room, where you can catch live sports on a big screen and play table soccer, and a superb beachside terrace. You can also watch films here, choosing a title from the extensive selection and watching it on a portable TV, set up on a private *beruga*.

Horizontal (10am-2am) Adjacent to a gorgeous stretch of beach, this super-stylin' place offers a radically different take on drinking culture compared with the usual drinking dens on Trawangan. Primarily an alfresco chillout zone, but with terrific food (see left), the cocktails are the best in Trawangan (try the raspberry margarita or Long Island ice tea). Also serves espresso and cappuccino.

Rudy's Pub (8am-4am Fri, 8am-11pm Sat-Thu) Run by the inimitable Joko, the friendliest and most entertaining barman in town, this place hosts a terrific Friday-night party.

NORTH & CENTRAL LOMBOK

☎ 0370

The sparsely populated northern part of Lombok is remarkably beautiful, with a variety of landscapes, few tourists and even fewer facilities. Public transport is not frequent though, nor does it detour from the main road. With a set of wheels, however, you can explore the shore, waterfalls and inland villages. The main coastal road is narrow but paved and in good condition.

Towering Gunung Rinjani is unquestionably the region's main attraction. But even if you don't attempt the cone itself, its southern slopes are well watered and lush, and offer scenic walks through rice fields and jungle. Most villages in central Lombok are traditional Sasak settlements, and several of them are known for their local handicrafts.

BANGSAL TO BAYAN

The port of Bangsal is run down and a hassle, see the boxed text, p299. Heading north of Bangsal, public transport isn't that frequent. Several minibuses a day go from Mandalika terminal in Bertais (Mataram) to Bayan, but you may have to get connections in Pemenang and/or Anyar. This area is best explored with your own wheels.

Sira

This peninsula has a glorious sweeping white-sand **beach**, some snorkelling offshore and Lombok's most luxurious hotel, the **Oberoi Lombok** (☎ 638444; www.oberoihotels.com; r from US$240, villas from US$350, plus 21% tax;). The rooms, villas and pavilions here are beyond commodious, with lashings of marble, teak floors, oriental rugs and astonishing garden-bathrooms

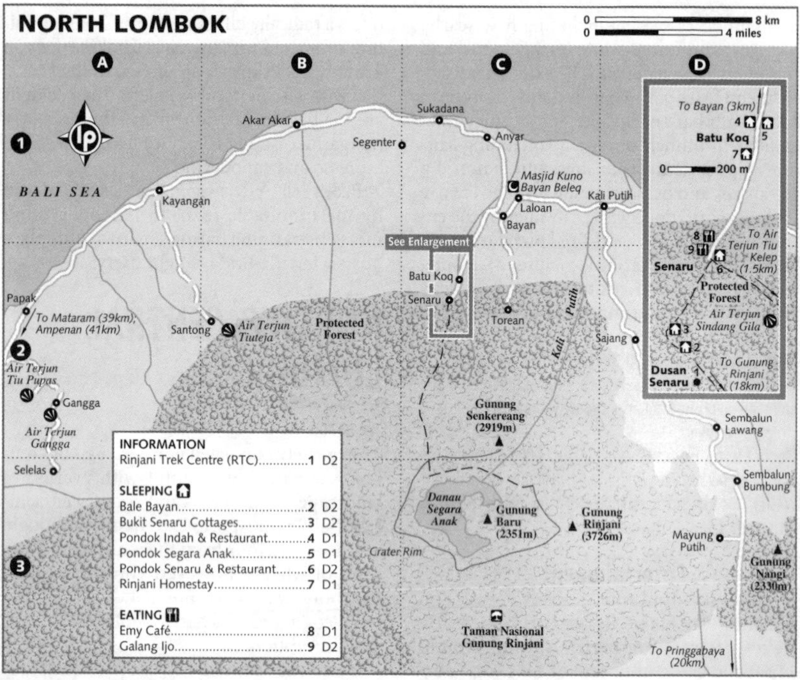

with sunken bathtubs. There's a fine spa and good sports facilities, including tennis courts, though beware the restaurant prices – a sandwich is 100,000Rp (plus tax).

Close by, signposted from the road south to Bangsal, the **Lombok Golf Kosaido Country Club** (☎ 640137; per round incl caddy & cart US$80) is an attractive 18-hole, 72-par course by the sea, laid with Bermuda grass. Hole 9 faces the waters of Sira Bay, while holes 10 to18 have great views of Rinjani. Manta Dive on Gili Trawangan can organise discounted rates here.

Gondang & Around

Just northeast of Gondang village, a 6km trail heads inland to **Air Terjun Tiu Pupas**, a 30m waterfall that's only really impressive in the wet season. Trails continue from here to other waterfalls including **Air Terjun Gangga**, the most beautiful of all. A guide is useful to navigate the confusing trails in these parts – speak to the owners of the **Pondok Pantai** (☎ 0812 375 2632; www.pontok-pantai.com; bungalows 50,000-90,000Rp) a welcoming Dutch-Indonesian–run guesthouse with lovely thatched bungalows, tip-top food (dishes 9000Rp to 22,000Rp) and a west-facing beachside setting that serves up blood-red sunsets. It's 2km north of Gondang.

Bayan

This northernmost part of Lombok is the birthplace of the Wektu Telu religion (p316), and also has some venerable mosques. One very fine example, **Masjid Kuno Bayan Beleq**, close to village of Laloan, is one of the oldest on Lombok, reputedly dating from 1634. Built on a square platform of river stones the structure has a pagoda-like upper section and inside there's a huge old drum. Access to the interior of the mosque is not permitted, and the structure is not actively used for worship. You may be asked to sign a visitor's book and make a donation for the mosque's upkeep.

Senaru & Batu Koq

These picturesque villages, merging into each other along a ridge with sweeping views to the east and south, are the main starting points for climbs up Gunung Rinjani. Even if you've not got your volcano-climbing head on, they're still worth a day or so, with some fine walking trails and dramatic waterfalls.

INFORMATION & ORIENTATION

Rinjani Trek Centre (RTC; ☎ satellite 0868 1210 4132; www.info2lombok.com), at the southern end of the village, has good information on Rinjani and the surrounding area.

The two villages are spread out along a single steep road which heads south to Rinjani. Batu Koq is about 3km south from Bayan, Senaru is a further 3km uphill.

SIGHTS & ACTIVITIES

Definitely visit **Air Terjun Sindang Gila** (2000Rp), a spectacular set of falls 20 minutes' walk from Senaru. The walk is partly through forest and partly alongside an irrigation canal that follows the contour of the hill, occasionally disappearing into tunnels where the cliffs are too steep.

A further 50 minutes or so up the hill is Air Terjun Tiu Kelep, another waterfall, where you can go swimming. The track is steep and tough at times, so it's a good idea to take a guide (15,000Rp).

Six kilometres south of Bayan is the traditional village of Dusun Senaru where locals will invite you to chew betel nut (or tobacco) and show you around.

Community tourism activities can be arranged in most guesthouses – they include a rice terraces and waterfalls walk (35,000Rp), which takes in Sindang Gila, some stunning vistas and a bemo ride back; and the Senaru Panorama Walk (45,000Rp), which is led by female guides and incorporates information about local lifestyles.

To recuperate, head to Emy Café (p313) for a posthike massage (25,000Rp).

SLEEPING & EATING

Some comfortable rooms have been built recently, but most of the dozen losmen here have basic rooms and shared cold-water mandi. As the climate's cooler, you won't need fans. All these places are dotted along the road from Bayan to Senaru.

Bukit Senaru Cottages (r 40,000Rp) Shortly before Dusan Senaru, this place has four well-constructed semidetached bungalows with verandas and bathrooms with Western toilets overlooking a leafy garden.

Pondok Indah & Restaurant (☎ 081 7578 8018; s/d 80,000/100,000Rp) A well-run friendly place with spacious accommodation in two blocks 3km south of Bayan. Many rooms share a communal balcony and have well-scrubbed showers and Western toilets. There's parking and a good restaurant (dishes 7000Rp to 18,000Rp).

Pondok Senaru & Restaurant (☎ 622868, 0868 1210 4141; r 150,000-300,000Rp) Well set-up place 4km from Bayan offering great easterly views of the valley from its recommended restaurant (dishes 11,000Rp to 21,000Rp) and spacious, spotless rooms – a little overpriced but the most comfortable digs in town. The superior rooms have TV, minibar and *hot* showers.

Also worth considering:

Rinjani Homestay (☎ 0817 5750 889; s/d 35,000/40,000Rp) A little further uphill it has plain clean rooms and a restaurant with Western and Indonesian dishes (7000Rp to 25,000Rp).

Bale Bayan (☎ 0817 5792 943; r 40,000Rp) Opposite Dusun Senaru village, this place has rustic bungalows and a restaurant in a nice garden.

Pondok Segara Anak (☎ 0817 5754 551; r 40,000Rp) Panoramic views and neat, clean good-value rooms. It's 3km from Bayak.

Head to **Emy Café** (dishes 5000-12,500Rp) or **Galang Ijo** (dishes 5000-8000Rp) both midway between Batu Koq and Senaru for simple food and some Sasak specials.

GETTING THERE & AWAY

From Mandalika terminal in Mataram catch a bus to Anyar (12,500Rp, 2½ hours). Bemo leave Anyar for Senaru (4000Rp) about every 20 minutes until 4.30pm. If you're coming from, or going to, eastern Lombok, get off at the junction near Bayan (your driver will know it), from where bemo go to Senaru.

THE SEMBALUN VALLEY

☎ 0376

High on the eastern side of Gunung Rinjani is the beautiful Sembalun Valley, whose inhabitants descend from the Hindu Javanese. The two main settlements are Sembalun Lawang and Sembalun Bumbung. The former is a popular starting point for treks up Gunung Rinjani. The statue of an enormous garlic bulb in the village is indicative of the area's main crop, which is harvested in October.

Sembalun Bumbung, 3km south of Sembalun Lawang and just off the main road, is a sprawling and relatively wealthy village. It's often referred to simply as Sembalun; the 'Bumbung' is used to differentiate its neighbour. However, Sembalun Lawang is the more convenient place to stay for organising treks.

Information & Activities

The staff at the **Rinjani Information Centre** (RIC; 6am-6pm) are well informed about the area and offer treks such as a not-too-demanding four-hour **Village Walk** (100,000Rp, minimum 2 people). The more strenuous **Wildflower Walk** (per person 560,000Rp for 2 people incl a guide, porters, meals and all camping gear) is a delightful two-day trek inside the national park past flowery grasslands; it costs less if there are more of you.

The RIC has also helped local women to revive traditional weaving in Sembalun Lawang. Follow the signs from the village centre to their workshops.

Sleeping & Eating

Sembalun Lawang is a more expensive place to stay than Senaru or Batu Koq, but the vistas are more impressive.

Bale Galeng (s/d with shared bathroom 30,000/45,000Rp) These basic, serviceable *lumbung* cottages are set in a rambling garden rich with scrubs and medicinal herbs. About 1km from the RIC.

Maria Guesthouse (r 50,000Rp) Try this homestay with two basic rooms; rates include breakfast and dinner.

Losman Lembah Rinjani (☎ 0818 0362 0918; s/d with shared bathroom 60,000/80,000Rp, s/d 130,000/160,000Rp) Head down a side road near the RIC to find this well-run place, the cheaper rooms have less impressive volcano views. There's a restaurant on site (dishes 8000Rp to 14,000Rp).

Sembalun Nauli (☎ 0818 362 040; sembalunnauli@lycos.com; r 120,000Rp) These smart, spacious rooms, with wonderful Rinjani views, are 3km before Sembalun Lawang on the road from Banyan. There's good local food here (dishes 6000Rp to 17,000Rp).

Getting There & Away

From Mandalika bus terminal take a bus to Aikmel (8000Rp) and change there for Sembalun Lawang (9000Rp). Hourly pick-ups connect Lawang and Bumbung.

There's no public transport between Sembalun Lawang and Senaru, you'll have to charter an *ojek*, or a bemo for around 100,000Rp. Roads to Sembalun are sometimes closed in the wet season due to landslides.

SAPIT

☎ 0376

On the southeastern slopes of Gunung Rinjani, Sapit is a tiny, very relaxed village with views across to Sumbawa. *Open*, tall red-brick tobacco-drying buildings, loom above the beautifully lush landscape, and 'baccy can be bought in blocks in the market.

Sights

Between Swela and Sapit, a side road leads to **Taman Lemor** (admission 3000Rp; 8am-4pm), a park with a refreshing spring-fed swimming pool and some pesky monkeys. Further towards Pringgabaya, **Makam Selaparang** is the burial place of ancient Selaparang kings.

You can also visit hot-water springs and small waterfalls near Sapit. Ask either homestay for directions.

Sleeping & Eating

Hati Suci Homestay (☎ 0818 545 655; www.hatisuci.tk; s 40,000-45,000Rp, d 75,000-85,000Rp) An efficiently run place with excellent budget bungalows with en-suite bathrooms set in a blossoming garden. The accommodation and restaurant (dishes 8000Rp to 18,000Rp) both offer stunning views over the sea to Sumbawa. Breakfast is included and hikes to Rinjani can be organised here.

Balelangga Bed & Breakfast (☎ 22197; s/d with shared bathroom 30,000/50,000Rp) Under the same management, this place has simpler rooms and good home cooking (dishes 6000Rp to 18,000Rp). It's sometimes closed in the low season.

Getting There & Away

To reach Sapit from Mataram or Central Lombok first head to Pringgabaya, which has frequent bemo connections to Sapit. Occasional bemo also go to Sapit from the Sembalun valley in the north.

GUNUNG RINJANI

Soaring over northern Lombok, the mighty Rinjani volcano is of immense cultural (and climatic) importance for Lombok's people, while climbing the peak is one of Indonesia's most exhilarating experiences. The great cone, which reaches 3726m, and its upper slopes were declared a national park in 1997. Thousands of pilgrims, for whom Rinjani is a sacred mountain, venture up to its crater lake and place offerings in the waters, bathe in the hot springs here and pay respects to Rinjani as an abode of deities.

Gunung Rinjani is the highest mountain on Lombok and Indonesia's highest outside Papua. Its caldera contains a cobalt crescent-

GUNUNG RINJANI

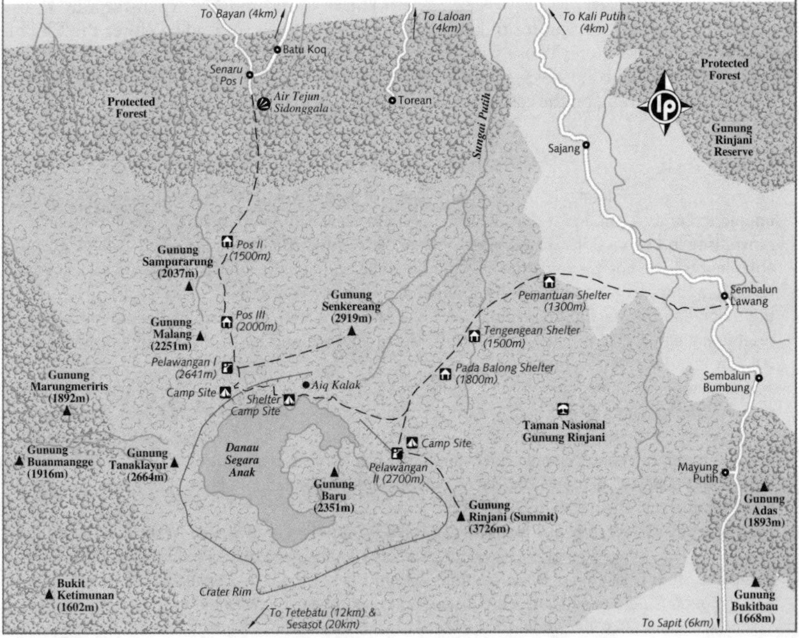

shaped lake, Danau Segara Anak (Child of the Sea), which is about 6km across at its widest point. The crater has a series of natural hot springs known as Aiq Kalak, whose waters locals take to blend with herbs to make medicinal treatments, particularly for skin diseases. The lake is 600m below the crater rim, and rising from its waters is a minor, newer cone, Gunung Baru (or Gunung Barujari), which only emerged a couple of hundred years ago. This ominously grey, highly active scarred peak erupted as recently as October 2004.

GUNUNG RINJANI SECURITY WARNING

There were incidents of armed robbery on Rinjani in 2000, though we have not received reports of any further incidents until another attack in July 2005. While this seems to have been an isolated incident, it's best to check safety advice locally before you set out.

There are plans to post police and mountain security guards inside the crater.

Both the Balinese and Sasaks revere Rinjani. To the Balinese, it is equal to Gunung Agung (p219), a seat of the gods, and many Balinese make an annual pilgrimage here. In a ceremony called *pekelan*, people throw jewellery into the lake and make offerings to the spirit of the mountain. Some Sasaks make several pilgrimages a year – full moon is their favourite time for paying respect to the mountain and for curing ailments by bathing in Aiq Kalak. Rinjani is particularly revered by the Wektu Telu (see the boxed text, p316) for whom the mountain has immense spiritual power.

The trek to the crater lake is not to be taken lightly and should only be undertaken as part of an organised trek due to the active status of Gunung Baru and, sadly, because there have been (very) occasional attacks on hikers (see left). Climbing Rinjani during the wet season (November to March), when the tracks are often treacherously slippy and there's a real risk of landslides, is not at all advisable – the National Park office often completely forbids access to Rinjani for the first three months of each year. June to August is the only time you are guaranteed (well, almost) no rain or cloud, but be prepared as it can still get very cold at the summit.

Senaru has the best services for trekkers so most start their treks there. Those who want the fastest summit climb, however, should start from Sembalun Lawang on the eastern side.

Organised Treks

The best and most inexpensive way to organise a trip is to head to either the Rinjani Trek Centre (p313) in Senaru or the Rinjani Information Centre (p313) in Sembalun Lawang. Anyone passing through Senggigi can

WEKTU TELU

Believed to have originated in the northern village of Bayan, Wektu Telu is an indigenous religion unique to Lombok, though it does bear many similarities with Agami Jawi, the Javanese Islamic syncretism. In the Sasak language, *wektu* means 'result' and *telu* means 'three'. The name probably denotes the complex mixture of Hindu, Islamic and animist influences that make up this religion; and the concept of a trinity is embodied in many Wektu Telu beliefs, such as the sun, the moon and the stars (representing heaven, earth and water); the head, body and limbs (representing creativity, sensitivity and control). Wektu laws are also based around three principles: religion, custom and governance.

The number of Wektu adherents is quite small (fewer than 30,000), although this is almost certainly understated as it is not a state recognised religion, and Wektu traditions and rituals continue under the unifying code of Islam. Nevertheless, numbers have been steadily declining as more and more young people now worship at orthodox Islamic mosques. You can recognise Wektu Telu believers by their *sapu puteq* (white headbands), tied in a knot at the front like Balinese Hindus, and their flowing white robes.

As recently as 1965 the vast majority of Sasaks in northern Lombok were Wektu Telu, but following the 1965 coup, Soeharto's New Order government decreed that all Indonesians must have an *agama*, an officially recognised religion – either Islam, Hinduism, Christianity or Buddhism – and indigenous religious beliefs were discouraged and decreed backward. In tense times, when 'godless' Communists were being slaughtered by the thousands, virtually all Lombok's Wektu Telu declared themselves to be Muslims on their state identity cards – many fearing that if they did not practise an official religion, they could be construed as being atheists. By 1967, as far as state records were concerned, virtually all Wektu Telu had become Wektu Lima – *lima* (five) refers to the five pillars of Islam that all orthodox Muslims strive to adhere to. (About 5000 villagers in Bentek, with strong Wektu Telu traditions, originally opted to be categorized as Buddhists, but later became Muslims).

The Wektu Telu observe only three days of fasting during Ramadan. They do not pray five times a day as dictated by Islamic law and some have no objection to eating pork. Their dead are buried with their heads facing Mecca, but Wektu Telu do not make pilgrimages there. In fact, the only fundamental tenets of Islam to which the Wektu Telu seem to hold firmly are the belief in Allah, and that Muhammad is Allah's prophet.

For the Wektu, death does not signify the end of a person's soul, and they believe that the departed return on important days in the calendar to provide ritual blessings. For this reason, much respect is paid to Wektu ancestors. Three rituals – the reading of sacred mantras, the offering of betel nut, and the placement of a bowl of spring water – are performed when the Wektu wish to invite their ancestors to a ceremony.

The Wektu also believe strongly that the spiritual world is firmly linked with the natural world – particularly springs, hilltops and mountains (of which Rinjani is most revered). Shaman called *pemangku* provide the contact between the two worlds, and act as guardians of pre-Islamic monuments called *gedeng lauq* and *gedeng daya,* sanctuaries of linga-shaped stones protected by bamboo roofs.

Most of the Wektu Telu religious festivals take place at the beginning of the rainy season (from October to December), or at harvest time (April to May), with celebrations in villages all over the island. Many of these ceremonies and rituals are annual events but, as they do not fall on specific days, getting to see one is a matter of luck and word of mouth. The Bayan area of northern Lombok remains a stronghold of the Wektu Telu community.

first contact the Rinjani Trek Centre's office there (p294). Funded by the New Zealand government, the centres use a rotation system so that all of the local trekking organisers get a slice of the hiking pie.

Whether you book through your losmen, or directly at the RTC or RIC, the same trek packages (at the same prices) are offered. The most popular is the three-day, two-night trek from Senaru to Sembalun Lawang via the summit and includes food, equipment, guide, porters, park fee and transport back to Senaru. This costs 1.6million rupiah for one, dropping to 966,000Rp per person for two hikers and 821,000Rp for three. An overnight trek to the crater rim from Senaru costs 1.19million rupiah for one, 714,000Rp for two and 606,900Rp for three. The deals are cheaper the more of you there are.

A number of agencies in Mataram, Senggigi and the Gili Islands can organise all-inclusive treks. Prices usually include everything outlined above, plus return transport from the point of origin. For example, **Perama** (www.peramatour.com), with offices in all of these locations, has a trekking package that leaves from any of the places above, via Senaru using official RTC guides for 1.6million rupiah per person (minimum two people).

Guides & Porters

Hiking independently is not recommended due to security and safety concerns (see the boxed text, opposite).

If you don't want to do an all-inclusive trekking package with RTC or RIC you can hire guides (100,000Rp per day) and porters (80,000Rp) from them independently, but make sure you take a radio (10,000Rp per day). Contract your guides and porters directly from the centres in Senaru and Sembalun Lawang, as they are licensed for your security. Guides are knowledgeable and informative, but won't carry anything for you, so take at least one porter. You also have to provide them with food, water and transport, and probably cigarettes as well.

Entrance Fee & Equipment

The entrance fee for the Rinjani National Park is 27,000Rp – register and pay at the RTC in Senaru or the RIC in Sembalun Lawang before you start your trek.

Sleeping bags and tents are essential and can be hired at either RTC or RIC. You'll also need solid footwear, layers of warm clothing, wet-weather gear, cooking equipment and a torch (flashlight), but these can also be hired from the RTC. Expect to pay about 50,000Rp a head per day for all your equipment.

Take a stove so you don't need to deplete the limited supply of firewood. Carry all rubbish out with you and make sure others in your party do the same.

Backpacks can be left at most losmen in Senaru or the RTC for around 5000Rp per day.

Food & Supplies

Trek organisers at RTC and RIC can arrange trekking food, or you can take your own. It's better to buy most supplies in Mataram or Senggigi, where it's cheaper and there's more choice, but some provisions are available in Senaru. Take plenty of water and a lighter.

Getting There & Away

For transport options from Sembalun Lawang to Senaru, see p314. If you've purchased a trekking package, transport back to the point of origin is usually included.

TETEBATU

☎ 0376

Nestling in the lower slopes of Gunung Rinjani, Tetebatu is an attractive rural retreat sitting at a high enough altitude (400m) to make the climate a tad more refreshing than down on the sticky coast. There are magnificent views across tobacco fields and rice paddies towards southern Lombok, east to the sea and north to Rinjani. The *open* (brick towers) that dot the landscape are used for drying tobacco, the major crop here. Tetebatu makes a fine setting for a few days hiking to nearby waterfalls or visiting the surrounding handicraft villages.

Tetebatu is quite spread out, with facilities on roads north and east (nicknamed 'waterfall road') of the *ojek* stop in the centre of the village. There's a **wartel** (9am-9pm) next to Salabuse Café.

Sights & Activities

TAMAN WISATA TETEBATU

A shady 4km track leading from the main road, just north of the mosque, heads into the Taman Wisata Tetebatu (Monkey Forest) with black monkeys and waterfalls – you will need a guide to find them. Alternatively, to get there you could take an *ojek* from the turn-off.

CLIMBING GUNUNG RINJANI

The two most popular ways to climb Gunung Rinjani are a five-day trek (described below) that starts at Senaru and finishes at Sembalun Lawang, or a strenuous dash from Senaru to the crater rim and back. A guide is essential from the hot springs to Sembalun Lawang, as the path is indistinct (see p312). This trek is outlined on the Gunung Rinjani map (p315). Another good map is the one from the Rinjani Trek Centre (RTC) – it is large, in colour, glossy and easy to understand.

It's often not possible to climb Rinjani during the wet season, particularly after heavy rainfall when the trail around the lake is very dangerous due to the threat of rock fall.

Day One: Senaru Pos I to Pos III (Five to Six Hours)

At the southern end of the village is the Rinjani Trek Centre (Pos I, 601m), where you register and pay the park fee. Just beyond the post, the trail forks – continue straight ahead on the right fork. The trail climbs steadily through scrubby farmland for about half an hour to the sign at the entrance to Gunung Rinjani National Park. The wide trail climbs for another 2½ hours until you reach Pos II (1500m), where there's a shelter. Water can be found 100m down the slopes from the trail, but it should be treated or boiled.

Another 1½ hours' steady walk uphill brings you to Pos III (2000m), where there are another two shelters in disrepair. Water is 100m off the trail to the right, but sometimes evaporates in the dry season. Pos III is usually the place to camp at the end of the first day.

Day Two: Pos III to Danau Segara Anak & Aiq Kalak (Four Hours)

From Pos III, it takes about 1½ hours to reach the rim, Pelawangan I, at an altitude of 2641m. Set off very early for the stunning sunrise. It's possible to camp at Pelawangan I, but there are drawbacks: level sites are limited, there's no water and it can be very blustery.

It takes about two hours to descend to Danau Segara Anak and around to the hot springs, Aiq Kalak. The first hour is a very steep descent and involves low-grade rock climbing in parts. From the bottom of the crater wall it's an easy 30-minute walk across undulating terrain around the lake's edge. There are several places to camp, but most locals prefer to be near the hot springs to soak their weary bodies and recuperate. There are also some caves nearby which are interesting, but not used for shelter. The nicest camp sites are at the lake's edge, and fresh water can be gathered from a spring near the hot springs. Some hikers spend two nights or even more at the lake, but most who are returning to Senaru from here head back the next day. The climb back up the rim is certainly taxing – allow at least three hours and start early to make it back to Senaru in one day. Allow five hours from the rim down to Senaru. Instead of retracing your steps, the best option is to complete the Rinjani trek by continuing to Sembalun Lawang and arranging transport back to Senaru (see p312).

Day Three: Aiq Kalak to Pelawangan II (Three to Four Hours)

The trail starts beside the last shelter at the hot springs and heads away from the lake for about 100m before veering right. It then traverses the northern slope of the crater, and it's an easy one-hour walk along the grassy slopes. It's then a steep and constant climb; from the lake it takes about three hours to reach the crater rim (2639m). At the rim, a sign points the way back to Danau Segara Anak. Water can be found down the slope near the sign. The trail forks here – go straight on to Lawang or continue along the rim to the camp site of Pelawangan II (2700m). It's only about 10 minutes more to the camp site which is on a bare ridge.

Day Four: Pelawangan II to Rinjani Summit (Five to Six Hours Return)

Gunung Rinjani stretches in an arc above the camp site at Pelawangan II and looks deceptively close. Start the climb at 3am in order to reach the summit in time for the sunrise and before the clouds roll in.

It takes about 45 minutes to clamber up a steep, slippery and indistinct trail to the ridge that leads to Rinjani. Once on the ridge it's a relatively easy walk uphill. After about an hour

LOMBOK

heading towards what looks like the peak, the real summit of Rinjani looms behind and towers above you.

The trail then gets steeper and steeper. About 350m before the summit, the scree is composed of loose, fist-sized rocks – it's easier to get along by scrambling on all fours. This section can take about an hour. The views from the top are truly magnificent on a clear day. The descent is much easier, but again, take it easy on the scree. In total it takes three hours or more to reach the summit, and two to get back down.

Day Four/Five: Pelawangan II to Sembalun Lawang (Five to Six Hours)

After negotiating the peak, it's still possible to reach Lawang the same day. After a two-hour descent, it's a long and hot three-hour walk back to the village. Head off early to avoid as much of the heat of the day as possible and make sure you've brought along plenty of water. From the camp site, head back along the ridge-crest trail. A couple of hundred metres past the turn-off to Danau Segara Anak there is a signposted right turn leading down a subsidiary ridge to Pada Balong and Sembalun Lawang. Once on the trail, it's easy to follow and takes around two hours to reach the bottom.

At the bottom of the ridge (where you'll find Pada Balong shelter; 1800m) the trail levels out and crosses undulating to flat grassland all the way to Sembalun Lawang. After about an hour you will hit the Tengengean shelter (1500m); it's then another 30 minutes to Pemantuan shelter (1300m). Early in the season, long grass obscures the trail until about 30 minutes beyond Pemantuan. The trail crosses many bridges; at the final bridge, just before it climbs uphill to a lone tree, the trail seems to fork; take the right fork and climb the rise. From here, the trail follows the flank of Rinjani before swinging around to Lawang at the end. A guide is essential for this part of the trip.

Variations

There are a few possible variations to the route to the top of Gunung Rinjani described above. They're outlined here:

- Compress the last two days into one (racking up a hefty 10 to 11 hours on the trail). On the plus side it's downhill all the way after the hard climb to the summit.
- Retrace your steps to Senaru after climbing to the summit, making a five-day circuit that includes another night at the hot springs.
- Another popular route, because the trail is well defined and (if you're experienced) can be trekked with only a porter, is a three-day trek from Senaru to the hot springs and back. The first night is spent at Pos III and the second at the hot springs. The return to Senaru on the final day takes eight to nine hours.
- For (almost) instant gratification (if you travel light and climb fast) you can reach the crater rim from Senaru in about six hours. You'll gain an altitude of approximately 2040m in 10km. Armed with a torch (flashlight), some moonlight and a guide, set off at midnight to arrive for sunrise. The return takes about five hours.
- If you reach Pelawangan I early in the day, consider taking a side trip along the crater rim, following it around to the east for about 3km to Gunung Senkereang (2919m). This point overlooks the gap in the rim where the stream that comes from the hot springs flows out of the crater and northeast towards the sea. It's not an easy walk, however, and the track is narrow and very exposed in places – if you do decide to give it a go, allow around two hours to get there and back.
- Start trekking from Sembalun Lawang (a guide is essential), from where it takes six or seven hours to get to Pelawangan II. This is a shorter walk to the rim than from Senaru, with only a three-hour trek up the ridge.

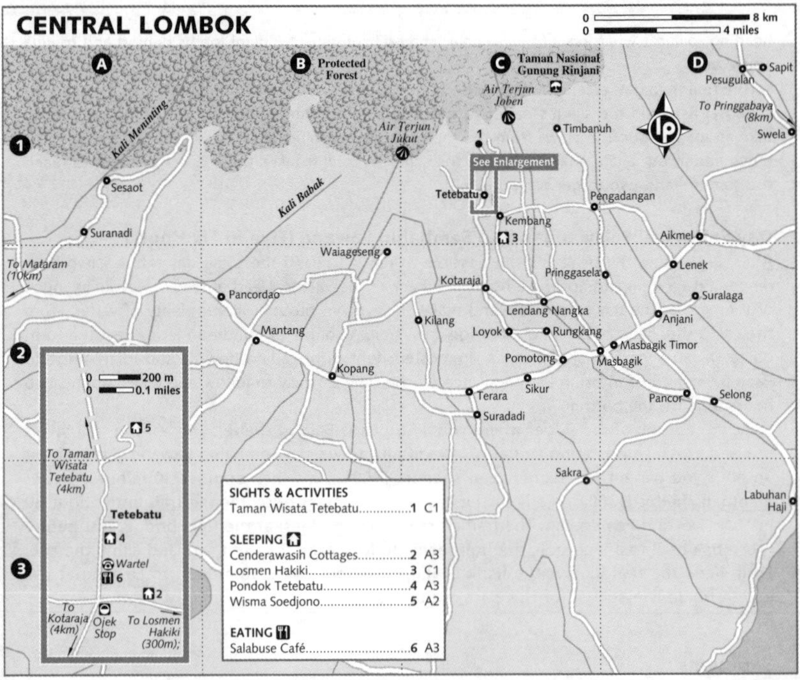

WATERFALLS

On the southern slopes of Gunung Rinjani National Park there are two waterfalls. Both are accessible by private transport, or a lovely 1½-hour walk (one way) through rice fields from Tetebatu. If walking, *be sure* to hire a reputable guide (ask at your losmen).

Locals believe that water from **Air Terjun Jukut** (Jeruk Manis, Air Temer; admission 2000Rp) will increase hair growth. The falls are a steep 2km walk from the car park at the end of the road.

Northwest of Tetebatu, **Air Terjun Joben** (Otak Kokok Gading; admission 2000Rp) is more of a public swimming pool, so less alluring.

Sleeping & Eating

Most accommodation in Tetebatu has a rustic charm. The losmen on Waterfall Rd tend to be more funky.

Pondok Tetebatu (☎ 632572; s/d 30,000/45,000Rp) North of the intersection this is a good choice with two rows of neat, spotless rooms, with Western toilets that face a pretty garden, plus a restaurant (dishes 8000Rp to 35,000Rp).

Losmen Hakiki (☎ 01808 0373 7407; cottages incl breakfast 50,000-70,000Rp) Enjoying a lovely aspect over rice fields, about 1km east of the intersection, this place has charming little *lumbung* with yellow window frames and serves tasty Indonesian and Sasak cuisine (7000Rp to 18,000Rp).

Cendrawasih Cottages (☎ 0818 0372 6709; r 65,000Rp) Four gorgeous little *lumbung* cottages, with bamboo walls and shower/mandi facing a pond and garden. Tuck into Sasak, Indonesian or Western grub (7000Rp to 22,000Rp) in the elevated octagonal lounge and eating area, which gives sweeping views of the surrounding area. It's about 500m east of the intersection.

Wisma Soedjono (☎ 21309; r 75,000-150,000Rp, cottages 125,000Rp;) About 2km north of the intersection, these slightly soulless but functional rooms (some with hot water) and lovely two-storey chalet-style cottages (with both balconies and verandas) are scattered around the grounds of a rambling family home. The large swimming pool is infrequently cleaned however. There's also a restaurant, with dishes from 10,000Rp to 28,000Rp.

Salabuse Café (☎ 0817 5731 143; dishes 6000-17,500Rp; 7am-10pm) Cheery, cheap place serving Western, Indonesian and Sasak meals.

Getting There & Around

Buses go from Mandalika to Pomotong (7000Rp), which is on the main east–west highway. From there, take a bemo to Kotaraja (2000Rp), then an *ojek* (3000Rp) or *cidomo* (4000Rp) to Tetebatu.

Bicycles and motorbikes can be rented at Pondok Tetebatu, and other losmen, for 15,000Rp and 50,000Rp per day, respectively.

SOUTH OF TETEBATU

The nearest market town to Tetebatu is **Kotaraja**, which is also the transport hub of the area. It's known for its skilled blacksmiths. There's a market on Monday and Wednesday mornings.

Loyok is noted for its fine basketry and **Rungkang** is known for its pottery, made from a local black clay. You'll find workshops in both villages.

Masbagik is a large town on Lombok's east–west highway with a daily morning market, a huge cattle market on Monday afternoon, and an imposing new mosque with elegant minarets. There's an ATM opposite the mosque. Masbagik Timur, 1km east, is a centre for black-clay pottery and ceramic production.

Lendang Nangka is a Sasak village surrounded by picturesque countryside, 3km north of the highway. In and around the village you can see blacksmiths who make knives, hoes and other tools using traditional techniques. A few silversmiths are also based here and there's a excellent homestay, **Radiah's** (☎ 0376 631463; per person incl meals 50,000Rp) run by English speaker Radiah and his wife Sannah, who make Western

SASAK LIFE

Lombok's indigenous Sasak people comprise about 90% of the island's population. Virtually all are now orthodox Muslims, though before 1965, many Sasaks in remote areas were Wektu Telu (see boxed text, p316), a subsect of Islam peculiar to Lombok.

The traditional Sasak village layout is a walled enclosure. Sasak houses are made of bamboo, and sit on a base of compacted mud; they have a steeply-angled thatched roof, fireplace and (usually) no windows. A dividing wall of bamboo or woven fibres separates the main living area in some houses. Each village will have *lumbung,* rice storage barns that sit on stilts (to keep rodents at bay) that look like little thatched cottages; their façades shaped like the letter omega, or a mosque's mihrab. (Many hotels in the Gili Islands and Tetebatunow offer *lumbung*-style cottage accommodation.) There are several examples of traditional villages in northern Lombok including Dusun Senaru (p312) on the slopes of Gunung Rinjani, while in the south, Sade and Rembitan (p322) near Kuta also have Sasak houses and *lumbung*. But across the island, modern concrete homes with tin roofs and windows containing several rooms are becoming more common.

Many Sasak villages, particularly on the north of the island, still maintain a caste system which heavily influences courtship and marriage – women are not allowed to marry a man from a lower caste by tradition. Weddings between the highest castes – *Datu* (men) and *Denek Bini* (women) – and lower castes are quite rare.

There are three kinds of marriage rituals in Sasak culture: arranged marriages, a union between cousins, and elopement. Until recently, the tradition of elopement was dying out, but with more contact between castes and travel between villages it has regained popularity. For a boy from a caste lower than his girlfriend, eloping with her for a specified period of days – whisking her away to a safe house before notifying the *kepala desa* (village chief) of his intent to marry her – may be the only route to marriage. The chief will talk with the couple, negotiate between the parents, consult elders from both villages, and fix a wedding dowry, and the fine to be paid for the boy's actions.

When romance has been blossoming for a while between a couple, it's not unknown for parents who disapprove of a daughter's suitor to surreptitiously arrange a marriage with another boy, confining their daughter to the family home under close supervision. But with many locals now having access to mobile phones and SMS, boyfriends are often able to 'kidnap' their sweethearts when she is alone in the family home (strict protocols apply, and for an elopement marriage to be valid he must take her from her house, not from the village well or by the roadside).

Dowries also reflect these caste differences: the lower his caste and the higher hers, the more money changes hands. For the ceremony the bride and groom usually dress in traditional costume and are carried through the village in sedan chairs to the accompaniment of gamelan music.

visitors very welcome and will explain all about Sasak traditions and local agriculture. Everyone knows their house in the village.

Pringgasela is a centre for traditional weaving on simple looms; the local textiles produced here feature coloured stripes. You can watch the weavers in action and buy sarongs and throws.

It's best to rent or charter private transport from Tetebatu to visit the craft villages in this area.

SOUTH LOMBOK

☎ 0370

South Lombok is blessed with the island's best beaches, from dramatic cliff-backed coves to oceanic expanses that catch world-class waves. The region is noticeably drier than the rest of Lombok and more sparsely populated, with limited roads and public transport. Most visitors head for Kuta – the antithesis of its Balinese namesake – a tranquil, relaxed base for exploring the terrific southern coastline.

PRAYA

pop 35,000

Praya is the south's main town. It's a very spread out place, with tree-lined streets and a few old **Dutch buildings**. There's nothing of much interest to visitors right now however, except perhaps a couple of ATMs on Jl Jend Sudirman, but by 2009 Lombok's new international **airport** should open close by, boosting the local economy. Meanwhile, the bemo terminal, on the northwest side of town, is the transport hub for the region.

Just up from the market, **Dienda Hayu Hotel** (☎ 654319; Jl Untung Surapati 28; r 50,000-80,000Rp; ❄) has rooms that are in fair shape, all with cold-water bathrooms.

AROUND PRAYA

Sukarara

The main street here is given over to touristy, commercial craft shops, but you may want to put up with the sales speak in order to see the various styles of weaving and watch the weavers at work. **Darnia Setia Artshop** (🕑 7am-6pm) has the widest range of textiles, including ikat, some coming from Sumba and elsewhere in Flores. To reach Sukarara, take a bemo to Puyung along the main road. From there, hire a *cidomo* or walk the 2km to Sukarara.

Penujak

Penujak is well known for its traditional *gerabah* pottery made from a local clay with the simplest of techniques. The pots range in size up to 1m high, and there are also various kitchen vessels and decorative figurines. The traditional pottery is a rich terracotta colour and is hand-burnished.

Penujak is on the main road from Praya to the south coast; any bemo to Sengkol or Kuta will drop you off.

Rembitan & Sade

The area from Sengkol down to Kuta is a centre for traditional Sasak culture. Regular bemo cover this route.

Rembitan is on a hill just west of the main road. It's a slightly sanitised 'traditional' Sasak village, but still boasts an authentic cluster of thatched houses and *lumbung*. On top of the hill is **Masjid Kuno**, an ancient thatched-roof mosque, a place of pilgrimage for Lombok's Muslims as one of the founding fathers of Islam in Indonesia is said to be buried here.

On the road between Rembitan and Sade are stores selling Javanese-style batik paintings (albeit painted by locals).

A little further south is Sade, another traditional, picturesque village that has been extensively renovated. It has informative guides who'll tell you about Sasak houses and village life. Donations are 'requested' by guides at both villages – 3000Rp to 7000Rp is enough, but expect to have to pay for photos too.

KUTA

Lombok's Kuta beach is a magnificent stretch of white sand and turquoise sea with rugged hills rising around it. Surfers are drawn here by the world-class waves, but the village has a languid charm of its own with some delightful hotels and a succession of dramatic bite-shaped bays nearby.

Long-slated plans for a succession of five-star resorts have failed to materialise, and this superb coast is still all but undeveloped, with far, far fewer facilities than the (in)famous Kuta Beach in Bali. Kuta comes alive during the annual Nyale fishing festival (in February or March; see the boxed text p324) and during the main tourist season (August), but for the rest of the year, it's very quiet.

Tourism dominates the local economy, but locals also harvest seaweed for the cosmetic industry in the dry season.

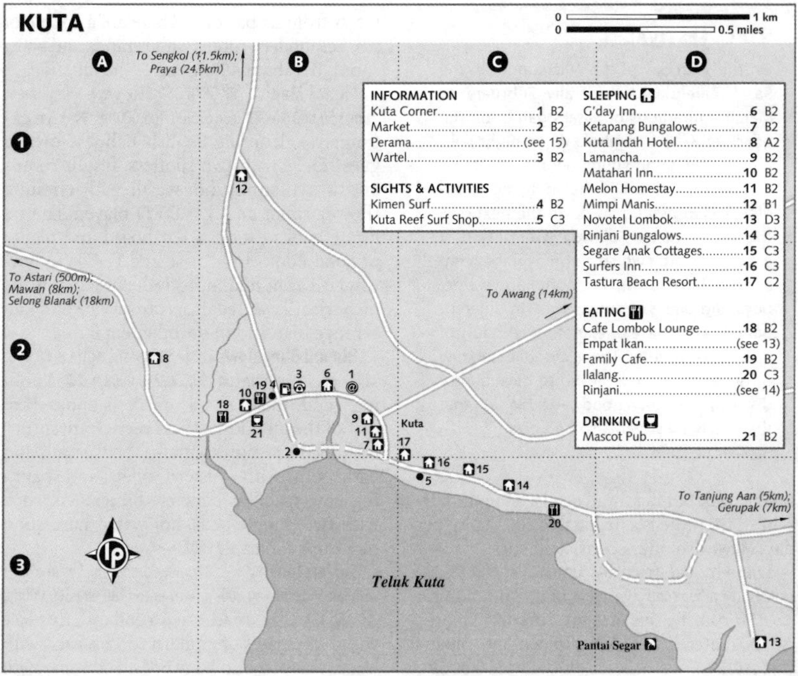

Information & Orientation

Several places change money, including the Kuta Indah Hotel and Segare Anak Cottages, which is also a postal agency.

There's a wartel in town and **Kuta Corner** (9am-7pm) has slow internet access and buys, sells or rents second-hand books. The **market** fires up on Sunday and Wednesday. **Perama** (☎ 654846), based at Segare Anak Cottages runs tourist buses to Mataram (75,000Rp) with connections to Senggigi and elsewhere.

Virtually everything in Kuta is on a single road that parallels the beach, either east or west of the junction where the road from Praya hits town.

> **SOUTH LOMBOK SECURITY WARNING**
>
> Tourists have been threatened and robbed at knifepoint on the back roads of South Lombok, in particular around Mawi. Ask around about the latest situation and do not leave your vehicle unattended – find a local to watch it for a tip.

Danger & Annoyances

If you decide to rent a bicycle or motorbike take care who you deal with – arrangements are informal and no rental contracts are exchanged. We have received reports of some visitors having motorbikes stolen, and then having to pay substantial sums of money as compensation to the owner (who may or may not have arranged the 'theft' himself). One recommended place that organises motorbike hire is the guesthouse Mimpi Manis (see p324).

See the security alert about Mawi beach in the boxed text left.

Activities

SURFING

Plenty of good waves break on the reefs, including lefts and rights, in the bay in front of Kuta, and some more on the reefs east of Tanjung Aan. As the waves break a long way from shore, use local boatmen to tow you out for around 50,000Rp. About 7km east of Kuta is the fishing village of **Gerupak**, where there are several breaks on the reefs at the entrance of Teluk Gerupak. There are plenty of breaks

NYALE FESTIVAL

On the 19th day of the 10th month in the Sasak calendar – generally February or March – hundreds of Sasaks gather on the beach at Kutain Lombok. When night falls, fires are built and young people sit around competing with each other in rhyming couplets called *pantun*. At dawn the next day, the first of millions of *nyale* (wormlike fish) are caught, after which it's time for the teenagers to have fun. In a colourful procession, boys and girls sail out to sea – in different boats – and chase one another with lots of noise and laughter. The *nyale* are eaten raw or grilled, and are believed to have aphrodisiac properties. A good catch is a sign that the rice harvest will also be good.

further out, but nearly all need a boat; the current charter rate is a negotiable 200,000Rp per day. **Mawi** also offers consistent surf.

Drop by the friendly **Kimen Surf** (☎ 655064; kimensurf@yahoo.com) just west of the junction for swell forecasts, tips and information. Boards can be rented here (30,000Rp per day), repairs undertaken, lessons are offered (310,000Rp for four hours) and day trips to Gerupak (240,000Rp) and Bangko Bangko (950,000Rp) organised.

Kuta Reef Surf Shop, a simple place on the beachfront, is another recommended place, offering surf and bodyboard rentals at similar rates.

LOMBOK

Sleeping

Breakfast is included at all the places listed here. All accommodation is virtually on or just behind the beach, except Mimpi Manis. Many places have plenty of character and are well spread out with no sense of overcrowding.

BUDGET

Segare Anak Cottages (☎ 654846; segareanakbungalows@yahoo.co.id; r 35,000-65,000Rp) Around 800m east of the junction. Overlooking a pretty garden the basic huts here have seen better days, but the newer concrete bungalows are a good deal and worth the extra rupiah. Also home to a moneychanger and the Perama office.

Melon Homestay (☎ 0817 367 892; angela_grannemann@web.de; r 50,000Rp, apt 65,000Rp) A terrific deal, this place has two gorgeous apartments with a lounge and self-catering facilities, one with sea views from its balcony. There are a couple of smaller modern rooms with veranda and bathroom. It's about 400m east of the junction.

Mimpi Manis (☎ 0818 369 950; www.mimpimanis.com; s 50,000-90,000Rp, d 65,000-105,000Rp; ⊠) An extremely welcoming English-Balinese-owned guesthouse with two spotless, bright rooms and a two-storey house, all with en-suite shower room and TV/DVD player. There's home-cooked food, a dartboard and plenty of good books to browse and DVDs to borrow. It's 2km inland from the beach, but the owners offer a free drop-off service and can arrange bike and motorbike rental.

Rinjani Bungalows (☎ 654849; s/d with fan 80,000/95,000Rp, s/d with air-con 200,000/250,000Rp; ⊠) Looking good, this well-run place is about 1km east of the junction. Offers very clean, spruce bamboo bungalows with ikat bedspreads and bathrooms with Western toilets, and spanking new spacious concrete bungalows, each with two double beds, hot water, hardwood furniture and cable TV.

Surfers Inn (☎ 655582; www.lombok-surfersinn.com; r with fan 100,000-160,000Rp, with air con 180,000-500,000Rp; ⊠ ⊠) A very smart, stylish and orderly place with five classes of modern rooms, each with huge windows and large beds, and some with sofas. Book ahead as it's very popular.

Also recommended:

Ketapang Bungalows (☎ 655194; s/d 30,000/40,000Rp) Has simple thatched-roof bungalows with verandas; it's 500m east of the junction.

Lamancha (☎ 655186; s/d 40,000/50,000Rp) Four basic but spotless semidetached huts with mandi and shower.

G'Day Inn (☎ 655432; s/d 40,000/60,000Rp) This friendly, family-run place offers clean, recently-renovated rooms, some with hot water as well as a café. Located about 300m east of the junction.

MIDRANGE

Matahari Inn (☎ 655000; www.matahariinn.com; r 180,000Rp-550,000Rp; ⊠ ⊠) This Balinese-themed hotel has an array of baroque rooms, each suffering somewhat from gaudy artefact overkill with an excess of reclining Buddhas and the like. Nevertheless, the garden, shaded by bamboo and palm trees is gorgeous.

Kutah Indah Hotel (☎ 653781; kutaindah@indonet.id; r US$17-30; ⊠ ⊠) Set around well-tended gardens with a clipped lawn, these cottages are spacious but slightly tired-looking – the pool's nice.

Tastura Beach Resort (☎ 655540; tastura@mataram.wasantara.net.id; r US$25-30; ⊠ ⊠) A bland, government-owned hotel with 20 distinctly average bungalows in expansive grounds 600m east of the junction. Cleanliness could be much better.

TOP END

Novotel Lombok (☎ 653333; www.novotel-lombok.com; r without/with terrace US$120/140, villa US$235, plus 21% tax; ✖ ◙) This attractive resort 3km east of the junction has appealing modern rooms, with coconut-wood flooring and furniture, that are set off less-than-attractive corridors. The spacious thatched Sasak-style villas are lovely however. Two pools face a superb beach and there's a wonderful spa, good restaurants and a plethora of activities on offer including catamaran sailing, fishing, scuba diving and even archery classes.

Eating & Drinking

All these places are on or just off the beach, though few actually have tables with sea views. For a really cheap bite, there are warung shacks on the beach opposite Surfers Inn and along the esplanade.

Family Cafe (☎ 653748; mains 6000-30,000Rp) Large thatched restaurant with a tempting menu including delicious *sate pusut* (satay served with coconut and chilli) and *urap urup* (mixed vegetables with *sambal* and coconut). Western dishes including chicken cordon bleu are tasty too. It also serves cocktails.

our pick **Astari** (dishes 8000-22,000Rp; ⏲ 8.30am-6pm) Perched on a mountaintop 2km west of town on the road to Mawan, this remarkable, mainly vegetarian lounge-restaurant has a to-die-for healthy menu that takes in winsome breakfasts, sandwiches, and creatively assembled mains. The blackboard always has a daily dish and drink of the day – perhaps focaccia bread with eggplant and tamarind cooler. The view at least matches the cuisine, and it's easy to lose hours up here daydreaming, enjoying the music, browsing magazines or playing backgammon, and gazing out over Kuta's low hump-backed hills to the distant ocean rollers.

Ilalang (dishes 11,000-35,000Rp) Right on the beach, this ramshackle-looking place scores for fresh seafood.

Cafe Lombok Lounge (☎ 655542; 12,000-30,000Rp) Inexpensive Indonesian food including *cumi cumi* (squid) and Western dishes like omelettes.

Mascot Pub (dishes 12,000-38,000Rp; ⏲ 11-2am) Virtually the only nightlife in town; though don't expect a rave – it's more a local band playing covers, and only on Friday and Saturday nights. Also serves Indonesian food.

Rinjani (dishes 13,000-39,000Rp; ⏲ 8am-11pm) This beachside place has a nice decked restaurant area, it serves both Western and Indonesian cuisine and also features live music some Saturdays.

Empat Ikan (Novotel Lombok; mains 75,000-175,000Rp) For something more fancy, this beachside hotel restaurant is strong on fish and seafood.

Getting There & Away

Kuta is a hassle to reach by public transport, from Mandalika terminal in Mataram you'll have to go via Praya (6000Rp), then to Sengkol (3500Rp) and finally to Kuta (2500Rp). You'll usually have to change buses at all these places. Many people opt for the Perama shuttle-bus option from Senggigi or the Gili Islands to Kuta.

Getting Around

Ojek congregate around the main junction as you enter Kuta. Bemo go east of Kuta to Awang and Tanjung Aan (2500Rp), and west to Selong Blanak (3000Rp), or can be charted to nearby beaches. See p323 for more information about bike-hire scams. The guesthouse Mimpi Manis rents bicycles for 20,000Rp and motorbikes for 35,000Rp a day.

EAST OF KUTA

Quite good roads traverse the coast to the east, passing a series of beautiful bays punctuated by headlands. There's public transport, but it's much easier with a motorbike.

Pantai Segar (Segar Beach) is about 2km east around the first headland, within walking distance of the town. The enormous rock of **Batu Kotak**, 2km further on divides two glorious white-sand beaches. Continuing east, **Tanjung Aan** is a very fine beach with chalk-white, powdery sand. Due to a spate of problems with stealing, there's a security guard keeping an eye on the place – even so, it's best not to bring valuables to the beach. The road continues another 2km to the fishing village and surfers' fave **Gerupak** where there's a market on Tuesday and a restaurant on the beach. Alternatively, turn northeast just before Tanjung Aan and go to **Awang**, a busy fishing village with a sideline in seaweed harvesting. You could take a boat from Awang across to Ekas (a charter costs around 120,000Rp) or to some of the other not-so-secret surf spots in this bay.

SASAK FESTIVALS & CEREMONIES

As more and more Sasaks have adopted orthodox Islam, many ancient cultural rituals and celebrations based on animist and Hindu traditions have dwindled in popularity. Nevertheless some festivals and events endure, and are being actively promoted by local authorities. In addition to these festivals, there are also important events celebrating the harvesting of a sea worm called *nyale* (p324) in Kuta, and the riotous Hindu–Wektu Telu 'rice war' known as Perang Topat held at Pura Lingsar (p291).

Lebaran Topat, held in the seven days after the end of the fasting month (Idul Fitri; Ramadan) in the Islamic calendar is a Sasak ceremony thought to be unique to West Lombok. Relatives gather in cemeteries to pour water over family graves, and add offerings of flowers, betel leaves and lime powder. A place to observe these ceremonies is Bintaro cemetery on the outskirts of Ampenan.

Malean Sampi (meaning 'cow chase' in Sasak) are highly competitive buffalo races held over a 100m waterlogged fields in Narmada (see p291), just east of Mataram. Two buffalo are yoked together and then driven along the course by a driver brandishing a whip. The event takes place in early April, and commemorates the beginning of the planting season.

Gendang Beleq (big drum) performances were originally performed before battles. Today many villages in central Lombok have a *gendang* battery, some with up to 40 drummers, who perform at festivals and ceremonies. The drums themselves are colossal, up to a metre in length and not unlike an oil drum in shape or size. The drummers support the drums using a sash around their necks.

Peresean (stick fighting) are martial art performances by two young men stripped to the waist, armed with rattan sticks and square shields made of cowhide. The Sasak believe that the more blood shed on the earth, the better the rainfall will be in the forthcoming wet season. In late July demonstrations can be seen in Senggigi and in late December there's a championship in Mataram.

WEST OF KUTA

West of Kuta are a succession of outstanding beaches that all have superb surf when conditions are right. It's possible that the region may eventually be developed when the new airport (p322) is completed, but for now it remains near-pristine and all but deserted. The road, which is potholed and very steep in places, doesn't follow the coast closely, so you'll need to detour slightly to find these beaches. **Mawan** (parking motorbike/car 2000/4000Rp) is the most impressive, a bite-shaped bay backed by steep green hills with a fine sandy beach below. **Tampa** is similar but a little wilder – you'll need to drive through rice fields on a grassy road, and past a tiny village to get there. **Mawi** (parking motorbike/car 2000/4000Rp), 16km from Kuta, is an absolutely stunning beach and surfing stronghold with a legendary barrel wave, but there can be a very strong riptide so be extra careful. Sadly, thefts have been reported here. **Selong Blanak** is another wonderfully expansive stretch of sand.

From **Pengantap**, the road climbs across a headland to descend to another superb bay; follow this around for about 1km then look out for the turn-off west to **Blongas**, which is a very steep, rough and winding road with breathtaking scenery.

EAST LOMBOK

☎ 0376

All that most travellers see of the east coast is Labuhan Lombok, the port for ferries to Sumbawa, but the road around the northeast coast is in fair shape, and a round-the-island trip is quite feasible. Similarly, the once-remote southeastern peninsula is becoming more accessible, particularly to those with their own transport.

LABUHAN LOMBOK

Labuhan Lombok (Labuhan Kayangan), is the port for ferries and boats to Sumbawa. The town centre of Labuhan Lombok, 3km west of the ferry terminal, is a scruffy place but it does have great views of Gunung Rinjani.

Sleeping & Eating

Try to avoid staying overnight as there's only one decent place – there are warung in town and around the ferry terminal.

Losmen Lima Tiga (☎ 23316; Jl Raya Kayangan; r 55,000Rp) About 2.5km inland from the port on the main road, this is a very clean family-run place with neat little rooms and spotless shared bathrooms.

Hotel Melati Munawar (r 30,000Rp) This one's filthy.

Getting There & Away

BUS & BEMO

Frequent buses and bemo travel between Labuhan Lombok and Mandalika terminal in Mataram (11,000Rp, two hours), and also head north from Labuhan Lombok to Anyar. Note that public transport to and from Labuhan Lombok is often marked 'Labuhan Kayangan' or 'Tanjung Kayangan'. Buses and bemo that don't go directly to Labuhan Lombok, but just travel the main road along the east coast, will only drop you off at the port entrance, from where you'll have to catch another bemo to the ferry terminal. Don't walk; it's too far.

FERRY

See p353 for details of ferry connections between Lombok and Sumbawa and p290 for bus connections between Mataram and Sumbawa.

NORTH OF LABUHAN LOMBOK

This road has limited public transport and becomes very steep and windy as you near Anyar. There are isolated black-sand beaches along the way, particularly at Obel Obel.

Leaving Labuhan Lombok, look out for the giant mahogany trees about 4km north of the harbour. From Labuhan Pandan, or from further north at Sugian, you can charter a boat to the uninhabited **Gili Sulat** and **Gili Pentangan**. Both islands have lovely white beaches and good coral for snorkelling, but no facilities.

Just before the village of Labuhan Pandan, 15km from Labuhan Lombok, the Swiss-run **Matahari Inn** (☎ 0812 3749 915; www.pondok-matahari.com; s/d 90,000/120,000Rp) is a peaceful place with clean, comfortable bungalows right on the beach and two rooms inland. There's good food (dishes 7000Rp to 26,000Rp), and snorkelling offshore. Fun dives (per dive US$31) and scuba-diving courses are offered by the instructor-owners.

SOUTH OF LABUHAN LOMBOK

The capital of the East Lombok administrative district, **Selong**, has some Dutch colonial buildings. The transport junction for the region is just to the west of Selong at **Pancor**, where you can catch bemo to most points south.

Labuhan Haji is on the coast where the black sand is a bit grubby, but the water is OK for swimming. The basic, isolated bungalows at **Melewi's Beach Hotel** (☎ 621241; r 40,000Rp) are almost on the beach and have great views across to Sumbawa.

Tanjung Luar is one of Lombok's main fishing ports and has lots of quaint Bugis-style houses on stilts. From there, the road swings west to **Keruak**, where wooden boats are built, and continues past the turn to **Sukaraja**, a traditional Sasak village where you can buy woodcarvings. Just west of Keruak a road leads south to **Jerowaru** and the southeastern peninsula. You'll need your own transport; be warned that it is easy to lose your way around here and that the roads go from bad to worse.

A sealed road branches west past Jerowaru – it gets pretty rough but eventually reaches **Ekas**, from where you can charter a boat to Awang across the bay. Offering a superb, if remote base in this part of Lombok, the spectacularly-sited **Heaven on the Planet** (☎ 0812 3705 393; www.heavenontheplanet.co.nz; basic chalets 100,000-150,000Rp, villas 300,000-500,000Rp; 🍽) is an ideal base for activity junkies with surfing, diving and abseiling facilities. There are two restaurants, and a well-stocked bar. Just a kilometre away from here, right by the Ekas surf break, a second resort to be called Ocean Heaven (formerly the Laut Surga), owned by the same Kiwi owners as Heaven on the Planet should be up and running by the time you read this.

The road to this region is really pretty terrible, so it's best to try to contact the hotel in advance and get them to come and pick you up, or you could consider chartering a boat from Awang (see p325).

Directory

CONTENTS

ACCOMMODATION

Bali has a huge range of accommodation, primarily in hotels of every shape, size and price. It has great value lodging no matter what your budget.

All accommodation attracts a combined tax and service (called 'plus plus') charge of 21%. In budget places, this is generally included in the price, but check first. Many midrange (but not all) and top-end places will add it on, which can add substantially to your bill.

In this guide, the rates quoted are those that travellers are likely to pay during the high season and include tax. With the ongoing downturn of business published rates are often whimsical at best.

The range of prices used in this book are as follows:

Budget Most rooms cost less than 250,000Rp (less than US$35) per night.
Midrange Most rooms cost between 250,000Rp (around US$35) and 800,000Rp (around US$75).
Top End Most rooms cost more than 800,000Rp (more than US$75).

Rates are almost always negotiable, especially outside the main peak season, and if you are staying for a few days, or longer, at midrange or top-end places, you should always seek a discount. In the low season, discounts between 30% and 50% aren't uncommon in many midrange and top-end hotels. Note that a high-season surcharge applies in many top-end hotels during holiday periods such as Christmas.

Rates are often given in US dollars (US$) as opposed to rupiah (Rp), especially at higher-end places. Sometimes rates are in both currencies, meaning you should offer to pay in the one offering the best deal based on current conversion rates.

Camping

The only camping ground on the whole island is at the headquarters of the Taman Nasional Bali Barat at Cekik in western Bali. It is only useful if you want to trek in the national park, and you will have to bring your own camping and cooking equipment.

Even if you're trekking in the central mountains, or in the national park, you will rarely find use for a tent – there are usually shelters of some sort, and most hikes can be completed in one day anyway.

Hotels

Pretty much every place to stay in Bali and Lombok will arrange tours, car rental and other services. Laundry service is universally available, sometimes for free.

BUDGET HOTELS

The cheapest accommodation n Bali is in small places that are simple, but clean and comfortable. A losmen is a small hotel, often family-run, which rarely has more than about a dozen rooms; names usually include the

PRACTICALITIES

- Current issues of English-language dailies (*Jakarta Post* and the *International Herald Tribune)* and major news magazines can be found at bookshops and minimarts in South Bali and Ubud. Don't buy either newspaper at more than cover price from street vendors, who are also the only source for Australian newspapers, which they sell for outrageous prices.
- Pop radio in Bali often has DJs jamming away in English. Short-wave broadcasts, such as Voice of America and the BBC World Service, can be picked up in Bali. Many hotels and some bars have satellite TV with all the international channels.
- Indonesia uses the PAL broadcasting standard, the same as Australia, New Zealand, the UK and most of Europe; for DVDs you buy here though, be aware that you may need a multi-region DVD player.
- Electricity is usually 220V to 240V AC in Bali. Wall plugs are the standard European variety – round with two pins. Service is usually reliable.
- Indonesia follows the metric system. There is a conversion table for the imperial system on the inside front cover.

word 'losmen', 'homestay,' 'inn' or '*pondok*'. Losmen are often built in the style of a Balinese home, ie a compound with an outer wall and separate buildings around an inner garden.

There are losmen all over Bali, and they vary widely in standards and price. In a few places you'll find a room for as little as 40,000Rp, but generally they're in the 50,000Rp to 150,000Rp range. Some of the cheap rooms are definitely on the dull side, but others are attractive, well kept and excellent value for money. A lush garden can be one of the most attractive features, even in very cheap places. The price usually includes a light breakfast, and rooms have an attached bathroom with a shower (cold water only), basin and generally a Western-style toilet and a fan.

Many budget places also resemble hotels and as competition in Bali has heated up, it's not uncommon to find amenities such as pools, hot water and air-con in budget places with rooms under 250,000Rp. Don't expect great levels of service in any of these places – although smiles abound.

MIDRANGE HOTELS

Midrange hotels are often constructed in Balinese bungalow style and set on spacious grounds with a pool. In the less expensive midrange hotels, rooms are priced from about 250,000Rp to 350,000Rp, which includes breakfast and a private bathroom. Midrange hotels may have a variety of rooms and prices, with the main difference being air-con and hot water versus a fan and cold water. Pools are common.

Upper-midrange hotels normally give their price in US dollars. Prices range from US$30 to US$75, and should include hot water, air-con, satellite TV and the like. Rooms at the top price end are likely to have a sunken bar in the swimming pool (usually unattended, but it looks good on the brochure). Many have a sense of style that is beguiling and which may help postpone your departure.

TOP-END HOTELS

Top-end hotels in Bali are world-class. You can find excellent places in Seminyak, Jimbaran, the resort strip of Nusa Dua and Tajung Benoa and Ubud. Exclusive properties can be found around the coast of East Bali and around Pemuteran in North Bali. Service is refined and you can expect décor that seems plucked from the pages of a glossy magazine. Views are superb – whether they're of the ocean or of lush valleys and rice paddies. At the best places you can expect daily deliveries of fresh fruit and flowers to your room. Bali regularly has several places in surveys of top hotels such as those done by *Conde Nast Traveller*.

Although top end in this book usually means a place where the average room costs at least US$75, you can multiply that by a factor of five at some of the world-class resorts. Great deals for these places can be found from many sources: hotel websites, internet booking services or as part of holiday packages. It pays to shop around.

Long-Term Accommodation

Like frangipani blossoms after a stiff breeze, villas litter the ground of South Bali. Often they land in the midst of rice paddies seemingly overnight. The villa boom has been quite controversial for environmental, aesthetic and economic reasons (see p61). Many skip collecting government taxes from guests which has raised the ire of their luxury hotel competitors.

Most villas are available for longer stays. At the minimum they have a kitchen, living room and private garden, and often two or more bedrooms, so they are suitable for a family or a group of friends.

But many villas go far beyond the norm. Some are literally straight out of the pages of *Architectural Digest* and other design magazines and come with pools, views, beaches and more. Often the houses are staffed and you have the services of a cook, driver etc. Some villas are part of developments – common in Seminyak – and may be linked to a hotel, which gives you access to additional services. Others are free-standing homes in rural areas such as the coast around Canggu.

Rates typically can range anywhere from US$500 for a modest villa to US$4000 per week and beyond for your own tropical estate. There are often deals, especially in the low-season. And for longer stays, you can find deals easily for US$700 a month. Look in the *Bali Advertiser* (www.baliadvertiser.biz) and on bulletin boards popular with expats such as the ones at Café Moka in Seminyak (p120) and Bali Buddha in Ubud (p195).

You can save quite a bit by waiting until the last minute, but during the high season the best villas can book up months in advance. The following agencies are among the many in Bali.

Bali Villas (☎ 0361-703060; www.balivillas.com)
Elite Havens (☎ 0361-731074; www.elitehavens.com)
Exotiq Real Estate (☎ 0361-737358; www.exotiqrealestate.com)
House of Bali (☎ 0361-739541; www.houseofbali.com)

Village Accommodation

In remote villages, you can often find a place to stay by asking the *kepala desa* (village chief or headman) and it will usually be a case of sleeping in a pavilion in a family compound. The price is negotiable, maybe about 25,000Rp per person per night. Your hosts may not even ask for payment, and in these cases you should definitely offer some gifts, like bottled water, sweets or fruit. If they give you a meal, it is even more important to make an offer of payment or gifts. It's a very good idea to take a Balinese friend or guide to help facilitate introductions, and to ensure that you make as few cultural faux pas as possible.

A good way to arrange a village stay is through the JED Village Ecotourism Network, see p348 for details.

BUSINESS HOURS

Government office hours in Bali and Lombok are roughly from 8am to 3pm Monday to Thursday and from 8am to noon on Friday, but they are not completely standardised. Postal agencies will often keep longer hours, and the main post offices are often open every day (from about 8am to 2pm Monday to Thursday and 8am to noon Friday; in the larger tourist centres, the main post offices are often open on weekends). Banking hours are generally from 8am to 2pm Monday to Thursday, from 8am to noon Friday and from 8am to about 11am Saturday. The banks enjoy many public holidays.

In this book it is assumed that restaurants and cafés are usually open about 8am to 10pm daily. Shops and services catering to tourists are open from 9am to about 8pm. Where the hours vary from these, they are noted in the text.

CHILDREN

Travelling with *anak-anak* (children) anywhere requires energy and organisation (see Lonely Planet's *Travel with Children* by Cathy Lanigan), but in Bali the problems are lessened by the Balinese affection for children. They believe that children come straight from God, and the younger they are, the closer they are to God. To the Balinese, children are considered part of the community and everyone, not just the parents, has a responsibility towards them. If a child cries, the Balinese get most upset and insist on finding a parent and handing the child over with a reproachful look. Sometimes they despair of uncaring Western parents, and the child will be whisked off to a place where it can be cuddled, cosseted and fed. In tourist areas this is less likely, but it's still common in traditional environments. A toddler may even get too much attention!

Children are a social asset when you travel in Bali, and people will display great interest in any Western child they meet. You will have to learn your child's age and sex in Bahasa Indonesia – *bulau* (month), *tahun* (year), *laki-laki* (boy) and *perempuan* (girl). You should also make polite inquiries about the other person's children, present or absent.

Lombok is generally quieter than Bali and the traffic is much less dangerous. People are fond of kids, but less demonstrative about it than the Balinese. The main difference is that services for children are much less developed.

Practicalities

ACCOMMODATION

A hotel with a swimming pool, air-con and a beachfront location is fun for kids and very convenient, and provides a good break for the parents. Sanur, Nusa Dua and Lovina are all good places for kids as the surf is placid and the streets quieter than the Kuta area.

Most places, at whatever price level, have a 'family plan', which means that children up to about 12 years old can share a room with their parents free of charge. The catch is that hotels may charge for extra beds, although some offer family rooms. If you need more space, just rent a separate room for the kids.

As noted in the text, many top-end hotels offer special programmes or supervised activities for kids, and where this isn't the case, most hotels can arrange a baby-sitter.

Hotel and restaurant staff are usually very willing to help and improvise, so always ask if you need something for your children.

FOOD

The same rules apply as for adults – kids should drink only clean water and eat only well-cooked food or fruit that you have peeled yourself. If you're travelling with a young baby, breast-feeding is much easier than bottles. For older babies, mashed bananas, eggs, peelable fruit and *bubur* (rice cooked to a mush in chicken stock) are all generally available. In tourist areas, supermarkets do sell jars of Western baby food and packaged UHT milk and fruit juice. Bottled drinking water is available everywhere. Bring plastic bowls, plates, cups and spoons for do-it-yourself meals.

SAFETY PRECAUTIONS

The main danger is traffic, so try to stay in less busy areas. If your children can't look after themselves in the water then they must be supervised – don't expect local people to act as life-savers.

On Bali, the sorts of facilities, safeguards and services that Western parents regard as basic may not be present. Not many restaurants provide a highchair; many places with great views have nothing to stop your kids falling over the edge and shops often have breakable things at kiddie height.

WHAT TO BRING

Apart from those items mentioned in the Health chapter (p364), bring some infant analgesic, antilice shampoo, a medicine measure and a thermometer.

You can take disposable nappies (diapers) with you, but they're widely available in Bali and to a lesser degree on Lombok.

For small children, bring a folding stroller or pusher, or you will be condemned to having them on your knee constantly, at meals and everywhere else. However, it won't be much use for strolling, as there are few paved footpaths that are wide and smooth enough. A papoose or a backpack carrier is a much easier way to move around with children.

Some equipment, such as snorkelling gear and boogie boards, can be rented easily in the tourist centres. A simple camera, or a couple of the throwaway ones, will help your child feel like a real tourist.

Sights & Activities

Many of the things that adults want to do on Bali will not interest their children. Have days when you do what they want, to offset the times you drag them to shops or temples. Encourage them to learn about the islands so they can understand and enjoy more of what they see.

Water play is always fun – you can often use hotel pools, even if you're not staying there. Waterbom Park in Tuban (p102) is a big hit with most kids. If your kids can swim, they can have a lot of fun with a mask and snorkel. Colourful kites are sold in shops and market stalls; get some string at a supermarket.

Other activities popular with kids include visiting Taman Burung Bali Bird Park and Rimba Reptil Park near Ubud (p205) and river rafting (p77). The water sports places in Tajung Benoa (p137) are very popular with the kids.

CLIMATE CHARTS

Just 8° south of the equator, the island of Bali has a tropical climate – the average temperature hovers around 30°C (86°F) all year round. Direct sun feels incredibly hot, especially in the middle of the day. In the wet season, from October to March, the humidity can be very high and quite oppressive. The almost daily tropical downpours come as a relief, but passes quickly, leaving flooded streets and renewed humidity. The dry season (April to September) is generally sunnier, less humid and, from a weather point of view, the best time to visit, though downpours can occur at any time.

There are marked variations across the island. The coast is hotter, but sea breezes can temper the heat. As you move inland you also move up, so the altitude works to keep things cool – at times it can get chilly up in the highlands, and a warm sweater or light jacket can be a good idea in mountain villages such as Kintamani and Candikuning. The northern slopes of Gunung Batur always seem to be wet and misty, while a few kilometres away, the east coast is nearly always dry and sunny.

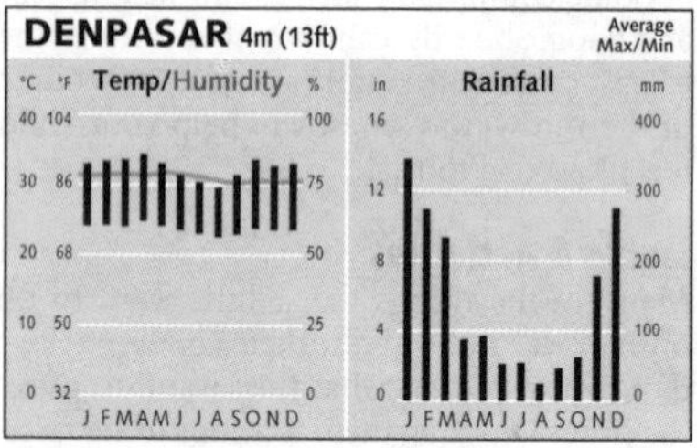

COURSES

More and more people are finding it rewarding to take one of the many courses available in Bali. The rich local culture and activities make for plenty of opportunities to learn something new. Whether it's exploring a food market, learning basic language skills, delving into the profusion of arts or honing your aquatic skills, you'll find plenty of options to expand your horizons.

Arts & Crafts

The Ubud area is the best place for art courses, see p185. A wide range of courses is available, including batik, jewellery making and painting.

Cooking

See p85 for information on learning how to exploit the fresh flavours of Balinese food for oral pleasure.

Language

Denpasar (p170) and Ubud (p186) have schools for learning Bahasa Indonesia.

Meditation & Spiritual Interests

For the Balinese, everything on the island is imbued with spiritual significance, and this ambience is an attraction for travellers looking for an alternative holiday experience. Ubud (p186) is a good place to go for spiritual enlightenment.

Music & Dance

Denpasar (p165), Sanur (see p139) and Ubud (p174) have schools where you can explore the rich traditions of Balinese music and dance.

Surfing & Diving

See the Bali & Lombok Outdoors chapter for more information on surf (p78) and dive schools (p75).

CUSTOMS

Indonesia has the usual list of prohibited imports, including drugs, weapons, fresh fruit and anything remotely pornographic.

Each adult can bring in 200 cigarettes (or 50 cigars or 100g of tobacco), a 'reasonable amount' of perfume and 1L of alcohol.

Officially, cameras, laptops and tape recorders must be declared to customs on entry, and you must take them with you when you leave. In practice, customs officials rarely worry about the usual gear tourists bring into Bali. Surfers with more than two or three boards may be charged a 'fee', and this could apply to other items if the officials suspect that you aim to sell them in Indonesia. If you have nothing to declare, customs clearance is quick and painless.

There is no restriction on foreign currency, but the import or export of rupiah is limited to five million rupiah. Amounts greater than that must be declared.

Indonesia is a signatory to the Convention on International Trade in Endangered Species (CITES), and as such bans the import and export of products made from endangered species. In particular, it is forbidden to export any product made from green sea turtles or turtle shells. In the interests of conservation,

TRAVEL ADVISORIES

Government departments charged with foreign affairs maintain websites with travel information and warnings for specific countries and regions. It's a good idea for travellers to check the following websites before a trip in order to confirm local conditions. But note that the advisories often are general to the point of meaninglessness and are guaranteed to allow for bureaucratic cover should trouble occur. Once in Bali, travellers may be able to get updated information through the local consulate (p335) or from embassies in Jakarta (p335).

- Australia Department of Foreign Affairs & Trade (www.dfat.gov.au)
- Canada Foreign Affairs (www.voyage.gc.ca)
- New Zealand Ministry of Foreign Affairs & Trade (www.mfat.govt.nz/travel)
- UK Foreign & Commonwealth Office (www.fco.gov.uk)
- US Department of State (www.travel.state.gov)

as well as conformity to customs laws, please don't buy turtle shell products. There may also be some ivory artefacts for sale in Bali, and the import and export of these is also banned in most countries.

DANGERS & ANNOYANCES

It's important to note that compared with many places in the world, Bali is fairly safe. There are some hassles from the avaricious, but most visitors face many more dangers at home. Petty theft occurs but it is not prevalent.

Security concerns have increased since the 2002 and 2005 bombings but these tend to fade after a while. The odds you will be caught up in such a tragedy are low. Note that large luxury hotels which are part of international chains tend to have the best security.

As for all destinations, you might want to check your government's travel advisories before you depart, and listen to local advice when you arrive. For more, see above.

In addition to the warnings following, see p94 for warnings specific to the Kuta region.

Outside the Mataram/Senggigi area on Lombok, emergency services may be nonexistent, or a long time coming. Don't expect an ambulance to collect injured surfers from the southwest coast. The Gili Islands don't have a formal police force.

For information on Bali's notorious dogs, see p68. See p364 for details on international clinics and medical care in Bali.

Begging

You may be approached by the occasional beggar in Kuta, Legian or Ubud – typically a woman with one or more young child. Pause and they might literally latch on.

Drugs

Numerous high-profile drug cases in Bali and on Lombok should be enough to dissuade anyone from having anything to do with illicit drugs. As little as two ecstasy tabs or a bit of pot has resulted in huge fines and multiyear jail sentences in Bali's notorious jail in Kerobokan. Try dealing and you may pay with your life.

You can expect to be offered pot, ecstasy, crystal meth (yabba), magic mushrooms and other drugs in nightclubs, beaches and while walking along tourist-area streets. Assume that such offers come from people who may be in cahoots with the police. That some foreigners have been able to buy their way out of jail by paying enormous fines (US$50,000 and up) should indicate that nabbing tourists for drugs is a cottage industry.

It's also worth noting that clubbers have been hit with random urine tests.

Hawkers, Pedlars & Touts

Many visitors regard the persistent attentions of people trying to sell as *the* number one annoyance in Bali (and in tourist areas of Lombok). These activities are officially restricted in many areas but hawkers will still work just outside the fence. Elsewhere, especially around many tourist attractions, visitors are frequently, and often constantly, hassled to buy things.

The best way to deal with hawkers is to completely ignore them from the first instance. Eye contact is crucial – don't make any! Even a polite '*tidak*' (no) seems to encourage them.

Never ask the price or comment on the quality unless you're interested in buying, or you want to spend half an hour haggling. It may seem very rude to ignore people who smile and greet you so cheerfully, but you might have to be a lot ruder to get rid of a hawker after you've spent a few minutes politely discussing his/her watches, rings and prices. Keep in mind though, that ultimately they're just people trying to make an honest living and if you don't want to buy anything then you are wasting their time trying to be polite.

Many touts employ fake, irritating Australian accents, eg 'Oi! Mate!'

Scams

Bali has such a relaxed atmosphere, and the people are so friendly, that you may not be on the lookout for scams. It's hard to say when an 'accepted' practice such as over-charging becomes an unacceptable rip-off, but be warned that there are some people in Bali (not always Balinese) who will engage in a practised deceit in order to get money from a visitor.

Most Balinese would never perpetrate a rip-off, but it seems that very few would warn a foreigner when one is happening. Be suspicious if you notice that bystanders are uncommunicative and perhaps uneasy, and one guy is doing all the talking.

Here is a rundown of the most common scams.

CAR CON

Friendly locals (often working in pairs) discover a 'serious problem' with your car or motorcycle – it's blowing smoke, leaking oil or petrol, or a wheel is wobbling badly (problems that one of the pair creates while the other distracts you). Coincidentally, he has a brother/cousin/friend nearby who can help, and before you know it they are demanding an outrageous sum for their trouble. Beware of anyone who tries to rush you into something without mentioning a price.

EASY MONEY

Friendly locals will convince a visitor that easy money can be made in a card game. Anyone falling for this one is a prime candidate for what happens to fools and their money.

HIGH RATES – NO COMMISSION

In the South Bali area especially, many travellers are ripped off by moneychangers, who use sleight of hand and rigged calculators. The moneychangers who offer the highest rates are usually the ones to look out for. Always count your money at least twice in front of the moneychanger, and don't let him touch the money again after you've finally counted it. The best defence is to use a bank-affiliated currency exchange or stick to ATMs.

Swimming

Kuta Beach and those to the north and south are subject to heavy surf and strong currents – always swim between the flags. Trained lifeguards do operate, but only at Kuta, Legian, Seminyak, Nusa Dua, Sanur and (sometimes) Senggigi. Most other beaches are protected by coral reefs, so they don't have big waves, but the currents can still be treacherous, especially along the coast running north and west from Seminyak. Currents can also cause problems off the Gilis.

Water pollution can also be a problem, especially after rains. Try to swim well away from any open streams you see flowing into the surf.

Be careful when swimming over coral, and never walk on it at all. It can be very sharp and coral cuts are easily infected. In addition, you are damaging a fragile environment.

Theft

Violent crime is relatively uncommon, but there is some bag-snatching, pickpocketing and theft from rooms and parked cars in the tourist centres. Don't leave anything exposed in a rental vehicle. Always carry money belts inside your clothes; and bags over your neck (not shoulder). Be sure to secure all your money *before* you leave the ATM, bank or moneychanger.

Beware of pickpockets in crowded places and bemo (small minibuses).

Hotel and guesthouse rooms are often not secure. Don't leave valuables in your room. Thieves will often enter through open-air bathrooms, so be sure to fasten the bathroom door. Most hotels offer some form of secure storage, such as in-room safes or central safety deposit boxes for guests – use it.

Many people lose things simply by leaving them on the beach while they go swimming.

On Lombok, theft and robbery are more common. Certainly there are hassles in Kuta, east of Kuta and west of Kuta around Mawi (see p322).

Traffic

Apart from the dangers of driving in Bali (see p359), the traffic in most tourist areas is often annoying, and frequently dangerous to pedestrians. Footpaths can be rough, even unusable, so you often have to walk on the road. Never expect traffic to stop because you think you're on a pedestrian crossing.

The traffic is much lighter on Lombok than in Bali, but there is still a danger of traffic accidents.

DISABLED TRAVELLERS

Bali is a difficult destination for those with limited mobility. While some of the airlines flying to Bali have a good reputation for accommodating people with disabilities, the airport is not well set up. Contact the airlines and ask them what arrangements can be made for disembarking and boarding at the airport.

Bemo, minibuses and buses that provide public transport are not accessible. The minibuses used by tourist shuttle bus and tour companies are similar. Upmarket hotels often have steps and lack ramps for wheelchairs, while the cheaper places usually have more accessible bungalows on ground level. Out on the street, the footpaths, where they exist at all, tend to be narrow, uneven, potholed and frequently obstructed.

The only hotels likely to be set up at all for disabled travellers are the big international chains in South Bali and Ubud. If you're keen to see Bali, your best bet is to contact these hotels and ask them what facilities they have for guests with disabilities. Sometimes this information can be found on their websites.

Bali is an enormously rewarding destination for people who are blind or vision impaired. Balinese music is heard everywhere, and the languages are fascinating to listen to. The smells of incense, spices, tropical fruit and flowers pervade the island, and are as exotic as you could wish for. With a sighted companion, most places should be reasonably accessible.

EMBASSIES & CONSULATES

Indonesian Embassies & Consulates

Indonesian embassies and consulates abroad include the following. For additional information see Indonesia's department of foreign affairs website (www.deplu.go.id).

Australia (☎ 02-6250 8600; www.kbri-canberra.org.au; 8 Darwin Ave, Yarralumla, ACT 2600)

Canada (☎ 613-724 1100; 55 Parkdale Ave, Ottawa, Ontario K1Y 1E5) Consulates: Toronto (☎ 416-360-4020; 129 Jarvis St); Vancouver (☎ 604-682-8855; 1630 Alberni St)

France (☎ 01-45 03 07 60; 47-49 Rue Cortambert, 75116 Paris); Consulate: Marseilles (☎ 04-9123-0160; 25 Blvd, Carmagnole)

Germany (☎ 030-478-070; Lehrter Str 16-17, 10557 Berlin) Consulates: Frankfurt (☎ 69-247-0908; Zeppelin Alle 23); Hamburg (☎ 40-512-071; Bebelalle 14)

Ireland (Honorary Consul; ☎ 353 852 491; 25 Kilvere Rathfarnham, Dublin)

Japan (☎ 03-3441 4201; 5-2-9 Higashi Gotanda, Shinagawa-ku, Tokyo) Consulates: Fukoka (☎ 092-761-3031; Kyuden Bldg 1-82, Watanabe–Dori–Chome, Chou-Ku, Fukuoka-Shi); Osaka (☎ 83-06-6252-9823; Daiwa Bank Semba Bldg 6th fl, 4-21 Minami Semba 4-Chome, Chuo-Ku); Sapporo (☎ 011-251-6002; 883-3 Chome 4-Jo, Miyayanomori, Chuo-Ku, Sapporo Shís)

Malaysia (☎ 03-2145-2011; 233 Jl Tun Razak, Kuala Lumpur) Consulates: Kota Kinabalu (☎ 60-088-218-600; Lorong Kemajuan, Karamunsing); Kuching (☎ 241734; 111 Jl Tun Abang Hj, Openg); Penang (☎ 04-2267-412; 467, Jl Burma)

Netherlands (☎ 070-310 8100; 8 Tobias Asserlaan, 2517 KC, The Hague)

New Zealand (☎ 04-4758 697; 70 Glen Rd, Kelburn, Wellington) Consular office: Auckland (☎ 09 300-9000; 2nd fl, 132 Vincent St)

Papua New Guinea (☎ 675-325 3116; 1+2/410, Kiroki St, Sir John Guise Dr, Waigani, Port Moresby) Consulate: Vanimo (☎ 675-857-1371; Sandaun Province)

Philippines (☎ 02-892-5061; 185 Salcedo St, Legaspi Village, Makati, Manila) Consulate: Davao (☎ 63-83-299-2930; Ecoland Subdivision, Davao City)

Singapore (☎ 737 7422; 7 Chatsworth Rd, Singapore)

Thailand (☎ 02-252 3135; 600-602 Petchburi Rd, Phyathai, Bangkok)

Timor Leste (☎ 670-312-333; Komplek Pertamina, Pantai Kelapa, Correios)

UK (☎ 020-7499 7661; 38 Grosvenor Square, London W1K 2HW)

USA (☎ 202-775-5200; 2020 Massachusetts Ave NW, Washington DC 20036) Consulates: Chicago (☎ 312-345-9300; 72 East Randolph St); Houston (☎ 713-785-1691; 10900 Richmond Ave); Los Angeles (☎ 213-383-5126; 3457 Wilshire Blvd); New York (☎ 212-879-0600; 5 East 68th St); San Francisco (☎ 415-474-9571; 1111 Columbus Ave)

Embassies & Consulates in Indonesia

Foreign embassies are in Jakarta, the national capital. Most of the foreign representatives in Bali are consular agents (or honorary consuls) who can't offer the same services as a full consulate or embassy. For some, this means a trek to Jakarta in the event of a lost passport.

BALI

The US, Australia and Japan (visitors from these countries together make up nearly half of all visitors) have formal consulates in Bali. Unless noted, the following offices are open from about 8.30am to noon, Monday to Friday. All telephone area codes are ☎ 0361.

Australia (Map pp166-7; ☎ 241118; www.dfat.gov.au/bali; Jl Hayam Wuruk 88B, Renon, Denpasar; 8am-noon, 12.30-4pm) The Australian consulate has a consular sharing agreement with Canada, and may also be able to help citizens of New Zealand, Ireland and Papua New Guinea.
France (Map p140; ☎ 285485; Jl Mertasari, Gang II 8, Sanur)
Germany (Map p140; ☎ 288535; Jl Pantai Karang 17, Batujimbar, Sanur)
Japan (Map pp166-7; ☎ 227628; konipdps@indo.net.id; Jl Raya Puputan 170, Renon, Denpasar)
Netherlands (Map pp96-7; ☎ 752777; Jl Raya Kuta 127/Imam Bonjol, Kuta)
Switzerland (Map pp96-7; ☎ 751735; Kuta Galleria, Blok Valet 2, 12, Kuta)
UK (Map p140; ☎ 270601; Jl Tirtanadi 20, Sanur)
USA (Map pp166-7; ☎ 233605; amcobali@indosat.net.id; Jl Hayam Wuruk 188, Renon, Denpasar; 8am-4.30pm)

JAKARTA

Most nations have an embassy in Jakarta (telephone area code ☎ 021), including the following:

Australia (☎ 2550 5555; www.indonesia.embassy.gov.au; Jl Rasuna Said Kav 15-16)
Brunei (☎ 3190 6080; Jl Tanjung Karang 7)
Canada (☎ 2550 7800; www.international.gc.ca/asia/jakarta; World Trade Centre, 6th fl, Jl Jend Sudirman Kav 29-31)
France (☎ 2355 7600; Jl MH Thamrin 20)
Germany (☎ 3985 5000; Jl MH Thamrin 1)
Japan (☎ 3192 4308; Jl MH Thamrin 24)
Netherlands (☎ 524 8200; Jl HR Rasuna Said Kav S-3)
New Zealand (☎ 570 9460; BRI II Bldg, 23rd fl, Jl Jend Sudirman Kav 44-46)
Papua New Guinea (☎ 7251218; 6th fl, Panin Bank Centre, Jl Jend Sudirman 1)
Philippines (☎ 310 0334; phjkt@indo.net.id; Jl Imam Bonjol 6-8)
Singapore (☎ 520 1489; Jl Rasuna Said, Block X/4 Kav 2)
Thailand (☎ 390 4052; Jl Imam Bonjol 74)
UK (☎ 315 6264; www.britain-in-indonesia.or.id; Jl. M.H. Thamrin 75)
USA (☎ 3435 9000; www.usembassyjakarta.org; Jl Medan Merdeka Selatan 4-5)

FESTIVALS & EVENTS

Try to obtain a *Calendar of Events* booklet – there are several versions published by the government. It lists every temple ceremony and village festival in Bali for the current (Western) year. You can also inquire at tourist offices or at your hotel.

Balinese Calendars, Holidays & Festivals

Apart from the usual Western calendar, the Balinese also use two local calendars, the *saka* calendar and the *wuku* calendar.

SAKA CALENDAR

The Hindu *saka* (or *caka*) calendar is a lunar cycle that is similar to the Western calendar in terms of the length of the year. Nyepi (see the boxed text, p338) is the major festival of the *saka* year – it's the last day of the year, ie the day after the new moon of the ninth month. Certain major temples celebrate their festivals by the *saka* calendar.

WUKU CALENDAR

The *wuku* calendar is used to determine festival dates. The calendar uses 10 different types of weeks between one and 10 days long, which all run simultaneously. The intersection of the various weeks determines auspicious days. The seven- and five-day weeks are of particular importance. A full year is made up of 30 individually named seven-day weeks (210 days).

Galungan, which celebrates the death of a legendary tyrant called Mayadenawa, is one of Bali's major festivals. During this 10-day period, held every 210 days, all the gods come down to earth for the festivities. Barong (mythical lion-dog creatures) prance from temple to temple and village to village, and locals rejoice with feasts and visits to families. The celebrations culminate with the Kuningan festival, when the Balinese say thanks and goodbye to the gods.

Every village in Bali will celebrate Galungan and Kuningan in grand style. Forthcoming dates are the following:

Year	Galungan	Kuningan
2007	27 Jun	7 Jul
2008	23 Jan	2 Feb
	20 Aug	30 Aug
2009	18 Mar	28 Mar

A GOOD DAY FOR...

Almost every Balinese home and business has a copy of the *Kalendar Cetakan* hanging on the wall. This annual publication tracks the various local religious calendars and overlays them upon your usual 365-day Western calendar. Details are extensive and most importantly, the calendar provides vital details on which days are most fortuitous for a myriad of activities such as bull castration, building a boat, laying a foundation, drilling a well, starting a long trip and having sex. Many Balinese would not think of scheduling any activity without checking the calendar first and this can lead to many inconveniences since many activities are only condoned for a few days a year (except sex which is called for at least 10 days a month – a real marketing tool!).

Bali Events

Besides the myriad of religious festivals, Bali has many organised events which have proven popular with locals and visitors alike. Be sure to confirm that the event will happen.

Bali Art Festival of Buleleng May or June, Singaraja (p259).
Bali Arts Festival Mid-June to mid-July, Denpasar (p170).
Kuta Karnival Late September and early October, Kuta (p104).
Ubud Writers & Readers Festival October, Ubud (p186).

Lombok Events

Many festivals take place at the start of the rainy season (around October to December) or at harvest time (around April to May). Most of them do not fall on specific days in the Western calendar, including Ramadan, so planning for them is not really possible.

Ramadan, the month of fasting, is the ninth month of the Muslim calendar. During this period, many restaurants are closed, and foreigners eating, drinking (especially alcohol) and smoking in public may attract a very negative reaction.

Other occasions observed on Lombok include the following:

Desa Bersih First Thursday in April – a harvest festival held in honour of Dewi Sri, the rice goddess in the region of Gunung Pengsong.
Nyale Fishing Festival Nineteenth day of the 10th month of the Sasak calendar (generally February/March) – commemorates the legend of a beautiful princess who went out to sea and drowned herself rather than choose between her many admirers – her long hair was transformed into the wormlike fish the Sasak call *nyale*.
Perang Topat November or December – a harvest festival featuring a mock battle with sticky rice held near Mataram (see p291).

Temple Festivals

Temple festivals in Bali are quite amazing, and you'll often come across them quite unexpectedly, even in the most remote corners of the island. The annual 'temple birthday' is known as an *odalan* and is celebrated once every Balinese year of 210 days. Since most villages have at least three temples, you're assured of at least five or six annual festivals in every village. In addition, there can be special festival days common throughout Bali; festivals for certain important temples and festivals for certain gods. The full moons which fall around the end of September to the beginning of October, or from early to mid-April, are often times for important temple festivals in Bali.

The most obvious sign of a temple festival is a long line of women in traditional costume, walking gracefully to the temple with beautifully arranged offerings of food, fruit and flowers piled in huge pyramids which they carry on their heads.

Meanwhile, the various *pemangku* (temple guardians and priests for temple rituals) suggest to the gods that they should come down for a visit. That's what those little thrones are for in the temple shrines – they are symbolic seats for the gods to occupy during festivals. Women dance the stately Pendet, an offering dance for the gods.

All night long on the island there's activity, music and dancing – it's like a great country fair, with food, amusements, games, stalls, gambling, noise, colour and confusion. Finally, as dawn approaches, the entertainment fades away, the *pemangku* suggest to the gods that it's time they made their way back to heaven and the people wind their weary way back home.

When you first arrive, it's well worth asking at a tourist office or your hotel what festivals will be held during your stay. Seeing one will be a highlight of your trip. Foreigners are welcome to watch the festivities and take photographs, but be unobtrusive and dress modestly.

NYEPI – THE DAY OF SILENCE

The major festival for the Hindu Balinese is Nyepi, usually falling around the end of March or early April. It celebrates the end of the old year and the start of the new one, according to the *saka* calendar, and usually coincides with the end of the rainy season.

Out with the Old Year...

In the weeks before Nyepi, much work goes into the making of *ogoh-ogoh* – huge monster dolls with menacing fingers and frightening faces – and into the preparation of offerings and rituals that will purify the island in readiness for the new year. The day before Nyepi, Tawur Agung Kesanga, is the 'Day of Great Sacrifices', with ceremonies held at town squares and sports grounds throughout the island. At about 4pm, the villagers, all dressed up in traditional garb, gather in the centre of town, playing music and offering gifts of food and flowers to the *ogoh-ogoh*. Then comes the *ngrupuk* – the great procession where the *ogoh-ogoh* figures are lifted on bamboo poles and carried through the streets, to frighten away all the evil spirits. This is followed by prayers and speeches and then, with flaming torches and bonfires, the *ogoh-ogoh* are burnt, and much revelry ensues. The biggest *ngrupuk* procession is in Denpasar (p170), but any large town will have a pretty impressive parade.

...And in with the New

The day of Nyepi itself officially lasts for 24 hours from sunrise, and is one of complete inactivity, so when the evil spirits descend they decide that Bali is uninhabited and leave the island alone for another year. All human activity stops – all shops, bars and restaurants close, no-one is allowed to leave their home and foreigners must stay in their hotels, and even Bali's international airport is closed down. No fires are permitted and at night all buildings must be blacked out – only emergency services are exempt.

Government offices, banks and many shops close the day before Nyepi, and some shops remain closed the day after. For visitors, Nyepi is a day for catching up on sleep, writing letters and remaining on their hotel's grounds or at some family-run places in their rooms. Most places will arrange for meals to be served to guests but should you wander off, the *pecalang* (village police) will politely but firmly send you home.

Future Dates of Nyepi

2007	19 Mar
2008	6 Apr
2009	26 Mar

FOOD

You can eat well with locals for under US$1 or in touristy places for under US$5. A fabulous meal prepared by a renowned chef will cost somewhat more but the constant is that at any price range the food is generally very fresh, often quite good and usually much cheaper than you would pay at home. See p85 for details.

In this book, restaurants are listed in order of cheapest to most expensive price for a meal.

GAY & LESBIAN TRAVELLERS

Gay travellers in Bali will experience few problems, and many of the island's most influential expatriate artists have been more-or-less openly gay. Physical contact between same-sex couples is acceptable and friends of the same sex often hold hands, though this does not indicate homosexuality.

There are many venues where gay men congregate, mostly in Kuta and Seminyak. There's nowhere that's exclusively gay, and nowhere that's even inconspicuously a lesbian scene. Hotels are happy to rent a room with a double bed to any couple. Homosexual behaviour is not illegal, and the age of consent for sexual activity is 16 years. Gay men in Indonesia are referred to as *homo*, or *gay*, and are quite distinct from the female impersonators called *waria*.

Many gays from other parts of the country come to live in Bali, as it is more tolerant, and also because it offers opportunities to meet foreign partners.

Gay prostitutes are mostly from Java, and some have been known to rip off their foreign clients. Gay Balinese men are usually just looking for nothing more than some adventures, though there is an expectation that the (relatively) wealthy foreign guy will pay for meals, drinks, hotels etc.

On Lombok, gay and lesbian travellers should definitely refrain from public displays of affection – advice that applies to straight couples as well. There are gay-friendly places in Senggigi (p293).

Organisations

Gaya Dewata (☎ 0361-234079; Denpasar) Bali's gay organisation.

Hanafi (see p101) Kuta-based gay-friendly tour operator and guide; good for the lowdown on the local scene.

Utopia Asia (www.utopia-asia.com) Not specific to Bali, but has excellent information about the Bali gay scene.

HOLIDAYS

The following holidays are celebrated throughout Indonesia. Many of these dates change according to the phase of the moon (not by month), and are estimates.

Tahun Baru Masehi (New Year's Day) 1 January

Idul Adha (Muslim festival of sacrifice) February

Muharram (Islamic New Year) February/March

Nyepi (Hindu New Year) March/April

Hari Paskah (Good Friday) April

Ascension of Christ April/May

Hari Waisak (Buddha's birth, enlightenment and death) April/May

Maulud Nabi Mohammed/Hari Natal (Prophet Mohammed's birthday) May

Hari Proklamasi Kemerdekaan (Indonesian Independence Day) 17 August

Isra Miraj Nabi Mohammed (Ascension of the Prophet Mohammed) September

Idul Fitri (End of Ramadan) November/December

Hari Natal (Christmas Day) 25 December

See Festivals & Events (p336) for additional holidays. The Muslim population in Bali observes Islamic festivals and holidays, including Ramadan. Religious and other holidays on Lombok are as follows.

Anniversary of West Lombok April 17 – government holiday

Ramadan Usually October

Founding of West Nusa Tenggara December 17 – public holiday

INSURANCE

Unless you are definitely sure that your health coverage at home will cover you in Bali and Lombok, you should take out travel insurance – bring a copy of the policy as evidence that you're covered. Get a policy that pays for medical evacuation if necessary.

Some policies specifically exclude 'dangerous activities', which can entail scuba diving, renting a local motorcycle and even trekking. Be aware that a locally acquired motorcycle licence isn't valid under some policies.

INTERNET ACCESS

Internet centres are common anywhere there are tourists in Bali. Expect to pay 200Rp to 500Rp per minute for access. Excellent places can be found in South Bali and Ubud (p175). At these centres you can download your digital camera or burn CDs. You can also network your laptop. Elsewhere, speed varies but is often slow.

Many hotels have internet centres for their guests. In-room broadband access, however, is limited to the newest of the international hotels, as noted in the individual reviews. In South Bali wi-fi access in cafés is increasingly common and is often free.

Internet access on Lombok tends to cost 400Rp to 500Rp per minute. However, outside of Mataram and Senggigi, wherever you go in Lombok, internet access is painfully slow.

LEGAL MATTERS

Gambling is illegal (although it's common, especially at cockfights), as is pornography. The government takes the smuggling, using and selling of drugs very, *very* seriously. Once you've been caught, and put in jail, there is very little that your consulate in Bali (if there's one) can do for you. You may have to wait for up to six months in jail before you even go to trial. See p333 for additional dire details.

Generally, you are unlikely to have any encounters with the police unless you are driving a rented car or motorcycle (see p350).

Some governments (including the Australian government) have laws making it illegal for their citizens to use child prostitutes or engage in other paedophiliac activities anywhere in the world. Foreigners have been prosecuted and penalties are severe.

There are police stations in all district capitals. If you have to report a crime or have other business at a police station, expect a lengthy and bureaucratic encounter. You should dress as respectably as possible, bring a fluent Indonesian-speaking friend for interpretation and moral support, arrive early and be very polite. You can also call the **Bali Tourist Police** (☎ 0361-224111) for advice. Call ☎ 112 in an emergency in Bali.

Police officers frequently expect to receive bribes, either to overlook some crime, misdemeanour or traffic infringement, or to provide a service that they should provide anyway. Generally, it's easiest to pay up – and the sooner you do it, the less it will cost. You may be told there's a 'fine' to pay on the spot or you can offer to a pay a 'fine' to clear things up. How much? Generally, 50,000Rp can work wonders and the officers are not proud. If things seem unreasonable however, ask for the officer's name and write it down.

If you're in trouble, contact your consulate as soon as you can – they can't get you out, but they can recommend English-speaking lawyers and may have useful contacts.

MAPS

For tourist resorts and towns, the maps in this guidebook are as good as you'll get. If you need a more detailed road map of the island, there are some OK sheet maps available in bookshops. The following are examples of good maps that are available. There are many more which are old and/or useless.

- Periplus Travel Maps has a decent *Bali* contour map (1:250,000), with a detailed section on southern Bali, plus maps of the main towns areas. However, the labelling and names used for towns are often incomprehensible. The *Lombok & Sumbawa* map is useful.
- The Periplus *Street Atlas Bali* may be more than you need, but it is more accurate than the sheet map. Again, there are inexplicable omissions.

MONEY

Indonesia's unit of currency is the rupiah (Rp). There are coins worth 50, 100, 500 and 1000Rp. Notes come in denominations of 500Rp (rare), 1000Rp, 5000Rp, 10,000Rp, 20,000Rp, 50,000Rp and 100,000Rp.

Check out the front cover of this book for an idea about current exchange rates of the rupiah. In recent times, the currency has been fairly stable. Many midrange hotels and all top-end hotels, along with some tourist attractions and tour companies, list their prices in US dollars, although you can usually pay in rupiah at a poorer exchange rate.

US dollars are usually the most negotiable currency.

Many travellers now rely mostly on ATMs for cash while in Bali. It is a good idea, however, to carry some backup funds in case your card is lost or the network goes down (usually just for a few hours).

Always carry a good supply of rupiah in small denominations with you. Throughout the island many will people will struggle to make change for a 50,000Rp note or larger.

ATMs

There are ATMs all over Bali. Most accept international ATM cards and major credit cards for cash advances. The exchange rates for ATM withdrawals are usually quite good, but check to see if your home bank will hit you with outrageous fees. Most ATMs in Bali allow a maximum withdrawal of 600,000Rp to 1.2 million rupiah. Try to avoid ones with a sticker saying '100,000Rp' as that's the denomination you'll get and you'll struggle to break those bills.

Major towns on Lombok have ATMs but there are none on the Gilis.

Banks

Major banks have branches in the main tourist centres and provincial capitals. Smaller towns may not have banks at all or have banks that don't exchange currency. Changing money can be time-consuming.

Cash

Changing money in Bali is not difficult in tourist areas. It's easiest to exchange US banknotes, especially US$100 bills. However, make certain that your money is new and recent. Older designs and damaged notes will often be refused.

Rupiah bills of 50,000Rp and larger can be hard to break. Always keep lots of small bills for public transport and other services.

Credit Cards

Visa, MasterCard and American Express (Amex) are accepted by most of the larger businesses that cater to tourists. You sign for the amount in rupiah – or dollars – and the bill is converted into your domestic currency. The conversion is at the interbank rate and is usually quite good, though some banks add various usage and exchange fees which are strictly for their own profit.

You can also get cash advances on major credit cards at many ATMs.

Moneychangers

Exchange rates offered by moneychangers are normally better than the banks, plus they offer quicker service and keep much longer hours. The exchange rates are advertised on boards along footpaths or on windows outside shops. It's worth looking around because rates vary a little, but beware of places advertising exceptionally high rates – they may make their profit by short-changing their customers (see p333). In the Kuta area, you can now find international banks with reliable exchange services (see p99). In hotels, the rates can be up to 20% less than a street moneychanger.

Tipping

Tipping a set percentage is not expected in Bali, but restaurant workers are poorly paid; if the service is good, it's appropriate to leave 4000Rp or more. Most midrange hotels and restaurants and all top-end hotels and restaurants add 21% to the bill for tax and service (known as 'plus plus'). This service component is distributed among hotel staff (one hopes), so you needn't tip under these circumstances.

It's also a nice thing to tip taxi drivers, guides, people giving you a massage, fetching you a beer on the beach etc.

Travellers Cheques

Travellers cheques are getting harder and harder to exchange, especially if they are not in US dollars. The exchange rates offered for travellers cheques are sometimes a little less than for cash, and small denominations usually get a lower rate.

PHOTOGRAPHY & VIDEO

Bali is one of the most photogenic places on earth, so be prepared.

Cameras

You can buy additional memory cards for digital cameras at photo shops in the major tourist centres, but you're really better off bringing what you need from home.

Basic 35mm film is available at reasonable prices – always check the expiry date first. Developing and printing (from film and digital) is available in tourist areas; it's cheap and good quality.

The best internet places (p339) will allow you to download your photos onto their computers for distribution to lucky friends and relatives worldwide or for burning onto a CD for storage or printing at a photo shop. It's also a good idea to bring along whatever cable your camera requires. The process is easiest for people who carry their own laptops.

Photographing People

Photograph with discretion and manners. It's always polite to ask first, and if they say no, then don't. A gesture, smile and nod are all that is usually necessary.

Restrictions

Military installations are not widespread in Bali, but you should be aware that these are sensitive subjects – if in doubt, ask before you shoot. You are usually welcome to take photos of ceremonies in the villages and temples, but try not to be intrusive. Ask before taking photos inside a temple.

There's one place where you must not take photographs at all – public bathing places. Balinese think of these places as private and do not 'see' one another when they're bathing. To intrude with a camera is very rude voyeurism.

Video

Bring any media you need from home in sealed packages – to avoid a customs search for prohibited material.

POST

Sending postcards and normal-sized letters (ie under 20g) by airmail is cheap, but not really fast. A postcard/letter to the USA costs 5000/10,000Rp (allow 13 days); to Australia costs 7500/15,000Rp (15 days); and to the UK costs 8000/18,000Rp (21 days).

For anything over 20g, the charge is based on weight. Sending large parcels is quite expensive, but at least you can get them properly wrapped and sealed at any post office.

Every substantial town has a *kantor pos* (post office). In tourist centres, there are also postal agencies. They are often open long hours and provide postal services. Many will also wrap and pack parcels.

Have poste restante mail sent to you via the post offices at Kuta (p99) and Ubud (p175).

Mail should be addressed to you with your surname underlined and in capital letters, then 'Kantor Pos', the name of the town, and then 'Bali, Indonesia'. You can also have mail sent to your hotel.

Express companies offer reliable, fast and expensive service.

FedEx (Map p128; ☎ 0361-701 727; Jl Bypass Nusa Dua 100X, Jimbaran) Located south of the airport.

UPS (Map p100; ☎ 0361-766 676; Jl Bypass Ngurah Rai 2005) Has a location near the Bali Galleria.

See opposite for how to ship large items.

SHOPPING

For some people Bali is a destination for shopping, for others it becomes their destiny. You will find a plethora of shops and stalls across the island. You can find everything from a cheap T-shirt and silly wooden carvings of penises to exquisite boutiques with alluring ranges of housewares and fashions by local designers.

Look in Kuta, Legian, Seminyak and Ubud for the widest range of goods, including what seems like millions of bead and necklace shops. Generally, Kuta is the place for huge, chain surf shops and Bintang T-shirts. Towards Legian things get more creative and as you go north through Seminyak shops become more exclusive and air-conditioned.

Western-style department stores and shopping centres in Denpasar and the Kuta area sell a large variety of clothing, shoes, leather goods, toys and scores of bead and necklace shops. Prices are mostly very good because of the low value of the rupiah.

The clothing industry has enjoyed spectacular growth from making beachwear for tourists – it now accounts for around half the value of Balinese exports. Furniture is a growth industry, with contemporary furniture and reproduction antiques being popular.

For details of where to buy arts and crafts, see p55.

The best buys on Lombok are handicrafts, such as boxes, basketware, pottery and handwoven textiles.

Ceramics

Nearly all local pottery is made from low-fired terracotta. Most styles are very ornate, even for functional items such as vases, flasks, ashtrays and lamp bases. Pejaten (p276) near Tabanan also has a number of pottery workshops producing small ceramic figures and glazed ornamental roof tiles. For details of where to buy ceramics, see p54.

Clothing

A variety of clothing is made locally, and sold in hundreds of small shops in all tourist centres, especially Kuta, Legian and Seminyak. It's mostly pretty casual, but it's not just beachwear – you can get just about anything you want, including tailor-made clothing, and there are many designer shops in Seminyak. Leatherwear is quite cheap and popular.

Fabrics & Weaving

Gianyar (p209), in eastern Bali, is a major textile centre with a number of factories where you can watch ikat (cloth in which a pattern

THE ART OF BARGAINING

Many everyday purchases in Bali require bargaining. This particularly applies to clothing, arts and crafts. Accommodation has a set price, but this is usually negotiable in the low season, or if you are staying at the hotel for several days.

In an everyday bargaining situation the first step is to establish a starting price – it's usually better to ask the seller for their price rather than make an initial offer. It also helps if you have some idea what the item is worth.

Generally, your first price could be anything from one-third to two-thirds of the asking price – assuming that the asking price is not completely over the top. Then, with offer and counteroffer, you'll move closer to an acceptable price. For example, the seller asks 60,000Rp for the handicraft, you offer 30,000Rp and so on, until eventually you both agree at somewhere around 45,000Rp. If you don't get to an acceptable price you're quite entitled to walk away – the vendor may even call you back with a lower price.

Note that when you name a price, you're committed – you have to buy if your offer is accepted. Remember, bargaining should be an enjoyable part of shopping on Bali, so maintain your sense of humour and keep things in perspective.

SHIPPING LARGE ITEMS

It might just be feasible to carry home a few folding chairs or artworks, but generally, if you buy large or heavy items you'll need to have them shipped home. For items that are shipped, you'll pay a 40% or 50% deposit and the balance (plus any taxes or import duties) when you collect the items at home. If possible, arrange for delivery to your door – if you have to pick the items up from the nearest port or freight depot you may be up for extra port charges.

Most places selling furniture or heavy artworks can arrange packing, shipping and insurance. Shipping costs for volumes less than a full container load vary greatly according to the company, destination and quantity – think in terms of around US$130 plus per cubic metre. Be aware that packing costs, insurance, fumigation and so on are included in some companies' prices but are charged as extras by others.

To get things home quickly and at great expense, see the express freight companies listed under Post, p341.

is produced by dyeing the individual threads before weaving) sarongs being woven on a hand-and-foot-powered loom. Any market will have a good range of textiles.

The village of Tenganan (p225) uses a double ikat process called *gringsing*, in which both the warp and weft are predyed – this is time-consuming and expensive. Belayu (p274), a small village in southwestern Bali is a centre for *songket* (silver- or gold-threaded cloth) weaving. Ubud (p174) is another good place for traditional weaving.

The village of Sukarara (p322) on Lombok is a good place for fabrics.

Furniture

Wood furniture is a big industry, though much of it is actually made in Java and sent to Bali for finishing and sale. Tourists are tempted by contemporary designs and reproduction antiques at much lower prices than they'd find at home. Some of the most attractive pieces are tropical-style interior furnishings. Outdoor furniture made from teak, mahogany and other rainforest timbers is often spectacular and better than you'd get at home for 10 times the price.

Harvesting timber for the local furniture industry and furniture manufacturing involves a high local value-added content and probably has a lesser impact on rainforests than large-scale clearing for export of logs and wood chips, which are much more significant causes of deforestation, and generate a lot less local employment.

The best places to look for furniture are the stores/warehouses along Jl Bypass Ngurah Rai in South Bali and in Kuta (p95). Mas (p174), south of Ubud, is also good. Many of these places will offer to make furniture to order, but if you're a one-off buyer on a short visit it's best to stick to items that are in stock, so you can see what you're getting.

Gamelan

If you are interested in seeing gamelan (Balinese orchestra) instruments being made, visit the village of Blahbatuh (p173) near Ubud.

In northern Bali, Sawan (p261), a small village southeast of Singaraja, is also a centre for the manufacture of gamelan instruments. Jembrana (p277), in western Bali, makes giant gamelan instruments.

Jewellery

Celuk (p205) has always been the village associated with silversmithing. The large shops that line the road into Celuk have imposing, bus-sized driveways and slick facilities. If you want to see the 'real' Celuk, go about 1km east of the road to visit family workshops. Other silverwork centres include Kamasan (p215), near Semarapura in eastern Bali.

Jewellery can be purchased ready-made or made-to-order – there's a wide range of earrings, bracelets and rings available, some using gemstones, which are imported from all over the world. Different design influences can be detected, from African patterning to the New Age preoccupation with dolphins and healing crystals.

Music & Video

Piracy is a major industry in Bali. CDs and DVDs featuring popular artists and entertainment cost as little as 10,000Rp and are widely sold in tourist areas. Quality is often bad (current release features are made with hand-held cameras in theatres!), the format may not work with your system and many of the disks are no good to begin with. You really will get what you pay for.

Legitimate DVDs are uncommon but authentic CDs are often sold in the same places offering fakes. They are good value at around 80,000Rp to 90,000Rp. The cost of CDs featuring Balinese and Indonesian artists is generally lower.

Paintings

There are a relatively small number of creative original painters in Bali today, and an enormous number of imitators who produce copies, or near copies, in well-established styles. Many of these imitative works are nevertheless very well-executed and attractive pieces. Originality is not considered as important in Balinese art as it is in the West. A painting is esteemed not for being new and unique but for taking a well-worn and popular idea and making a good reproduction of it. Some renowned artists will simply draw out the design, decide the colours and then employ apprentices to actually apply the paint. This leads to the mass production of similar works that is so characteristic of Balinese art.

Unfortunately, much of the painting today is churned out for the tourist market and much of that market is extremely undiscriminating about what it buys. Thus, the shops are packed full of paintings in the various popular styles – some of them quite good, a few of them really excellent, and many of them uniformly alike and uniformly poor in quality (think doe-eyed puppies in garish colours).

Before making a purchase, visit the museums and galleries of Ubud (p175) to see the best of Balinese art and some of the European influences that have shaped it. At the galleries you will get an idea of how to value truly deserving Balinese paintings.

Sculpture

Balinese stone is surprisingly light and it's not at all out of the realms of possibility to bring a friendly stone demon back with you in your airline baggage. A typical temple door guardian weighs around 10kg. The stone, however, is very fragile so packing must be done carefully if you're going to get it home without damage. Some of the Batubulan workshops will pack figures quickly and expertly, often suspending the piece in the middle of a wooden framework and packing around it with shredded paper. There are also many capable packing and forwarding agents, though the shipping costs will almost certainly be more than the cost of the article.

Batubulan, on the main highway from South Bali to Ubud (p204), is a major stone-carving centre. Workshops are found further north along the road in Tegaltamu and Silakarang. Stone figures from 25cm to 2m tall line both sides of the road, and stone carvers can be seen in action in the many workshops here.

Wayang Kulit

Wayang kulit (leather puppets) are made in the village of Puaya (p206) near Sukawati, south of Ubud, and in Peliatan (p198) a village near Ubud.

Woodcarvings

As with paintings, try to see some of the best-quality woodcarvings in museums and galleries before you consider buying. Again, many standard pieces are produced in the same basic designs, and craft shops are full of them. Even with a basic frog, hand or fisherman design, some are much better than others. Look for quality first, then look at the price – you may see the same article vary in price by anything from 10% to 1000%!

Apart from the retail mark-up and your bargaining skills, many factors determine costs, including the artist, the type of wood used, the originality of the item and the size. The simplest small carvings start at around 15,000Rp, while many fine pieces can be found for under 100,000Rp; there's no upper limit.

Ubud (p174) and Mas (p206) are good places to look for woodcarvings. For more details on where to buy these arts and crafts, see p55.

SOLO TRAVELLERS

Bali (and to a lesser degree Lombok) is a good place for solo travellers. Both locals and other travellers tend to be open and friendly, making it easy to hook up with others while exploring the island.

Most places to stay have accommodation for single travellers for a price at least a little cheaper than pairs. Women travelling alone should refer to the Women Travellers section (p347).

TELEPHONE

The telecommunications service within Indonesia is provided by Telkom, a government monopoly. All of Indonesia is covered by a domestic satellite telecommunications network. To call any country direct from Indonesia dial 001 plus the country code followed by the number, or make a call via the international operator (☎ 101).

The country code for Indonesia is ☎ 62. The area code for Jakarta is ☎ 021 and for Lombok it's ☎ 0370. Bali has six telephone area codes, listed in the relevant chapters of this book. Phone numbers beginning with ☎ 08 are usually mobile (cell) phones.

Telkom publishes a good phone book for Bali that includes yellow pages in English. Local directory assistance operators (☎ 108) are very helpful and some of them speak English. If you call directory assistance and have to spell out a name, try to use the 'Alpha, Bravo, Charlie' system of saying the letters.

Calling internationally can easily cost from US$0.25 to US$1 or more a minute no matter which of the methods you choose to opt for as outlined in the text following.

Some foreign telephone companies issue cards that enable you to make calls from Indonesian phones and have the cost billed to your home phone account. However, the catch is that most public telephones, wartel (public telephone offices) and hotels won't allow you to call the toll-free ☎ 008 or ☎ 001 access numbers needed to use these phonecards or other home-billing schemes, and the few hotels and wartel that do permit it charge a particular fee for doing so.

Internet connections fast enough to support Voice Over Internet (VOI) services like Skype are uncommon. Internet centres that allow this charge 3000Rp or more.

Mobile Phones

The cellular service in Indonesia is GSM. There are several local providers. If your phone company offers international roaming in Indonesia, you can use your own mobile telephone in Bali – check with the company to find out how much they charge.

Alternatively, a mobile phone (called a handphone in Indonesia) using the GSM system can be used more cheaply if you purchase a prepaid SIM card that you insert into your phone in Bali. This will cost about 50,000Rp from shops in the Kuta area and will give you your own local telephone number. However make certain the phone you bring is both unlocked and able to take SIM cards. Basic phones bought locally start at US$30.

Usually the person selling you your SIM card will install it and make certain things are working. There is also a requirement that you show some ID so your number can be registered with the government but often busy clerks will suggest you return 'some other time' thus saving you this formality.

Long-distance and international calls from a mobile can be less expensive than through the regular phone system. When you buy your SIM card and usage credit ask about special access codes that can result in international calls for as low as US$0.25 per minute.

Phonecards

The vast majority of public phones use phonecards. Some use the regular *kartu telepo* (phonecards) with a magnetic strip. Others use a *kartu chip*, which has an electronic chip embedded in it. You can buy phonecards in denominations of 5000Rp, 10,000Rp, 25,000Rp, 50,000Rp and 100,000Rp at wartel, moneychangers, post offices and many shops. An international call from a card phone costs about the same per minute as a call from a wartel.

Telephone Offices

A *kantor telekomunikasi* (telecommunications office) is a main telephone office operated by Telkom, usually only found in bigger towns. Wartel are sometimes run by Telkom, but the vast majority are private, and there's a lot of them. You can make local, *inter-lokal* (long-distance) and international calls from any wartel.

The charge for international calls is the same from all parts of Bali, but may be cheaper in Telkom offices than in private ones. In most areas you dial the number yourself, and the cost increases in *pulsa* – a unit of time that varies according to the destination.

The official Telkom price of a one-minute call is about the equivalent of US$1 to most parts of the world. Many wartel, however, will charge higher per-minute rates.

You can sometimes make reverse-charge (collect) calls from a Telkom wartel, though most private ones don't allow it and those that do will charge a set fee.

TIME

Bali, Lombok and the islands of Nusa Tenggara to the east are all on Waktu Indonesian Tengah or WIT (Central Indonesian Standard Time), which is eight hours ahead of Greenwich Mean Time/Universal Time or two hours behind Australian Eastern Standard Time. Java is another hour behind Bali and Lombok.

Not allowing for variations due to daylight-saving time in foreign countries, when it's noon on Bali and Lombok, it's 11pm the previous day in New York and 8pm in Los Angeles, 4am in London, 5am in Paris and Amsterdam, noon in Perth, 1pm in Tokyo, and 2pm in Sydney and Melbourne. See the World Time Zones map (p394-5).

'Bali time' is an expression that refers to the Balinese reluctance to be obsessed by punctuality.

TOILETS

You'll still encounter Asian-style toilets in the cheapest losmen around Bali (particularly in the far west). These toilets have two footrests and a hole in the floor – you squat down and aim. In almost every place catering for tourists, Western-style sit-down toilets are the norm. At some tourist attractions in Bali, there are public toilets that cost about 500Rp per visit.

Apart from tourist cafés and restaurants, and midrange and top-end accommodation, you won't find toilet paper, so bring your own. If there is a bin next to the toilet, it's for toilet paper. Where public toilets exist they are often horrible.

TOURIST INFORMATION

The tourist office in Ubud is an excellent source of information on cultural events. Otherwise the tourist offices in this book are largely hit or miss (mostly the latter). It helps to have a specific question and don't bother asking about tourist services like tours. Hotels are often good sources of info.

Some of the best information is found in the many free publications aimed at tourists and expats which are distributed in South Bali and Ubud. These include the following:

Bali Advertiser Newspaper and website (www.bali advertiser.biz) with voluminous ads and comprehensive information; idiosyncratic columnists.

Bali Tourist Advertiser An informative tourist-oriented companion of the *Bali Advertiser*.

Hello Bali Big and glossy with good features, restaurant and entertainment reviews.

Lombok Times Newspaper and website (www.lombok times.com) with tourist news and features.

What's Up Bali Useful weekly brochure with entertainment listings.

Yak Glossy mag celebrating the expat swells of Seminyak and Ubud.

The website **Bali Discovery** (www.balidiscovery.com) has a first-rate Bali news section and a wealth of other island information. Use the handy search feature.

VISAS

The visa situation in Indonesia seems to be constantly in flux. It is essential that you confirm current formalities before you arrive in Bali or Lombok. Failure to meet all the entrance requirements can see you on the first flight out.

No matter what type of visa you are going to use, your passport *must* be valid for at least six months from the date of your arrival.

The main visa options for visitors to Bali and Lombok follow:

- Visa in Advance – citizens of countries not eligible for Visa Free or Visa on Arrival must apply for a visa before they arrive in Indonesia. Typically this is a visitors visa, which comes in two flavours: 30 or 60 days. Details vary by country, so you should contact the nearest Indonesian embassy or consulate in order to determine processing fees and time. Note this is the only way people from any country can obtain a 60-day visitor visa.
- Visa on Arrival – citizens of over 50 countries may apply for a visa when they arrive at the airport in Bali. There are special lanes for this at immigration in the arrivals area. The cost is US$25, collectable on the spot. You can pay by credit card or major currency, which will be converted (but it's easiest to hand them the exact amount in US currency). This visa is only good for 30 days and cannot be extended. Note that only EU citizens who carry passports issued by the countries listed opposite can use visa on arrival. You can also obtain a seven-day visa this way for US$10 but go with the 30-day one unless you know for sure you'll be out of Indonesia in less than seven days. Eligible countries include Argentina, Australia, Austria, Bahrain, Belgium, Brazil, Bulgaria, Cambodia, Canada, Cyprus, Den-

mark, Egypt, Estonia, Finland, France, Germany, Greece, Hungary, Iceland, India, Iran, Ireland, Italy, Japan, Kuwait, Laos, Liechtenstein, Luxembourg, Maldives, Malta, Mexico, Monaco, New Zealand, Norway, Oman, People's Republic of China, Poland, Portugal, Qatar, Russia, Saudi Arabia, South Africa, South Korea, Spain, Suriname, Switzerland, Sweden, Taiwan, The Netherlands, United Arab Emirates, UK and the USA.
- Visa Free – citizens of Brunei, Chile, Hong Kong, Macau, Malaysia, Morocco, Peru, Philippines, Singapore, Thailand and Vietnam may receive a nonextendable 30-day visa for free when they arrive at the airport in Bali.

Whichever type of visa you use to enter Bali or Lombok, you'll be issued with a tourist card that is valid for a 30- or 60-day stay according to your visa (if you have obtained one of the coveted 60-day visas in advance, be sure the immigration official at the airport gives you a 60-day card). Keep the tourist card with your passport, as you'll have to hand it back when you leave the country. Note that some travellers have been fined for overstaying by only a day or so (officially it is US$20 per day for up to 60 days past your visa, after which it can mean jail) or for losing their tourist card.

The vast majority of visitors to Lombok first pass through Bali or another Indonesian city such as Jakarta so they already have tourist cards. There are, however, a few direct flights to Lombok from other countries so in these instances the same visa rules outlined above apply.

Other Requirements

Officially, an onward/return ticket is a requirement for a tourist card (and visitors visa), and visitors are frequently asked to show their ticket on arrival. If you look scruffy or broke, you may also be asked to present evidence of sufficient funds to support yourself during your stay – US$1000 in cash or travellers cheques (or the equivalent in other currencies) should be sufficient. A credit card in lieu of cash or travellers cheques may not satisfy these requirements, although this is rare.

It's not possible to extend a tourist card, unless there's a medical emergency or you have to answer legal charges. If you want to spend more time in Indonesia you have to leave the country and then re-enter – some long-term foreign residents have been doing this for years. Singapore is the destination of choice for obtaining a new visa.

There are two main *kantor imigrasi* (immigration offices) in Bali. The **Denpasar office** (Map pp166-7; ☎ 0361-227828; ⌚ 8am-2pm Mon-Thu, 8am-11am Fri, 8am-noon Sat) is just up the street from the main post office in Renon. The airport **immigration office** (☎ 0361-751038) has similar hours.

On Lombok, the **immigration office** (Map p289; ☎ 632520; Jl Udayana 2; ⌚ 7am-2pm Mon-Thu, 7am-11am Fri, 7am-12.30am Sat) is in Mataram. If you have to apply for changes to your visa, make sure you're neatly dressed, but don't be overly optimistic.

For visa advice and service, many expats in South Bali use the services of **Bali Mode** (☎ 0361-765162; balimode@hotmail.com). Visa extensions (on legally extendable visas) average 400,000Rp to 500,000Rp.

Social Visas

If you have a good reason for staying longer (eg study or family reasons), you can apply for a *sosial/budaya* (social/cultural) visa. You will need an application form from an Indonesian embassy or consulate, and a letter of introduction or promise of sponsorship from a reputable person or school in Indonesia. It's initially valid for three months, but it can be extended for one month at a time at an immigration office within Indonesia for a maximum of six months. There are fees for the application and for extending the visa too.

WOMEN TRAVELLERS

Women travelling solo on Bali will get a lot of attention from Balinese guys, but Balinese men are, on the whole, fairly benign. Generally, Bali is safer for women than most areas of the world and, with the usual care, women should feel secure travelling alone.

Some precautions are simply the same for any traveller, but women should take extra care not to find themselves alone on empty beaches, down dark streets or in other situations where help might not be available. Late at night in the tourist centres, solo women should take a taxi, and sit in the back. Note that problems do occur and it is a good idea to practise the same precautions you use at home.

If you are going to stay in Bali for longer than a short holiday, the **Bali International Women's Association** (BIWA; ☎ 0361-285 552; www.biwabali.org) can prove essential. It was established by expats to 'foster friendship and mutual understanding' and meets monthly to organise support for local charities. It also works to help members integrate into local life.

Kuta Cowboys

In tourist areas of Bali (and Lombok), you'll encounter young men who are keen to spend time with visiting women. Commonly called Kuta Cowboys, beach boys, bad boys, guides or gigolos, these guys think they're super cool, with long hair, lean bodies, tight jeans and lots of tattoos. While they don't usually work a straight sex-for-money deal, the visiting woman pays for the meals, drinks and accommodation, and commonly buys the guy presents.

It's not uncommon for them to form long-term relationships, with the guy hopeful of finding a new and better life with his partner in Europe, Japan, Australia or the US. While most of these guys around Bali are genuinely friendly and quite charming, some are predatory con artists who practise elaborate deceits. Many of them now come from outside Bali, and have a long succession of foreign lovers. Be healthily sceptical about what they tell you, particularly if it comes down to them needing money. Always insist on using condoms.

Lombok

Traditionally, women on Lombok are treated with respect, but in the touristy areas, harassment of single foreign women may occur. Would-be guides/boyfriends/gigolos are often persistent in their approaches, and can be aggressive when ignored or rejected. Clothes that aren't too revealing are a good idea – beachwear should be reserved for the beach, and the less skin you expose the better. Two or more women together are less likely to experience problems, and women accompanied by a man are unlikely to be harassed. It is better not to walk alone at night.

WORK

Quite a lot of foreigners own businesses in Bali – mostly hotels, restaurants and tour agencies. To do so legally, foreigners need the appropriate work or business visa, which requires sponsorship from an employer, or evidence of a business that brings investment to Indonesia. Many foreigners are engaged in buying and exporting clothing, handicrafts or furniture, and stay for short periods – within the limits of a 30- or 60-day tourist card. It's illegal to work if you've entered Indonesia on a tourist card, and you'll have to leave the country to change your visa status. Even if you do get work, typically teaching English, payment is often in rupiah, which doesn't convert into a lot of foreign currency. Under-the-table work, such as dive shop and bar jobs, is typically poorly paid .

Volunteer & Aid Work

LOCAL ORGANISATIONS

Ubud is a hub for nonprofit and volunteer organisations. **Bali Spirit** (☎ 0361-970 992; www.balispirit.com; 44 Jl Hanoman) is part of a café (Kafe, see p196). It has information on a number of non-profit and volunteer groups located in Ubud, including the Indonesian Development of Education & Permaculture (IDEP), Sumatran Orangutan Society (SOS) and Volunteers & Interns for Balinese Education (VIBE) which are listed below. The **Pondok Pecak Library & Learning Centre** (Map p188; ☎ 0361-976 194; pondok@indo.net.id; Monkey Forest Rd) also has info on local charities.

BIWA (see p347) is a useful clearing house for information on local charities.

The following organisations have need for donations, supplies and often volunteers. Check their websites to see their current status.

East Bali Poverty Project (www.eastbalipovertyproject.org) Works to help children in the impoverished mountain villages of East Bali.

IDEP (Indonesian Development of Education & Permaculture; www.idepfoundation.org) A large Ubud-based organisation that works on environmental projects, disaster planning and community improvement. Runs the Bali Cares shop (p198).

JED (Village Ecotourism Network; ☎ 0361-735320; www.jed.or.id) Organises highly regarded tours (p363) of small villages. Often needs volunteers to improve its services and work with the villagers.

PPLH Bali (☎ 0361 281684; www.pplhbali.or.id; Jl Danau Tamblingan 148, Sanur) Located with the Hotel Santai (see p142), organises a broad range of environmental and education programs.

SOS (Sumatran Orangutan Society; www.orangutans-sos.org) An Ubud-based group that works to save endangered species throughout Indonesia.

VIBE (Volunteers & Interns for Balinese Education; www.vibefoundation.org) An Ubud-based group that works to support English-language courses in Bali schools. It regularly needs volunteers to teach English and art as well as manage projects.

Yakkum Bali (Yayasan Rama Sesana; www.yrsbali.org) Dedicated to improving reproductive health for women across Bali.
YKIP (Humanitarian Foundation of Mother Earth; www.ykip.org) Established after the 2002 bombings, it organises health and education projects for Bali's children.

INTERNATIONAL ORGANISATIONS

Another possible source for long-term paid or volunteer work in Bali or Lombok are the following agencies.

Australian Volunteers International (www.australianvolunteers.com) Organises professional contracts for Australians.
Global Volunteers (www.globalvolunteers.org) Arranges professional and paid volunteer work for US citizens.
Voluntary Service Overseas (www.vso.org.uk) British overseas volunteer programme accepts qualified volunteers from other countries. Branches in Canada (www.vsocanada.org) and the Netherlands (www.vso.nl).
Volunteer Service Abroad (www.vsa.org.nz) Organises professional contracts for New Zealanders.

Transport

CONTENTS

GETTING THERE & AWAY

Most international visitors to Bali will arrive by air, either directly or via Jakarta. For island-hoppers, there are frequent ferries between eastern Java and Bali, and between Bali and Lombok, as well as domestic flights between the islands. Most people visit Lombok via Bali.

ENTERING THE COUNTRY

Arrival procedures at Bali's airport are fairly painless, although it can take some time for a whole planeload of visitors to clear immigration. At the baggage claim area, porters are keen to help get your luggage to the customs tables and beyond, and they've been known to ask up to US$20 for their services – if you want help with your bags, agree on a price beforehand. The formal price is 4000Rp per piece.

Once through customs, you're out with the tour operators, touts and taxi drivers. The touts will be working hard to convince you to come and stay at some place in the Kuta area. Most have contacts at a few places, and if you're not sure where you intend to stay, they may be worth considering, but you'll likely pay more for accommodation if a tout or a taxi driver takes you there without a reservation.

Passport

Your passport must be valid for six months after your date of arrival in Indonesia.

AIR

Although Jakarta, the national capital, is the gateway airport to Indonesia, there are also many direct international flights to Bali and a few to Lombok.

Airports & Airlines

BALI AIRPORT

The only airport in Bali, Ngurah Rai Airport (DPS) is just south of Kuta, however it is sometimes referred to internationally as Denpasar or on some internet flight booking sites as Bali.

The **international terminal** (☎ 0361-751011) and **domestic terminal** (☎ 0361-751011) are a few hundred metres apart. In the first you'll find internet centres and shops with high prices.

International airlines flying to and from Bali regularly change.

Air Asia (airline code AK; ☎ 0361-760116; www.airasia.com) Serves Kuala Lumpur.

Cathay Pacific Airways (airline code CX; ☎ 0361-766 931; www.cathaypacific.com) Serves Hong Kong.

China Airlines (airline code CI; ☎ 0361-754856; www.china-airlines.com) Serves Taipei.

Continental Airlines (airline code CO; ☎ 0361-768 358; www.continental.com) Service from the US via Hawaii and Guam.

Eva Air (airline code BR; ☎ 0361-751011; www.evaair.com) Serves Taipei.

THINGS CHANGE...

The information in this chapter is particularly vulnerable to change. Check directly with the airline or a travel agent to make sure you understand how a fare (and ticket you may buy) works and be aware of the security requirements for international travel. Shop carefully. The details given in this chapter should be regarded as pointers and are not a substitute for your own careful, up-to-date research.

DEPARTURE TAX

The Departure Tax from Bali and Lombok is 20,000Rp domestic and 100,000Rp international. It's best to have the exact amount for the officer.

Garuda Indonesia (airline code GA; ☎ 0361-227824; www.garuda-indonesia.com) Serves Australia, Japan, Korea and Singapore direct.
Japan Airlines (airline code JL; ☎ 0361-757077; www.jal.co.jp) Serves Tokyo.
Korean Air (airline code KE; ☎ 0361-768377; www.koreanair.com) Serves Seoul.
Malaysia Airlines (airline code MH; ☎ 0361-764995; www.mas.com.my) Serves Kuala Lumpur.
Qantas Airways (airline code QF; ☎ 0361-288331; www.qantas.com.au) Extensive Australian service; plans to rebrand flights to Bali as Jetstar.
Singapore Airlines (airline code SQ; ☎ 0361-768388; www.singaporeair.com) Several Singapore flights daily.
Thai Airways International (airline code TG; ☎ 0361-288141; www.thaiair.com) Serves Bangkok.

Domestic airlines serving Bali from other parts of Indonesia change frequently. The ones listed below serve Jakarta, Surabaya and many more places.
Air Asia (airline code AK; ☎ 0361-760116; www.airasia.com)
Adam Air (airline code KI; ☎ 0361-227999; www.adamair.co.id)
Garuda Indonesia (airline code GA; ☎ 0361-227824; www.garuda-indonesia.com)
Lion Air (airline code JT; ☎ 0361-763872; www.lionairlines.com)
Mandala Airlines (airline code RI; ☎ 0361-751011; www.mandalaair.com)
Merpati Airlines (airline code MZ; ☎ 0361-235358; www.merpati.co.id)

Money

The rates offered at the exchange counters at the international and domestic terminals are competitive, and as good as the moneychangers in Kuta and the tourist centres. There are ATMs in both terminals as well as before and after immigration.

Luggage

The **left-luggage room** (per piece per day 10,000Rp; 24hr) is in the international terminal, behind the McDonald's near the departures area.

LOMBOK AIRPORT

Lombok's Selaparang Airport (AMI) is just north of Mataram. The airport has hotel reservations desks, cafés, ATMs, moneychangers and internet access.

Airlines flying to and from Lombok include the following:
Garuda Indonesia (airline code GA; ☎ 0370-638259; www.garuda-indonesia.com) Jakarta, Surabaya and Bali.
Lion Air (airline code JT; ☎ 0370-629111, 0370-692222; www.lionairlines.com) Surabaya.
Merpati Airlines (airline code MZ; ☎ 0370-621111; www.merpati.co.id) Flies to Bali and Sumbawa.
Silk Air (airline code MI; ☎ 0370-628254; www.silkair.com) Serves Singapore direct.

Tickets

Deregulation in the Indonesian and the Asian aviation markets means that there are frequent deals to Bali.

ROUND-THE-WORLD TICKETS

Round-the-world (RTW) tickets that include Bali are usually offered by an alliance of several airlines such as **Star Alliance** (www.staralliance.com) and **One World** (www.oneworld.com). These tickets come in many flavours, but most let you visit several continents over a period of time that can be as long as a year. It's also worth investigating Circle Pacific–type tickets which are similar to RTW tickets but limit you to the Pacific region.

These tickets can be great deals. Prices for RTW tickets are usually under US$2000 – not much different from what you'll pay to Bali alone from North America or Europe.

Asia

Bali is well connected to Asian cities. Lombok is now linked to Singapore.

STA Travel proliferates in Asia, with branches in **Bangkok** (☎ 02-236 0262; www.statravel.co.th), **Singapore** (☎ 6737 7188; www.statravel.com.sg), **Hong Kong** (☎ 2736 1618; www.statravel.com.hk) and **Japan** (☎ 03 5391 2922; www.statravel.co.jp). Another resource in Japan is **No 1 Travel** (☎ 03 3205 6073; www.no1-travel.com); in Hong Kong try **Four Seas Tours** (☎ 2200 7760; www.fourseastravel.com/english).

Australia

Australia is well-served with numerous direct flights from Bali to all major cities.

STA Travel (☎ 1300 733 035; www.statravel.com.au) is a well-known agenciey for discount fares nationwide. **Flight Centre** (☎ 133 133;

TRANSPORT

www.flightcentre.com.au) has offices throughout Australia. For online bookings, try www.travel.com.au.

Canada

From Canada, you'll change planes at an Asian hub.

Travel Cuts (☎ 800-667-2887; www.travelcuts.com) is Canada's national student travel agency. For online bookings try the websites listed under USA (right). Replace the '.com' with a '.ca.'

Continental Europe

None of the major European carriers fly to Bali at present. Singapore is the most likely place to change planes coming from Europe, with Bangkok, Hong Kong and Kuala Lumpur also being popular.

FRANCE

Recommended agencies:

Anyway (☎ 08 92 89 38 92; www.anyway.fr)
Lastminute (☎ 08 92 0 50 00; www.lastminute.fr)
Nouvelles Frontières (☎ 08 25 00 07 47; www.nouvelles-frontieres.fr)
OTU Voyages (☎ 08 20 81 78 17; www.otu.fr) This agency specialises in student and youth travellers.
Voyageurs du Monde (☎ 01 40 15 11 15; www.vdm.com)

GERMANY

Recommended agencies:

Expedia (www.expedia.de)
Just Travel (☎ 089 747 3330; www.justtravel.de)
Lastminute (☎ 01805 284 366; www.lastminute.de)
STA Travel (☎ 01805 456 422; www.statravel.de) For travellers under the age of 26.

THE NETHERLANDS

One recommended agency is **Airfair** (☎ 020 620 5121; www.airfair.nl).

New Zealand

Garuda Indonesia has infrequent flights from Bali to Auckland. Otherwise you will have to change planes in Australia or Singapore.

Both **Flight Centre** (☎ 0800 243 544; www.flightcentre.co.nz) and **STA Travel** (☎ 0508 782 872; www.statravel.co.nz) have branches throughout the country. The site www.travel.co.nz is recommended for online bookings.

Other Indonesian Islands

From Bali, you can get flights to major Indonesian cities, often for under US$50 but definitely not much more than US$100. The ticket area at the domestic terminal is a bit of a bazaar. Specials posted in windows often offer great deals. Deals to Jakarta put the price of a plane ticket in the same class as the bus – with a savings of about 22 hours in transit time.

From Lombok, you can get some decent deals but direct service is mostly limited to Bali, Surabaya and Jakarta.

UK & Ireland

From London, the most direct service to Bali is on Singapore Airlines through Singapore. Other transit points include Bangkok, Hong Kong and Kuala Lumpur.

Recommended travel agencies include the following:

Flight Centre (☎ 0870 890 8099; www.flightcentre.co.uk)
Flightbookers (☎ 0870 010 7000; www.ebookers.com)
Quest Travel (☎ 0870 442 3542; www.questtravelcom)
STA Travel (☎ 0870 160 0599; www.statravel.co.uk)
Trailfinders (☎ 0845 05 05 891; www.trailfinders.co.uk)

USA

Continental Airlines is the sole American carrier to serve Bali, however it does so as part of its local Pacific service which means you will hopscotch through Hawaii and Guam on your way. Often quicker connections can be had through any of the major Asian hubs with nonstop service to Bali.

The following websites are recommended for online bookings:

Expedia (www.expedia.com)
Kayak (www.kayak.com)
Orbitz (www.orbitz.com)
STA Travel (www.sta.com)
Travelocity (www.travelocity.com)

SEA

You can reach Java, just west of Bali, and Sumbawa, just west of Lombok, via ferries. Through buses can take you all the way to Jakarta. Longer distance boats serve Indonesia's eastern islands.

Java

When visiting Java from Bali and Lombok, some land travel is necessary.

FERRY

Ferries (adult/child 4300/2900Rp, car and driver 81,500Rp; every 30 minutes) run 24 hours, crossing the Bali Strait between Gilimanuk in western Bali and Ketapang (Java). The actual crossing takes under 30 minutes, but you'll spend longer than this loading, unloading and waiting around. Car rental contracts usually prohibit rental vehicles being taken out of Bali, but it may be possible to take a rented motorcycle across, by arrangement with the owner.

From Ketapang, bemo (small minibuses) travel 4km north to the terminal, where buses leave for Baluran, Probolingo (for Gunung Bromo), Surabaya, Yogyakarta and Jakarta. There's a train station near the ferry port, with trains to Probolingo, Surabaya, Yogyakarta and Jakarta. Contact the **Train Information Service** (☎ 0361-227131) for more information.

BUS

To/From Bali

The ferry crossing is included in the services to/from Ubung terminal in Denpasar offered by numerous bus companies, many of which travel overnight. It's advisable to buy your ticket at least one day in advance, at travel agents in the tourist centres or at the Ubung terminal. Note too that fierce air competition has put tickets to Jakarta and Surabaya in the range of bus prices.

Fares vary between operators; it's worth paying extra for a decent seat and air-con. For a comfortable bus ride, typical fares and travel times are Surabaya (120,000Rp, 10 hours), Yogyakarta (180,000Rp, 16 hours) and Jakarta (275,000Rp, 24 hours). Some companies travel directly between Java and Singaraja, via Lovina, on the north coast of Bali.

To/From Lombok

Public buses go daily from Mandalika terminal to major cities on Java. Most buses are comfortable, with air-con and reclining seats. Destinations include Surabaya (179,000Rp, 20 hours), Yogyakarta (272,000Rp, 30 hours) and Jakarta (375,000Rp, 38 hours).

Sumbawa

Ferries travel between Labuhan Lombok and Poto Tano on Sumbawa every 45 minutes (passenger 12,500Rp; motorcycle 32,000Rp; car 253,000Rp). They run 24 hours a day and the trip takes 1½ hours. There are direct buses from Mandalika terminal to Bima (135,000Rp, 12 hours) and Sumbawa Besar (77,000Rp, six hours).

Other Indonesian Islands

Services to other islands in Indonesia are often in flux, although Pelni is reliable. Check for other services at Benoa Harbour.

PELNI

The national shipping line is **Pelni** (www.pelni.co.id), which schedules large boats on long-distance runs throughout Indonesia.

To/From Bali

Three ships from Pelni stop at Benoa Harbour as part of their regular loops throughout Indonesia. *Dobonsolo* with Java, Nusa Tenggara, Maluku and northern Papua; and *Awu* and *Tilongkabila* with Nusa Tenggara and southern Sulawesi. Prices are dependent on the route and the class of travel, and this can range widely in price. Check for details locally but in general fares, even in 1st class, are very low, eg Benoa Harbour to Surabaya on Java is US$35.

You can inquire and book at the **Pelni offices** in Tuban (Map p103; ☎ 0361-763963; www.pelni.co.id; Jl Raya Kuta 299; 🕑 8am-noon & 1-4pm Mon-Thu, 8am-11.30am & 1-4pm Fri, 8am-1pm Sat) and at Benoa Harbour (Map p128; ☎ 0361-721377; 🕑 8am-4pm Mon-Fri, 8am-12.30pm Sat).

To/From Lombok

Pelni ships link Lembar with other parts of Indonesia. The *Awu* heads to Waingapu, Ende, Kupang and Kalabahi; the *Kelimutu* goes to Bima, Makassar and Papua; and the *Tilongkabila* to Bima, Labuanbajo and Sulawesi. Tickets can be bought at the **Pelni office** (Map p289; ☎ 0370-637212; Jl Industri 1; 🕑 8am-noon & 1pm-3.30pm Mon-Thu & Sat, 8am-11am Fri) in Mataram.

GETTING AROUND

Especially on Bali, the best way to get around is with your own transport whether you drive or you hire a driver. This gives you the flexibility to explore at will and allows you to reach many places that are otherwise inaccessible.

Public transport is cheap but can be cause for very long journeys if you are not sticking to a major route. In addition, some places may be impossible to reach.

There are also tourist shuttle buses and these combine economy with convenience.

TRANSPORT

TO/FROM THE AIRPORT

Bali's Ngurah Rai Airport is immediately south of Tuban and Kuta. From the official counters, just outside the terminals, there are usually hassle-free prepaid airport taxis. The costs are (depending on drop-off point):

Destination	Cost
Denpasar	70,000Rp
Jimbaran	60,000Rp
Kuta Beach	45,000Rp
Legian	50,000Rp
Nusa Dua	85,000Rp
Sanur	85,000Rp
Seminyak	60,000Rp
Ubud	175,000Rp

If you have a surfboard, you'll be charged at least 35,000Rp extra, depending on its size. Ignore any touts that aren't part of the official scheme. Many hotels will offer to pick you up at the airport however there's no need to use this service if costs more than the above rates.

The thrifty can walk across the airport car park to the right (northeast) from the international and domestic terminals and continue a couple of hundred metres through the vehicle exit to the airport road (ignoring any touts along the way), where you can hail a regular cab for about half the above amounts.

If you are really travelling light, Kuta Beach is less than a 30 minute-walk north.

Any taxi will take you to the airport at a metered rate that should be about half what we have listed.

AIR

Garuda Indonesia, Lion Air and Merpati Airlines have several flights daily between Bali and Lombok. The route is competitive and fares hover around about 280,000Rp, although new entrants in the market may offer better deals.

BEMO

The main form of public transport in Bali and on Lombok is the bemo. A generic term for any vehicle used as public transport, it's normally a minibus or van with a row of low seats down each side. Bemo usually hold about 12 people in very cramped conditions.

Riding bemo can be part of your Bali adventure or a major nightmare depending on your outlook at the moment in time. Certainly you can expect journeys to be rather lengthy and you'll find that getting to many places is both time-consuming and inconvenient. It's rather uncommon to see visitors on bemo in Bali.

On Lombok, bemo are minibuses or pick-up trucks and are a major means of transport for visitors.

See p334 for information on pickpocketing on public bemo.

Fares

Bemo operate on a standard route for a set (but unwritten) fare. Unless you get on at a regular starting point, and get off at a regular finishing point, the fares are likely to be fuzzy. The cost per kilometre is pretty variable, but is cheaper on longer trips. The minimum fare is about 4000Rp. The fares listed in this book reflect what a tourist should reasonably expect to pay.

Bemo are justly famous for overcharging tourists, and finding out the *harga biasa* ('correct' fare) requires local knowledge and subtlety. The best procedure is to hand over the correct fare as you get off, as the locals do, no questions asked. To find out the correct fare, consult a trusted local before you get on. Note what other passengers pay when they get off, bearing in mind that schoolchildren and the driver's friends pay less. If you speak Bahasa Indonesia, you can ask your fellow passengers, but in a dispute they will probably support the bemo jockey.

The whole business of overcharging tourists is a bit of a game; bemo drivers and jockeys are usually good-humoured about it, but some tourists take it very seriously and have unpleasant arguments over a few thousand rupiah. Sometimes you will be charged extra (perhaps double the passenger price) if you have a big bag, as you will be taking up space where otherwise a paying passenger could squeeze in.

Make sure you know where you're going, and accept that the bemo normally won't leave until it's full and will usually take a roundabout route to collect and deliver as many passengers as possible. If you get into an empty bemo, always make it clear that you do not want to charter it. (The word 'charter' is understood by all drivers.)

Terminals & Routes

Every town has at least one terminal *(terminal bis)* for all forms of public transport. There are often several terminals in larger towns, according to the direction the bus or bemo is heading. For example, Denpasar, the hub of Bali's transport system has four main bus/bemo terminals and three minor ones. Terminals can be confusing, but most bemo and buses have signs and, if in doubt, you will be told where to go by a bemo jockey or driver anyway.

To go from one part of Bali to another, it is often necessary to go via one or more of the terminals in Denpasar, or via a terminal in one of the other larger regional towns. For example, to get from Sanur to Ubud by public bemo, you go to the Kereneng terminal in Denpasar, transfer to the Batubulan terminal, and then take a third bemo to Ubud. This is circuitous and time-consuming, so many visitors prefer the tourist shuttle buses or charter vehicle or taxi.

BICYCLE

A famous temple carving shows the Dutch artist WOJ Nieuwenkamp pedalling through Bali in 1904. Bali's roads have improved greatly since then, but surprisingly few people tour the island on a *sepeda* (bicycle). Many visitors, however, are using bikes around the towns and for day trips in Bali and on Lombok; good quality rental bikes are available, and several companies organise full-day cycle trips in the back country, including the following:

Atlantis Adventure (☎ 0361-284312; www.atlantis-adventures-bali.com) Rides start from US$35.
Bali Bintang (☎ 0361-973138; bintangtours@hotmail.com)
Bali Eco & Educational Cycling Tour (☎ 0361-975557, 081-833 6580)

Popular tours start high up in the central mountains at places such as Kintamani or Bedugal. The tour company takes you to the top and then you ride down relatively quiet mountain roads soaking up the lush scenery and tropical scents. The costs with bicycle, gear and lunch is US$25 to US$40.

Some people are put off cycling by tropical heat, heavy traffic, frequent showers and high mountains. But when you're riding on level or downhill, the breeze really moderates the heat.

Multigear mountain bikes make it possible to get up the higher mountains in Bali or on Lombok, but with a bit of negotiating and patience, you can get a bemo or minibus to take you and your bike up the steepest sections.

The main advantage of touring Bali by bike is the quality of the experience. By bicycle you can be totally immersed in the environment – you can hear the wind rustling in the rice paddies, the sound of a gamelan (traditional Balinese orchestra) practising, and catch the scent of the flowers. Even at the height of the tourist season, cycle tourers on the back roads experience the friendliness that seems all but lost on the usual tourist circuit. Once you get away from the congested south, the roads are more relaxed and the experience sublime.

Lombok is ideal for touring by bicycle. In the populated areas, the roads are flat and the traffic everywhere is less dangerous than in Bali. East of Mataram are several attractions that would make a good day trip, or you could go south to Banyumulek via Gunung Pengsong and return. Some of the coastal roads have hills and curves like a roller coaster – try going north from Mataram, via Senggigi, to Pemenang, and then (if you feel energetic) return via the steep climb over the Pusuk Pass.

Hire

There are plenty of bicycles for rent in the tourist areas, but many of them are in poor condition. The best place to rent good quality mountain bikes in Bali is in the south and Ubud. On Lombok you can find good bikes in Senggigi.

Ask at your accomodation about where you can rent a good bike, often hotels have their own. Generally prices range from 20,000Rp to 30,000Rp per day.

Touring

See Road Conditions (p359) for more information, and make sure your bike is equipped for these conditions. Even the smallest village has some semblance of a bike shop – a flat tyre should cost about 4000Rp to fix.

The Periplus Bali and Lombok maps are a good place to start your planning. Pick the smallest roads for real peace and remember that no matter how lost you get, locals are always happy to help with directions.

BOAT

Public ferries (adult/child 21,000/14,000Rp) travel nonstop between Padangbai in Bali and Lembar on Lombok. Motorcycles cost 155,000Rp and cars cost 330,000Rp – go through the weighbridge at the west corner of the Padangbai car park. Depending on conditions the trip can take three to five hours.

Boats run 24 hours and leave about every 90 minutes; food and drink is sold on board.

Anyone who carries your luggage on or off the ferries at both ports will expect to be paid, so agree on the price first or carry your own stuff. Also, watch out for scams where the porter may try to sell you a ticket you've already bought. Lembar is worse for this.

Perama (Padangbai ☎ 0363-41419; Café Dona, Jl Pelabuhan; 🕑 7am-8pm; Senggigi ☎ 0370-693007; 🕑 6am-10pm) has a 40-passenger boat that takes about four hours to travel from Padangbai to Senggigi (200,00Rp; departs 9am, returns 1.30pm), where you can get another boat to the Gilis. Snacks are sold on board.

BUS

Distances in Bali and on Lombok are relatively short so you won't have cause to ride many large buses unless you are transferring between islands or going from one side to another. Note that bemo are usually minibuses seating about 12 in cramped uncomfort.

Public Bus

BALI

Larger minibuses and full-size buses ply the longer routes, particularly on routes linking Denpasar, Singaraja, and Gilimanuk. They operate out of the same terminals as the bemo. Buses are faster than bemo because they do not make as many stops along the way.

LOMBOK

Buses and bemo of various sizes are the cheapest and most common way of getting around Lombok. On rough roads in remote areas, trucks may be used as public transport. Mandalika is the main bus terminal for all of Lombok. There are also regional terminals at Praya and Pancor (near Selong). You may have to go via one or more of these transport hubs to get from one part of Lombok to another.

Public transport fares are fixed by the provincial government, and displayed on a noticeboard outside the terminal office of Mandalika terminal. You may have to pay more if you have a large bag or surfboard.

Tourist Shuttle Bus

Shuttle buses are quicker, more comfortable and more convenient than public transport, and though more expensive, they are very popular with budget and midrange travellers. If you're with a group of three or more people (or sometimes even two), it will probably be cheaper to charter a vehicle, however.

Perama (www.peramatour.com) has a near monopoly on this service in Bali. It has offices or agents in Kuta, Sanur, Ubud, Lovina, Padangbai and Candidasa. At least one bus a day links these Bali tourist centres with more frequent services to the airport. There are also services to Kitimani and along the east coast from Lovina to/from Candidasa via Amed by demand.

Fares are reasonable (for example Kuta to Lovina is 70,000Rp). Be sure to book your trip at least a day ahead in order to confirm schedules. It is also important to understand where Perama buses will pick you up and drop you off as you may need to pay an extra 5000Rp to get to/from your hotel.

Note that shuttle buses often do not provide a direct service – those from Kuta to Candidasa may stop en route at Sanur, Ubud and Padangbai, and maybe other towns on request.

Perama also operates on Lombok. Currently, this service only links Mataram (p286) with Kuta, Senggigi (p293), Bangsal (p311) and Tetebatu (p317) – so you can't travel from Kuta to Bangsal without changing in Mataram, but you can normally connect on the same day. From Senggigi, there are also shuttle boats to the Gili Islands (p299).

CAR & MOTORCYCLE

Renting a car or motorcycle can open up Bali and Lombok for exploration and can also leave you counting the minutes until you return it. It gives you the freedom to explore the myriad of back roads and lets you set your own schedule. Most people don't rent a car for their entire visit but rather get one for a few days of wandering. In Bali it is common to get a car in the south or Ubud and circumnavigate at least part of the island.

See Road Conditions (p351) for details of the at times harrowing driving conditions on the islands.

Driving Licence

If you plan to drive a car, you *must* have an International Driving Permit (IDP). It's easy to obtain one from your national motoring organisation if you have a normal driving licence. Bring your home licence as well – it's supposed to be carried in conjunction with the IDP.

BALI ROAD DISTANCES (KM)

	Amed	Bangli	Bedugul	Candidasa	Denpasar	Gilimanuk	Kintamani	Kuta	Lovina	Negara	Nusa Dua	Padangbai	Sanur	Semarapura	Singaraja	Tirtagangga	Ubud
Amed	---																
Bangli	59	---															
Bedugul	144	97	---														
Candidasa	32	52	88	---													
Denpasar	57	47	78	31	---												
Gilimanuk	197	181	148	165	134	---											
Kintamani	108	20	89	71	67	135	---										
Kuta	73	57	57	41	10	144	77	---									
Lovina	89	86	41	139	89	79	70	99	---								
Negara	161	135	115	126	95	33	163	104	107	---							
Nusa Dua	81	81	102	55	24	158	91	14	113	109	---						
Padangbai	45	39	75	13	18	178	58	28	126	154	42	---					
Sanur	64	40	85	38	7	141	78	15	96	102	22	37	---				
Semarapura	37	26	61	27	47	181	46	57	112	124	71	14	52	---			
Singaraja	78	75	30	128	78	90	59	88	11	118	92	115	85	105	---		
Tirtagangga	14	65	101	13	84	212	85	95	112	179	108	26	91	44	142	---	
Ubud	68	29	35	54	23	157	29	33	40	120	47	41	30	29	95	67	---

MOTORCYCLE LICENCE

If you have a motorcycle licence at home, get your IDP endorsed for motorcycles too.

If you have an IDP endorsed for motorcycles you will have no problems. If not, you should obtain a local licence, which is valid for one month in Bali only. It's not worth getting a motorcycle licence for a day or two – rent or charter a car or minibus instead.

The person renting the bike may not check your licence or IDP, and the cop who stops you may be happy with a nonendorsed IDP or bribe. You might get away without a motorcycle endorsement, but you *must* have an IDP. Officially there's a two million rupiah fine for riding without a proper licence, and the motorcycle can be impounded – unofficially, the cop may expect a substantial 'on-the-spot' payment. If you have an accident without a licence, your insurance company might refuse coverage.

To get a local motorcycle licence in Bali, go independently (or have the rental agency/owner take you) to the **Poltabes Denpasar** (Police Station; Map p128; ☎ 0361-1427352; Jl Gunung Sanhyang; 8am-1pm Mon-Sat) for a Temporary Permit, which is valid for three months. When you arrive you will see a mobbed main hall filled with confusion. However step around to a side entrance and look for the sign reading 'Foreigner License Applicant.' Here you will find cheery English-speaking officials who for a sum of 200,000Rp will take your picture, give you the required written test (in English, answers available) and see that you are ready to ride in under two hours. Sure it costs more than in the hall of chaos, but who can argue with the service? Just be sure to bring your passport and a photocopy of same.

Fuel & Spare Parts

Bensin (petrol) is sold by the government-owned Pertamina company, and currently costs about 5000Rp per litre. Bali has numerous petrol stations but there are gaps in their coverage notably along the east coast north of Amlapura and in the mountains. In that case, look for the little roadside fuel shops that fill your tank from a plastic container. It's the same on Lombok, petrol stations are found in major towns.

Petrol pumps usually have a meter, which records the litres and a table that shows how much to pay for various amounts. Make sure to check that the pump is reset to zero before the attendant starts to put petrol in your vehicle, and check the total amount that goes in before the pump is reset for the next customer.

Tyre repair services can be found in almost every town.

Hire

Very few agencies in Bali will allow you to take their rental cars or motorcycles to Lombok – the regular vehicle insurance is not valid outside Bali.

See Insurance (opposite) for details or rental insurance.

CAR

By far the most popular rental vehicle is a small jeep – they're compact, have good ground clearance and the low gear ratio is well suited to exploring Bali's back roads, although the bench seats at the back are uncomfortable on a long trip. The main alternative is the larger Toyota Kijang, which seats six. Automatic transmission is uncommon in rental cars.

Rental and travel agencies at all tourist centres advertise cars for hire. A Suzuki jeep costs about 100,000Rp per day, with unlimited kilometres and very limited insurance – maybe less per day for longer rentals. A Toyota Kijang costs from around 140,000Rp per day. These costs will vary considerably according to demand, the condition of the vehicle, length of hire and your bargaining talents. It's common for extra days to cost much less than the first day.

There's no reason to book rental cars in advance over the internet or with a tour package, and it will almost certainly cost more than arranging it locally. Look to the tourist centres in Bali and on Lombok for car-hire agencies. In fact rental touts will look for you. Hotels are usually a good source of options.

Shop around for a good deal, and check the car carefully before you sign up. Rental cars usually have to be returned to the place from where they are rented – you can't do a one-way rental, but some operators will let you leave a car at the airport.

Big international rental operators in Bali have a presence and may be worth investigating if you're not travelling on a budget – vehicle quality and condition will likely be of high standard. Typical rates run well more than US$60 per day with another US$40 per day for a driver.

Europcar (☎ 0361-705030; www.europcar.com)
Hertz (☎ 0361-7462627; www.hertz.com)

MOTORCYCLE

Motorcycles are a popular way of getting around Bali and Lombok, locals ride pillion on a *sepeda motor* (motorcycle) almost from birth. Motorcycling is just as convenient and as flexible as driving and the environmental impact and the cost are much less.

Motorcycles are ideal for Lombok's tiny, rough roads, which may be difficult or impassable by car. Once you get out of the main centres there's not much traffic, apart from people, dogs and water buffalo.

But think carefully before renting a motorcycle. It is dangerous and every year a number of visitors go home with lasting damage – Bali and Lombok are no places to learn to ride a motorcycle.

Motorcycles for rent in Bali and on Lombok are almost all between 90cc and 200cc, with 100cc the usual size. You really don't need anything bigger, as the distances are short and the roads are rarely suitable for travelling fast. In beach areas, many come equipped with a rack on the side for a surfboard.

Rental charges vary with the motorcycle and the period of rental – bigger, newer motorcycles cost more, while longer rental periods attract lower rates. A newish 125cc Honda in good condition might cost 30,000Rp to 40,000Rp a day, but for a week or more you might get the same motorcycle for as little as 25,000Rp per day. This should include minimal insurance for the motorcycle (probably with a US$100 excess), but not for any other person or property.

Individual owners rent out the majority of motorcycles. Generally it's travel agencies, restaurants, losmen (basic accommodation) or shops with a sign advertising 'motorcycle for rent'. In Bali, the Kuta region is the easiest and cheapest place to rent a motorcycle, but you'll have no trouble finding one anywhere tourists regularly visit including on Lombok.

See Insurance opposite for details on rental insurance.

Riding Considerations

Check the motorcycle over before riding off – some are in very bad condition. You must carry the motorcycle's registration papers with you while riding. Make sure the agency/owner gives them to you before you ride off.

Helmets are compulsory and this requirement is enforced in tourist areas, but less so in the countryside. You can even be stopped for not having the chin-strap fastened – a favourite of policemen on the lookout for some extra cash. The standard helmets you get with rental bikes are pretty lightweight. You may want to bring something more substantial from home.

Despite the tropical climate, it's still wise to dress properly for motorcycling. Thongs, shorts and a T-shirt are poor protection. And when it rains in Bali, it really rains. A poncho is handy, but it's best to get off the road and sit out the storm.

Insurance

Rental agencies and owners usually insist that the vehicle itself is insured, and minimal insurance should be included in the basic rental deal – often with an excess of as much as US$100 for a motorcycle and US$500 for a car (ie the customer pays the first US$100/500 of any claim). The more formal motorcycle and car-hire agencies may offer additional insurance to reduce the level of the excess, and cover damage to other people or their property, ie 'third-party' or 'liability' cover.

Especially with cars, the owner's main concern is insuring the vehicle. In some cases, a policy might cover the car for 30 million rupiah, but provide for only 10 million rupiah third-party cover. Your travel insurance may provide some additional protection, although liability for motor accidents is specifically excluded from many policies. The third-party cover might seem inadequate, but if you do cause damage or injury, it's usually enough for your consulate to get you out of jail.

A private owner renting a motorcycle may not offer any insurance at all. Ensure that your personal travel insurance covers injuries incurred while motorcycling. Some policies specifically exclude coverage for motorcycle riding, or have special conditions.

Road Conditions

Bali traffic can be horrendous in the south, around Denpasar and up to Ubud, and is usually quite heavy as far as Padangbai to the east and Tabanan to the west. Finding your way around the main tourist sites can be a challenge, as roads are only sometimes signposted and maps are often out of date. Off the main routes, roads can be rough, but they are usually surfaced – there are few dirt roads on Bali. Driving is most difficult in the large towns, where streets are congested, traffic can be awful, and one-way streets are infuriating.

CHARTERING A VEHICLE & DRIVER

An excellent way to travel anywhere around Bali is by chartered vehicle. It literally allows you to leave the driving and inherent frustrations to others. If you are part of a group it can make sound economic sense as well. This is also possible on Lombok but less common.

It's easy to arrange a charter: just listen for one of the frequent offers of 'transport?' in the streets around the tourist centres; approach a driver yourself; or ask at your hotel. Many car-hire places will also supply a driver as well.

Chartering a vehicle costs about 350,000Rp to 500,000Rp per day – although this depends greatly on the distance and, more importantly, your negotiating skills. Shorter times – say from Kuta to Ubud will cost less (one to two hours for about 100,000Rp). If you are planning to start early, finish late and cover an awful lot of territory, then you will have to pay more. Although a driver may reasonably ask for an advance for petrol, never pay the full fare until you have returned. For day trips, you will be expected to buy meals for the driver (*nasi campur* – rice with meat and vegetables – and water is standard), particularly if you stop to eat yourself. Tipping for a job well done is expected.

Drivers that hang around tourist spots and upmarket hotels will tend to charge more and are rarely interested in negotiating or bargaining. Beware of tactics like claiming you must hire the vehicle for a minimum of five hours, or assertions that your destination is 'very far' or that 'the roads are very rough'. Agree clearly on a route beforehand.

You can sometimes arrange to charter an entire bemo for your trip at a bemo terminal. The cost is about the same as for chartering a vehicle and you will enjoy the adventure of a bemo without the crowds – or chickens.

Roads in Lombok are often very rough but traffic is lighter than Bali.

Avoid driving at night or at dusk. Many bicycles, carts and horse-drawn vehicles do not have proper lights, and street lighting is limited.

POLICE

Police will stop drivers on some very slender pretexts, and it's fair to say that they're not motivated by a desire to enhance road safety. If a cop sees your front wheel half an inch over the faded line at a stop sign, if the chinstrap of your helmet isn't fastened, or if you don't observe one of the ever changing and poorly signposted one-way traffic restrictions, you may be waved down. They also do spot checks of licences and vehicle registrations, especially before major holiday periods. It's not uncommon to see cops stopping a line of visitors on motorcycles while locals fly past sans helmets.

The cop will ask to see your licence and the vehicle's registration papers, and he will also tell you what a serious offence you've committed. He may start talking about court appearances, heavy fines and long delays. Stay cool and don't argue. Don't offer him a bribe. Eventually he'll suggest that you can pay him some amount of money to deal with the matter. If it's a very large amount, tell him politely that you don't have that much. These matters can be settled for something between 10,000Rp and 60,000Rp; although it will be more like 100,000Rp if you don't have an IDP or if you argue. Always make sure you have the correct papers, and don't have too much visible cash in your wallet. If things deteriorate, ask for the cop's name and talk about contacting your consulate.

Road Rules

Visiting drivers commonly complain about crazy Balinese drivers, but often it's because the visitors don't understand the local conventions of road use. The following rules are very useful.

- Watch your front – it's your responsibility to avoid anything that gets in front of your vehicle. A car, motorcycle or anything else pulling out in front of you, in effect, has the right of way. Often drivers won't even look to see what's coming when they turn left at a junction – they listen for the horn.
- Use your horn to warn anything in front that you're there, especially if you're about to overtake.
- Drive on the left side of the road, although it's often a case of driving on whatever side of the road is available.

HITCHING

You can hitchhike in Bali and on Lombok, but it's not a very useful option for getting around, as public transport is so cheap and frequent and private vehicles are often full.

Bear in mind, also, that hitching is never entirely safe in any country. Travellers who decide to hitch should understand that they are taking a small but potentially serious risk.

LOCAL TRANSPORT

Dokar & Cidomo

Small *dokar* (pony carts) still provide local transport in some remote areas, and even in areas of Denpasar, but they're uncommon, extremely slow and are not particularly cheap. Prices start at 4000Rp per person for a short trip, but are negotiable, depending on demand, number of passengers, nearby competition, and your bargaining skills. The tourist price can be high if the driver thinks the tourist will pay big-time for the novelty value.

The pony cart used on Lombok is known as a *cidomo* – a contraction of *cika* (a traditional handcart), *dokar* and *mobil* (because car wheels and tyres are used). They are often brightly coloured and the horses decorated with coloured tassels and jingling bells. A typical *cidomo* has a narrow bench seat on either side. The ponies appear to some visitors to be heavily laden and harshly treated, but they are usually looked after reasonably well, if only because the owners depend on them for their livelihood. *Cidomo* are a very popular form of transport in many parts of Lombok, and often go to places that bemo don't, won't or can't.

Lombok fares are not set by the government. The price will always depend on demand, the number of passengers, the destination and your negotiating skills – maybe 2000Rp to 4000Rp per passenger for a short trip.

Ojek

Around some major towns, and along roads where bemo rarely or never venture, transport may be provided by an *ojek* (a motorcycle that takes a paying passenger). However, with increased vehicle ownership in Bali, *ojek* are becoming increasingly less common. They're OK on quiet country roads, but a high-risk option in the big towns. You will find them in remote places like Nusa Lembongan and Nusa Penida. *Ojek* are more common on Lombok.

Fares are negotiable, but about 8000Rp for 5km is fairly standard.

Taxi

BALI

Metered taxis are common in South Bali and Denpasar. They are essential for getting around Kuta and Seminyak, where you can easily flag one down. Elsewhere, they're often a lot less hassle than haggling with bemo jockeys and charter drivers.

The usual rate for a taxi is 5000Rp flag fall and 2000Rp per kilometre, but the rate is higher in the evening. If you phone for a taxi, the minimum charge is 10,000Rp. Any driver that claims meter problems or who won't use it should be avoided.

The most reputable taxi agency is **Bali Taxi** (☎ 0361-701111), which uses distinctive blue vehicles with the words 'Bluebird Group' over the windshield. Drivers speak reasonable English, won't offer you illicit opportunities and use the meter at all times. There's even a number to call with complaints (☎ 0361-701621).

After Bali Taxi, standards decline rapidly. Some are acceptable, although you may have a hassle getting the driver to use the meter after dark. Others may claim that their meters are often 'broken' or nonexistent, and negotiated fees can be over the odds (all the more reason to tip Bali Taxi drivers about 10%).

Taxis can be annoying with their constant honking to attract patrons. And men, especially single men, will find that some taxi drivers may promote a 'complete massage' at a 'spa'. Drivers will enthusiastically pantomime some of the activities that this entails. At the very least, insist that they keep their hands on the wheel.

LOMBOK

There are plenty of bemo and taxis around Mataram and Senggigi. In Lombok, **Lombok Taksi** (☎ 0370-627000), also owned by the Bluebird Group, always use the meter without you having to ask; they are the best choice. The only place where you would need to negotiate a taxi fare is if you get in a taxi at the harbour at Bangsal (but not on the main road in Pemenang). See the boxed text, p299 for more details.

TOURS

Many travellers end up taking one or two organised tours because it can be such a quick and convenient way to visit a few places in Bali, especially where public transport is limited (eg Pura Besakih) or nonexistent (eg Ulu Watu after sunset). All sorts of tours are available from the tourist centres – the top-end hotels can arrange expensive day tours for their guests, while tour companies along the main streets in the tourist centres advertise cheaper trips for those on a budget.

BOAT TOURS BETWEEN LOMBOK & FLORES

Travelling by sea between Lombok and Labuanbajo is a popular way to get to Flores, as you get to see far more of the region's spectacular coastline and dodge some seriously lengthy bus journeys and nonentity towns. Typical itineraries from Lombok take in snorkelling at Pulau Satonda off the coast of Sumbawa, a dragon-spotting hike in Komodo and other stops for swimming and partying along the way. From Labuanbajo, it's a similar story, but usually with stops at Rinca and Pulau Moyo.

However, be aware that this kind of trip is no luxury cruise – a lot depends on the boat, the crew and your fellow travellers, who you are stuck with for the duration. Some shifty operators have reneged on 'all-inclusive' agreements en route, and others operate decrepit old tugs without life jackets or radio. The seas in this part of Indonesia can be extremely hazardous, especially during rainy season when trips can be cancelled – and this journey is certainly not one to embark upon with some dodgy set-up.

Given these safety concerns, the well-organised tours on decent boats run by **Perama** (see Gili Trawangan, p305; Mataram, p290; or Senggigi, p298 for contact details) are recommended. Current charges for cabin/deck are 1.5 million rupiah/1.05 million rupiah for the three-day trip to Labuanbajo and one million/700,000Rp for the two-day Labuanbajo–Lombok journey.

LOMBOK ROAD DISTANCES (KM)

	Bangsal	Bayan	Kuta	Labuhan Lombok	Labuhanhaji	Lembar	Mataram	Pemenang	Praya	Pringgabaya	Sapit	Senaru	Senggigi	Tetebatu
Bangsal	---													
Bayan	57	---												
Kuta	86	143	---											
Labuhan Lombok	101	66	75	---										
Labuhanhaji	157	100	57	39	---									
Lembar	54	121	64	109	77	---								
Mataram	32	96	54	69	64	27	---							
Pemenang	1	56	79	109	105	53	26	---						
Praya	54	121	26	66	39	39	27	53	---					
Pringgabaya	102	74	83	8	26	102	75	101	62	---				
Sapit	106	47	101	25	43	120	92	119	80	18	---			
Senaru	54	102	140	68	106	116	86	63	117	81	54	---		
Senggigi	18	81	64	79	74	40	10	25	40	88	106	72	---	
Tetebatu	76	120	50	45	32	98	44	75	29	46	63	130	54	---

There is an extraordinarily wide range of prices for the same sorts of tours. The cheaper ones may have less comfortable vehicles, less-qualified guides and be less organised, but the savings can be considerable. Higher priced tours may include buffet lunch, English-speaking guides and air-con, but generally a higher price is no guarantee of higher quality. Some tours make long stops at craft shops, so you can buy things and the tour company can earn commissions for the tour operator. Tours are typically in eight- to 12-seat minibuses, which pick you up and drop you off.

Tours can be booked at the desk of any large hotel, but these will often be more expensive than a similar tour booked at a tour agency with the price in rupiah. If you can get together a group of four or more, most tour agencies will arrange a tour to suit you. It's much better to create your own tour and itinerary by chartering a vehicle.

Day Tours

The following are the usual tours sold around Bali. They are available from most hotels and shops selling services to tourists. Typically you will be picked up in the morning along with other travellers at nearby hotels. You may then go to a central area where you are re-distributed to the minibus doing *your* tour.

Prices can range from 20,000Rp to 100,000Rp even if standards seem similar, so it pays to shop around.

Bedugul Tour Includes Sangeh or Alas Kedaton, Mengwi, Jatiluwih, Candikuning and sunset at Tanah Lot.

Besakih Tour Includes craft shops at Celuk, Mas and Batuan, Gianyar, Semarapura (Klungkung), Pura Besakih, and return via Bukit Jambal.

Denpasar Tour Takes in the arts centre, markets, museum and perhaps a temple or two.

East Bali Tour Includes the usual craft shops, Semarapura (Klungkung), Kusamba, Goa Lawah, Candidasa and Tenganan.

Kintamani–Gunung Batur Tour Takes in the craft shops at Celuk, Mas and Batuan, a dance at Batubulan, Tampaksiring and views of Gunung Batur. Alternatively, the tour may go to Goa Gajah, Pejeng, Tampaksiring and Kintamani.

Singaraja–Lovina Tour Goes to Mengwi, Bedugul, Gitgit, Singaraja, Lovina, Banjar and Pupuan.

Sunset Tour Includes Mengwi, Marga, Alas Kedaton and the sunset at Tanah Lot.

Other Tours

There a number of Bali tour operators that offer tours that vary from the norm. Often these can be excellent ways to see things that are otherwise hard for a visitor to find such as religious ceremonies like cremations. Trips to remote areas or villages can be a fine way to see aspects of rural life in Bali. Many come with local guides who take joy in describing customs, how crops such as rice are grown and other details of day-to-day life.

Look to the following tour operators for more creative and inventive tours. Prices span the gamut but tend to be more expensive than the bog-standard tours aimed at tourists.

Bali Discovery Tours (☎ 0361-286283; www.balidiscovery.com) Offers numerous and customisable tours that differ from the norm. One visits a small rice-growing village in the west near Tabanan for hands-on demonstrations of cultivation.

JED (Village Ecotourism Network; ☎ 0361-735320; www.jed.or.id) Organises highly regarded tours of small villages, including coffee-growing Pelaga in the mountains, fruit-growing Sibetan in the east, seaweed farms on Nusa Ceningan and ancient Tenganan. You can make arrangements to stay with a family in the villages.

Suta Tours (☎ 0361-465249; www.sutatour.com) Arranges trips to see cremation ceremonies and special temple festivals; market tours and other custom plans.

Ubud Tourist Information (Map p188; ☎ 973285; Jl Raya Ubud; 8am-8pm) They organise simple yet effective cultural tours, especially around special religious events.

Waka Land Cruise (☎ 0361-426972; www.wakaexperience.com) Luxurious tours deep into rice terraces and tiny villages.

Lombok

Some companies organise day tours around Lombok from Bali, which cost US$100 or more and involve tearing through Senggigi and a few villages by minibus. A longer tour, with more time for sightseeing and relaxing, will be more expensive but more satisfying.

Tours originating on Lombok are based in Senggigi. You can usually book market visits in Mataram, a jaunt out to the Gilis or a trip down the south coast.

Health

Dr Trish Batchelor

CONTENTS

Treatment for minor injuries and common traveller's health problems is easily accessed in Bali and to a lesser degree on Lombok (see p285). But be aware that for serious conditions, you will need to leave the islands.

Travellers tend to worry about contracting infectious diseases when in the tropics, but infections are a rare cause of serious illness or death in travellers. Pre-existing medical conditions such as heart disease, and accidental injury (especially traffic accidents), account for most life-threatening problems. Becoming ill in some way, however, is relatively common. Fortunately most common illnesses can either be prevented with some common-sense behaviour or be treated easily with a well-stocked traveller's medical kit.

The following advice is a general guide only and does not replace the advice of a doctor trained in travel medicine.

BEFORE YOU GO

Make sure all medications are packed in their original, clearly labelled, containers. A signed and dated letter from your physician describing your medical conditions and medications (including generic names), is also a good idea. If you are carrying syringes or needles, be sure to have a physician's letter documenting their medical necessity. If you have a heart condition ensure you bring a copy of your electrocardiogram taken just prior to travelling.

If you happen to take any regular medication bring double your needs in case of loss or theft. In most Southeast Asian countries, excluding Singapore, you can buy many medications over the counter without a doctor's prescription, but it can be difficult to find some of the newer drugs, particularly the latest antidepressant drugs, blood pressure medications and contraceptive pills.

INSURANCE

Even if you are fit and healthy, don't travel without health insurance – accidents do happen. Declare any existing medical conditions you have – the insurance company will check if your problem is pre-existing and will not cover you if it is undeclared. You may require extra cover for adventure activities such as rock climbing. If your health insurance doesn't cover you for medical expenses abroad, consider getting extra insurance. If you're uninsured, emergency evacuation is expensive – bills of more than US$100,000 are not uncommon.

Find out in advance if your insurance plan will make payments directly to providers or reimburse you later for overseas health expenditures. (In many countries doctors expect payment in cash at the time of treatment.) Some policies offer lower and higher

HEALTH ADVISORIES

It's usually a good idea to consult your government's travel-health website before departure, if one is available:

Australia (www.smartraveller.gov.au)
Canada (www.phac-aspc.gc.ca/tmp-pmv/pub_e.html)
New Zealand (www.safetravel.govt.nz)
UK (www.dh.gov.uk/PolicyAndGuidance/HealthAdviceForTravellers/fs/en)
US (www.cdc.gov/travel/)

medical-expense options; the higher ones are chiefly for countries that have extremely high medical costs, such as the USA. You may prefer a policy that pays doctors or hospitals directly rather than you having to pay on the spot and claim later. If you have to claim later, make sure you keep all documentation. Some policies ask you to call back (reverse charges) to a centre in your home country where an immediate assessment of your problem is made.

RECOMMENDED VACCINATIONS

Specialised travel-medicine clinics are your best source of information; they stock all available vaccines and will be able to give specific recommendations for you and your trip. The doctors will take into account factors such as past vaccination history, the length of your trip, activities you may be undertaking and underlying medical conditions, such as pregnancy.

Most vaccines don't produce immunity until at least two weeks after they're given, so visit a doctor four to eight weeks before departure. Ask your doctor for an International Certificate of Vaccination (otherwise known as the yellow booklet), which will list all the vaccinations you've received.

The World Health Organization recommends the following vaccinations for travellers to Southeast Asia:

Adult diphtheria & tetanus Single booster recommended if none in the previous 10 years. Side effects include sore arm and fever.

Hepatitis A Provides almost 100% protection for up to a year, a booster after 12 months provides at least another 20 years protection. Mild side effects such as headache and sore arm occur in 5% to 10% of people.

Hepatitis B Now considered routine for most travellers. Given as three shots over six months. A rapid schedule is also available, as is a combined vaccination with Hepatitis A. Side effects are mild and uncommon, usually headache and sore arm. Lifetime protection occurs in 95% of people.

Measles, mumps & rubella (MMR) Two doses of MMR are required unless you have had the diseases. Occasionally a rash and flulike illness can develop a week after receiving the vaccine. Many young adults require a booster.

Polio In 2002, no countries in Southeast Asia reported cases of polio. Only one booster is required as an adult for lifetime protection. Inactivated polio vaccine is safe during pregnancy.

Typhoid Recommended unless your trip is less than a week and only to developed cities. The vaccine offers around 70% protection, lasts for two to three years and comes as a single shot. Tablets are also available, however the injection is usually recommended as it has fewer side effects. Sore arm and fever may occur.

Varicella If you haven't had chickenpox, discuss this vaccination with your doctor.

These immunisations are recommended for long-term travellers (more than one month) or those at special risk:

Japanese B Encephalitis Three injections in all. Booster recommended after two years. Sore arm and headache are the most common side effects. Rarely an allergic reaction comprising hives and swelling can occur up to 10 days after any of the three doses.

Meningitis Single injection. There are two types of vaccination: the quadrivalent vaccine gives two to three years protection; meningitis group C vaccine gives around 10 years protection. Recommended for long-term backpackers aged under 25.

Rabies Three injections in all. A booster after one year will then provide 10 years protection. Side effects are rare – occasionally headache and sore arm.

Tuberculosis (TB) A complex issue. Adult long-term travellers are usually recommended to have a TB skin test before and after travel, rather than vaccination. Only one vaccine given in a lifetime.

REQUIRED VACCINATIONS

The only vaccine required by international regulations is yellow fever. Proof of vaccination will only be required if you have visited a country in the yellow-fever zone within the six days prior to entering Southeast Asia. If you are travelling to Southeast Asia from Africa or South America you should check to see if you require proof of vaccination.

MEDICAL CHECKLIST

Recommended items for a personal medical kit:

- antifungal cream (eg clotrimazole)
- antibacterial cream (eg muciprocin)
- antibiotic for skin infections (eg amoxicillin/clavulanate or cephalexin)
- antibiotics for diarrhoea include norfloxacin or ciprofloxacin; for bacterial diarrhoea azithromycin; for giardiasis or amoebic dysentery tinidazole
- antihistamine – there are many options (eg cetirizine for daytime and promethazine for night)
- antiseptic (eg Betadine)
- antispasmodic for stomach cramps (eg buscopan)
- contraceptives
- decongestant (eg pseudoephedrine)

- DEET-based insect repellent
- diarrhoea treatment – consider an oral rehydration solution (eg Gastrolyte), diarrhoea 'stopper' (eg loperamide) and antinausea medication (eg prochlorperazine)
- first-aid items such as scissors, Elastoplasts, bandages, gauze, thermometer (but not mercury), sterile needles and syringes, safety pins and tweezers
- ibuprofen or another anti-inflammatory
- indigestion medication (eg Quick Eze or Mylanta)
- laxative (eg Coloxyl)
- migraine medication – take your personal medicine
- paracetamol
- steroid cream for allergic/itchy rashes (eg 1% to 2% hydrocortisone)
- sunscreen and hat
- throat lozenges
- thrush (vaginal yeast infection) treatment (eg clotrimazole pessaries or diflucan tablet)
- Ural or equivalent if you're prone to urine infections

INTERNET RESOURCES

There is a wealth of travel health advice on the internet. The **World Health Organization** (WHO; www.who.int/ith/) publishes a superb book called *International Travel & Health,* which is revised annually and is available online at no cost. Another website of general interest is **MD Travel Health** (www.mdtravelhealth.com), which provides travel health recommendations for every country. The **Centers for Disease Control & Prevention** (CDC; www.cdc.gov) website also has good general information. For further information, **LonelyPlanet.com** (www.lonelyplanet.com) is a good place to start. You can also check the websites of various foreign embassies in Indonesia (see p335).

FURTHER READING

Lonely Planet's *Healthy Travel – Asia & India* is a handy pocket-sized book that is packed with useful information including pretrip planning, emergency first aid, immunisation and disease information and what to do if you get sick on the road. Other recommended references include *Traveller's Health* by Dr Richard Dawood and *Travelling Well* by Dr Deborah Mills – check out the website (www.travellingwell.com.au).

IN TRANSIT

DEEP VEIN THROMBOSIS (DVT)

Deep vein thrombosis (DVT) occurs when blood clots form in the legs during plane flights, chiefly because of prolonged immobility. The longer the flight, the greater the risk. Although most blood clots are reabsorbed uneventfully, some may break off and travel through the blood vessels to the lungs, where they may cause life-threatening complications.

The chief symptom of DVT is swelling or pain of the foot, ankle, or calf, usually but not always on just one side. When a blood clot travels to the lungs, it may cause chest pain and difficulty in breathing. Travellers with any of these symptoms should immediately seek medical attention.

To prevent the development of DVT on long flights you should walk about the cabin, perform isometric compressions of the leg muscles (ie contract the leg muscles while sitting), drink plenty of fluids, and avoid alcohol and tobacco.

JET LAG & MOTION SICKNESS

Jet lag is common when crossing more than five time zones; it results in insomnia, fatigue, malaise or nausea. To avoid jet lag try drinking plenty of fluids (nonalcoholic) and eating light meals. Upon arrival, seek exposure to natural sunlight and re-adjust your schedule (for meals, sleep etc) as soon as possible.

Antihistamines such as dimenhydrinate (Dramamine) and meclizine (Antivert, Bonine) are usually the first choice for treating motion sickness. Their main side effect is drowsiness. A herbal alternative is ginger, which works like a charm for some people.

IN BALI & LOMBOK

AVAILABILITY & COST OF HEALTH CARE

Bali's best public hospitals are in Denpasar and Singaraja. In the first instance, foreigners would be best served in one of two private clinics that cater mainly to tourists and expats.

BIMC (Map p100; ☎ 761263; www.bimcbali.com; Jl Ngurah Rai 100X; 24hr) is on the bypass road just east of Kuta near the Bali Galleria and easily accessible from most of southern Bali. It's a modern Australian-run clinic that can do

DRINKING WATER

- Never drink tap water.
- Bottled water is generally safe – check the seal is intact at purchase.
- Avoid ice.
- Avoid fresh juices – they may have been watered down.
- Boiling water is the most efficient method of purifying it.
- The best chemical purifier is iodine. It should not be used by pregnant women or those people who suffer from thyroid problems.
- Water filters should also filter out viruses. Ensure your filter has a chemical barrier such as iodine and a small pore size, eg less than four microns.

tests, hotel visits and arrange medical evacuation. A basic consultation costs 600,000Rp.

International SOS (Map p100; ☎ 710505; www.sos-bali.com; Jl Ngurah Rai 505X; 24hr) is near BIMC and offers similar services at similar prices.

At both these places you should confirm that your health and/or travel insurance will cover you. In cases where your medical condition is considered serious you may well be evacuated by air ambulance to top-flight hospitals in Jakarta or Singapore. Here's where proper insurance is vital as these flights can cost more than US$10,000.

In Kuta, Nusa Dua and Ubud there are also locally owned clinics catering to tourists and just about any hotel can put you in touch with an English-speaking doctor.

In more remote areas, facilities are basic; generally a small public hospital, doctor's surgery or *puskesmas* (community health care centre). Specialist facilities for neurosurgery and heart surgery are nonexistent, and the range of available drugs (including painkillers) is limited. Travel insurance policies often have an emergency assistance phone number, which might be able to recommend a doctor or clinic, or use its contacts to find one in a remote area.

Health care is not free in Bali, and you will get more prompt attention if you can pay cash up-front for treatment, drugs, surgical equipment, drinking water, food and so on. Try to get receipts and paperwork so you can claim it all later on your travel insurance.

In government-run clinics and hospitals, services such as meals, washing and clean clothing are normally provided by the patient's family. If you are unfortunate enough to be on your own in a Bali hospital, contact your consulate – you need help.

The best hospital on Lombok is in Mataram, and there are more basic ones in Praya and Selong. There are pharmacies in the main towns and tourist centres, but the choice of medicines is limited.

Self-treatment may be appropriate if your problem is minor (eg traveller's diarrhoea), you are carrying the appropriate medication and you cannot attend a recommended clinic. If you think you may have a serious disease, especially malaria, do not waste time – travel to the nearest quality facility to receive attention. It is always better to be assessed by a doctor than to rely on self-treatment.

Outside of tourist centres, buying medication over the counter is not recommended, as fake medications and poorly stored or out-of-date drugs are common. Check with a large international hotel for a recommendation of a good local pharmacy.

INFECTIOUS DISEASES

Bird Flu

Otherwise known as Avian Influenza, the H5N1 had claimed more than 50 victims in Indonesia by mid-2006. Most of the cases have been in Java, west of Bali. The infection was not showing any signs of diminishing and treatment has proven to be very difficult. Travellers to Bali and Lombok – neither of which had had a confirmed case by mid-2006 – may wish to check the latest conditions before their journey. See Internet Resources (see opposite) for some good sources of current information.

Dengue Fever

This mosquito-borne disease is becomingly increasingly problematic throughout Southeast Asia, especially in the cities. As there is no vaccine available it can only be prevented by avoiding mosquito bites. The mosquito that carries dengue bites day and night, so use insect avoidance measures at all times. Symptoms include high fever, severe headache and body ache (dengue was previously known as 'breakbone fever'). Some people develop a rash and experience diarrhoea. The southern islands of Thailand are particularly high risk.

There is no specific treatment, just rest and paracetamol – do not take aspirin as it increases the likelihood of haemorrhaging. See a doctor to be diagnosed and monitored.

Hepatitis A

A problem throughout the region, this food- and waterborne virus infects the liver, causing jaundice (yellow skin and eyes), nausea and lethargy. There is no specific treatment for hepatitis A, you just need to allow time for the liver to heal. All travellers to Southeast Asia should be vaccinated against hepatitis A.

Hepatitis B

The only sexually transmitted disease that can be prevented by vaccination, hepatitis B is spread by body fluids, including sexual contact. In some parts of Southeast Asia up to 20% of the population are carriers of hepatitis B, and usually are unaware of this. The long-term consequences can include liver cancer and cirrhosis.

Hepatitis E

Hepatitis E is transmitted through contaminated food and water and has similar symptoms to hepatitis A, but is far less common. It is a severe problem in pregnant women and can result in the death of both mother and baby. There is currently no vaccine, and prevention is by following safe eating and drinking guidelines.

HIV

HIV is a major problem in many Asian countries, and Bali has one of the highest rates of HIV infection in Indonesia. Official HIV figures in Indonesia are unrealistically low and it's believed the incidence of the disease will increase significantly unless hospital procedures are improved and safe sex is promoted. The main risk for most travellers is sexual contact with locals, prostitutes and other travellers – in Indonesia the spread of HIV is primarily through heterosexual activity.

The risk of sexual transmission of the HIV virus can be dramatically reduced by the use of a *kondom* (condom). These are available from supermarkets, street stalls and drugstores in tourist areas, and from the *apotik* (pharmacy) in almost any town (from about 1500Rp to 3000Rp each – it's worth getting the more expensive brands).

Japanese B Encephalitis

While a rare disease in travellers, at least 50,000 locals are infected each year. This viral disease is transmitted by mosquitoes. Most cases occur in rural areas and vaccination is recommended for travellers spending more than one month outside of cities. There is no treatment, and one-third of infected people will die while another third will suffer permanent brain damage. Highest risk areas include Vietnam, Thailand and Indonesia.

Malaria

The risk of contracting malaria in Bali is extremely low, but Lombok is viewed as a malaria risk area. During and just after the wet season (October to March), there is a very low risk of malaria in northern Bali, and a slightly higher risk in far western Bali, particularly in and around Gilimanuk. So, if you are staying in budget accommodation anywhere outside of southern Bali, or trekking in northern or western Bali during, or just after, the rainy season, you should consider taking antimalarial drugs and seek medical advice about this. However, it is not currently considered necessary to take antimalarial drugs if you are sticking to the tourist centres in southern Bali, regardless of the season – but confirm this with your doctor prior to departure.

If you are going away from the main tourist areas (Senggigi, the Gilis) of Lombok, or further afield in Indonesia, you should take preventative measures, even though significant progress has been made in reducing the number of mosquitoes in Lombok, and therefore the risk of malaria and other insect-borne diseases. The risk is greatest in the wet months and in remote areas. The very serious Plasmodium falciparum strain causes cerebral malaria and may be resistant to many drugs.

For such a serious and potentially deadly disease, there is an enormous amount of misinformation concerning malaria. You must get expert advice as to whether your trip actually puts you at risk. Many parts of Southeast Asia, particularly city and resort areas, have minimal to no risk of malaria, and the risk of side effects from the tablets may outweigh the risk of getting the disease. For most rural areas, however, the risk of contracting the disease far outweighs the risk of any tablet side effects. Remember that malaria can be fatal. Before you travel, seek medical advice on the right medication and dosage for you.

Malaria is caused by a parasite transmitted by the bite of an infected mosquito. The most important symptom of malaria is fever, but general symptoms such as headache, diarrhoea, cough, or chills may also occur. Diagnosis can only be made by taking a blood sample.

Two strategies should be combined to prevent malaria – mosquito avoidance, and antimalarial medications. Most people who catch malaria are taking inadequate or no antimalarial medication.

Travellers are advised to prevent mosquito bites by taking these steps:

- Use a DEET-containing insect repellent on exposed skin. Wash this off at night, as long as you are sleeping under a mosquito net. Natural repellents such as Citronella can be effective, but must be applied more frequently than products containing DEET.
- Sleep under a mosquito net impregnated with Permethrin.
- Choose accommodation with screens and fans (if not air-conditioned).
- Impregnate clothing with Permethrin in high-risk areas.
- Wear long sleeves and trousers in light colours.
- Use mosquito coils.
- Spray your room with insect repellent before going out for your evening meal.

There are a variety of medications available:

Artesunate Derivatives of Artesunate are not suitable as a preventive medication. They are useful treatments under medical supervision.

Chloroquine & Paludrine The effectiveness of this combination is now limited in most of Southeast Asia. Common side effects include nausea (40% of people) and mouth ulcers. Generally not recommended.

Doxycycline This daily tablet is a broad-spectrum antibiotic that has the added benefit of helping to prevent a variety of tropical diseases, including leptospirosis, tick-borne disease, typhus and melioidosis. The potential side effects include photosensitivity (a tendency to sunburn), thrush in women, indigestion, heartburn, nausea and interference with the contraceptive pill. More serious side effects include ulceration of the oesophagus – you can help prevent this by taking your tablet with a meal and a large glass of water, and never lying down within half an hour of taking it. Must be taken for four weeks after leaving the risk area.

Lariam (Mefloquine) Lariam has received much bad press, some of it justified, some not. This weekly tablet suits many people. Serious side effects are rare but include depression, anxiety, psychosis and having fits. Anyone with a history of depression, anxiety, other psychological disorder, or epilepsy should not take Lariam. It is considered safe in the second and third trimesters of pregnancy. It is around 90% effective in most parts of Southeast Asia, but there is significant resistance in parts of northern Thailand, Laos and Cambodia. Tablets must be taken for four weeks after leaving the risk area.

Malarone This new drug is a combination of Atovaquone and Proguanil. Side effects are uncommon and mild, most commonly nausea and headache. It is the best tablet for scuba divers and for those on short trips to high-risk areas. It must be taken for one week after leaving the risk area.

A final option is to take no preventive medication but to have a supply of emergency medication should you develop the symptoms of malaria. This is less than ideal, and you'll need to get to a good medical facility within 24 hours of developing a fever. If you choose this option the most effective and safest treatment is Malarone (four tablets once daily for three days). Other options include Mefloquine and Quinine but the side effects of these drugs at treatment doses make them less desirable. Fansidar is no longer recommended.

Rabies

Still a common problem in most parts of Southeast Asia. Rabies is a uniformly fatal disease spread by the bite or lick of an infected animal – most commonly a dog or monkey. You should seek medical advice immediately after any animal bite and commence post-exposure treatment. Having pretravel vaccination means the postbite treatment is greatly simplified. If an animal bites you, gently wash the wound with soap and water, and apply an iodine-based antiseptic. If you are not pre-vaccinated you will need to receive rabies immunoglobulin as soon as possible.

STDs

Sexually transmitted diseases most common in Southeast Asia include herpes, warts, syphilis, gonorrhoea and chlamydia. People carrying these diseases often have no signs of infection. Condoms will prevent gonorrhoea and chlamydia but not warts or herpes. If after a sexual encounter you develop any rash, lumps, discharge or pain when passing urine seek immediate medical attention. If you have been sexually active during your travels have an STD check on your return home.

Tuberculosis

While rare in travellers, medical and aid workers and long-term travellers who have significant contact with the local population should take precautions. Vaccination is usually only given to children under the age of five, but adults at risk are recommended pre- and post-travel TB testing. The main symptoms are fever, cough, weight loss, night sweats and tiredness.

Typhoid

This serious bacterial infection is also spread via food and water. It gives a high and slowly progressive fever, headache and may be accompanied by a dry cough and stomach pain. It is diagnosed by blood tests and treated with antibiotics. Vaccination is recommended for all travellers spending more than a week in Southeast Asia, or travelling outside of the major cities. Be aware that vaccination is not 100% effective so you must still be careful with what you eat and drink.

Typhus

Murine typhus is spread by the bite of a flea whereas scrub typhus is spread via a mite. These diseases are rare in travellers. Symptoms include fever, muscle pains and a rash. You can avoid these diseases by following general insect-avoidance measures. Doxycycline will also prevent them.

TRAVELLER'S DIARRHOEA

Traveller's diarrhoea is by far the most common problem affecting travellers – between 30% and 50% of people will suffer from it within two weeks of starting their trip. In over 80% of cases, traveller's diarrhoea is caused by bacteria (there are numerous potential culprits), and therefore responds promptly to treatment with antibiotics. Treatment with antibiotics will depend on your situation – how sick you are, how quickly you need to get better, where you are etc.

Traveller's diarrhoea is defined as the passage of more than three watery bowel-actions within 24 hours, plus at least one other symptom such as fever, cramps, nausea, vomiting or feeling generally unwell.

Treatment consists of staying well-hydrated; rehydration solutions such as Gastrolyte are the best for this. Antibiotics such as Norfloxacin, Ciprofloxacin or Azithromycin will kill the bacteria quickly.

Loperamide is just a 'stopper' and doesn't get to the cause of the problem. It can be helpful, for example if you have to go on a long bus ride. Don't take Loperamide if you have a fever, or blood in your stools. Seek medical attention quickly if you do not respond to an appropriate antibiotic.

Amoebic Dysentery

Amoebic dysentery is very rare in travellers but is often misdiagnosed by poor quality labs in Southeast Asia. Symptoms are similar to bacterial diarrhoea, ie fever, bloody diarrhoea and generally feeling unwell. You should always seek reliable medical care if you have blood in your diarrhoea. Treatment involves two drugs; Tinidazole or Metroniadzole to kill the parasite in your gut and then a second drug to kill the cysts. If left untreated complications such as liver or gut abscesses can occur.

Giardiasis

Giardia lamblia is a parasite that is relatively common in travellers. Symptoms include nausea, bloating, excess gas, fatigue and intermittent diarrhoea. 'Eggy' burps are often attributed solely to giardiasis, but work in Nepal has shown that they are not specific to this infection. The parasite will eventually go away if left untreated but this can take months. The treatment of choice is Tinidazole, with Metronidazole being a second-line option.

ENVIRONMENTAL HAZARDS

Diving

Divers and surfers should seek specialised advice before they travel to ensure their medical kit contains treatment for coral cuts and tropical ear infections, as well as the standard problems. Divers should ensure their insurance covers them for decompression illness – get specialised dive insurance through an organisation such as **Divers Alert Network** (DAN; www.danseap.org). Have a dive medical before you leave your home country – there are certain medical conditions that are incompatible with diving and economic considerations may override health considerations for some dive operators in Southeast Asia.

Food

Eating in restaurants is the biggest risk factor for contracting traveller's diarrhoea. Ways to avoid it include eating only freshly cooked food, avoiding shellfish and food that has been sitting around in buffets. Peel all fruit, cook vegetables, and soak salads in iodine water for at least 20 minutes. Eat in busy restaurants with a high turnover of customers.

Heat

Many parts of Southeast Asia are hot and humid throughout the year. For most people it takes at least two weeks to adapt to the hot climate. Swelling of the feet and ankles is common, as are muscle cramps caused by excessive sweating. Prevent these by avoiding dehydration and excessive activity in the heat. Take it easy when you first arrive. Don't eat salt tablets (they aggravate the gut) but drinking rehydration solution or eating salty food helps. Treat cramps by stopping activity, resting, rehydrating with double-strength rehydration solution and gently stretching.

Dehydration is the main contributor to heat exhaustion. Symptoms include feeling weak, headache, irritability, nausea or vomiting, sweaty skin, a fast, weak pulse and a normal or slightly elevated body temperature. Treatment involves getting out of the heat and/or sun, fanning the victim and applying cool wet cloths to the skin, laying the victim flat with their legs raised and rehydrating with water containing one-quarter of a teaspoon of salt per litre. Recovery is usually rapid and it is common to feel weak for some days afterwards.

Heat stroke is a serious medical emergency. Symptoms come on suddenly and include weakness, nausea, a hot dry body with a body temperature of over 41°C, dizziness, confusion, loss of coordination, fits and eventually collapse and loss of consciousness. Seek medical help and commence cooling by getting the person out of the heat, removing their clothes, fanning them and applying cool wet cloths or ice to their body, especially to the groin and armpits.

Prickly heat is a common skin rash in the tropics, caused by sweat being trapped under the skin. The result is an itchy rash of tiny lumps. Treat by moving out of the heat and into an air-conditioned area for a few hours and by having cool showers. Creams and ointments clog the skin so they should be avoided. Locally bought prickly-heat powder can be helpful.

Tropical fatigue is common in long-term expats based in the tropics. It's rarely due to disease and is caused by the climate, inadequate mental rest, excessive alcohol intake and the demands of daily work in a different culture.

Insect Bites & Stings

Bedbugs don't carry disease but their bites are very itchy. They live in the cracks of furniture and walls and then migrate to the bed at night to feed on you. You can treat the itch with an antihistamine. Lice inhabit various parts of your body but most commonly your head and pubic area. Transmission is via close contact with an infected person. They can be difficult to treat and you may need numerous applications of an antilice shampoo such as Permethrin. Pubic lice are usually contracted from sexual contact.

Ticks are contracted after walking in rural areas. Ticks are commonly found behind the ears, on the belly and in armpits. If you have had a tick bite and experience symptoms such as a rash at the site of the bite or elsewhere, fever, or muscle aches you should see a doctor. Doxycycline prevents tick-borne diseases.

Leeches are found in humid rainforest areas. They do not transmit any disease but their bites are often intensely itchy for weeks afterwards and can easily become infected. Apply an iodine-based antiseptic to any leech bite to help prevent infection.

Bee and wasp stings mainly cause problems for people who are allergic to them. Anyone with a serious bee or wasp allergy should carry an injection of adrenaline (eg an Epipen) for emergency treatment. For others pain is the main problem – apply ice to the sting and take painkillers.

Most jellyfish in Southeast Asian waters are not dangerous, just irritating. Some jellyfish, including the Portuguese man-of-war, occur on the north coast of Bali, especially in July and August, and also between the Gili Islands and Lombok. The sting is extremely painful but rarely fatal. First aid for jellyfish stings involves pouring vinegar onto the affected area to neutralise the poison. Do not rub sand or water onto the stings. Take painkillers, and anyone who feels ill in any way after being stung should seek medical advice. Take local advice if there are dangerous jellyfish around and keep out of the water.

Parasites

Numerous parasites are common in local populations in Southeast Asia; however, most of these are rare in travellers. The two rules to follow if you wish to avoid parasitic infections are to wear shoes and to avoid eating raw food, especially fish, pork and vegetables.

A number of parasites are transmitted via the skin by walking barefoot including strongyloides, hookworm and cutaneous *larva migrans*.

Skin Problems

Fungal rashes are common in humid climates. There are two common fungal rashes that affect travellers. The first occurs in moist areas that get less air such as the groin, armpits and between the toes. It starts as a red patch that slowly spreads and is usually itchy. Treatment involves keeping the skin dry, avoiding chafing and using an antifungal cream such as Clotrimazole or Lamisil. *Tinea versicolor* is also common – this fungus causes small, light-coloured patches, most commonly on the back, chest and shoulders. Consult a doctor.

Cuts and scratches become easily infected in humid climates. Take meticulous care of any cuts and scratches to prevent complications such as abscesses. Immediately wash all wounds in clean water and apply antiseptic. If you develop signs of infection (increasing pain and redness) see a doctor. Divers and surfers should be particularly careful with coral cuts as they become easily infected.

Snakes

Southeast Asia is home to many species of both poisonous and harmless snakes. Although you are unlikely to run into snakes in Bali or on Lombok (you may come across the black-and-white stripy sea snakes on Lombok), assume all snakes are poisonous and never touch one.

Sunburn

Even on a cloudy day sunburn can occur rapidly. Always use a strong sunscreen (at least factor 30), making sure to reapply after a swim, and always wear a wide-brimmed hat and sunglasses outdoors. Avoid lying in the sun during the hottest part of the day (10am to 2pm). If you become sunburnt stay out of the sun until you have recovered, apply cool compresses and take painkillers for the discomfort. One per cent hydrocortisone cream applied twice daily is also helpful.

WOMEN'S HEALTH

Pregnant women should receive specialised advice before travelling. The ideal time to travel is in the second trimester (between 16 and 28 weeks), when the risk of pregnancy-related problems are at their lowest and pregnant women generally feel at their best. During the first trimester there is a risk of miscarriage and in the third trimester complications such as premature labour and high blood pressure are possible. It's wise to travel with a companion. Always carry a list of quality medical facilities available at your destination and ensure you continue your standard antenatal care at these facilities. Avoid rural travel in areas with poor transportation and medical facilities. Most of all, ensure travel insurance covers all pregnancy-related possibilities, including premature labour.

Malaria is a high-risk disease in pregnancy. The WHO recommends that pregnant women do *not* travel to areas with Chloroquine-resistant malaria. None of the more effective antimalarial drugs are completely safe in pregnancy.

Traveller's diarrhoea can quickly lead to dehydration and result in inadequate blood flow to the placenta. Many of the drugs used to treat various diarrhoea bugs are not recommended in pregnancy. Azithromycin is considered safe.

In the tourist areas of Bali, supplies of sanitary products and brands that are familiar are readily available. On Lombok the major brand sanitary towels are not a problem to get hold of and are reasonably priced. Tampons, however, are like gold dust, they are hard to find and super expensive! Try and bring you own from home or stock up on them in Hero supermarket in Mataram or in the supermarkets in Senggigi. Tampax and Lillets are available.

Birth-control options may be limited so bring adequate supplies of your own form of contraception.

Heat, humidity and antibiotics can all contribute to thrush. Treatments are antifungal creams and pessaries such as Clotrimazole. An alternative is a tablet of fluconazole (Diflucan). Urinary tract infections can be precipitated by dehydration or long journeys without toilet stops; bring suitable antibiotics.

Language

CONTENTS

WHO SPEAKS WHAT WHERE?

Bali

The indigenous language, Bahasa Bali, has various forms based on traditional caste distinctions. The average traveller needn't worry about learning Balinese, but it can be fun to learn a few words. For practical purposes, it probably makes better sense to concentrate your efforts on learning Bahasa Indonesia.

Bahasa Indonesia is the national language, used in the education system and for all legal and administrative purposes. It's becoming more and more widely used, partly because of its official language status and partly because it serves as a lingua franca (a linking language), allowing the many non-Balinese now living and working in Bali to communicate – and avoid the intricacies of the caste system inherent in Bahasa Bali.

A good phrasebook is a wise investment. Lonely Planet's *Indonesian Phrasebook* is a handy, pocket-sized introduction to the language. The *Bali Pocket Dictionary* can be found at a few bookshops in Bali. It lists grammar and vocabulary in English, Indonesian, and low, polite and high Balinese.

English is common in the tourist areas, and is usually spoken very well. Many Balinese in the tourist industry also have a smattering (or more) of German, Japanese, French and/or Italian. A few older people speak Dutch and are often keen to practise it, but if you want to travel in remote areas, and communicate with people who aren't in the tourist business, it's a good idea to learn some Bahasa Indonesia.

Lombok

Most people on Lombok speak their own indigenous language (Sasak) and Bahasa Indonesia, which they are taught at school and use as their formal and official mode of communication. Apart from those working in the tourist industry, few people on Lombok speak English, and this includes police and other officials. English is becoming more widely spoken, but is still rare outside the main towns and tourist centres.

BAHASA BALI

The national language of Indonesia, Bahasa Indonesia, is widely used in Bali, but it isn't Balinese. Balinese, or Bahasa Bali, is another language entirely. It has a completely different vocabulary and grammar, and the rules governing its use are much more complex. It's a difficult language for a foreigner to come to grips with. Firstly, it isn't a written language, so there's no definitive guide to its grammar or vocabulary, and there is considerable variation in usage from one part of the island to another. Bahasa Bali isn't taught in schools either, and dictionaries and grammars that do exist are attempts to document current or historical usage, rather than set down rules for correct syntax or pronunciation.

Balinese is greatly complicated by its caste influences. In effect, different vocabularies and grammatical structures are used, depending on the relative social position of the speaker, the person being spoken to and the person being spoken about. Even traditional usage has always been somewhat arbitrary, because of the intricacies of the caste system.

The various forms of the language (or languages) and their respective uses are categorised as follows:

- Basa Alus is used among educated people, and is derived from the Hindu-Javanese court languages of the 10th century.
- Basa Lumrah (also called Biasa or Ketah) is used when talking to people of the same caste or level, and between friends and family. It is an old language of mixed origin, with words drawn from Malayan, Polynesian and Australasian sources.
- Basa Madia (also called Midah), a mixture of Basa Lumrah and Basa Alus, is used as a polite language for speaking to or about strangers, or people to whom one wishes to show respect.
- Basa Singgih, virtually a separate language, is used to address persons of high caste, particularly in formal and religious contexts. Even the Balinese are not always fluent in this language. It is based on the ancient Hindu Kawi language, and can be written using a script that resembles Sanskrit, as seen in the *lontar* (palm) books where it's inscribed on strips of leaf (see the boxed text on p45). Written Basa Singgih is also seen on the signs that welcome you to, and farewell you from, most villages in Bali.
- Basa Sor (also called Rendah) is used when talking with people of a lower caste, or to people who are noncaste.

The different vocabularies only exist for about 1000 basic words, mostly relating to people and their actions. Other words (in fact, an increasing proportion of the modern vocabulary), are the same regardless of relative caste levels.

Usage is also changing with the decline of the traditional caste system and modern tendencies towards democratisation and social equality. It is now common practice to describe the language in terms of only three forms:

- Low Balinese (Ia), equivalent to Basa Lumrah, is used between friends and family, and also when speaking with persons of equal or lower caste, or about oneself.
- Polite Balinese (Ipun), the equivalent of Basa Madia, is used for speaking to superiors or strangers, and is becoming more widespread as a sort of common language that isn't so closely linked to caste.
- High Balinese (Ida), a mixture of Basa Alus and Basa Singgih, is used to indicate respect for the person being addressed or the person being spoken about.

The polite and high forms of the language frequently use the same word, while the low form often uses the same word as Bahasa Indonesia. The polite form, Basa Madia or Midah, is being used as a more egalitarian language, often combined with Bahasa Indonesia to avoid the risk of embarrassment in case the correct caste distinctions aren't made.

So how does one Balinese know at which level to address another? Initially, a conversation between two strangers would commence in the high language. At some point the question of caste would be asked and then the level adjusted accordingly. Among friends, however, a conversation is likely to be carried on in low Balinese, no matter what the caste of the speakers may be.

Bahasa Bali uses very few greetings and civilities on an everyday basis. There are no equivalents for 'please' and 'thank you'. Nor is there a usage that translates as 'good morning' or 'good evening', although the low Balinese *kenken kebara?* (how are you?/how's it going?) is sometimes used. More common is *lunga kija?*, which literally means 'where are you going?' (in low, polite and high Balinese).

BAHASA INDONESIA

Like most languages, Indonesian has a simplified colloquial form and a more developed literary form. It's among the easiest of all spoken languages to learn – there are no tenses, plurals or genders and, even better, it's easy to pronounce.

Apart from ease of learning, there's another very good reason for trying to pick up at least a handful of Indonesian words and phrases: few people are as delighted with visitors learning their language as Indonesians. They won't criticise you if you mangle your pronunciation or tangle your grammar and they make you feel like you're an expert even if you only know a dozen or so words. Bargaining also seems a whole lot easier and more natural when you do it in their language.

Written Indonesian can be idiosyncratic, however, and there are often inconsistent spellings of place names. Compound names are written as one word or two, eg Airsanih or Air Sanih, Padangbai or Padang Bai. Words starting with 'Ker' sometimes lose the 'e', as in Kerobokan/Krobokan.

In addition, some Dutch variant spellings remain in common use. These tend to occur in business names, with 'tj' instead of the modern **c** (as in Tjampuhan/Campuan), and 'oe' instead of the **u** (as in Soekarno/Sukarno).

PRONUNCIATION

Most letters have a pronunciation more or less the same as their English counterparts. Nearly all the syllables carry equal emphasis, but a good approximation is to stress the second to last syllable. The main exception to the rule is the unstressed **e** in words such as *besar* (big), pronounced 'be-sarr'.

a	as in 'father'
e	as in 'bet' when unstressed, although sometimes it's hardly pronounced at all, as in the greeting *selamat*, which sounds like 'slamat' if said quickly. When stressed, **e** is like the 'a' in 'may', as in *becak* (rickshaw), pronounced 'baycha'. There's no set rule as to when **e** is stressed or unstressed.
i	as in 'unique'
o	as in 'hot'
u	as in 'put'
ai	as in 'Thai'
au	as the 'ow' in 'cow'
ua	as 'w' when at the start of a word, eg *uang* (money), pronounced 'wong'
c	as the 'ch' in 'chair'
g	as in 'get'
ng	as the 'ng' in 'sing'
ngg	as the 'ng' in 'anger'
j	as in 'jet'
r	slightly rolled
h	a little stronger than the 'h' in 'her'; almost silent at the end of a word
k	like English 'k', except at the end of a word when it's like a closing of the throat with no sound released, eg *tidak* (no/not), pronounced 'tee-da'
ny	as the 'ny' in canyon

ACCOMMODATION

I'm looking for a ...	*Saya mencari ...*
campground	*tempat kemah*
guesthouse	*rumah yang disewakan*
hotel	*hotel*
youth hostel	*losmen pemuda*

MAKING A RESERVATION

(for written and phone inquiries)

I'd like to book ...	*Saya mau pesan ...*
in the name of ...	*atas nama ...*
date	*tanggal*
from ... (date)	*dari ...*
to ... (date)	*sampai ...*
credit card	*kartu kredit*
number	*nomor*
expiry date	*masa berlakunya sampai*
Please confirm availability and price.	*Tolong dikonfirmasi mengenai ketersediaan kamar dan harga.*

Where is a cheap hotel?
Hotel yang murah di mana?
What is the address?
Alamatnya di mana?
Could you write it down, please?
Anda bisa tolong tuliskan?
Do you have any rooms available?
Ada kamar kosong?

How much is it ... ?	*Berapa harganya ... ?*
per day	*sehari*
per person	*seorang*
one night	*satu malam*
one person	*satu orang*
room	*kamar*
bathroom	*kamar mandi*
I'd like a ...	*Saya cari ...*
bed	*tempat tidur*
single room	*kamar untuk seorang*
double bedroom	*tempat tidur besar satu kamar*
room with two beds	*kamar dengan dua tempat tidur*
room with a bathroom	*kamar dengan kamar mandi*
I'd like to share a dorm.	*Saya mau satu tempat tidur di asrama.*

Is breakfast included?	*Apakah harganya termasuk makan pagi/sarapan?*
May I see it?	*Boleh saya lihat?*
Where is the bathroom?	*Kamar mandi di mana?*
Where is the toilet?	*Kamar kecil di mana?*
I'm/we're leaving today.	*Saya/Kami berangkat hari ini.*

CONVERSATION & ESSENTIALS

Addressing People

Pronouns, particularly 'you', are rarely used in Indonesian. When speaking to an older man (or anyone old enough to be a father), it's common to call them *bapak* (father) or simply *pak*. Similarly, an older woman is *ibu* (mother) or simply *bu*. *Tuan* is a respectful term for a man, like 'sir'. *Nyonya* is the equivalent for a married woman, and *nona* for an unmarried woman. *Anda* is the egalitarian form designed to overcome the plethora of words for the second person.

To indicate negation, *tidak* is used with verbs, adjectives and adverbs; *bukan* with nouns and pronouns.

Welcome.	*Selamat datang.*
Good morning.	*Selamat pagi.* (before 11am)
Good day.	*Selamat siang.* (noon to 2pm)
Good day.	*Selamat sore.* (3pm to 6pm)
Good evening.	*Selamat malam.* (after dark)
Good night.	*Selamat tidur.* (to someone going to bed)
Goodbye.	*Selamat tinggal.* (to person staying)
Goodbye.	*Selamat jalan.* (to person leaving)
Yes.	*Ya.*
No. (not)	*Tidak.*
No. (negative)	*Bukan.*
Maybe.	*Mungkin.*
Please.	*Tolong.* (asking for help)
Please.	*Silahkan.* (giving permission)
Thank you (very much).	*Terima kasih (banyak).*
You're welcome.	*Kembali.*
Sorry.	*Maaf.*
Excuse me.	*Permisi.*
Just a minute.	*Tunggu sebentar*
How are you?	*Apa kabar?*
I'm fine.	*Kabar baik.*
What's your name?	*Siapa nama Anda?*
My name is ...	*Nama saya ...*
Are you married?	*Sudah kawin?*
Not yet.	*Belum.*
How old are you?	*Berapa umur Anda?*
I'm ... years old.	*Umur saya ... tahun.*
Where are you from?	*Anda dari mana?*
I'm from ...	*Saya dari ...*
I like ...	*Saya suka ...*
I don't like ...	*Saya tidak suka ...*
Good.	*Bagus.*
Good, fine, OK.	*Baik.*

LANGUAGE

DIRECTIONS

Where is ...?	*Di mana ...?*
How many kilometres?	*Berapa kilometer?*
Which way?	*Ke mana?*
Go straight ahead.	*Jalan terus.*
Turn left/right.	*Belok kiri/kanan.*
Stop!	*Berhenti!*
at the corner	*di sudut*
at the traffic lights	*di lampu merah*
here/there/over there	*di sini/situ/sana*
behind	*di belakang*
in front of	*di depan*
opposite	*di seberang*
far (from)	*jauh (dari)*
near (to)	*dekat (dengan)*
north	*utara*
south	*selatan*
east	*timur*
west	*barat*
beach	*pantai*
island	*pulau*
lake	*danau*
main square	*alun-alun*
market	*pasar*
sea	*laut*

SIGNS

Masuk	Entrance
Keluar	Exit
Informasi	Information
Buka	Open
Tutup	Closed
Dilarang	Prohibited
Ada Kamar Kosong	Rooms Available
Penuh (Tidak Ada Kamar Kosong)	Full (No Vacancies)
Polisi	Police
Kamar Kecil/Toilet	Toilets/WC
Pria	Men
Wanitai	Women

EMERGENCIES

Help!	*Tolong saya!*
There's been an accident!	*Ada kecelakaan!*
I'm lost.	*Saya tersesat.*
Leave me alone!	*Jangan ganggu saya!*
Call ...!	*Panggil ...!*
a doctor	*dokter*
the police	*polisi*

HEALTH

I'm ill.	*Saya sakit.*
It hurts here.	*Sakitnya di sini.*
I'm ...	*Saya sakit...*
asthmatic	*asma*
diabetic	*kencing manis*
epileptic	*epilepsi*
I'm allergic to ...	*Saya alergi...*
antibiotics	*antibiotik*
aspirin	*aspirin*
penicillin	*penisilin*
bees	*tawon/kumbang*
nuts	*kacang*
antiseptic	*penangkal infeksi/antiseptik*
condoms	*kondom*
contraceptive	*kontrasepsi*
diarrhoea	*mencret/diare*
medicine	*obat*
nausea	*mual*
sunblock cream	*sunscreen/tabir surya/sunblock*
tampons	*tampon*

LANGUAGE DIFFICULTIES

I (don't) understand.
Saya (tidak) mengerti.
Do you speak English?
Bisa berbicara Bahasa Inggris?
Does anyone here speak English?
Ada yang bisa berbicara Bahasa Inggris di sini?
How do you say ... in Indonesian?
Bagaimana mengatakan ... dalam Bahasa Indonesia?
What does ... mean?
Apa artinya ...?
I can only speak a little (Indonesian).
Saya hanya bisa berbicara (Bahasa Indonesia) sedikit.
Please write that word down.
Tolong tuliskan kata itu.
Can you show me (on the map)?
Anda bisa tolong tunjukkan pada saya (di peta)?

NUMBERS

1	*satu*
2	*dua*
3	*tiga*
4	*empat*
5	*lima*
6	*enam*
7	*tujuh*
8	*delapan*
9	*sembilan*
10	*sepuluh*

A half is *setengah,* which is pronounced 'stenger', eg *stenger kilo* (half a kilo). 'Approximately' is *kira-kira*. After the numbers one to 10, the 'teens' are *belas,* the 'tens' are *puluh,* the 'hundreds' are *ratus,* the 'thousands' are *ribu* and 'millions' are *juta* – but as a prefix *satu* (one) becomes *se-*, eg *seratus* (one hundred). Thus:

11	*sebelas*
12	*duabelas*
13	*tigabelas*
20	*dua puluh*
21	*dua puluh satu*
25	*dua puluh lima*
30	*tiga puluh*
99	*sembilan puluh sembilan*
100	*seratus*
150	*seratus limapuluh*
200	*dua ratus*
888	*delapan ratus delapan puluh delapan*
1000	*seribu*

PAPERWORK

name	*nama*
nationality	*kebangsaan*
date of birth	*tanggal kelahiran*
place of birth	*tempat kelahiran*
sex/gender	*jenis kelamin*
passport	*paspor*
visa	*visa*

QUESTION WORDS

Who?	*Siapa?*
What?	*Apa?*
What is it?	*Apa itu?*
When?	*Kapan?*
Where?	*Di mana?*
Which?	*Yang mana?*
Why?	*Kenapa?*
How?	*Bagaimana?*

SHOPPING & SERVICES

What is this?	*Apa ini?*
How much is it?	*Berapa (harganya)?*
I'd like to buy ...	*Saya mau beli ...*
I don't like it.	*Saya tidak suka.*
May I look at it?	*Boleh saya lihat?*
I'm just looking.	*Saya lihat-lihat saja.*
I'll take it.	*Saya beli.*
this/that	*ini/itu*
big	*besar*
small	*kecil*
more	*lebih*
less	*kurang*
bigger	*lebih besar*
smaller	*lebih keci*
expensive	*mahal*
another/one more	*satu lagi*
Do you accept ...?	*Bisa bayar pakai ...?*
credit cards	*kartu kredit*
travellers cheques	*cek perjalanan*
What time does it open/close?	*Jam berapa buka/tutup?*
May I take photos?	*Boleh saya potret?*
I'm looking for a/the ...	*Saya cari ...*
bank	*bank*
church	*gereja*
city centre	*pusat kota*
embassy	*kedutaan*
food stall	*warung*
hospital	*rumah sakit*
market	*pasar*
museum	*museum*
police	*kantor polisi*
post office	*kantor pos*
public phone	*telepon umum*
public toilet	*WC* ('way say') *umum*
restaurant	*rumah makan*
telephone centre	*wartel*
tourist office	*kantor pariwisata*

TIME & DATES

What time is it?	*Jam berapa sekarang?*
When?	*Kapan?*
What time?	*Jam berapa?*
seven o'clock	*jam tujuh*
How many hours?	*Berapa jam?*
five hours	*lima jam*
in the morning	*pagi*
in the afternoon	*siang*
in the evening	*malam*
today	*hari ini*
tomorrow	*besok*
yesterday	*kemarin*
hour	*jam*
day	*hari*
week	*minggu*
month	*bulan*
year	*tahun*
Monday	*hari Senin*
Tuesday	*hari Selasa*
Wednesday	*hari Rabu*
Thursday	*hari Kamis*
Friday	*hari Jumat*
Saturday	*hari Sabtu*
Sunday	*hari Minggu*
January	*Januari*
February	*Februari*
March	*Maret*
April	*April*
May	*Mei*
June	*Juni*
July	*Juli*
August	*Agustus*
September	*September*
October	*Oktober*
November	*Nopember*
December	*Desember*

TRANSPORT
Public Transport

What time does the ... leave/arrive?	*Jam berapa ... berangkat/datang?*
boat/ship	*kapal*
bus	*bis*
plane	*kapal terbang*
I'd like a ... ticket.	*Saya mau tiket ...*
one-way	*sekali jalan*
return	*pulang pergi*
1st class	*kelas satu*
2nd class	*kelas dua*
I want to go to ...	*Saya mau ke ...*
The train has been delayed/cancelled.	*Kereta terlambat/dibatalkan.*
the first	*pertama*
the last	*terakhir*
ticket	*karcis*
ticket office	*loket*
timetable	*jadwal*

Private Transport

Where can I hire a ...?	*Di mana saya bisa sewa ...?*
I'd like to hire a ...	*Saya mau sewa ...*
bicycle	*sepeda*
car	*mobil*
4WD	*gardan ganda*
motorcycle	*sepeda motor*

ROAD SIGNS

Beri Jalan	Give Way
Bahaya	Danger
Dilarang Parkir	No Parking
Jalan Memutar	Detour
Masuk	Entry
Dilarang Mendahului	No Overtaking
Kurangi Kecepatan	Slow Down
Dilarang Masuk	No Entry
Satu Arah	One Way
Keluar	Exit
Kosongkan	Keep Clear

Is this the road to ...?	*Apakah jalan ini ke ... ?*
Where's a service station?	*Di mana pompa bensin?*
Please fill it up.	*Tolong isi sampai penuh.*
I'd like ... litres.	*Minta ... liter bensin.*
diesel	*disel*
leaded petrol	*bensin bertimbal*
unleaded petrol	*bensin tanpa timbal*
I need a mechanic.	*Saya perlu montir.*
The car has broken down at ...	*Mobil mogok di...*
The motorcycle won't start.	*Motor tidak bisa jalan.*
I have a flat tyre.	*Ban saya kempes.*
I've run out of petrol.	*Saya kehabisan bensin.*
I had an accident.	*Saya mengalami kecelakaan.*
(How long) Can I park here?	*(Berapa lama) Saya boleh parkir di sini?*
Where do I pay?	*Saya membayar di mana?*

TRAVEL WITH CHILDREN

Is there a/an ...?	*Ada .....?*
I need a ...	*Saya perlu....*
baby change room	*tempat ganti popok kamar*
car baby seat	*kursi anak untuk di mobil*
child-minding service	*tempat penitipan anak*
children's menu	*menu untuk anak-anak*
disposable nappies/diapers	*popok sekali pakai*
formula	*susu kaleng*
(English-speaking) babysitter	*suster yang bisa berbicara (Bahasa Inggris)*
highchair	*kursi anak*
potty	*pispot*
stroller	*kereta anak/dorongan anak*

Are children allowed?
Boleh bawa anak-anak?

Glossary

For food and drink terms, see Eat Your Words, p91.

adat – tradition, customs and manners
aling aling – gateway backed by a small wall
alus – identifiable 'goodies' in an *arja* drama
anak-anak – children
angker – evil power
angklung – portable form of the *gamelan*
anjing – dogs
apotik – pharmacy
arja – refined operatic form of Balinese theatre; also a dance-drama, comparable to Western opera
Arjuna – a hero of the *Mahabharata* epic and a popular temple gate guardian image

bahasa – language; Bahasa Indonesia is the national language of Indonesia
bale – an open-sided pavilion with a steeply pitched thatched roof
bale banjar – communal meeting place of a *banjar;* a house for meetings and *gamelan* practice
bale gede – reception room or guesthouse in the home of a wealthy Balinese
bale kambang – floating pavilion; a building surrounded by a moat
bale tani – family house in Lombok; see also *serambi*
balian – see *dukun*
banjar – local division of a village consisting of all the married adult males
banyan – a type of ficus tree, often considered holy; see also *waringin*
bapak – father; also a polite form of address to any older man; also *pak*
Barong – mythical lion-dog creature
Barong Tengkok – portable *gamelan* used for wedding processions and circumcision ceremonies on Lombok
baten tegeh – decorated pyramids of fruit, rice cakes and flowers
batik – process of colouring fabric by coating part of the cloth with wax, dyeing it and melting the wax out; the waxed part is not coloured, and repeated waxing and dyeing builds up a pattern
batu bolong – rock with a hole
Bedaulu, Dalem – legendary last ruler of the Pejeng dynasty
belalu – quick-growing, light wood
bemo – popular local transport in Bali and on Lombok; usually a small minibus but often a small pick-up in rural areas
bensin – petrol (gasoline)
beruga – communal meeting hall in Bali; open-sided pavilion on Lombok
bhur – world of demons
bhwah – world of humans
Bima Suarga – a hero of the *Mahabharata* epic
bioskop – cinema
bokor – artisans; they produce the silver bowls used in traditional ceremonies
Brahma – the creator; one of the trinity of Hindu gods
Brahmana – the caste of priests and the highest of the Balinese castes; all priests are Brahmanas, but not all Brahmanas are priests
bu – mother; shortened form of *ibu*
bukit – hill; also the name of Bali's southern peninsula
bulau – month
bupati – government official in charge of a *kabupaten*
buruga – thatched platforms on stilts

cabang – large tanks used to store water for the dry season
camat – government official in charge of a *kecamatan*
candi – shrine, originally of Javanese design; also known as *prasada*
candi bentar – gateway entrance to a temple
caste – hereditary classes into which Hindu society is divided. There are four castes: three branches of the 'nobility' *(Brahmana, Ksatriyasa* and *Wesia)*, and the common people *(Sudra)*
cendrawasih – birds of paradise
cengceng – cymbals
cidomo – pony cart with car wheels (Lombok)
cucuk – gold headpieces

dalang – puppet master and storyteller in a *wayang kulit* performance
danau – lake
dangdut – pop music
desa – village
dewa – deity or supernatural spirit
dewi – goddess
Dewi Danau – goddess of the lakes
Dewi Sri – goddess of rice
dokar – pony cart; known as a *cidomo* on Lombok
dukun – 'witch doctor'; faith healer and herbal doctor; also *balian*
Durga – goddess of death and destruction, and consort of *Shiva*
dusun – local divisions of a village

Dwarpala – guardian figure who keeps evil spirits at bay in temples

endek – elegant fabric, like *songket,* but the weft threads are predyed

Gajah Mada – famous *Majapahit* prime minister who defeated the last great king of Bali and extended *Majapahit* power over the island
Galungan – great Balinese festival; an annual event in the 210-day Balinese *wuku* calendar
gamelan – traditional Balinese orchestra, with mostly percussion instruments like large xylophones and gongs; also called a *gong*
Ganesha – *Shiva's* elephant-headed son
gang – alley or footpath
gangsa – xylophone-like instrument
Garuda – mythical man-bird creature, vehicle of *Vishnu;* modern symbol of Indonesia and the national airline
gedong – shrine
gendang beleq – a war dance; like the Oncer dance
gendong – street vendors who sell *jamu,* said to be a cure-all tonic
gili – small island (Lombok)
goa – cave; also spelt *gua*
gong – see *gamelan*
gong gede – large orchestra; traditional form of the *gamelan* with 35 to 40 musicians
gong kebyar – modern, popular form of a *gonge gede,* with up to 25 instruments
gringsing – rare double *ikat* woven cloth
gua – cave; also spelt *goa*
gunung – mountain
gunung api – volcano
gusti – polite title for members of the *Wesia* caste

Hanuman – monkey god who plays a major part in the *Ramayana*
harga biasa – standard price
harga turis – inflated price for tourists
homestay – small, family-run *losmen*

ibu – mother; also a polite form of address to any older woman
Ida Bagus – honourable title for a male *Brahmana*
iders-iders – long painted scrolls used as temple decorations
ikat – cloth where a pattern is produced by dyeing the individual threads before weaving; see also *gringsing*
Indra – king of the gods

jalak putih – local name for Bali starling
jalan – road or street; abbreviated to *Jl*
jalan jalan – to walk around
jamu – a cure-all tonic; see also *gendong*
Jepun – frangipani trees
jidur – large cylindrical drums played throughout Lombok
Jimny – small, jeeplike Suzuki vehicle; the usual type of rental car
Jl – *jalan;* road or street
jukung – see *prahu*

kabupaten – administrative districts (known as regencies during Dutch rule)
kahyangan jagat – directional temples
kain – a length of material wrapped tightly around the hips and waist, over a sarong
kain poleng – black-and-white chequered cloth
kaja – in the direction of the mountains; see also *kelod*
kaja-kangin – corner of the courtyard
kaki lima – food carts
kala – demonic face often seen over temple gateways
Kalendar Cetakan – Balinese calendar used to plan a myriad of activities
kamben – a length of *songket* wrapped around the chest for formal occasions
kampung – village or neighbourhood
kangin – sunrise
kantor – office
kantor imigrasi – immigration office
kantor pos – post office
Kawi – classical Javanese; the language of poetry
kebyar – a type of dance
Kecak – traditional Balinese dance; tells a tale from the *Ramayana* about Prince Rama and Princess Sita
kecamatan – subdistrict; see also *camat*
kedais – coffee house
kelod – opposite of *kaja;* in the direction away from the mountains and towards the sea
kelurahan – local government area
kemban – woman's breast-cloth
kempli – gong
kendang – drums
kepala desa – village head
kepeng – old Chinese coins with a hole in the centre
kori agung – gateway to the second courtyard in a temple
kota – city
kras – identified 'baddies' in an *arja* drama
kris – traditional dagger
Ksatriyasa – second Balinese caste
kuah – sunset side
kulkul – hollow tree-trunk drum used to sound a warning or call meetings

labuhan – harbour; also called *pelabuhan*
laki-laki – boy
lamak – long, woven palm-leaf strips used as decorations in festivals and celebrations
lambung – long black sarongs worn by *Sasak* women; see also *sabuk*

langse – rectangular decorative hangings used in palaces or temples
Legong – classic Balinese dance
legong – young girls who perform the *Legong*
leyak – evil spirit that can assume fantastic forms by the use of black magic
lingam – phallic symbol of the Hindu god *Shiva*
lontar – specially prepared palm leaves
losmen – small Balinese hotel, often family-run
lukisan antic – antique paintings
lulur – body mask
lumbung – rice barn with a round roof; an architectural symbol of Lombok

madia – the body
Mahabharata – one of the great Hindu holy books, the epic poem tells of the battle between the Pandavas and the Korawas
Majapahit – last great Hindu dynasty on Java
makan Padang – Padang food
mandi – Indonesian 'bath' consisting of a large water tank from which you ladle cold water over yourself
manusa yadnya – ceremonies which mark the various stages of Balinese life from before birth to after cremation
mapadik – marriage by request, as opposed to *ngrorod*
mata air panas – natural hot springs
meditasi – swimming and sunbathing
mekepung – traditional water buffalo races
meru – multiroofed shrines in Balinese temples; the name comes from the Hindu holy mountain Mahameru
mobil – car
moksa – freedom from earthly desires
muncak – mouse deer

naga – mythical snakelike creature
ngrorod – marriage by elopement; see also *mapadik*
ngrupuk – great procession where *ogoh-ogoh* figures are used to ward off evil spirits
nista – the legs
nusa – island; also called *pulau*
Nusa Tenggara Barat (NTB) – West Nusa Tenggara; a province of Indonesia comprising the islands of Lombok and Sumbawa
nyale – wormlike fish caught off Kuta, Lombok
Nyepi – major annual festival in the Hindu *saka* calendar, this is a day of complete stillness after a night of chasing out evil spirits

odalan – Balinese 'temple birthday' festival; held in every temple annually, according to the *wuku* calendar, ie once every 210 days
ogoh-ogoh – huge monster dolls used in the *Nyepi* festival
ojek – motorcycle that carries paying pillion passengers
oong – Bali's famed magic mushrooms

padi – growing rice plant
padmasana – temple shrine resembling a vacant chair; a throne for the supreme god Sanghyang Widhi in the manifestation of Siwa Raditya
pak – father; shortened form of *bapak*
pal ungan – shallow trough
palinggihs – temple shrines consisting of a simple, little throne
panca dewata – centre and four cardinal points in a temple
pande – blacksmiths; they are treated somewhat like a caste in their own right
pantai – beach
pantun – ancient Malay poetical verse in rhyming couplets
paras – a soft, grey volcanic stone used in stone carving
pasar – market
pasar malam – night market
pecalang – village or *banjar* police
pedanda – high priest
pekelan – ceremony where gold trinkets and objects are thrown into the lake
pelabuhan – harbour; also called *labuhan*
Pelni – the national shipping line
pemangku – temple guardians and priests for temple rituals
penjor – long bamboo pole with decorated end, arched over the road or pathway during festivals or ceremonies
perbekel – government official in charge of a *desa*
perempuan – girl
pesmangku – priest for temple rituals
pitra yadna – cremation
plus plus – a combined tax and service charge of 21% added by midrange and top-end accommodation and restaurants
pondok – simple lodging or hut
prada – cloth highlighted with gold leaf, or gold or silver paint and thread
prahu – traditional Indonesian boat with outriggers
prasada – shrine; see also *candi*
prasasti – inscribed copper plates
pria – man; male
propinsi – province; Indonesia has 27 *propinsi* – Bali is a *propinsi*, Lombok and its neighbouring island of Sumbawa comprise *propinsi Nusa Tenggara Barat (NTB)*
puasa – to fast, or a fast
pulau – island; also called *nusa*
puputan – warrior's fight to the death; an honourable but suicidal option when faced with an unbeatable enemy
pura – temple
pura dalem – temple of the dead
pura desa – village temple for everyday functions
pura puseh – temple of the village founders or fathers, honouring the village's origins
pura subak – temple of the rice growers' association

puri – palace
pusit kota – used on road signs to indicate the centre of town
puskesmas – community health centre

rajah – lord or prince
Ramadan – Muslim month of fasting
Ramayana – one of the great Hindu holy books; these stories form the keystone of many Balinese dances and tales
Rangda – widow-witch who represents evil in Balinese theatre and dance
rebab – bowed lute
RRI – Radio Republik Indonesia; Indonesia's national radio broadcaster
RSU or RSUP – Rumah Sakit Umum or Rumah Sakit Umum Propinsi; a public hospital or provincial public hospital
rumah makan – restaurant; literally 'eating place'

sabuk – Four-metre-long scarf that holds the *lambung* in place
sadkahyangan – 'world sanctuaries'; most sacred temples
saiban – temple or shrine offering
saka – Balinese calendar based on the lunar cycle; see also *wuku*
sampian – palm-leaf decoration
Sasak – native of Lombok; also the language
sawah – individual rice field; see also *subak*
selandong – traditional scarf
selat – strait
sepeda – bicycle
sepeda motor – motorcycle
serambi – open veranda on a *bale tani,* the traditional Lombok family house
Shiva – the creator and destroyer; one of the three great Hindu gods
sinetron – soap operas
songket – silver- or gold-threaded cloth, hand-woven using a floating weft technique
stupas – domes for housing Buddha relics
subak – village association that organises rice terraces and shares out water for irrigation
Sudra – common caste to which the majority of Balinese belong
sungai – river
swah – world of gods

tahun – year
taksu – divine interpreter for the gods
tambulilingan – bumblebees
tanjung – cape or point
tektekan – ceremonial procession
teluk – gulf or bay
tiing – bamboo
tirta – water
toya – water
transmigrasi – government programme of trans-migration
trimurti – Hindu trinity
triwangsa – caste divided into three parts *(Brahmana, Ksatriyasa* and *Wesia)*; means three people
trompong – drums
TU – Telepon Umum; a public telephone
tugu – lord of the ground
tukang prada – group of artisans who make temple umbrellas
tukang wadah – group of artisans who make cremation towers

undagi – designer of a building, usually an architect-priest
utama – the head

Vishnu – the preserver; one of the three great Hindu gods

wanita – woman; female
wantilan – large *bale* pavilion used for meetings, performances and cockfights
waria – female impersonator, transvestite or transgendered; combination of the words *wanita* and *pria*
waringin – large shady tree with drooping branches which root to produce new trees; see *banyan*
warnet – *warung* with internet access
wartel – public telephone office; contraction of *warung telekomunikasi*
warung – food stall
wayang kulit – leather puppet used in shadow puppet plays; see also *dalang*
wayang wong – masked drama playing scenes from the *Ramayana*
Wektu Telu – religion peculiar to Lombok; originated in Bayan and combines many tenets of Islam and aspects of other faiths
Wesia – military caste and most numerous of the Balinese noble castes
WIB – Waktu Indonesia Barat; West Indonesia Time
wihara – monastery
WIT – Waktu Indonesia Tengah; Central Indonesia Time
wuku – Balinese calendar made up of 10 different weeks, between one and 10 days long, all running concurrently; see also *saka*

yeh – water; also river
yoni – female symbol of the Hindu god *Shiva*

Behind the Scenes

THIS BOOK

This is the 11th edition of Lonely Planet's *Bali & Lombok*. We first visited Bali, the Island of the Gods, way back in the early '70s, when a floral-shirted Tony Wheeler came through while researching the inaugural *Across Asia on the Cheap,* wondering even then at the island's steadily increasing tourism industry. Since then an army of Lonely Planet authors have returned time and time again: Following in Tony's sandalled footprints have been Mary Coverton (who worked with Tony on *Bali & Lombok 1*, 1984), Alan Samagalski, James Lyon, Paul Greenway, Kate Daly, Ryan Ver Berkmoes and Lisa Steer-Guérard.

For this edition, Ryan Ver Berkmoes returned again to Bali, while the intrepid island-hopping Iain Stewart researched and wrote the Lombok chapter. Meanwhile, local foodie Janet de Neefe wrote the new Food & Drink chapter, while expert medico Dr Trish Batchelor wrote Health. Prof Philip Goad wrote the Contemporary Hotel Design boxed text.

This guidebook was commissioned in Lonely Planet's Melbourne office, and produced by the following:

Commissioning Editors Marg Toohey, Jessa Boanas-Dewes
Coordinating Editor Elizabeth Anglin
Coordinating Cartographer Ross Butler
Coordinating Layout Designer Jacqueline McLeod, Margie Jung
Managing Editor Gabbi Stefanos, Melanie Dankel
Managing Cartographers Corie Waddell, Julie Sheridan
Assisting Editors Elisa Arduca, Margedd Heliosz, Kate Evans, Cathryn Game
Assisting Cartographers Karina Vitiritti
Assisting Layout Designer Cara Smith
Cover Designer Yukiyoshi Kamimura
Language Content Coordinator Quentin Frayne
Project Manager Chris Love
Terima kasih banyak Errol Hunt

Thanks to Carol Chandler, Sally Darmody, Nicole Hansen, Laura Jane, Katie Lynch, Celia Wood

THANKS

RYAN VER BERKMOES

This list just seems to grow. Many thanks to friends like Jeremy Allan, Eliot Cohen, Jamie James, Hanafi, Kerry and Milton Turner (what a lunch!), Nicoline Dolman, Jack Daniels, John Taylor, Marilyn, Wayan Suarnata, Karen McClellan, Kahar Salamun, Liv Gusing (the best writer I know who should be writing), Ove Sandstrom, John Taylor and many, many more. The wonderful thing about Bali is that it inspires so much affection that people just can't stop sharing their favourite places, secrets and more.

At Lonely Planet, thanks to Marg Toohey, a stellar Commissioning Editor, with or without gin and tonics. Jessa Boanas-Dewes carried the book forward, right into the waiting arms of Errol Hunt. Thanks to all for guidance, understanding and inspiration.

Finally, there's Annah who always gives me a welcome 'merp' and Erin Corrigan, who discovered Bali for herself and proved that paradise begins at home.

THE LONELY PLANET STORY

The story begins with a classic travel adventure: Tony and Maureen Wheeler's 1972 journey across Europe and Asia to Australia. There was no useful information about the overland trail then, so Tony and Maureen published the first Lonely Planet guidebook to meet a growing need.

From a kitchen table, Lonely Planet has grown to become the largest independent travel publisher in the world, with offices in Melbourne (Australia), Oakland (USA) and London (UK). Today Lonely Planet guidebooks cover the globe. There is an ever-growing list of books and information in a variety of media. Some things haven't changed. The main aim is still to make it possible for adventurous travellers to get out there – to explore and better understand the world.

At Lonely Planet we believe travellers can make a positive contribution to the countries they visit – if they respect their host communities and spend their money wisely. Every year 5% of company profit is donated to charities around the world.

IAIN STEWART

I'd like to thank my wife Fiona above all for holding the fort at home and coping so admirably during the lengthy research trip that this job necessitated – you're remarkable. My family in Ashley and Tyneside also chipped in considerably with child care, attention and affection for our boys Louis and Monty. In Lombok I was aided and abetted by many Indonesians and *bule* including Barbara and Mel in Senggigi, Guy & Nadine, Simon of the Blue Marlin, Chris of Irish bar fame, Marcus Stevens at Manta Dive, Jo and Marta, Seanster in Gili T, Christine Barnes and Made in Kuta – thanks to you all.

OUR READERS

Many thanks to the travellers who used the last edition and wrote to us with helpful hints, useful advice and interesting anecdotes:

A Vicky Adams, Luca Altea, Guido Amkreutz, Patrick Andre, Federico Arrizabalaga, Marie Augustsson, **B** Alexandra Brown, Lynn Bell, Leong Benjamin, Neil Beswick, David Bishop, Martin Bode, Thijs Bosch, Andrew Bratt, David Bulluss, **C** Geoffrey Carliez, Helen & Gil Carroll, Paolo Cassese, Clive & Gwen Clements, Dara Conlan, Scott Crosby, Dugan Cummings, **D** Francesco D'alessandro, Maurits Daub, Jane de la Fosse, Marian de Vaan, **E** Bea en Aat Kars, Sonya Englisch, Marius Ernsting, **F** Kelvin Fong, Jeanette Fries, Jeanette Friggebo, **G** Daniela Gherguta, Wendy Glamocak, Jess Glanfield, Ursula Goedhart, Nick Goetzfridt, Sharon Greenspan, Christine Greiser, David Grossman, Barbara Guthrie, **H** Ingo Hanke, Julia Hansen, Lucas Harms, Tony Hobbs, Clare Holland, Judith Holmes, David Houliston, Frank & Betty Hughes, Ronelle Hutchinson, Trine Hxvset, **J** Alan Jacobs, John & Jasmine Jenks, Martin John, Wayne Johnson, **K** Irene Kawahara, Sue Kellerman, Julia Kovacs, Peter Kunkel, **L** Danai Lamb, Julianne le Shana, R Leduc, Regis Levesque, Ann Lindvall, Sascha Loeffler, Adam Love, **M** Maharani Maharani, Anna Marti, Melanie Miles, Shan Miller, Mette Munk, **N** Chris Naylor, Eddy & Sheryl Neo, Gaetan Nicodeme, Nadia Nicolini, Peter Norment, **O** John O'Halloran, Simo Ollila, Dieneke Oostindier, **P** Andrea Panzoni, Derek Peggs, Roger & Cloudia Pelzer, Omar Pestoni, Elizabeth Pittman, **R** David Ragg, Elin Rauum, Kees Roelse, Jacqui Rutten, **S** Marcia Scheepers, Mark Seldon, Alan Siegel, Chew Siong, Nyoman Smeenk, Kees Smetsers, Raymond Smith, Shawn Smith, Carolyn Stewart, **T** Stanley & Christine Tonkins, **V** Frans van der Burg, Monique van Griensven, Tom van Leemputten, Yves Vantomme, Carina Vega, Rob Vermay, Paul Vuhu, **W** Tamara Wiher, Simon Wilhelm, Peter, Ana & Thomas Williams, Ian Wilton, Beatrice Wong, Franklin Wong, Jen Woolard, **Y** Yumiko, Moingeon & Yves-Marie Yanagi

SEND US YOUR FEEDBACK

We love to hear from travellers – your comments keep us on our toes and help make our books better. Our well-travelled team reads every word on what you loved or loathed about this book. Although we cannot reply individually to postal submissions, we always guarantee that your feedback goes straight to the appropriate authors, in time for the next edition. Each person who sends us information is thanked in the next edition – and the most useful submissions are rewarded with a free book.

To send us your updates – and find out about Lonely Planet events, newsletters and travel news – visit our award-winning website: **www.lonelyplanet.com/contact**.

Note: we may edit, reproduce and incorporate your comments in Lonely Planet products such as guidebooks, websites and digital products, so let us know if you don't want your comments reproduced or your name acknowledged. For a copy of our privacy policy visit www.lonelyplanet.com/privacy.

Index

INDEX

000 Map pages
000 Photograph pages

INDEX

000 Map pages
000 Photograph pages

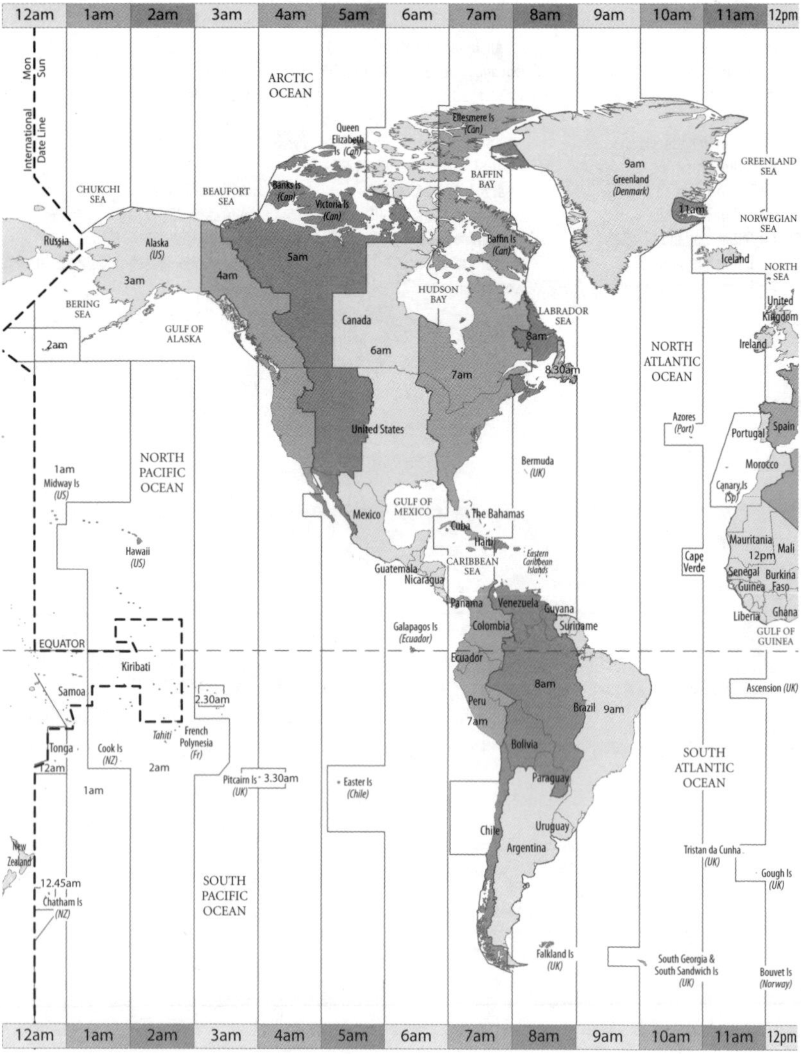
12am
1am
2am
3am
4am
5am
6am
7am
8am
9am
10am
11am
12pm
Mon
Sun
International Date Line
ARCTIC OCEAN
Queen Elizabeth Is (Can)
Ellesmere Is (Can)
9am
Greenland (Denmark)
GREENLAND SEA
BAFFIN BAY
CHUKCHI SEA
BEAUFORT SEA
Banks Is (Can)
Victoria Is (Can)
11am
NORWEGIAN SEA
Russia
Alaska (US)
5am
Baffin Is (Can)
Iceland
4am
NORTH SEA
3am
HUDSON BAY
BERING SEA
LABRADOR SEA
United Kingdom
GULF OF ALASKA
Canada
8am
2am
6am
Ireland
NORTH ATLANTIC OCEAN
8.30am
7am
Azores (Port)
United States
Portugal
Spain
NORTH PACIFIC OCEAN
Bermuda (UK)
1am
Midway Is (US)
Morocco
Canary Is (Sp)
GULF OF MEXICO
Mexico
The Bahamas
Cuba
Hawaii (US)
Haiti
Mauritania
Mali
12pm
Cape Verde
Eastern Caribbean Islands
Guatemala
CARIBBEAN SEA
Nicaragua
Senegal
Burkina Faso
Guinea
Panama
Venezuela
Guyana
Galapagos Is (Ecuador)
Colombia
Suriname
Liberia
Ghana
GULF OF GUINEA
EQUATOR
Ecuador
Kiribati
8am
Ascension (UK)
Samoa
2.30am
Peru
Brazil
9am
7am
Tahiti
French Polynesia (Fr)
Bolivia
SOUTH ATLANTIC OCEAN
Tonga
Cook Is (NZ)
2am
12am
Pitcairn Is (UK)
3.30am
Easter Is (Chile)
Paraguay
1am
Chile
Uruguay
Argentina
New Zealand
Tristan da Cunha (UK)
12.45am
Chatham Is (NZ)
Gough Is (UK)
SOUTH PACIFIC OCEAN
Falkland Is (UK)
South Georgia & South Sandwich Is (UK)
Bouvet Is (Norway)

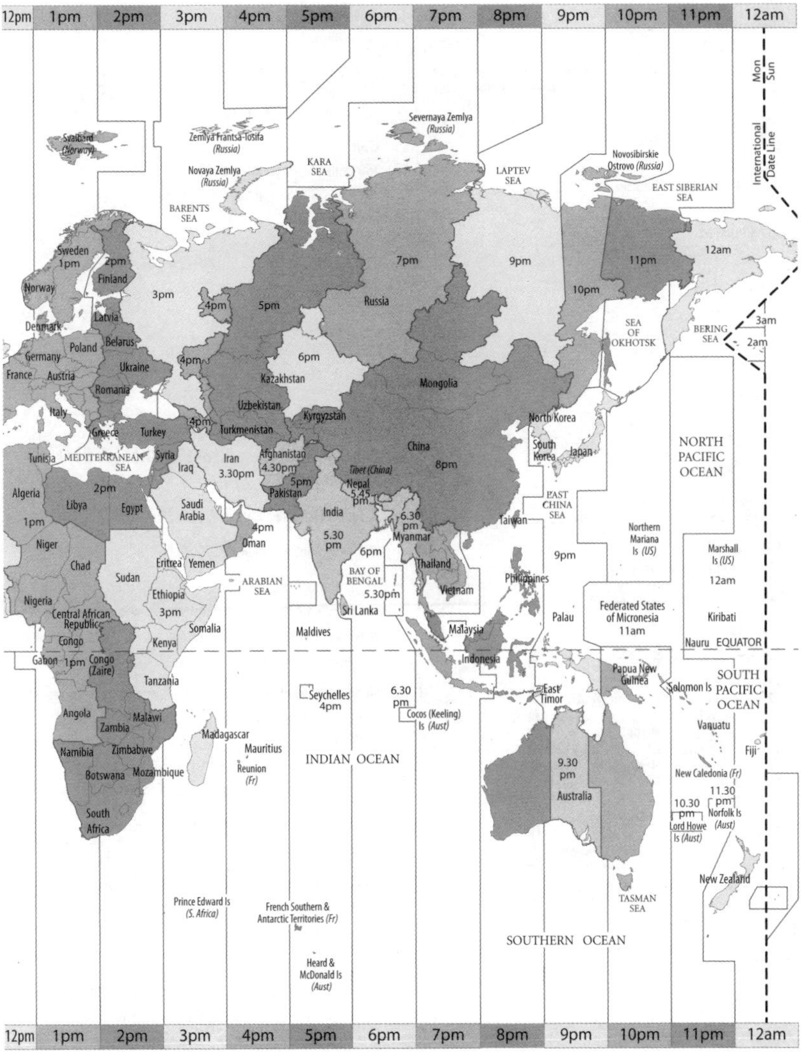
12pm
1pm
2pm
3pm
4pm
5pm
6pm
7pm
8pm
9pm
10pm
11pm
12am
Mon
Sun
International Date Line
Svalbard (Norway)
Zemlya Frantsa-Iosifa (Russia)
Novaya Zemlya (Russia)
Severnaya Zemlya (Russia)
KARA SEA
BARENTS SEA
LAPTEV SEA
Novosibirskie Ostrovo (Russia)
EAST SIBERIAN SEA
Sweden 1pm
Norway
Finland
Denmark
Latvia
Poland
Belarus
Germany
Ukraine
France
Austria
Romania
Italy
Greece
Turkey
Russia
Kazakhstan
Uzbekistan
Turkmenistan
Kyrgyzstan
Mongolia
China
North Korea
South Korea
Japan
SEA OF OKHOTSK
BERING SEA
3am
2am
Tunisia
MEDITERRANEAN SEA
Syria
Iraq
Iran 3.30pm
Afghanistan 4.30pm
Pakistan
Tibet (China)
Nepal 5.45 pm
Algeria
Libya
Egypt
Saudi Arabia
India 5.30 pm
6.30 pm
Myanmar
Taiwan
EAST CHINA SEA
NORTH PACIFIC OCEAN
Niger
Chad
Sudan
Eritrea
Yemen
Oman
ARABIAN SEA
BAY OF BENGAL
Thailand
Vietnam
Philippines
Northern Mariana Is (US)
Marshall Is (US)
Nigeria
Central African Republic
Ethiopia
Somalia
Sri Lanka
Maldives
Malaysia
Palau
Federated States of Micronesia 11am
Kiribati
Congo
Gabon
Congo (Zaire)
Kenya
Tanzania
Indonesia
Papua New Guinea
Nauru EQUATOR
Solomon Is
SOUTH PACIFIC OCEAN
Seychelles 4pm
Cocos (Keeling) Is (Aust)
East Timor
Angola
Malawi
Zambia
Madagascar
Mauritius
Reunion (Fr)
INDIAN OCEAN
Vanuatu
Fiji
Namibia
Zimbabwe
Botswana
Mozambique
South Africa
9.30 pm
Australia
New Caledonia (Fr)
11.30 pm
Norfolk Is (Aust)
10.30 pm
Lord Howe Is (Aust)
New Zealand
TASMAN SEA
Prince Edward Is (S. Africa)
French Southern & Antarctic Territories (Fr)
Heard & McDonald Is (Aust)
SOUTHERN OCEAN

MAP LEGEND

ROUTES

Tollway	One-Way Street
Freeway	Street Mall/Steps
Primary Road	Tunnel
Secondary Road	Walking Tour
Tertiary Road	Walking Tour Detour
Lane	Walking Trail
Track	Walking Path
Unsealed Road	Pedestrian Overpass

TRANSPORT

Ferry	Rail
Bus Route	

HYDROGRAPHY

River, Creek	Water
Swamp	Mudflats
Mangrove	Reef

BOUNDARIES

International	Regional, Suburb
State, Provincial	Ancient Wall
Marine Park	Cliff

AREA FEATURES

Airport	Land
Area of Interest	Mall
Beach, Desert	Market
Building	Park
Cemetery, Christian	Rocks
Cemetery, Other	Sports
Forest	Urban

POPULATION

● CAPITAL (NATIONAL)	◉ CAPITAL (STATE)
● Large City	● Medium City
● Small City	● Town, Village

SYMBOLS

Sights/Activities

- Beach
- Buddhist
- Christian
- Diving, Snorkelling
- Hindu
- Islamic
- Monument
- Museum, Gallery
- Point of Interest
- Pool
- Ruin
- Snorkelling
- Surfing, Surf Beach
- Zoo, Bird Sanctuary

Eating

- Eating

Drinking

- Drinking
- Café

Entertainment

- Entertainment

Shopping

- Shopping

Sleeping

- Sleeping
- Camping

Transport

- Airport, Airfield
- Bus Station
- General Transport
- Parking Area
- Petrol Station
- Taxi Rank

Information

- Bank, ATM
- Embassy/Consulate
- Hospital, Medical
- Information
- Internet Facilities
- Police Station
- Post Office, GPO
- Telephone

Geographic

- Lighthouse
- Lookout
- Mountain, Volcano
- National Park
- Pass, Canyon
- Shelter, Hut
- Waterfall

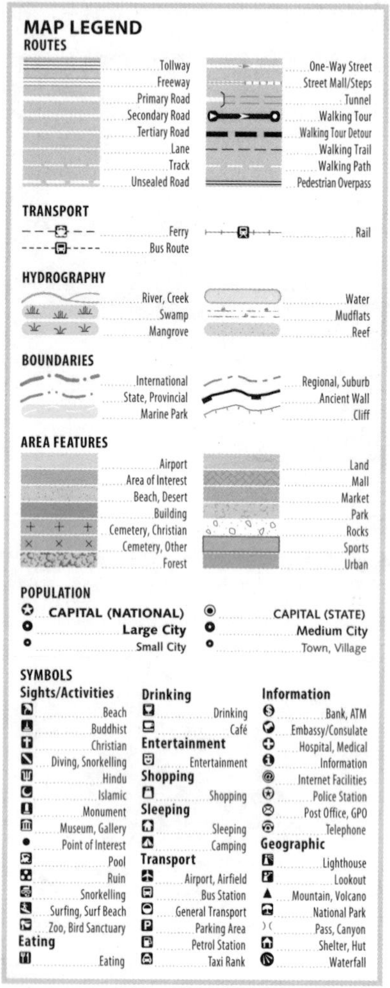

LONELY PLANET OFFICES

Australia
Head Office
Locked Bag 1, Footscray, Victoria 3011
☎ 03 8379 8000, fax 03 8379 8111
talk2us@lonelyplanet.com.au

USA
150 Linden St, Oakland, CA 94607
☎ 510 893 8555, toll free 800 275 8555
fax 510 893 8572
info@lonelyplanet.com

UK
72–82 Rosebery Ave,
Clerkenwell, London EC1R 4RW
☎ 020 7841 9000, fax 020 7841 9001
go@lonelyplanet.co.uk

Published by Lonely Planet Publications Pty Ltd
ABN 36 005 607 983